The Globalization Reader

The Globalization Reader

Second edition

Edited by

Frank J. Lechner
and
John Boli

Blackwell
Publishing

BLACKWELL PUBLISHING
350 Main Street, Malden, MA 02148-5020, USA
9600 Garsington Road, Oxford OX4 2DQ, UK
550 Swanston Street, Carlton, Victoria 3053, Australia

First edition published 2000
Second edition published 2004 by Blackwell Publishing Ltd

6   2006

Library of Congress Cataloging-in-Publication Data

The globalization reader / edited by Frank J. Lechner and John Boli. —2nd ed.
     p.   cm.
   This new edition has been thoroughly revised and updated, with thirty new essays
and a new section on anti-globalization movement.
   Includes bibliographical references and index.
   ISBN 1-4051-0279-9 (alk. paper) — ISBN 1-4051-0280-2 (pbk. : alk. paper)
   1. International economic relations.   2. International economic relations—Social
aspects.   3. International economic integration.   4. Globalization.   5. Anti-
globalization movement.   I. Lechner, Frank.   II. Boli, John, 1948–

HF1359.G59   2003
337–dc21

                                                    2003056025

ISBN-13: 978-1-4051-0279-7 (alk. paper) — ISBN-13: 978-1-4051-0280-3 (pbk. : alk. paper)

A catalogue record for this title is available from the British Library.

Set in 10 on 11.5 pt Galliard
by SNP Best-set Typesetter Ltd, Hong Kong
Printed and bound in the United Kingdom
by TJ International, Padstow, Cornwall

The publisher's policy is to use permanent paper from mills that operate a sustainable
forestry policy, and which has been manufactured from pulp processed using acid-
free and elementary chlorine-free practices. Furthermore, the publisher ensures that
the text paper and cover board used have met acceptable environmental
accreditation standards.

For further information on Blackwell Publishing, visit our website:
www.blackwellpublishing.com

Contents

Sources and Acknowledgments

1. John Micklethwait and Adrian Wooldridge, excerpted from "A Future Perfect: The Essentials of Globalization" © John Micklethwait and Adrian Wooldridge 2000, pp. 332–42. Reprinted by permission of The Wylie Agency, Inc., and The Wylie Agency (UK) Ltd.

2. Amartya Sen, excerpted from "How to Judge Globalism," reprinted with permission from *The American Prospect*, 13, 1, January 1–January 14, 2002. *The American Prospect*, 5 Broad Street, Boston, MA 02109. All rights reserved.

3. John Gray, excerpted from *False Dawn: The Delusions of Global Capitalism*, The New Press, 1998, pp. 1–7, 17–21. Reproduced with permission of Curtis Brown Ltd., London, on behalf of John Gray. Copyright © John Gray.

4. Benjamin Barber, excerpted from "Introduction," in *Jihad vs. McWorld*, pp. 3–8, 9–10, 17–20. Published originally by Times Books 1995. Benjamin R. Barber is Kekst Professor of Civil Society at the University of Maryland, Director, New York office, The Democracy Collaborative and the author of many books including *Strong Democracy* (1984), *Jihad vs. McWorld* (Times Books, 1995), *A Place for Us* (Farrar, Straus & Giroux, 1998), *A Passion for Democracy: American Essays* (Princeton University Press, 1998), and *The Truth of Power: Intellectual Affairs in the Clinton White House* (W. W. Norton & Co.).

5. Samuel Huntington, excerpted from "The Clash of Civilizations?," pp. 22–3, 25–32, 39–41, 49. Reprinted by permission of *Foreign Affairs*, 72, 3, Summer 1993. Copyright © 1993 by the Council on Foreign Relations, Inc.

6. Hans Küng, excerpted from *A Global Ethic for Global Politics and Economics*, Oxford University Press, 1998, pp. 91–3, 105, 108–11, 223–6. Reprinted by permission of Hans Küng.

7. E. J. Hobsbawm, excerpted from "The World Unified," in *The Age of Capital 1848–1875*, Weidenfeld & Nicolson, 1975, pp. 48–50, 51–3, 65–7, 68. Reprinted by permission of The Orion Publishing Group Ltd.

8. Immanuel Wallerstein, excerpted from "The Rise and Future Demise of the World Capitalist System: Concepts for Comparative Analysis," *Comparative Studies in Society and History*, 16, 1974, pp. 390–2, 399–406. © Society for Comparative Study of Society and History. Reprinted by permission of Cambridge University Press.

9. Leslie Sklair, edited from Chapter 5 of *Globalization: Capitalism and its Alternatives* (3rd edn.), 2002. Reprinted by permission of Oxford University Press.

10. Robert O. Keohane and Joseph S. Nye, excerpted from "Realism and Complex Interdependence," in *Power and Interdependence* by Robert O. Keohane and Joseph S. Nye, 3rd ed., pp. 3–7. Copyright © 2000 by Robert O. Keohane and Joseph S. Nye. Reprinted by permission of Addison-Wesley Educational Publishers, Inc.

11. John Meyer et al., excerpted from "World Society and the Nation-State," *American Journal of Sociology*, 1997, pp. 144–6, 150–1, 152–3, 157–61, 173–5. Reprinted by permission of The University of Chicago Press.

12. Roland Robertson, excerpted from *Globalization: Social Theory and Global Culture*. Reprinted by permission of Sage Publishing Ltd. Copyright © Roland Robertson 1992, pp. 8–9, 25–9, 174–80.

13. Arjun Appadurai, excerpted from "Disjuncture and Difference in the Global Cultural Economy," in *Modernity at Large: Cultural Dimensions of Globalization*, University of Minnesota Press, 1996, pp. 27–30, 32–43. Reprinted by permission of Arjun Appadurai.

14. Ulf Hannerz, excerpted from *Cultural Complexity: Studies in the Social Organization of Meaning*, Columbia University Press, 1992, pp. 217–22, 228–31, 239–45, 261–2, 266–7. Reprinted by permission of Columbia University Press.

15. James L. Watson, excerpted from *Golden Arches East: McDonald's in East Asia*. Copyright © 1997 by the Board of the Trustees of the Leland Stanford Jr. University. With the permission of Stanford University Press, www.sup.org

16. Martin Albrow, excerpted from "Travelling Beyond Local Cultures," in John Eade (ed.), *Living the Global City: Globalization as a Local Process*, Routledge, 1997, pp. 43–51. Reprinted by permission of Taylor & Francis Books Ltd.

17. Bruce Fuller, excerpted from "Strong States, Strong Teachers?" Copyright © 1991. In *Growing-Up Modern: The Western State Builds Third-World Schools* by Bruce Fuller, pp. 111–13, 115–27. Reproduced by permission of Routledge, Inc., part of the Taylor & Francis Group.

18. Timothy Taylor, excerpted from *Global Pop: World Music, World Markets*, Routledge, 1997, pp. 127–8, 129–30, 134–5, 142–3. Copyright © 1997. Reproduced by permission of Routledge, Inc., part of the Taylor & Francis Group.

19. William Greider, excerpted from "Wawasan 2020." Reprinted with permission of Simon & Schuster Adult Publishing Group, from *One World, Ready or Not* by William Greider, pp. 81–6, 91–2, 100–2. Copyright © 1997 by William Greider.

20. Miguel Korzeniewicz, excerpted from "Commodity Chains and Marketing Strategies: Nike and the Global Athletic Footwear Industry," pp. 247–61 in Gary Gereffi and Miguel Korzeniewicz (eds.), *Commodity Chains and Global Capitalism*. Copyright © 1994 by Gary Gereffi and Miguel Korzeniewicz. Reproduced by permission of Greenwood Publishing Group, Inc., Westport, CT.

21. David Dollar and Aart Kraay, excerpted from "Growth is Good for the Poor," reprinted by permission of *Foreign Affairs*, 81, 1, January/February 2002. Copyright © 2002 by the Council on Foreign Relations, Inc.

22. Oxfam, excerpted from "Growth with Equity is Good for the Poor," *Oxfam Policy Papers* 6/00. Reproduced with permission from Oxfam Publishing, 274 Banbury Road, Oxford, OX2 7DZ.

23. Mary Robinson (UN High Commissioner for Human Rights), excerpted from "Beyond Good Intentions: Corporate Citizenship for a New Century," RSA World Leaders Lecture, May 7, 2002. Reprinted by permission of United Nations Publications.

24. David Henderson, excerpted from "The Case Against 'Corporate Social Responsibility'," reprinted with permission from *Policy*, 17, 2, Winter 2001. Copyright © 2001 by the Centre for Independent Studies, Sydney, www.cis.org.au. Based on the essay, *Misguided Virtue: False Notions of Corporate Social Responsibility* by David Henderson, published in 2001 by the New Zealand Business Roundtable and in London by the Institute of Economic Affairs.

25. Joseph E. Stiglitz, excerpted from "Globalism's Discontents," reprinted with permission from *The American Prospect*, 13, 1, January 1–14, 2002. The American Prospect, 5 Broad Street, Boston, MA 02109. All rights reserved.

26. Kenichi Ohmae, excerpted from *The End of the Nation State: The Rise of Regional Economies*, pp. 7, 11–16, 141–2. Reprinted with the permission of The Free Press, a division of Simon & Schuster Adult Publishing Group. Copyright © 1995 by McKinsey & Co., Inc.

27. Susan Strange, excerpted from *The Retreat of the State*, Cambridge University Press, 1996, pp. 3–8, 9–10, 12–14. Reprinted by permission of Cambridge University Press.

28. Dani Rodrik, excerpted from *Has Globalization Gone Too Far?* pp. 2, 4–7, 77–81. Copyright © 1997 Institute for International Economics, Washington, DC. All rights reserved.

29. Geoffrey Garrett, excerpted from "Introduction," in *Partisan Politics in the Global Economy*, Cambridge University Press, 1998, pp. 1–11. Reprinted by permission of Cambridge University Press.

30. Kofi Annan, excerpted from "The Role of the State in the Age of Globalisation," keynote address to Conference on Globalisation and International Relations in the 21st Century, June 2002. Reprinted by permission of United Nations Publications.

31. Nitza Berkovitch, excerpted from "The Emergence and Transformation of the International Women's Movement," in John Boli and George M. Thomas (eds.), *Constructing World Culture: International Nongovernmental Organizations since 1875*, pp. 109–10, 119–21, 124–6. Copyright © 1999 by the Board of Trustees of the Leland Stanford Jr. University. With the permission of Stanford University Press, www.sup.org

32. Beijing Declaration, excerpted from United Nations Fourth World Conference on Women, 1995, #1–27, 35. Reprinted by permission of United Nations Publications.

33. John Boli and George Thomas, excerpted from "World Culture in the World Polity: A Century of International Non-Governmental Organization," *American Sociological Review*, 1997, pp. 172–3, 174, 179–82, 187–8. Reprinted by permission of the American Sociological Association.

34. Peter Eigen, excerpted from "Closing the Corruption Casino: The Imperatives of a Multilateral Approach," opening address at Global Forum II, The Hague, Netherlands, May 28, 2001. Reprinted by permission of Peter Eigen, Chairman, Transparency International, http://www.transparency.org

35.   Jessica Matthews, excerpted from "Power Shift." Reprinted by permission of *Foreign Affairs*, 76, 1, January/February 1997. Copyright © 1997 by the Council on Foreign Relations, Inc.

36.   Michael Bond, "The Backlash Against NGOs." Originally published in *Prospect*, April 2000, www.prospect-magazine.co.uk

37.   Sean MacBride and Colleen Roach, excerpted from "The New International Information Order," pp. 3–10. From *International Encyclopedia of Communications*, 4 Vols., ed. Erik Barnouw, copyright © 1989 by Trustees of the University of Pennsylvania. Used by permission of Oxford University Press, Inc.

38.   John Sinclair, Elizabeth Jacka, and Stuart Cunningham (eds.), excerpted from "Peripheral Vision," in *New Patterns in Global Television: Peripheral Vision*, ed. John Sinclair, Elizabeth Jacka, and Stuart Cunningham (Oxford University Press, 1996), pp. 5–10, 18–21, 25. Reprinted by permission of Oxford University Press.

39.   John Tomlinson, excerpted from *Cultural Imperialism: A Critical Introduction*, 1991, pp. 45–50, 108–13. By permission of Continuum International Publishing Group Ltd., The Tower Building, 11 York Road, London, SE1 7NX, England.

40.   Heather Tyrrell, excerpted from "Bollywood versus Hollywood: Battle of the Dream Factories," in Tracey Skelton and Tim Allen (eds.), *Culture and Global Change*, Routledge, 1999, pp. 260–6, 272–3. Reprinted by permission of Taylor & Francis Books Ltd.

41.   Frank Lechner, excerpted from "Global Fundamentalism," in William H. Swatos (ed.), *A Future for Religion?* pp. 19, 27–32, copyright © 1993 by William H. Swatos. Reprinted by permission of Sage Publications, Inc.

42.   Mustapha Kamal Pasha, excerpted from "Globalization, Islam and Resistance," in Barry K. Gills (ed.), *Globalization and the Politics of Resistance*, Macmillan Press, 2000. Reproduced with permission of Palgrave Macmillan.

43.   Bassam Tibi, excerpted from *The Challenge of Fundamentalism: Political Islam and the New World Disorder*, pp. 2–3, 15–17, 65–7. Copyright © 1998 The Regents of the University of California. Reprinted by permission of the University of California Press.

44.   Ann Elizabeth Mayer, excerpted from "The Fundamentalist Impact on Law, Politics, and Constitutions in Iran, Pakistan, and the Sudan," in Martin E. Marty and R. Scott Appleby (eds.), *Fundamentalisms and the State*, University of Chicago Press, 1993, pp. 115–23. Reproduced by permission of University of Chicago Press.

45.   Shahla Haeri, excerpted from "Obedience Versus Autonomy: Women and Fundamentalism in Iran and Pakistan," in Martin E. Marty and R. Scott Appleby (eds.), *Fundamentalisms and Society*, University of Chicago Press, 1993, pp. 182–91. Reproduced by permission of University of Chicago Press.

46.   Salman Rushdie, "Yes, This Is About Islam," *The New York Times*, November 2, 2001. © 2001 by Salman Rushdie. Reprinted by permission of The Wylie Agency, Inc., and The Wylie Agency (UK) Ltd.

47.   Excerpted from *World Commission on Environment and Development: Our Common Future*, pp. 1–9. Oxford University Press (1987). Reprinted by permission of Oxford University Press.

48. United Nations Conference on Environment and Development, excerpted from "Rio Declaration on Environment and Development" and "Agenda 21," 1992, #1–25. Reprinted by permission of United Nations Publications.

49. Excerpted from Paul Wapner, "Greenpeace and Political Globalism," in Paul Wapner, *Environmental Activism and World Civic Politics*, pp. 41–3, 47–54. © 1996, State University of New York. Reprinted by permission of the State University of New York Press. All rights reserved.

50. Excerpted from Margaret E. Keck and Kathryn Sikkink, "Environmental Advocacy Networks," in Margaret E. Keck and Kathryn Sikkink (eds.), *Activists Beyond Borders: Advocacy Networks in International Politics* (Cornell University Press, 1998), pp. 150–62. Copyright © 1998 by Cornell University. Used by permission of the publisher, Cornell University Press.

51. Excerpted from Abigail Abrash, "The Amungme, Kamoro & Freeport: How Indigenous Papuans Have Resisted the World's Largest Gold and Copper Mine," *Cultural Survival Quarterly*, Spring 2001. Reprinted by permission of Cultural Survival.

52. Excerpted from Wolfgang Sachs, *Planet Dialectics: Explorations in Environment and Development* (Zed Books, 1999), pp. 129–31, 149–55. Reprinted by permission of Zed Books Ltd., London.

53. Excerpted from Gustavo Esteva and Madhu Suri Prakash, *Grassroots Post-Modernism: Remaking the Soil of Cultures* (Zed Books, 1998), pp. 19–26, 27–8, 32–3. Reprinted by permission of Zed Books Ltd., London.

54. Excerpted from James Harding, "Counter-Capitalism: Globalisation's Children Strike Back," *Financial Times*, September 2001. Reprinted by permission of the *Financial Times*.

55. Excerpted from Vandana Shiva, "Ecological Balance in an Era of Globalization," in Paul Wapner and Lester Edwin J. Ruiz (eds.), *Principled World Politics: The Challenge of Normative International Relations* (Rowman & Littlefield, 2000), pp. 130–1, 132–3, 135–7, 139–41, 145–7, 148–9. Reprinted by permission of the Rowman & Littlefield Publishing Group.

56. Excerpted from Subcomandante Marcos, *Our Word is Our Weapon* ("Tomorrow Begins Today"), Closing Remarks at the First Intercontinental *Encuentro* for Humanity and against Neoliberalism, August 3, 1996 (Seven Stories Press, 2001), pp. 115–23. Reprinted by permission of Seven Stories Press.

57. Excerpted from World Social Forum, "Porto Alegre Call for Mobilization," 2001. Reprinted by permission of World Social Forum, www.movsoc.org

58. Excerpted from the International Forum on Globalization, *A Better World Is Possible!*, report summary, 2002. Reprinted by permission of the International Forum on Globalization.

Preface to the Second Edition

Globalization is still going strong. In many different fields, the world is drawing together as a single society, marked by common institutions and organizations, by a shared culture and consciousness. But globalization is also ever more contested. Policy makers struggle with problems attributed to globalization. Public debate about the process, already strong in the 1990s, has intensified. Academic studies critical of globalization continue to proliferate. Opposition has crystallized into movements of resistance that have taken to the streets. In the second edition of this reader, we try to capture not only enduring features of globalization but also new debates reflecting new developments.

Some events that took place while we prepared this second edition illustrate the enduring features of globalization. At the 2002 World Cup, teams representing Asian countries competed effectively, marking their arrival on the global football scene. In spite of opposition from the United States, the International Criminal Court was established in The Hague. An international conference in Barcelona addressed the intensifying spread of AIDS. In a period of turmoil in financial markets, communications and media conglomerates had to rethink their strategies. As the campaign against Islamic terrorism continued, a UN report criticized Arab states for their isolation. In sports and law, in economics and public health, in religion and geopolitics we see forms of global integration, organization, and consciousness emerging.

Yet these examples also illustrate that globalization does not point toward a smoothly unified world society. Though football may be a global game, it also inspires divisive nationalist fervor. Whether the International Criminal Court will be able effectively to prosecute war crimes and crimes against humanity without superpower support remains to be seen. However impressive the mobilization against AIDS may be, both individual countries and international institutions have yet to contain the epidemic. Visions of a single world market for cultural products may suffer a setback if integrated media companies fall apart. Not just Arab countries but the world as a whole now face the question of whether, and how, predominantly Islamic societies will participate in globalization. The terrorist events in the first years of the new century only made that question more urgent. In each instance mentioned above, and indeed in many responses to terrorism, the depth and direction of globalization are at issue.

In most respects, globalization early in the twenty-first century continues trends of the late twentieth century. We have accordingly retained several features of the first edition:

- *Structure*: Like its predecessor, this edition is organized into sections covering numerous aspects of globalization, from theoretical to experiential, from economic to cultural.

- *Issues*: Among the problems the Reader illustrates are the integration of world markets and its consequences, the viability of the nation-state in relation to new forms of power, the likelihood of greater cultural homogeneity, and the institutionalization of global efforts to deal with global problems.
- *Purpose*: Our goal remains to provide a variety of perspectives on different dimensions of globalization, and thereby to convey its importance and complexity.

In recognition of the new realities of globalization and the expanded debate on the subject, our coverage has also changed in some ways:

- *New themes*: This edition has a new section on the proliferating anti-globalization movements. The section on constructing identities focuses more explicitly on the problem of Islamic fundamentalism, while the section on reorganizing the globe now more directly addresses the growth of global civil society. The economic globalization section adds more material on debates about world poverty and the role of corporations in global development.
- *New selections*: This edition includes, among other new items, different excerpts from the work of Roland Robertson and Ulf Hannerz; readings by James Watson on globalization in food, by Timothy Taylor on world music, by Heather Tyrrell on Bollywood, and by Salman Rushdie on Islam; an excerpt from Susan Strange on the "retreat of the state"; statements by NGOs such as Oxfam and Transparency International; and new case studies of cultural globalization and global environmentalism.
- *New voices*: Additional prominent figures in the global discussion of globalization are represented in this edition, ranging from UN Secretary General Kofi Annan and UN High Commissioner for Human Rights Mary Robinson, to economists Amartya Sen and Joseph Stiglitz and globalization critics Wolfgang Sachs and Vandana Shiva.

In all, about half of the selections in this edition are new. In deciding which selections from the first edition to eliminate to make room for these replacements, we especially considered how well they served the needs of students. We hope this updated edition will help new readers to make sense of globalization – both what it is and how it is being debated in world society.

Frank Lechner and John Boli

General Introduction

At the end of the twentieth century, globalization became an all-purpose catchword in public and scholarly debate. Government officials could attribute their country's economic woes to the onslaught of globalization, business leaders justified downsizing of their companies as necessary to prepare for globalization, environmentalists lamented the destructive impact of unrestrained globalization, and advocates for indigenous peoples blamed the threatened disappearance of small cultures on relentless globalization. As different parties used the term in highly disparate ways and the concept itself became a global symbol, its meaning became inflated. Globalization risked becoming a global cliché. One purpose of this reader is to show that, worn though it may be, the concept still usefully captures significant worldwide changes that have continued into the twenty-first century. Indeed, underlying the various nuances of the term, as used strategically by many groups, is a shared awareness that the world itself is changing. We think that awareness is correct. We are witnessing the consolidation of a new global society. The selections compiled in this reader aim to describe and explain the course of globalization and the shape of its outcomes.

What does globalization involve? After World War II, the infrastructure for communication and transportation improved dramatically, connecting groups, institutions, and countries in new ways. More people can travel, or migrate, more easily to distant parts of the globe; satellite broadcasts bring world events to an increasingly global audience; the Internet begins to knit together world-spanning interest groups of educated users. Such links are the raw material of globalization. They are molded into new organizational forms as regional institutions go global or new ones take shape on the world stage. Increasing international trade and investment bring more countries into the global capitalist system; democracy gains strength as a global model for organizing nation-states; numerous international organizations take on new responsibilities in addressing issues of common concern. These institutions, in turn, are crystallizing into a comprehensive world society. The world is becoming a single place, in which different institutions function as parts of one system and distant peoples share a common understanding of living together on one planet. This world society has a culture; it instills in many people a budding consciousness of living in a world society. To links and institutions we therefore add culture and consciousness. Globalization is the process that fitfully brings these elements of world society together.

Is globalization new? Many scholars point to sixteenth-century Europe as the original source of globalization. After all, the Europeans established worldwide trade connections on their own terms, brought their culture to different regions by settling vast areas, and defined the ways in which different peoples were to interact with each other. Economically and culturally, the modern world system already existed nearly five centuries ago. Others point to the late nineteenth century as a period of intense globalization, when millions migrated, trade greatly expanded, and new norms and organizations came to govern international conduct. At the beginning of the twentieth century, such scholars would stress, the movement of people, goods, and finance across national borders was at least as free and significant as it is today. We agree that globalization has been happening for a long time. We also agree that specific features of world society have their roots in earlier periods. We add, however, that the second half of the twentieth century was a significant period of globalization in its own right. World War II gave globalization a new impetus. Obscured by Cold War divisions, the transformation of world society in the past six decades – in terms of linkages, institutions, and culture and consciousness – was nevertheless profound. This reader includes selections from scholars skeptical of this claim, but it also illustrates by many examples that globalization has entered a new phase.

Is globalization driven by the expanding market? The pursuit of economic opportunity has long sent merchants around the globe, and powerful states have supported their profit-seeking activities. Capitalism knows no bounds, as Marx noted more than a century ago. Marx expected the European economy to become a truly global system, and in many ways it has. In recent years, the integration of financial markets has added a new kind of interdependence. To us, this does not mean that globalization is first and foremost an economic project. While an economic system operating along capitalist lines now encompasses most regions of the world, and economic motives always have been important in creating global linkages, globalization takes place in many spheres for many reasons. The economy may be a driving force in creating global change in some periods, but its effects depend on what happens outside of world markets. To understand the world economy, then, one also needs to understand world society. Accordingly, this reader presents a comprehensive picture of globalization, covering economic, political, cultural, and experiential dimensions.

Does globalization make the world more homogeneous? This question would seem to answer itself: If certain activities or institutions become global, they must displace existing, locally variable activities and institutions. If there are more global linkages, global institutions, and global values, presumably this means that more people will have more in common. To many critics of globalization, this seemingly neutral description is nefarious. Globalization is the work of the West, they argue. Markets set western rules for economic activity; one kind of western state has taken hold around the world; by controlling information flows, western media companies shape global consciousness; the popular culture of "McWorld" is of mostly western origin. Globalization thus entails cultural imperialism.

We agree that some things become more similar around the world as globalization proceeds. There is only one World Trade Organization and it enforces one set of trade rules; there is only one kind of bureaucratic state that societies can legitimately adopt. But we do not think this leads to a homogeneous world, for three reasons. First, general rules and models are interpreted in light of local circumstances. Thus, regions respond to similar economic constraints in different ways; countries still have great leeway in structuring their own policies; the same television program means different things to different audiences; McDonald's adapts its menu and marketing to local tastes. Second, growing similarity provokes reactions. Advocates for many cultures seek to protect their heritage or assert their identity: witness the efforts of fundamentalists to reinstate what they consider orthodoxy, the actions of indigenous peoples to claim their right to cultural survival, and the attempt of Asian leaders to put forth a distinctive Asian model of human rights. Third, cultural and political differences have themselves become globally valid. The notion that people and countries are entitled to their particularity or distinctiveness is itself part of global culture. The tension between homogeneity and heterogeneity is integral to globalization, and this reader illustrates it in several ways.

Does globalization determine local events? In 2002, Afghan girls returned to school after the United States defeated the Taliban regime; a war crimes tribunal in The Hague handed down convictions for atrocities committed during the war in Bosnia; African countries struggled to achieve progress as parts of their educated classes succumbed to AIDS; and melting glaciers raised concern about the impact of global warming. Around the world, local events bear the imprint of global processes. It would be easy to infer that local autonomy and local tradition must fall by the wayside, but globalization is not a one-way street. To be sure, local and global events become more and more intertwined, as illustrated by the way a global "war on terror" enhances the educational opportunities of some Muslim women, by the role of global institutions in dealing with the aftermath of major regional conflicts, by the domestic reverberations of a global epidemic, and by the way global climate change alters the habitat of specific groups. But the local feeds into the global as well: both the Taliban's failures and their own desires helped to change the fortunes of Afghan women; the Bosnian war provoked the innovative establishment of a war crimes tribunal to vindicate global principles; domestic hesitations and constraints contribute to the spread of HIV/AIDS in many countries; global warming results from the release of greenhouse gases in specific manufacturing centers and high-consumption countries. Yet, even if globalization does not necessarily "determine" local events, there is no escaping it. As world society integrates, individuals become conscious of being enveloped in global networks, subject to global forces, governed by global rules. Some of our selections concretely illustrate this local–global connection.

Is globalization harmful? Implicit in the questions we have raised is a widespread sense that globalization may be harmful to the well-being of individuals, countries, and cultures. If the market is the driving force in globalization, many fear, it is bound to exacerbate inequality by creating winners and losers. If globalization makes the world more homogeneous, others fear, many cultures are in trouble. Loss of local autonomy may mean that more people will be vulnerable to economic swings, environmental degradation, and epidemics. For these and other reasons, globalization has become an extremely contentious process. Indeed, the debate about the merits and direction of globalization is itself an important component of global culture. As we already indicated above, we are skeptical of the most sweeping critiques of globalization. But our purpose in this reader is not to offer definitive judgments; the subject is too complex for a clear-cut assessment in any case. Rather, we present a variety of perspectives that convey the thrust of actual debates and ongoing research so that readers can understand the varied consequences of globalization and make their own informed judgments.

The Globalization Reader aims to convey the complexity, importance, and contentiousness of globalization. This is an exciting time in social science scholarship, as many creative minds try to discern the outlines of a new era. The reader includes some of their best work. But making sense of globalization is not just a task for scholars and students. It is a public concern. We hope this reader will assist a diverse audience in understanding the patterns and problems of globalization, which is likely to remain a dominant concern of the twenty-first century.

Note on Selections

Footnotes, citations, and sources of quoted passages have been excised. Omitted text is indicated by "[. . .]".

Part I

Debating Globalization

Introduction

When the Cold War drew to a close in the late 1980s, some in the West proclaimed the "end of history": from now on, there would be no more deep conflicts about how to organize societies, no more ideological divisions in the world. In the "new world order" heralded by the American president at the time, George H. W. Bush, countries would cooperate peacefully as participants in one worldwide market, pursuing their interests while sharing commitments to basic human values. These triumphant responses to the new global situation heartily embraced economic liberalization and the prosperity and democratization it supposedly entailed. As global trade and investment expanded, more and more people could share in the bounty of a growing economy. Economic and political interdependence would create shared interests that would help prevent destructive conflict and foster support for common values. As vehicles of globalization, international organizations could represent such common values for the benefit of humanity. Globalization, in this rosy scenario, created both wealth and solidarity. The spread of market-oriented policies, democratic polities, and individual rights promised to promote the well-being of billions of people.

This influential perspective on globalization has been challenged by critics who see globalization as a juggernaut of untrammeled capitalism. They fear a world ruled by profit-seeking global corporations. They see economic interdependence as making countries more vulnerable to the destructive impact of market shifts. The social fabric – the ties among people all across the globe – is strained when winners in the global game become disconnected from losers. "By allowing market values to become all-important," said George Soros, himself a significant player in world financial markets, in 1998, "we actually narrow the space for moral judgment and undermine public morality. . . . Globalization has increased this aberration, because it has actually reduced the power of individual states to determine their destiny." The process, other critics add, is lopsided because it imposes the political and cultural standards of one region in the world, namely the West, on all other regions. Globalization is westernization by another name. It undermines the cultural integrity of other cultures and is therefore repressive, exploitative, and harmful to most people in most places.

Our selections in this part illustrate the major positions in the global debate about the merits and direction of globalization. John Micklethwait and Adrian Wooldridge, journalists at *The Economist*, represent the positive view of globalization by arguing that it not only produces greater economic efficiency and prosperity but also extends the "idea of liberty." Globalization opens up societies and reduces the "tyranny of place." In a more globalized world, more people can freely exercise their talents, decide where they want to live, and fashion their own identities. Like Micklethwait and Wooldridge, Amartya Sen, winner of the Nobel Memorial Prize in Economics, recognizes the potential benefits of global integration. Briefly illustrating worldwide contributions to the process, he refutes the idea that globalization is a "new Western curse." Yet he agrees with critics of globalization that it is profoundly unjust in its consequences. To him, however, the central question is not whether to use the global market economy, but how to create institutions that can lead to a more equitable distribution of its benefits.

John Gray, a British scholar, criticizes globalization more strongly as the attempted imposition of a single utopian economic model, American-style free-market capitalism, on the rest of the world. This brutal process creates insecurity and inequality. It fosters geopolitical rivalry and resists democratic control. But because it ignores human needs for diversity and security, it is also unsustainable, and Gray therefore expects globalization in its contemporary form to be a "false dawn." Benjamin Barber, an American political scientist, similarly questions the impact of economic globalization. He espies an increasingly homogeneous "McWorld" in which American-inspired popular culture overwhelms all others and societies lose the capacity to govern themselves democratically. He emphasizes that McWorld evokes a defense of indigenous national or religious traditions around the world, producing a variety of movements he captures with the label "Jihad." Pushing Barber's ideas still further, Samuel Huntington, another American scholar, argues that the defense of distinct cultural values is not merely reactive; rather, he points out, the globe is now divided into several civilizations with often irreconcilable worldviews. Resisting incorporation into one world society, these civilizations struggle with one another in profound conflicts that ultimately will reduce the influence of the West.

While Barber and Huntington sketch culturally divisive responses to globalization, Hans Küng, a German theologian, holds out hope for a more unifying or universal resolution of the problems created by globalization. He envisions a world society that serves common human interests. Küng proposes a global ethic, consisting of principles potentially shared by all human beings, as a moral restraint on states and markets and as a foundation for a global "civil society."

The critics thus share a fear of the unrestrained capitalist system. Some lament its imperial obliteration of cultural distinctions and advocate preserving or reviving traditional cultural distinctions. Others are more concerned about the impact on solidarity within societies and advocate stronger self-governance in democratic states. Still others worry most about the economic, political, and cultural divisions that result from globalization and advocate the cosmopolitan pursuit of a unified but just world. Such critical views of globalization themselves affect the course of the process. The increasingly deliberate efforts from many quarters to define the proper shape of world society also contribute significantly to its formation, an issue to which we return in the last section of this book. At the very least, the debate expresses a common global consciousness, though not, of course, a global consensus.

1 The Hidden Promise: Liberty Renewed

John Micklethwait and Adrian Wooldridge

[. . .] Karl Marx's tomb in Highgate Cemetery is a sorry place. The sculpture of his great bearded head is sometimes soiled with pigeon droppings; the army of celebrated intellectuals and communist dignitaries that used to come to pay its respects to the master has dwindled into a tiny band of eccentrics. In one way, this is a pity. As a prophet of socialism. Marx may be kaput; but as a prophet of "the universal interdependence of nations," as he called globalization, he can still seem startlingly relevant.

For all his hatred of the Victorian bourgeoisie, Marx could not conceal his admiration for its ability to turn the world into a single marketplace. Some of this admiration was mere schadenfreude, to be sure, born of his belief that in creating a global working class the bourgeoisie was also creating its very own grave diggers; but a surprising amount of this respect was genuine, like a prizefighter's respect for his muscle-bound opponent. In less than a hundred years, Marx argued, the bourgeoisie had "accomplished wonders far surpassing Egyptian pyramids, Roman aqueducts and Gothic cathedrals"; had conducted "expeditions that put in the shade all former exoduses of nations and crusades"; and had "created more massive and more colossal productive forces" than all preceding generations put together. In achieving all this, it had begun to transform an agglomeration of warring nations and petty principalities into a global marketplace.

Marx was at his most expansive on globalization in *The Communist Manifesto*, which he cowrote with Friedrich Engels, a factory owner turned revolutionary, and published in 1848, a year in which ancien régimes were tottering throughout Europe.

> The need of a constantly expanding market for its products chases the bourgeoisie over the entire surface of the globe. It must nestle everywhere, settle everywhere, establish connections everywhere.
>
> The bourgeoisie has through its exploitation of the world market given a cosmopolitan character to production and consumption in every country. . . . In place of the old wants, satisfied by the production of the country, we find new wants, requiring for their satisfaction the products of distant land and climes. In place of the old local and national seclusion and self-sufficiency, we have intercourse in every direction, universal interdependence of nations.

Original publication details: Excerpted from John Micklethwait and Adrian Wooldridge, "A Future Perfect: The Essentials of Globalization" (2000), pp. 332–42. © John Micklethwait and Adrian Wooldridge 2000. Reprinted by permission of the Wylie Agency, Inc., and the Wylie Agency (UK) Ltd.

Even Marx's final resting place is, to some extent, a vindication of this great insight. Opposite him in Highgate lies William Nassar Kennedy, a colonel of the Winnipeg Rifles who was "called home" in 1885 while returning to Canada from Egypt, where he was in command of the Nile Voyageurs. A little further down there is John MacKinlay and his wife, Caroline Louisa, "late of Bombay." Highgate Cemetery is strewn with the graves of Victorian soldiers, bureaucrats, and merchants who devoted their lives to turning the world into a single market.

What would Marx make of the world today? Imagine for a moment that the prayers of the faithful were answered and the great man awoke from his slumber. Having climbed out of his mausoleum, dusted himself off, and taken a frustrated sniff at the bottle of scotch, what would Marx find? There would, of course, be the shock of discovering that, on all the big issues, he had been proved hopelessly wrong. It was communism that succumbed to its own internal contradictions and capitalism that swept all before it. But he might at least console himself with the thought that his description of globalization remains as sharp today as it was 150 years ago.

Wandering down Highgate Hill, Marx would discover the Bank of Cyprus (which services the three hundred thousand Cypriots that live in London), several curry houses (now England's most popular sort of eatery), and a Restaurante do Brazil. He might be less surprised to find a large Irish community. But the sign inviting him to watch "Irish Sports Live," thanks to a pub's satellite-television linkup, might intrigue him. On the skyline, he would soon spot the twin towers of Canary Wharf, built by Canadian developers with money borrowed from Japanese banks and now occupied mostly by American investment banks.

Marx would hear Asian voices and see white schoolchildren proudly wearing T-shirts with pictures of black English soccer stars. Multicultural London (which is now home to thirty-three ethnic communities, each with a population of more than ten thousand) might well exhilarate a man who was called "the Moor" by his own children because of his dark complexion. He could stop at almost any newsstand and pick up a copy of the *Frankfurter Allgemeine Zeitung* that would be no more than a day old. Nearly swept off his feet by a passing Rolls-Royce, he might be more surprised to discover that the vehicle, like the rest of Britain's car industry, was now owned by a German company.

If Marx were to venture back to his old haunts in Soho, he would find a cluster of video-production companies and advertising agencies that sells its services to the world. If he climbed up to Hampstead Heath, the Marx family's favorite picnic spot, he might be surprised to discover that the neighborhood's most expensive house is now owned by an Indian, Lakshmi Mittal, who has built up one of the world's biggest steel companies. London is home to around a quarter of Europe's five hundred biggest companies. Its financial-services industry alone employs directly or indirectly 850,000 people, more than the population of the city of Frankfurt.

Yet even as Marx marveled at these new creations of the bourgeoisie and perhaps applauded its meritocratic dynamism, it is hard to believe that some of the old revolutionary fires would not burn anew. Poverty of the grinding sort that inspired Engels to write *The Condition of the Working Class in England* (1845) might have disappeared; the rigid class system of the Victorians might have evaporated: Marx might even have been slightly shocked by the absence of domestic servants. But the founder of communism would have no trouble tracking down inequality and sensing that it was on the increase.

Barely ten miles separate elegant Chelsea (where ironically enough the Marx family lived when they first came to London, before being evicted for not paying the rent) from the crumbling wasteland of Newham, but they seem like two different countries. In one, you might be forgiven for thinking that the biggest problem is the availability of residential parking permits; in the other, two thirds of the sixteen-year-olds fail their basic high-school exams, and the mortality rate for people under twenty-five is 50 percent above the national average. As he studied the newspaper and looked at the pictures on the flashing television screens of, say, Somalia or even parts of Los Angeles, Marx might well see globalization as a process that is only just beginning – a job half done. Once again, he might consider, the world is hurtling toward a "crisis of capitalism" – not unlike the last one that his own theories did so much to make ruinous.

The Priority of Liberty

This, then, is the beginning of the future, perfect or not, that we have tried to describe in this book. The fact that it has much in common with the world of yesterday (and especially the world of a century ago) is not surprising. History condemns us to repeat ourselves, though not necessarily to repeat all our mistakes.

. . . we have tried to build a measured defense of globalization. Yes, it does increase inequality, but it does not create a winner-take-all society, and the winners hugely outnumber the losers. Yes, it leaves some people behind, but it helps millions more to leap ahead. Yes, it can make bad government worse, but the onus should be on crafting better government, not blaming globalization. Yes, it curtails some of the power of nation-states, but they remain the fundamental unit of modern politics. Globalization is not destroying geography, merely enhancing it.

In most cases, the bulwarks of our defense have been economic. The simple fact is that globalization makes us richer – or makes enough of us richer to make the whole process worthwhile. Globalization clearly benefits producers by giving them greater choice over their raw materials, production techniques, and human talent, not to mention over the markets where they sell their goods. Equally clearly, globalization benefits consumers by providing them with better goods at better prices. Globalization increases efficiency and thus prosperity.

These economic arguments need to be made, and with far more eloquence, by our leaders. Too many politicians take the Clintonesque tack of defending the easy bits of globalization – typically, the successes of their own country's exports – and shying away from talking about the benefits that flow, say, from imports or foreign takeovers of "their" companies. This is not only economically illiterate but dangerous, because it allows myths to emerge, such as the idea that globalization is a zero-sum game. But there is also a broader need to wrench globalization from all the dry talk of markets penetrated, currencies depreciated, and GDPs accelerated and to place the process in its proper political context: as an extension of the idea of liberty and as a chance to renew the fundamental rights of the individual. [. . .]

The Open Society

Globalization redresses this balance in two ways. The most obvious is that it puts limits on the power of government. This advantage is most obvious in commerce. Free trade makes it easier for businesspeople to escape from interfering officials by moving their money and operations abroad. As we have pointed out, companies seldom want to flee, but the very fact that they might acts as a brake on those officials. The sullen fury of a Bangalore bureaucrat staring at the satellite dishes that allow "his" software companies to export their products without his grasping fingers interfering would delight Mill (even though he worked for the often more extortionate East India Company). More important still, free trade allows ordinary people to buy products from companies who make the best of their kind rather than from those that enjoy cozy relationships with governments. Similarly, they can put their retirement money in pension funds that are not tied to schemes of national aggrandizement.

Governments are not retreating from this easily. They can still slap controls on the flow of capital (as Malaysia did in the wake of the Asian crisis) or even on the flow of information. (Singapore employs a staff of censors whose job is to surf the Internet ceaselessly looking for objectionable information to block.) But the world is nevertheless a lot freer today than it was just a few decades ago, before globalization got into high gear. In 1966, for example, the British Labour government imposed a travel allowance that virtually confined Britons to their own country except for two weeks' worth of penny-pinching foreign vacation. Today, any politician who suggested such a restriction would be carted off to an asylum.

Indeed, the recent history of globalization can be written as a story, albeit an uneven story, of spreading a political culture that is based on individual liberty to areas that have been longing to embrace it for years. The last dozen years of the twentieth century saw not only the spectacular death of the biggest alternative to liberal democracy, totalitarian communism, but also the slow death of other collectivist models. Around the world, countries have abandoned attempts to plan their way to prosperity. Even the Asian crisis, in its own awful way, has made it more difficult for the continent's authoritarians to boast that they had discovered a nondemocratic way to generate growth.

Many on the left would argue that globalization has merely involved a change of master. Globalization may have liberated us from the onus of having to get our television programs – or our health care and pensions – from our governments, but it has forced us to get the same things from giant companies that are just as remote and even less accountable. The gentleman in Whitehall has been replaced by the knucklehead in the boardroom or, if you work in the Académie Française, by the illiterate in Hollywood.

This suspicion is healthy and should be encouraged. But so far the evidence is that it is misplaced. Of course, businesses will try to control markets, but that does not mean that they will be able to. As we have seen, one of the wonders of global capitalism is its capacity to hurl challenges at incumbent champions. Most of the forces of globalization – particularly the availability of capital and technology – favor small companies. In parts of Europe and Asia, commercial oligarchies are clinging to power, but only because governments collude with them. There is nothing global about, say, the importance of *guanxi* in Asia – quite the opposite. By the same token, the Department of Justice campaign to restrain Microsoft's power, no matter how misguided, has a legitimately global aim of trying to open up a market.

In fact, many of the most vengeful howls directed at globalization come from self-interested business elites who are being forced to surrender to consumer choice. Globalization does not mean homogenization. People want to consume books, movies, even potato chips, that reflect their own identities, and those identities remain primarily national. When politicians complain that globalization is changing society, they are correct, but they seldom bother to ask whose society it is. When society is defined by a fairly compact national economy, an elite has a chance of co-opting it.

But when society is an open-ended international system, it becomes increasingly difficult for any elite to identify their values with the common good.

The Individual's Prayer

Restricting overmighty states and elites is all very well, but globalization increases the basic freedom of individuals as well. We have already talked about the tyranny of place: Most people's lots in life are determined by where they were born, something illiberal regimes everywhere have done their best to reinforce. As Leszek Kolakawski, a Polish intellectual, points out, one of the defining features of communist regimes is their refusal to allow people to move from city to city without official permission; they even made short journeys difficult, providing few road signs or decent street maps. Even today, the lives of half the world's population are bounded by local villages, and local markets.

Travel and migration have long provided a fraction of the world's population with freedom from the tyranny of place. The printing press and the television have allowed others a more imaginary form of escape. Globalization is now making these freedoms more pervasive. The impact of the Internet, particularly as it goes wireless, will also be dramatic. The World Wide Web allows people to gain access to information anywhere at any time. And it allows them to do so in a way that undermines local elites and expensive middlemen. People will never escape the pull of geography entirely, as the tendency of business to cluster in particular places shows. But those clusters only survive if they work with the grain of globalization. And the penalty for being born a long way from those clusters is diminishing. Remember the Bangladeshi farmers using their cell phones to check the proper prices for their produce rather than having to accept the diktats of local grain merchants.

The more these ties weaken, the more people can exercise what used to be called God-given talents. Again, businesspeople are the most obvious beneficiaries: If you have a good idea and the entrepreneurial vim to pursue it, you can take it anywhere you want. If, like Michael Skok of AlphaBlox, you think that your business belongs in Silicon Valley, not the Thames valley, you can take it there. But there are also more spiritual, artistic reasons to believe that globalization is a good thing. The thousands of Miltons who remain "mute and inglorious" in their villages often begin to sing only after they move to the "mansion houses of liberty" that are the world's great cities. Bustling centers of trade from fifteenth-century Venice to twentieth-century New York have usually been centers of creativity, too. Even if your God-given talents are more prosaic, it is becoming ever easier to study abroad, and, thanks again to the Internet, you will soon be able to do so (more or less) without leaving home.

Somewhere behind the freedom to exercise our talents lies the most fundamental freedom of all: the freedom to define our own identities. This can sound like the moan of a petulant teenager, but it is at the heart of what is becoming one of the main debates of our time, between liberals and the growing band of communitarians. (To the extent that "the third way" means anything at all, its adherents are probably on the side of the communitarians.) Communitarians, as their name suggests, worry about the effect of things like globalization on communities. John Gray, one of globalization's most searching critics, has argued that human beings' "deepest need is a home, a network of common practices and inherited traditions that confers on them the blessings of a settled identity."

There can be no doubt that people need a home and a network. But does this home have to be the one they were born in? And does this network have to be the one provided by their ancestors? People also have a drive to better themselves, to extend their identities, to cross traditional boundaries, and to try out new experiences. John Gray himself happily abandoned the Newcastle working class into which he was born for the metropolitan intelligentsia. One of the many benefits of globalization is that it increases the number of people who can exercise Gray's privilege of fashioning his own identity.

This is not to say that conservative and communitarian worries about individualism run wild are empty. In the same breath that he praised America's faith in individualism, Tocqueville warned of the danger that each man may be "shut up in the solitude of his own heart." One of the great risks of globalization is that it fosters anomie – the normlessness that comes from having your ties with the rest of society weakened. Anybody who spends long periods of time on business trips knows the loneliness of the long-distance traveler. Ex-pats complain that their children grow up not knowing their grandparents. The most common complaint among Internet addicts is that they end up feeling (rather like the compulsive masturbators of Victorian medical treatises) isolated, lonely, and depressed.

All too true. Yet the issue that separates liberals from communitarians is not the desirability of human ties but the question of coercion. For liberals, the best communities are the spontaneous creations of free individuals rather than the products of bossy politicians, and one of the many cases for globalization is that it lets a million of these spontaneous communities bloom. The smaller the world becomes, the more communities are defined by common interests and outlooks rather than by the mere accident of physical proximity.

The idea of spontaneous communities will hardly placate globalization's harshest critics. For some people, the idea that individuals take precedence over society is nothing more than Western cultural imperialism. Wee Kim Wee, the former president of Singapore, argues that "placing society above the self" is one of his country's "core values." It is all very well for the egomaniacs of Manhattan and Los Angeles to abandon their gods in pursuit of self-fulfillment. But everybody else knows that such selfishness leads inexorably to the wasteland.

Yet the yearning for freedom is no more peculiar to the West than the yearning for prosperity. Other parts of the world have been quieter on the subject not because their peoples are wedded to collectivism but because their rulers have been less fussy about the methods they have used to hold onto power. Singaporeans bitterly resent the fact that their government gives them a superb education but then proceeds to treat them like children. The students who were brutally crushed at Tiananmen Square constructed replicas of the Statue of Liberty.

An Empire without End

Look around the world, and it is not hard to find examples of people for whom this message may seem a little empty. What does Reginaldo Gobetti care about the freedom to create his own identity; he just wants a job. Our argument is not that globalization is delivering the liberal dream, with billions of people gradually becoming the wired (or wireless) equivalent of Jefferson's yeoman farmers. Our argument is merely that globalization is delivering enough of that dream to make it worth pressing forward and to make it worth defending on more than just narrow economic grounds.

In fact, the two arguments should run in tandem. Globlization is helping to give birth to an economy that is closer to the classic theoretical model of capitalism, under which rational individuals pursue their interests in the light of perfect information, relatively free from government and geographical obstacles. It is also helping to create a society that is closer to the model that liberal political theorists once imagined, in which power lies increasingly in the hands of individuals rather than governments, and in which people are free, within reasonable bounds, to pursue the good life wherever they find it.

It would be nice if we could end on that optimistic, perhaps even slightly utopian, note. Yet we have also stressed the importance of vigilance and the need for not just politicians but also those who have prospered from globalization – particularly the cosmocrats – to help those who have done less well.

The trouble is that the devil has all the best tunes. One reason why globalization's enemies are so much more persuasive than its friends is that they are more visible: The victims are usually concentrated in particular places, whereas its beneficiaries are spread out all over the place. But supporters have also done a lousy job of making their case. We have already lamented the shortage of Peels and Rockefellers. But consider once again whether any modern leader would stand up and argue that "by encouraging freedom of intercourse between the nations of the world we are promoting the separate welfare of each and are fulfilling the beneficent designs of an all-seeing Creator" or invite his audience to celebrate "commerce, the happy instrument of promoting civilization, of abating national jealousies and prejudices and of encouraging the maintenance of general peace by every consideration as well as every obligation of Christian duty." [. . .]

2 How to Judge Globalism

Amartya Sen

Globalization is often seen as global Westernization. On this point, there is substantial agreement among many proponents and opponents. Those who take an upbeat view of globalization see it as a marvelous contribution of Western civilization to the world. There is a nicely stylized history in which the great developments happened in Europe: First came the Renaissance, then the Enlightenment and the Industrial Revolution, and these led to a massive increase in living standards in the West. And now the great achievements of the West are spreading to the world. In this view, globalization is not only good, it is also a gift from the West to the world. The champions of this reading of history tend to feel upset not just because this great benefaction is seen as a curse but also because it is undervalued and castigated by an ungrateful world.

From the opposite perspective, Western dominance – sometimes seen as a continuation of Western imperialism – is the devil of the piece. In this view, contemporary capitalism, driven and led by greedy and grabby Western countries in Europe and North America, has established rules of trade and business relations that do not serve the interests of the poorer people in the world. The celebration of various non-Western identities – defined by religion (as in Islamic fundamentalism), region (as in the championing of Asian values), or culture (as in the glorification of Confucian ethics) – can add fuel to the fire of confrontation with the West.

Is globalization really a new Western curse? It is, in fact, neither new nor necessarily Western; and it is not a curse. Over thousands of years, globalization has contributed to the progress of the world through travel, trade, migration, spread of cultural influences, and dissemination of knowledge and understanding (including that of science and technology). These global interrelations have often been very productive in the advancement of different countries. They have not necessarily taken the form of increased Western influence. Indeed, the active agents of globalization have often been located far from the West.

To illustrate, consider the world at the beginning of the last millennium rather than at its end. Around 1000 A.D., global reach of science, technology, and mathematics was changing the nature of the old world, but the dissemination then was, to a great extent, in the opposite direction of what we see today. The high technology in the world of 1000 A.D. included paper, the printing press, the crossbow, gunpowder, the iron-chain suspension bridge, the kite, the magnetic compass, the wheelbarrow, and the rotary fan. A millennium ago, these items were used extensively in

Original publication details: Excerpted from Amartya Sen, "How to Judge Globalism," *The American Prospect*, 13, 1, January 1–14, 2002. Reprinted by permission of *The American Prospect*, 5 Broad Street, Boston, MA 02109, USA. All rights reserved.

China – and were practically unknown elsewhere. Globalization spread them across the world, including Europe.

A similar movement occurred in the Eastern influence on Western mathematics. The decimal system emerged and became well developed in India between the second and sixth centuries; it was used by Arab mathematicians soon thereafter. These mathematical innovations reached Europe mainly in the last quarter of the tenth century and began having an impact in the early years of the last millennium, playing an important part in the scientific revolution that helped to transform Europe. The agents of globalization are neither European nor exclusively Western, nor are they necessarily linked to Western dominance. Indeed, Europe would have been a lot poorer – economically, culturally, and scientifically – had it resisted the globalization of mathematics, science, and technology at that time. And today, the same principle applies, though in the reverse direction (from West to East). To reject the globalization of science and technology because it represents Western influence and imperialism would not only amount to overlooking global contributions – drawn from many different parts of the world – that lie solidly behind so-called Western science and technology, but would also be quite a daft practical decision, given the extent to which the whole world can benefit from the process. [...]

Global Interdependences and Movements

The misdiagnosis that globalization of ideas and practices has to be resisted because it entails dreaded Westernization has played quite a regressive part in the colonial and postcolonial world. This assumption incites parochial tendencies and undermines the possibility of objectivity in science and knowledge. It is not only counterproductive in itself; given the global interactions throughout history, it can also cause non-Western societies to shoot themselves in the foot – even in their precious cultural foot.

Consider the resistance in India to the use of Western ideas and concepts in science and mathematics. In the nineteenth century, this debate fitted into a broader controversy about Western education versus indigenous Indian education. The "Westernizers," such as the redoubtable Thomas Babington Macaulay, saw no merit whatsoever in Indian tradition. "I have never found one among them [advocates of Indian tradition] who could deny that a single shelf of a good European library was worth the whole native literature of India and Arabia," he declared. Partly in retaliation, the advocates of native education resisted Western imports altogether. Both sides, however, accepted too readily the foundational dichotomy between two disparate civilizations.

European mathematics, with its use of such concepts as sine, was viewed as a purely "Western" import into India. In fact, the fifth-century Indian mathematician Aryabhata had discussed the concept of sine in his classic work on astronomy and mathematics in 499 A.D., calling it by its Sanskrit name, *jya-ardha* (literally, "half-chord"). This word, first shortened to *jya* in Sanskrit, eventually became the Arabic *jiba* and, later, *jaib*, which means "a cove or a bay." In his history of mathematics, Howard Eves explains that around 1150 A.D., Gherardo of Cremona, in his translations from the Arabic, rendered *jaib* as the Latin *sinus*, the corresponding word for a cove or a bay. And this is the source of the modern word *sine*. The concept had traveled full circle – from India, and then back.

To see globalization as merely Western imperialism of ideas and beliefs (as the rhetoric often suggests) would be a serious and costly error, in the same way that any European resistance to Eastern influence would have been at the beginning of the last millennium. Of course, there are issues related to globalization that do connect with imperialism (the history of conquests, colonialism, and alien rule remains relevant today in many ways), and a postcolonial understanding of the world has its merits. But it would be a great mistake to see globalization primarily as a feature of imperialism. It is much bigger – much greater – than that.

The issue of the distribution of economic gains and losses from globalization remains an entirely separate question, and it must be addressed as a further – and extremely relevant – issue. There is extensive evidence that the global economy has brought prosperity to many different areas of the globe. Pervasive poverty dominated the world a few centuries ago; there were only a few rare pockets of affluence. In overcoming that penury, extensive economic interrelations and modern technology have been and remain influential. What has happened in Europe, America, Japan, and East Asia has important messages for all other regions, and we cannot go very far into understanding the nature of globalization today without first acknowledging the positive fruits of global economic contacts.

Indeed, we cannot reverse the economic predicament of the poor across the world by withholding from them the great advantages of contemporary technology, the well-established efficiency of international trade and exchange, and the social as well as economic merits of living in an open society. Rather, the main issue is how to make good use of the remarkable benefits of economic intercourse and technological progress in a way that pays adequate attention to the interests of the deprived and the underdog. That is, I would argue, the constructive question that emerges from the so-called antiglobalization movements.

Are the Poor Getting Poorer?

The principal challenge relates to inequality – international as well as intranational. The troubling inequalities include disparities in affluence and also gross asymmetries in political, social, and economic opportunities and power.

A crucial question concerns the sharing of the potential gains from globalization – between rich and poor countries and among different groups within a country. It is not sufficient to understand that the poor of the world need globalization as much as the rich do; it is also important to make sure that they actually get what they need. This may require extensive institutional reform, even as globalization is defended.

There is also a need for more clarity in formulating the distributional questions. For example, it is often argued that the rich are getting richer and the poor poorer. But this is by no means uniformly so, even though there are cases in which this has happened. Much depends on the region or the group chosen and what indicators of economic prosperity are used. But the attempt to base the castigation of economic globalization on this rather thin ice produces a peculiarly fragile critique.

On the other side, the apologists of globalization point to their belief that the poor who participate in trade and exchange are mostly getting richer. Ergo – the argument runs – globalization is not unfair to the poor; they too benefit. If the central relevance of this question is accepted, then the whole debate turns on determining which side is correct in this empirical dispute. But is this the right battleground in the first place? I would argue that it is not.

Global Justice and the Bargaining Problem

Even if the poor were to get just a little richer, this would not necessarily imply that the poor were getting a fair share of the potentially vast benefits of global economic interrelations. It is not adequate to ask whether international inequality is getting marginally larger or smaller. In order to rebel against the appalling poverty and the staggering inequalities that characterize the contemporary world – or to protest against the unfair sharing of benefits of global cooperation – it is not necessary to show that the massive inequality or distributional unfairness is also getting marginally larger. This is a separate issue altogether.

When there are gains from cooperation, there can be many possible arrangements. As the game theorist and mathematician John Nash discussed more than half a century ago (in "The Bargaining Problem," published in *Econometrica* in 1950, which was cited, among other writings, by the Royal Swedish Academy of Sciences when Nash was awarded the Nobel Prize in economics), the central issue in general is not whether a particular arrangement is better for everyone than no cooperation at all would be, but whether that is a fair division of the benefits. One cannot rebut the criticism that a distributional arrangement is unfair simply by noting that all the parties are better off than they would be in the absence of cooperation; the real exercise is the choice *between* these alternatives. [. . .]

Likewise, one cannot rebut the charge that the global system is unfair by showing that even the poor gain something from global contacts and are not necessarily made poorer. That answer may or may not be wrong, but the question certainly is. The critical issue is not whether the poor are getting marginally poorer or richer. Nor is it whether they are better off than they would be had they excluded themselves from globalized interactions.

Again, the real issue is the distribution of globalization's benefits. Indeed, this is why many of the antiglobalization protesters, who seek a better deal for the underdogs of the world economy, are not – contrary to their own rhetoric and to the views attributed to them by others – really "antiglobalization." It is also why there is no real contradiction in the fact that the so-called antiglobalization protests have become among the most globalized events in the contemporary world.

Altering Global Arrangements

However, can those less-well-off groups get a better deal from globalized economic and social relations without dispensing with the market economy itself? They certainly can. The use of the market economy is consistent with many different ownership patterns, resource availabilities, social opportunities, and rules of operation (such as patent laws and antitrust regulations). And depending on these conditions, the market economy would generate different prices, terms of trade, income distribution, and, more generally, diverse overall outcomes. The arrangements for social security and other public interventions can make further modifications to the outcomes of the market processes, and together they can yield varying levels of inequality and poverty.

The central question is not whether to use the market economy. That shallow question is easy to answer, because it is hard to achieve economic prosperity without making extensive use of the opportunities of exchange and specialization that market relations offer. Even though the operation of a given market economy can be significantly defective, there is no way of dispensing with the institution of markets in general as a powerful engine of economic progress.

But this recognition does not end the discussion about globalized market relations. The market economy does not work by itself in global relations – indeed, it cannot operate alone even within a given country. It is not only the case that a market-inclusive system can generate very distinct results depending on various enabling conditions (such as how physical resources are distributed, how human resources are developed, what rules of business relations prevail, what social-security arrangements are in place, and so on). These enabling conditions themselves depend critically on economic, social, and political institutions that operate nationally and globally.

The crucial role of the markets does not make the other institutions insignificant, even in terms of the results that the market economy can produce. As has been amply established in empirical studies, market outcomes are massively influenced by public policies in education, epidemiology, land reform, microcredit facilities, appropriate legal protections, et cetera; and in each of these fields, there is work to be done through public action that can radically alter the outcome of local and global economic relations.

Institutions and Inequality

Globalization has much to offer; but even as we defend it, we must also, without any contradiction, see the legitimacy of many questions that the antiglobalization protesters ask. There may be a misdiagnosis about where the main problems lie (they do not lie in globalization, as such), but the ethical and human concerns that yield these questions call for serious reassessments of the adequacy of the national and global institutional arrangements that characterize the contemporary world and shape globalized economic and social relations.

Global capitalism is much more concerned with expanding the domain of market relations than with, say, establishing democracy, expanding elementary education, or enhancing the social opportunities of society's underdogs. Since globalization of markets is, on its own, a very inadequate approach to world prosperity, there is a need to go beyond the priorities that find expression in the chosen focus of global capitalism. As George Soros has pointed out, international business concerns often have a strong preference for working in orderly and highly organized autocracies rather than in activist and less-regimented democracies, and this can be a regressive influence on equitable development. Further, multinational firms can exert their influence on the priorities of public expenditure in less secure third-world countries by giving preference to the safety and convenience of the managerial classes and of privileged workers over the removal of widespread illiteracy, medical deprivation, and other adversities of the poor. These possibilities do not, of course, impose any insurmountable barrier to development, but it is important to make sure that the surmountable barriers are actually surmounted. [. . .]

Fair Sharing of Global Opportunities

To conclude, the confounding of globalization with Westernization is not only ahistorical, it also distracts attention from the many potential benefits of global integration. Globalization is a historical process that has offered an abundance of opportunities and rewards in the past and continues to do so today. The very existence of potentially large benefits makes the question of fairness in sharing the benefits of globalization so critically important.

The central issue of contention is not globalization itself, nor is it the use of the market as an institution, but the inequity in the overall balance of institutional arrangements – which produces very unequal sharing of the benefits of globalization.

The question is not just whether the poor, too, gain something from globalization, but whether they get a fair share and a fair opportunity. There is an urgent need for reforming institutional arrangements – in addition to national ones – in order to overcome both the errors of omission and those of commission that tend to give the poor across the world such limited opportunities. Globalization deserves a reasoned defense, but it also needs reform.

3 From the Great Transformation to the Global Free Market

John Gray

The collapse of the global marketplace would be a traumatic event with unimaginable consequences. Yet I find it easier to imagine than the continuation of the present regime.

George Soros

The origins of the catastrophe lay in the Utopian endeavour of economic liberalism to set up a self-regulating market system.

Karl Polanyi

Mid-nineteenth century England was the subject of a far-reaching experiment in social engineering. Its objective was to free economic life from social and political control and it did so by constructing a new institution, the free market, and by breaking up the more socially rooted markets that had existed in England for centuries. The free market created a new type of economy in which prices of all goods, including labour, changed without regard to their effects on society. In the past, economic life had been constrained by the need to maintain social cohesion. It was conducted in social markets – markets that were embedded in society and subject to many kinds of regulation and restraint. The goal of the experiment that was attempted in mid-Victorian England was to demolish these social markets, and replace them by deregulated markets that operated independently of social needs. The rupture in England's economic life produced by the creation of the free market has been called the Great Transformation.

The achievement of a similar transformation is the overriding objective today of transnational organizations such as the World Trade Organisation, the International Monetary Fund and the Organisation for Economic Cooperation and Development. In advancing this revolutionary project they are following the lead of the world's last great Enlightenment regime, the United States. The thinkers of the Enlightenment, such as Thomas Jefferson, Tom Paine, John Stuart Mill and Karl Marx never doubted that the future for every nation in the world was to accept some version of western institutions and values. A diversity of cultures was not a permanent condition of human life. It was a stage on the way to a universal civilization. All such thinkers advocated the creation of a single worldwide civilization, in which the varied traditions and cultures of the past were superseded by a new, universal community founded on reason.

The United States today is the last great power to base its policies on this enlightenment thesis. According to the 'Washington consensus', 'democratic capitalism' will soon be accepted throughout the world. A global free market will become a reality. The manifold economic cultures and systems that the world has always contained will be redundant. They will be merged into a single universal free market.

Transnational organizations animated by this philosophy have sought to impose free markets onto the economic life of societies throughout the world. They have implemented programmes of policies whose ultimate objective is to incorporate the world's diverse economies into a single global free market. This is a Utopia that can never be realized; its pursuit has already produced social dislocation and economic and political instability on a large scale.

In the United States free markets have contributed to social breakdown on a scale unknown in any other developed country. Families are weaker in America than in any other country. At the same time, social order has been propped up by a policy of mass incarceration. No other advanced industrial country, aside from post-communist Russia, uses imprisonment as a means of social control on the scale of the United States. Free markets, the desolation of families and communities and the use of the sanctions of criminal law as a last recourse against social collapse go in tandem.

Free markets have also weakened or destroyed other institutions on which social cohesion depends in the US. They have generated a long economic boom from which the majority of Americans has hardly benefited. Levels of inequality in the United States resemble those of Latin American countries more than those of any European society. Yet such direct consequences of the free market have not weakened support for it. It remains the sacred cow of American politics and has become identified with America's claim to be a model for a universal civilization. The Enlightenment project and the free market have become fatefully intertwined.

A single global market is the Enlightenment's project of a universal civilization in what is likely to be its final form. It is not the only variant of that project to have been attempted in a century that is littered with false Utopias. The former Soviet Union embodied a rival Enlightenment Utopia, that of a universal civilization in which markets were replaced by central planning. The human costs of that defunct Utopia were incalculable. Millions of lives were lost through totalitarian terror, ubiquitous corruption and apocalyptic environmental degradation. An immeasurable price in human suffering was exacted by the Soviet project – yet it failed to deliver the modernization it promised for Russia. At the close of the Soviet era Russia was in some ways further from modernity than it had been in late Tsarist times.

The Utopia of the global free market has not incurred a human cost in the way that communism did. Yet over time it may come to rival it in the suffering that it inflicts. Already it has resulted in over a hundred million peasants becoming migrant labourers in China, the exclusion from work and participation in society of tens of millions in the advanced societies, a condition of near-anarchy and rule by organized crime in parts of the post-communist world, and further devastation of the environment.

Even though a global free market cannot be reconciled with any kind of planned economy, what these Utopias have in common is more fundamental than their differences. In their cult of reason and efficiency, their ignorance of history and their contempt for the ways of life they consign to poverty or extinction, they embody the same rationalist hubris and cultural imperialism that have marked the central traditions of Enlightenment thinking throughout its history.

A global free market presupposes that economic modernization means the same thing everywhere. It interprets the globalization of the economy – the spread of industrial production into interconnected market economies throughout the world – as the inexorable advance of a singular type of western capitalism: the American free market.

The real history of our time is nearer the opposite. Economic modernization does not replicate the American free market system throughout the world. It works against the free market. It spawns indigenous types of capitalism that owe little to any western model.

The market economies of east Asia diverge deeply from one another, with those of China and Japan exemplifying different varieties of capitalism. Equally, Russian capitalism differs fundamentally from capitalism in China. All that these new species of capitalism have in common is that they are not converging on any western model.

The emergence of a truly global economy does not imply the extension of western values and institutions to the rest of humankind. It means the end of the epoch of western global supremacy. The original modern economies in England, western Europe and north America are not models for the new types of capitalism created by global markets. Most countries which try to refashion their economies on the model of Anglo-Saxon free markets will not achieve a sustainable modernity.

Today's Utopia of a single global market assumes that the economic life of every nation can be refashioned in the image of the American free market. Yet in the United States the free market has ruptured the liberal capitalist civilization, founded on Roosevelt's New Deal, on which its post-war prosperity rested. The United States is only the limiting case of a general truth. Wherever deregulated markets are promoted in late modern societies they engender new varieties of capitalism.

In China they have spawned a new variant of the capitalism practised by the Chinese diaspora throughout the world. In Russia the collapse of Soviet institutions has not produced free markets but instead a novel variety of post-communist anarcho-capitalism.

Nor is the growth of a world economy promoting the universal spread of western liberal democracy. In Russia it has produced a hybrid type of democratic government in which strong presidential power is central. In Singapore and Malaysia economic modernization and the growth have been achieved without loss of social cohesion by governments that reject the universal authority of liberal democracy. With luck, a similar government may emerge in China when it becomes fully post-communist.

A world economy does not make a single regime – 'democratic capitalism' – universal. It propagates new types of regimes as it spawns new kinds of capitalism. The global economy that is presently under construction will not assure the free market's future. It will trigger a new competition between remaining social market economies and free markets in which social markets must reform themselves profoundly or be destroyed. Yet, paradoxically, free market economies will not be the winners in this contest. For they too are being transformed out of all recognition by global competition.

The free market governments of the 1980s and 1990s failed to achieve many of their objectives. In Britain, levels of taxation and state spending were as high, or higher, after eighteen years of Thatcherite rule than they were when Labour fell from power in 1979.

Free market governments model their policies on the era of *laissez-faire* – the mid-nineteenth century period in which government claimed that it did not intervene in economic life. In reality a *laissez-faire* economy – that is to say, an economy in which markets are deregulated and put beyond the possibility of political or social control – cannot be reinvented. Even in its heyday it was a misnomer. It was created by state coercion, and depended at every point in its workings on the power of government. By the First World War the free market had ceased to exist in its most extreme form because it did not meet human needs – including the need for personal freedom.

Yet, without diminishing the size of the state or reinstating the social institutions that supported the free market in its Victorian heyday, free market policies have encouraged new inequalities in income, wealth, access to work and quality of life that rival those found in the vastly poorer world of the mid-nineteenth century. [. . .]

Economic globalization – the worldwide spread of industrial production and new technologies that is promoted by unrestricted mobility of capital and unfettered freedom of trade – actually threatens the stability of the single global market that is being constructed by American-led transnational organizations.

The central paradox of our time can be stated thus: economic globalization does not strengthen the current regime of global *laissez-faire*. It works to undermine it. There is nothing in today's global market that buffers it against the social strains arising from highly uneven economic development within and between the world's diverse societies. The swift waxing and waning of industries and livelihoods, the sudden shifts of production and capital, the casino of currency speculation – these conditions trigger political counter-movements that challenge the very ground rules of the global free market.

Today's worldwide free market lacks the political checks and balances which allowed its mid-Victorian precursor in England to wither away. It can be made more humanly tolerable for the citizens of states which pursue innovative and resourceful policies, but such reforms at the margin will not render the global free market much less unstable. Today's regime of global *laissez-faire* will be briefer than even the *belle époque* of 1870 to 1914, which ended in the trenches of the Great War. [. . .]

The False Dawn of the Global Free Market

[. . .] The natural counterpart of a free market economy is a politics of insecurity. If 'capitalism' means 'the free market', then no view is more deluded than the belief that the future lies with 'democratic capitalism'. In the normal course of democratic political life the free market is always short-lived. Its social costs are such that it cannot for long be legitimated in any democracy. This truth is demonstrated by the history of the free market in Britain, and it is well understood by more far-sighted neo-liberal thinkers who plan to make the free market global.

Those who seek to design a free market on a worldwide scale have always insisted that the legal framework which defines and entrenches it must be placed beyond the reach of any democratic legislature. Sovereign states may sign up to membership of the World Trade Organisation; but it is that organization, not the legislature of any sovereign state, which determines what is to count as free trade, and what a restraint of it. The rules of the game of the market must be elevated beyond any possibility of revision through democratic choice.

The role of a transnational organization such as the WTO is to project free markets into the economic life of every society. It does so by trying to compel adherence to the rules which release free markets from the encumbered or embedded markets that exist in every society. Transnational organizations can get away with this only insofar as they are immune from the pressures of democratic political life.

Polanyi's description of the legislation that was required to create a market economy in the nineteenth century applies with equal force to the project of the global free market today, as has been advanced through the World Trade Organisation and similar bodies.

> Nothing must be allowed to inhibit the formation of markets, nor must incomes be permitted to form other than through sales. Neither must there be any interference with the adjustment of prices to changed market conditions – whether the prices are those of goods, labour, land, or money. Hence there must not only be markets for all elements of industry, but no measure or policy must be countenanced that would influence the action of these markets. Neither price, nor supply, nor demand must be fixed or regulated; only such policies and measures are in order which help to ensure the self-regulation of the market by creating conditions which make the market the only organizing power in the economic sphere.

To be sure, this is an unrealizable fantasy; its pursuit by transnational bodies has produced economic dislocation, social chaos and political instability in hugely different countries throughout the world.

In the conditions in which it has been attempted in the late twentieth century, reinventing the free market has involved ambitious social engineering on a massive scale. No reformist programme today has a chance of success unless it understands that many of the changes produced, accelerated or reinforced by New Right policies are irreversible. Equally, no political reaction against the consequences of free-market policies will be effective that does not grasp the technological and economic transformations that such policies were able to harness.

Reinventing the free market has effected profound ruptures in the countries in which it has been attempted. The social and political settlements which it has destroyed – the Beveridge settlement in Britain and the Roosevelt New Deal in the United States – cannot now be recreated. The social market economies of continental Europe cannot be renewed as recognizable variants of post-war social or Christian democracy. Those who imagine that there can be a return to the 'normal politics' of post-war economic management are deluding themselves and others.

Even so, the free market has not succeeded in establishing the hegemonic power that was envisaged for it. In all democratic states the political supremacy of the free market is incomplete, precarious and soon undermined. It cannot easily survive periods of protracted economic setback. In Britain the unintended consequences of neo-liberal policies themselves weakened the New Right's hold on political power. The delicate coalition of electoral and economic constituencies that the New Right mobilized in support of its policies was soon scattered.

It was dissolved partly by the effects of New Right policies and partly by the forces that are loose in the world economy at large. New Right policies offered those who voted for them a chance of upward social mobility. Over time they undid the social structures in which such aspirations were framed. Moreover, they imposed heavy costs and risks on some aspirants to property-ownership. Those who have been immobilized by negative equity in their homes can hardly be expected to be enthusiastic about the regime of deregulation that landed them in their difficulties. The economic insecurities which New Right policies exacerbate were bound to weaken the initial coalitions that supported and benefited from these policies. Labour's landslide victory in May 1997 resulted partly from these self-undermining effects of the Tories' New Right policies.

However, the dislocations of social and economic life today are not caused solely by free markets. Ultimately they arise from the banalization of technology. Technological innovations made in advanced western countries are soon copied everywhere. Even without free-market policies the managed economies of the post-war period could not have survived – technological advance would have made them unsustainable.

New technologies make full employment policies of the traditional sort unworkable. The effect of information technologies is to throw the social division of labour into a flux. Many occupations are disappearing and all jobs are less secure. The division of labour in society is now less stable than it has been since the Industrial Revolution. What global markets do is to transmit this instability to every economy in the world, and in doing so they make a new politics of economic insecurity universal.

The free market cannot last in an age in which economic security for the majority of people is being reduced by the world economy. The regime of *laissez-faire* is bound to trigger counter-movements which reject its constraints. Such movements – whether populist and xenophobic, fundamentalist or neo-communist – can achieve few of their goals; but they can still rattle to pieces the brittle structures that support global *laissez-faire*. Must we accept that the world's economic life cannot be organized as a universal free market and that better forms of governance by global regulation are unachievable? Is a late modern anarchy our historical fate?

A reform of the world economy is needed that accepts a diversity of cultures, regimes and market economies as a permanent reality. A global free market belongs to a world in which western hegemony seemed assured. Like all other variants of the Enlightenment Utopia of a universal civilization it presupposes western supremacy. It does not square with a pluralist world in which there is no power that can hope to exercise the hegemony that Britain, the United States and other western states possessed in the past. It does not meet the needs of a time in which western institutions and values are no longer universally authoritative. It does not allow the world's manifold cultures to achieve modernizations that are adapted to their histories, circumstances and distinctive needs.

A global free market works to set sovereign states against one another in geopolitical struggles for dwindling natural resources. The effect of a *laissez-faire* philosophy which condemns state intervention in the economy is to impel states to become rivals for control of resources that no institution has any responsibility for conserving.

Nor, evidently, does a world economy that is organized as a global free market meet the universal human need for security. The *raison d'être* of governments everywhere is their ability to protect citizens from insecurity. A regime of global *laissez-faire* that prevents governments from discharging this protective role is creating the conditions for still greater political, and economic, instability.

In advanced economies that are competently and resourcefully governed, ways may be found in which the risks imposed on citizens by world markets can be mitigated. In poorer countries, global *laissez-faire* produces fundamentalist regimes and works as a catalyst for the disintegration of the modern state. At the global level, as at that of the nation-state, the free market does not promote stability or democracy. Global democratic capitalism is as unrealizable a condition as worldwide communism.

4 Jihad vs. McWorld

Benjamin Barber

History is not over. Nor are we arrived in the wondrous land of techné promised by the futurologists. The collapse of state communism has not delivered people to a safe democratic haven, and the past, fratricide and civil discord perduring, still clouds the horizon just behind us. Those who look back see all of the horrors of the ancient slaughterbench reenacted in disintegral nations like Bosnia, Sri Lanka, Ossetia, and Rwanda and they declare that nothing has changed. Those who look forward prophesy commercial and technological interdependence – a virtual paradise made possible by spreading markets and global technology – and they proclaim that everything is or soon will be different. The rival observers seem to consult different almanacs drawn from the libraries of contrarian planets.

Yet anyone who reads the daily papers carefully, taking in the front page accounts of civil carnage as well as the business page stories on the mechanics of the information superhighway and the economics of communication mergers, anyone who turns deliberately to take in the whole 360-degree horizon, knows that our world and our lives are caught between what William Butler Yeats called the two eternities of race and soul: that of race reflecting the tribal past, that of soul anticipating the cosmopolitan future. Our secular eternities are corrupted, however, race reduced to an insignia of resentment, and soul sized down to fit the demanding body by which it now measures its needs. Neither race nor soul offers us a future that is other than bleak, neither promises a polity that is remotely democratic.

The first scenario rooted in race holds out the grim prospect of a retribalization of large swaths of humankind by war and bloodshed: a threatened balkanization of nation-states in which culture is pitted against culture, people against people, tribe against tribe, a Jihad in the name of a hundred narrowly conceived faiths against every kind of interdependence, every kind of artificial social cooperation and mutuality: against technology, against pop culture, and against integrated markets; against modernity itself as well as the future in which modernity issues. The second paints that future in shimmering pastels, a busy portrait of onrushing economic, technological, and ecological forces that demand integration and uniformity and that mesmerize peoples everywhere with fast music, fast computers, and fast food – MTV, Macintosh, and McDonald's – pressing nations into one homogeneous global theme park, one McWorld tied together by communications, information, entertainment,

Original publication details: Excerpted from Benjamin Barber, "Introduction," in Benjamin Barber, *Jihad vs. McWorld* (Times Books, 1995), pp. 3–8, 9–10, 17–20. Benjamin R. Barber is Kekst Professor of Civil Society at the University of Maryland; Director of the New York office of the Democracy Collaborative; and the author of many books, including *Strong Democracy* (1984), *A Place for Us* (1998), *A Passion for Democracy: American Essays* (1998), and *The Truth of Power: Intellectual Affairs in the Clinton White House* (2001).

and commerce. Caught between Babel and Disneyland, the planet is falling precipi-
tously apart and coming reluctantly together at the very same moment.

Some stunned observers notice only Babel, complaining about the thousand newly
sundered "peoples" who prefer to address their neighbors with sniper rifles and
mortars; others – zealots in Disneyland – seize on futurological platitudes and the
promise of virtuality, exclaiming "It's a small world after all!" Both are right, but
how can that be?

We are compelled to choose between what passes as "the twilight of sovereignty"
and an entropic end of all history; or a return to the past's most fractious and de-
moralizing discord; to "the menace of global anarchy," to Milton's capital of hell,
Pandaemonium; to a world totally "out of control."

The apparent truth, which speaks to the paradox at the core of this book, is that
the tendencies of both Jihad *and* McWorld are at work, both visible sometimes
in the same country at the very same instant. Iranian zealots keep one ear tuned
to the mullahs urging holy war and the other cocked to Rupert Murdoch's Star
television beaming in *Dynasty, Donahue,* and *The Simpsons* from hovering satellites.
Chinese entrepreneurs vie for the attention of party cadres in Beijing and simultaneously pursue KFC franchises in cities like Nanjing, Hangzhou, and Xian where
twenty-eight outlets serve over 100,000 customers a day. The Russian Orthodox
church, even as it struggles to renew the ancient faith, has entered a joint venture
with California businessmen to bottle and sell natural waters under the rubric
Saint Springs Water Company. Serbian assassins wear Adidas sneakers and listen to
Madonna on Walkman headphones as they take aim through their gunscopes at
scurrying Sarajevo civilians looking to fill family watercans. Orthodox Hasids and
brooding neo-Nazis have both turned to rock music to get their traditional messages
out to the new generation, while fundamentalists plot virtual conspiracies on the
Internet.

Now neither Jihad nor McWorld is in itself novel. History ending in the triumph
of science and reason or some monstrous perversion thereof (Mary Shelley's Doctor
Frankenstein) has been the leitmotiv of every philosopher and poet who has regret-
ted the Age of Reason since the Enlightenment. Yeats lamented "the center will not
hold, mere anarchy is loosed upon the world," and observers of Jihad today have
little but historical detail to add. The Christian parable of the Fall and of the possibilities of redemption that it makes possible captures the eighteenth-century ambivalence – and our own – about past and future. I want, however, to do more than dress
up the central paradox of human history in modern clothes. It is not Jihad and
McWorld but the relationship between them that most interests me. For, squeezed
between their opposing forces, the world has been sent spinning out of control. Can
it be that what Jihad and McWorld have in common is anarchy: the absence of
common will and that conscious and collective human control under the guidance
of law we call democracy?

Progress moves in steps that sometimes lurch backwards; in history's twisting
maze, Jihad not only revolts against but abets McWorld, while McWorld not only
imperils but re-creates and reinforces Jihad. They produce their contraries and need
one another. My object here then is not simply to offer sequential portraits of
McWorld and Jihad, but while examining McWorld, to keep Jihad in my field of
vision, and while dissecting Jihad, never to forget the context of McWorld. Call it a
dialectic of McWorld: a study in the cunning of reason that does honor to the radical
differences that distinguish Jihad and McWorld yet that acknowledges their powerful and paradoxical interdependence.

There is a crucial difference, however, between my modest attempt at dialectic and that of the masters of the nineteenth century. Still seduced by the Enlightenment's faith in progress, both Hegel and Marx believed reason's cunning was on the side of progress. But it is harder to believe that the clash of Jihad and McWorld will issue in some overriding good. The outcome seems more likely to pervert than to nurture human liberty. The two may, in opposing each other, work to the same ends, work in apparent tension yet in covert harmony, but democracy is not their beneficiary. In East Berlin, tribal communism has yielded to capitalism. In Marx-Engelsplatz, the stolid, overbearing statues of Marx and Engels face east, as if seeking distant solace from Moscow: but now, circling them along the streets that surround the park that is their prison are chain eateries like TGI Friday's, international hotels like the Radisson, and a circle of neon billboards mocking them with brand names like Panasonic, Coke, and GoldStar. New gods, yes, but more liberty?

What then does it mean in concrete terms to view Jihad and McWorld dialectically when the tendencies of the two sets of forces initially appear so intractably antithetical? After all, Jihad and McWorld operate with equal strength in opposite directions, the one driven by parochial hatreds, the other by universalizing markets, the one re-creating ancient subnational and ethnic borders from within, the other making national borders porous from without. Yet Jihad and McWorld have this in common: they both make war on the sovereign nation-state and thus undermine the nation-state's democratic institutions. Each eschews civil society and belittles democratic citizenship, neither seeks alternative democratic institutions. Their common thread is indifference to civil liberty. Jihad forges communities of blood rooted in exclusion and hatred, communities that slight democracy in favor of tyrannical paternalism or consensual tribalism. McWorld forges global markets rooted in consumption and profit, leaving to an untrustworthy, if not altogether fictitious, invisible hand issues of public interest and common good that once might have been nurtured by democratic citizenries and their watchful governments. Such governments, intimidated by market ideology, are actually pulling back at the very moment they ought to be aggressively intervening. What was once understood as protecting the public interest is now excoriated as heavy-handed regulatory browbeating. Justice yields to markets, even though, as Felix Rohatyn has bluntly confessed, "there is a brutal Darwinian logic to these markets. They are nervous and greedy. They look for stability and transparency, but what they reward is not always our preferred form of democracy." If the traditional conservators of freedom were democratic constitutions and Bills of Rights, "the new temples to liberty," George Steiner suggests, "will be McDonald's and Kentucky Fried Chicken."

In being reduced to a choice between the market's universal church and a re-tribalizing politics of particularist identities, peoples around the globe are threatened with an atavistic return to medieval politics where local tribes and ambitious emperors together ruled the world entire, women and men united by the universal abstraction of Christianity even as they lived out isolated lives in warring fiefdoms defined by involuntary (ascriptive) forms of identity. This was a world in which princes and kings had little real power until they conceived the ideology of nationalism. Nationalism established government on a scale greater than the tribe yet less cosmopolitan than the universal church and in time gave birth to those intermediate, gradually more democratic institutions that would come to constitute the nation-state. Today, at the far end of this history, we seem intent on re-creating a world in which our only choices are the secular universalism of the cosmopolitan market and the everyday particularism of the fractious tribe.

In the tumult of the confrontation between global commerce and parochial ethnicity, the virtues of the democratic nation are lost and the instrumentalities by which it permitted peoples to transform themselves into nations and seize sovereign power in the name of liberty and the commonweal are put at risk. Neither Jihad nor McWorld aspires to resecure the civic virtues undermined by its denationalizing practices; neither global markets nor blood communities service public goods or pursue equality and justice. Impartial judiciaries and deliberative assemblies play no role in the roving killer bands that speak on behalf of newly liberated "peoples," and such democratic institutions have at best only marginal influence on the roving multinational corporations that speak on behalf of newly liberated markets. Jihad pursues a bloody politics of identity, McWorld a bloodless economics of profit. Belonging by default to McWorld, everyone is a consumer; seeking a repository for identity, everyone belongs to some tribe. But no one is a citizen. Without citizens, how can there be democracy? [. . .]

Jihad is, I recognize, a strong term. In its mildest form, it betokens religious struggle on behalf of faith, a kind of Islamic zeal. In its strongest political manifestation, it means bloody holy war on behalf of partisan identity that is metaphysically defined and fanatically defended. Thus, while for many Muslims it may signify only ardor in the name of a religion that can properly be regarded as universalizing (if not quite ecumenical), I borrow its meaning from those militants who make the slaughter of the "other" a higher duty. I use the term in its militant construction to suggest dogmatic and violent particularism of a kind known to Christians no less than Muslims, to Germans and Hindis as well as to Arabs. The phenomena to which I apply the phrase have innocent enough beginnings: identity politics and multicultural diversity can represent strategies of a free society trying to give expression to its diversity. What ends as Jihad may begin as a simple search for a local identity, some set of common personal attributes to hold out against the numbing and neutering uniformities of industrial modernization and the colonizing culture of McWorld.

America is often taken as the model for this kind of benign multiculturalism, although we too have our critics like Arthur Schlesinger, Jr., for whom multiculturalism is never benign and for whom it signals the inaugural logic of a long-term disintegration. Indeed, I will have occasion to write about an "American Jihad" being waged by the radical Right. The startling fact is that less than 10 percent (about twenty) of the modern world's states are truly homogeneous and thus, like Denmark or the Netherlands, can't get smaller unless they fracture into tribes or clans. In only half is there a single ethnic group that comprises even 75 percent of the population. As in the United States, multiculturalism is the rule, homogeneity the exception. Nations like Japan or Spain that appear to the outside world as integral turn out to be remarkably multicultural. And even if language alone, the nation's essential attribute, is made the condition for self-determination, a count of the number of languages spoken around the world suggests the community of nations could grow to over six thousand members.

The modern nation-state has actually acted as a cultural integrator and has adapted well to pluralist ideals: civic ideologies and constitutional faiths around which their many clans and tribes can rally. It has not been too difficult to contrive a civil religion for Americans or French or Swiss, since these "peoples" actually contain multitudes of subnational factions and ethnic tribes earnestly seeking common ground. But for Basques and Normans? What need have they for anything but blood and memory? And what of Alsatians, Bavarians, and East Prussians? Kurds, Ossetians, East Timorese, Quebecois, Abkhazians, Catalonians, Tamils, Inkatha Zulus, Kurile Islander Japanese – peoples without countries inhabiting nations they cannot call their own? Peoples trying to seal themselves off not just from others but from modernity? These are frightened tribes running not to but from civic faith in search of something more palpable and electrifying. How will peoples who define themselves by the slaughter of tribal neighbors be persuaded to subscribe to some flimsy artificial faith organized around abstract civic ideals or commercial markets? Can advertising divert warriors of blood from the genocide required by their ancient grievances? [. . .]

McWorld is a product of popular culture driven by expansionist commerce. Its template is American, its form style. Its goods are as much images as matériel, an aesthetic as well as a product line. It is about culture as commodity, apparel as ideology. Its symbols are Harley-Davidson motorcycles and Cadillac motorcars hoisted from the roadways, where they once represented a mode of transportation, to the marquees of global market cafés like Harley-Davidson's and the Hard Rock where they become icons of lifestyle. You don't drive them, you feel their vibes and rock to the images they conjure up from old movies and new celebrities, whose personal appearances are the key to the wildly popular international café chain Planet Hollywood. Music, video, theater, books, and theme parks – the new churches of a commercial civilization in which malls are the public squares and suburbs the neighborless neighborhoods – are all constructed as image exports creating a common world taste around common logos, advertising slogans, stars, songs, brand names, jingles, and trademarks. Hard power yields to soft, while ideology is transmuted into a kind of videology that works through sound bites and film clips. Videology is fuzzier and less dogmatic than traditional political ideology: it may as a consequence be far more successful in instilling the novel values required for global markets to succeed.

McWorld's videology remains Jihad's most formidable rival, and in the long run it may attenuate the force of Jihad's recidivist tribalisms. Yet the information revolution's instrumentalities are also Jihad's favored weapons. Hutu or Bosnian Serb identity was less a matter of real historical memory than of media propaganda by a leadership set on liquidating rival clans. In both Rwanda and Bosnia, radio broadcasts whipped listeners into a killing frenzy. As *New York Times* rock critic Jon Pareles has noticed, "regionalism in pop music has become as trendy as microbrewery beer and narrowcasting cable channels, and for the same reasons." The global culture is what gives the local culture its medium, its audience, and its aspirations. Fascist pop and Hasid rock are not oxymorons; rather they manifest the dialectics of McWorld in particularly dramatic ways. Belgrade's radio includes stations that broadcast Western pop music as a rebuke to hard-liner Milosevic's supernationalist government and stations that broadcast native folk tunes laced with antiforeign and anti-Semitic sentiments. Even the Internet has its neo-Nazi bulletin boards and Turk-trashing Armenian "flamers" (who assail every use of the word *turkey*, fair and fowl alike, so to speak), so that the abstractions of cyberspace too are infected with a peculiar and rabid cultural territoriality all their own.

The dynamics of the Jihad–McWorld linkage are deeply dialectical. Japan has, for example, become more culturally insistent on its own traditions in recent years even as its people seek an ever greater purchase on McWorld. In 1992, the number-one restaurant in Japan measured by volume of customers was McDonald's, followed in the number-two spot by the Colonel's Kentucky Fried Chicken. In France, where cultural purists complain bitterly of a looming Sixième République ("la République Américaine"), the government attacks "franglais" even as it funds EuroDisney park just outside of Paris. In the same spirit, the cinema industry makes war on American film imports while it bestows upon Sylvester Stallone one of France's highest honors, the Chevalier des arts et lettres. Ambivalence also stalks India. Just outside of Bombay, cheek by jowl with villages still immersed in poverty and notorious for the informal execution of unwanted female babies or, even, wives, can be found a new town known as SCEEPZ – the Santa Cruz Electronic Export Processing Zone – where Hindi-, Tamil-, and Mahratti-speaking computer programmers write software for Swissair, AT&T, and other labor-cost-conscious multinationals. India is thus at once a major exemplar of ancient ethnic and religious tensions and "an emerging power in the international software industry." To go to work at SCEEPZ, says an employee, is "like crossing an international border." Not into another country, but into the virtual nowhere-land of McWorld.

More dramatic even than in India, is the strange interplay of Jihad and McWorld in the remnants of Yugoslavia. In an affecting *New Republic* report, Slavenka Drakulic told the brief tragic love story of Admira and Bosko, two young star-crossed lovers from Sarajevo: "They were born in the late 1960s," she writes. "They watched Spielberg movies; they listened to Iggy Pop; they read John le Carré; they went to a disco every Saturday night and fantasized about traveling to Paris or London." Longing for safety, it seems they finally negotiated with all sides for safe passage, and readied their departure from Sarajevo. Before they could cross the magical border that separates their impoverished lane from the seeming sanctuary of McWorld, Jihad caught up to them. Their bodies lay along the riverbank, riddled with bullets from anonymous snipers for whom safe passage signaled an invitation to target practice. The murdered young lovers, as befits émigrés to McWorld, were clothed in jeans and sneakers. So too, one imagines, were their murderers.

Further east, tourists seeking a piece of old Russia that does not take them too far from MTV can find traditional Matryoshka nesting dolls (that fit one inside the other) featuring the nontraditional visages of (from largest to smallest) Bruce Springsteen, Madonna, Boy George, Dave Stewart, and Annie Lennox.

In Russia, in India, in Bosnia, in Japan, and in France too, modern history then leans both ways: toward the meretricious inevitability of McWorld, but also into Jihad's stiff winds, heaving to and fro and giving heart both to the Panglossians and the Pandoras, sometimes for the very same reasons. The Panglossians bank on EuroDisney and Microsoft, while the Pandoras await nihilism and a world in Pandaemonium. Yet McWorld and Jihad do not really force a choice between such polarized scenarios. Together, they are likely to produce some stifling amalgam of the two suspended in chaos. Antithetical in every detail, Jihad and McWorld nonetheless conspire to undermine our hard-won (if only half-won) civil liberties and the possibility of a global democratic future. In the short run the forces of Jihad, noisier and more obviously nihilistic than those of McWorld, are likely to dominate the near future, etching small stories of local tragedy and regional genocide on the face of our times and creating a climate of instability marked by multimicrowars inimical to global integration. But in the long run, the forces of McWorld are the forces underlying the slow certain thrust of Western civilization and as such may be unstoppable. Jihad's microwars will hold the headlines well into the next century, making predictions of the end of history look terminally dumb. But McWorld's homogenization is likely to establish a macropeace that favors the triumph of commerce and its markets and to give to those who control information, communication, and entertainment ultimate (if inadvertent) control over human destiny. Unless we can offer an alternative to the struggle between Jihad and McWorld, the epoch on whose threshold we stand – postcommunist, postindustrial, postnational, yet sectarian, fearful, and bigoted – is likely also to be terminally postdemocratic.

5 The Clash of Civilizations?

Samuel P. Huntington

The Next Pattern of Conflict

World politics is entering a new phase, and intellectuals have not hesitated to prolif-erate visions of what it will be – the end of history, the return of traditional rivalries between nation states, and the decline of the nation state from the conflicting pulls of tribalism and globalism, among others. Each of these visions catches aspects of the emerging reality. Yet they all miss a crucial, indeed a central, aspect of what global politics is likely to be in the coming years.

It is my hypothesis that the fundamental source of conflict in this new world will not be primarily ideological or primarily economic. The great divisions among humankind and the dominating source of conflict will be cultural. Nation states will remain the most powerful actors in world affairs, but the principal conflicts of global politics will occur between nations and groups of different civilizations. The clash of civilizations will dominate global politics. The fault lines between civilizations will be the battle lines of the future.

Conflict between civilizations will be the latest phase in the evolution of conflict in the modern world. For a century and a half after the emergence of the modern international system with the Peace of Westphalia, the conflicts of the Western world were largely among princes – emperors, absolute monarchs and constitutional monarchs attempting to expand their bureaucracies, their armies, their mercantilist economic strength and, most important, the territory they ruled. In the process they created nation states, and beginning with the French Revolution the principal lines of conflict were between nations rather than princes. In 1793, as R. R. Palmer put it, "The wars of kings were over; the wars of peoples had begun." This nineteenth-century pattern lasted until the end of World War I. Then, as a result of the Russian Revolution and the reaction against it, the conflict of nations yielded to the conflict of ideologies, first among communism, fascism-Nazism and liberal democracy, and then between communism and liberal democracy. During the Cold War, this latter conflict became embodied in the struggle between the two superpowers, neither of which was a nation state in the classical European sense and each of which defined its identity in terms of its ideology.

These conflicts between princes, nation states and ideologies were primarily conflicts within Western civilization, "Western civil wars," as William Lind has labeled them. This was as true of the Cold War as it was of the world wars and the

Original publication details: Excerpted from Samuel Huntington, "The Clash of Civilizations?," *Foreign Affairs*, 72, 3, Summer 1993, pp. 22–3, 25–32, 39–41, 49. Copyright © 1993 by the Council on Foreign Relations, Inc. Reprinted by permission of *Foreign Affairs*.

earlier wars of the seventeenth, eighteenth and nineteenth centuries. With the end of the Cold War, international politics moves out of its Western phase, and its centerpiece becomes the interaction between the West and non-Western civilizations and among non-Western civilizations. In the politics of civilizations, the peoples and governments of non-Western civilizations no longer remain the objects of history as targets of Western colonialism but join the West as movers and shapers of history. [...]

Why Civilizations Will Clash

Civilization identity will be increasingly important in the future, and the world will be shaped in large measure by the interactions among seven or eight major civilizations. These include Western, Confucian, Japanese, Islamic, Hindu, Slavic-Orthodox, Latin American and possibly African civilizations. The most important conflicts of the future will occur along the cultural fault lines separating these civilizations from one another.

Why will this be the case?

First, differences among civilizations are not only real; they are basic. Civilizations are differentiated from each other by history, language, culture, tradition and, most important, religion. The people of different civilizations have different views on the relations between God and man, the individual and the group, the citizen and the state, parents and children, husband and wife, as well as differing views of the relative importance of rights and responsibilities, liberty and authority, equality and hierarchy. These differences are the product of centuries. They will not soon disappear. They are far more fundamental than differences among political ideologies and political regimes. Differences do not necessarily mean conflict, and conflict does not necessarily mean violence. Over the centuries, however, differences among civilizations have generated the most prolonged and the most violent conflicts.

Second, the world is becoming a smaller place. The interactions between peoples of different civilizations are increasing; these increasing interactions intensify civilization consciousness and awareness of differences between civilizations and commonalities within civilizations. North African immigration to France generates hostility among Frenchmen and at the same time increased receptivity to immigration by "good" European Catholic Poles. Americans react far more negatively to Japanese investment than to larger investments from Canada and European countries. Similarly, as Donald Horowitz has pointed out, "An Ibo may be . . . an Owerri Ibo or an Onitsha Ibo in what was the Eastern region of Nigeria. In Lagos, he is simply an Ibo. In London, he is a Nigerian. In New York, he is an African." The interactions among peoples of different civilizations enhance the civilization-consciousness of people that, in turn, invigorates differences and animosities stretching or thought to stretch back deep into history.

Third, the processes of economic modernization and social change throughout the world are separating people from longstanding local identities. They also weaken the nation state as a source of identity. In much of the world religion has moved in to fill this gap, often in the form of movements that are labeled "fundamentalist." Such movements are found in Western Christianity, Judaism, Buddhism and Hinduism, as well as in Islam. In most countries and most religions the people active in fundamentalist movements are young, college-educated, middle-class technicians, professionals and business persons. The "unsecularization of the world," George Weigel has remarked, "is one of the dominant social facts of life in the late twentieth century." The revival of religion, "la revanche de Dieu," as Gilles Kepel labeled it, provides a basis for identity and commitment that transcends national boundaries and unites civilizations.

Fourth, the growth of civilization-consciousness is enhanced by the dual role of the West. On the one hand, the West is at a peak of power. At the same time, however, and perhaps as a result, a return to the roots phenomenon is occurring among non-Western civilizations. Increasingly one hears references to trends toward a turning inward and "Asianization" in Japan, the end of the Nehru legacy and the "Hinduization" of India, the failure of Western ideas of socialism and nationalism and hence "re-Islamization" of the Middle East, and now a debate over Westernization versus Russianization in Boris Yeltsin's country. A West at the peak of its power confronts non-Wests that increasingly have the desire, the will and the resources to shape the world in non-Western ways.

In the past, the elites of non-Western societies were usually the people who were most involved with the West, had been educated at Oxford, the Sorbonne or Sandhurst, and had absorbed Western attitudes and values. At the same time, the populace in non-Western countries often remained deeply imbued with the indigenous culture. Now, however, these relationships are being reversed. A de-Westernization and indigenization of elites is occurring in many non-Western countries at the same time that Western, usually American, cultures, styles and habits become more popular among the mass of the people.

Fifth, cultural characteristics and differences are less mutable and hence less easily compromised and resolved than political and economic ones. In the former Soviet Union, communists can become democrats, the rich can become poor and the poor rich, but Russians cannot become Estonians and Azeris cannot become Armenians. In class and ideological conflicts, the key question was "Which side are you on?" and people could and did choose sides and change sides. In conflicts between civilizations, the question is "What are you?" That is a given that cannot be changed. And as we know, from Bosnia to the Caucasus to the Sudan, the wrong answer to that question can mean a bullet in the head. Even more than ethnicity, religion discriminates sharply and exclusively among people. A person can be half-French and half-Arab and simultaneously even a citizen of two countries. It is more difficult to be half-Catholic and half-Muslim.

Finally, economic regionalism is increasing. The proportions of total trade that were intraregional rose between 1980 and 1989 from 51 percent to 59 percent in Europe, 33 percent to 37 percent in East Asia, and 32 percent to 36 percent in North America. The importance of regional economic blocs is likely to continue to increase in the future. On the one hand, successful economic regionalism will reinforce civilization-consciousness. On the other hand, economic regionalism may succeed only when it is rooted in a common civilization. The European Community rests on the shared foundation of European culture and Western Christianity. The success of the North American Free Trade Area depends on the convergence now underway of Mexican, Canadian and American cultures. Japan, in contrast, faces difficulties in creating a comparable economic entity in East Asia because Japan is a society and civilization unique to itself. However strong the trade and investment links Japan may develop with other East Asian countries, its cultural differences with those countries inhibit and perhaps preclude its promoting regional economic integration like that in Europe and North America.

Common culture, in contrast, is clearly facilitating the rapid expansion of the economic relations between the People's Republic of China and Hong Kong, Taiwan,

Singapore and the overseas Chinese communities in other Asian countries. With the Cold War over, cultural commonalities increasingly overcome ideological differences, and mainland China and Taiwan move closer together. If cultural commonality is a prerequisite for economic integration, the principal East Asian economic bloc of the future is likely to be centered on China. This bloc is, in fact, already coming into existence. As Murray Weidenbaum has observed,

> Despite the current Japanese dominance of the region, the Chinese-based economy of Asia is rapidly emerging as a new epicenter for industry, commerce and finance. This strategic area contains substantial amounts of technology and manufacturing capability (Taiwan), outstanding entrepreneurial, marketing and services acumen (Hong Kong), a fine communications network (Singapore), a tremendous pool of financial capital (all three), and very large endowments of land, resources and labor (mainland China) ... From Guangzhou to Singapore, from Kuala Lumpur to Manila, this influential network – often based on extensions of the traditional clans – has been described as the backbone of the East Asian economy.

Culture and religion also form the basis of the Economic Cooperation Organization, which brings together ten non-Arab Muslim countries: Iran, Pakistan, Turkey, Azerbaijan, Kazakhstan, Kyrgyzstan, Turkmenistan, Tadjikistan, Uzbekistan and Afghanistan. One impetus to the revival and expansion of this organization, founded originally in the 1960s by Turkey, Pakistan and Iran, is the realization by the leaders of several of these countries that they had no chance of admission to the European Community. Similarly, Caricom, the Central American Common Market and Mercosur rest on common cultural foundations. Efforts to build a broader Caribbean-Central American economic entity bridging the Anglo-Latin divide, however, have to date failed.

As people define their identity in ethnic and religious terms, they are likely to see an "us" versus "them" relation existing between themselves and people of different ethnicity or religion. The end of ideologically defined states in Eastern Europe and the former Soviet Union permits traditional ethnic identities and animosities to come to the fore. Differences in culture and religion create differences over policy issues, ranging from human rights to immigration to trade and commerce to the environment. Geographical propinquity gives rise to conflicting territorial claims from Bosnia to Mindanao. Most important, the efforts of the West to promote its values of democracy and liberalism as universal values, to maintain its military predominance and to advance its economic interests engender countering responses from other civilizations. Decreasingly able to mobilize support and form coalitions on the basis of ideology, governments and groups will increasingly attempt to mobilize support by appealing to common religion and civilization identity.

The clash of civilizations thus occurs at two levels. At the micro-level, adjacent groups along the fault lines between civilizations struggle, often violently, over the control of territory and each other. At the macro-level, states from different civilizations compete for relative military and economic power, struggle over the control of international institutions and third parties, and competitively promote their particular political and religious values.

The Fault Lines between Civilizations

The fault lines between civilizations are replacing the political and ideological boundaries of the Cold War as the flash points for crisis and bloodshed. The Cold War began when the Iron Curtain divided Europe politically and ideologically. The Cold War ended with the end of the Iron Curtain. As the ideological division of Europe has disappeared, the cultural division of Europe between Western Christianity, on the one hand, and Orthodox Christianity and Islam, on the other, has reemerged. The most significant dividing line in Europe, as William Wallace has suggested, may well be the eastern boundary of Western Christianity in the year 1500. This line runs along what are now the boundaries between Finland and Russia and between the Baltic states and Russia, cuts through Belarus and Ukraine separating the more Catholic western Ukraine from Orthodox eastern Ukraine, swings westward separating Transylvania from the rest of Romania, and then goes through Yugoslavia almost exactly along the line now separating Croatia and Slovenia from the rest of Yugoslavia. In the Balkans this line, of course, coincides with the historic boundary between the Hapsburg and Ottoman empires. The peoples to the north and west of this line are Protestant or Catholic; they shared the common experiences of European history – feudalism, the Renaissance, the Reformation, the Enlightenment, the French Revolution, the Industrial Revolution; they are generally economically better off than the peoples to the east; and they may now look forward to increasing involvement in a common European economy and to the consolidation of democratic political systems. The peoples to the east and south of this line are Orthodox or Muslim; they historically belonged to the Ottoman or Tsarist empires and were only lightly touched by the shaping events in the rest of Europe; they are generally less advanced economically; they seem much less likely to develop stable democratic political systems. The Velvet Curtain of culture has replaced the Iron Curtain of ideology as the most significant dividing line in Europe. As the events in Yugoslavia show, it is not only a line of difference; it is also at times a line of bloody conflict.

Conflict along the fault line between Western and Islamic civilizations has been going on for 1,300 years. After the founding of Islam, the Arab and Moorish surge west and north only ended at Tours in 732. From the eleventh to the thirteenth century the Crusaders attempted with temporary success to bring Christianity and Christian rule to the Holy Land. From the fourteenth to the seventeenth century, the Ottoman Turks reversed the balance, extended their sway over the Middle East and the Balkans, captured Constantinople, and twice laid siege to Vienna. In the nineteenth and early twentieth centuries as Ottoman power declined Britain, France, and Italy established Western control over most of North Africa and the Middle East.

After World War II, the West, in turn, began to retreat; the colonial empires disappeared; first Arab nationalism and then Islamic fundamentalism manifested themselves; the West became heavily dependent on the Persian Gulf countries for its energy; the oil-rich Muslim countries became money-rich and, when they wished to, weapons-rich. Several wars occurred between Arabs and Israel (created by the West). France fought a bloody and ruthless war in Algeria for most of the 1950s; British and French forces invaded Egypt in 1956; American forces went into Lebanon in 1958; subsequently American forces returned to Lebanon, attacked Libya, and engaged in various military encounters with Iran; Arab and Islamic terrorists, supported by at least three Middle Eastern governments, employed the weapon of the weak and bombed Western planes and installations and seized Western hostages. This warfare between Arabs and the West culminated in 1990, when the United States sent a massive army to the Persian Gulf to defend some Arab countries against aggression by another. In its aftermath NATO planning is increasingly directed to potential threats and instability along its "southern tier."

This centuries-old military interaction between the West and Islam is unlikely to decline. It could become more virulent. The Gulf War left some Arabs feeling proud that Saddam Hussein had attacked Israel and stood up to the West. It also left many feeling humiliated and resentful of the West's military presence in the Persian Gulf, the West's overwhelming military dominance, and their own apparent inability to shape their destiny. Many Arab countries, in addition to the oil exporters, are reaching levels of economic and social development where autocratic forms of government become inappropriate and efforts to introduce democracy become stronger. Some openings in Arab political systems have already occurred. The principal beneficiaries of these openings have been Islamist movements. In the Arab world, in short, Western democracy strengthens anti-Western political forces. This may be a passing phenomenon, but it surely complicates relations between Islamic countries and the West. [. . .]

The West versus the Rest

The west is now at an extraordinary peak of power in relation to other civilizations. Its superpower opponent has disappeared from the map. Military conflict among Western states is unthinkable, and Western military power is unrivaled. Apart from Japan, the West faces no economic challenge. It dominates international political and security institutions and with Japan international economic institutions. Global political and security issues are effectively settled by a directorate of the United States, Britain and France, world economic issues by a directorate of the United States, Germany and Japan, all of which maintain extraordinarily close relations with each other to the exclusion of lesser and largely non-Western countries. Decisions made at the UN Security Council or in the International Monetary Fund that reflect the interests of the West are presented to the world as reflecting the desires of the world community. The very phrase "the world community" has become the euphemistic collective noun (replacing "the Free World") to give global legitimacy to actions reflecting the interests of the United States and other Western powers. Through the IMF and other international economic institutions, the West promotes its economic interests and imposes on other nations the economic policies it thinks appropriate. In any poll of non-Western peoples, the IMF undoubtedly would win the support of finance ministers and a few others, but get an overwhelmingly unfavorable rating from just about everyone else, who would agree with Georgy Arbatov's characterization of IMF officials as "neo-Bolsheviks who love expropriating other people's money, imposing undemocratic and alien rules of economic and political conduct and stifling economic freedom."

Western domination of the UN Security Council and its decisions, tempered only by occasional abstention by China, produced UN legitimation of the West's use of force to drive Iraq out of Kuwait and its elimination of Iraq's sophisticated weapons and capacity to produce such weapons. It also produced the quite unprecedented action by the United States, Britain and France in getting the Security Council to demand that Libya hand over the Pan Am 103 bombing suspects and then to impose sanctions when Libya refused. After defeating the largest Arab army, the West did not hesitate to throw its weight around in the Arab world. The West in effect is using international institutions, military power and economic resources to run the world in ways that will maintain Western predominance, protect Western interests and promote Western political and economic values.

That at least is the way in which non-Westerners see the new world, and there is a significant element of truth in their view. Differences in power and struggles for military, economic and institutional power are thus one source of conflict between the West and other civilizations. Differences in culture, that is basic values and beliefs, are a second source of conflict. V. S. Naipaul has argued that Western civilization is the "universal civilization" that "fits all men." At a superficial level much of Western culture has indeed permeated the rest of the world. At a more basic level, however, Western concepts differ fundamentally from those prevalent in other civilizations. Western ideas of individualism, liberalism, constitutionalism, human rights, equality, liberty, the rule of law, democracy, free markets, the separation of church and state, often have little resonance in Islamic, Confucian, Japanese, Hindu, Buddhist or Orthodox cultures. Western efforts to propagate such ideas produce instead a reaction against "human rights imperialism" and a reaffirmation of indigenous values, as can be seen in the support for religious fundamentalism by the younger generation in non-Western cultures. The very notion that there could be a "universal civilization" is a Western idea, directly at odds with the particularism of most Asian societies and their emphasis on what distinguishes one people from another. Indeed, the author of a review of 100 comparative studies of values in different societies concluded that "the values that are most important in the West are least important worldwide." In the political realm, of course, these differences are most manifest in the efforts of the United States and other Western powers to induce other peoples to adopt Western ideas concerning democracy and human rights. Modern democratic government originated in the West. When it has developed in non-Western societies it has usually been the product of Western colonialism or imposition.

The central axis of world politics in the future is likely to be, in Kishore Mahbubani's phrase, the conflict between "the West and the Rest" and the responses of non-Western civilizations to Western power and values. Those responses generally take one or a combination of three forms. At one extreme, non-Western states can, like Burma and North Korea, attempt to pursue a course of isolation, to insulate their societies from penetration or "corruption" by the West, and, in effect, to opt out of participation in the Western-dominated global community. The costs of this course, however, are high, and few states have pursued it exclusively. A second alternative, the equivalent of "bandwagoning" in international relations theory, is to attempt to join the West and accept its values and institutions. The third alternative is to attempt to "balance" the West by developing economic and military power and cooperating with other non-Western societies against the West, while preserving indigenous values and institutions; in short, to modernize but not to Westernize. [. . .]

Western civilization is both Western and modern. Non-Western civilizations have attempted to become modern without becoming Western. To date only Japan has fully succeeded in this quest. Non-Western civilizations will continue to attempt to acquire the wealth, technology, skills, machines and weapons that are part of being modern. They will also attempt to reconcile this modernity with their traditional culture and values. Their economic and military strength relative to the West will increase. Hence the West will increasingly have to accommodate these non-Western modern civilizations whose power approaches that of the West but whose values and interests differ significantly from those of the West. This will require the West to maintain the economic and military power necessary to protect its interests in relation to these civilizations. It will also, however, require the West to develop a more profound understanding of the basic religious and philosophical assumptions underlying other civilizations and the ways in which people in those civilizations see their interests. It will require an effort to identify elements of commonality between Western and other civilizations. For the relevant future, there will be no universal civilization, but instead a world of different civilizations, each of which will have to learn to coexist with the others.

6 A Global Ethic as a Foundation for Global Society

Hans Küng

An ethical consensus – an agreement on particular values, criteria, attitudes – as a basis for the world society that is coming into being: is that not a great, beautiful illusion? In view of the differences which have always existed between nations, cultures and religions; in view of the current tendencies and trends towards cultural, linguistic and religious self-assertion; in view even of the widespread cultural nationalism, linguistic chauvinism and religious fundamentalism, is it possible to envisage any ethical consensus at all, let alone in global dimensions? However, one can also argue in the opposite direction: precisely in view of this oppressive situation, a basic ethical consensus is necessary.

Challenges and Responses

Key questions and principles

(1) We live in a world and time in which we can observe new dangerous tensions and polarizations between believers and non-believers, church members and those who have been secularized, the clerical and the anti-clerical – not only in Russia, Poland and Germany but also in France, in Algeria and Israel, in North and South America, Asia and Africa.

My response to this challenge is: there will be no survival of democracy without a coalition of believers and non-believers in mutual respect!

However, many people will say: do we not also live in a period of new cultural confrontations? That is true.

(2) We live in a world and a time in which humankind is threatened by what S. Huntington has called a "clash of civilizations", for example between Muslim or Confucian civilization and Western civilization. However, we are threatened not so much by a new world war as by every possible conflict between two countries or within one country, in a city, even a street or school.

My response to this challenge is: There will be no peace between the civilizations without a peace between the religions!

And there will be no peace between the religions without a dialogue between the religions.

However, many people will object: are there not so many dogmatic differences and obstacles between the different religions which make a real dialogue a naive illusion? That is true.

Original publication details: Excerpted from Hans Küng, *A Global Ethic for Global Politics and Economics* (Oxford University Press, 1998), pp. 91–3, 105, 108–11, 223–6. Reprinted by permission of Hans Küng.

(3)   We live in a world and a time when better relations between the religions are often blocked by every possible dogmatism, which can be found not only in the Roman Catholic Church but in all churches and religions and also in modern ideologies.

My response to this challenge is: There will be no new world order without a new world ethic, a global or planetary ethic despite all dogmatic differences.

What should the precise function of such a global ethic be? I can only repeat that a global ethic is not a new ideology or superstructure; it does not seek to make the specific ethics of the different religions and philosophies superfluous. Thus it is no substitute for the Torah, the Sermon on the Mount, the Qur'an, the Bhagavadgita, the discourses of the Buddha or the sayings of Confucius. The one global ethic does not mean a single global culture, far less a single global religion. To put it positively, a global ethic, a world ethic is none other than the necessary minimum of common human values, criteria and basic attitudes. Or, to be more precise: the global ethic is a basic consensus on binding values, irrevocable criteria and basic attitudes which are affirmed by all religions despite their dogmatic differences, and which can indeed also be contributed by non-believers. [. . .]

A First Formulation of a Global Ethic

To avoid misunderstandings I should repeat here: a global ethic does not mean a new global ideology, far less a uniform world religion beyond all existing religions; least of all does it mean the domination of one religion over all others. As I have indicated, a global ethic means a basic consensus on binding values, irrevocable criteria and personal basic attitudes, without which any community is sooner or later threatened with anarchy or a new dictatorship. But if the question is one of a basic ethical consensus, I will certainly be expected not to keep to universal programmatic words (truth, justice, humanity) and the Golden Rule, but to define the content of this consensus more closely. However, if one is to make the global ethic more concrete, first of all the formal question must be clarified. [. . .]

How should a global ethic be made specific? Content

For the first time in the history of the religions, the Council of the Parliament of the World's Religions, which met for the first time in Chicago between 28 August and 4 September 1993 with the participation of 6,500 people from every possible religion, ventured to commission and present a declaration on a global ethic: the author of this book had the honour and the burden of drafting this declaration and has given an account of the whole history of its origin and the broad international and inter-religious process of consultation in a publication of his own. As was only to be expected, this declaration provoked vigorous discussions during the Parliament. But the welcome thing was that at a time when so many religions are entangled in political conflicts, indeed in bloody wars, adherents of very different religions, great and small, made this declaration their own by signing it, as representatives of countless believers on this earth. This declaration is now the basis for an extensive process of discussion and acceptance which will certainly last a long time. It is to be hoped that despite all the obstacles the discussion will take place in all religions. For of course this first declaration on human obligations – like the first Declaration on the Rights of Man in 1776 in connection with the American Revolution – is not an end but a beginning.

One of the many hopeful signs for this acceptance is the firm confirmation of the Chicago Declaration by a report of the InterAction Council of former Presidents of State and Prime Ministers under the chairmanship of the former German Federal Chancellor Helmut Schmidt. This report was discussed under the title *In Search of Global Ethical Standards* in Vienna from March 22–24, 1996 with experts from the various religions, and approved in a plenary assembly of the InterAction Council in Vancouver on May 22, 1996.

Of course these statesmen are also aware of the negative role which the religions have often played and still play in the world: "The world is also afflicted by religious extremism and violence preached and practised in the name of religion." But that does not prevent them from also taking note of the positive role of the religions, particularly in respect of a common human ethic: "Religious institutions still command the loyalty of hundreds of millions of people," and do so despite all secularization and all consumerism: "The world's religions constitute one of the great traditions of wisdom for humankind. This repository of wisdom, ancient in its origins, has never been needed more." The minimal standards which make a collective life possible at all are important. Without an ethic and self-restraint humankind would revert to the jungle. "In a world of unprecedented change humankind has a desperate need of an ethical base on which to stand."

The statements on the priority of ethics over politics are encouragingly clear: "Ethics should precede politics and the law, because political action is concerned with values and choice. Ethics, therefore, must inform and inspire our political leadership." In response to the epoch-making change that is taking place, our institutions need a rededication to ethical norms: "We can find the sources of such a rededication in the world's religions and ethical traditions. They have the spiritual resources to give an ethical lead to the solution of our ethnic, national, social, economic and religious tensions. The world's religions have different doctrines but they all advocate a common ethic of basic standards. What unites the world's faiths is far greater than what divides them."

The InterAction Council positively adopted the Chicago Declaration on a Global Ethic: "We are therefore grateful that the Parliament of the World's Religions, which assembled in Chicago in 1993, proclaimed a Declaration towards a Global Ethic which we support in principle." The legal and ethical levels are clearly distinguished, and it is emphasized that what the United Nations proclaimed in its Declaration on Human Rights and the two supplementary conventions is confirmed and deepened by the Declaration of the World's Religions from the perspective of human responsibility: the full realization of the intrinsic dignity of the human person, the inalienable freedom and equality in principle of all humans, and the necessary solidarity and interdependence of all humans with each other, both as individuals and as communities. The statesmen are also convinced "that there will be no better global order without a global ethic".

Of course the politicians are also very well aware that a global ethic is no substitute for the Torah, the Gospels, the Qur'an, the Bhagavadgita, the Discourses of the Buddha or the Teachings of Confucius and others. It is concerned simply with "a minimal basic consensus relating to binding values, irrevocable standards and moral attitudes which can be affirmed by all religions despite their dogmatic differences, and can also be supported by non-believers". The alliance of believers and non-believers (also including that of theologians, philosophers, religious and social scientists) in the matter of an ethic is important. What is it aimed at?

The core of a global ethic

The basic ethical demand of the Chicago Declaration is the most elementary that one can put to human beings, though it is by no means a matter of course: true humanity: "Now as before, women and men are treated inhumanely all over the world. They are robbed of their opportunities and their freedom; their human rights are trampled underfoot; their dignity is disregarded. But might does not make right! In the face of all humanity our religions and ethical convictions demand that every human being must be treated humanely! That means that every human being without distinction of age, sex, race, skin colour, physical or mental ability, language, religion, political view, or national or social origin possesses an inalienable and untouchable dignity."

In this way, modern men and women with their "will to power" are shown quite clearly that even in our time they in no way stand "above good and evil", that rather the criterion of humanity has to be respected by all: "Everyone, the individual as well as the state, is therefore obliged to honour this dignity and protect it. Humans must always be the subjects of rights, must be ends, never mere means, never objects of commercialization and industrialization in economics, politics and media, in research institutes, and industrial corporations. No one stands 'above good and evil' – no human being, no social class, no influential interest group, no cartel, no police apparatus, no army, and no state. On the contrary; possessed of reason and conscience, every human is obliged to behave in a genuinely human fashion, to do good and avoid evil!"

Would not only Woodrow Wilson, but also Hans Morgenthau, who had endured so much inhumanity in his life and at the same time was always in search of universal criteria, have been in agreement with such basic demands? At all events it is a sign of the times that today a body of proven and completely realistic statesmen have expressly adopted as the basis of a global ethic the two basic principles:

- Every human being must be treated humanely!
- What you wish done to yourself, do to others.

These two principles should be the irrevocable, unconditional norm for all spheres of life, for family and communities, for races, nations and religions. Moreover on the basis of them the InterAction Council also affirms four irrevocable directives on which all religions agree. (Here they can be given only by title, without further elaboration; one could also render them, recalling the demonstrators in Prague or Rangoon, with ethical imperatives like "justice", "truth", humanity or whatever):

- Commitment to a culture of non-violence and respect for all life: the age-old directive: You shall not kill! Or in positive terms: Have respect for life!
- Commitment to a culture of solidarity and a just economic order: the age-old directive: You shall not steal! Or in positive terms: Deal honestly and fairly!
- Commitment to a culture of tolerance and a life of truthfulness: the age-old directive: You shall not lie! Or in positive terms: Speak and act truthfully!
- Commitment to a culture of equal rights and partnership between men and women: the age-old directive: You shall not commit sexual immorality! Or in positive terms: Respect and love one another! [. . .]

Human rights and human obligations:
The International Commission on Global Governance

The report by The Commission on Global Governance appointed by UNO bears the title *Our Global Neighbourhood*. The term "global governance" can be misunderstood as indicating a "global government"; such a thing is neither realistic nor worth striving for. It would be all too remote from the citizens of the world, nor could it be legitimated democratically. Moreover a world government is already firmly ruled out by the co-chairmen of the distinguished twenty-five member commission, the former Swedish Prime Minister Ingvar Carlsson and the former Commonwealth General Secretary Shridath Ramphal, in their introduction: "We are not proposing movement towards world government"; this could lead to "an even less democratic world than we have", indeed to "one more accommodating to power". But on the other hand the goal is not a "world without systems or rules"; this would be "a chaotic world" and "it would pose equal or even greater danger". So the challenge is "to strike the balance in such a way that the management of global affairs is responsive to the interests of all people in a sustainable future, that it is guided by basic human values, and that it makes global organization conform to the reality of global diversity." Indeed, the growing number of people who are committed to a global ethic will find themselves supported by this report: "This is a time for the international community to be bold, to explore new ideas, to develop new visions and to demonstrate commitment to values in devising new governance arrangements."

The phenomenon of globalization in all its dimensions forms the starting point for this analysis of "a new world" which takes several hundred pages: "Never before has change come so rapidly, on such a global scale, and with such global visibility." This is true:

- of the military transformations and the total change in the strategic setting: a new arms race, the arms trade, the rise in civil conflict, widespread violence;
- of the economic trends, in which the economic rise of several developing countries is distracting attention from the still rising number of the poorest of all;
- of the social and environmental change, in which people are beginning to assert their right to participate in their own governance; this urgently calls for an enlightened leadership which represents all countries and peoples and not just the most powerful.

After this analysis of the situation in the first chapter of the report, there follow a wealth of analyses, reflections and proposals on the great problem areas of a policy for world governance today:

- the advancement of global security (avoiding, recognizing and settling crises);
- the management of economic interdependence;
- the strengthening of the rule of law world-wide (international law);
- the reform of the United Nations.

What is surprising here from the perspective of a global ethic is that before all these problem areas, immediately after the analysis of the situation, in a whole chapter the question of "values for the Global Neighbourhood" is raised and in view of the increased neighbourhood tensions in all spheres, a "neighbourhood ethic" is called for. Why? Without a global ethic the frictions and tensions in life together in the one world would multiply: "Without leadership (a courageous leadership infused with that ethic at all levels of society) even the best-designed institutions and strategies will fail." There is then the terse comment that "global values must be the cornerstone of global governance". And anyone who asks doubtfully whether enough of today's political leaders are steeped in this ethic is given hope by the remark that "many people world-wide, particularly the young, are more willing to respond to these issues than their governments, for whom the short term in the context of political expediency tends to take preference".

But let us leave aside speculation as to which politicians in particular will stand out in respect for the "ethical dimension of the world political order". More important is the question how it can be made concrete. And here, too, it is amazing that this document gives the Golden Rule as the main basic principle: "People should treat others as they would themselves wish to be treated." On this foundation the basic values of respect for life, freedom, justice, mutual respect, readiness to help, and integrity are developed: "All these values derive in one way or another from the principle, which is in accord with religious teaching around the world, that people should treat others as they would themselves wish to be treated."

And the report goes very much further in explicitly requiring "these values to be expressed in the form of a global civic ethic with specific rights and responsibilities", in which "all citizens, as individuals and as members of different private groups and associations, should accept the obligation to recognize and help protect the rights of others". This ethic should be incorporated into the developing "fabric of international norms". For such a global ethic "would help humanize the impersonal workings of bureaucracies and markets and constrain the competitive and self-serving instincts of individuals and groups". Indeed, without this global ethic the new wider global civil society which is coming into being could "become unfocused and even unruly".

It would be hard to think of a finer confirmation of the global ethic project than these statements by the commission. Finally, the commission even makes an explicit request. The authors were presumably unaware that, as I remarked earlier, it had already been made in a discussion in the Revolutionary Parliament of 1789 in Paris, but could not be met at that time: "Rights need to be joined with responsibilities." For the "tendency to emphasize rights while forgetting responsibilities" has "deleterious consequences". "We therefore urge the international community to unite in support of a global ethic of common rights and shared responsibilities. In our view, such an ethic – reinforcing the fundamental rights that are already part of the fabric of international norms, would provide the moral foundation for constructing a more effective system of global governance."

It cannot be repeated often enough that all human beings have rights, human rights: the right to a secure life, equitable treatment, an opportunity to earn a fair living and provide for their own welfare, the definition and preservation of their differences through peaceful means, participation in governance at all levels, free and fair petition for redress of gross injustices, equal access to information and to the global commons.

But hardly ever has it been stated in an official international document that concrete responsibilities, human responsibilities, are associated with human rights: "At the same time, all people share a responsibility to:

- contribute to the common good;
- consider the impact of their actions on the security and welfare of others;
- promote equity, including gender equity;
- protect the interests of future generations by pursuing sustainable development and safeguarding the global commons;
- preserve humanity's cultural and intellectual heritage;
- be active participants in governance; and
- work to eliminate corruption."

Moreover it is remarkable that this fundamental section of the UN Commission Report on a civil ethic ends with a very concrete hope, that "over time, these principles could be embodied in a more binding international document – a global charter of Civil Society – that could provide a basis for all to agree on rules that should govern the global neighbourhood". [. . .]

Questions

1 What is the "hidden promise" of globalization, according to Micklethwait and Wooldridge? How do they counter the "vengeful howls" against globalization? What kinds of globalization gains, in addition to the ones they mention, could you cite in support of their position?

2 How does Sen show that globalization is not a western "curse"? By what criteria should "globalism" be judged? What is the "central issue of contention" in the debate about globalization?

3 Gray begins his chapter with a quote from the economic historian Karl Polanyi about the "catastrophe" of traditional economic liberalism. How does this point apply to contemporary globalization? What makes globalization an "unrealizable fantasy," according to Gray? What kinds of reforms of the world economy does he envision?

4 What are the key features of "McWorld" and " Jihad"? How does McWorld provoke and support Jihad? What does Barber find most threatening about globalization?

5 What is new about world politics today, according to Huntington? Does this image of a world embroiled in clashes of civilizations contradict the conventional view that globalization is a process that creates new bonds across cultural boundaries? Does he demonstrate that civilizations are now the primary forms of identity and organization in world society?

6 Why does the world need a "global ethic," according to Küng, and what does it consist of? Do you think people around the world can agree on such an ethic? Must such an ethic be biased in favor of certain cultures, e.g., western or European cultures?

Part II

Explaining Globalization

Introduction

How can we best explain globalization? The question is not easy to answer. After all, as we suggested in our introduction, globalization has many layers and dimensions. A good explanation must come to grips with this complexity. In addition, a new world society, still under formation, presents a moving target, so any theory must be adaptable in defining globalization itself. And explanation is all the more difficult because, as globalization re-creates the world, tools once used to make sense of earlier historical periods may no longer be adequate. The "global age," Martin Albrow argued in his book by that title, calls for new theory, new thinking, and new departures in social science, especially if the discontinuity between old and new is as profound as many observers claim. In this part, we illustrate important work in progress on these issues drawn from four major perspectives.

Each of these perspectives proposes a different account of globalization. We can illustrate the differences between them by comparing their answers to a hypothetical question (taken from the excerpt by John Meyer and colleagues): How would a newly discovered island society be incorporated into world society? One group of scholars would reply that corporations would stake a claim to the island's natural resources, send engineers to create infrastructure, and build plants to take advantage of cheap labor. Another group of scholars would argue that representatives of major powers would assist the society in building a capable state and tempt it to form alliances; international organizations would provide support and advice so that the society can be a stable participant in global politics. A third group of scholars would stress that the island would be invaded by experts helping it build the institutions any proper country must have, so that it can function like any other society. A final group would focus on the way the society would balance its own heritage against the intrusions of world culture, aided by organizations concerned about preserving its unique culture. Incorporation can thus take the form of economic exploitation, political agreements and alliances, institutional reform according to global models, or self-reflexive cultural identification. The selections show that such answers derive from different views of the motive forces and characteristic features of globalization.

1   World-System Theory

To scholars inspired by Marx, globalization is expansion of the capitalist system around the globe. The selection by Eric Hobsbawm sets the stage with the historical claim that, in an important sense, the world first became unified around the middle of the nineteenth century. Networks of communication and economic exchange were thickening. A world economy, guided by liberal philosophy with global aspirations, constituted a single world that since has grown more integrated and standardized. Immanuel Wallerstein, author of a multivolume study of *The Modern World-System*, puts this historical claim in context. What happened in the mid-nineteenth century, he implies, was a phase in a centuries-old process. The capitalist world-system originated in the sixteenth century, when European traders established firm connections with Asia, Africa, and the Americas. From the outset, this system consisted of a single economy – a market and a regional division of labor – but many states. In the "core" of the system, the dominant classes were supported by strong states as they exploited labor, resources, and trade opportunities, most notably in "peripheral" areas. The "semiperiphery" lessened polarization between core and periphery and thus helped to keep the system remarkably stable. Leslie Sklair complements this long-term perspective by stressing the role of transnational corporations and classes as the prime movers in the contemporary global system. He argues that a global consumerist ideology supports the exploitative structure commanded by transnational corporations and helps the dominant transnational class get ever stronger.

2   Neorealism/Neoliberal Institutionalism

The states that play a supporting role in Wallerstein's world-system analysis move center stage in the work of students of international relations. In the classic neorealist view, the focus is on independent states pursuing their interests – security and power – constrained only by the power of others. Many scholars now see this "realistic" picture as too simple. As Robert Keohane and Joseph Nye illustrate, globalization produces a more complex system of interdependent states in which transnational rules and organizations have gained influence. States pursuing their interests are still a major force, and study of this global system must still focus on the way states respond to constraints. But in an interdependent system, new organizations besides states critically influence world politics, no clear hierarchy of issues common to all states exists, and the use of force has become less effective. World society therefore contains many centers of power and has no single power hierarchy. Even as power disperses and goals diverge, new common rules for dealing with issues gain strength. "Complex interdependence" is but one label for the more nuanced picture that emerges.

3   World Polity Theory

Other scholars agree that states are an important component of world society but give greater attention to the global context in which states are immersed. What is new in world society, they argue, is the all-encompassing "world polity" and its associated world culture, which supplies a set of cultural rules or scripts that specify how institutions around the world should deal with common problems. Globalization is the formation and enactment of this world polity and culture. One of the world polity's key elements, as John Meyer and colleagues explain, is a general, globally legitimated model of how to form a state. Guided by this model, particular states in widely varying circumstances organize their affairs in surprisingly similar fashion. Because world society is organized as a polity with an intensifying global culture, new organizations – business enterprises, educational institutions, social movements, leisure and hobby groups, and so on – spring up to enact its precepts. As carriers of global principles, these organizations then help to build and elaborate world society further.

4 World Culture Theory

In this perspective, world culture indeed is new and important, but it is less homogeneous than world-polity scholars imply. Globalization is a process of relativization, as Roland Robertson puts it. Societies relate to a single system of societies, while individuals relate to a single sense of humanity. World society, thus, consists of a complex set of relationships among multiple units in the "global field." In this model, world society is not governed by a particular set of values but by the confrontation of different ways of organizing these relationships. Globalization compresses the world into a single entity, and people necessarily become more and more aware of their new global existence. But what is important about this process is the problem of "globality": how to make living together in one global system meaningful or even possible. Not surprisingly, religious traditions take on new significance insofar as they address the new global predicament that compels societies and individuals to "identify" themselves in new ways. Robertson concludes that a "search for fundamentals" is inherent in globalization.

Arjun Appadurai analyzes the cultural compression of the globe by showing how ideas, money, and people flow through disjoint "scapes." These flows intersect in different ways in particular societies, where identity construction becomes a matter of making local sense of the collision. While the flows homogenize the world to some extent, the disjunctures in globalization also produce heterogeneity. Sameness and difference "cannibalize" each other. Like Robertson and Appadurai, Ulf Hannerz thinks that all cultures are becoming subcultures within a larger entity. This "global ecumene" is marked by its "organization of diversity," not by homogenization, for transnational flows are themselves diverse and particular societies adapt those flows in distinct ways. Though the distribution of culture is affected by the unequal power of center and periphery, Hannerz shows with Nigerian examples that globalization is a process of "interaction" that produces a "creolized world."

As even this brief sketch of theories makes clear, scholars thus far have offered different views on the key dimensions, sources, and consequences of globalization. These theories have made substantial advances in accounting for transformations of the world. They all express a distinctly global point of view, even though they also still rely on ideas familiar from earlier social theory. As orienting perspectives, they guide much current research. But explaining globalization is necessarily work in progress, a collective effort to clarify the problems posed by the rise of a new world society as much as an attempt to produce satisfying accounts of how the world has become a global whole.

7 The World Unified

E. J. Hobsbawm

> The bourgeoisie, by the rapid improvement of all instruments of production, by the immensely facilitated means of communication, draws all, even the most barbarian nations into civilisation . . . In one word, it creates a world after its own image.
>
> K. Marx and F. Engels, 1848

> As commerce, education, and the rapid transition of thought and matter, by telegraph and steam have changed everything, I rather believe that the great Maker is preparing the world to become one nation, speaking one language, a consummation which will render armies and navies no longer necessary.
>
> President Ulysses S. Grant, 1873

> "You should have heard all he said – I was to live on a mountain somewhere, go to Egypt or to America."
>
> "Well, what of it?" Stolz remarked coolly. "You can be in Egypt in a fortnight and in America in three weeks."
>
> "Whoever goes to America or Egypt? The English do, but then that's the way the Lord God made them and besides, they have no room to live at home. But which of us would dream of going? Some desperate fellow, perhaps, whose life is worth nothing to him."
>
> I. Goncharov, 1859

I

When we write the "world history" of earlier periods, we are in fact making an addition of the histories of the various parts of the globe, but which, in so far as they had knowledge of one another, had only marginal and superficial contacts, unless the inhabitants of some region had conquered or colonized another, as the west Europeans did the Americas. It is perfectly possible to write the earlier history of Africa with only a casual reference to that of the Far East, with (except along the west coast and the Cape) little reference to Europe, though not without fairly persistent reference to the Islamic world. What happened in China was, until the eighteenth century, irrelevant to the political rulers of Europe, other than the Russians, though not to some of their specialized groups of traders; what happened in Japan was beyond the direct knowledge of all except the handful of Dutch merchants who were allowed to maintain a foothold there between the sixteenth and the mid-nineteenth centuries. Conversely, Europe was for the Celestial Empire merely a region of outer barbarians fortunately remote enough to pose no problem of assessing the precise degree of their undoubted subservience to the Emperor, though raising some minor problems of administration for the officials in charge of some ports. For that matter, even within the regions in which there was significant inter-

Original publication details: Excerpted from E. J. Hobsbawm, "The World Unified," in *The Age of Capital 1848–1875* (Weidenfeld & Nicolson, 1975), pp. 48–50, 51–3, 65–7, 68. Reprinted by permission of the Orion Publishing Group Ltd.

action, much could be ignored without inconvenience. For whom in western Europe – merchants or statesmen – was it of any consequence what went on in the mountains and valleys of Macedonia? If Libya had been entirely swallowed by some natural cataclysm, what real difference would it have made to anybody, even in the Ottoman Empire of which it was technically a part, and among the Levant traders of various nations?

The lack of interdependence of the various parts of the globe was not simply a matter of ignorance, though of course, outside the region concerned and often within it, ignorance of "the interior" was still considerable. Even in 1848 large areas of the various continents were marked in white on even the best European maps – notably in Africa, central Asia, the interior of South and parts of North America and Australia, not to mention the almost totally unexplored Arctic and Antarctic. The maps which might have been drawn up by any other cartographers would certainly have shown even vaster spaces of the unknown; for if the officials of China or the illiterate scouts, traders and *coureurs de bois* of each continental hinterland knew a great deal more about some areas, large or small, than Europeans did, the sum total of their geographical knowledge was much more exiguous. In any case, the mere arithmetical addition of everything that any expert knew about the world would be a purely academic exercise. It was not generally available: in fact, there was not, even in terms of geographical knowledge, *one* world.

Ignorance was a symptom rather than a cause of the lack of the world's unity. It reflected both the absence of diplomatic, political and administrative relations, which were indeed slender enough, and the weakness of economic links. It is true that the "world market", that crucial pre-condition and characteristic of capitalist society, had long been developing. International trade had more than doubled in value between 1720 and 1780. In the period of the Dual Revolution (1780–1840) it had increased more than threefold – yet even this substantial growth was modest by the standards of our period. By 1870 the value of foreign trade for every citizen of the United Kingdom, France, Germany, Austria and Scandinavia was between four and five times what it had been in 1830, for every Dutchman and Belgian about three times as great, and even for every citizen of the United States – a country for which foreign commerce was only of marginal importance – well over double. During the 1870s an annual quantity of about 88 million tons weight of seaborne merchandise were exchanged between the major nations, as compared with 20 million in 1840. Thirty-one million tons of coal crossed the seas, compared to 1.4 million; 11.2 million tons of grain, compared to less than 2 million; 6 million tons of iron, compared to 1 million; even – anticipating the twentieth century – 1.4 million tons of petroleum, which had been unknown to overseas trade in 1840.

Let us measure the tightening of the net of economic interchanges between parts of the world remote from each other more precisely. British exports to Turkey and the Middle East rose from 3.5 million pounds in 1848 to a peak of almost 16 million in 1870; to Asia from 7 million to 41 million (1875); to Central and South America from 6 million to 25 million (1872); to India from around 5 million to 24 million (1875); to Australasia from 1.5 million to almost 20 million (1875). In other words in, say, thirty-five years, the value of the exchanges between the most industrialized economy and the most remote or backward regions of the world had increased about sixfold. Even this is of course not very impressive by present standards, but in sheer volume it far surpassed anything that had previously been conceived. The net which linked the various regions of the world was visibly tightening. [. . .]

Indeed, what we call the "explorers" of the mid-nineteenth century were merely one well-publicized, but numerically not very important, sub-group of a very large body of men who opened the globe to knowledge. They were those who travelled in areas in which economic development and profit were not yet sufficiently active to replace the "explorer" by the (European) trader, the mineral prospector, the surveyor, the builder of railway and telegraph, in the end, if the climate were to prove suitable, the white settler. "Explorers" dominated the cartography of inner Africa, because that continent had no very obvious economic assets for the west between the abolition of the Atlantic slave-trade and the discovery, on the one hand of precious stones and metals (in the south), on the other of the economic value of certain primary products which could only be grown or collected in tropical climates, and were still far from synthetic production. Neither was yet of great significance or even promise until the 1870s, though it seemed inconceivable that so large and under-utilized a continent should not, sooner rather than later, prove to be a source of wealth and profit. (After all, British exports to sub-Saharan Africa had risen from about 1.5 million pounds in the late 1840s to about 5 million in 1871 – they doubled in the 1870s to reach about 10 million in the early 1880s – which was by no means unpromising.) "Explorers" also dominated the opening of Australia, because the interior desert was vast, empty and, until the mid-twentieth century, devoid of obvious resources for economic exploitation. On the other hand, the oceans of the world ceased, except for the Arctic – the Antarctic attracted little interest during our period – to preoccupy the "explorers". Yet the vast extension of shipping, and above all the laying of the great submarine cables, implied a great deal of what can properly be called exploration.

The world in 1875 was thus a great deal better known than ever before. Even at the national level, detailed maps (mostly initiated for military purposes) were now available in many of the developed countries: the publication of the pioneer enterprise of this kind, the Ordnance Survey maps of England – but not yet of Scotland and Ireland – was completed in 1862. However, more important than mere knowledge, the most remote parts of the world were now beginning to be linked together by means of communication which had no precedent for regularity, for the capacity to transport vast quantities of goods and numbers of people, and above all, for speed: the railway, the steamship, the telegraph.

By 1872 they had achieved the triumph chronicled by Jules Verne: the possibility of travelling round the world in eighty days, even allowing for the numerous mishaps which dogged the indomitable Phileas Fogg. Readers may recall the imperturbable traveller's route. He went by rail and channel steamer across Europe from London to Brindisi and thence by boat through the newly opened Suez Canal (an estimated seven days). The journey from Suez to Bombay by boat was to take him thirteen days. The rail journey from Bombay to Calcutta should, but for the failure to complete a stretch of the line, have taken him three days. Thence by sea to Hong Kong, Yokohama and across the Pacific to San Francisco was still a long stretch of forty-one days. However, since the railroad across the American continent had been completed by 1869, only the still not wholly controlled perils of the West – herds of bison, Indians etc. – stood between the traveller and a normal journey of seven days to New York. The remainder of the trip – Atlantic crossing to Liverpool and railway to London – would have posed no problems but for the requirements of fictional suspense. In fact, an enterprising American travel agent offered a similar round-the-world trip not long after.

How long would such a journey have taken Fogg in 1848? It would have had to be almost entirely by sea, since no railway lines as yet crossed the continent, while virtually none existed anywhere else in the world except in the United States, where they hardly yet went further inland than two hundred miles. The speediest of sailing ships, the famous tea clippers, would most usually take an average of 110 days for the journey to Canton around 1870, when they were at the peak of their technical achievement; they could not do it in less than ninety days but had been known to take 150. We can hardly suppose a circumnavigation in 1848 to have taken, with anything but the best of fortunes, much less than eleven months, or say four times as long as Phileas Fogg, not counting time spent in port. [. . .]

II

We are today more familiar than the men of the mid-nineteenth century with this drawing together of all parts of the globe into a single world. Yet there is a substantial difference between the process as we experience it today and that in the previous century. What is most striking about it in the later twentieth century is an international standardization which goes far beyond the purely economic and technological. In this respect our world is more massively standardized than Phileas Fogg's, but only because there are more machines, productive installations and businesses. The railroads, telegraphs and ships of 1870 were not less recognizable as international "models" wherever they occurred than the automobiles and airports of 1970. What hardly occurred then was the international, and interlinguistic standardization of culture which today distributes, with at best a slight time-lag, the same films, popular music-styles, television programmes and indeed styles of popular living across the world. Such standardization did affect the numerically modest middle classes and some of the rich, up to a point, or at least in so far as it was not brought up against the barriers of language. The "models" of the developed world were copied by the more backward in the handful of dominant versions – the English throughout the Empire, in the United States and, to a much smaller extent, on the European continent, the French in Latin America, the Levant, and parts of eastern Europe, the German–Austrian throughout central and eastern Europe, in Scandinavia and also to some extent in the United States. A certain common visual style, the overstuffed and overloaded bourgeois interior, the public baroque of theatres and operas, could be discerned, though for practical purposes only where Europeans or colonists descended from Europeans had established themselves. Nevertheless, except in the United States (and Australia) where high wages democratized the market, and therefore the lifestyles, of the economically more modest classes, this remained confined to a comparative few.

There is no doubt that the bourgeois prophets of the mid-nineteenth century looked forward to a single, more or less standardized, world where all governments would acknowledge the truths of political economy and liberalism carried throughout the globe by impersonal missionaries more powerful than those Christianity or Islam had ever had; a world reshaped in the image of the bourgeoisie, perhaps even one from which, eventually, national differences would disappear. Already the development of communications required novel kinds of international coordinating and standardizing organisms – the International Telegraph Union of 1865, the Universal Postal Union of 1875, the International Meteorological Organization of 1878, all of which still survive. Already it had posed – and for limited purposes solved by means of the International Signals Code of 1871 – the problem of an internationally standardized "language". Within a few years attempts to devise artificial cosmopolitan languages were to become fashionable, headed by the oddly named *Volapük* ("world-speak") excogitated by a German in 1880. (None of these succeeded, not even the most promising contender, *Esperanto*, another product of the 1880s.) Already the labour movement was in the process of establishing a global organization which was to draw political conclusions from the growing unification of the world – the International.

Nevertheless international standardization and unification in this sense remained feeble and partial. Indeed, to some extent the rise of new nations and new cultures with a democratic base, i.e. using separate languages rather than the international idioms of educated minorities, made it more difficult, or rather, more circuitous. Writers of European or global reputation had to become so through translation. And while it is significant that by 1875 readers of German, French, Swedish, Dutch, Spanish, Danish, Italian, Portuguese, Czech and Hungarian were able to enjoy some or all of Dickens's works (as Bulgarian, Russian, Finnish, Serbo–Croat, Armenian and Yiddish ones were to before the end of the century), it is equally significant that this process implied an increasing linguistic division. Whatever the long-term prospects, it was accepted by contemporary liberal observers that, in the short and medium term, development proceeded by the formation of different and rival nations. The most that could be hoped was that these would embody the same type of institutions, economy and beliefs. The unity of the world implied division. The world system of capitalism was a structure of rival "national economies". The world triumph of liberalism rested on its conversion of all peoples, at least among those regarded as "civilized". No doubt the champions of progress in the third quarter of the nineteenth century were confident enough that this would happen sooner or later. But their confidence rested on insecure foundations.

They were indeed on safe ground in pointing to the ever-tightening network of global communications, whose most tangible result was a vast increase in the flow of international exchanges of goods and men – trade and migration. Yet even in the most plainly international field of business, global unification was not an unqualified advantage. For if it created a world economy, it was one in which all parts were so dependent on each other that a pull on one thread would inevitably set all others into movement. [. . .]

All these developments affected only that sector of the world which was already drawn into the international economy. Since vast areas and populations – virtually all of Asia and Africa, most of Latin America, and quite substantial parts even of Europe – still existed outside any economies but those of purely local exchange and remote from port, railway and telegraph, we ought not to exaggerate the unification of the world achieved between 1848 and 1875. After all, as an eminent chronicler of the time pointed out, "The *world economy* is only at its beginning"; but, as he also added, correctly, "even these beginnings allow us to guess at its future importance, inasmuch as the present stage already represents a truly amazing transformation in the productivity of humanity". [. . .]

8 The Rise and Future Demise of the World Capitalist System

Immanuel Wallerstein

We take the defining characteristic of a social system to be the existence within it of a division of labor, such that the various sectors or areas within are dependent upon economic exchange with others for the smooth and continuous provisioning of the needs of the area. Such economic exchange can clearly exist without a common political structure and even more obviously without sharing the same culture.

A mini-system is an entity that has within it a complete division of labor, and a single cultural framework. Such systems are found only in very simple agricultural or hunting and gathering societies. Such mini-systems no longer exist in the world. Furthermore, there were fewer in the past than is often asserted, since any such system that became tied to an empire by the payment of tribute as "protection costs" ceased by that fact to be a "system", no longer having a self-contained division of labor. For such an area, the payment of tribute marked a shift, in Polanyi's language, from being a reciprocal economy to participating in a larger redistributive economy.

Leaving aside the now defunct mini-systems, the only kind of social system is a world-system, which we define quite simply as a unit with a single division of labor and multiple cultural systems. It follows logically that there can, however, be two varieties of such world-systems, one with a common political system and one without. We shall designate these respectively as world-empires and world-economies.

It turns out empirically that world-economies have historically been unstable structures leading either towards disintegration or conquest by one group and hence transformation into a world-empire. Examples of such world-empires emerging from world-economies are all the so-called great civilizations of pre-modern times, such as China, Egypt, Rome (each at appropriate periods of its history). On the other hand, the so-called nineteenth-century empires, such as Great Britain or France, were not world-empires at all, but nation-states with colonial appendages operating within the framework of a world-economy.

World-empires were basically redistributive in economic form. No doubt they bred clusters of merchants who engaged in economic exchange (primarily long-distance trade), but such clusters, however large, were a minor part of the total economy and not fundamentally determinative of its fate. Such long-distance trade tended to be, as Polanyi argues, "administered trade" and not market trade, utilizing "ports of trade".

Original publication details: Excerpted from Immanuel Wallerstein, "The Rise and Future Demise of the World Capitalist System: Concepts for Comparative Analysis," *Comparative Studies in Society and History*, 16, 1974, pp. 390–2, 399–406. © Society for Comparative Study of Society and History. Reprinted by permission of Cambridge University Press.

It was only with the emergence of the modern world-economy in sixteenth-century Europe that we saw the full development and economic predominance of market trade. This was the system called capitalism. Capitalism and a world-economy (that is, a single division of labor but multiple polities and cultures) are obverse sides of the same coin. One does not cause the other. We are merely defining the same indivisible phenomenon by different characteristics.

How and why it came about that this particular European world-economy of the sixteenth century did not become transformed into a redistributive world-empire but developed definitively as a capitalist world-economy has been explained elsewhere. The genesis of this world-historical turning-point is marginal to the issues under discussion in this paper, which is rather what conceptual apparatus one brings to bear on the analysis of developments within the framework of precisely such a capitalist world-economy.

Let us therefore turn to the capitalist world-economy. We shall seek to deal with two pseudo-problems, created by the trap of not analyzing totalities: the so-called persistence of feudal forms, and the so-called creation of socialist systems. In doing this, we shall offer an alternative model with which to engage in comparative analysis, one rooted in the historically specific totality which is the world capitalist economy. We hope to demonstrate thereby that to be historically specific is not to fail to be analytically universal. On the contrary, the only road to nomothetic propositions is through the historically concrete, just as in cosmology the only road to a theory of the laws governing the universe is through the concrete analysis of the historical evolution of this same universe.

On the "feudalism" debate, we take as a starting-point Frank's concept of "the development of underdevelopment", that is, the view that the economic structure of contemporary underdeveloped countries is not the form which a "traditional" society takes upon contact with "developed" societies, not an earlier stage in the "transition" to industrialization. It is rather the result of being involved in the world-economy as a peripheral, raw material-producing area, or as Frank puts it for Chile, "underdevelopment . . . is the necessary product of four centuries of capitalism itself".

This formulation runs counter to a large body of writing concerning the underdeveloped countries that was produced in the period 1950–70, a literature which sought the factors that explained "development" within non-systems such as "states" or "cultures" and, once having presumably discovered these factors, urged their reproduction in underdeveloped areas as the road to salvation. [. . .]

What was happening in Europe from the sixteenth to the eighteenth centuries is that over a large geographical area going from Poland in the northeast westwards and southwards throughout Europe and including large parts of the Western Hemisphere as well, there grew up a world-economy with a single division of labor within which there was a world market, for which men produced largely agricultural products for sale and profit. I would think the simplest thing to do would be to call this agricultural capitalism.

This then resolves the problems incurred by using the pervasiveness of *wage*-labor as a defining characteristic of capitalism. An individual is no less a capitalist exploiting labor because the state assists him to pay his laborers low wages (including wages in kind) and denies these laborers the right to change employment. Slavery and so-called "second serfdom" are not to be regarded as anomalies in a capitalist system. Rather the so-called serf in Poland or the Indian on a Spanish *encomienda* in New Spain in this sixteenth-century world-economy were working for landlords who "paid" them (however euphemistic this term) for cash-crop production. This is a relationship in which labor-power is a commodity (how could it ever be more so than under slavery?), quite different from the relationship of a feudal serf to his lord in eleventh-century Burgundy, where the economy was not oriented to a world market, and where labor-power was (therefore?) in no sense bought or sold.

Capitalism thus means labor as a commodity to be sure. But in the era of agricultural capitalism, wage-labor is only one of the modes in which labor is recruited and recompensed in the labor market. Slavery, coerced cash-crop production (my name for the so-called "second feudalism"), share-cropping, and tenancy are all alternative modes. It would be too long to develop here the conditions under which differing regions of the world-economy tend to specialize in different agricultural products.

What we must notice now is that this specialization occurs in specific and differing geographic regions of the world-economy. This regional specialization comes about by the attempts of actors in the market to avoid the normal operation of the market whenever it does not maximize their profit. The attempts of these actors to use non-market devices to ensure short-run profits makes them turn to the political entities which have in fact power to affect the market – the nation-states. (Again, why at this stage they could not have turned to city-states would take us into a long discursus, but it has to do with the state of military and shipping technology, the need of the European land-mass to expand overseas in the fifteenth century if it was to maintain the level of income of the various aristocracies, combined with the state of political disintegration to which Europe had fallen in the Middle Ages.)

In any case, the local capitalist classes – cash-crop landowners (often, even usually, nobility) and merchants – turned to the state, not only to liberate them from non-market constraints (as traditionally emphasized by liberal historiography) but to create new constraints on the new market, the market of the European world-economy.

By a series of accidents – historical, ecological, geographic – northwest Europe was better situated in the sixteenth century to diversify its agricultural specialization and add to it certain industries (such as textiles, shipbuilding, and metal wares) than were other parts of Europe. Northwest Europe emerged as the core area of this world-economy, specializing in agricultural production of higher skill levels, which favored (again for reasons too complex to develop) tenancy and wage-labor as the modes of labor control. Eastern Europe and the Western Hemisphere became peripheral areas specializing in export of grains, bullion, wood, cotton, sugar – all of which favored the use of slavery and coerced cash-crop labor as the modes of labor control. Mediterranean Europe emerged as the semi-peripheral area of this world-economy specializing in high-cost industrial products (for example, silks) and credit and specie transactions, which had as a consequence in the agricultural arena share-cropping as the mode of labor control and little export to other areas.

The three structural positions in a world-economy – core, periphery, and semi-periphery – had become stabilized by about 1640. How certain areas became one and not the other is a long story. The key fact is that given slightly different starting-points, the interests of various local groups converged in northwest Europe, leading to the development of strong state mechanisms, and diverged sharply in the peripheral areas, leading to very weak ones. Once we get a difference in the strength of the state-machineries, we get the operation of "unequal exchange" which is enforced by strong states on weak ones, by core states on peripheral areas. Thus capitalism involves not only appropriation of the surplus-value by an owner from a laborer, but an appropriation of surplus of the whole world-economy by core areas.

And this was as true in the stage of agricultural capitalism as it is in the stage of industrial capitalism.

In the early Middle Ages, there was to be sure trade. But it was largely either "local", in a region that we might call the "extended" manor, or "long-distance", primarily of luxury goods. There was no exchange of "bulk" goods, of "staples" across intermediate-size areas, and hence no production for such markets. Later on in the Middle Ages, world-economies may be said to have come into existence, one centering on Venice, a second on the cities of Flanders and the Hanse. For various reasons, these structures were hurt by the retractions (economic, demographic, and ecological) of the period 1300–1450. It is only with the creating of a *European* division of labor after 1450 that capitalism found firm roots.

Capitalism was from the beginning an affair of the world-economy and not of nation-states. It is a misreading of the situation to claim that it is only in the twentieth century that capitalism has become "world-wide", although this claim is frequently made in various writings, particularly by Marxists. Typical of this line of argument is Charles Bettelheim's response to Arghiri Emmanuel's discussion of unequal exchange:

> The tendency of the capitalist mode of production to become worldwide is manifested not only through the constitution of a group of national economies forming a complex and hierarchical structure, including an imperialist pole and a dominated one, and not only through the antagonistic relations that develop between the different "national economies" and the different states, but also through the constant "transcending" of "national limits" by big capital (the formation of "international big capital", "world firms", etc. . . .).

The whole tone of these remarks ignores the fact that capital has never allowed its aspirations to be determined by national boundaries in a capitalist world-economy, and that the creation of "national" barriers – generically, mercantilism – has historically been a defensive mechanism of capitalists located in states which are one level below the high point of strength in the system. Such was the case of England *vis-à-vis* the Netherlands in 1660–1715, France *vis-à-vis* England in 1715–1815, Germany *vis-à-vis* Britain in the nineteenth century, the Soviet Union *vis-à-vis* the US in the twentieth. In the process a large number of countries create national economic barriers whose consequences often last beyond their initial objectives. At this later point in the process the very same capitalists who pressed their national governments to impose the restrictions now find these restrictions constraining. This is not an "internationalization" of "national" capital. This is simply a new political demand by certain sectors of the capitalist classes who have at all points in time sought to maximize their profits within the real economic market, that of the world-economy.

If this is so, then what meaning does it have to talk of structural positions within this economy and identify states as being in one of these positions? And why talk of three positions, inserting that of "semi-periphery" in between the widely-used concepts of core and periphery? The state-machineries of the core states were strengthened to meet the needs of capitalist landowners and their merchant allies. But that does not mean that these state-machineries were manipulable puppets. Obviously any organization, once created, has a certain autonomy from those who pressed it into existence for two reasons. It creates a stratum of officials whose own careers and interests are furthered by the continued strengthening of the organization itself, however the interests of its capitalist backers may vary. Kings and bureaucrats wanted to stay in power and increase their personal gain constantly. Secondly, in the process of creating the strong state in the first place, certain "constitutional" compromises had to be made with other forces within the state-boundaries and these institutionalized compromises limit, as they are designed to do, the freedom of maneuver of the managers of the state-machinery. The formula of the state as "executive committee of the ruling class" is only valid, therefore, if one bears in mind that executive committees are never mere reflections of the wills of their constituents, as anyone who has ever participated in any organization knows well.

The strengthening of the state-machineries in core areas has as its direct counterpart the decline of the state-machineries in peripheral areas. The decline of the Polish monarchy in the sixteenth and seventeenth centuries is a striking example of this phenomenon. There are two reasons for this. In peripheral countries, the interests of the capitalist landowners lie in an opposite direction from those of the local commercial bourgeoisie. Their interests lie in maintaining an open economy to maximize their profit from world-market trade (no restrictions in exports and access to lower-cost industrial products from core countries) and in elimination of the commercial bourgeoisie in favor of outside merchants (who pose no local political threat). Thus, in terms of the state, the coalition which strengthened it in core countries was precisely absent.

The second reason, which has become ever more operative over the history of the modern world-system, is that the strength of the state-machinery in core states is a function of the weakness of other state-machineries. Hence intervention of outsiders via war, subversion, and diplomacy is the lot of peripheral states.

All this seems very obvious. I repeat it only in order to make clear two points. One cannot reasonably explain the strength of various state-machineries at specific moments of the history of the modern world-system primarily in terms of a genetic-cultural line of argumentation, but rather in terms of the structural role a country plays in the world-economy at that moment in time. To be sure, the initial eligibility for a particular role is often decided by an accidental edge a particular country has, and the "accident" of which one is talking is no doubt located in part in past history, in part in current geography. But once this relatively minor accident is given, it is the operations of the world-market forces which accentuate the differences, institutionalize them, and make them impossible to surmount over the short run.

The second point we wish to make about the structural differences of core and periphery is that they are not comprehensible unless we realize that there is a third structural position: that of the semi-periphery. This is not the result merely of establishing arbitrary cutting-points on a continuum of characteristics. Our logic is not merely inductive, sensing the presence of a third category from a comparison of indicator curves. It is also deductive. The semi-periphery is needed to make a capitalist world-economy run smoothly. Both kinds of world-system, the world-empire with a redistributive economy and the world-economy with a capitalist market economy, involve markedly unequal distribution of rewards. Thus, logically, there is immediately posed the question of how it is possible politically for such a system to persist. Why do not the majority who are exploited simply overwhelm the minority who draw disproportionate benefits? The most rapid glance at the historic record shows that these world-systems have been faced rather rarely by fundamental system-wide insurrection. While internal discontent has been eternal, it has usually taken quite long before the accumulation of the erosion of power has led to the decline of a world-system, and as often as not, an external force has been a major factor in this decline.

There have been three major mechanisms that have enabled world-systems to retain relative political stability (not in terms of the particular groups who will play the leading roles in the system, but in terms of systemic survival itself). One obviously is the concentration of military strength in the hands of the dominant forces. The modalities of this obviously vary with the technology, and there are to be sure political prerequisites for such a concentration, but nonetheless sheer force is no doubt a central consideration.

A second mechanism is the pervasiveness of an ideological commitment to the system as a whole. I do not mean what has often been termed the "legitimation" of a system, because that term has been used to imply that the lower strata of a system feel some affinity with or loyalty towards the rulers, and I doubt that this has ever been a significant factor in the survival of world-systems. I mean rather the degree to which the staff or cadres of the system (and I leave this term deliberately vague) feel that their own well-being is wrapped up in the survival of the system as such and the competence of its leaders. It is this staff which not only propagates the myths; it is they who believe them.

But neither force nor the ideological commitment of the staff would suffice were it not for the division of the majority into a larger lower stratum and a smaller middle stratum. Both the revolutionary call for polarization as a strategy of change and the liberal encomium to consensus as the basis of the liberal polity reflect this proposition. The import is far wider than its use in the analysis of contemporary political problems suggests. It is the normal condition of either kind of world-system to have a three-layered structure. When and if this ceases to be the case, the world-system disintegrates.

In a world-empire, the middle stratum is in fact accorded the role of maintaining the marginally-desirable long-distance luxury trade, while the upper stratum concentrates its resources on controlling the military machinery which can collect the tribute, the crucial mode of redistributing surplus. By providing, however, for an access to a limited portion of the surplus to urbanized elements who alone, in pre-modern societies, could contribute political cohesiveness to isolated clusters of primary producers, the upper stratum effectively buys off the potential leadership of coordinated revolt. And by denying access to political rights for this commercial-urban middle stratum, it makes them constantly vulnerable to confiscatory measures whenever their economic profits become sufficiently swollen so that they might begin to create for themselves military strength.

In a world-economy, such "cultural" stratification is not so simple, because the absence of a single political system means the concentration of economic roles vertically rather than horizontally throughout the system. The solution then is to have three *kinds* of states, with pressures for cultural homogenization within each of them – thus, besides the upper stratum of core-states and the lower stratum of peripheral states, there is a middle stratum of semi-peripheral ones.

This semi-periphery is then assigned as it were a specific economic role, but the reason is less economic than political. That is to say, one might make a good case that the world-economy as an economy would function every bit as well without a semi-periphery. But it would be far less *politically* stable, for it would mean a polarized world-system. The existence of the third category means precisely that the upper stratum is not faced with the *unified* opposition of all the others because the *middle* stratum is both exploited and exploiter. It follows that the specific economic role is not all that important, and has thus changed through the various historical stages of the modern world-system.

Where then does class analysis fit in all of this? And what in such a formulation are nations, nationalities, peoples, ethnic groups? First of all, without arguing the point now, I would contend that all these latter terms denote variants of a single phenomenon which I will term "ethno-nations".

Both classes and ethnic groups, or status-groups, or ethno-nations are phenomena of world-economies and much of the enormous confusion that has surrounded the concrete analysis of their functioning can be attributed quite simply to the fact that they have been analyzed as though they existed within the nation-states of this world-economy, instead of within the world-economy as a whole. This has been a Procrustean bed indeed.

The range of economic activities being far wider in the core than in the periphery, the range of syndical interest groups is far wider there. Thus, it has been widely observed that there does not exist in many parts of the world today a proletariat of the kind which exists in, say, Europe or North America. But this is a confusing way to state the observation. Industrial activity being disproportionately concentrated in certain parts of the world-economy, industrial wage-workers are to be found principally in certain geographic regions. Their interests as a syndical group are determined by their collective relationship to the world-economy. Their ability to influence the political functioning of this world-economy is shaped by the fact that they command larger percentages of the population in one sovereign entity than another. The form their organizations take have, in large part, been governed too by these political boundaries. The same might be said about industrial capitalists. Class analysis is perfectly capable of accounting for the political position of, let us say, French skilled workers if we look at their structural position and interests in the world-economy. Similarly with ethno-nations. The meaning of ethnic consciousness in a core area is considerably different from that of ethnic consciousness in a peripheral area precisely because of the different class position such ethnic groups have in the world-economy.

Political struggles of ethno-nations or segments of classes within national boundaries of course are the daily bread and butter of local politics. But their significance or consequences can only be fruitfully analyzed if one spells out the implications of their organizational activity or political demands for the functioning of the world-economy. This also incidentally makes possible more rational assessments of these politics in terms of some set of evaluative criteria such as "left" and "right".

The functioning then of a capitalist world-economy requires that groups pursue their economic interests within a single world market while seeking to distort this market for their benefit by organizing to exert influence on states, some of which are far more powerful than others but none of which controls the world-market in its entirety. Of course, we shall find on closer inspection that there are periods where one state is relatively quite powerful and other periods where power is more diffuse and contested, permitting weaker states broader ranges of action. We can talk then of the relative tightness or looseness of the world-system as an important variable and seek to analyze why this dimension tends to be cyclical in nature, as it seems to have been for several hundred years. [. . .]

9 Sociology of the Global System

Leslie Sklair

The Conceptual Space for Transnational Practices (TNP)

The concept of transnational practices refers to the effects of what people do when they are acting within specific institutional contexts that cross state borders. Transnational practices create globalizing processes. TNPs focus attention on observable phenomena, some of which are measurable, instead of highly abstract and often very vague relations between conceptual entities. [. . .]

The global system is most fruitfully conceptualized as a system that operates at three levels, and knowledge about which can be organized in three spheres, namely the economic, the political, and the culture-ideology. Each sphere is typically characterized by a representative institution, cohesive structures of practices, organized and patterned, which can only be properly understood in terms of their transnational effects. The dominant form of globalization in the present era is undoubtedly capitalist globalization. This being the case, the primary agents and institutional focus of economic transnational practices are the transnational corporations.

However, there are others. The World Bank, the IMF, WTO, commodity exchanges, the G7 (political leaders of the seven most important economies), the US Treasury and so on are mostly controlled by those who share the interests of the major TNCs and the major TNCs share their interests. In a revealing report on 'IMF: Efforts to Advance U.S. Policies at the Fund' by the US General Accounting Office (GAO-01-214, January 23, 2001) we discover that the US Treasury and the Executive Director actively promoted US policies on sound banking, labour issues, and audits of military expenditures. The report concluded that it was difficult to determine the precise significance of US influence, because other countries generally support the same policies. This phenomenon is widely known as the Washington Consensus, a term coined by John Williamson of the Institute for International Economics.

> By 'Washington' Williamson meant not only the US government, but all those institutions and networks of opinion leaders centered in the world's defacto capital – the IMF, World Bank, think-tanks, politically sophisticated investment bankers, and worldly finance ministers, all those who meet each other in Washington and collectively define the conventional wisdom of the moment . . . [One may roughly] summarize this consensus as . . . the belief that Victorian virtue and economic policy – free markets and sound money – is the key to economic development.

Original publication details: Edited from Leslie Sklair, "Transnational Practices, Corporations, Class and Consumerism," in *Globalization: Capitalism and its Alternatives*, 3rd edn. (Oxford University Press, 2002). Reprinted by permission of Oxford University Press.

This is the transnational capitalist class at work. The underlying goal of keeping global capitalism on course is in constant tension with the selfish and destabilizing actions of those who cannot resist system-threatening opportunities to get rich quick or to cut their losses. It is, however, the direct producers, not the transnational capitalist class who usually suffer most when this occurs as, for example, the tin miners of Bolivia and the rest of the world found out when the London Metal Exchange terminated its tin contract in 1985 and when the Association of Coffee Producing Countries collapsed late in 2001. [. . .]

It may be helpful to spell out who determine priorities for economic, political and culture-ideology transnational practices, and what they actually do. Those who own and control the TNCs organize the production of commodities and the services necessary to manufacture and sell them. The state fraction of the transnational capitalist class produces the political environment within which the products and services can be successfully marketed all over the world irrespective of their origins and qualities. Those responsible for the dissemination of the culture-ideology of consumerism produce the values and attitudes that create and sustain the need for the products. These are analytical rather than empirical distinctions. In the real world they are inextricably mixed. TNCs get involved in host country politics, and the culture-ideology of consumerism is largely promulgated through the transnational corporations involved in mass media and advertising. Members of the transnational capitalist class often work directly for TNCs, and their life styles are exemplary for the spread of consumerism. Nevertheless, it is useful to make these analytical distinctions, particularly where the apparent and real empirical contradictions are difficult to disentangle.

The thesis on which this conceptual apparatus rests and on which any viable theory of the current dominant global system depends is that capitalism is changing qualitatively from an international to a globalizing system. This is the subject of a heated debate in academic, political and cultural circles. The idea that capitalism has entered a new global phase (whether it be organized or disorganized) clearly commands a good deal of support though, unsurprisingly, there are considerable differences on the details. The conception of capitalism of Ross and Trachte convincingly locates the emergence of global capitalism in a series of technological revolutions (primarily in transportation, communications, electronics, biotechnology), and this provides a key support to the global system theory being elaborated here. My focus on transnational corporations draws on a large and rich literature on the global corporation, again full of internal disputes, but based on the premise, well expressed by Howells and Wood that 'the production processes within large firms are being decoupled from specific territories and being formed into new global systems'. [. . .]

Economic Transnational Practices

Economic transnational practices are economic practices that transcend state boundaries. These may seem to be entirely contained within the borders of a single country even though their effects are transnational. For example, within one country there are consumer demands for products that are unavailable, in general or during particular seasons, from domestic sources. Retailers place orders with suppliers who fill the orders from foreign sources. Neither the retailer nor the consumer needs to know or care where the product comes from, though some countries now have country of origin rules making mandatory the display of this information. Many campaigning groups make sure that customers know, for example, that some products come from sweatshops in Asia or the USA. There may be a parallel situation in the supplier country. Local producers may simply sell their products to a domestic marketing board or wholesaler and neither know nor care who the final consumer is. Transnational corporations, big or small, enter the scene when sellers, intermediaries, and buyers are parts of the same transnational network.

Hundreds of thousands of companies based all over the world export goods and services. In the US alone in the late 1990s there were more than 200,000 exporting companies according to the website of the US Department of Commerce. Of this large number of exporters only about 15 percent operated from multiple locations, but these accounted for about 80 percent of exports from the US and almost half of manufacturing exports were from the top 50 firms. They, of course, are the major TNCs, comprising the less than one percent of US manufacturers that export to 50 or more countries. Over half of all US export value derives from their transnational economic practices and, significantly, much of their business is comprised of intra-firm transactions. The picture is similar in many other countries with firms that export manufactured goods. The global economy is dominated by a few gigantic transnational corporations marketing their products, many of them global brands, all over the world, some medium-sized companies producing in a few locations and selling in multiple markets, while many many more small firms sell from one location to one or a few other locations.

One important consequence of the expansion of the capitalist world economy has been that individual economic actors (like workers and entrepreneurs) and collective economic actors (like trade unions and TNCs) have become much more conscious of the transnationality of their practices and have striven to extend their global influence. As capitalist globalization spread, anti-globalization researchers and activists focused on imports and exports, and vested some products with great political and culture-ideology significance. Increasing numbers of consumers now register where what they are buying comes from, and producers now register where what they are producing will go to, and this knowledge may affect their actions. An important example of this process is the rapid growth of ethical and organic marketing between Third World producers and First World consumers. These transnational practices must be seen within the context of an unprecedented increase in the volume of economic transnational practices since the 1950s, as evidenced by the tremendous growth of cross-border trade. According to the World Bank, global exports rose from US$94 billion in 1965, to $1,365 billion in 1986, $3,500 billion in 1993 and over $5,400 billion in 1999. Foreign investment and other types of capital flows have increased even more rapidly. This means that even some quite poor people in some poor countries now have access to many non-local consumer goods, and through their use of the mass media are becoming more aware of the status-conferring advantages that global branded goods and services have over others. [. . .]

The Transnational Capitalist Class

The transnational capitalist class is not made up of capitalists in the traditional Marxist sense. Direct ownership or control of the means of production is no longer the exclusive criterion for serving the interests of capital, particularly not the global interests of capital.

The transnational capitalist class (TCC) is transnational in at least five senses. Its members tend to share global as well as local economic interests; they seek to exert economic control in the workplace, political control in domestic and international politics, and culture-ideology control in everyday life; they tend to have global rather than local perspectives on a variety of issues; they tend to be people from many countries, more and more of whom begin to consider themselves citizens of the world as well as of their places of birth; and they tend to share similar lifestyles, particularly patterns of luxury consumption of goods and services. In my formulation, the transnational capitalist class includes the following four fractions:

- TNC executives and their local affiliates (corporate fraction);
- globalizing state and inter-state bureaucrats and politicians (state fraction);
- globalizing professionals (technical fraction); and
- merchants and media (consumerist fraction).

This class sees its mission as organizing the conditions under which its interests and the interests of the global system (which usually but do not always coincide) can be furthered within the transnational, inter-state, national and local contexts. The concept of the transnational capitalist class implies that there is one central transnational capitalist class that makes system-wide decisions, and that it connects with the TCC in each community, region and country.

Political transnational practices are not primarily conducted within conventional political organizations. Neither the transnational capitalist class nor any other class operates primarily through transnational political parties. However, loose transnational political groupings do exist and they do have some effects on, and are affected by, the political practices of the TCC in most countries. There are no genuine transnational political parties, though there appears to be a growing interest in international associations of parties, which are sometimes mistaken for transnational parties. [. . .]

There are, however, various transnational political organizations through which fractions of the TCC operate locally, for example, the Rotary Club and its offshoots and the network of American, European and Japan-related Chambers of Commerce that straddles the globe. As Errington and Gewertz show in their study of a Rotary Club in Melanesia as well as my own research on AmCham in Mexico, these organizations work as crucial transmission belts and lines of communication between global capitalism and local business. [. . .]

At a more elevated level are the Trilateral Commission of the great and good from the United States, Europe and Japan whose business is 'Elite Planning for World Management'; the World Economic Forum which meets at Davos in Switzerland and the annual global conferences organized by *Fortune* magazine that bring together the corporate and the state fractions of the TCC. Many other similar but less well-known networks for capitalist globalization exist, for example the Bilderberg Group and Caux Round Table of senior business leaders. There are few major cities in any First or Third World (and now New Second World) country that do not have members of or connections with one or more of these organizations. They vary in strength from the major First World political and business capitals, through important Third World cities like Cairo, Singapore and Mexico City, to nominal presences in some of the poorer countries in Africa, Asia and Latin America. They are backed up by many powerful official bodies, such as foreign trade and economics departments of the major states. Specialized agencies of the World Bank and the IMF, WTO, US Agency for International Development (USAID), development banks, and the

UN work with TNCs, local businesses, and NGOs (willing and not so willing) in projects that promote the agenda of capitalist globalization. [. . .]

Labour and the Transnational Capitalist Class

The relative strength of the transnational capitalist class can be understood in terms of the relative weakness of transnational labour. Labour is represented by some genuinely transnational trade unions. . . . In addition, there are some industrially based transnational union organizations, for example the International Metalworkers Federation, and the International Union of Food and Allied Workers' Associations. These have been involved in genuine transnational labour struggles, and have gained some short-term victories. However, they face substantial difficulties in their struggles against organized capital, locally and transnationally, and they have little influence. [. . .]

While most TNCs in most countries will follow the local rules regarding the unions, host governments, particularly those promoting export processing industries (not always under pressure from foreign investors), have often suspended national labour legislation in order to attract TNCs and/or to keep production going and foreign currency rolling in. With very few exceptions, most globalizing bureaucrats and politicians wanting to take advantage of the fruits of capitalist globalization will be unhelpful towards labour unions, if not downright hostile to them when they dare to challenge the transnational capitalist class. [. . .]

Culture-Ideology Transnational Practices

[. . .] Bagdikian characterized those who control this system [world media] as the lords of the global village. They purvey their product (a relatively undifferentiated mass of news, information, ideas, entertainment and popular culture) to a rapidly expanding public, eventually the whole world. He argued that national boundaries are growing increasingly meaningless as the main actors (five groups at the time he was writing) strive for total control in the production, delivery, and marketing of what we can call the culture-ideology goods of the capitalist global system. Their goal is to create a buying mood for the benefit of the global troika of media, advertising and consumer goods manufacturers. 'Nothing in human experience has prepared men, women and children for the modern television techniques of fixing human attention and creating the uncritical mood required to sell goods, many of which are marginal at best to human needs'. Two symbolic facts: by the age of 16, the average North American youth has been exposed to more than 300,000 television commercials; and the former Soviet Union sold advertising slots on cosmonaut suits and space ships! In order to connect and explain these facts, we need to generate a new framework, namely the culture-ideology of consumerism.

The Culture-Ideology of Consumerism

The transformation of the culture-ideology of consumerism from a sectional preference of the rich to a globalizing phenomenon can be explained in terms of two central factors, factors that are historically unprecedented. First, capitalism entered a qualitatively new globalizing phase in the 1960s. . . . [I]n the second half of the twentieth century, for the first time in human history, the dominant economic system, capitalism, was sufficiently productive to provide a basic package of material possessions and services to almost everyone in the First World and to privileged groups elsewhere. . . . A rapidly globalizing system of mass media was also geared up to tell everyone what was available and, crucially, to persuade people that this culture-ideology of consumerism was what a happy and satisfying life was all about. . . .

Mass media perform many functions for global capitalism. They speed up the circulation of material goods through advertising, which reduces the time between production and consumption. They begin to inculcate the dominant ideology into the minds of viewers, listeners and readers from an early age, in the words of Esteinou Madrid, 'creating the political/cultural demand for the survival of capitalism'. The systematic blurring of the lines between information, entertainment, and promotion of products lies at the heart of this practice. This has not in itself created consumerism, for consumer cultures have been in place for centuries. What it has created is a reformulation of consumerism that transforms all the mass media and their contents into opportunities to sell ideas, values, products, in short, a consumerist worldview. [. . .]

Contemporary consumer culture would not be possible without the shopping mall, both symbolically and substantively. As Crawford argued, the merging of the architecture of the mall with the culture of the theme park has become the key symbol and the key spatial reference point for consumer capitalism, not only in North America but increasingly all over the world. What Goss terms the magic of the mall has to be understood on several levels, how the consuming environment is carefully designed and controlled, the seductive nature of the consuming experience, the transformation of nominal public space into actual private terrain. Although there are certainly anomalies of decaying city districts interspersed with gleaming malls bursting with consumer goods in the First World, it is in the poorer parts of the Third World that these anomalies are at their most stark. Third World malls until quite recently catered mainly to the needs and wants of expatriate TNC executives and officials, and local members of the transnational capitalist class. The success of the culture-ideology of consumerism can be observed all over the world in these malls, where now large numbers of workers and their families flock to buy, usually with credit cards, thus locking themselves into the financial system of capitalist globalization. [. . .]

The Theory of the Global System: A Summary

The theory of the global system can be summarized, graphically, as follows. All global systems rest on economic transnational practices and at the highest level of abstraction these are the building blocks of the system. Concretely, in the capitalist global system they are mainly located in the major transnational corporations. Transnational political practices are the principles of organization of the system. Members of the transnational capitalist class drive the system, and by manipulating the design of the system they can build variations into it. Transnational culture-ideology practices are the nuts and bolts and the glue that hold the system together. Without them, parts of the system would drift off into space. This is accomplished through the culture-ideology of consumerism. [. . .]

In order to work properly the dominant institutions in each of the three spheres have to take control of key resources. Under the conditions of capitalist globalization, the transnational corporations strive to control global capital and material resources, the transnational capitalist class strives to control global power, and the transnational agents and institutions of the culture-ideology of consumerism strive to control the realm of ideas. Effective corporate control of global capital and resources is almost complete. There are few important natural resources that are entirely exempt from the formal or effective control of the TNCs or official agencies with whom they have strategic alliances. The transnational capitalist class and its local affiliates exert their rule through its connections with globalizing bureaucrats and politicians in pro-capitalist political parties or social democratic parties that choose not to fundamentally challenge the global capitalist project. The local affiliates of the TCC exert authority in non-capitalist states indirectly to a greater or lesser extent. This is the price levied as a sort of entrance fee into the capitalist global system. In the last resort, it is the corporate control of capital and labour that is the decisive factor for those who do not wish to be excluded from the system.

The struggle for control of ideas in the interests of capitalist consumerism is fierce, the goal is to create the one-dimensional man within the apparently limitless vistas of consumerism that Marcuse prophesied. Ideas that are antagonistic to the global capitalist project can be reduced to one central counter-hegemonic idea, the rejection of the culture-ideology of consumerism itself, and they get little exposure in the mass media, as opposed to alternative media where they are at the core of an exciting cultural diversity for minority groups all over the world. Without consumerism, the rationale for continuous capitalist accumulation dissolves. It is the capacity to commercialize and commodify all ideas and the products in which they adhere, television programmes, advertisements, newsprint, books, tapes, CDs, videos, films, the Internet and so on, that global capitalism strives to appropriate. [. . .]

10 Realism and Complex Interdependence

Robert O. Keohane and Joseph S. Nye

One's assumptions about world politics profoundly affect what one sees and how one constructs theories to explain events. We believe that the assumptions of political realists, whose theories dominated the postwar period, are often an inadequate basis for analyzing the politics of interdependence. The realist assumptions about world politics can be seen as defining an extreme set of conditions or *ideal type*. One could also imagine very different conditions. In this chapter, we shall construct another ideal type, the opposite of realism. We call it *complex interdependence*. After establishing the differences between realism and complex interdependence, we shall argue that complex interdependence sometimes comes closer to reality than does realism. When it does, traditional explanations of change in international regimes become questionable and the search for new explanatory models becomes more urgent.

For political realists, international politics, like all other politics, is a struggle for power but, unlike domestic politics, a struggle dominated by organized violence. In the words of the most influential postwar textbook, "All history shows that nations active in international politics are continuously preparing for, actively involved in, or recovering from organized violence in the form of war." Three assumptions are integral to the realist vision. First, states as coherent units are the dominant actors in world politics. This is a double assumption: states are predominant; and they act as coherent units. Second, realists assume that force is a usable and effective instrument of policy. Other instruments may also be employed, but using or threatening force is the most effective means of wielding power. Third, partly because of their second assumption, realists assume a hierarchy of issues in world politics, headed by questions of military security: the "high politics" of military security dominates the "low politics" of economic and social affairs.

These realist assumptions define an ideal type of world politics. They allow us to imagine a world in which politics is continually characterized by active or potential conflict among states, with the use of force possible at any time. Each state attempts to defend its territory and interests from real or perceived threats. Political integration among states is slight and lasts only as long as it serves the national interests of the most powerful states. Transnational actors either do not exist or are politically unimportant. Only the adept exercise of force or the threat of force permits states to survive, and only while statesmen succeed in adjusting their interests, as in a well-functioning balance of power, is the system stable.

Original publication details: Excerpted from Robert O. Keohane and Joseph S. Nye, "Realism and Complex Interdependence," in Robert O. Keohane and Joseph S. Nye, *Power and Interdependence* (Addison-Wesley, 2001), 3rd ed., pp. 3–7. Copyright © 2001 by Robert O. Keohane and Joseph S. Nye. Reprinted by permission of Addison-Wesley Educational Publishers, Inc.

Each of the realist assumptions can be challenged. If we challenge them all simultaneously, we can imagine a world in which actors other than states participate directly in world politics, in which a clear hierarchy of issues does not exist, and in which force is an ineffective instrument of policy. Under these conditions – which we call the characteristics of complex interdependence – one would expect world politics to be very different than under realist conditions.

We will explore these differences in the next section of this chapter. We do not argue, however, that complex interdependence faithfully reflects world political reality. Quite the contrary: both it and the realist portrait are ideal types. Most situations will fall somewhere between these two extremes. Sometimes, realist assumptions will be accurate, or largely accurate, but frequently complex interdependence will provide a better portrayal of reality. Before one decides what explanatory model to apply to a situation or problem, one will need to understand the degree to which realist or complex interdependence assumptions correspond to the situation.

The Characteristics of Complex Interdependence

Complex interdependence has three main characteristics:

1   *Multiple channels* connect societies, including: informal ties between governmental elites as well as formal foreign office arrangements; informal ties among nongovernmental elites (face-to-face and through telecommunications); and transnational organizations (such as multinational banks or corporations). These channels can be summarized as interstate, transgovernmental, and transnational relations. *Interstate* relations are the normal channels assumed by realists. *Transgovernmental* applies when we relax the realist assumption that states act coherently as units; *transnational* applies when we relax the assumption that states are the only units.

2   The agenda of interstate relationships consists of multiple issues that are not arranged in a clear or consistent hierarchy. This *absence of hierarchy among issues* means, among other things, that military security does not consistently dominate the agenda. Many issues arise from what used to be considered domestic policy, and the distinction between domestic and foreign issues becomes blurred. These issues are considered in several government departments (not just foreign offices), and at several levels. Inadequate policy coordination on these issues involves significant costs. Different issues generate different coalitions, both within governments and across them, and involve different degrees of conflict. Politics does not stop at the waters' edge.

3   Military force is not used by governments toward other governments within the region, or on the issues, when complex interdependence prevails. It may, however, be important in these governments' relations with governments outside that region, or on other issues. Military force could, for instance, be irrelevant to resolving disagreements on economic issues among members of an alliance, yet at the same time be very important for that alliance's political and military relations with a rival bloc. For the former relationships this condition of complex interdependence would be met; for the latter, it would not.

Traditional theories of international politics implicitly or explicitly deny the accuracy of these three assumptions. Traditionalists are therefore tempted also to deny the relevance of criticisms based on the complex interdependence ideal type. We believe, however, that our three conditions are fairly well approximated on some global issues of economic and ecological interdependence and that they come close to characterizing the entire relationship between some countries. One of our purposes here is to prove that contention and to try to convince you to take these criticisms of traditional assumptions seriously.

Multiple channels

A visit to any major airport is a dramatic way to confirm the existence of multiple channels of contact among advanced industrial countries; there is a voluminous literature to prove it. Bureaucrats from different countries deal directly with one another at meetings and on the telephone as well as in writing. Similarly, nongovernmental elites frequently get together in the normal course of business, in organizations such as the Trilateral Commission, and in conferences sponsored by private foundations.

In addition, multinational firms and banks affect both domestic and interstate relations. The limits on private firms, or the closeness of ties between government and business, vary considerably from one society to another; but the participation of large and dynamic organizations, not controlled entirely by governments, has become a normal part of foreign as well as domestic relations.

These actors are important not only because of their activities in pursuit of their own interests, but also because they act as transmission belts, making government policies in various countries more sensitive to one another. As the scope of governments' domestic activities has broadened, and as corporations, banks, and (to a lesser extent) trade unions have made decisions that transcend national boundaries, the domestic policies of different countries impinge on one another more and more. Transnational communications reinforce these effects. Thus, foreign economic policies touch more domestic economic activity than in the past, blurring the lines between domestic and foreign policy and increasing the number of issues relevant to foreign policy. Parallel developments in issues of environmental regulation and control over technology reinforce this trend.

Absence of hierarchy among issues

Foreign affairs agendas – that is, sets of issues relevant to foreign policy with which governments are concerned – have become larger and more diverse. No longer can all issues be subordinated to military security. As Secretary of State Kissinger described the situation in 1975:

> progress in dealing with the traditional agenda is no longer enough. A new and unprecedented kind of issue has emerged. The problems of energy, resources, environment, population, the uses of space and the seas now rank with questions of military security, ideology and territorial rivalry which have traditionally made up the diplomatic agenda.

Kissinger's list, which could be expanded, illustrates how governments' policies, even those previously considered merely domestic, impinge on one another. The extensive consultative arrangements developed by the OECD, as well as the GATT, IMF, and the European Community, indicate how characteristic the overlap of domestic and foreign policy is among developed pluralist countries. The organization within nine major departments of the United States government (Agriculture,

Commerce, Defense, Health, Education and Welfare, Interior, Justice, Labor, State, and Treasury) and many other agencies reflects their extensive international commitments. The multiple, overlapping issues that result make a nightmare of governmental organization.

When there are multiple issues on the agenda, many of which threaten the interests of domestic groups but do not clearly threaten the nation as a whole, the problems of formulating a coherent and consistent foreign policy increase. In 1975 energy was a foreign policy problem, but specific remedies, such as a tax on gasoline and automobiles, involved domestic legislation opposed by auto workers and companies alike. As one commentator observed, "virtually every time Congress has set a national policy that changed the way people live . . . the action came after a consensus had developed, bit by bit, over the years, that a problem existed and that there was one best way to solve it." Opportunities for delay, for special protection, for inconsistency and incoherence abound when international politics requires aligning the domestic policies of pluralist democratic countries.

Minor role of military force

Political scientists have traditionally emphasized the role of military force in international politics. Force dominates other means of power: *if* there are no constraints on one's choice of instruments (a hypothetical situation that has only been approximated in the two world wars), the state with superior military force will prevail. If the security dilemma for all states were extremely acute, military force, supported by economic and other resources, would clearly be the dominant source of power. Survival is the primary goal of all states, and in the worst situations, force is ultimately necessary to guarantee survival. Thus military force is always a central component of national power.

Yet particularly among industrialized, pluralist countries, the perceived margin of safety has widened: fears of attack in general have declined, and fears of attacks *by one another* are virtually nonexistent. France has abandoned the *tous azimuts* (defense in all directions) strategy that President de Gaulle advocated (it was not taken entirely seriously even at the time). Canada's last war plans for fighting the United States were abandoned half a century ago. Britain and Germany no longer feel threatened by each other. Intense relationships of mutual influence exist between these countries, but in most of them force is irrelevant or unimportant as an instrument of policy.

Moreover, force is often not an appropriate way of achieving other goals (such as economic and ecological welfare) that are becoming more important. It is not impossible to imagine dramatic conflict or revolutionary change in which the use or threat of military force over an economic issue or among advanced industrial countries might become plausible. Then realist assumptions would again be a reliable guide to events. But in most situations, the effects of military force are both costly and uncertain.

Even when the direct use of force is barred among a group of countries, however, military power can still be used politically. Each superpower continues to use the threat of force to deter attacks by other superpowers on itself or its allies; its deterrence ability thus serves an indirect, protective role, which it can use in bargaining on other issues with its allies. This bargaining tool is particularly important for the United States, whose allies are concerned about potential Soviet threats and which has fewer other means of influence over its allies than does the Soviet Union over its Eastern European partners. The United States has, accordingly, taken advantage of the Europeans' (particularly the Germans') desire for its protection and linked the issue of troop levels in Europe to trade and monetary negotiations. Thus, although the first-order effect of deterrent force is essentially negative – to deny effective offensive power to a superpower opponent – a state can use that force positively – to gain political influence.

Thus, even for countries whose relations approximate complex interdependence, two serious qualifications remain: (1) drastic social and political change could cause force again to become an important direct instrument of policy; and (2) even when elites' interests are complementary, a country that uses military force to protect another may have significant political influence over the other country.

In North–South relations, or relations among Third World countries, as well as in East–West relations, force is often important. Military power helps the Soviet Union to dominate Eastern Europe economically as well as politically. The threat of open or covert American military intervention has helped to limit revolutionary changes in the Caribbean, especially in Guatemala in 1954 and in the Dominican Republic in 1965. Secretary of State Kissinger, in January 1975, issued a veiled warning to members of the Organization of Petroleum Exporting Countries (OPEC) that the United States might use force against them "where there is some actual strangulation of the industrialized world."

Even in these rather conflictual situations, however, the recourse to force seems less likely now than at most times during the century before 1945. The destructiveness of nuclear weapons makes any attack against a nuclear power dangerous. Nuclear weapons are mostly used as a deterrent. Threats of nuclear action against much weaker countries may occasionally be efficacious, but they are equally or more likely to solidify relations between one's adversaries. The limited usefulness of conventional force to control socially mobilized populations has been shown by the United States' failure in Vietnam as well as by the rapid decline of colonialism in Africa. Furthermore, employing force on one issue against an independent state with which one has a variety of relationships is likely to rupture mutually profitable relations on other issues. In other words, the use of force often has costly effects on nonsecurity goals. And finally, in Western democracies, popular opposition to prolonged military conflicts is very high.

It is clear that these constraints bear unequally on various countries, or on the same countries in different situations. Risks of nuclear escalation affect everyone, but domestic opinion is far less constraining for communist states, or for authoritarian regional powers, than for the United States, Europe, or Japan. Even authoritarian countries may be reluctant to use force to obtain economic objectives when such use might be ineffective and disrupt other relationships. Both the difficulty of controlling socially mobilized populations with foreign troops and the changing technology of weaponry may actually enhance the ability of certain countries, or nonstate groups, to use terrorism as a political weapon without effective fear of reprisal.

The fact that the changing role of force has uneven effects does not make the change less important, but it does make matters more complex. This complexity is compounded by differences in the usability of force among issue areas. When an issue arouses little interest or passion, force may be unthinkable. In such instances, complex interdependence may be a valuable concept for analyzing the political process. But if that issue becomes a matter of life and death – as some people thought oil might become – the use or threat of force could become decisive again. Realist assumptions would then be more relevant. [. . .]

The Political Processes of Complex Interdependence

Role of international organizations

Finally, the existence of multiple channels leads one to predict a different and significant role for international organizations in world politics. Realists in the tradition of Hans J. Morgenthau have portrayed a world in which states, acting from self-interest, struggle for "power and peace." Security issues are dominant; war threatens. In such a world, one may assume that international institutions will have a minor role, limited by the rare congruence of such interests. International organizations are then clearly peripheral to world politics. But in a world of multiple issues imperfectly linked, in which coalitions are formed transnationally and transgovernmentally, the potential role of international institutions in political bargaining is greatly increased. In particular, they help set the international agenda, and act as catalysts for coalition-formation and as arenas for political initiatives and linkage by weak states.

Governments must organize themselves to cope with the flow of business generated by international organizations. By defining the salient issues, and deciding which issues can be grouped together, organizations may help to determine governmental priorities and the nature of interdepartmental committees and other arrangements within governments. The 1972 Stockholm Environment Conference strengthened the position of environmental agencies in various governments. The 1974 World Food Conference focused the attention of important parts of the United States government on prevention of food shortages. The September 1975 United Nations special session on proposals for a New International Economic Order generated an intragovernmental debate about policies toward the Third World in general. The International Monetary Fund and the General Agreement on Tariffs and Trade have focused governmental activity on money and trade instead of on private direct investment, which has no comparable international organization.

By bringing officials together, international organizations help to activate potential coalitions in world politics. It is quite obvious that international organizations have been very important in bringing together representatives of less developed countries, most of which do not maintain embassies in one another's capitals. Third World strategies of solidarity among poor countries have been developed in and for a series of international conferences, mostly under the auspices of the United Nations. International organizations also allow agencies of governments, which might not otherwise come into contact, to turn potential or tacit coalitions into explicit transgovernmental coalitions characterized by direct communications. In some cases, international secretariats deliberately promote this process by forming coalitions with groups of governments, or with units of governments, as well as with nongovernmental organizations having similar interests.

International organizations are frequently congenial institutions for weak states. The one-state-one-vote norm of the United Nations system favors coalitions of the small and powerless. Secretariats are often responsive to Third World demands. Furthermore, the substantive norms of most international organizations, as they have developed over the years, stress social and economic equity as well as the equality of states. Past resolutions expressing Third World positions, sometimes agreed to with reservations by industrialized countries, are used to legitimize other demands. These agreements are rarely binding, but up to a point the norms of the institution make opposition look more harshly self-interested and less defensible.

Table 10.1 *Political processes under conditions of realism and complex interdependence*

	Realism	Complex interdependence
Goals of actors	Military security will be the dominant goal.	Goals of states will vary by issue area. Transgovernmental politics will make goals difficult to define. Transnational actors will pursue their own goals.
Instruments of state policy	Military force will be most effective, although economic and other instruments will also be used.	Power resources specific to issue areas will be most relevant. Manipulation of interdependence, international organizations, and transnational actors will be major instruments.
Agenda formation	Potential shifts in the balance of power and security threats will set the agenda in high politics and will strongly influence other agendas.	Agenda will be affected by changes in the distribution of power resources within issue areas; the status of international regimes; changes in the importance of transnational actors; linkages from other issues and politicization as a result of rising sensitivity interdependence.
Linkages of issues	Linkages will reduce differences in outcomes among issue areas and reinforce international hierarchy.	Linkages by strong states will be more difficult to make since force will be ineffective. Linkages by weak states through international organizations will erode rather than reinforce hierarchy.
Roles of international organizations	Roles are minor, limited by state power and the importance of military force.	Organizations will set agendas, induce coalition-formation, and act as arenas for political action by weak states. Ability to choose the organizational forum for an issue and to mobilize votes will be an important political resource.

International organizations also allow small and weak states to pursue linkage strategies. In the discussions on a New International Economic Order, Third World states insisted on linking oil price and availability to other questions on which they had traditionally been unable to achieve their objectives. Small and weak states have also followed a strategy of linkage in the series of Law of the Sea conferences sponsored by the United Nations.

Complex interdependence therefore yields different political patterns than does the realist conception of the world. (Table 10.1 summarizes these differences.) Thus, one would expect traditional theories to fail to explain international regime change in situations of complex interdependence. But, for a situation that approximates realist conditions, traditional theories should be appropriate.

11   World Society and the Nation-State

John W. Meyer, John Boli, George M. Thomas, and Francisco O. Ramirez

This essay reviews arguments and evidence concerning the following proposition: *Many features of the contemporary nation-state derive from worldwide models constructed and propagated through global cultural and associational processes.* These models and the purposes they reflect (e.g., equality, socioeconomic progress, human development) are highly rationalized, articulated, and often surprisingly consensual. Worldwide models define and legitimate agendas for local action, shaping the structures and policies of nation-states and other national and local actors in virtually all of the domains of rationalized social life – business, politics, education, medicine, science, even the family and religion. The institutionalization of world models helps explain many puzzling features of contemporary national societies, such as structural isomorphism in the face of enormous differences in resources and traditions, ritualized and rather loosely coupled organizational efforts, and elaborate structuration to serve purposes that are largely of exogenous origins. World models have long been in operation as shapers of states and societies, but they have become especially important in the postwar era as the cultural and organizational development of world society has intensified at an unprecedented rate.

The operation of world society through peculiarly cultural and associational processes depends heavily on its statelessness. The almost feudal character of parcelized legal-rational sovereignty in the world has the seemingly paradoxical result of diminishing the causal importance of the organized hierarchies of power and interests celebrated in most "realist" social scientific theories. The statelessness of world society also explains, in good measure, the lack of attention of the social sciences to the coherence and impact of world society's cultural and associational properties. Despite Tocqueville's well-known analysis of the importance of cultural and associational life in the nearly stateless American society of the 1830s, the social sciences are more than a little reluctant to acknowledge patterns of influence and conformity that cannot be explained solely as matters of power relations or functional rationality. This reluctance is most acute with respect to global development. Our effort here represents, we hope, a partial corrective for it.

We are trying to account for a world whose societies, organized as nation-states, are structurally similar in many unexpected dimensions and change in unexpectedly similar ways. A hypothetical example may be useful to illustrate our arguments, and

Original publication details: Excerpted from John W. Meyer, John Boli, George M. Thomas, and Francisco O. Ramirez, "World Society and the Nation-State," *American Journal of Sociology*, 1997, pp. 144–6, 150–1, 152–3, 157–61, 173–5. Reprinted by permission of the University of Chicago Press.

we shall carry the example throughout the essay. If an unknown society were "discovered" on a previously unknown island, it is clear that many changes would occur. A government would soon form, looking something like a modern state with many of the usual ministries and agencies. Official recognition by other states and admission to the United Nations would ensue. The society would be analyzed as an economy, with standard types of data, organizations, and policies for domestic and international transactions. Its people would be formally reorganized as citizens with many familiar rights, while certain categories of citizens – children, the elderly, the poor – would be granted special protection. Standard forms of discrimination, especially ethnic and gender based, would be discovered and decried. The population would be counted and classified in ways specified by world census models. Modern educational, medical, scientific, and family law institutions would be developed. All this would happen more rapidly, and with greater penetration to the level of daily life, in the present day than at any earlier time because world models applicable to the island society are more highly codified and publicized than ever before. Moreover, world-society organizations devoted to educating and advising the islanders about the models' importance and utility are more numerous and active than ever.

What would be unlikely to happen is also clear. Theological disputes about whether the newly discovered *Indios* had souls or were part of the general human moral order would be rare. There would be little by way of an imperial rush to colonize the island. Few would argue that the natives needed only modest citizenship or human rights or that they would best be educated by but a few years of vocational training.

Thus, without knowing anything about the history, culture, practices, or traditions that obtained in this previously unknown society, we could forecast many changes that, upon "discovery," would descend on the island under the general rubric of "development." Our forecast would be imprecise because of the complexity of the interplay among various world models and local traditions, but the likely range of outcomes would be quite limited. We can identify the range of possibilities by using the institutionalist theoretical perspective underlying the analysis in this essay to interpret what has already happened to practically all of the societies of the world after their discovery and incorporation into world society. [. . .]

Explanatory Models

Most analyses see nation-states as collective actors – as products of their own histories and internal forces. We emphasize instead models of the sort depicted in figure 11.1.

Figure 11.1 presents the view that nation-states are more or less exogenously constructed entities – the many individuals both inside and outside the state who engage in state formation and policy formulation are enactors of scripts rather more than they are self-directed actors. The social psychology at work here is that of Goffman or Snow, emphasizing dramaturgical and symbolic processes in place of the hard-boiled calculation of interests assumed by rationalistic actor-centric approaches.

We have deliberately oversimplified figure 11.1 because the proposition we are examining focuses on the enactment dimension of world-societal development. Of course, states, organizations, and individuals also contribute to the content and structure of world culture, and much world-cultural change and elaboration occur within transnational organizations and associations independent of lower-level units. A more

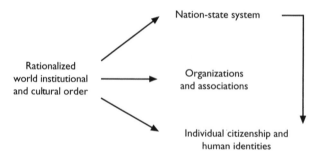

Figure 11.1   *The world as enactment of culture*

complete figure would depict recursive processes among the constituent parts of world society, but here we concentrate on enactment processes.

The exogenous cultural construction of the nation-state model makes it easy and "natural" for standard sociopolitical forms to arise in our island society. Models and measures of such national goals as economic progress and social justice are readily available and morally compelling. Also available are model social problems, defined as the failure to realize these goals, that make it easy to identify and decry such failures as inefficient production methods or violations of rights. Alongside these are prescriptions about standardized social actors and policies that are to be engaged in the effort to resolve these newly recognized problems. All this is widely known and ready for implementation. [. . .]

Isomorphism and Isomorphic Change

Given other perspectives' emphases on the heterogeneity of economic and political resources (realist theories) or on local cultural origins (microphenomenological theories), most lines of thought anticipate striking diversity in political units around the world and in these units' trajectories of change. Our argument accounts for the similarities researchers often are surprised to find. It explains why our island society, despite all the possible configurations of local economic forces, power relationships, and forms of traditional culture it might contain, would promptly take on standardized forms and soon appear to be similar to a hundred other nation-states around the world.

Take the example of women in higher education. Microrealist or functional actor-centric models suggest that female enrollments in universities would increase in developed economies much more than elsewhere. Macrorealist arguments imply that female enrollments would expand in the core much more than the periphery, while microphenomenological arguments point to rising female enrollments in Western but not Islamic countries. However, female enrollments have expanded rapidly everywhere, and in about the same time period – a period in which world societal discourse has emphasized female equality. This finding makes sense only if common world forces are at work.

Isomorphic developments leading to the same conclusion are reported in studies of many other nation-state features: constitutional forms emphasizing both state power and individual rights, mass schooling systems organized around a fairly standard curriculum, rationalized economic and demographic record keeping and data systems, antinatalist population control policies intended to enhance national development, formally equalized female status and rights, expanded human rights in general, expansive environmental policies, development-oriented economic policy, universalistic welfare systems, standard definitions of disease and health care, and even some basic demographic variables. Theories reasoning from the obviously large differences among national economies and cultural traditions have great difficulty accounting for these observed isomorphisms, but they are sensible outcomes if nation-states are enactments of the world cultural order. [. . .]

Processes of World Society's Impact on Nation-States

So far we have argued that the observable isomorphism among nation-states supports our proposition that these entities derive from models embedded in an overarching world culture. What processes in world society construct and shape these "actors" to produce such isomorphism? The usual approach to answering this question would seek to identify mechanisms whereby actors rationally pursuing their interests make similar choices and decisions. This approach implicitly assumes that actor definitions and interests are largely fixed and independent of culture. We find it more useful and revealing to focus on processes that produce or reconstruct the actors themselves. We identify three processes by which world-societal elements authorize and fashion national states: the construction of identity and purpose, systemic maintenance of actor identity, and legitimation of the actorhood of such subnational units as individuals and organized interests.

Construction of nation-state identity and purpose

World society contains much cultural material authoritatively defining the nation-state as the preferred form of sovereign, responsible actor. The external recognition and construction of sovereign statehood has been a crucial dimension of the Western system for centuries, with new claimants especially dependent on obtaining formal recognition from dominant powers. With the anticolonial and self-determination movements of the twentieth century, all sorts of collectivities have learned to organize their claims around a nation-state identity, and the consolidation of the United Nations system has provided a central forum for identity recognition that diminishes the importance of major states. Entry into the system occurs, essentially, via application forms (to the United Nations and other world bodies) on which the applicant must demonstrate appropriately formulated assertions about sovereignty and control over population and territory, along with appropriate aims and purposes.

More than 130 new nation-state entities have formed since 1945. They consistently proclaim, both internally and externally, their conformity to worldwide models of national identity and state structure. So, too, would our island society. But older states, too, have learned to adapt to changes in these models. Thus, through both selection and adaptation, the system has expanded to something close to universality of the nation-state form. Realist theories, grounding their analyses in each country's particular resources and history, would predict a much wider variety of forms, including the retention of older statuses such as formal dependency or indirect incorporation of small or weak entities.

World-cultural models of sovereign identity take concrete form in particular state structures, programs, and policies. As described above, worldwide models of the rationalized nation-state actor define appropriate constitutions, goals, data systems, organization charts, ministry structures, and policies. Models also specify standard forms for the cultural depiction of national identity. Methods of constructing national culture through traditions, museums, tourism, and national intellectual culture are highly stylized. Nation-states are theorized or imagined communities drawing on models that are lodged at the world level.

Often, copying world models or conventions amounts to simple mimesis that has more to do with knowing how to fill in forms than with managing substantive problems. For instance, to compile comparable educational enrollment data in the 1950s, UNESCO statisticians chose to report enrollments for a six-year primary level and three-year junior and senior secondary levels. In ensuing decades, many countries structured their mass schooling systems around this six-year/three-year/three-year model, generally without investigating whether it would best meet any of the presumed purposes of schooling.

Strang shows the extraordinary impact of the legitimized identity system on the survival and stability of states. Throughout modern history, dependent territories have moved to sovereign statehood at a steadily increasing rate that accelerated rapidly in the postwar period. Once sovereign, countries almost never revert to dependence. Even the breakup of the Soviet Union produced not dependent territories but formally sovereign nation-states, unprepared as some of the former republics were for this status. Thus, it is highly unlikely that our island society would be incorporated as a dependent territory of an extant nation-state; this would be too great a violation of the legitimized right to self-determination. Moreover, establishing the island society's sovereign status in the international system would stabilize its new state, though it would not preclude, and might even increase, instability in the state's government.

Orientation to the identity and purposes of the nation-state model increases the rate at which countries adopt other prescribed institutions of modernity. Having committed themselves to the identity of the rationalizing state, appropriate policies follow – policies for national development, individual citizenship and rights, environmental management, foreign relations. These policies are depicted as if they were autonomous decisions because nation-states are defined as sovereign, responsible, and essentially autonomous actors. Taking into account the larger culture in which states are embedded, however, the policies look more like enactments of conventionalized scripts. Even if a state proclaims its opposition to the dominant world identity models, it will nevertheless pursue many purposes within this model. It will develop bureaucratic authority and attempt to build many modern institutions, ranging from a central bank to an educational system. It will thereby find itself modifying its traditions in the direction of world-cultural forms.

Systemic maintenance of nation-state actor identity

If a specific nation-state is unable to put proper policies in place (because of costs, incompetence, or resistance), world-society structures will provide help. This process operates more through authoritative external support for the legitimate purposes of states than through authoritarian imposition by dominant powers or interests. For example, world organizations and professionalized ideologies actively encourage countries to adopt population control policies that are justified not as good for the world as a whole but as necessary for national development. National science policies are also promulgated as crucial to national development; before this link was theorized, UNESCO efforts to encourage countries to promote science failed to diffuse. As this example illustrates, international organizations often posture as objective disinterested others who help nation-states pursue their exogenously derived goals.

Resistance to world models is difficult because nation-states are formally committed, as a matter of identity, to such self-evident goals as socioeconomic development, citizen rights, individual self-development, and civil international relations. If a particular regime rhetorically resists world models, local actors can rely on legitimacy myths (democracy, freedom, equality) and the ready support of activist external groups to oppose the regime. Nation-state "choices" are thus less likely to conflict with world-cultural prescriptions than realist or microphenomenological theories anticipate because both nation-state choices and world pressures derive from the same overarching institutions.

Legitimation of subnational actors and practices

World-cultural principles license the nation-state not only as a managing central authority but also as an identity-supplying nation. Individual citizenship and the sovereignty of the people are basic tenets of nationhood. So too are the legitimacy and presumed functional necessity of much domestic organizational structure, ranging from financial market structures to organizations promoting individual and collective rights (of labor, ethnic groups, women, and so on). World-society ideology thus directly licenses a variety of organized interests and functions. Moreover, in pursuing their externally legitimated identities and purposes by creating agencies and programs, nation-states also promote the domestic actors involved. Programs and their associated accounting systems increase the number and density of types of actors, as groups come forward to claim newly reified identities and the resources allocated to them.

A good example is the rise of world discourse legitimating the human rights of gays and lesbians, which has produced both national policy changes and the mobilization of actors claiming these rights. As nation-states adopt policies embodying the appropriate principles, they institutionalize the identity and political presence of these groups. Of course, all these "internally" generated changes are infused with world-cultural conceptions of the properly behaving nation-state.

Hence, if a nation-state neglects to adopt world-approved policies, domestic elements will try to carry out or enforce conformity. General world pressures favoring environmentalism, for example, have led many states to establish environmental protection agencies, which foster the growth of environmental engineering firms, activist groups, and planning agencies. Where the state has not adopted the appropriate policies, such local units and actors as cities, schools, scout troops, and religious groups are likely to practice environmentalism and call for national action. Thus, world culture influences nation-states not only at their centers, or only in symbolic ways, but also through direct connections between local actors and world culture. Such connections produce many axes of mobilization for the implementation of world-cultural principles and help account for similarities in mobilization agendas and strategies in highly disparate countries.

Explicit rejection of world-cultural principles sometimes occurs, particularly by nationalist or religious movements whose purported opposition to modernity is seen as a threat to geopolitical stability. While the threat is real enough, the analysis is mistaken because it greatly underestimates the extent to which such movements conform to rationalized models of societal order and purpose. These movements mobilize around principles inscribed in world-cultural scripts, derive their organizing capacity from the legitimacy of these scripts, and edit their supposedly primordial claims to maximize this legitimacy. By and large, they seek an idealized modern community undergoing broad-based social development where citizens (of the right sort) can fully exercise their abstract rights. While they violate some central elements of world-cultural ideology, they nonetheless rely heavily on other elements. For example, religious "fundamentalists" may reject the extreme naturalism of modernity by making individuals accountable to an unchallengeable god, but they nevertheless exhort their people to embrace such key world-cultural elements as nation building, mass schooling, rationalized health care, and professionalization. They also are apt to reformulate their religious doctrine in accordance with typical modern conceptions of rational-moral discipline. In general, nationalist and religious movements intensify isomorphism more than they resist it. [. . .]

Conclusion

A considerable body of evidence supports our proposition that world-society models shape nation-state identities, structures, and behavior via worldwide cultural and associational processes. Carried by rationalized others whose scientific and professional authority often exceeds their power and resources, world culture celebrates, expands, and standardizes strong but culturally somewhat tamed national actors. The result is nation-states that are more isomorphic than most theories would predict and change more uniformly than is commonly recognized. As creatures of exogenous world culture, states are ritualized actors marked by extensive internal decoupling and a good deal more structuration than would occur if they were responsive only to local cultural, functional, or power processes.

As the Western world expanded in earlier centuries to dominate and incorporate societies in the larger world, the penetration of a universalized culture proceeded hesitantly. Westerners could imagine that the locals did not have souls, were members of a different species, and could reasonably be enslaved or exploited. Inhabiting a different moral and natural universe, non-Western societies were occasionally celebrated for their noble savagery but more often cast as inferior groups unsuited for true civilization. Westerners promoted religious conversion by somewhat parochial and inconsistent means, but broader incorporation was ruled out on all sorts of grounds. Education and literacy were sometimes prohibited, rarely encouraged, and never generally provided, for the natives were ineducable or prone to rebellion. Rationalized social, political, and economic development (e.g., the state, democracy, urban factory production, modern family law) was inappropriate, even unthinkable. Furthermore, the locals often strongly resisted incorporation by the West. Even Japan maintained strong boundaries against many aspects of modernity until the end of World War II, and Chinese policy continues a long pattern of resistance to external "aid."

The world, however, is greatly changed. Our island society would obviously become a candidate for full membership in the world community of nations and individuals. Human rights, state-protected citizen rights, and democratic forms would become natural entitlements. An economy would emerge, defined and measured in rationalized terms and oriented to growth under state regulation. A formal national polity would be essential, including a constitution, citizenship laws, educational structures, and open forms of participation and communication. The whole apparatus of rationalized modernity would be mobilized as necessary and applicable; internal and external resistance would be stigmatized as reactionary unless it was couched in universalistic terms. Allowing the islanders to remain imprisoned in their society, under the authority of their old gods and chiefs and entrapped in primitive economic technologies, would be unfair and discriminatory, even though the passing of their traditional society would also occasion nostalgia and regret.

Prevailing social theories account poorly for these changes. Given a dynamic socio-cultural system, realist models can account for a world of economic and political absorption, inequality, and domination. They do not well explain a world of formally equal, autonomous, and expansive nation-state actors. Microcultural or phenomenological lines of argument can account for diversity and resistance to homogenization, not a world in which national states, subject to only modest coercion or control, adopt standard identities and structural forms.

We argue for the utility of recognizing that rationalized modernity is a universalistic and inordinately successful form of the earlier Western religious and post-religious system. As a number of commentators have noted, in our time the religious elites of Western Christendom have given up on the belief that there is no salvation outside the church. That postulate has been replaced by the belief among almost all elites that salvation lies in rationalized structures grounded in scientific and technical knowledge – states, schools, firms, voluntary associations, and the like. The new religious elites are the professionals, researchers, scientists, and intellectuals who write secularized and unconditionally universalistic versions of the salvation story, along with the managers, legislators, and policymakers who believe the story fervently and pursue it relentlessly. This belief is worldwide and structures the organization of social life almost everywhere.

The colossal disaster of World War II may have been a key factor in the rise of global models of nationally organized progress and justice, and the Cold War may well have intensified the forces pushing human development to the global level. If the present configuration of lowered systemic (if not local) tensions persists, perhaps both the consensuality of the models and their impact on nation-states will decline. On the other hand, the models' rationalized definitions of progress and justice (across an ever broadening front) are rooted in universalistic scientific and professional definitions that have reached a level of deep global institutionalization. These definitions produce a great deal of conflict with regard to their content and application, but their authority is likely to prove quite durable.

Many observers anticipate a variety of failures of world society, citing instances of gross violations of world-cultural principles (e.g., in Bosnia), stagnant development (e.g., in Africa), and evasion of proper responsibility (in many places). In our view, the growing list of perceived "social problems" in the world indicates not the weakness of world-cultural institutions but their strength. Events like political torture, waste dumping, or corruption, which not so long ago were either overlooked entirely or considered routine, local, specific aberrations or tragedies, are now of world-societal significance. They violate strong expectations regarding global integration and propriety and can easily evoke world-societal reactions seeking to put things right. A world with so many widely discussed social problems is a world of Durkheimian and Simmelian integration, however much it may also seem driven by disintegrative tendencies.

12   Globalization as a Problem

Roland Robertson

The Crystallization of a Concept and a Problem

Globalization as a concept refers both to the compression of the world and the intensification of consciousness of the world as a whole. The processes and actions to which
the concept of globalization now refers have been proceeding, with some interrup-
tions, for many centuries, but the main focus of the discussion of globalization is on
relatively recent times. In so far as that discussion is closely linked to the contours
and nature of modernity, globalization refers quite clearly to recent developments.
In the present book globalization is conceived in much broader terms than that, but
its main empirical focus is in line with the increasing acceleration in both concrete
global interdependence and consciousness of the global whole in the twentieth
century. But it is necessary to emphasize that globalization is not equated with or
seen as a direct consequence of an amorphously conceived modernity.

Use of the noun 'globalization' has developed quite recently. Certainly in academic circles it was not recognized as a significant concept, in spite of diffuse and intermittent usage prior to that, until the early, or even middle, 1980s. During the second
half of the 1980s its use increased enormously, so much so that it is virtually impossible to trace the patterns of its contemporary diffusion across a large number of areas
of contemporary life in different parts of the world. By now, even though the term
is often used very loosely and, indeed, in contradictory ways, it has *itself* become part
of 'global consciousness,' an aspect of the remarkable proliferation of terms centred
upon 'global.' Although the latter adjective has been in use for a long time (meaning,
strongly, worldwide; or, more loosely, 'the whole'), it is indicative of our contemporary concern with globalization that the *Oxford Dictionary of New Words* (1991) actually includes 'global' as a *new* word, focusing specifically, but misleadingly, on its use
in 'environmental jargon.' That same *Dictionary* also defines 'global consciousness'
as 'receptiveness to (and understanding) of cultures other than one's own, often as
part of an appreciation of world socio-economic and ecological issues.' It maintains
that such a use has been much influenced by Marshall McLuhan's idea of 'the global
village,' introduced in his book *Explorations in Communication* (1960). The notion
of compression, or 'shrinking,' is indeed present in that influential book about the
shared simultaneity of media, particularly televisual, experience in our time. There
can be little doubt that McLuhan both reflected and shaped media trends, so much
so that in time we have come to witness (self-serving) media attempts to consolidate
the idea of the global *community*. On the other hand the media fully acknowledge

Original publication details: Excerpted from Roland Robertson, *Globalization: Social Theory and Global Culture*
(Sage, 1992), pp. 8–9, 25–9, 174–80. Copyright © Roland Robertson 1992. Reprinted by permission of
Sage Publishing Ltd.

the 'nationality' of particular media systems, and report at length on the tough realities of international relations, wars and so on. Such realities are far from the communal connotations which some have read into McLuhan's imagery. In the same period when McLuhan's notion of the global village was becoming influential there occurred the 'expressive revolution' of the 1960s. That was, to put it very simply, a 'revolution' in consciousness among the young in numerous parts of the world, centred upon such themes as liberation and love, in both individual and collective terms. In fact the *Oxford Dictionary of New Words* maintains that the current term 'global consciousness . . . draws on the fashion for *consciousness-raising* in the sixties' (1991).

Undoubtedly the 1960s 'revolution' in consciousness had an important effect in many parts of the world, in its sharpening of the sense of what was supposedly common to all in an increasingly tight-knit world. Yet, as we will see more fully, this sense of global interdependence has rapidly become recognized in numerous other, relatively independent, domains and fora. World wars, particularly World War II with its 'humanity-shaking' events and its aftermath, the rise of what became known as the Third World, the proliferation of international, transnational and supranational institutions and the attempts to coordinate what has become known as the global economy have played crucial parts in the twofold process of 'objective' and 'subjective' 'globalization.' And surely McLuhan's own Catholic-tinged observations concerning the media-centred 'global village' were partly shaped by such developments. [. . .]

Coming to Terms with the World as a Whole

[. . .] My model of what, in the most flexible terms, may be called the global field is centred on the way(s) in which we think about globality in relation to the basic makeup of that field. My formulation is more multifaceted than that of Dumont, in that I think in terms of four major aspects, or reference points, rather than two. These are *national societies*, *individuals*, or more basically, *selves*, *relationships between national societies*, or *the world system of societies*; and, in the generic sense, *mankind*, which, to avoid misunderstanding, I frequently call *humankind*. [. . .]

In the broadest sense I am concerned with the way(s) in which the world is ordered. Whereas I am setting out this model of order in what may appear to be formal terms, the intent which actually guides it is to inject *flexibility* into our considerations of 'totality.' In so far as we think about the world as a whole, we are inevitably involved in a certain kind of what is sometimes pejoratively called totalistic analysis. But even though my scheme does involve a 'totalizing' tendency, it does so partly in order to comprehend *different* kinds of orientation to the global circumstance. It will be seen in Chapter 4 that movements, individuals and other actors perceive and construct the order (or disorder) of the world in a number of different ways. In *that* sense what my model does is to facilitate interpretation and analysis of such variation. So there is a crucial difference between imposing a model of the global field on all the present and potential actors in that field and setting out a model which facilitates comprehension of variation in that field. The latter is an important consideration. My interest is in how order is, so to speak, *done*; including order that is 'done' by those seeking explicitly to establish legal principles for the ordering of the world. To put it yet another way, my model is conceived as an attempt to make analytical and interpretive sense of how quotidian actors, collective or individual, go about the business of conceiving of the world, including attempts to *deny* that the world is one.

Nevertheless, in spite of my acknowledgment of certain denials of global wholeness, I maintain that the trends towards the unicity of the world are, when all is said and done, inexorable. [. . .]

Globalization refers in this particular sense to the coming into, often problematic, conjunction of different forms of life. This cannot be accurately captured in the simple proposition that globalization is 'a consequence of modernity,' which I consider specifically towards the end of this volume. Present concern with globality and globalization cannot be comprehensively considered simply as an aspect or outcome of the Western 'project' of modernity or, except in very broad terms, enlightenment. In an increasingly globalized world there is a heightening of civilizational, societal, ethnic, regional and, indeed individual, self-consciousness. There are constraints on social entities to locate themselves within world history and the global future. Yet globalization in and of itself also involves the diffusion of the *expectation* of such identity declarations.

This model, which is presented diagrammatically in Figure 12.1, gives the basic outline of what I here call the global field but which for other purposes I call the global-human condition. The figure indicates the four major components, or reference points, of the conception of globality, the basic way in which we are able as empirically informed analysts to 'make sense' of globality, as well as the form in terms of which globalization has in the last few centuries actually proceeded. Discussion of different, or alternative, forms in terms of which globalization *might* have occurred or, indeed, did partially occur are discussed in later chapters. To provide an example at this stage, it is clear that Islam historically has had a general 'globalizing' thrust; but had that potential form of globalization succeeded we would now almost certainly comprehend contemporary 'globality' differently. There would be a need for a different kind of model.

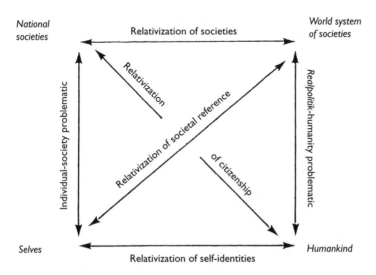

Figure 12.1   *The global field*

The model is presented in primary reference to twentieth-century developments. In that it partly summarizes such developments it draws attention to increasing, interrelated thematizations of societies, individual selves, international relations and humankind. At the same time, it opens the way to the discussion and study of the ways in which the general pattern came historically to prevail. It also allows for different, indeed conflicting, empirical emphases within 'the field' [. . .]

First, while I have emphasized that my perspective allows for empirical variation with respect to what later I call images of world order and that my primary task in analyzing globalization is to lay bare and open up relatively neglected aspects of that theme, there are clearly moral and critical dimensions of my approach to globalization. I will only mention the most general here. There is certainly a sense in which I am trying to tackle directly the problem of *global complexity*, a point which will become even clearer when I address the question of the shifting contents of the four major components of my model. It will, I hope, also become clear that I am arguing for the moral acceptance of that complexity. In other words, complexity becomes something like a moral issue in its own right. Specifically, the way in which I tackle the issues of globality and globalization suggests that in order for one to have a 'realistic' view of the world as a whole one must, at least in the contemporary circumstance, accept in principle the relative autonomy of each of the four main components and that, by the same token, one should acknowledge that each of the four is in one way or another constrained by the other three. In one sense, then, overemphasis on one to the expense of attention to the other three constitutes a form of 'fundamentalism.' Simply put, one cannot and should not wish away the reality of one or more aspects of the terms in which globalization has been proceeding. This certainly does not exhaust the issue of the extent to which my approach to globalization is moral and critical. But it must suffice for the moment.

Second, there is the issue of the processes which bring about globalization – the 'causal mechanisms' or the 'driving forces.' What happens here to arguments about the dynamics of capitalism and the forces of imperialism which have undoubtedly played a large part in bringing the world into an increasingly compressed condition? In arguing that mine is a cultural perspective on globalization I do not wish to convey the idea that I consider the matter of 'the forces' or 'the mechanisms' of globalization unimportant. However, I am well aware that that is well-trodden ground. The spread of Western capitalism and the part played by imperialism have been addressed at great length, as has the increasingly complex crystallization of the contemporary global economy. In contrast, the discussion of the disputed terms in which globalization has occurred and is occurring has been greatly neglected. It is that and directly related issues which form the main concern . . . , and it is hoped that such a cultural focus will place work in the more traditional vein in a new light. While the use of the term 'culture' here is certainly not as broad and all-embracing as is to be found in some tendencies within the relatively new field of cultural studies, it is employed much more fluidly and adventurously than in conventional sociological work. In particular, my approach is used to demonstrate discontinuities and differences, rather than the traditional sociological view of culture as integrating. It is also meant to indicate a particular way of doing sociology, rather than a sociology that concentrates on culture as such.

Third, in my representation of the global field I have emphasized a number of processes of *relativization*. That term is meant to indicate the ways in which, as globalization proceeds, challenges are increasingly presented to the stability of particular perspectives on, and collective and individual participation in, the overall globalization process. As I have said, this picture of the global field has been produced in primary reference to contemporary globality and globalization. It is an ideal-typical representation of what is meant here by global complexity. In one important respect it indicates overall processes of differentiation in so far as global complexity is concerned. Broadly speaking, application of the model involves the view that processes of differentiation of the main spheres of globality increase over time. Thus differentiation between the spheres was much lower in earlier phases of globalization; while the effects of such differentiation have been encountered unevenly and with different responses in different parts of the world. [. . .]

Globalization and the Search for Fundamentals

The approach to globalization which I have been advocating takes its departure from empirical generalizations concerning the rapidly increasing compression of the entire world into a single, global field and conceptual ideas about the ways in which the world as a whole should be 'mapped' in broadly sociological terms. The two strands of elaboration are, of course, closely linked. In the relatively early stage of my attempts to theorize the topic of globalization the issue of 'fundamentalism' was conspicuous. Indeed it was partly in order to account for the resurgence of religious fundamentalism in the late 1970s and early 1980s that I revitalized my longstanding interest in 'international' phenomena. Coming to terms with fundamentalism and related issues has been a prominent aspect of my work on globalization, even though over the last ten years or so I have revised my thinking about the relationship between globalization and fundamentalism (more generally 'the search for fundamentals'). Whereas my first formulations tended to see politicoreligious fundamentalism as resulting largely from compression of the *inter-societal system* (fundamentalism as an attempt to express society identity), my more recent attempts to grasp analytically the more general problem of the assertion of 'deep particularity' on the global scene have centred upon the global construction and dissemination of ideas concerning the value of particularism. The first perspective involves an emphasis on space-time compression leading to the felt necessity for societies (and regions and civilizations, as well as 'subnational' entities) to declare their identities for both internal and external purposes. It tends to involve a focus on fundamentalism as a *reaction* to, rather than as an aspect – or, indeed, a creation – of, globalization; although that was not the exclusive focus of my earlier perspective. The second approach involves a more definite stress on the idea that the expectation of identity declaration is built into the general process of globalization. This does not mean that the notion of fundamentalism as reaction or resistance is thereby relinquished, but that that possibility is now viewed in a more general frame.

There have been four major focal points of the dominant globalization process since the sixteenth century: *nationally constituted societies; the international system of societies; individuals;* and *humankind.* At the risk of repetition, my argument in this respect can be restated. It is largely in terms of the enhancement of each of these reference points, in the sense of their being tangibly crystallized, and the raising of problems about the relationships between them that the globalization process has proceeded in recent centuries. At the same time there have been changes in the ways in which each of these major components of the overall global circumstance has been operatively constructed. All of this means that we have to conceive of the concept of globalization as having primarily to do with *the form* in terms of which the world has moved towards unicity. So when we speak of globalization we must realize that we are referring above all to a relatively specific path that the world has taken in the direction of it becoming singular. The world could in theory, as I have argued, have become a single entity along different trajectories – without, for example, involving the salience of the national society which has *actually* been a vital ingredient of the overall globalization process. [. . .]

Universalism and Particularism Globalized

In my perspective globalization in what I call its primary sense is a relatively autonomous process. Its central *dynamic* involves the twofold process of the particularization of the universal and the universalization of the particular. The particularization of the universal, defined as the global concretization of the problem of universality, has become the occasion for the search for *global* fundamentals. In other words, the current phase of very rapid globalization facilitates the rise of movements concerned with the 'real meaning' of the world, movements (and individuals) searching for the meaning of the world as a whole. The universalization of the particular refers to the global universality of the search for the particular, for increasingly fine-grained modes of identity presentation. To put it as sharply as possible, I propose that 'fundamentalism' is a mode of thought and practice which has become almost globally institutionalized, in large part, as far as the twentieth century is concerned, in terms of the norm of national self-determination, announced after World War I by Woodrow Wilson, given new life after World War II with respect to what became known as the Third World, and then expanded on a global scale to all manner of 'entities' from the 1960s onwards. In so far as analysts see 'the search' entirely in terms of an atavistic response to globalization they are failing to deal with the participatory aspect of globalization. This does not mean that there are no atavistic, isolationist or anti-global responses to globalization. But we have to be very careful in delineating these. They are by no means self-evident. [. . .]

In addressing globalization I have paid particular attention to what I have called the take-off period of modern globalization, lasting from about 1870 through to the mid-1920s; and I have been struck by the extent to which in that period the general issue of the coordination of the particular and the universal received widespread practical and political attention. This was a time when there was great emphasis on the need to invent tradition and national identity within the context of an increasingly compressed, globalized world. Indeed much of the desire to invent tradition and identity derived from the contingencies of global compression and the concomitant spread of expectations concerning these. During the period lasting from about 1870 to 1925 basic geohuman contingencies were formally worked out in such terms as the time-zoning of the world and the establishment of the international dateline; the near-global adoption of the Gregorian calendar and the adjustable seven-day week; and the establishment of international telegraphic and signaling codes. At the same time, there arose movements which were specifically concerned with the relationship between the local and the panlocal, one of the most notable being the ecumenical movement which sought to bring the major 'world' religious traditions into a coordinated, concultural discourse. On the secular front, the international socialist movement had parallel aims, but it was even more ambitious in that it sought to overcome *strong* particularism in the name of internationalism. A more specific case is provided by the rise at the end of the nineteenth century of the International Youth Hostel movement, which attempted an international coordination of particularistic, 'back to nature' ventures. Other particular–universal developments of the time include the modern Olympic Games and Nobel prizes. The contemporary use of such terms as 'fundamentals' and 'fundamentalism' was also established, mainly in the USA, in the same period.

What is particularly significant about this period is that the material circumstance of the world (as a heliocentric globe) was, as it were, dealt with in relationship to the rapidly spreading consciousness of the global world as such, greatly facilitated by recently developed rapid means of travel and communication, such as the airplane and the wireless. One crucial aspect of these trends was that events and circumstances previously segregated in space and time increasingly came to be considered as simultaneous in terms of categories which were universalistically particular and particularistically universal. Spatial and temporal categories and measures were globally institutionalized so as to both accentuate consciousness of difference and to universalize difference.

Needless to say, such developments did not emerge *de novo* during the period in question. The steady growth in map-making and its globalization, the interpenetration of modes of 'travelers' tales,' the growth of postal services, the increase in the spread of travel, the early rise of tourism – all these, and still other, developments lay in the background to the rapid trends of the crucial take-off period of modern globalization. One particularly important development of a somewhat different kind concerned what has been called the politicization of archeology in the mid-nineteenth century. As we have seen, in that earlier period the monuments of classical and biblical civilization in Egypt, Mesopotamia, Greece and other areas of the Near and Middle East became national quests, within the context of increasingly international and industrialized society. In turn these monuments have become the bases of the official national symbols of the peoples of the Middle East and the eastern Mediterranean. Now in those areas both local and non-local archeologists are shaping 'a new past for the peoples of that region.' All of this began, it should be remembered, in a period of great (often imperial) concern with the unification of humankind.

In sum I argue that the search for fundamentals – in so far as it exists on any significant scale – is to a considerable degree both a contingent feature of globalization and an aspect of global culture. In a sense 'fundamentalism within limits' makes globalization work. [. . .]

13 Disjuncture and Difference in the Global Cultural Economy

Arjun Appadurai

It takes only the merest acquaintance with the facts of the modern world to note that it is now an interactive system in a sense that is strikingly new. Historians and sociologists, especially those concerned with translocal processes and the world systems associated with capitalism, have long been aware that the world has been a congeries of large-scale interactions for many centuries. Yet today's world involves interactions of a new order and intensity. Cultural transactions between social groups in the past have generally been restricted, sometimes by the facts of geography and ecology, and at other times by active resistance to interactions with the Other (as in China for much of its history and in Japan before the Meiji Restoration). Where there have been sustained cultural transactions across large parts of the globe, they have usually involved the long-distance journey of commodities (and of the merchants most concerned with them) and of travelers and explorers of every type. The two main forces for sustained cultural interaction before this century have been warfare (and the large-scale political systems sometimes generated by it) and religions of conversion, which have sometimes, as in the case of Islam, taken warfare as one of the legitimate instruments of their expansion. Thus, between travelers and merchants, pilgrims and conquerors, the world has seen much long-distance (and long-term) cultural traffic. This much seems self-evident.

But few will deny that given the problems of time, distance, and limited technologies for the command of resources across vast spaces, cultural dealings between socially and spatially separated groups have, until the past few centuries, been bridged at great cost and sustained over time only with great effort. The forces of cultural gravity seemed always to pull away from the formation of large-scale ecumenes, whether religious, commercial, or political, toward smaller-scale accretions of intimacy and interest.

Sometime in the past few centuries, the nature of this gravitational field seems to have changed. Partly because of the spirit of the expansion of Western maritime interests after 1500, and partly because of the relatively autonomous developments of large and aggressive social formations in the Americas (such as the Aztecs and the Incas), in Eurasia (such as the Mongols and their descendants, the Mughals and Ottomans), in island Southeast Asia (such as the Buginese), and in the kingdoms of precolonial Africa (such as Dahomey), an overlapping set of ecumenes began to emerge, in which congeries of money, commerce, conquest, and migration began to create durable cross-societal bonds. This process was accelerated by the technology

Original publication details: Excerpted from Arjun Appadurai, "Disjuncture and Difference in the Global Cultural Economy," in *Modernity at Large: Cultural Dimensions of Globalization* (University of Minnesota Press, 1996), pp. 27–30, 32–43. Reprinted by permission of Arjun Appadurai.

transfers and innovations of the late eighteenth and nineteenth centuries, which created complex colonial orders centered on European capitals and spread throughout the non-European world. This intricate and overlapping set of Eurocolonial worlds (first Spanish and Portuguese, later principally English, French, and Dutch) set the basis for a permanent traffic in ideas of peoplehood and selfhood, which created the imagined communities of recent nationalisms throughout the world.

With what Benedict Anderson has called "print capitalism," a new power was unleashed in the world, the power of mass literacy and its attendant large-scale production of projects of ethnic affinity that were remarkably free of the need for face-to-face communication or even of indirect communication between persons and groups. The act of reading things together set the stage for movements based on a paradox – the paradox of constructed primordialism. There is, of course, a great deal else that is involved in the story of colonialism and its dialectically generated nationalisms, but the issue of constructed ethnicities is surely a crucial strand in this tale.

But the revolution of print capitalism and the cultural affinities and dialogues unleashed by it were only modest precursors to the world we live in now. For in the past century, there has been a technological explosion, largely in the domain of transportation and information, that makes the interactions of a print-dominated world seem as hard-won and as easily erased as the print revolution made earlier forms of cultural traffic appear. For with the advent of the steamship, the automobile, the airplane, the camera, the computer, and the telephone, we have entered into an altogether new condition of neighborliness, even with those most distant from ourselves. Marshall McLuhan, among others, sought to theorize about this world as a "global village," but theories such as McLuhan's appear to have overestimated the communitarian implications of the new media order. We are now aware that with media, each time we are tempted to speak of the global village, we must be reminded that media create communities with "no sense of place." The world we live in now seems rhizomic, even schizophrenic, calling for theories of rootlessness, alienation, and psychological distance between individuals and groups on the one hand, and fantasies (or nightmares) of electronic propinquity on the other. Here, we are close to the central problematic of cultural processes in today's world.

Thus, the curiosity that drove Pico Iyer to Asia (in 1988) is in some ways the product of a confusion between some ineffable McDonaldization of the world and the much subtler play of indigenous trajectories of desire and fear with global flows of people and things. Indeed, Iyer's own impressions are testimony to the fact that, if *a* global cultural system is emerging, it is filled with ironies and resistances, sometimes camouflaged as passivity and a bottomless appetite in the Asian world for things Western.

Iyer's own account of the uncanny Philippine affinity for American popular music is rich testimony to the global culture of the hyperreal, for somehow Philippine renditions of American popular songs are both more widespread in the Philippines, and more disturbingly faithful to their originals, than they are in the United States today. An entire nation seems to have learned to mimic Kenny Rogers and the Lennon sisters, like a vast Asian Motown chorus. But *Americanization* is certainly a pallid term to apply to such a situation, for not only are there more Filipinos singing perfect renditions of some American songs (often from the American past) than there are Americans doing so, there is also, of course, the fact that the rest of their lives is not in complete synchrony with the referential world that first gave birth to these songs.

In a further globalizing twist on what Fredric Jameson has called "nostalgia for the present," these Filipinos look back to a world they have never lost. This is one of the central ironies of the politics of global cultural flows, especially in the arena of entertainment and leisure. [. . .]

The central problem of today's global interactions is the tension between cultural homogenization and cultural heterogenization. A vast array of empirical facts could be brought to bear on the side of the homogenization argument, and much of it has come from the left end of the spectrum of media studies, and some from other perspectives. Most often, the homogenization argument subspeciates into either an argument about Americanization or an argument about commoditization, and very often the two arguments are closely linked. What these arguments fail to consider is that at least as rapidly as forces from various metropolises are brought into new societies they tend to become indigenized in one or another way: this is true of music and housing styles as much as it is true of science and terrorism, spectacles and constitutions. The dynamics of such indigenization have just begun to be explored systemically, and much more needs to be done. But it is worth noticing that for the people of Irian Jaya, Indonesianization may be more worrisome than Americanization, as Japanization may be for Koreans, Indianization for Sri Lankans, Vietnamization for the Cambodians, and Russianization for the people of Soviet Armenia and the Baltic republics. Such a list of alternative fears to Americanization could be greatly expanded, but it is not a shapeless inventory: for polities of smaller scale, there is always a fear of cultural absorption by polities of larger scale, especially those that are nearby. One man's imagined community is another man's political prison.

This scalar dynamic, which has widespread global manifestations, is also tied to the relationship between nations and states. For the moment let us note that the simplification of these many forces (and fears) of homogenization can also be exploited by nation-states in relation to their own minorities, by posing global commoditization (or capitalism, or some other such external enemy) as more real than the threat of its own hegemonic strategies.

The new global cultural economy has to be seen as a complex, overlapping, disjunctive order that cannot any longer be understood in terms of existing center–periphery models (even those that might account for multiple centers and peripheries). Nor is it susceptible to simple models of push and pull (in terms of migration theory), or of surpluses and deficits (as in traditional models of balance of trade), or of consumers and producers (as in most neo-Marxist theories of development). Even the most complex and flexible theories of global development that have come out of the Marxist tradition are inadequately quirky and have failed to come to terms with what Scott Lash and John Urry have called disorganized capitalism. The complexity of the current global economy has to do with certain fundamental disjunctures between economy, culture, and politics that we have only begun to theorize.

I propose that an elementary framework for exploring such disjunctures is to look at the relationship among five dimensions of global cultural flows that can be termed (a) *ethnoscapes*, (b) *mediascapes*, (c) *technoscapes*, (d) *financescapes*, and (e) *ideoscapes*. The suffix -*scape* allows us to point to the fluid, irregular shapes of these landscapes, shapes that characterize international capital as deeply as they do international clothing styles. These terms with the common suffix -*scape* also indicate that these are not objectively given relations that look the same from every angle of vision but, rather, that they are deeply perspectival constructs, inflected by the historical, linguistic, and political situatedness of different sorts of actors: nation-states, multinationals, diasporic communities, as well as subnational groupings and movements (whether religious, political, or economic), and even intimate face-to-face groups, such as villages, neighborhoods, and families. Indeed, the individual actor is the last locus of this perspectival set of landscapes, for these landscapes are eventually navigated by agents who both experience and constitute larger formations, in part from their own sense of what these landscapes offer.

These landscapes thus are the building blocks of what (extending Benedict Anderson) I would like to call *imagined worlds*, that is, the multiple worlds that are constituted by the historically situated imaginations of persons and groups spread around the globe. An important fact of the world we live in today is that many persons on the globe live in such imagined worlds (and not just in imagined communities) and thus are able to contest and sometimes even subvert the imagined worlds of the official mind and of the entrepreneurial mentality that surround them.

By *ethnoscape*, I mean the landscape of persons who constitute the shifting world in which we live: tourists, immigrants, refugees, exiles, guest workers, and other moving groups and individuals constitute an essential feature of the world and appear to affect the politics of (and between) nations to a hitherto unprecedented degree. This is not to say that there are no relatively stable communities and networks of kinship, friendship, work, and leisure, as well as of birth, residence, and other filial forms. But it is to say that the warp of these stabilities is everywhere shot through with the woof of human motion, as more persons and groups deal with the realities of having to move or the fantasies of wanting to move. What is more, both these realities and fantasies now function on larger scales, as men and women from villages in India think not just of moving to Poona or Madras but of moving to Dubai and Houston, and refugees from Sri Lanka find themselves in South India as well as in Switzerland, just as the Hmong are driven to London as well as to Philadelphia. And as international capital shifts its needs, as production and technology generate different needs, as nation-states shift their policies on refugee populations, these moving groups can never afford to let their imaginations rest too long, even if they wish to.

By *technoscape*, I mean the global configuration, also ever fluid, of technology and the fact that technology, both high and low, both mechanical and informational, now moves at high speeds across various kinds of previously impervious boundaries. Many countries now are the roots of multinational enterprise: a huge steel complex in Libya may involve interests from India, China, Russia, and Japan, providing different components of new technological configurations. The odd distribution of technologies, and thus the peculiarities of these technoscapes, are increasingly driven not by any obvious economies of scale, of political control, or of market rationality but by increasingly complex relationships among money flows, political possibilities, and the availability of both un- and highly-skilled labor. So, while India exports waiters and chauffeurs to Dubai and Sharjah, it also exports software engineers to the United States – indentured briefly to Tata-Burroughs or the World Bank, then laundered through the State Department to become wealthy resident aliens, who are in turn objects of seductive messages to invest their money and know-how in federal and state projects in India. [. . .]

It is useful to speak as well of *financescapes*, as the disposition of global capital is now a more mysterious, rapid, and difficult landscape to follow than ever before, as currency markets, national stock exchanges, and commodity speculations move megamonies through national turnstiles at blinding speed, with vast, absolute implications for small differences in percentage points and time units. But the critical point is that the global relationship among ethnoscapes, technoscapes, and financescapes is deeply disjunctive and profoundly unpredictable because each of these landscapes is subject to its own constraints and incentives (some political, some informational, and some technoenvironmental), at the same time as each acts as a constraint and a parameter for movements in the others. Thus, even an elementary model of global political economy must take into account the deeply disjunctive relationships among human movement, technological flow, and financial transfers.

Further refracting these disjunctures (which hardly form a simple, mechanical global infrastructure in any case) are what I call *mediascapes* and *ideoscapes*, which are closely related landscapes of images. *Mediascapes* refer both to the distribution of the electronic capabilities to produce and disseminate information (newspapers, magazines, television stations, and film-production studios), which are now available to a growing number of private and public interests throughout the world, and to the images of the world created by these media. These images involve many complicated inflections, depending on their mode (documentary or entertainment), their hardware (electronic or preelectronic), their audiences (local, national, or transnational), and the interests of those who own and control them. What is most important about these mediascapes is that they provide (especially in their television, film, and cassette forms) large and complex repertoires of images, narratives, and ethnoscapes to viewers throughout the world, in which the world of commodities and the world of news and politics are profoundly mixed. What this means is that many audiences around the world experience the media themselves as a complicated and interconnected repertoire of print, celluloid, electronic screens, and billboards. The lines between the realistic and the fictional landscapes they see are blurred, so that the farther away these audiences are from the direct experiences of metropolitan life, the more likely they are to construct imagined worlds that are chimerical, aesthetic, even fantastic objects, particularly if assessed by the criteria of some other perspective, some other imagined world. [. . .]

Ideoscapes are also concatenations of images, but they are often directly political and frequently have to do with the ideologies of states and the counterideologies of movements explicitly oriented to capturing state power or a piece of it. These ideoscapes are composed of elements of the Enlightenment worldview, which consists of a chain of ideas, terms, and images, including *freedom, welfare, rights, sovereignty, representation*, and the master term *democracy*. The master narrative of the Enlightenment (and its many variants in Britain, France, and the United States) was constructed with a certain internal logic and presupposed a certain relationship between reading, representation, and the public sphere. But the diaspora of these terms and images across the world, especially since the nineteenth century, has loosened the internal coherence that held them together in a Euro-American master narrative and provided instead a loosely structured synopticon of politics, in which different nation-states, as part of their evolution, have organized their political cultures around different keywords. [. . .]

This globally variable synaesthesia has hardly even been noted, but it demands urgent analysis. Thus *democracy* has clearly become a master term, with powerful echoes from Haiti and Poland to the former Soviet Union and China, but it sits at the center of a variety of ideoscapes, composed of distinctive pragmatic configurations of rough translations of other central terms from the vocabulary of the Enlightenment. This creates ever new terminological kaleidoscopes, as states (and the groups that seek to capture them) seek to pacify populations whose own ethnoscapes are in motion and whose mediascapes may create severe problems for the ideoscapes with which they are presented. The fluidity of ideoscapes is complicated in particular by the growing diasporas (both voluntary and involuntary) of intellectuals who continuously inject new meaning-streams into the discourse of democracy in different parts of the world.

This extended terminological discussion of the five terms I have coined sets the basis for a tentative formulation about the conditions under which current global flows occur: they occur in and through the growing disjunctures among ethnoscapes, technoscapes, financescapes, mediascapes, and ideoscapes. This formulation, the core of my model of global cultural flow, needs some explanation. First, people, machinery, money, images, and ideas now follow increasingly nonisomorphic paths; of course, at all periods in human history there have been some disjunctures in the flows of these things, but the sheer speed, scale, and volume of each of these flows are now so great that the disjunctures have become central to the politics of global culture. The Japanese are notoriously hospitable to ideas and are stereotyped as inclined to export (all) and import (some) goods, but they are also notoriously closed to immigration, like the Swiss, the Swedes, and the Saudis. Yet the Swiss and the Saudis accept populations of guest workers, thus creating labor diasporas of Turks, Italians, and other circum-Mediterranean groups. Some such guest-worker groups maintain continuous contact with their home nations, like the Turks, but others, like high-level South Asian migrants, tend to desire lives in their new homes, raising anew the problem of reproduction in a deterritorialized context.

Deterritorialization, in general, is one of the central forces of the modern world because it brings laboring populations into the lower-class sectors and spaces of relatively wealthy societies, while sometimes creating exaggerated and intensified senses of criticism or attachment to politics in the home state. Deterritorialization, whether of Hindus, Sikhs, Palestinians, or Ukrainians, is now at the core of a variety of global fundamentalisms, including Islamic and Hindu fundamentalism. In the Hindu case, for example, it is clear that the overseas movement of Indians has been exploited by a variety of interests both within and outside India to create a complicated network of finances and religious identifications, by which the problem of cultural reproduction for Hindus abroad has become tied to the politics of Hindu fundamentalism at home.

At the same time, deterritorialization creates new markets for film companies, art impresarios, and travel agencies, which thrive on the need of the deterritorialized population for contact with its homeland. Naturally, these invented homelands, which constitute the mediascapes of deterritorialized groups, can often become sufficiently fantastic and one-sided that they provide the material for new ideoscapes in which ethnic conflicts can begin to erupt. The creation of Khalistan, an invented homeland of the deterritorialized Sikh population of England, Canada, and the United States, is one example of the bloody potential in such mediascapes as they interact with the internal colonialisms of the nation-state. The West Bank, Namibia, and Eritrea are other theaters for the enactment of the bloody negotiation between existing nation-states and various deterritorialized groupings.

It is in the fertile ground of deterritorialization, in which money, commodities, and persons are involved in ceaselessly chasing each other around the world, that the mediascapes and ideoscapes of the modern world find their fractured and fragmented counterpart. For the ideas and images produced by mass media often are only partial guides to the goods and experiences that deterritorialized populations transfer to one another. In Mira Nair's brilliant film *India Cabaret*, we see the multiple loops of this fractured deterritorialization as young women, barely competent in Bombay's metropolitan glitz, come to seek their fortunes as cabaret dancers and prostitutes in Bombay, entertaining men in clubs with dance formats derived wholly from the prurient dance sequences of Hindi films. These scenes in turn cater to ideas about Western and foreign women and their looseness, while they provide tawdry career alibis for these women. Some of these women come from Kerala, where cabaret clubs and the pornographic film industry have blossomed, partly in response to the purses and tastes of Keralites returned from the Middle East, where their diasporic lives away from women distort their very sense of what the relations between men and women might be. These tragedies of displacement could certainly be replayed in a more detailed analysis of the relations between the Japanese and German sex tours to Thailand and the tragedies of the sex trade in Bangkok, and in other similar loops that tie together fantasies about the Other, the conveniences and seductions of travel, the economics of global trade, and the brutal mobility fantasies that dominate gender politics in many parts of Asia and the world at large. [. . .]

One important new feature of global cultural politics, tied to the disjunctive relationships among the various landscapes discussed earlier, is that state and nation are at each other's throats, and the hyphen that links them is now less an icon of conjuncture than an index of disjuncture. This disjunctive relationship between nation and state has two levels: at the level of any given nation-state, it means that there is a battle of the imagination, with state and nation seeking to cannibalize one another. Here is the seedbed of brutal separatisms – majoritarianisms that seem to have appeared from nowhere and microidentities that have become political projects within the nation-state. At another level, this disjunctive relationship is deeply entangled with various global disjunctures: ideas of nationhood appear to be steadily increasing in scale and regularly crossing existing state boundaries, sometimes, as with the Kurds, because previous identities stretched across vast national spaces or, as with the Tamils in Sri Lanka, the dormant threads of a transnational diaspora have been activated to ignite the micropolitics of a nation-state. [. . .]

States find themselves pressed to stay open by the forces of media, technology, and travel that have fueled consumerism throughout the world and have increased the craving, even in the non-Western world, for new commodities and spectacles. On the other hand, these very cravings can become caught up in new ethnoscapes, mediascapes, and, eventually, ideoscapes, such as democracy in China, that the state cannot tolerate as threats to its own control over ideas of nationhood and peoplehood. States throughout the world are under siege, especially where contests over the ideoscapes of democracy are fierce and fundamental, and where there are radical disjunctures between ideoscapes and technoscapes (as in the case of very small countries that lack contemporary technologies of production and information); or between ideoscapes and financescapes (as in countries such as Mexico or Brazil, where international lending influences national politics to a very large degree); or between ideoscapes and ethnoscapes (as in Beirut, where diasporic, local, and translocal filiations are suicidally at battle); or between ideoscapes and mediascapes (as in many countries in the Middle East and Asia) where the lifestyles represented on both national and international TV and cinema completely overwhelm and undermine the rhetoric of national politics. In the Indian case, the myth of the law-breaking hero has emerged to mediate this naked struggle between the pieties and realities of Indian politics, which has grown increasingly brutalized and corrupt.

The transnational movement of the martial arts, particularly through Asia, as mediated by the Hollywood and Hong Kong film industries is a rich illustration of the ways in which long-standing martial arts traditions, reformulated to meet the fantasies of contemporary (sometimes lumpen) youth populations, create new cultures of masculinity and violence, which are in turn the fuel for increased violence in national and international politics. Such violence is in turn the spur to an increasingly rapid and amoral arms trade that penetrates the entire world. The worldwide spread of the AK-47 and the Uzi, in films, in corporate and state security, in terror, and in police and military activity, is a reminder that apparently simple technical uniformities often conceal an increasingly complex set of loops, linking images of violence to aspirations for community in some imagined world.

Returning then to the ethnoscapes with which I began, the central paradox of ethnic politics in today's world is that primordia (whether of language or skin color or neighborhood or kinship) have become globalized. That is, sentiments, whose greatest force is in their ability to ignite intimacy into a political state and turn locality into a staging ground for identity, have become spread over vast and irregular spaces as groups move yet stay linked to one another through sophisticated media capabilities. This is not to deny that such primordia are often the product of invented traditions or retrospective affiliations, but to emphasize that because of the disjunctive and unstable interplay of commerce, media, national policies, and consumer fantasies, ethnicity, once a genie contained in the bottle of some sort of locality (however large), has now become a global force, forever slipping in and through the cracks between states and borders.

But the relationship between the cultural and economic levels of this new set of global disjunctures is not a simple one-way street in which the terms of global cultural politics are set wholly by, or confined wholly within, the vicissitudes of international flows of technology, labor, and finance, demanding only a modest modification of existing neo-Marxist models of uneven development and state formation. There is a deeper change, itself driven by the disjunctures among all the landscapes I have discussed and constituted by their continuously fluid and uncertain interplay, that concerns the relationship between production and consumption in today's global economy. Here, I begin with Marx's famous (and often mined) view of the fetishism of the commodity and suggest that this fetishism has been replaced in the world at large (now seeing the world as one large, interactive system, composed of many complex subsystems) by two mutually supportive descendants, the first of which I call production fetishism and the second, the fetishism of the consumer.

By *production fetishism* I mean an illusion created by contemporary transnational production loci that masks translocal capital, transnational earning flows, global management, and often faraway workers (engaged in various kinds of high-tech putting-out operations) in the idiom and spectacle of local (sometimes even worker) control, national productivity, and territorial sovereignty. To the extent that various kinds of free-trade zones have become the models for production at large, especially of high-tech commodities, production has itself become a fetish, obscuring not social relations as such but the relations of production, which are increasingly transnational. The locality (both in the sense of the local factory or site of production and in the extended sense of the nation-state) becomes a fetish that disguises the globally dispersed forces that actually drive the production process. This generates alienation (in Marx's sense) twice intensified, for its social sense is now compounded by a complicated spatial dynamic that is increasingly global.

As for the *fetishism of the consumer*, I mean to indicate here that the consumer has been transformed through commodity flows (and the mediascapes, especially of advertising, that accompany them) into a sign, both in Baudrillard's sense of a simulacrum that only asymptotically approaches the form of a real social agent, and in the sense of a mask for the real seat of agency, which is not the consumer but the producer and the many forces that constitute production. Global advertising is the key technology for the worldwide dissemination of a plethora of creative and culturally well-chosen ideas of consumer agency. These images of agency are increasingly distortions of a world of merchandising so subtle that the consumer is consistently helped to believe that he or she is an actor, where in fact he or she is at best a chooser.

The globalization of culture is not the same as its homogenization, but globalization involves the use of a variety of instruments of homogenization (armaments, advertising techniques, language hegemonies, and clothing styles) that are absorbed into local political and cultural economies, only to be repatriated as heterogeneous dialogues of national sovereignty, free enterprise, and fundamentalism in which the state plays an increasingly delicate role: too much openness to global flows, and the nation-state is threatened by revolt, as in the China syndrome; too little, and the state exits the international stage, as Burma, Albania, and North Korea in various ways have done. In general, the state has become the arbitrageur of this *repatriation of difference* (in the form of goods, signs, slogans, and styles). But this repatriation or export of the designs and commodities of difference continuously exacerbates the internal politics of majoritarianism and homogenization, which is most frequently played out in debates over heritage.

Thus the central feature of global culture today is the politics of the mutual effort of sameness and difference to cannibalize one another and thereby proclaim their successful hijacking of the twin Enlightenment ideas of the triumphantly universal and the resiliently particular. This mutual cannibalization shows its ugly face in riots, refugee flows, state-sponsored torture, and ethnocide (with or without state support). Its brighter side is in the expansion of many individual horizons of hope and fantasy, in the global spread of oral rehydration therapy and other low-tech instruments of well-being, in the susceptibility even of South Africa to the force of global opinion, in the inability of the Polish state to repress its own working classes, and in the growth of a wide range of progressive, transnational alliances. Examples of both sorts could be multiplied. The critical point is that both sides of the coin of global cultural process today are products of the infinitely varied mutual contest of sameness and difference on a stage characterized by radical disjunctures between different sorts of global flows and the uncertain landscapes created in and through these disjunctures. [. . .]

14   The Global Ecumene

Ulf Hannerz

Ethnology is in the sadly ludicrous, not to say tragic, position, that at the very moment when it begins to put its workshop in order, to forge its proper tools, to start ready for work on its appointed task, the material of its study melts away with hopeless rapidity.

(Bronislaw Malinowski)

We can easily now conceive of a time when there will be only one culture and one civilization on the entire surface of the earth. I don't believe this will happen, because there are contradictory tendencies always at work – on the one hand towards homogenization and on the other towards new distinctions.

(Claude Lévi-Strauss)

Each year in the spring, the countries of Europe meet in a televised song contest, a media event watched by hundreds of millions of people. There is first a national contest in each country to choose its own entry for the international competition. A few years ago, a controversy erupted in Sweden after this national contest. It was quite acceptable that the tune which was first runner-up had been performed by a lady from Finland, and the second runner up by an Afro-American lady who was by now a naturalized Swede. Both were highly thought of and somehow represented that new heterogeneity of Swedish society which had evolved over the last couple of decades. What was controversial was the winning tune, the refrain of which was "Four Buggs and a Coca Cola"; Bugg, like the name of the soft drink, was a brand name (for a chewing gum). Many people thought it improper that the national entry in the European contest should revolve around two brand names. But of the two, Coca Cola was much the more controversial, as it was widely understood as a central symbol of "cultural imperialism." Indeed, a synonym for the latter is "the cocacolonization of the world." Under the circumstances, what drew much less attention was the fact that the winning tune was a calypso, not something one would conventionally think of as typically Swedish, either.

In the end, the text was changed before the European finals, where the Swedish entry finished in the lower end of the field. But that is neither here nor there. For our purposes, what matters is what an incident like this tells us about the kind of cultures we make now.

Long ago, Alfred Kroeber suggested on the one hand that "probably the greater part of every culture has percolated into it," on the other hand that "as soon as a culture has accepted a new item, it tends to lose interest in [its] foreignness of origin." The former seems to be a culture-historical fact. The latter of Kroeber's claims is perhaps at this point more debatable. The interrelatedness of cultures may nowadays

Original publication details: Excerpted from Ulf Hannerz, *Cultural Complexity: Studies in the Social Organization of Meaning* (Columbia University Press, 1992), pp. 217–22, 228–31, 239–45, 261–2, 266–7. Reprinted by permission of Columbia University Press.

force itself upon our awareness more than before, due to its intensity and perhaps its particular current forms. Increasingly, cultural debates around the world are about a loss of integrity in national cultures, about the impact of communication satellites, about the internationalization of youth cultures, about the new cultural diversity created within national boundaries as the natives are joined by migrants and refugees. The origin of new cultural items is becoming a core aspect of the meanings they have to us.

It must now be more difficult than ever, or at least more unreasonable, to see the world (in terms of that metaphor scrutinized earlier) as a cultural mosaic, of separate pieces with hard, well-defined edges. Cultural interconnections increasingly reach across the world. More than ever, there is a global ecumene. The entities we routinely call cultures are becoming more like subcultures within this wider entity, with all that this suggests in terms of fuzzy boundaries and more or less arbitrary delimitation of analytical units. To grasp this fact of globalization, in its wide range of manifestations and implications, is the largest task at present confronting a macroanthropology of culture.

Centers and Peripheries in Cultural Flow

Until the 1960s or so, acknowledgments of the fact that "we are all in the same world" were mostly pieties, with uncertain political and intellectual implications. Since then, in the social sciences, understandings of globalization have usually involved a view of asymmetry; key conceptual pairs have been center (or core) and periphery, metropolis and satellite.

Asymmetries are present in the global social organization of meaning as well. But what kind of asymmetries are they? How closely aligned are the asymmetries of culture with those of economy, politics, or military might? How do center/periphery relationships in the world affect structures of meaning and cultural expression?

In political and military terms, the world during much of the twentieth century had two superpowers, and whatever freedom of movement other countries exercised, whether great or small, it tended ultimately to be constrained by this arrangement. In economic terms, the century has by and large seen the United States in a dominant position, with a number of lesser powers grouped around it, varyingly in ascent or decline. In cultural terms, would we recognize other powers than these?

As we understand things now, the question has two sides (which may be to simplify matters). There is that cultural production in the periphery which is somehow in response to the political and economic dominance of the center. Here the world system as defined in political and/or economic terms is obviously given cultural recognition of one kind or other. On the other hand, there is the issue of cultural diffusion. What defines the center/periphery relationship here are above all asymmetries, in the terms used before, of input quantity and scale. When the center speaks, the periphery listens, and mostly does not talk back.

In this case, the cultural centers of the world are not by definition identical with political and economic centers. Are they in practice? To begin with, let us just consider this in gross terms, as an issue of the overall cultural influence of nations. It can be argued that the center/periphery relationships of culture are not, at least at any particular point in time, a mere reflection of political and economic power. In the

American case, the congruence is undeniable. The general cultural influence of the Soviet Union in the world in the decades of its greatest strength, on the other hand, remained modest compared with its political and military power. Among the lesser powers, Britain and France may at present be stronger as cultural than as economic and political centers; this is perhaps debatable. Japan, on the whole, has at least so far kept a rather lower cultural profile in the world, despite its economic success (and with some exceptions). Most of what it exports does not seem to be identifiably marked by Japaneseness.

If the global pattern of center/periphery relationships in culture thus has some degree of separateness, it is easy to see in some instances what is behind a greater cultural influence. To a degree the present cultural influence of Britain and France still reflects the fact that old-style colonial powers could more or less monopolize the center/periphery cultural flow to its domains. In large parts of the world this even now makes London or Paris not just *a* center but *the* center. In old settler colonies, historical ties are yet closer, as links of kinship and ancestry also connect the periphery to a specific center. In Australia, when critics refer to "the cultural cringe," it is the deference to things English they have in mind. Language is obviously also a factor which may convert political power into cultural influence, and then conserve the latter. As people go on speaking English, French, and Portuguese in postcolonial lands, in postcolonial times, old center/periphery relationships get a prolonged lease on life. If all this means that the center/periphery relationships of culture tend to exhibit some lag relative to present and emergent structures of political and economic power, it might also mean that Japan may well yet come into a position of greater cultural influence in the world.

One might speculate that people also make different assumptions, in a metacultural fashion, about the nature of the relationship between themselves and their culture. By and large, Americans may not expect that the meanings and the cultural forms they invent are only for themselves; possibly because they have seen at home over the years that practically anybody can become an American. The French may see their culture as a gift to the world. There is a *mission civilisatrice*. The Japanese, on the other hand – so it is said – find it a strange notion that anyone can "become Japanese," and they put Japanese culture on exhibit, in the framework of organized international contacts, as a way of displaying irreducible distinctiveness rather than in order to make it spread. (Notably, many of those who engage in introducing aspects of Japanese culture to the world are alien cultural brokers.)

Staying with the conception of cultural centers as places where culture is invented and from which it is diffused, however, one cannot be satisfied with only the very generalized picture of the relative standing of a handful of countries as wholes. Too much is missing, and too much is assumed. Countries do not always exercise their influence at the same level across the gamut of cultural expressions. American influence is at present very diverse, but perhaps most conspicuous in science, technology, and popular culture; French influence on world culture is rather of the high culture variety, and in related fields such as sophisticated food and fashion; there is widespread interest in the organization and internal cultural engineering of Japanese corporations. In such more specialized ways, places like the Vatican or the Shia holy city of Qom also organize parts of the world into center/periphery relationships of culture, for certain purposes.

In this context, one should also keep in mind that particularly in such fields as science and technology, the spread of knowledge between nations can be actively prevented, for reasons of economic, political, and military advantage. Indeed, there are signs that such large-scale restrictive management of knowledge is on the increase. Often, it is primarily a part of competitive relationships between centers, but it constrains the cultural flow between center and periphery as well, maintaining the advantage of the former.

It is another characteristic of the structure of center/periphery relationships that it has many tiers. Some countries have a strong influence in their regions, due to a well-developed cultural apparatus – Mexico in Latin America, for example, and Egypt in the Arab world. A shared language and cultural tradition can be important in this way, at the same time as a sizable domestic market for cultural products can give one country an advantageous position in having something to export to the rest of the region. Such regional centers may base their production on meanings and forms wholly internal to the region, or they may operate as cultural brokers, translating influences from first-tier-centers into something more adapted to regional conditions.

World cultural process, it appears, has a much more intricate organization of diversity than is allowed in a picture of a center/periphery structure with just a handful of all-purpose centers. A further issue, obviously, if one tries to arrive at a kind of present-day global cultural flow chart is to what extent the peripheries indeed talk back, which would in large part be a question of the influence of the Third World on the Occident.

Reggae music, swamis, and Latin American novels exemplify the kind of counter-currents from more or less recent cultural history that may first enter one's mind; culture coming fully developed, as it were, from periphery to center, and at the same time culture which the periphery can give away, and keep at the same time. There are indeed instances like these, and while they are not new, they may well be on the increase. A little more will be said about them toward the end of the chapter. Yet desirable as one might find it to be able to speak of world culture in terms of more equal exchange, the conclusion can at present hardly be avoided that asymmetry rules. [. . .]

Bush and Beento: The World in the Third World

I come back to Nigeria once more. No single Third World country can perfectly exemplify all the variations in center/periphery cultural interrelations and local implications at the periphery. Any one of them, on the other hand, allows us the opportunity to identify some of the variables, and some recurrent tendencies.

When I first became acquainted with Nigeria, several decades ago, I encountered in the local version of English a couple of words which, when put together, now strike me as especially revealing: "bush" and "beento." The latter had become the term for a Nigerian who had been to England, or possibly somewhere else overseas, and returned. During the sojourn abroad, the beento had acquired an advanced education, and so he (for there were rather fewer she beentos) could claim a privileged position in an expanding, at least in part conspicuously meritocratic, national social structure. But hardly less important for the definition of the beento as a social type was the general sophistication which he had acquired abroad, a savoir-faire with regard to the way of life of the metropolis, and an intimate appreciation of its finer points. "Bush," on the other hand, could be used descriptively but would ring in Nigerian ears especially as a denunciation hurled, in richly varying combinations, at adversaries and wrongdoers: an epithet for ignorance and rustic, unsophisticated,

uncouth conduct. To be labeled bush in one way or other was to have one's rightful place in modern society put in question.

Beento and bush indeed seem to demarcate, in an embryonic folk model, the space
in which contemporary Nigerian national culture has grown. This is not a national
culture in the sense of a structure of meaning which is uniform and generally shared
within, and distinctive toward the outside. I have in mind rather the entire cultural
inventory actually available within the boundaries of the state, the universe of
meaning and cultural form within which people live, and which through their lives
they give some kind of social organization. At one end of this space, then, with its
varied connections and cleavages, there is the openness to the world, more especially
to the influence of western Europe and North America. London and New York are
by now parts of Nigerian culture, if not as situated experiences, then at least as vibrant
images. And metropolitanism is embodied in that figure of a migrant returning home
laden with cultural capital. The beento stands, as it were, at the intersection where
Wallerstein meets Bourdieu.

In cultural terms, it is at least partly true that what center/periphery relationships
order is a charismatic geography, arranged around the bright lights of the metropolis. "Bengal's cultural center of gravity became located in Calcutta," writes Poddar,
one of the interpreters of the Bengal Renaissance; but, moreover, "Calcutta's intellectual center of gravity became located in London. If the promise of Bengal's and
also India's regeneration was imported from there, the fatal constraints to its fulfill-
ment were also unloaded from the same ship."

Whatever the consequences may be, places such as London, Paris, New York, and
Miami continue to be, or grow into, expatriate capitals of parts of the Third World.
It may even seem as if many national cultures now have their centers, their cyno-
sures, outside the territory of the state. In these places, more than elsewhere, their
beentos become beentos, not just immigrants in the societies of the center, but also
extensions of those societies of the periphery in which they hold continued membership. Such cities are also the centers of a cultural apparatus reaching into Third
World national cultures; and not merely because the people of the periphery are
allowed in on what the center produces mostly for itself, but also because a considerable part of the production of capital-C and popular culture for the periphery likewise takes place there, or its works are disseminated from there. *Presence Africaine*,
the publishing house of Negritude, was a Left Bank phenomenon, and many of the
current generation of glossy newsmonthlies for the Third World are edited in London
or Paris, by partly Third World staffs. As yet another aspect of the integral role of
the metropoles in the national cultures of the periphery, these are the places where
exiles go, where shadow politics is conducted, where protest meetings are held, plots
hatched, battles over extradition fought. It is where cultural critics can be heard after
their voices have been silenced at home.

Within national boundaries, the global center/periphery relationships are linked
directly to those of nation and region. To an extent, one may look at all this again
in spatial terms (although now a little more close up than we began by doing), as
territories are organized by way of hierarchies of urban centers. Capitals – in the
Nigerian instance, Lagos – and other large cities become the bridgeheads of transnational cultural influences, through the concentration there of particular institutional and occupational structures, and of groups of people who through their
life-styles serve on the national scene as cultural models of metropolitanism. Here
are the national jet set, the larger clusters of technocrats and professionals, as well
as the representatives from the global center; and here, indeed, one finds in the

most complete version what I have sketched as the typical contemporary complex culture.

At the other end of a national cultural spectrum one may find the thousands of rural hamlets to which transnational cultural influences tend to reach in a more fragmented, and perhaps indirect, manner. They are the contemporary approximations of "bush," where the cultural flows within state and market frameworks, and the division of knowledge depending on a division of labor drawn to a great extent from the center, are still weak as compared to that social organization of meaning which belongs mostly within a form of life framework of a pronounced local character. [. . .]

Popular Culture: The Call of the Center, the Response of the Periphery

As one attempts to get a sense of the management of meaning between center and periphery, in Nigeria as elsewhere in the world, one can hardly ignore popular culture. Hardly any other area of contemporary culture is as strongly associated with the market framework generally, and the transnational flow of cultural commodities particularly. Established assumptions about cultural purity and authenticity come readily to the surface here. Not least among intellectuals and policymakers, the influx of popular culture from the global centers into the peripheries is described rather unremittingly in terms of its destructive and distracting powers. And this is as true in debate in the Third World (or on behalf of the Third World, among interested outsiders) as in a country like Sweden which, if finer distinctions are to be made, would probably be described as part of the semi-periphery (but hardly, on the other hand, of the semi-center) as far as transnational cultural flow is concerned. It is said that local products are threatened with extinction through the importation of "cheap foreign junk." One may detect some hypocrisy here, insofar as it is implied that all local products are of great intellectual or aesthetic merit, never merely cheap local junk.

Produced by the relatively few for a great many consumers, popular culture fits well with a center/periphery structure. Indeed, it may model it. The institutions and the performers of Nigerian popular culture are mostly based in those major urban centers which are at the same time bridgeheads of transnational culture. *Lagos Weekend*, the scandal sheet much enjoyed by the young men-about-town in Kafanchan during my early field periods there, literally placed the capital at the center of their attention. The major sports events occur in the larger cities, and young men have color pictures of British soccer teams on their walls. As popular music groups tour middle-sized and small towns all over the country, they display not only the newest in sounds and in dance but also in fashion and argot. The local commercial artists often draw on the more metropolitan media for ideas. One tailor in Kafanchan had a signboard outside his shop showing his nickname, Ringo Star (sic). In the personal photo albums of young people, pictures of themselves and their friends, in their best outfits and striking sophisticated poses, mix with cutout pictures of athletes, musicians, and movie stars.

Intensely reflexive, popular culture often tells us something about how its producers as well as its consumers see themselves, and in what directions they would like their lives to move. And in Nigeria, popular culture seems fairly permeated with meanings and meaningful forms drawn, or deriving in some other way, from the center. The most relevant contrast to popular culture here, I would suggest, is not, or perhaps only secondarily, high culture, the symbolic forms produced and largely consumed within a cultural elite. It is rather, once more, "bush." Involvement with popular culture in Nigeria appears to be above all a manifestation of metropolis-oriented sophistication and modernity. In a way, it may be more like popular culture as it was in early modern Europe, as described by the historian Peter Burke – a field of activity more or less uniting elites and masses in shared pastimes and pleasures. Perhaps this quality of metropolitan-orientedness also accounts for some of what is often referred to as the philistinism of Third World elites. One can reach toward the charisma of the center at least as well through a greater investment in popular culture as through involvement with a more differentiated, less widely understood high culture.

For all this, the center/periphery relationships of popular culture in Nigeria are not of an altogether simple kind. They are asymmetrical, but not free of contradictions, and they do not relegate the periphery to that entirely passive role in cultural construction which the preoccupation with popular culture in the global homogenization scenario seems to suggest.

One aspect of this is that the transnational flow of culture, by giving the periphery access to a wider cultural inventory, provides it with new resources of technology and symbolic expression to refashion and quite probably integrate with what exists of more locally rooted materials. Local cultural entrepreneurs have thus gradually mastered the alien cultural forms, taking them apart to investigate their potentialities in terms of symbolic modes, genres, and organizations of performance. Thus new competences are acquired, and the resulting new forms are more responsive to, and at the same time in part outgrowths of, local everyday life: examples of what I just outlined as the tendency toward maturation, and also of the possibilities of import substitution.

There are good examples of this in music. Popular Nigerian music stars such as Fela Anikulapo-Kuti, Sunny Ade, and Ebenezer Obey have hardly had to fear the foreign competition, and do not enact pale copies of it but perform in styles they have created themselves. Juju music, for example, for some time the dominant popular music form in Western Nigeria, has combined inspirations from more traditional Yoruba music and from high-life, another and rather earlier established popular music form. From modest origins in palm wine bars, it has moved up to large bands performing in night clubs and selling their record albums in large editions. The texts often have their roots in Yoruba praise singing, and likewise show affinities with the religious music of the syncretistic Aladura churches.

In this connection, I should return to the doubts I expressed initially about the sense of time, or more precisely the lacking sense of time, in the scenario of global homogenization. The onslaught of transnational influences, as often described or hinted at, seems rather too sudden. In West Africa, such influences have been filtering into the coastal societies for centuries already, although in earlier periods on a smaller scale and by modest means. There has been time to absorb the foreign influences, to modify the modifications in turn, and to fit shifting cultural forms to developing social structures, to situations and emerging audiences. This is not a scene where the peripheral culture is utterly defenseless, but rather one where locally evolving alternatives to imports are available, and where there are people at hand to perform innovative acts of cultural brokerage.

It is another aspect of the complicated nature of the center/periphery relationships of culture that there is both close attention to the center and what comes out of it and rather ambivalent responses to it. While the celebratory stance toward the center may be dominant, and have logical priority, the typical expressions and personifications of center influence cannot escape unfavorable notice, implicit or explicit. Nigerian popular writing, of which for almost half a century there has been a considerable amount, makes fun both of metropolitan English, too preciously pronounced, and of its corruptions and innovative adaptations in Nigerian everyday discourse. Extreme pidgin forms may be put in the mouth of some characters to define them as country bumpkins, while semiliterate crooks and ruffians make use of big English words. Metropolitan-style honorifics, not least abbreviations of academic credentials, are also much in evidence, mostly for comical effect.

What surely contributes to a certain cultural ambivalence is the fact that the cultural manifestations of center/periphery relationships frequently become inextricably entangled with matters of class. To have wealth and power is to have easier access to the metropolis; and it is through one's relationship to the metropolis that one often gains wealth and power in the periphery. To repeat, like so many Third World countries, Nigeria is a highly meritocratic, credentialist society, where one can carry metropolitan culture on one's sleeve and gain great and very visible advantage from it. The view of the beento, one of the main symbols of the center/periphery relationship in the Nigerian imagination, from below is thus not always sympathetic. Popular writers may describe him as arrogant, distant, and unfriendly. Yet it is another recurrent theme that the returning beento turns into a tragic figure. He has lost touch, his formal skills are not practical, his new universalist morality does not fit into the Nigerian rough-and-tumble. At the same time, in a populist vein, even "bush" can sometimes be used rhetorically to draw attention to a quality of down-to-earth sincerity and lack of affectation.

Then again, there are those television antennae over the roofs of Kafanchan. *Charlie's Angels* are in town, and the Ewings of *Dallas* as well. But they are not alone, and it is not obvious what they accomplish.

One problem with the global homogenization scenario tends to be the quality of the evidence for it. Quite frequently it is anecdotal – "I switched on the television set in my hotel room in Lagos (or Manila, or Tel Aviv, or Geneva), and found that *Dallas* was on." In a more sophisticated version, quantitative evidence is provided that on one Third World television channel or other, some high percentage of the programming is imported.

To be more completely persuasive, arguments about the impact of the transnational cultural flow would have to say something about how people respond to it. The mere fact that Third World television stations buy a lot of imported programs, for example, often has more to do with the fact that they are cheap, instances of cultural dumping, than that audiences are necessarily enthralled with them. We may have little idea about how many television sets are actually on when they are shown, and even less what is the quality of attention to them.

At least as problematic is the sense that people make of the transnational cultural flow. Even when we refer to it as a "flow of meaning," we must keep in mind the uncertainties built into the communicative process. If one cannot be too sure of perfect understanding even in a face-to-face interaction in a local context with much cultural redundancy, the difficulties (or the opportunities for innovative interpretations, if one wants to turn things around) multiply where communication is largely one way, between people whose perspectives have been shaped in very different contexts, in places very distant from one another. The meaning of the transnational cultural flow is thus in the eye of the beholder: what he sees, we generally know little about.

One intricate issue here is the relationship between different symbolic modes and the global diversity of culture. Do some symbolic forms, in some modes, travel better than others? We know well enough where the barriers of incomprehension are in the linguistic mode. How is the transnational spread of popular culture affected by varying sensibilities with respect to other modes, such as music, or gestures and body movement? One may rather facilely explain the spread of Indian and Hong Kong movies over much of the Third World by referring to the fact that they are cheap (which appeals to distributors) and action-packed (which appeals to somewhat unsophisticated audiences). But the latter point in particular may hide as much as it reveals. What kind, or degree, of precision is there in the audience appreciation of the symbolic forms of another country?

In any case, the beginnings of serious media research by Nigerian scholars show that the most popular series have been those made in the country. And much of the earthy humor of these series is again generated by local responses to metropolitan influences, as well as by exaggerated displays of metropolitan-derived culture. They regularly show people making fools of themselves as they embrace alien cultural items, and make inept use of them. In one, a prominent business woman is depicted as a member of "the American Dollar Club." In another, when someone tries to change the eating habits of the main character, a local chief, to include European dishes, he stares at the spaghetti and asks what are those worms on his plate.

Current conceptions of cultural imperialism exemplify on the largest imaginable scale the curious fact that according to the economics of culture, to receive may be to lose. In that way, they are a useful antidote to old "white man's burden" notions of the gifts of culture from center to periphery as unadulterated benefaction. Yet it would seem impossible to argue that the transnational cultural influences are generally deleterious. In the areas of scholarship and intellectual life, we hardly take a conflict for granted between the transnational flow of culture and local cultural creativity. Without a certain openness to impulses from the outside world, we would expect science, art, and literature to become impoverished anywhere. Obviously, Nigerian literary life could hardly exist were it not for the importation of literacy and a range of literary forms. But there would not have been a Nigerian Nobel Prize winner in literature in 1986 if Wole Soyinka had not creatively drawn on both a literary expertise drawn mostly from the Occident and an imagination rooted in a Nigerian mythology, and turned them into something unique. [. . .]

Conclusion: A Creolizing World

During the twentieth century – and especially in its latter part – the global ecumene has indeed been an organization of diversity, and one which has also been characterized by diversity in organization. The point of view which I have tried to develop in this chapter can perhaps be summarized as follows:

1   The autonomy and boundedness of cultures must nowadays be understood as a matter of degree;
2   The distribution of culture within the world is affected by a structure of asymmetrical, center/periphery, relationships;
3   These relationships affect cultures, to different degrees, particularly in two analytically distinguishable ways – by shaping the material and power conditions to which cultures adapt, even in their more autonomous cultural processes, and through the more direct influx of initially alien meanings and cultural forms;

4   That influx does not enter into a vacuum, or inscribe itself on a cultural tabula
     rasa, but enters into various kinds of interaction with already existing meanings
     and meaningful forms, however these may be socially distributed, in cumulative
     historical processes;
5   The transnational cultural flow is internally diverse;
6   Market, state, form of life, and movement frameworks for the organization of
     cultural flow all have their own, somewhat diverse, ways of organizing (which
     may include promoting, regulating, or preventing) the transnational cultural flow;
7   Not all cultures are local, in the sense of being territorially bounded;
8   And it is hardly self-evident that the end result of the cultural processes connected
     to transnational center/periphery relationships must be a global homogenization
     of culture.

Is there, then, any other scenario, any alternative overall conceptualization, which
may give us a better grasp of the current interplay between world culture and the
national cultures of the periphery?

Whatever anthropologists and their neighbors in other disciplines have been up
to in constructing more general points of view toward complexity and change in the
Third World, they have hardly ever done justice to the particular qualities of cultural
phenomena and cultural processes, as these occur within structures of social relationships. And frameworks which seemed satisfactory at one time have by now been
overtaken by events. [. . .]

The flow of culture between countries and continents may result in another diversity of culture, based more on interconnections than on autonomy. It also allows the
sense of a complex culture as a network of perspectives, or as an ongoing debate.
People can come into it from the diaspora, as consultants and advisors, or they can
come into it from the multiform local cultures, from the bush. The outcome is not
predicted. Creolization though is openended; the tendencies toward maturation and
saturation are understood as quite possibly going on side by side, or interweaving.
There may come a time of decreolization, the metropolitan Standard eventually
becoming dominant, but a creole culture could also stabilize, or the interplay of
center and periphery could go on and on, never settling into a fixed form precisely
because of the openness of the global whole. What matters is that we are sensitized,
through the creolist view, to what general kind of culture this is.

As the world turns, today's periphery may be tomorrow's center. The historian
Bernard Bailyn has suggested, in his book *The Peopling of British North America* that
American culture as it was by the beginning of the eighteenth century "becomes
most fully comprehensible when seen as the exotic far Western periphery, a march-
land, of the metropolitan European culture system." It is an anachronism, according
to Bailyn, to look, as many American historians have done, at colonial America as a
frontier, looking forward and outward, anticipating progress, rather than as "a ragged
outer margin of a central world, a backward-looking diminishment of metropolitan
accomplishment." This may be a controversial point of view. The fact remains,
however, that a new culture did grow out of that management of meaning which
occurred in this periphery, a culture which went on to turn the tables on the world
but which in its internal processes has continued to show the continued fluidity of a
creolizing continuum. Anglo culture, the culture of the WASPs, may have provided
the metropolis, the Standard, the mainstream, but as it reaches out toward every
corner of society, it becomes creolized itself. Ethnic boundaries remain noticeable,
yet cultural meanings and forms flow across them. American music with African

sources is not necessarily Black music, it may be mountain music or symphony music. You do not have to be Jewish to have *chutzpah*; it may be enough to be a New Yorker.

If some peripheries – in time – become centers, and some old centers pass them as they move in the other direction, what seems unlikely to change, given the way things are, is the organization of the world by way of center/periphery relationships. And as cultural traffic plays its part in this, something like creole cultures may have a larger part in our future than cultures designed, each by itself, to be pieces of a mosaic. Toward the end of the twentieth century, and during the twenty-first, it would seem to be through our grasp of the flux of the global ecumene that we can best make sense of *Homo sapiens*.

Questions

1   How, and to what extent, did the world become "unified" in the mid-nineteenth century? Would Immanuel Wallerstein agree that this period marks a key stage in globalization?

2   What does the world of the twentieth century have in common with that of the sixteenth? How does Wallerstein explain the remarkable stability of an economically unequal and politically divided world system? What concepts does he contribute to the study of globalization?

3   Although Sklair notes that the current global system is "not synonymous with the global capitalist system," he regards specific features of world capitalism as driving forces of globalization. What are these features, and what do they add to Wallerstein's analysis of world capitalism?

4   How does "complex interdependence" constrain the behavior of states interested in enhancing their power and security, according to Keohane and Nye? What traditional assumptions about world politics does this new situation call into question? How can international organizations transform world politics?

5   What do Meyer and his colleagues mean when they say that nation-states are not "collective actors"? What surprising similarities among nation-states do they note, and how do they account for them? Do they identify a driving force in globalization?

6   How does Robertson define globalization, and how does his "model of order" capture its key features? What is the "take-off period of modern globalization"? How does globalization trigger debate about world order and a "search for fundamentals"?

7   What views of cultural globalization does Appadurai challenge when he describes the process as an "infinitely varied contest of sameness and difference" in a complex "disjunctive order"? How can (or must) any group draw on the flows in different "scapes" to construct its identity?

8   For Hannerz, does the emerging "global ecumene" have a single, entirely homogeneous culture? What globalization processes contribute to cultural creolization? Do you see these same processes at work in your own culture? Do you see parallels to the notions of "bush" and "beento" in your culture?

Part III

Experiencing Globalization

Introduction

In *Golden Arches East*, James Watson reports that, as older residents of Hong Kong revel in the quality of Cantonese cuisine, their offspring avidly consume Big Macs, pizza, and Coca-Cola. Not long ago, travelers on British Rail's first-class Pullman service could enjoy dishes from India, the Middle East, China, Greece, and so on, as Allison James reports in a volume on *Cross-Cultural Consumption*. From personal experience, we can attest that, in urban areas of the American South, Thai cuisine successfully competes with traditional fare and supermarkets abound with produce from most continents. To be sure, these examples refer to privileged areas of the world. They are not unprecedented, as the earlier European adoption of New World potatoes and sugar demonstrates. Yet they illustrate one way in which globalization affects people concretely, namely through changes in diet and taste. Such changes express new linkages, new transnational structures, a new global culture. More and more people can literally get a taste of what it means to be part of world society.

No one experiences globalization in all its complexity, but globalization is significant insofar as it reshapes the daily lives of billions of people. Increasingly, the larger world is present locally. This obviously applies to a Kofi Annan (the UN Secretary General) or a Bill Gates (the Chairman of Microsoft), conscious contributors to globalization, but it is also true for the Thai prostitutes, minions in a global industry, who are now suffering from AIDS. American textile workers know it as they feel the impact of intense foreign competition and outsourcing to overseas companies. Soccer fans regard it as routine when a large portion of the world's population directs its attention to the World Cup every four years. Business people traveling internationally see it daily in the media offerings in their hotel rooms.

Experiencing globalization, as some of these examples indicate, is not a one-way process, in the sense that large structural change is bound to overwhelm individuals. People participate and respond in different ways. They can shape, resist, absorb, or try to avoid globalization. They can seek opportunity in it, feel the harm of it, or lament the power of it. For some, globalization is a central reality; for others, it is still on the margins of their lives. In short, there is no one experience of globalization. That, in itself, is an important aspect of the process. The formation of a new world society does not involve all people in the same way and it does not create the same texture in everyone's everyday life. But there are some commonalities in the global experience of globalization. To one degree or another, globalization is real to almost everyone. It transforms the prevailing sense of time and space, now globally standardized. It envelops everyone in new institutions. It poses a challenge, in the sense that even marginally affected groups must take a stance toward the world. And globalization, as we will see again in Part VIII, raises identity problems for societies and individuals alike.

The selections in this part illuminate the experience of globalization from different vantage points. They show that the experience of globalization involves creative adaptation to global processes, new mixtures of cultural frameworks, and the growth of a variable global consciousness. James Watson describes McDonald's customers in Hong Kong, including children, as critical consumers to whose expectations about food and service the multinational corporation must adapt. Far from imposing a new dietary standard, McDonald's blended into an already heterogeneous urban landscape. Watson concludes that in places like Hong Kong the transnational is the local. Martin Albrow studies the lives of various groups in London, showing that for many the place where they live is no longer connected to a sense of community through local culture. Rather, many groups, notably immigrants and their offspring, extend their relations and allegiances transnationally, as far as their resources can carry them. The global city thus harbors many global actors. Bruce Fuller studies one aspect of globalization – the expansion of formal education as a world institution – as it unfolds in Malawi. In one of the poorest countries in the world, bureaucratically organized and classroom-based public education is regarded as the way to "become modern." Malawi tries to do what any proper state must. But as Fuller observed classes in action, he found that teachers keeping control of large classes with few resources necessarily deviated from the global ideology that legitimates their position. The last selection finds Timothy Taylor using the experience of one musician to show how a new kind of "global pop" is developing. Youssou N'Dour, a world music star from Senegal, has brought a mixture of commercialized African music styles to western audiences while also reaching African audiences as a traditional praise-singer. Musicians like N'Dour, Taylor argues, are not interested in preserving an artificial authenticity; rather, they strive to be "global citizens" by creatively blending the many sounds they hear.

15 McDonald's in Hong Kong

James L. Watson

[...] how does one explain the phenomenal success of American-style fast food in Hong Kong and, increasingly, in Guangzhou – the two epicenters of Cantonese culture and cuisine? Seven of the world's ten busiest McDonald's restaurants are located in Hong Kong. When McDonald's first opened in 1975, few thought it would survive more than a few months. By January 1, 1997, Hong Kong had 125 outlets, which means that there was one McDonald's for every 51,200 residents, compared to one for every 30,000 people in the United States. Walking into these restaurants and looking at the layout, one could well be in Cleveland or Boston. The only obvious differences are the clientele, the majority of whom are Cantonese-speakers, and the menu, which is in Chinese as well as English.

Transnationalism and the Fast Food Industry

Does the roaring success of McDonald's and its rivals in the fast food industry mean that Hong Kong's local culture is under siege? Are food chains helping to create a homogeneous, "global" culture better suited to the demands of a capitalist world order? Hong Kong would seem to be an excellent place to test the globalization hypothesis, given the central role that cuisine plays in the production and maintenance of a distinctive local identity. Man Tso-chuen's great-grandchildren are today avid consumers of Big Macs, pizza, and Coca-Cola; does this somehow make them less "Chinese" than their grandfather?

It is my contention that the cultural arena in places like Hong Kong is changing with such breathtaking speed that the fundamental assumptions underlining such questions are themselves questionable. Economic and social realities make it necessary to construct an entirely new approach to global issues, one that takes the consumers' own views into account. Analyses based on neomarxian and dependency (center/periphery) models that were popular in the 1960s and 1970s do not begin to capture the complexity of emerging transnational systems.

This chapter represents a conscious attempt to bring the discussion of globalism down to earth, focusing on one local culture. The people of Hong Kong have embraced American-style fast foods, and by so doing they might appear to be in the vanguard of a worldwide culinary revolution. But they have not been stripped of their cultural traditions, nor have they become "Americanized" in any but the most superficial of ways. Hong Kong in the late 1990s constitutes one of the world's most

Original publication details: Excerpted from James L. Watson, *Golden Arches East: McDonald's in East Asia* (Stanford University Press, 1997). Copyright © 1997 by the Board of the Trustees of the Leland Stanford Jr. University. Reprinted by permission of Stanford University Press, www.sup.org

heterogeneous cultural environments. Younger people, in particular, are fully conversant in transnational idioms, which include language, music, sports, clothing, satellite television, cybercommunications, global travel, and – of course – cuisine. It is no longer possible to distinguish what is local and what is not. In Hong Kong, as I hope to show in this chapter, the transnational *is* the local. [. . .]

Mental Categories: Snack Versus Meal

As in other parts of East Asia, McDonald's faced a serious problem when it began operation in Hong Kong: Hamburgers, fries, and sandwiches were perceived as snacks (Cantonese *siu sihk*, literally "small eats"); in the local view these items did not constitute the elements of a proper meal. This perception is still prevalent among older, more conservative consumers who believe that hamburgers, hot dogs, and pizza can never be "filling." Many students stop at fast food outlets on their way home from school; they may share hamburgers and fries with their classmates and then eat a full meal with their families at home. This is not considered a problem by parents, who themselves are likely to have stopped for tea and snacks after work. Snacking with friends and colleagues provides a major opportunity for socializing (and transacting business) among southern Chinese. Teahouses, coffee shops, bakeries, and ice cream parlors are popular precisely because they provide a structured yet informal setting for social encounters. Furthermore, unlike Chinese restaurants and banquet halls, snack centers do not command a great deal of time or money from customers.

Contrary to corporate goals, therefore, McDonald's entered the Hong Kong market as a purveyor of snacks. Only since the late 1980s has its fare been treated as the foundation of "meals" by a generation of younger consumers who regularly eat non-Chinese food. Thanks largely to McDonald's, hamburgers and fries are now a recognized feature of Hong Kong's lunch scene. The evening hours remain, however, the weak link in McDonald's marketing plan; the real surprise was breakfast, which became a peak traffic period (more on this below).

The mental universe of Hong Kong consumers is partially revealed in the everyday use of language. Hamburgers are referred to, in colloquial Cantonese, as *han bou bao* – *han* being a homophone for "ham" and *bao* the common term for stuffed buns or bread rolls. *Bao* are quintessential snacks, and however excellent or nutritious they might be, they do not constitute the basis of a satisfying (i.e., filling) meal. In South China that honor is reserved for culinary arrangements that rest, literally, on a bed of rice (*fan*). Foods that accompany rice are referred to as *sung*, probably best translated as "toppings" (including meat, fish, and vegetables). It is significant that hamburgers are rarely categorized as meat (*yuk*); Hong Kong consumers tend to perceive anything that is served between slices of bread (Big Macs, fish sandwiches, hot dogs) as *bao*. In American culture the hamburger is categorized first and foremost as a meat item (with all the attendant worries about fat and cholesterol content), whereas in Hong Kong the same item is thought of primarily as bread.

From Exotic to Ordinary: McDonald's Becomes Local

Following precedents in other international markets, the Hong Kong franchise promoted McDonald's basic menu and did not introduce items that would be more recognizable to Chinese consumers (such as rice dishes, tropical fruit, soup noodles). Until recently the food has been indistinguishable from that served in Mobile, Alabama, or Moline, Illinois. There are, however, local preferences: the best-selling items in many outlets are fish sandwiches and plain hamburgers; Big Macs tend to be the favorites of children and teenagers. Hot tea and hot chocolate outsell coffee, but Coca-Cola remains the most popular drink.

McDonald's conservative approach also applied to the breakfast menu. When morning service was introduced in the 1980s, American-style items such as eggs, muffins, pancakes, and hash brown potatoes were not featured. Instead, the local outlets served the standard fare of hamburgers and fries for breakfast. McDonald's initial venture into the early morning food market was so successful that Mr. Ng hesitated to introduce American-style breakfast items, fearing that an abrupt shift in menu might alienate consumers who were beginning to accept hamburgers and fries as a regular feature of their diet. The transition to eggs, muffins, and hash browns was a gradual one, and today most Hong Kong customers order breakfasts that are similar to those offered in American outlets. But once established, dietary preferences change slowly: McDonald's continues to feature plain hamburgers (but not the Big Mac) on its breakfast menu in most Hong Kong outlets.

Management decisions of the type outlined above helped establish McDonald's as an icon of popular culture in Hong Kong. From 1975 to approximately 1985, McDonald's became the "in" place for young people wishing to associate themselves with the laid-back, nonhierarchical dynamism they perceived American society to embody. The first generation of consumers patronized McDonald's precisely because it was *not* Chinese and was *not* associated with Hong Kong's past as a backward-looking colonial outpost where (in their view) nothing of consequence ever happened. Hong Kong was changing and, as noted earlier, a new consumer culture was beginning to take shape. McDonald's caught the wave of this cultural movement and has been riding it ever since.

Anthropological conventions and methodologies do not allow one to deal very well with factors such as entrepreneurial flair or managerial creativity. Ethnographers are used to thinking in terms of group behavior, emphasizing coalitions and communities rather than personalities. In studies of corporate culture, however, the decisive role of management – or, more precisely, individual managers – must be dealt with in a direct way. This takes us into the realm of charisma, leadership, and personality.

Thanks largely to unrelenting efforts by Mr. Ng and his staff, McDonald's made the transition from an exotic, trendy establishment patronized by self-conscious status seekers to a competitively priced chain offering "value meals" to busy, preoccupied consumers. Today, McDonald's restaurants in Hong Kong are packed – wall-to-wall – with people of all ages, few of whom are seeking an American cultural experience. Twenty years after Mr. Ng opened his first restaurant, eating at McDonald's has become an ordinary, everyday experience for hundreds of thousands of Hong Kong residents. The chain has become a local institution in the sense that it has blended into the urban landscape; McDonald's outlets now serve as rendezvous points for young and old alike. [. . .]

Sanitation and the Invention of Cleanliness

Besides offering value for money, another key to McDonald's success was the provision of extra services, hitherto unavailable to Hong Kong consumers. Until the mid-1980s, a visit to any Hong Kong restaurant's toilet (save for those in fancy hotels) could best be described as an adventure. Today, restaurant toilets all over the territory are in good working order and, much to the surprise of visitors who remember the past, they are (relatively) clean. Based on conversations with people representing the full range of social strata in Hong Kong, McDonald's is widely perceived as the catalyst of this dramatic change. The corporation maintained clean facilities and did not waver as new outlets opened in neighborhoods where public sanitation had never been a high priority. Daniel Ng recalled how, during the early years of his business, he had to re-educate employees before they could even begin to comprehend what corporate standards of cleanliness entailed. Many workers, when asked to scrub out a toilet, would protest that it was already cleaner than the one in their own home, only to be told that it was not clean enough. McDonald's set what was perceived at the time to be an impossible standard and, in the process, raised consumers' expectations. Rivals had to meet these standards in order to compete. Hong Kong consumers began to draw a mental equation between the state of a restaurant's toilets and its kitchen. In pre-1980s public eateries (and in many private homes), the toilet was located inside the kitchen. One was not expected to see any contradiction in this arrangement; the operative factor was that both facilities had to be near the water supply. Younger people, in particular, have begun to grow wary of these arrangements and are refusing to eat at places they perceive to be "dirty."

Without exception my informants cited the availability of clean and accessible toilets as an important reason for patronizing McDonald's. Women, in particular, appreciated this service; they noted that, without McDonald's, it would be difficult to find public facilities when they are away from home or office. A survey of one Hong Kong outlet in June 1994 revealed that 58 percent of the consumers present were women. For many Hong Kong residents, therefore, McDonald's is more than just a restaurant; it is an oasis, a familiar rest station, in what is perceived to be an inhospitable urban environment.

What's in a Smile? Friendliness and Public Service

American consumers expect to be served "with a smile" when they order fast food, but . . . this is not true in all societies. In Hong Kong people are suspicious of anyone who displays what is perceived to be an excess of congeniality, solicitude, or familiarity. The human smile is not, therefore, a universal symbol of openness and honesty. "If you buy an apple from a hawker and he smiles at you," my Cantonese tutor once told me, "you know you're being cheated."

Given these cultural expectations, it was difficult for Hong Kong management to import a key element of the McDonald's formula – service with a smile – and make it work. Crew members were trained to treat customers in a manner that approximates the American notion of "friendliness." Prior to the 1970s, there was not even an indigenous Cantonese term to describe this form of behavior. The traditional notion of friendship is based on loyalty to close associates, which by definition cannot be extended to strangers. Today the concept of *public* friendliness is recognized – and verbalized – by younger people in Hong Kong, but the term many of them use to express this quality is "friendly," borrowed directly from English. McDonald's, through its television advertising, may be partly responsible for this innovation, but to date it has had little effect on workers in the catering industry.

During my interviews it became clear that the majority of Hong Kong consumers were uninterested in public displays of congeniality from service personnel. When shopping for fast food most people cited convenience, cleanliness, and table space as primary considerations; few even mentioned service except to note that the food should be delivered promptly. Counter staff in Hong Kong's fast food outlets (including McDonald's) rarely make great efforts to smile or to behave in a manner Americans would interpret as friendly. Instead, they project qualities that are admired in the local culture: competence, directness, and unflappability. In a North American setting the facial expression that Hong Kong employees use to convey these qualities would likely be interpreted as a deliberate attempt to be rude or indifferent. Workers who smile on the job are assumed to be enjoying themselves at the consumer's (and management's) expense: In the words of one diner I overheard while standing in a queue, "They must be playing around back there. What are they laughing about?"

Consumer Discipline?

[A] hallmark of the American fast food business is the displacement of labor costs from the corporation to the consumers. For the system to work, consumers must be educated – or "disciplined" – so that they voluntarily fulfill their side of an implicit bargain: We (the corporation) will provide cheap, fast service, if you (the customer) carry your own tray, seat yourself, and help clean up afterward. Time and space are also critical factors in the equation: Fast service is offered in exchange for speedy consumption and a prompt departure, thereby making room for others. This system has revolutionized the American food industry and has helped to shape consumer expectations in other sectors of the economy. How has it fared in Hong Kong? Are Chinese customers conforming to disciplinary models devised in Oak Brook, Illinois?

The answer is both yes and no. In general Hong Kong consumers have accepted the basic elements of the fast food formula, but with "localizing" adaptations. For instance, customers generally do not bus their own trays, nor do they depart immediately upon finishing. Clearing one's own table has never been an accepted part of local culinary culture, owing in part to the low esteem attaching to this type of labor. [. . .]

Perhaps the most striking feature of the American-inspired model of consumer discipline is the queue. Researchers in many parts of the world have reported that customers refuse, despite "education" campaigns by the chains involved, to form neat lines in front of cashiers. Instead, customers pack themselves into disorderly scrums and jostle for a chance to place their orders. Scrums of this nature were common in Hong Kong when McDonald's opened in 1975. Local managers discouraged this practice by stationing queue monitors near the registers during busy hours and, by the 1980s, orderly lines were the norm at McDonald's. The disappearance of the scrum corresponds to a general change in Hong Kong's public culture as a new generation of residents, the children of refugees, began to treat the territory as their home. Courtesy toward strangers was largely unknown in the 1960s: Boarding a bus during rush hour could be a nightmare and transacting business at a bank teller's window required brute strength. Many people credit McDonald's with being the first public institution in Hong Kong to enforce queuing, and thereby helping to create a more "civilized" social order. McDonald's did not, in fact, introduce the queue to Hong Kong, but this belief is firmly lodged in the public imagination.

Hovering and the Napkin Wars

Purchasing one's food is no longer a physical challenge in Hong Kong's McDonald's but finding a place to sit is quite another matter. The traditional practice of "hovering" is one solution: Choose a group of diners who appear to be on the verge of leaving and stake a claim to their table by hovering nearby, sometimes only inches away. Seated customers routinely ignore the intrusion; it would, in fact, entail a loss of face to notice. Hovering was the norm in Hong Kong's lower- to middle-range restaurants during the 1960s and 1970s, but the practice has disappeared in recent years. Restaurants now take names or hand out tickets at the entrance; warning signs, in Chinese and English, are posted: "Please wait to be seated." Customers are no longer allowed into the dining area until a table is ready.

Fast food outlets are the only dining establishments in Hong Kong where hovering is still tolerated, largely because it would be nearly impossible to regulate. Customer traffic in McDonald's is so heavy that the standard restaurant design has failed to reproduce American-style dining routines: Rather than ordering first and finding a place to sit afterward, Hong Kong consumers usually arrive in groups and delegate one or two people to claim a table while someone else joins the counter queues. Children make ideal hoverers and learn to scoot through packed restaurants, zeroing in on diners who are about to finish. It is one of the wonders of comparative ethnography to witness the speed with which Hong Kong children perform this reconnaissance duty. Foreign visitors are sometimes unnerved by hovering, but residents accept it as part of everyday life in one of the world's most densely populated cities. It is not surprising, therefore, that Hong Kong's fast food chains have made few efforts to curtail the practice.

Management is less tolerant of behavior that affects profit margins. In the United States fast food companies save money by allowing (or requiring) customers to collect their own napkins, straws, plastic flatware, and condiments. Self-provisioning is an essential feature of consumer discipline, but it only works if the system is not abused. In Hong Kong napkins are dispensed, one at a time, by McDonald's crew members who work behind the counter; customers who do not ask for napkins do not receive any. This is a deviation from the corporation's standard operating procedure and adds a few seconds to each transaction, which in turn slows down the queues. Why alter a well-tested routine? The reason is simple: napkins placed in public dispensers disappear faster than they can be replaced. [. . .]

Children as Consumers

[. . .] McDonald's has become so popular in Hong Kong that parents often use visits to their neighborhood outlet as a reward for good behavior or academic achievement. Conversely, children who misbehave might lose their after-school snacking privileges or be left at home while their siblings are taken out for a McDonald's brunch on Sunday. During interviews parents reported that sanctions of this type worked better than anything they could think of to straighten out a wayward child: "It is my nuclear deterrent," one father told me, in English.

Many Hong Kong children of my acquaintance are so fond of McDonald's that they refuse to eat with their parents or grandparents in Chinese-style restaurants or *dim sam* teahouses. This has caused intergenerational distress in some of Hong Kong's more conservative communities. In 1994, a nine-year-old boy, the descendant of illustrious ancestors who settled in the New Territories eight centuries ago, talked about his concerns as we consumed Big Macs, fries, and shakes at McDonald's: "A-bak [uncle], I like it here better than any place in the world. I want to come here every day." His father takes him to McDonald's at least twice a week, but his grandfather, who accompanied them a few times in the late 1980s, will no longer do so. "I prefer to eat *dim sam*," the older man told me later. "That place [McDonald's] is for kids." Many grandparents have resigned themselves to the new consumer trends and take their preschool grandchildren to McDonald's for mid-morning snacks – precisely the time of day that local teahouses were once packed with retired people. Cantonese grandparents have always played a prominent role in child minding, but until recently the children had to accommodate to the proclivities of their elders. By the 1990s grandchildren were more assertive and the mid-morning *dim sam* snack was giving way to hamburgers and Cokes.

The emergence of children as full-scale consumers has had other consequences for the balance of domestic power in Hong Kong homes. Grade school children often possess detailed knowledge of fast foods and foreign (non-Chinese) cuisines. Unlike members of the older generation, children know what, and how, to eat in a wide variety of restaurants. Specialized information is shared with classmates: Which chain has the best pizza? What is ravioli? How do you eat a croissant? Food, especially fast food, is one of the leading topics of conversation among Hong Kong school children. Grandchildren frequently assume the role of tutors, showing their elders the proper way to eat fast food. Without guidance, older people are likely to disassemble the Big Mac, layer by layer, and eat only those parts that appeal to them. Hong Kong adults also find it uncomfortable to eat with their hands and devise makeshift finger guards with wrappers. Children, by contrast, are usually expert in the finer points of fast food etiquette and pay close attention to television ads that feature young people eating a variety of foods. It is embarrassing, I was told by an 11-year-old acquaintance, to be seen at McDonald's with a grandfather who does not know how to eat "properly."

Many Hong Kong kindergartens and primary schools teach culinary skills, utilizing the lunch period for lessons in flatware etiquette, menu reading, and food awareness (taste-testing various cuisines, including Thai, European, and Indian). Partly as a consequence, Hong Kong's youth are among the world's most knowledgeable and adventurous eaters. One can find a wide range of cuisines in today's Hong Kong, rivaling New York City for variety. South Asian, Mexican, and Spanish restaurants are crowded with groups of young people, ages 16 to 25, sharing dishes as they graze their way through the menu. Culinary adventures of this nature are avoided by older residents (people over 50), who, in general, have a more restricted range of food tolerance.

Ronald McDonald and the Invention of Birthday Parties

Until recently most people in Hong Kong did not even know, let alone celebrate, their birthdates in the Western calendrical sense; dates of birth according to the lunar calendar were recorded for divinatory purposes but were not noted in annual rites. By the late 1980s, however, birthday parties, complete with cakes and candles, were the rage in Hong Kong. Any child who was anyone had to have a party, and the most popular venue was a fast food restaurant, with McDonald's ranked above all competitors. The majority of Hong Kong people live in overcrowded flats, which means that parties are rarely held in private homes.

Except for the outlets in central business districts, McDonald's restaurants are packed every Saturday and Sunday with birthday parties, cycled through at the rate of one every hour. A party hostess, provided by the restaurant, leads the children in games while the parents sit on the sidelines, talking quietly among themselves. For a small fee celebrants receive printed invitation cards, photographs, a gift box containing toys and a discount coupon for future trips to McDonald's. Parties are held in a special enclosure, called the Ronald Room, which is equipped with low tables and tiny stools – suitable only for children. Television commercials portray Ronald McDonald leading birthday celebrants on exciting safaris and expeditions. The clown's Cantonese name, Mak Dong Lou Suk-Suk ("Uncle McDonald"), plays on the intimacy of kinship and has helped transform him into one of Hong Kong's most familiar cartoon figures. [. . .]

Conclusions: Whose Culture Is it?

[. . .] Having watched the processes of culture change unfold for nearly thirty years, it is apparent to me that the ordinary people of Hong Kong have most assuredly *not* been stripped of their cultural heritage, nor have they become the uncomprehending dupes of transnational corporations. Younger people – including many of the grandchildren of my former neighbors in the New Territories – are avid consumers of transnational culture in all of its most obvious manifestations: music, fashion, television, and cuisine. At the same time, however, Hong Kong has itself become a major center for the *production* of transnational culture, not just a sinkhole for its *consumption*. Witness, for example, the expansion of Hong Kong popular culture into China, Southeast Asia, and beyond: "Cantopop" music is heard on radio stations in North China, Vietnam, and Japan; the Hong Kong fashion industry influences clothing styles in Los Angeles, Bangkok, and Kuala Lumpur; and, perhaps most significant of all, Hong Kong is emerging as a center for the production and dissemination of satellite television programs throughout East, Southeast, and South Asia.

A lifestyle is emerging in Hong Kong that can best be described as postmodern, postnationalist, and flamboyantly transnational. The wholesale acceptance and appropriation of Big Macs, Ronald McDonald, and birthday parties are small, but significant aspects of this redefinition of Chinese cultural identity. In closing, therefore, it seems appropriate to pose an entirely new set of questions: Where does the transnational end and the local begin? Whose culture is it, anyway? In places like Hong Kong the postcolonial periphery is fast becoming the metropolitan center, where local people are consuming and simultaneously producing new cultural systems. [. . .]

16 Travelling Beyond Local Cultures

Martin Albrow

Globalization, Culture and Locality

In the last thirty years transformations of industrial organization in the advanced societies, accompanied by the acceptance of the ideas of post-industrialism and post-modernity, mean that the problem-setting for community analysis has shifted. In the last decade globalization theory has brought issues of time, space and territorial organization into the centre of the frame of argument. We have to look again at the way social relations are tied to place and re-examine issues of locality and culture.

Our data about people in one small area suggest that locality has a much less absolute salience for individuals and social relations than older paradigms of research allow. They live in a global city, London, which has already been the focus for much globalization research. However, research has largely focused on links with international finance, on urban development and on the more emphatically international lifestyles of jet-setters and yuppies. Scant attention has been paid to everyday life. Thus Knight and Gappert's useful volume on cities in a global society contains twenty-three papers, but not one considers everyday life in the city. Yet the volume already implies quite different patterns of living for those caught up in global processes and takes us far outside notions of locality as the boundary for meaningful social relations.

Yet the theorization of everyday life under global conditions effectively introduces a range of considerations which takes us beyond ideas of post-modernity and post-industrialism. These ideas evolved out of earlier mass society concerns and the notion of the fragmentation of industrial society. To that extent post-modernity theory lent credence to the idea of a dissolution of concepts without effectively advocating an alternative frame. Indeed very often the claim was implicit that the search for an alternative was a doomed project from the beginning.

Globalization theory, on the other hand, does commit itself to propositions about the trajectory of social change which do not envisage a collapse into chaos or a meaningless juxtaposition of innumerable and incommensurable viewpoints. It puts on the agenda a recasting of the whole range of sociological concepts which were forged for the period of nation-state sociology.

We do not have to begin from scratch. For our purposes in this chapter we can draw on a number of core propositions about globalization based on earlier work.

Original publication details: Excerpted from Martin Albrow, "Travelling Beyond Local Cultures," in John Eade (ed.), *Living the Global City: Globalization as a Local Process* (Routledge, 1997), pp. 43–51. Reprinted by permission of Taylor & Francis Books Ltd.

In exploring their relevance for local social relations we will find that we develop them further and discover the need to advance additional ones. Our starting points to which we will return are:

1   The values informing daily behaviour for many groups in contemporary society relate to real or imagined material states of the globe and its inhabitants (*globalism*).
2   Images, information and commodities from any part of the earth may be available anywhere and anytime for ever-increasing numbers of people worldwide, while the consequences of worldwide forces and events impinge on local lives at any time (*globality*).
3   Information and communication technology now make it possible to maintain social relationships on the basis of direct interaction over any distance across the globe (*time–space compression*).
4   Worldwide institutional arrangements now permit mobility of people across national boundaries with the confidence that they can maintain their lifestyles and life routines wherever they are (*disembedding*).

We could add to this list but for the moment it is sufficient to permit us to turn to our local studies and identify the patterns of social life which call out for new sociological conceptualizations. Before doing so we ought to add that while these propositions are associated with the general theory of globalization, the extent to which they necessarily implicate the globe as a whole, or require the unicity of the world, is open to an argument which does not have to be resolved here in order to show their relevance for studies of local social relations.

Social and Cultural Spheres in an Inner London Locality

The transformations of the last sixty years now make it difficult to capture anything in London like the picture of locality you will find in a study such as Hoggart's. The paradigmatic equivalent of his account in empirical research was the work of Willmott and Young at the Institute of Community Studies in 1957. But they were capturing a world imminently dissolving. The variety of possibilities now evident extend our conceptual capacities to the extreme. They certainly burst the bounds of nation-state sociology.

Our research on locality and globalization is based in the inner London borough of Wandsworth, south of the river, west of centre, formed from the amalgamation of seven or eight nineteenth-century villages, which give their names to the local areas within what is a largely continuous residential belt. In terms of race politics headlines Wandsworth has led a quiet life in comparison with neighbouring Lambeth. Its press image is mainly associated with the policies of the Conservative-controlled local council which has been known as the "flagship" authority of the Thatcher years for its advocacy of low local taxation, contracting out of local services and the sale of council houses.

This image of tranquil continuity through change is maintained even for the area of Tooting which has a large Asian immigrant population. Yet even a cursory visit suggests that the concept of local culture is unlikely to fit new conditions. Given that the task of reconceptualization and documenting new realities is long term, I will not attempt to prejudge our findings by a premature characterization of Tooting. However, if we turn to our respondents in Tooting and, instead of seeking

to fit them to pre-given sociological categories, listen to their own references to
locality, culture and community, we already detect the possibility of new cultural
configurations occupying the same territorial area.

Adopting an individualistic methodology as one strategy for penetrating the new
social relations, we can identify a range of responses which take us beyond the notion
of local culture and community without suggesting any corollary of anomie or social
disorganization as the old conceptual frames tended to assume. At this stage we are
not offering a holistic account of social relations in this area of London, but we can
already say that globalization theory is going to allow us to interpret our respondents
in a quite different way from older sociologies which focused on place rather than
space.

True we can find old-established "locals", benchmarks for analysis, but if we let
them speak, the nuances of a new age come through. Take 73-year-old Grace Angel,
who was born in Wandsworth and has lived in her house in Tooting for over fifty
years, who met her husband when they carried stretchers for the injured during the
air raids on London in the Second World War. He is now disabled but she benefits
from the support of her own age group, mainly white women, who meet at a Day
Centre three times a week. She engages in all the traditional activities of a settled life,
visiting family, knitting and enjoying crafts. She rarely leaves Wandsworth; she enjoys
the sense of community.

At the same time her life is not confined by the locality. She tells how she writes
letters to France and the United States. She also wrote "to Terry Waite all the time
he was held hostage and to his wife. I actually got a letter from him, thanking me
for my support." Into her local frame enters a mass media symbol of the conflict
between the West and militant Islam. We have to ask where that fits in with
the concept of local culture, not simply an ephemeral image cast on a screen as
diversion or even information, but a global figure who becomes a personal
correspondent.

Mrs Angel would hardly recognize the image of Tooting another resident provides. True, Reginald Scrivens only moved to Tooting seventeen years ago but he
has lived in London for thirty-two years and works in a City bank. He reads the
broadsheet Conservative newspapers, has a drink with his colleagues after work and
watches television with his wife in the evening. They don't socialize locally and he
doesn't enjoy living in Tooting any more:

> It's very mixed these days, with the Asians and the blacks, and a lot of the area is quite
> run down. It's not a nice place to walk through. There isn't any real community either.
> I still know a few people along my street, but most of the people I used to know moved
> out, because Tooting got so bad. . . .
>
> Families come and go. Neighbours don't care about each other any more. The
> foreigners all stick together though. I'll say this about them – they look after their
> own. That's more than you can say about most of our lot these days.

His wife goes to local shops. He goes to a local church. They are not going to move.
It is an easy journey to work in Central London.

Mr Scrivens lives in Tooting but is alienated from it, or rather Tooting falls short
of an image of community which he thinks it might have had or ought to have. Yet
it still is convenient enough to remain there. Convenience, however, can also combine
with indifference. Forty-four-year-old Ted North came to Tooting from Yorkshire
ten years ago and has worked as a traffic warden ever since, feels settled, belongs to

the local Conservative club, rarely goes out of the area, but doesn't really notice whether there is a community as such.

A Londoner, who moved to Tooting three years ago at the age of 22 and became a postman, Gary Upton, is even more detached:

> Locality isn't all that important to me, but I don't really feel affected by the rest of the world either. I have my life to lead and I'll lead it wherever I am.

Even a much older man, Harry Carter, a 62-year-old taxi driver, who has lived in Tooting for twenty-two years, would move anywhere and feels community spirit has totally disappeared almost everywhere in London. For him globalization is "common sense" and "obviously happening". And if you are a young unemployed man like Dean Garrett, born in Tooting the year Harry arrived, living with your girlfriend and her parents, you are used to the Asians because you were brought up with them but stick with your own. You stay in Tooting and use its library and shops but not because of community feeling.

This indifference to place, however, can be transvalued into a positive desire for constant mobility and into an estimation of locality as a consumer good. Keith Bennett is 25, works in a shop and came to Tooting six months ago. He has travelled through the United States, his mother lives abroad, he has completed a degree, reckons travel has changed his life and would love to go all over the world. He has never had a sense of community but values Tooting:

> because it's got a mixed feel . . . it helps to make people aware of other people . . . it's close enough to fun places like Brixton and Streatham, and it's easy to get into town from here.

He is white but lives with an Asian family and has an Asian girlfriend. His Asian friends tell him "that they have a good community feel among other Asians but not with the whites". For an older widow living alone, like 77-year-old Agnes Cooper, the issues of culture and community cannot be transvalued into spectacle as they are with Keith. She responds directly to their messages. The Asians are close-knit "with no room for outsiders" and she was plainly baffled by a Sikh who could not understand the meaning of hot cross buns at Easter when she tried to explain them to him. She has lived for fourteen years in Tooting and her social network and activity are as local as Grace Angel's, but she notices a lack of true community feeling. She remarked on people buying properties in the area just for resale.

Eight white residents of Tooting, each one with a different orientation to the local area, easily generalized into a different type, potentially raising a series of conceptual distinctions which render the question of the presence or absence of local community simplistic. This question makes more sense in the case of our older respondents, but their answers are quite different. For Grace it is there, Agnes is not sure, for Reginald it has gone and for Harry it went a long time ago everywhere in London. Ted is younger than them and came later. He does not know whether community is there and is unconcerned as he gets on with his local life.

Our three young men have different responses again. As with Ted "community" has lost salience, and locality has become facility. Globalist Keith finds Tooting a useful point from which to enjoy the world, for Gary its generalizable qualities are what counts, it could be anywhere and that suits him, while for Dean it's a question of necessity rather than values. There is nowhere else to go.

At one time a sociologist might have held that these were all different perspectives on the same phenomenon, partial points of view which could be composited into the social reality of Tooting. Later these views would have been held to justify a sociological relativism – perspectives which simply co-existed without any way of reconciling them. A later post-modernist view would find in them a fragmented, dislocated reality.

There is another (at least one) alternative. The Deans co-exist with the Agneses, the Reginalds with the Keiths. If they do not meet each other at least they encounter many others who are similar. These people inhabit co-existing social spheres, coeval and overlapping in space, but with fundamentally different horizons and time-spans. The reality of Tooting is constituted by the intermeshing and interrelating of these spheres. Grace's community is no more the authentic, original Tooting than is Ted's.

There is an additional vital point. Apart from Grace these white Tooting residents are all immigrants, they all moved into the area, respectively seventeen, ten, three, twenty-two, a half and fourteen years ago. It is an area which is always on the move and in that sense in- and out-migration is normal. Yet this does not preclude a sense of the "other" in Tooting, namely the Asians, often perceived as holding together, as constituting a community in the sense that the whites are not. To that extent we can see the Asian community acquires in the eyes of the whites the qualities which they consider themselves to have lost. Instead of seeking to assimilate the incoming ethnic group, which in any case has lived there longer than them, whites like Keith, with Asian friends and living in an Asian family, may seek to be assimilated themselves. We may then be tempted to apply the concept of local culture, not to the white residents but to the Asians.

Our oldest Asian respondent, Naranjan, is 65 years old and has lived in Tooting for nineteen years. She came from Tanzania but met her husband in India and nearly all her family live there apart from sons who live just outside London. She is in constant touch with her family in India and a sister in New York, usually by letter, and returns to India every year. Yet she and her husband are fond of Germany and Switzerland and she enjoys travelling. Otherwise she is very busy locally, sings in her temple, attends the elderly day centre and has friends in all ethnic groups.

Here the point which comes through strongly is that Indian culture is as much a family culture as a local one. Religious occasions encourage the maintenance of family ties across space. The disembedding Giddens associates with modernity effectively sustains pre-modern kin relations and permits a form of reverse colonization.

The same is the case with a much younger Pakistani woman, Zubdha, aged 26, born in Bradford, who came to Tooting three years ago. She is married and works in a social agency, maintains constant touch by telephone with family in Pakistan and visited over 120 friends and relatives there earlier in the year. However, she likes Tooting as a place where she is comfortable with her ethnic culture, can buy *halal* meat, has plenty of friends and no wish to leave.

For the white population, looking in from the outside, the Asians in Tooting appear to constitute a community. From the inside the orientations are varied. One thing is clear, racial segregation is apparent to both sides, but its meaning varies from person to person. In some cases it is a matter of feeling safer rather than any deep identification with an ethnic group. Such was the case with a 28-year-old shop owner, born in Birmingham, who moved to Tooting four years ago and who has no contact with aunts and uncles in India. His experience in both Birmingham and Tooting was that Asian youths stuck together for safety but he feels a sense of community in

Tooting, too, which does not extend to cover blacks and whites. He thinks he will stay in Tooting so that his daughter can settle in somewhere. Settling seems a matter of contingent considerations rather than anything deeper.

A much more recent newcomer is Ajit, also 28 years old, who came to Tooting from Delhi three years ago and brought his wife, but has broken off relations with his family in India. He has set up a small business and his contacts are other businessmen. He notices no real community but has no intention of returning to India either. He sees signs of racial barriers breaking down for young people and considers this process as providing hope for the future.

These hopes might be borne out by the experience of 18-year-old Kuldeep, who helps in his parents' shop. He came to Britain from Bombay with them six years ago and says that he could not now return to India because he feels "too English". He considers most white people to be very open but his friends are almost all Asian and they spend a lot of time together out in clubs or playing football.

The same questioning of his Indian identity arises for a 35-year-old Asian pharmacist, Kishor, who was born in East Africa and has lived in Tooting for ten years. He finds no real community and strong racial segregation but he appreciates Tooting for its convenient location for work and his sports club. He has distant cousins in the United States whom he occasionally calls and when he has a holiday he usually goes to Portugal.

In sum, our Asian respondents have orientations to community as varied as those of the whites. They all acknowledge the barriers between Asian and white but their orientations to other Asians are not as the whites imagine. For a start the most intense felt identification with the Asian community comes from women and their local involvements are matched by the strength of their ties with the sub-continent. The men have a more instrumental relationship with other Asians, one of mutual protection and business opportunity, but not one which leads them to celebrate cultural difference.

Out of these interviews emerge both real differences in involvement in local culture and quite refined conscious distinctions about the nature of community. Most observant of all is possibly a Jamaican-born black community worker, Michael, who has lived with his parents in Tooting for eighteen years and works in Battersea, the other side of Wandsworth. For him nothing happens in Tooting which could be called community life. He contrasts it with Battersea, but even there what goes on he attributes to boredom rather than real involvement. His own friends are spread across London and everything he does revolves around the telephone. He calls Jamaica and the United States every week, and has been back to Jamaica every year for the last ten years. He sees Britain as just another American state but does not believe that the world is becoming a smaller place. Somehow for him the very strength of his Caribbean ties and the barriers coming down between people also push other people away.

New Concepts for Local/Global Conditions

We have cited individual cases at some length, not to confirm a general picture, nor to find a common thread. Indeed it would be possible to construct a different general type of orientation to living in the global city for each of our respondents. Equally we are not concerned to identify where some are right and others wrong. Our initial hypothesis is that each may be right for his or her own circumstances and social network.

Grace Angel and Naranjan both find active lives in a local community, one white the other Asian, and we have no reason to think that these are not reliable respondents. It is just that their worlds co-exist without impinging on each other.

Similarly the much-travelled Keith Bennett and Michael, the Jamaican community worker, agree that there is no community life in Tooting. Each finds it a convenient base for a London life and links with the rest of the world. But just because they agree there is no reason to take their view to be of more weight than anyone else's.

Let us suppose that this is not a matter of perspectives; rather that our interviews represent different realities, linked by their co-existence in a locality but not thereby creating a local culture or community. If that were the case the local area of Tooting would be characterized by a co-present diversity of lifestyles and social configurations. This diversity would then *constitute* the reality, not some average of a set of dispersed readings of the same phenomenon.

Yet this diversity would not represent chaos. Broadly there is no sense from our interviews of a collapsing world, even if there is regret for a world that is past. Each respondent makes sense of a situation, each relating in a different way to the local area. Certainly there is no sense of a Tooting community which comprises the population of the local area. Nor even is there a configuration in Elias' sense, except in so far as there is substantial agreement on the importance of the ethnic divide between whites and Asians. Yet ethnicity provides only one of the conditions for the lives of our respondents and in no sense creates an overall framework in the way Elias and Scotson's "established" and "outsiders" model encapsulates and co-ordinates the lives of the inhabitants of Winston Parva.

In other words our material is suggestive of a different order of things, which requires different conceptualizations from those available even only twenty years ago. Note the word "suggestive" – we are talking about empirical possibilities. Their realization is not yet demonstrated by these few interviews. Further research will need to adopt a variety of methodologies and take account of contextual factors, such as the possible effects of local state policies, before it can conclude that the globalized locality exists in Tooting. Moreover the impact of any future political mobilization can never be discounted. None the less, we have enough evidence to warrant the close examination of an alternative theoretical framework for future research.

We can make sense of these interviews by drawing on globalization theory. In particular by taking account of the different time horizons and spatial extent of our respondents' social networks we can specify the new elements of regularly constituted social relations in a locality in a global city. Let us now advance four new propositions about locality paralleling the four on globalization we set out above:

1   The locality can sustain as much globalist sentiment as there are sources of information for and partners in making sense of worldwide events.
2   A locality can exhibit the traces of world events (e.g. the expulsion of East African Asians) which remove any feeling of separation from the wider world.
3   The networks of individuals in a locality can extend as far as their resources and will to use the communications at their disposal. Time–space compression allows the maintenance of kin relations with India or Jamaica as much as with Birmingham or Brentford.
4   The resources and facilities of a locality may link it to globally institutionalized practices. It is convenient both to be there if you want to use the products of global culture and as good as anywhere else as a base from which to travel. As

such both transients and permanent residents can equally make a life which is open to the world.

Let us now bring these four propositions about a globalized locality together. In sum they suggest the possibility that individuals with very different lifestyles and social networks can live in close proximity without untoward interference with each other. There is an old community for some, for others there is a new site for a community which draws its culture from India. For some Tooting is a setting for peer group leisure activity, for others it provides a place to sleep and access to London. It can be a spectacle for some, for others the anticipation of a better, more multicultural community. [. . .]

17 Strong States, Strong Teachers?

Bruce Fuller

My friend Chimtali, age 14, moved 10 kilometers from her small village nestled against the Zomba plateau to just outside the trading post of the same name. She had recently entered a government boarding school to pursue her secondary studies. She liked her teachers and her subjects. It was the foreign-seeming customs that she found amusing. Chimtali now was required to wear pajamas at night. And she was relearning how to eat. Growing up in the village she simply used her hands, but now she was required to use utensils imported from London. Nor was she allowed to eat fried *ngumbi*, those plentiful and tasty African bugs resembling winged roaches. While Chimtali obviously enjoyed becoming modern, she had not suspected that secondary school would require such deep changes in daily habits.

State Penetration of the School's Boundaries

Administrative rituals

State regulation of teacher action is often not very subtle within Malawi. Each teacher is expected to speak in English, or in the dominant tribe's language, after grade 4, to move through three textbooks page by page, to write down a lesson plan for each day's activities, and to hand this book over for inspection whenever requested by the headmaster (this is termed a "modern educational reform"). But the lack of subtlety I discovered that cool morning I sat in the back of a damp classroom outside Lilongwe was still surprising. Instructing grade 7 civics, the teacher was eliciting choral responses as pupils looked at a list written on the blackboard. He began with the question:

T: "How does government get money?"
Ps (in unison): "Income tax, customs duties . . ."

Then, he asked individual children:

T: "What is the work of police?"
P1: "To arrest kids."
P2: "To protect houses."

Getting the attention of the class, the teacher (through his intonation) then elicited everyone to repeat what he said:

Original publication details: Excerpted from Bruce Fuller, "Strong States, Strong Teachers?," in Bruce Fuller, *Growing-Up Modern: The Western State Builds Third-World Schools* (Routledge, 1991), pp. 111–13, 115–27. Copyright © 1991. Reproduced by permission of Routledge, Inc., part of the Taylor & Francis Group.

T: "The police work to maintain peace and order."
Ps   (in unison): "To maintain peace and order."

The teacher then called on individual pupils to recite the six types of police in Malawi (as he wrote each type on the blackboard). Then reviewing each branch, he continued:

T: "If the PMF police came here, what will (*sic*) they do?"
P3:   "They will deal with a riot or a strike."
T: "Now the special branch . . . when you go to public meetings and see well-dressed men, they are checking on whether the situation is okay. If it is not, they take away the leaders."

> My note: of the forty-seven pupils in the room, about ten are visibly fading from the conversation. The teacher then erases the six types of police, proceeding to call on individual pupils asking the functions of each type. This serves to get the attention of previously disinterested youngsters.

The education ministry can not afford to write and publish a civics textbook for primary school pupils. Only in the past decade have texts become available for arithmetic, English, and Chichewa. But this factual material on police was pulled from a modest secondary school text which serves as this primary teacher's curriculum guide. [. . .]

Competing clubs: limits to the state's penetration

Political elites – with clear intent or through inadvertent mimicry of modern organizing – shape the social rules and knowledge that are transmitted into the classroom. Yet how does the teacher respond to this pressure to construct bureaucratic social rules and to express modern symbols? I see three basic factors that limit the state's actual influence over the classroom teacher.

First, *the state's capacity to provide material resources is constrained*, which eats into the state's own authority. Despite limited resources, Third World governments have been very effective in constructing school buildings, often collaborating with traditional local leaders and drawing on villagers' eagerness to build even simple structures. But the second injection of resources, necessary for deepening the school's effect on children's achievement, either never comes or is very modest. In most Third World countries teachers remain in short supply. Our Malawi school survey found an average of 119 pupils enrolled in grade 1 classes (with about eighty-five attending each day); attendance falls to about forty-five pupils per classroom by grade 6. Most primary school teachers in this African nation have not completed secondary school. Many come from families that are still engaged in subsistence farming. Almost two-thirds of the teachers we surveyed had no desks for pupils in their classrooms. Over half the teachers received fewer than ten textbooks for their entire class each year. With this questionable level of teacher quality and extreme shortage of instructional materials, should we expect the state, via the school, to have much impact on children's learning?

On the other hand, the scarcity of instructional material may inadvertently strengthen the state's authority over what legitimate knowledge is presented to pupils. In the Third World, teachers must rely heavily on state-written textbooks. [. . .] Books other than texts are rarely found in African classrooms; libraries in primary schools are non-existent. The central state's influence – in casting official knowledge and communicating modern symbols via textbooks – goes unchallenged. [. . .]

Second, the state's influence on teachers is constrained by the *inconsistent character of ideological messages emanating from political elites*. This is especially true as fragile (or stumbling) states struggle to rapidly build (or reinforce) institutions that will incorporate diverse groups. [. . .] Schools, for instance, can teach high-status languages, talk about math and science, and rhetorically link schooling to higher paying jobs. Of course, *signaling opportunity* to enter the modern world does not guarantee material gains for the masses. Where schooling expands more quickly than jobs in the cash economy, political elites must contend with disenchanted youths and parents. And if the state moves too quickly, ignoring tribal traditions and forms of authority, secular elites lose legitimacy.

The fragile state's tendency to emit mixed messages was crisply illustrated one day as I observed two energetic teachers in a southern Malawi primary school, close to the Mozambique border. Walking into the grade 4 classroom, I noticed that the day's attendance was written on the blackboard: "48 girls and 52 boys." A science teacher accompanied the regular teacher in presenting a talk on different types of soil. In large urban schools – this primary had over two thousand pupils attending each day – it is common to see a teacher with specific training in mathematics or science. The fact that a specialist joins the regular teacher adds to the status of the subject. And this specialist came with some hands-on material: canisters filled with five different types of dirt. In rapid succession, the two teachers gave each pair of children a dash of brown soil, red soil, sandy soil, and rain soil. The science teacher pursued tangents on how to read a rain gauge and on which soils would support more crops. The science teacher talked at this batch of one hundred pupils, eliciting choral pronunciation of terms in English: "milliliter," "this is clay soil," "rocks lay beneath this kind of soil."

The content of this lesson was quite relevant, especially to children who spent part of each day working on the family plot. Yet the pieces of knowledge (facts) were simply spoken at this densely packed group of children. This was science – a high-status topic that required a special authority to explain the topic in English. This modern set of codes was delivered within a mass setting. Dishing out dirt to one hundred kids must be done quickly; information is attached to each pile; children repeat these fragments of knowledge; the teacher moves on quickly to the next chunk of information. Marking the class period's end, the teacher ordered everyone to engage in quick calisthenics, "Stand up! . . . hands up, forward, side, sit down." All one hundred obediently responded, although several had to lift their drowsy heads off their desks before popping up. The science specialist launched into the next topic: "germs and pests that live in dirty houses."

Teachers' ideologies

When we examine teachers' own beliefs about schooling and socialization the third constraint on the state's local penetration arises. *Teachers' own beliefs and behaviors vary*, spawned either within the school's own institutional boundaries or determined by the state's mixed messages. [. . .]

Our initial findings on the educational ideologies of teachers in Malawi, as well as their perceptions of their classroom behavior are quite interesting. We asked teachers, for instance, about the importance they place on three possible goals of schooling. Seventy percent of the teachers reported that improving "pupils' ways of thinking" is a very important goal. Just 47 percent believed that assistance in getting a better job is very important. We also asked about more specific teaching practices related to how children should be socialized. Fifty-one percent said that they "strongly agreed" with the statement: "schools should teach children rules and how to fit into society." Fewer (38 percent) strongly agreed that "pupils learn more when they listen and ask fewer questions." But only 19 percent strongly agreed that "school should teach children how to pursue their own individual goals and interests." The greatest consensus was on a statement that fell between a liberal-individualistic versus a strong fitting-in view of socialization. Sixty percent of all teachers strongly agreed that "school should teach children to cooperate and respect other people." In short, ideologies held by the typical teacher are not clear-cut, often reflecting a mix of educational philosophy.

Mass Conditions and the Teacher's Pursuit of Authority

Romantic or functionalist beliefs are one thing. But when the teacher actually is faced with sixty or seventy children in the classroom, how does he or she structure action? Reports by teachers of what they do are not always reliable. Teachers' perceptions in Malawi, however, closely matched the observational findings from other work, including the recent studies in Nigeria and Thailand, and my ongoing work in Botswana (with Wes Snyder and David Chapman).

Teachers in Malawi report spending 45 percent of their class time lecturing and interacting with the entire class (including presentation of material, reading aloud from textbooks, asking for choral recitations, and asking questions of individual pupils while the class listens). Thirty percent of teachers' time was reportedly spent supervising pupils working silently on exercises (in Malawi, usually writing out arithmetic problems or short vocabulary lists in their exercise books). These teacher actions commonly occur in a thirty-five-minute sequence like that which I observed in a four-room school close to Lunzu:

- The fourth-grade teacher begins the period by writing a multiplication problem on the board (.252 kilograms times 3). (Note: since this is math, the teacher shifts to speaking English.)
- The teacher asks for a choral response (from all seventy-two pupils) to each calculation: "3 times 2 is? . . . 3 times 5 is? . . ." Whenever the response is not loud and crisp, the teacher speaks more sharply, "3 times 2 is what?!"
- After working through three such problems with the entire class, the teacher writes another problem on the board and directs all pupils to calculate it in their exercise books. (Note: all pupils have an exercise book and a pencil.)
- As pupils finish the problem they eagerly wave their books, remaining seated on the cold concrete floor. One by one the teacher circulates to each pupil, checking answers. Getting to seventy-two pupils requires only 20 minutes. (Note: pupil attention drifts as the teacher continues to circulate.)
- The teacher then goes back to the blackboard, asking individual pupils to stand and work through the problem. When a pupil makes a mistake, the teacher quickly interrupts and moves to another pupil, many of whom are emphatically waving their hands and snapping their fingers. Those pupils who made a mistake, four in all, remain standing until a correct answer is given.

This sequence of talking at the entire class, eliciting choral responses, then assigning an individually-performed exercise is quite common, regardless of the subject being taught. The important point here is that the *conditions of mass schooling* drive teacher action, not the more complex and diverse ideologies that teachers hold in their heads. This pedagogical sequence aims at keeping the attention of the entire class and demanding that each child work alone on an exercise (at least for a very brief time). [. . .]

Sounds of clashing symbols

Under the fragile state, the teacher is the arbiter between central elites seeking uniform socialization and plural tribes which resist or ignore this pursuit of hegemony. In attending to the classroom's "maintenance system" the teacher must accommodate these local differences. To build cohesion teachers must depart from the central state's socialization agenda. For instance, teachers in Malawi are expected to teach all subjects in English after grade 4. In addition, the language spoken by the dominant tribe – which controls the national government – is taught beginning in the first grade. Once you leave the towns and the central region dominated by the Chewa tribe, few children will understand Chichewa or English. So teachers commonly speak in Yao, Tumbuka, or one of the other thirty-five tribal languages spoken. Instruction in English holds enormous status among the political elite; but the teacher must obviously speak in the children's tribal language if any camaraderie is to be built inside the classroom.

In remote rural schools, headmasters are apologetic that Chichewa and English are not spoken by their teachers. These schools enroll children of subsistence farmers, living in sparsely populated villages often a day's walk from the nearest paved road. The only government official they see is the district education officer, once a month when he brings teachers' salaries in cash. If teachers pressed the language of a foreign tribe (be it the language of Chewa political elites or of British economic elites), children would understand little and the school would alienate parents. In this case the central government would be seen as too ideological and irrelevant. But by delivering subjects in the indigenous language, the state's socialization agenda appears less obtrusive.

At times, even the state will attempt to accommodate local forms of authority within textbooks and the curriculum. Early one morning we arrived at a primary school close to rural Dowa. The rains had come two weeks prior. The morning air was cool and damp. Entering the dark, stark classroom I saw just eleven youngsters, all sitting on the floor, which my butt soon told me was cold and wet. Embarrassed, the teacher flew out the door, returning with an old chair . . . a scarce but strong symbol of respect for his strange white visitor. The teacher continued reading a passage from the government's grade 7 English textbook ". . . Mkandawire, the local headman, sat talking to his fellow villagers. The rains had not come that season, and the villagers were worried about their crops and the health of their children. The headman had thought much about why the rain had not come. He was presenting possible explanations. . . ."

Interestingly, the story goes on to present several spiritual and traditional explanations for why the rains had not come. After reading the story, the teacher asked pupils questions in English, practicing their reading comprehension. But the traditional wisdom of village headmen continued to receive respect throughout the discussion. This section of the textbook provides a collection of traditional stories, at times blended with Western knowledge and symbols. One historical story deals with a woman who allegedly fools slave traders by pretending she's a witch. Another tells of a middle-class man who uses a clock to make sure he catches his bus on time, and features pictures of him jumping from bed dressed in pajamas running to the bus stop. Very few Malawians can afford to ride a bus, and fewer sleep in beds. Pajamas are seen as an incredibly funny artifact worn only by the British.

Many teachers are quite active within their classrooms. The life and pace of inter-action between these teachers and their many pupils is remarkable. Their common lesson sequence does engage the majority of pupils: presenting a chunk of material, eliciting choral responses, assigning short twenty-minute exercises, then reviewing the material by working out the problems on the blackboard. The resulting cohesion maintains the teacher's authority and sanctions the discrete bits of information contained within the official curriculum. This routine also allows the teacher to demonstrate to the headmaster, in a standardized way, how far the class has progressed in the textbook. Whether this regimen effectively imparts literacy or useful social skills is rarely asked. The teacher's legitimacy is simply rein-forced by following institutionalized rules for how he or she is supposed to act. There is ample faith that these actions will lead to desired socialization and academic outcomes.

Occasionally Malawian teachers set down social rules that contradict the other-wise mass structure of the classroom. Maintaining order and discipline remains a concern. Yet the teacher relinquishes control, encouraging pupils to engage in more complex individual activities or to work cooperatively in groups. This combination of high energy, engagement, and more lateral interaction among children was illus-trated by the following sequence observed in one classroom not far from the capital city of Lilongwe:

- The teacher begins the Chichewa period (grade 3) by passing out textbooks. Few pupils own their own. I noted that on the blackboard was written, "67 on roll, 59 present." The teacher commanded all children to stand and touch their toes, raise their arms over their heads, and clap their hands. The morning is warm, but the children seem keen on getting off the concrete floor for a few moments. These sudden calisthenics signal the beginning of the next thirty-five-minute period.
- The teacher writes twelve Chichewa words on the board and begins pointing to each word. This prompts a wild waving of hands and snapping of fingers – a styl-ized snapping that results from a sharp simultaneous flicking of the wrist and fingers. Performed by this batch of kids, it sounds like a muffled orchestra of crickets. (I think to myself that Victorian missionary teachers would have been shocked to witness this audible African sign of eagerness in the classroom.)
- A five-sentence paragraph containing these new words is read by the teacher from the Chichewa text. She then bangs an aluminum pot with a broad stick . . . like a metal drum. This sends the children scurrying around, forming into familiar groups of three or four. As the dust (literally) settles, one child in each group begins reading the passage out loud to the other group members. The teacher circles around the class, listening to recitations within each group, for about 15 minutes.
- The teacher grabs the pot and stick once more; the same piercing percussion sends pupils back into their tidy columns, as if they were sitting one behind each other in desks (but in this classroom there are no desks).

- Again, the pupils are told to stand and run through their well-learned exercises. This round includes turning in circles, jumping up and down, pointing to the blackboard, the door, and the windows (where no glass remains). The names of these classroom features are shouted out in English.
- The teacher then reads ten Chichewa words which pupils write in their exercise books. They exchange books to read how their partner wrote the words. The teacher again circulates around to all fifty-nine, checking their spelling.

I recall my initial fright in seeing the instinctive compliance exhibited by these small children, quickly replying to the teacher's every command. But within the routine, children were encouraged to interact with each other. First, reading to each other. Later, reading their partner's written Chichewa words. The content and form of this cooperative action was certainly prescribed by the teacher. But this horizontal interaction between small groups or pairs of children departed strongly from the usual pattern where the teacher constantly interacts with the entire mass of pupils, or where pupils work in isolation from one another. [. . .]

The teacher's strong authority

Most African teachers are members of the small class of people who are literate and who receive a steady wage in cash. The teacher also holds the power to allocate forms of secular merit and virtue to children. Relatively few children persist through primary school and enter secondary school. But those that do persist gain a shot at entering the modern economic sector to make a steady wage. This institutionalized role as gate-keeper, legitimated by the state, brings enormous status to the teacher. Yet day to day in the classroom, many teachers feel that they must demonstrate their strict authority. This is particularly true in settings like Malawi, where colonial schools historically reflected deference to authoritarian officialdom, and the overcrowded conditions of mass schooling create uncertainty for which tight control appears to be an effective antidote.

Whenever a Malawian pupil must urinate, he or she is required to seek out the teacher, who is usually standing at the front of the class. Before all, the pupil bows down onto one knee, folds his or her hands, and requests a leave. Two or three children during each class period will typically go through this rather fluid motion, with little apparent embarrassment. But as a ritual, signaling control over the child's most basic movements, the exercise is significant.

Often when a thirty-five-minute class period has been completed, the teacher will signal to a pupil to pick up a rag and erase the blackboard, as the teacher moves to the back of the classroom. The teacher will just stand, scanning over the pupils, until the blackboard is spotless. This crisply signals the shift to a new subject, as well as the teacher's authority to assign a routine chore while he or she simply waits. Similarly, when the headmaster or a visitor enters the classroom, the teacher bows and clasps one wrist as they shake hands. The teacher is thereby displaying his or her deference to persons that are higher in the status order. I have often thought about how pupils, who are subordinated daily to the teacher's authority, view their own teacher's self-subordination to the headmaster or the occasional government representative.

These rituals reinforce the hierarchical form of authority found in the "modern" African school. In fact, the severe asymmetry of authority found in Malawian schools suggests that Dreeben's emphasis on achievement and individualism may not apply in many Third World settings. The modern state may preach the virtues of self-reliance, higher productivity, and entrepreneurial initiative. But the structure of authority and status previously found in colonial schools (be they operated by imperial administrations or by missions) continues to be reproduced. Here the liberal, romantic side of the Western state can not be operationalized in the face of classrooms spilling over with children. Note again, the *post-colonial* state is attempting to broaden opportunity to achieve higher status and higher income by opening access to the school institution. But the mass conditions and uncertainty which result inside the classroom push the teacher to seek control, and to engage in rituals that signal authority but which do very little to encourage learning. [. . .]

18   Strategic Inauthenticity

Timothy D. Taylor

[. . .]

Youssou N'Dour: "A Modern Griot"

Youssou N'Dour (1959–) is one of a handful but growing number of nonwestern pop stars from the African continent born around or after the independence of their homeland. He is probably the biggest international nonwestern pop star appearing in this book and has been written about extensively by the U.S. music press. N'Dour sings many of the typical stories of those who are trying to be subjects of modernity and not its objects: stories about the dangers of being overrun by tourism, the degradation of the environment, moving from the country to the city, and nostalgia for the ancestors and their wisdom. This modernization, however, in the form of the colonial machine, left N'Dour and his fellow Senegalese few options. The stories of modernization and colonialism/postcolonialism intersect time and again in his music, as, I have been arguing, they do in the "real world."

N'Dour, like Rhoma Irama, expresses the desire to make a new popular music that incorporates elements of indigenous traditional musics and uses the local language. At the same time, N'Dour acknowledges the influence of musics from around the world on him. "It's just a natural process of evolution," N'Dour says. "My style evolves depending on what other musics I've heard." He explains his mix of musics and sounds in explicitly politico-historical terms.

> The process of modernisation began relatively late in Senegambia. Ghana and Nigeria had developed their hi-life and such styles much earlier. The hit sounds in Senegal in the Fifties and Sixties were still the Cuban dance songs of [Orquesta] Aragon and Johnny Pacheco. For those of us who wanted to form a purely Senegalese pop sound, this Cuban music was rhythmically acceptable, but harmonically foreign. And of course there was the problem of language. We wanted to sing in our own Wolof language. The Gambian group, Super Eagles, later called I Fang Bondi, who were pioneering their Afro Manding jazz, and the Senegalese groups, Baobab and Sahel, had already begun to translate local traditional songs and rhythms to the instruments of pop music. Perhaps I had more of what we call in Wolof, *fit*, or courage. When I started with the Star Band, we went even further, developing a dance music which I called mbalax. The dancers at the Miami [a night club in Dakar] were no longer content with the pachanga or the cha cha cha, but followed the tama drum and the other sabars [drums] into their own natural dances.

Original publication details: Excerpted from Timothy D. Taylor, *Global Pop: World Music, World Markets* (Routledge, 1997), pp. 127–8, 129–30, 134–5, 142–3. Copyright © 1997. Reproduced by permission of Routledge, Inc., part of the Taylor & Francis Group.

The traditional stylistic and musical aspects of mbalax, which means "the rhythm of the drum" in Wolof, are mostly concerned with rhythm.

> That drum [mbung mbung], along with others like the talmbeut, ndende, bougarabu, djembe, nder, tunge, gorong and tama, creates the rhythm. When they say in Dakar, 'C'est très mbalax', they mean it's got a very strong, distinctive rhythm. So the base of mbalax is the drums, collectively known as sabars. There could be up to eight in any traditional line-up. In my group, I gave some of those drum parts to guitars and keyboards. The rhythms can change within songs – that is always a big attraction. This diversity comes from many tribal sources: Toucouleur, Peul, Bambara, Djola, Serer, as well as Wolof. We could make ten songs and they'd all sound different, unusual to people in the West. So I created this modern style, but the Senegalese quickly recognised it as their own popular music, and when it was recorded in France under favourable conditions it made even better sense to them.

The resulting sound brought N'Dour to the attention of western musicians such as Peter Gabriel and Paul Simon (both of whom recorded with him on some of their albums). N'Dour's album *The Guide* (*Wommat*) of 1994 was nominated for a Grammy (ultimately losing to Ali Farka Toure and Ry Cooder) and features guest appearances by black British American pop star Neneh Cherry and American jazz great Branford Marsalis. "Leaving (Dem)" opens *The Guide* and is the most upbeat song on the album, although the melancholy tale of the lyrics might indicate otherwise. The trajectory of "Leaving" isn't much different from a contemporary U.S. rock song: a brief guitar introduction followed by the rhythm track, then the vocals in N'Dour's amazing voice, supple, grainy, high, muscular. But the guitar sound owes more to South African *mbaqanga* than anything else; it may be *très* mbalax, but it makes use of African popular musics from all over, including soukous, highlife, Afrobeat, reggae, salsa, soul, and disco according to one commentator. Once the rhythm starts, the song inhabits an ecstatic groove, emphasized by N'Dour's conversational yet melodic singing style, and the horns (saxophone, trombones, trumpet). N'Dour further adds to the effect produced by the song by stepping down from it with an improvised, metrically free harmonica solo at the song's conclusion – bringing Stevie Wonder's brand of joyous music to mind – and including applause and whistles, even though this song was recorded in a studio without a live audience. There is also a background chorus that vocalizes along with N'Dour near the end of the song, adding to the celebratory sound. [. . .]

The lyrics of the song illustrate the kind of movement in the global postmodern that might take those at the traditional metropoles by surprise. Rather than becoming modern and moving, as did so many European moderns from the country to the city, N'Dour instead tells of wanting to move the other direction: he has had enough of modernity, thank you very much. He is interested in cultivating older ways of interaction, through one's friends and family, rather than the faceless, impersonal postcolonial city. "I am a modern man," he says. "I love traditional things, but I think African music must be popular. We have to go forward." So he built a 24-track recording studio in Dakar, naming it Xippi, or "eyes open," also the title of one of his albums.

With songs such as "Leaving," N'Dour's music mounts a different kind of resistance – or different kinds of resistances – than those we have examined so far. *The Guide* does offer songs that rage against the European colonial machine, such as "How you are (No mele)," which incorporates a rap in English. At the same time, however, N'Dour addresses more local concerns, most of which sound familiar to western listeners: "There is a lot of joblessness here [in Senegal]. Many kids here have dreams, but the opportunities are limited."

Although N'Dour is clearly a modern western musician of sorts, he evidently still views himself as a griot, or, a *gawulo*, literally, "the one who is always singing praises," a Tukulor people version of the better-known griot. One of the most revealing statements about him wasn't made by the extremely private musician himself, but by an associate who refused to let *Rolling Stone* use his name.

> Remember, he knows how to use power but not how to give it away. That is a very hard thing for anyone, but especially an African, knowing who to trust and who to give responsibility to. The only people Youssou really trusts are members of his family and the friends he's had since childhood. It's a very insular world. And you also have to remember that first and foremost, he's a griot.
>
> Traditionally, griots are always supported by the king and the country and are paid to sing. The idea that he has to pay someone [to do sound or lights or to produce or accompany him] so that he can sing and perform is very confusing.

N'Dour is a Muslim, though, unlike Rhoma Irama, his music and lyrics have not taken on specifically Islamic issues. But his music is still informed by a strong sense of right and wrong. "You know," he told interviewer Brian Cullman, "when you are walking with a girl, you have to make sure you walk along the right path, that you watch your step. You have a certain responsibility to be very proper." The idea of "propriety" recurs throughout his songs, which exhort youths to behave respectfully toward their parents, caution the west to behave respectfully toward its former colonies, and ask tourists to treat his country well.

Because of his fame, N'Dour realizes the extent to which he, as an international star and local *gawulo*, can help his more provincial listeners understand the events in the larger world. "In my society where there are those who cannot read or write, I was able to tell them in song just what was happening in South Africa. My own mother had seen pictures on TV but she didn't fully understand the situation. I could make a link between the situation in South Africa today and a famous, bloody battle in our own history – the battle of N'Der in the nineteenth century."

The international success N'Dour has achieved leaves him mindful of his roots in the family tradition of musicians and *gawulos*. "Before the radio," he says, "griots gathered the people together and gave them the news, the information from the king. He helped them understand the world, he was their voice. That's what I am, a modern griot." Before that he was a premodern griot, singing for various traditional rituals, including circumcision ceremonies. N'Dour's current duties are thus those of a griot: telling stories, giving admonitions, keeping watch. [. . .]

N'Dour doesn't use his status just to educate people from the African continent, however; much of his music is aimed at the west. Just as "Leaving" might turn some westerners' ideas about Africa upside down – it is a song about leaving the city for the country, not the other way around – N'Dour is also bent on demonstrating to his growing worldwide listeners that Africa is modern already.

> I'm really defending a cause: the cause of a new image of Africa. For me, the measure of success is more than anything how well I arrive at exposing my music as a representation of not only African music but of African life and the whole image of Africa.
>
> I think Americans are more and more interested in Africa but they have a long way to go. The day that people in the West understand how much we understand about the workings of the rest of the planet will be a happy day for us.

Like so many stars outside the North American/U.K. rock music circuit, N'Dour was "discovered" by an influential western musician, in this case, Peter Gabriel, resulting in much collaboration since they met in 1984 and leading to other collaborations, such as on Paul Simon's *Graceland*, as well as with Sting, Bruce Springsteen, and Tracy Chapman. By 1990, N'Dour dropped his musicologist manager Verna Gillis for a New York lawyer, Thomas Rome, symbolizing his departure from *mbalax* to pop/rock. (His latest album, however, lists Gillis as the manager and executive producer, a switch back that has not yet been commented on in the music press.) He lives in London and drives a BMW but hasn't cut ties to Senegal, or his hometown of Dakar, the capital. "I love Dakar, but I am very visible here, I am an example. Everything I do, it's seen."

Now, as a star, N'Dour realizes the role he may be able to play in the globalization of African popular musics such as *mbalax*: "The new generation of African musicians really has a chance to have an impact on American audiences. That has not yet happened, but I think it will, soon." His artistic advisor, Canadian Michael Brook (known for his own syncretic musics), seems to have gotten into the habit of filling in the silences of the taciturn N'Dour.

> What's exciting for me is that the band is right on the edge of establishing a personal music. It has traditional African and Senegalese elements in it, and it also has pop elements in it, but it feels like they're going into a new stage of musical maturity, one where the influences become less relevant. They're Africans making music, but you wouldn't necessarily label it *African music*. It's something altogether new [emphasis in original].

As his fame and popularity have grown, N'Dour has had to face criticisms that his music, which was, early on, a conscious attempt to re-Africanize Senegalese music, has become too slick, too commercial, too western. "Well," N'Dour says, "it was first made Senegalese and then opened to show the side of modern Africa, of towns like Dakar and Abidjan. I think my music has really evolved. It's true that it's lost a bit for older people but then it's gained popularity with younger people. That's life. I don't make music for such and such a person; I do it because it's me – what I feel." [. . .]

N'Dour, in the meantime, continues patiently to explain his position. "In Dakar we hear many different recordings. We are open to these sounds. When people say my music is too Western, they must remember that we, too, hear this music over here. We hear the African music with the modern." [. . .]

Whose Authenticity?

Given western listeners' concern for authenticity and the desire of musicians from around the world to be stars and make it in the global music industry, N'Dour's and Kidjo's clear lack of concern with authenticity is striking at first. It seems to me there are two reasons for the lack of interest in authenticity by these musicians. One, more prevalent in the west, is aesthetic: these musicians, like Peter Gabriel, are artists, they make art, and in art, anything goes: the aesthetic is by its very nature, voracious. But N'Dour and Kidjo view western demands for authenticity as concomitant with demands that they and their countries remain premodern, or modern, while the rest of the globe moves further toward a postindustrial, late capitalist, postmodern culture. N'Dour and Kidjo are concerned with becoming global citizens and do this by showing that their countries and their continent are neither backward nor premodern, that they can make cultural forms as (post)modern as the west's. They hear many sounds – in Kidjo's case, she grew up with lots of sounds, lots of musics – and pull these into their music, to the chagrin of some western critics. [. . .]

Questions

1   How does the experience of McDonald's customers in Hong Kong resemble and differ from that of their counterparts in the West? How does Watson use his case study to argue that "the transnational *is* the local"? What assumptions about cultural globalization does he challenge?

2   In what ways is everyday local life in metropolitan areas like London becoming more profoundly "global," according to Albrow? How does globalization affect people's attachment to their local community?

3   In what respects is the school experience of the students and teachers observed by Fuller similar to your own, and how does it differ from yours? What does their experience tell you about the difficulties developing countries face in implementing a global institution? Do schools in Malawi strengthen the state? Do they make individual students more independent thinkers?

4   How does Taylor describe the distinctive features of Youssou N'Dour's world music? Is N'Dour mainly interested in preserving authentic African musical styles? What does it mean to say that artists like N'Dour are "concerned with becoming global citizens"?

Part IV

Economic Globalization

Introduction

The 1990s witnessed a wave of economic globalization. By 1997, the countries of Southeast Asia had decidedly become an integral part of the world economy. Successful exporters, they had enjoyed high growth rates for many years, and the promise of these "emerging markets" attracted increasing amounts of foreign capital. Then, quite unexpectedly, the pattern reversed. As Japan's recession translated into diminished Japanese investment in and imports from the region, the growth prospects of other countries dimmed. In Thailand, South Korea, and Indonesia, banks and companies had trouble paying their debts. As foreign capital fled, even high interest rates could not prevent a slide in currencies, which further exacerbated the debt problems. With exports to Europe and the United States absorbing only part of the excess production capacity in Asia, failing companies had to lay off workers. Since its own financial sector was burdened by bad debts, Japan could not be an engine for regional growth. Thus, the Asian "miracle" gave way to the Asian "contagion."

Asia's problems had global ramifications. Western financial markets came under severe pressure as profit expectations declined. The Asian contagion contributed to a loss of confidence in Russia's economic reform efforts, halting though they were in any case. The ruble went into free fall, defaults on foreign debts ensued, and economic misery spread widely within Russia. Latin America was not immune either; its largest economy, Brazil, became the focus of an intense international effort to prevent the contagion from spreading there. As Asian demand declined, commodity prices fell in world markets, adding to the difficulties of countries dependent on raw material exports. In the United States, the contagion helped to dampen inflation; gasoline prices, for example, fell to their lowest levels since World War II.

The widespread use of the contagion metaphor indicated to worldwide audiences that the world indeed had become a single, integrated economy in which everyone was dependent on everyone else. For government officials and business leaders, consumers and investors, Korean workers and IMF strategists, Russian farmers and Brazilian retirees, the Asian contagion revealed the reality and danger of globalization. It was not the first shock to the world economy, since the oil crisis of the 1970s and the subsequent debt crisis in many developing countries had already exposed the extent of modern global interdependence. Yet in the decades prior to the Asian crisis, economic globalization had been generally welcomed. For many years, leaders and economists cheered as world trade grew faster than world GDP, foreign direct investment outstripped domestic investment, and the volume of international currency transactions increased exponentially. Many formerly marginal "Third World" countries became growing, exporting tigers. The production of many goods once monopolized by the industrialized West spread across the globe, linking companies, workers, and whole countries in transnational "commodity chains." Not only did actual economic exchanges intensify, they also were increasingly managed by international organizations, such as the GATT and its successor, the World Trade Organization, that promulgated global rules. By many standards, then, economic integration had become a hallmark of globalization, deliberately promoted by governments, corporations, and international organizations alike. So closely intertwined had parts of the world economic system become that they now all became vulnerable to distant troubles.

At the same time, various skeptical voices began to challenge what had quickly become conventional wisdom among opinion leaders. Like Immanuel Wallerstein in Part II, scholars question the uniqueness of the late twentieth century. The sixteenth and the nineteenth centuries, they argue, already witnessed dramatic integration that set the stage for all subsequent developments. Financial markets may operate differently due to new computer technology, and the geopolitical context may be different due to the demise of the Soviet Union, but these are not qualitative changes. Other skeptics, by contrast, argue not that capitalism has always been global but that it is not yet fully globalized. For example, they suggest that the real roots of economic troubles, from Asia to Russia to Brazil, lie in bad domestic decisions. International markets can exploit and aggravate such errors but they are not the primary cause of a contagious crisis. The involvement of countries in the world economy varies greatly in any case. While some small economies, such as the Netherlands, are highly dependent on exports, for large countries, especially the United States, imports and exports still represent only a small portion of total GDP. The whole notion of integration is misleading for these skeptics, since the core of the world economy is only perhaps 30 of the world's 200 countries – a few countries of the Asian Pacific, western Europe, and North America, which account for the vast bulk of world capital and nearly all of the largest multinational corporations. Globalization, from this perspective, amounts to only modestly more intense ties among countries, corporations, and consumers in the industrialized democracies.

We think the skeptics make some good empirical points but underestimate the significance of recent qualitative changes. Our purpose, however, is not to settle these debates. Instead, we present illustrations of integration, contrasting views of its implications for inequality, and a discussion of possible new forms of regulation of global economic activity. This part concludes with a provocative assessment of economic globalization by an influential economist.

In the first selection, William Greider illustrates how Malaysia attracted investment by offering tax-free economic zones to foreign companies, notably in the semiconductor industry. While Malaysian growth accelerated as a result, Greider is concerned about the "global jobs auction" that such policies engender as countries compete to provide the lowest-wage workforce. He bemoans this "manic logic of capitalism," in the words of his book's subtitle. At the same time, he shows that Malaysian women who work at plants such as Motorola's derive real benefits from their new-found employment. Next, Miguel Korzeniewicz demonstrates how global production actually works in one prominent sector. The Nike Corporation relied on Asian production and American marketing from the outset, but production in Asia diversified as Korean producers began to manage sites in Vietnam and Indonesia. The Nike commodity chain thus pulled in cheaper workers in new countries while most profits still flowed to corporate owners in the West. In recent years, this disparity has motivated various groups to protest the treatment of Asian workers producing Nike shoes.

David Dollar and Aart Kraay, economists at the World Bank, argue that globalization is good for the poor. Greater openness to trade and investment translates into greater growth, which generally lifts the income of the very poor and reduces the inequality between rich and poor countries. China and India, in particular, have had success with their globalization strategy. While noting that such success is not inevitable, Dollar and Kraay conclude that trends since the 1970s refute the critiques of antiglobalization activists. The response by Oxfam, a British relief and development organization, takes issue with their conclusion by arguing that they analyze data selectively. While poverty has declined in some Asian countries, Latin America has not enjoyed similar progress. Current growth patterns actually reinforce inequality. The key issue is whether gains from growth are fairly distributed, a point made by Sen in Part I. While growth is necessary for dealing with poverty and inequality, Oxfam believes real equity requires broader reforms.

Mary Robinson, speaking as UN High Commissioner for Human Rights, advocates one such reform, namely the adoption of a "global compact" for corporate responsibility. She makes the case that multinational corporations have a responsibility to respect human rights and protect the environment. While the compact she describes is voluntary in principle, her argument illustrates one way in which people concerned about the consequences of economic globalization search for new rules to regulate global economic activity. David Henderson opposes such regulation. He thinks advocates of corporate social responsibility wrongly assume that there are agreed-upon solutions to global problems and that companies have a special role to play in helping to bring them about. Imposing such a code is also costly. This effort to remake the capitalist world economy is a form of "global salvationism" that undermines economic freedom and competition.

Joseph Stiglitz, formerly chief economist at the World Bank, concludes this part with his argument that thus far economic globalization has been unjust, undemocratic, and disadvantageous to developing nations. Capital liberalization has created undue volatility and trade liberalization has put large groups of workers at risk. He attributes the downside of globalization especially to the policies of international financial institutions, which he accuses of advocating "market fundamentalism." Stiglitz calls for a new global economic agenda and a new form of global governance.

19   Wawasan 2020

William Greider

The process of global economic integration is broadly driven by market forces, in particular the competitive price pressures to reduce costs, but the actual events of industrial movement depend crucially upon political transactions – irregular deals that often offend the reigning principles of free-market enterprise. When a multinational corporation seeks to shift production to low-wage labor markets, a process of political bargaining ensues with the governments competing for the new factories. Concessions are offered, deals are made, investment follows.

Given the worldwide thirst for economic development and the abundance of willing governments, these political arrangements are now so commonplace that almost everyone regards them as normal. The multinational companies usually have the leverage to stipulate terms for their capital investments, but the leverage is reversed in some important cases and nations can dictate terms to the firms.

A corporation's power is naturally strongest if it is dealing with a small, very poor country desperate for industrial development. The terms typically involve special political favors not available to others in commerce: state subsidies, exemption from taxation, government suppression of workers, special status as export enclaves free of import duties.

With these protective benefits, commerce is able to leap across the deepest social and economic divisions, bringing advanced production systems to primitive economies, disturbing ancient cultures with startling elements of modernity. Governments of developing nations may be nervous about the cultural disruption, but they usually suppress doubts and dissent. Starting from positions of weakness, the poor states hope this exchange will start them on an upward track toward higher levels of industrialization and an escape from general poverty. Some are succeeding in those terms and with spectacular results; many others eagerly offer themselves as the new greenfields for migrating production.

Even successful nations discover, however, that a basic insecurity lingers in their economic advance. A prosperity based on the strategies of multinational corporations remains hostage to them. If a country manages to graduate from low-wage status and establish a self-sustaining industrial base, its achievement may become permanent. But the very process of moving up also threatens to drive away the global investors. If capital does eventually move on, a relationship intended to be a mutually rewarding symbiosis may prove to have been parasitic.

Original publication details: Excerpted from William Greider, "Wawasan 2020," from William Greider, *One World, Ready or Not* (Simon & Schuster, 1997), pp. 81–6, 91–2, 100–2. Copyright © 1997 by William Greider. Reprinted by permission of Simon & Schuster Adult Publishing Group.

An ironic and debilitating form of global convergence is under way between rich and poor: a global jobs auction. The irregular political leverage that commerce first employed in the weak countries is now being applied to the wealthy and powerful as well, especially the United States. Multinationals are, in effect, conducting a peripatetic global jobs competition, awarding shares of production to those who make the highest bids – that is, the greatest concessions by the public domain. If a poor country like Malaysia grants public favors to capital in exchange for scarce jobs, then so will Ohio or Alabama.

In the industrial zone at Petaling Jaya outside Kuala Lumpur, a line of dingy blue buses began delivering workers for the 2 P.M. shift change at the Motorola plant. Motorola's blue logo was visible from the freeway, along with some other celebrated names of electronics like Canon, Sanyo, Panasonic and Minolta. Its factory looked like a low-slung office building facing an asphalt parking lot that was bordered by palms and giant yews. The white facade was temporarily decorated with dozens of red paper lanterns and gilded banners in honor of the Chinese New Year. Above the front entrance, a billboard invited workers to enter the "Motorola 10 K Run," winners to compete at the US Austin marathon.

The arriving workers passed through glass doors and headed down a long gleaming corridor toward the changing room, past the library and health center and an automatic banking machine. All of them were women, and most were young, small and delicate by American standards. They were dressed in the modesty of Islam – flowing ankle-length dresses, heads and shoulders draped by the Muslim *tundjung*, silken scarves of pale blue, orange and brown. A few wore the fuller, more conservative black veils that closely framed their faces like pale brown hearts and encased the upper body like shrouds.

"Good afternoon, ladies." Roger Bertelson, Motorola's country manager, was showing me around, and the two of us towered above the stream of women. They passed by, eyes down, barely nodding. Bertelson had brush-cut hair and a sunny American forwardness, like a taller version of Ross Perot. He was explaining the "I Recommend" board on the wall, a display covered with snapshots of employees who had made successful suggestions.

"We had to change the culture," Bertelson said, "because the Malay home does not encourage women to speak out. The daughter is supposed to have babies and take care of her husband. The idea was to break down the resistance to speaking out. We use positive reinforcement, just like you would work with schoolchildren. First, convince them that you are going to listen to them. Then have them stand up before their peers for recognition."

The automatic teller machine also disturbed the culture. "We had to change the pattern," he said. "She had to go home and tell her father: 'I'm not going to bring my money home in a pay envelope any more. It's going into the bank.'"

Farther along the hallway, the women passed by a collection of Norman Rockwell paintings – warm, nostalgic scenes of American life – each accompanied by an inspirational aphorism in English. "People Will Take Note of Excellent Work." "You'll Be Prepared for Anything with Enthusiasm." "What We Say Is as Important as How We Say It." It was hard to know what meaning these homey American images might have in this setting.

At the changing room, the women removed shoes and veils and proceeded to the gowning room across the hall. A few minutes later they emerged cloaked in ghostly white jumpsuits, wearing surgical masks and hooded bonnets. They looked like otherworldly travelers, more chaste than they would appear in the most severe Islamic garments. At the air shower, blasts of purified air cleansed them of any remaining particles of dust. Then they entered the sealed operations room, where the rows of complex machines and monitors awaited the next shift.

Once inside, the women in space suits began the exacting daily routines of manufacturing semiconductor chips. They worked in a realm of submicrons, attaching leads on devices too small to see without the aid of the electronic monitors. Watching the women through an observation window, Bertelson remarked: "She doesn't really do it, the machine does it."

The manufacturing process for semiconductors literally bounced around the world. Larger silicon wafers that included the circuitry for multiple chips had been designed and fabricated back in the States (or perhaps in Scotland, where the industry had also located a major production base). Then the wafers were flown by 747 to Malaysia (or perhaps Singapore or the Philippines or elsewhere in Asia) for final assembly – sawed into individual chips, wired, tested and packaged. The finished chips were shipped back to North America, Asia and Europe to become the functional guts of TV sets, computers, cars, portable phones, missile control systems and countless other products.

The spectacle of cultural transformation at Motorola was quite routine – three times a day, seven days a week – but it conveyed the high human drama of globalization: a fantastic leap across time and place, an exchange that was banal and revolutionary, vaguely imperial and exploitative, yet also profoundly liberating. In the longer sweep of history, the social intrusions of modern technology might be as meaningful as the economic upheavals. Motorola and the other semiconductor companies settled in Malaysia have managed to unite the leading edge of technological complexity with shy young women from the *kampong*, rural villages where destiny was defined as helping peasant fathers and husbands harvest the rice or palm oil.

At lunch in the company cafeteria, Bertelson and his management staff talked about the complexity. "We improve our productivity 15 percent a year, that's company policy," he said. "We have a road map for each one of our operations that calls for a 10x improvement by the year 2000, by automating and by improving worker efficiency. We will do that."

Malaysian production was not exempt from the same steep "learning curve" that drove price competition throughout the global industry, a standing assumption that costs and prices will fall by roughly 30 percent every time the volume doubles. To defend market share, every producer must continuously squeeze out more waste and imperfection or develop the new materials and production methods that could keep up with the curve. "Our technology, the miniaturization, is growing so fast that we really need to get the human element out of the process as fast as we can," Bertelson said.

Around the lunch table Bertelson's department managers looked like a visionary's ideal of multicultural cooperation. Chinese, Malay, Indian, black, yellow, pale brown, Christian, Buddhist, Muslim, Hindu. The only white guys were Bertelson and a Scottish engineer named Dave Anderson, hired from Singapore. Longinus Bernard, an Indian from Johore whose father had worked on colonial estates, described the early days in 1974 when Motorola started up. "We were so small, everybody knows everybody," he said. "It was really – how do you call it – a good feeling."

Hassim Majid, manager of government affairs, explained how the racial diversity had been achieved. "We were advised by the government to play an active role in restructuring the ethnic composition of the company," he said. "We were told to hire x number of Malay people like me, Chinese and Indians, just like your affirmative action in the United States. Motorola did well in meeting the government requirement."

The Kuala Lumpur operations, Motorola's largest outside the United States, had 5,000 employees, 80 percent Malay and 3,900 ladies, as the managers called them. The company had plans to double this facility, though not its employment. It represented one of the ripe anomalies of global economic revolution: while conservative ideologues in America fiercely contested the threat of multiculturalism, conservative American corporations were out around the world doing it. In the global context, the preoccupation of American politics with race and cultural superiority seemed ludicrous, out of touch and perhaps also dangerous.

At night, downtown Kuala Lumpur looked a little like a theme park celebrating postcolonial Asian prosperity. Some important buildings were fancifully lit with streamers of sparkling lights, giving outline to an eclectic collection of architecture. The clock tower of an old British administrative building was reminiscent of Westminster, but with oriental grace notes. The railway station looked like a Moorish fantasy imported from some other colonial outpost, as indeed its design was. Dozens of modern office towers formed a dense cluster that dwarfed remnants of the past. The city's oldest mosque, Bandaraya, one of its pale domes in collapse, sat at the foot of the thirty-story Bank Bumiputra.

By the river, the old central market hall had been renovated into artisans' stalls and tourist boutiques, with a US fast-food franchise nearby that sold "Prosperity Burgers." In the early evening, young professionals from the office towers gathered at the outdoor cafes for beer or tea. One night I watched six Malay boys entertaining the sidewalk patrons with an acrobatic hip-hop routine that seemed straight out of Compton, California, the lyrics in Bahasa.

On the headquarters building of the state-owned television station, the Malaysian national imperative – "2020" – was spelled out in huge red lights two stories high and framed by two glittering butterflies. The full slogan, *"Wawasan 2020,"* appeared frequently around the city and was otherwise embedded in everyday consciousness. It stood for the shared "vision" of what Malaysia intended to become: a self-sufficient industrial nation, with an economy that will grow eight times larger by 2020, with a people who will be, as Prime Minister Mahathir Mohamad often emphasized, "psychologically subservient to none."

To that end, the government in the last decade force-fed the development of a national car, the Proton Saga, a smart-looking sedan that relied heavily on Mitsubishi of Japan for design and components, but now claimed 70 percent local content. Mahathir rode in one with "2020" on the license plate. Proton was selling 102,000 cars a year at home and abroad, and has spawned an infant components industry. It was moving into Vietnam with a co-production venture, and a second national car, the Kancil, named for a small jungle deer, was planned with Daihatsu.

The essence of *"Wawasan 2020"* was rapid growth – 7 percent a year, every year for the next twenty-five years – and government industrial strategies to foster homegrown industries and a new middle class of talented managers and professionals. Per capita income was supposed to quadruple by 2020. Mahathir talked somewhat airily about launching ventures in telecommunications and aerospace, forming industrial consortia with Asian neighbors like Indonesia or Thailand that could become freestanding rivals to the most advanced economies.

That was the plan. It sounded improbably optimistic, even for the dynamic economies of Southeast Asia, and grandiose in some elements. But Malaysia had earned its self-confidence. Since 1971 its economy had expanded yearly at about the same phenomenal pace: GNP rose from 13 million ringgits in 1971 to 123 million twenty years later. Per capita income had exploded from an impoverished level of $410 a year to more than $3,000. In more basic terms, Malaysian life expectancy increased in two decades from 62.3 to 70.5 years.

In some ways Malaysia was the best-case illustration of globalization, though it was also unrepresentative because its development was more mature than others and the country was quite small, only twenty million people in territory the size of Florida and Georgia combined. The spectacular growth occurred under a one-party regime that Mahathir had led for nearly fifteen years. [. . .]

Malaysia, in order to secure its status as a major export platform, had offered the semiconductor industry, among other things, a lengthy holiday from taxes. Plants in the economic zones were given "pioneer" status for five to ten years. That meant no taxation on earnings in the country, exemptions from import duties and other forms of state subsidies. These tax holidays would eventually expire, but could be renewed and extended if a company made new investments. Other tax breaks kicked in later.

A more controversial benefit was the government's guarantee that electronics workers would be prohibited from organizing independent unions. Though organized labor functioned with some freedom in other sectors, including electrical manufacturing, the government decreed that the goal of national development required a union-free environment for the "pioneers" in semiconductors. The original restriction, supposedly temporary, was regularly protested by groups of workers, but nearly twenty-five years later the ban was still enforced. It now covered not just semiconductors but every other electronics product as well, including at the Japanese firms, which, unlike the American firms, were unionized at home.

Whenever the labor rights issue arose, leading companies professed not to care one way or the other, but the same message always got delivered to the government: unions will jeopardize investment. The government always backed off. On one occasion in the 1980s a delegation from American companies warned the minister of labor: "If unionization is forced upon them, some companies that are already operating here will close down their local operations while others would cease to continue investment, thereby moving to obsolescence."

In 1988, pressured by complaints from the AFL-CIO and the threat of trade sanctions, the labor minister announced an opening. Given the robust growth in Malaysia's electronics sector, he was lifting the restrictions and would recognize a new national union of electronics workers. Five hundred workers gathered from Kuala Lumpur factories to begin an organizing drive. A few days later a delegation from the Malaysian-American Electronics Industry Association met with the labor minister to express their disappointment. Simultaneously, US executives collared Mahathir at a trade conference he was attending in New York. The policy change was rescinded. The labor minister retired.

Instead of the national union, the government offered a weaker alternative, company-by-company "in-house unions." When workers organized one at Harris Electronics, the twenty-one leaders were fired and the new union evaporated. The French-owned Thomson Electronics, which had acquired elements of the old RCA from General Electric, inherited a factory with a union with three thousand members. It closed the plant and moved to Vietnam.

Bruno Petera, a forty-two-year-old supervisor at Harris and one of the union organizers who lost his job, thought the union movement would eventually persevere,
regardless of the obstacles, as Malaysians became more confident about themselves.
The nation was building not only a new middle class, but also a new working class.
In time, he said, people would object to their own powerlessness.

"Once you meet your material needs, you want the dignity," Bruno said. "The
dignity to ask a question, to file a complaint, to speak for yourself. It will happen,
little by little. Nothing is given free without a struggle." [. . .]

The strategy of pursuing rapid growth was more plausible when only a limited
number of Asian nations were pursuing it, but it became less so as the poker game
was widened to take in many more players. Malaysia was now surrounded by struggling nations engaged in a fierce competition for capital, for any industries that would
move them up the ladder.

Malaysia's economic vulnerability had two dimensions. First, the domestic
shortage of labor put upward pressure on wages at all skill levels, despite one
million foreign workers brought in temporarily from Indonesia and elsewhere. If
wage levels were allowed to rise too rapidly, it would drive capital elsewhere.
Yet reformers on the other end of the global system in America and Europe
were pushing in that direction: campaigning for labor rights in countries like Malaysia
in order to foster rising wages that might lessen the downward pressures on
high-wage nations and also increase worldwide consumer demand for everyone's
products.

In Malaysia, the low wages were frankly regarded as a national asset. Mahathir
complained about the Western intruders: "They know very well this is the sole
comparative advantage of the developing countries. They know that all the other
comparative advantages – technology, capital, rich domestic markets, legal framework,
management and marketing network – are with the developed countries."

Those qualities of advancement were the other dimension of Malaysia's vulnerability: the frustrating struggle to acquire higher levels of technological development
for the domestic economy. The threat was crisply summarized in a December 1993
economics report cabled from the US Embassy: The "concern is waning foreign interest in Malaysia as a site for investment, especially in high-tech, capital intensive industries. . . . The issue is technology transfer. Unless Malaysia manages to attract
increasingly sophisticated manufacturers, it risks getting caught in a medium-tech
trap, finding itself saddled with a low-growth industrial base."

The poker game continued, but on a more sophisticated level. American companies like Motorola and Intel were regarded as cooperative players because they were
locating software design centers in Malaysia and spreading technological competence
to the local population. The Japanese, on the other hand, "are very, very difficult,"
Anwar said. "No technology transfers, no locals hired for management, no research
centers. The Americans are very different."

Malaysia's supposed "comparative advantage" of cheap labor did not help much
in the advanced fields. Malaysian engineers with master's degrees were in over-
abundance and cost only one fourth of US engineers. But the Indian engineers in
Bangalore were twice as cheap as the Malaysians. There were too many bidders for
too few jobs.

"These guys are competing for the best airports," Jeffrey Garten remarked in
Washington. "It sounds crazy, but this is going to boil down to infrastructure and
which country provides the most convenient modern airport for businesses."

In broader outline, the political insecurities of a Malaysia were not as different from Alabama or Ohio or industrial countries in general as people in those places wished to imagine. All were stuck in different aspects of the same poker game. The global revolution put labor wages in play, but it also put governments in play. The shift in power that drove the irregular bargaining was eroding the public realm, as well as private incomes, and stimulated a race to the bottom: lower wages, lower taxes, less accountability. To borrow an old cliché from the ideology of laissez-faire capitalism, the multinationals were freely pursuing beggar-thy-neighbor politics.

That debilitating process would continue until nations found the sovereign means to confront the marketplace or collaborated on asserting new terms for how commerce was allowed to function. Or the process would continue until the system broke down, destabilized by its own freewheeling behavior.

In the meantime, the major powers, led by the United States, promoted further liberalization of the global trading regime, encouraged the competence of their own multinationals and promoted the objective of greater globalization. Increasing numbers of citizens were unconvinced. The US government, among others, lacked a coherent, concrete vision of how this globalization was expected to benefit the general population.

The Malaysian government at least had its own "*Wawasan 2020*," a concrete plan for what the nation intended to become. Americans might ask, What was the American *wawasan*?

20 Commodity Chains and Marketing Strategies: Nike and the Global Athletic Footwear Industry

Miguel Korzeniewicz

The world-economic trends and cycles of the past two decades have made it increasingly apparent that the production and distribution of goods take place in complex global networks that tie together groups, organizations, and regions. The concept of commodity chains is helpful in mapping these emerging forms of capitalist organization. Most often, analysts depict global commodity chains (GCCs) by focusing primarily on production processes and their immediate backward and forward linkages. Less attention has been paid to the crucial role played by the design, distribution, and marketing nodes within a GCC. These nodes are important because they often constitute the epicenter of innovative strategies that allow enterprises to capture greater shares of wealth within a chain. Furthermore, a GCC perspective helps us understand how marketing and consumption patterns in core areas of the world shape production patterns in peripheral and semiperipheral countries. Thus an analysis of the design, distribution, and marketing segments within a commodity chain can provide unique insights into the processes through which core-like activities are created, and competitive pressures are transferred elsewhere in the world-economy.

To provide such an analysis, this chapter focuses on the distribution segment of a particular commodity chain: athletic footwear. In particular, this chapter examines the marketing strategy of one corporation within the global athletic shoe industry (Nike) to refine our understanding of the dynamic nature of global commodity chains. The example of athletic footwear is useful in exploring how commodity chains are embedded in cultural trends. The social organization of advertising, fashion, and consumption shapes the networks and nodes of global commodity chains. The athletic footwear case shows that the organization of culture itself is an innovative process that unevenly shapes patterns of production and consumption in core, semiperipheral, and peripheral areas of the world-economy. [. . .]

Original publication details: Excerpted from Miguel Korzeniewicz, "Commodity Chains and Marketing Strategies: Nike and the Global Athletic Footwear Industry," in Gary Gereffi and Miguel Korzeniewicz (eds.), *Commodity Chains and Global Capitalism*, pp. 247–61. Copyright © 1994 by Gary Gereffi and Miguel Korzeniewicz. Reproduced by permission of Greenwood Publishing Group, Inc., Westport, CT.

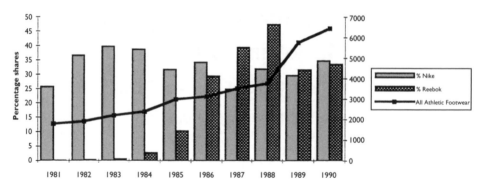

Figure 20.1   *Total wholesale revenues of athletic footwear and Nike's and Reebok's shares, 1981–90*
Source: National Sporting Goods Association.

Trends in the US Athletic Shoe Market

The athletic footwear market in the United States has been characterized over the past two decades by phenomenal rates of growth. As indicated by figure 20.1, wholesale revenues of athletic shoes in the United States tripled between 1980 and 1990. In the past six years, consumers in the United States more than doubled their expenditures on athletic shoes: In 1985 they spent $5 billion and bought 250 million pairs of shoes, whereas by the end of 1991 retail sales totaled $12 billion for nearly 400 million pairs of shoes. Three-fourths of all Americans bought athletic shoes in 1991, compared with two-thirds in 1988. In 1990, athletic shoes accounted for about a third of all shoes sold. The athletic footwear industry today generates $12 billion in retail sales, with at least twenty-five companies earning $20 million or more in annual sales. From the point of view of Schumpeterian innovations, the trajectory of the athletic footwear commodity chain over recent times provides valuable insights into the creation of a modern consumer market.

Retail markets for athletic shoes are highly segmented according to consumer age groups. Teenagers are the most important consumers of athletic shoes. A study sponsored by the Athletic Footwear Association found that the average American over twelve years of age owns at least two pairs of athletic shoes, worn for both athletic and casual purposes. As experienced by many parents and youngsters during the 1980s and 1990s, athletic shoes have been constructed and often promoted among teenagers as an important and visible symbol of social status and identity.

The products in this commodity chain also are highly differentiated according to models and the particular sport for which they are purportedly designed. By 1989, Nike was producing shoes in 24 footwear categories, encompassing 300 models and 900 styles. Reebok sold 175 models of shoes in 450 colors, and planned to add 250 new designs. Adidas and LA Gear sell 500 different styles each. The two fastest-growing segments of athletic shoes in the late 1980s were basketball shoes and walking shoes, while the volume of sales for tennis and running shoes declined. In 1991, basketball shoes accounted for 22 percent of sales, and cross trainers for 14 percent of sales. Product differentiation provides an important vehicle both for competition among enterprises and price stratification.

Finally, the sports footwear market is highly segmented according to price. Indicative of this segmentation, the price distribution of athletic shoes has a very wide range.

In 1989 the average cost of basketball, walking, and running shoes was between $40 and $47, while top-of-the-line shoes cost about $175. The bulk of production is oriented toward sales of the lower-priced shoes, while the market for the higher-priced commodities is substantially smaller. In 1990, more than 80 percent of athletic shoe purchases were priced under $35, with only 1.4 percent of shoes bought costing more than $65. Price rather than appearance or functionality often constitutes the primary matrix differentiating athletic shoes as status symbols.

Since displacing Adidas in the early 1980s, and after falling behind Reebok in the mid-1980s, Nike Corporation has become the largest and most important athletic shoe company in the United States. Nike's sales have grown from $2 million in 1972 to $270 million in 1980, and to over $3 billion in 1991. Reebok, the number two brand in the United States today, experienced similar rates of growth – in fact, Reebok has been the fastest-growing company in the history of American business. Between 1981 and 1987, Reebok's sales grew from $1.5 million to $1.4 billion, experiencing an average annual growth rate of 155 percent. Similarly, LA Gear grew at a dazzling rate, from $11 million in 1985 to $535 million in 1989. Between 1985 and 1990, Nike's share of the athletic footwear market in the United States declined from 30 to 25 percent, Reebok's rose from 14 to 24 percent; LA Gear's increased from a minimal share to 11 percent, and Converse's share declined from 9 to 5 percent. These data suggest that a limited number of large firms compete within the athletic footwear market in the United States, but also that the organization of the market provides considerable permeability for successful entry and competition by new enterprises.

What are the factors that explain the enormous growth of the athletic shoe industry? The evidence suggests, in part, that the most important enterprises within this commodity chain have grown by increasing their control over the nodes involved in the material production of athletic shoes. The most fundamental innovation of these enterprises, however, has been the *creation* of a market, and this has entailed the construction of a convincing world of symbols, ideas, and values harnessing the desires of individuals to the consumption of athletic shoes. By focusing on the marketing and circulation nodes of a commodity chain, greater analytical precision can be gained in identifying the crucial features of these innovations.

Rather than analyzing the athletic footwear chain as a whole, the next section focuses on a single enterprise, Nike Corporation. Although a comparative analysis of other enterprises would yield greater insights into possible differences in organizational trajectories, the focus on a single firm allows a more detailed exploration of the innovative strategies that have characterized the athletic footwear commodity chain. This approach also highlights the relevance of world-systems theory, and the concept of commodity chains, to the study of economic and social processes at a microlevel of observation. Nike's rise to prominence has been based on its ability to capture a succession of nodes along the commodity chain, increasing its expertise and control over the critical areas of design, distribution, marketing, and advertising. This strategy also involved a fundamental reshaping of production and consumption, hence contributing to the recent transformation of the athletic footwear commodity chain.

Nike Corporation: Competition, Upgrading and Innovation in a Commodity Chain

The activities of Nike Corporation created a quintessential American product that has captured a large share of the giant US athletic footwear market. Nike

Corporation increased its revenues tenfold in the past ten years, from $270 million in 1980 to an estimated $3 billion in 1991. Nike sells tens of millions of athletic shoes in the United States every year, yet all of the firm's manufacturing operations are conducted overseas, making the company an archetype of a global sourcing strategy. Nike Corporation never relocated domestic production abroad, as many American companies have done, because the firm actually originated by importing shoes from Japan. It has subcontracted nearly all of its production overseas ever since: currently, "all but 1 percent of the millions of shoes Nike makes each year are manufactured in Asia." In the United States, Nike has developed essentially as a design, distribution, and marketing enterprise.

Nike's successful implementation of its overseas sourcing strategy can best be understood as part of the firm's effort to retain control over highly profitable nodes in the athletic footwear commodity chain, while avoiding the rigidity and pressures that characterize the more competitive nodes of the chain. "We don't know the first thing about manufacturing," says Neal Lauridsen, Nike's vice-president for Asia-Pacific. "We are marketers and designers." Nike's practice of overseas sourcing provides strategic and geographical mobility to the firm by developing a complex division of labor among the components of a global subcontracting network. The way these characteristics are linked to consumer demand and marketing strategies helps explain the tremendous growth and success of Nike. [. . .]

Marketing as an upgrading strategy (1976–1984)

During this second period, Nike Corporation introduced major innovations in marketing, distribution, and subcontracting for the production of athletic footwear. First, between 1976 and 1984, Nike was shaped by (and helped to shape) the "fitness boom" – the phenomenal growth of jogging, running, and exercise as a common activity by millions of Americans. Nike was part of this phenomenon by implementing a marketing strategy that involved the development of a vast and visible network of endorsement contracts with basketball, baseball, and football players and coaches. Second, Nike's distribution network was enhanced by the establishment of a strategic alliance with Foot Locker, a rapidly growing chain of retail stores marketing athletic products. Finally, Nike Corporation sought to further enhance its control over subcontractors and lower production costs by shifting most manufacturing activities from Japan to South Korea and (to a lesser extent) Taiwan. Combined, these innovations provided a significant competitive edge to Nike Corporation.

Beginning in the mid-1970s, running, jogging, and exercise in general became part of mainstream American culture. Nike Corporation was in the right place at the right time to capitalize on this phenomenon by outperforming competing brands and becoming the most important athletic shoe company in the United States. But the ability to gain from this phenomenon required a major reorientation in the marketing of the company's products: Nike Corporation's main customer base had to shift, as one observer puts it, from "running geeks to yuppies." To achieve this shift, Nike's promotional efforts in the 1970s moved slowly but consistently away from amateur sports to professional sports, and from lesser-known track and field runners to highly visible sports figures. In 1977 and 1978 Nike developed a strategy to sign visible college basketball coaches; by 1979 it had signed over fifty college coaches. One measure of Nike's promotional success was the cover of *Sports Illustrated* of

March 26, 1979, which showed Larry Bird (at the time a player in the NCAA tournament) wearing Nike shoes. In the late 1970s, Nike also began to promote heavily in baseball, and by 1980 a Nike representative had signed over fifty players in different baseball teams – as well as eight players in the Tampa Bay team that made it to the 1980 Super Bowl. This new marketing strategy enhanced Nike's image in its new market niche.

Nike's rise as the largest athletic shoe company in the United States also involved creating a more effective distribution network. Foot Locker, an emerging chain of sport equipment retailers, became the most important distributor of Nike shoes. As a way to solve inventory and financial bottlenecks, Nike people devised an advance-order purchase system they called "futures." The system required major distributors to commit themselves to large orders six months in advance, in return for a 5–7 percent discount and a guaranteed delivery schedule. Foot Locker was one of the first dealers to try the futures contracts, and to benefit from them, eventually becoming Nike's most important retailer. Another reason for Foot Locker's close relationship with Nike was the latter's flexibility, and its willingness to change design specifications on request from dealers. This responsiveness of Nike contrasted with Adidas' generally inflexible approach to their supply of shoes, and further extended the company's competitive edge.

Finally, the phenomenal growth in the demand for athletic shoes changed Nike's subcontracting patterns. Nike now needed larger outputs, lower labor prices, and more control over the manufacturing process. In 1974 the great bulk of BRS's [Blue Ribbon Sports'] $4.8 million in sales was still coming from Japan. Phil Knight, aware of rising labor costs in Japan, began to look for sourcing alternatives. One of these alternatives was the United States. In early 1974, BRS rented space in an empty old factory in Exeter, New Hampshire, and later opened a second factory in Saco, New Hampshire. Domestic facilities also fulfilled a critical R&D function that Nike would later use to gain greater control over production processes abroad. However, by 1984 imported shoes (mostly from Korea and Taiwan) rose to 72 percent of the US shoe market, and US-based factories were forced to close. The collapse of the US production base was due primarily to its limited manufacturing capacity and its economic implausibility. Product timelines lagged and American-based manufacturing found itself unable to compete with lower Asian labor costs.

While Nippon Rubber (Nike's Japanese supplier) reportedly made the decision to relocate part of its production to South Korea and Taiwan, Nike also began to look for new sources of its own. In October 1975, Phil Knight flew to Asia to search for alternative supply sources to lessen his dependency on both Nissho Iwai and Nippon Rubber without losing either company. In Japan, Knight met a Chinese trader who agreed to set up a Nike-controlled corporation called Athena Corporation that established production facilities in Taiwan. In South Korea the Sam Hwa factory of Pusan became the main partner, which began 1977 making 10,000 pairs of Nike shoes a month, and ending the year by making about 100,000 pairs a month. By 1980, nearly 90 percent of Nike's shoe production was located in Korea and Taiwan.

The consolidation of South Korea and Taiwan as the main geographical centers of manufacturing also involved the emergence of a complex system of stratification among Nike's suppliers. Donaghu and Barff identify three main classes of factories supplying Nike: developed partners, volume producers, and developing sources.

"Developed partners" are the upper tier of Nike suppliers, responsible for the most innovative and sophisticated shoes. "Volume producers" are those that manufacture a specific type of product in large quantities. These factories are typically less flexible than developed partners in their manufacturing organization. Finally, "developing sources" are the newer factories that attracted Nike because of their low labor costs, entering into a series of tutelary arrangements both with Nike and the more experienced Nike suppliers.

The geographical dynamism of Nike's shifts in subcontracting arrangements interacted with this complex stratification system in interesting ways. As labor costs in Japan rose in the 1970s, Nike Corporation shifted production to emerging semiperipheral countries such as South Korea and Taiwan. As labor costs in the established semiperipheral supply locations began to rise in the 1980s, Nike tried to shift some of the labor-intensive, technologically less advanced segments of its production to new locations in peripheral areas (such as China). It is interesting to note, however, that linkages with developed partners remained critical for two reasons. First, several of Nike's more sophisticated models required the expertise and flexibility of older, more reliable partners. Second, the technological expertise and capital of the older partners was often necessary to bring newer production facilities up to Nike standards, leading to joint ventures between the older, more established sources and the newer ones. From this point of view, centralization and decentralization of subcontracting arrangements were constrained by marketing requirements.

Design, advertising, and the return to the semiperiphery (post-1985)

After 1985, Nike entered into another period of high growth, based on innovations in product design (the creation of the "Air Nike" models, which quickly became immensely popular) and advertising strategies (signing its most popular endorser, Michael Jordan). Also, Nike Corporation continued to target new market niches, entering the aerobics segment of the market, where Reebok had become increasingly dominant, and the growing and profitable athletic apparel markets. Finally, Nike Corporation altered its subcontracting arrangements, shifting important segments in the manufacture of Nike's athletic shoes to the People's Republic of China, Thailand, and Indonesia. However, the need for specialized and sophisticated production runs once again forced Nike to return to more experienced manufacturers in South Korea and Taiwan.

The ability to produce high-performance, sophisticated footwear models became critical to Nike because the company was able to pull out of its early 1980s stagnation through its "Nike Air" technological innovation. By 1984 the phenomenal growth of a mass market for jogging shoes began to stabilize, particularly in the men's segment of the market. Other companies, like Reebok and LA Gear, were becoming more effective in selling to the female and aerobics segments of the market. Nike Corporation, accustomed to years of high growth, was in crisis. Many endorsement contracts were canceled, the Athletics West program cut down its sponsored athletes from 88 to 50, and by the end of 1984, Nike had laid off 10 percent of its 4,000-person work force. Another indication of Nike's bad fortunes was its declining influence among sports coaches and agents. To reverse this decline, Nike Corporation once again turned toward introducing a drastic product innovation.

Nike's declining fortunes in the mid-1980s were reversed by the introduction of Air Nike (a new technology that allowed a type of gas to be compressed and stored within the sole) and by the phenomenal success of its "Air Jordan" line of basketball shoes, as well as the success of the endorser they were named after, Michael Jordan. In Nike's Los Angeles store, the first two shipments of Air Jordans sold out in three days. By 1985 it was clear that Air Jordan shoes were a huge success. Nike sold in three months what had been projected for the entire year. The first contract between Nike Corporation and Michael Jordan was worth $2.5 million over five years, and it included (among other things) a royalty to the athlete on all Air Jordan models sold by the company.

The several advertising campaigns featuring Michael Jordan highlight Nike's capacity to influence market demand for its shoes. Nike's video and print advertisements have been among the most innovative and controversial in recent years, adding to Nike's visibility and undoubtedly contributing to its phenomenal growth. Part of the appeal of Nike advertising is its success in tapping and communicating a consistent set of values that many people in the 1970s and 1980s identified with: hipness, irreverence, individualism, narcissism, self-improvement, gender equality, racial equality, competitiveness, and health.

But there also have been several allegations made that by targeting inner-city youths in its advertising and marketing campaigns, Nike has profited substantially from sales directly related to drug and gang money, showing little concern for the social and financial stability of the predominantly black, poor communities, where sales account for 20 percent of the total athletic footwear market. The relationship between the athletic footwear industry and drug money has become increasingly evident by the alarming rate of robberies and killings over expensive sports shoes. Some store owners claim that Nike is not only aware that drug money contributes heavily to its sales, but that Nike representatives adamantly encourage distributors in the inner cities to specifically target and cater to this market.

Nike commercials tend to be subtle. The trademark "swoosh" logo is often far more prominent than dialogue or a straightforward pitch. They are also controversial. Nike's use of the Beatles' song "Revolution" to advertise its new "Nike Air" was startling, and so has been its recent use of John Lennon's song "Instant Karma." Some of the most distinctive Nike advertisements contain themes that can best be described as postmodern: the rapid succession of images, image self-consciousness, and "ads-within-ads" themes. The "Heritage" Nike commercial, showing a white adult runner training in an urban downtown area while images of sports heroes are projected on the sides of buildings, is particularly striking because it seeks to identify the viewer with an idealized figure (the runner) who is in turn identifying with idealized figures (the sports heroes). This ninety-second advertisement cost over $800,000 to run once in its entirety during the 1991 Superbowl. Though there is no dialogue, the product is identifiable (it is seen almost subliminally several times), and the message of the commercial is clear. Postmodern theory, given its sensitivity to new cultural phenomena, can be helpful in understanding advertising as a crucial element in the athletic footwear global commodity chain. An understanding of consumption must be based on commodity aesthetics because consumption is increasingly the consumption of signs. Similarly, Featherstone has noted the increasing importance of the production of symbolic goods and images. In a sense, Nike represents an archetype of a firm selling to emerging postmodern consumer markets that rest on segmented, specialized, and dynamic features.

As in the previous periods, these drastic changes in marketing and distribution strategies were accompanied by shifts in the firm's subcontracting strategy. In 1980 Nike began a process of relocation to the periphery (particularly China, Indonesia, and Thailand) that most other companies would gradually follow in the course of the decade. This relocation was driven by cost advantages: "a mid-priced shoe made in South Korea which costs Nike US $20 when it leaves the docks of Pusan will only cost about US $15 to make in Indonesia or China." Nike Corporation was one of the very first companies to enter the People's Republic of China. In 1980, Phil Knight began to set up a manufacturing base in China. Soon an agreement between Nike Corporation and the Chinese government was finalized, and shoes began to be produced in the PRC. This rapid success can be explained by the fact that Nike used a Chinese-born representative (David Chang) who was thoroughly familiar with the local environment, which meant that proposals were quickly translated into Chinese and attuned to the negotiating style and objectives of the Chinese government. Also, Nike's objectives were long-term and the volumes of production being negotiated were significant, which coincided with the development priorities of the Chinese government at the time.

Just as Nike led the trend of entry into China, later in the mid-1980s it led a reevaluation of the benefits and disadvantages of associating directly with developing partners. By late 1984, production in Chinese factories totaled 150,000 pairs a month, one-seventh of the originally projected 1 million pairs a month. The early 1980s also signaled a slowdown in the rapid growth of conventional athletic footwear markets at a time when competition from other athletic footwear firms (LA Gear, Reebok) was increasing. By 1983 Nike terminated its subcontracting arrangement with the Shanghai factory, and in 1984 negotiated an early termination of its contract with the Tianjin factory.

In the mid-1980s Nike briefly considered shifting production back to established manufacturing sources in South Korea and Taiwan. The advantages of lower labor costs in the developing manufacturing areas had to be weighed against disadvantages in production flexibility, quality, raw material sourcing, and transportation. The development of a new shoe model from technical specifications to shoe production was four months in South Korea, compared to eight months in China. The ratio of perfect-quality (A-grade) shoes to aesthetically flawed, but structurally sound (B-grade) shoes was 99 : 1 in Korea, 98 : 2 in Taiwan, and 80 : 20 in China. While Taiwan and South Korea sourced 100 percent of the raw materials needed for production, China was only able to source 30 percent. Finally, shipping from Taiwan and South Korea was 20–25 days; from Shanghai it was 35–40 days.

The mid-1980s also marked the introduction of the "Nike Air" technology and especially the "Air Jordan" model. Being more sophisticated, secretive, and expensive, this model required more experienced and trustworthy suppliers of the "developed partners" type that had been developed in South Korea over the years. One Reebok executive argued that "as the complexity of our product increases, it continues to go to [South Korea]. The primary reason is that product development out of Korean factories is quick and accurate for athletic footwear, better than any place in the world." An observer concluded in the mid-1980s that after the trend of relocation to low-wage locations like Thailand, Indonesia, and China, "buyers are starting to return [to Pusan] after finding that the extra cost of doing business in South Korea is offset by reliability and the large capacity of its factories." This need for more established suppliers coincided with the adjustments that the Korean shoe producers themselves made in an effort to adapt to rising labor costs and the migration of many firms to other countries. Many Pusan firms shrunk in size but also increased the unit value of their production.

However, the relative importance of South Korean firms has continued to decline. Thus, "at least one-third of the lines in Pusan have shut down in the past three years. Only a handful of South Korean companies are expected to remain significant shoe exporters in a couple of years." Similar changes have affected shoe-producing firms in Taiwan, where "since 1988, the number of footwear companies has fallen from 1,245 to 745. Athletic shoe exports slipped from US$1.5 billion in 1988 to US$ 1 billion (in 1991)." Taiwanese and South Korean-based firms, on the other hand, are used for managing and mediating the relocation of production facilities to the periphery.

The shift of Nike's production to the periphery has become significant. "In the fiscal year to 31 May 1988, Nike bought 68 percent of its shoes from South Korea but only 42 percent in 1991–92. China, Indonesia and Thailand produced 44 percent of Nike's shoes last fiscal year; against less than 10 percent in 1987–88." This same trend is expected to continue in the future: "now, Vietnam looks like the next country on the list. Two major Taiwanese suppliers, Feng Tay and Adi Corporation, are interested in starting production in Vietnam if and when the U.S. trade embargo of its old adversary is lifted."

The advantages of Nike Corporation that have enabled it to become a powerful and profitable link in the athletic footwear commodity chain are the expertise of its designers in finding technological advances in shoe comfort and performance, the distribution networks built over the past twenty-five years, and the effectiveness of its marketing, promotion and advertising campaigns.

Overall assessment

To summarize the arguments made in this section, Nike's development of its twin strategies of overseas subcontracting and domestic marketing can best be understood as involving three distinct periods, each corresponding to different patterns of market demand, geographical locus of production, and marketing strategies. In the first period, between 1962 and 1975, Nike Corporation emphasized control over the import and distribution nodes of its commodity chain. Between 1976 and 1984, Nike Corporation enhanced its relative competitive position by extending control to marketing, and by redesigning its subcontracting strategy to take advantage of new opportunities in Southeast Asia (in South Korea and Taiwan initially, later in China, Thailand, and Indonesia). Finally, beginning in the mid-1980s, Nike Corporation successfully extended control to product design and advertising, further upgrading the firm's organizational structure. As a whole, these three periods suggest that Nike Corporation has sustained and enhanced its competitive edge through the implementation of frequent innovations in the nodes and networks of its commodity chain.

Conclusions

This chapter has examined the organizational strategies of Nike Corporation within the global athletic shoe industry. Nike's uncommon success and growth is due in part to social and cultural trends that have made leisure and fitness more important in our contemporary society. It is also the outcome of Nike's strategy of responding to these trends by accumulating expertise and control over the increasingly important service nodes of the athletic footwear commodity chain: import, distribution, marketing, and advertising.

Nike Corporation (and the athletic footwear industry in general) are excellent case studies of how goods emerge from complex, transnational linkages at different stages of production and distribution. Nike Corporation was born a globalized company. The study confirms a division of labor between core or postindustrial societies (that will presumably specialize in services over time) and noncore societies at different levels of industrialization (that will increasingly specialize in manufacturing). While Korean and Chinese firms are producing the actual shoe, US-based Nike promotes the symbolic nature of the shoe and appropriates the greater share of the value resulting from its sales.

Nike and the athletic shoe industry show that there are emerging patterns of consumption that have enormous consequences for social and economic organization. Linkages between consumption and production must be explored in greater detail. While a consensus has been building for some time that there are new patterns in the organization of production (alternatively called flexible specialization, flexible production, or post-Fordist production), we also need a better understanding of what may be called "post-Fordist consumption" – that is, the emerging patterns of consumption and distribution that are the counterpart to transformations in the realm of production.

21   Growth is Good for the Poor

David Dollar and Aart Kraay

A Rising Tide

One of the main claims of the antiglobalization movement is that globalization is widening the gap between the haves and the have-nots. It benefits the rich and does little for the poor, perhaps even making their lot harder. As union leader Jay Mazur put it in these pages, "globalization has dramatically increased inequality between and within nations". The problem with this new conventional wisdom is that the best evidence available shows the exact opposite to be true. So far, the current wave of globalization, which started around 1980, has actually promoted economic equality and reduced poverty.

Global economic integration has complex effects on income, culture, society, and the environment. But in the debate over globalization's merits, its impact on poverty is particularly important. If international trade and investment primarily benefit the rich, many people will feel that restricting trade to protect jobs, culture, or the environment is worth the costs. But if restricting trade imposes further hardship on poor people in the developing world, many of the same people will think otherwise.

Three facts bear on this question. First, a long-term global trend toward greater inequality prevailed for at least 200 years; it peaked around 1975. But since then, it has stabilized and possibly even reversed. The chief reason for the change has been the accelerated growth of two large and initially poor countries: China and India. Second, a strong correlation links increased participation in international trade and investment on the one hand and faster growth on the other. The developing world can be divided into a "globalizing" group of countries that have seen rapid increases in trade and foreign investment over the last two decades – well above the rates for rich countries – and a "nonglobalizing" group that trades even less of its income today than it did 20 years ago. The aggregate annual per capita growth rate of the globalizing group accelerated steadily from one percent in the 1960s to five percent in the 1990s. During that latter decade, in contrast, rich countries grew at two percent and nonglobalizers at only one percent. Economists are cautious about drawing conclusions concerning causality, but they largely agree that openness to foreign trade and investment (along with complementary reforms) explains the faster growth of the globalizers.

Third, and contrary to popular perception, globalization has not resulted in higher inequality within economies. Inequality has indeed gone up in some countries (such as China) and down in others (such as the Philippines). But those changes are not

Original publication details: Excerpted from David Dollar and Aart Kraay, "Growth is Good for the Poor," *Foreign Affairs*, 81, 1, January/February 2002. Copyright © 2002 by the Council on Foreign Relations, Inc. Reprinted by permission of *Foreign Affairs*.

systematically linked to globalization measures such as trade and investment flows, tariff rates, and the presence of capital controls. Instead, shifts in inequality stem more from domestic education, taxes, and social policies. In general, higher growth rates in globalizing developing countries have translated into higher incomes for the poor. Even with its increased inequality, for example, China has seen the most spectacular reduction of poverty in world history – which was supported by opening its economy to foreign trade and investment.

Although globalization can be a powerful force for poverty reduction, its beneficial results are not inevitable. If policymakers hope to tap the full potential of economic integration and sustain its benefits, they must address three critical challenges. A growing protectionist movement in rich countries that aims to limit integration with poor ones must be stopped in its tracks. Developing countries need to acquire the kinds of institutions and policies that will allow them to prosper under globalization, both of which may be different from place to place. And more migration, both domestic and international, must be permitted when geography limits the potential for development.

The Great Divide

Over the past 200 years, different local economies around the world have become more integrated while the growth rate of the global economy has accelerated dramatically. Although it is impossible to prove causal linkage between the two developments – since there are no other world economies to be tested against – evidence suggests the arrows run in both directions. As Adam Smith argued, a larger market permits a finer division of labor, which in turn facilitates innovation and learning by doing. Some of that innovation involves transportation and communications technologies that lower costs and increase integration. So it is easy to see how integration and innovation can be mutually supportive.

Different locations have become more integrated because of increased flows of goods, capital, and knowledge. From 1820 to 1914, international trade increased faster than the global economy. Trade rose from about 2 percent of world income in 1820 to 18 percent in 1914. The globalization of trade took a step backward during the protectionist period of the Great Depression and World War II, and by 1950 trade (in relation to income) was lower than it had been in 1914. But thanks to a series of multilateral trade liberalizations under the General Agreement on Tariffs and Trade (GATT), trade dramatically expanded among industrialized countries between 1960 and 1980. Most developing countries remained largely isolated from this trade because of their own inward-focused policies, but the success of such notable exceptions as Taiwan and South Korea eventually helped encourage other developing economies to open themselves up to foreign trade and investment.

International capital flows, measured as foreign ownership of assets relative to world income, also grew during the first wave of globalization and declined during the Great Depression and World War II; they did not return to 1914 levels until 1980. But since then, such flows have increased markedly and changed their nature as well. One hundred years ago, foreign capital typically financed public infrastructure projects (such as canals and railroads) or direct investment related to natural resources. Today, in contrast, the bulk of capital flows to developing countries is direct investments tied to manufacturing and services.

The change in the nature of capital flows is clearly related to concurrent advances in economic integration, such as cheaper and faster transportation and revolutionary changes in telecommunications. Since 1920, seagoing freight charges have declined by about two-thirds and air travel costs by 84 percent; the cost of a three-minute call from New York City to London has dropped by 99 percent. Today, production in widely differing locations can be integrated in ways that simply were not possible before.

Another aspect of integration has been the movement of people. Yet here the trend is reversed: there is much more international travel than in the past but much less permanent migration. Between 1870 and 1910, about ten percent of the world's population relocated permanently from one country to another; over the past 25 years, only one to two percent have done so.

As economic integration has progressed, the annual growth rate of the world economy has accelerated, from 1 percent in the mid-nineteenth century to 3.5 percent in 1960–2000. Sustained over many years, such a jump in growth makes a huge difference in real living standards. It now takes only two to three years, for example, for the world economy to produce the same amount of goods and services that it did during the entire nineteenth century. Such a comparison is arguably a serious understatement of the true difference, since most of what is con- sumed today – airline travel, cars, televisions, synthetic fibres, life-extending drugs – did not exist 200 years ago. For any of these goods or services, therefore, the growth rate of output since 1820 is infinite. Human productivity has increased almost unimaginably.

All this tremendous growth in wealth was distributed very unequally up to about 1975, but since then growing equality has taken hold. One good measure of inequal- ity among individuals worldwide is the mean log deviation – a measure of the gap between the income of any randomly selected person and a general average. It takes into account the fact that income distributions everywhere are skewed in favor of the rich, so that the typical person is poorer than the group average; the more skewed the distribution, the larger the gap. Per capita income in the world today, for example, is around $5,000, whereas a randomly selected person would most likely be living on close to $1,000 – 80 percent less. That gap translates into a mean log deviation of 0.8.

Taking this approach, an estimate of the world distribution of income among individuals shows rising inequality between 1820 and 1975. In that period, the gap between the typical person and world per capita income increased from about 40 percent to about 80 percent. Since changes in income inequality within countries were small, the increase in inequality was driven mostly by differences in growth rates across countries. Areas that were already relatively rich in 1820 (notably, Europe and the United States) grew faster than poor areas (notably, China and India). Global inequality peaked sometime in the 1970s, but it then stabilized and even began to decline, largely because growth in China and India began to accelerate.

Another way of looking at global inequality is to examine what is happening to the extreme poor – those people living on less than $1 per day. Although the per- centage of the world's population living in poverty has declined over time, the absolute number rose fairly steadily until 1980. During the Great Depression and World War II, the number of poor increased particularly sharply, and it declined somewhat immediately thereafter. The world economy grew strongly between 1960 and 1980, but the number of poor rose because growth did not occur in the places where the worst-off live. But since then, the most rapid growth has occurred in poor locations. Consequently the number of poor has declined by 200 million since 1980. Again, this trend is explained primarily by the rapid income growth in China and India, which together in 1980 accounted for about one-third of the world's population and more than 60 percent of the world's extreme poor.

Upward Bound

The shift in the trend in global inequality coincides with the shift in the economic strategies of several large developing countries. Following World War II, most developing regions chose strategies that focused inward and discouraged integration with the global economy. But these approaches were not particularly successful, and throughout the 1960s and 1970s developing countries on the whole grew less rapidly than industrialized ones. The oil shocks and U.S. inflation of the 1970s created severe problems for them, contributing to negative growth, high inflation, and debt crises over the next several years. Faced with these disappointing results, several developing countries began to alter their strategies starting in the 1980s.

For example, China had an extremely closed economy until the mid-1970s. Although Beijing's initial economic reform focused on agriculture, a key part of its approach since the 1980s has involved opening up foreign trade and investment, including a drop in its tariff rates by two-thirds and its nontariff barriers by even more. These reforms have led to unprecedented economic growth in the country's coastal provinces and more moderate growth in the interior. From 1978 to 1994 the Chinese economy grew annually by 9 percent, while exports grew by 14 percent and imports by 13 percent. Of course, China and other globalizing developing countries have pursued a wide range of reforms, not just economic openness. Beijing has strengthened property rights through land reform and moved from a planned economy toward a market-oriented one, and these measures have contributed to its integration as well as to its growth.

Other developing countries have also opened up as a part of broader reform programs. During the 1990s, India liberalized foreign trade and investment with good results; its annual per capita income growth now tops four percent. It too has pursued a broad agenda of reform and has moved away from a highly regulated, planned system. Meanwhile, Uganda and Vietnam are the best examples of very low-income countries that have increased their participation in trade and investment and prospered as a result. And in the western hemisphere, Mexico is noteworthy both for signing its free-trade agreement with the United States and Canada in 1993 and for its rapid growth since then, especially in the northern regions near the U.S. border.

These cases illustrate how openness to foreign trade and investment, coupled with complementary reforms, typically leads to faster growth. India, China, Vietnam, Uganda, and Mexico are not isolated examples; in general, countries that have become more open have grown faster. The best way to illustrate this trend is to rank developing countries in order of their increases in trade relative to national income over the past 20 years. The top third of this list can be thought of as the "globalizing" camp, and the bottom two-thirds as the "nonglobalizing" camp. The globalizers have increased their trade relative to income by 104 percent over the past two decades, compared to 71 percent for rich countries. The nonglobalizers, meanwhile, actually trade less today than they did 20 years ago. The globalizers have also cut their import tariffs by 22 percentage points on average, compared to only 11 percentage points for the nonglobalizers.

How have the globalizers fared in terms of growth? Their average annual growth rates accelerated from 1 percent in the 1960s to 3 percent in the 1970s, 4 percent in the 1980s, and 5 percent in the 1990s. Rich countries' annual growth rates, by comparison, slowed to about 2 percent in the 1990s, and the nonglobalizers saw their growth rates decline from 3 percent in the 1970s to 1 percent in the 1980s and 1990s.

The same pattern can be observed on a local level. Within both China and India, the locations that are integrating with the global economy are growing much more rapidly than the disconnected regions. Indian states, for example, vary significantly in the quality of their investment climates as measured by government efficiency, corruption, and infrastructure. Those states with better investment climates have integrated themselves more closely with outside markets and have experienced more investment (domestic and foreign) than their less-integrated counterparts. Moreover, states that were initially poor and then created good investment climates had stronger poverty reduction in the 1990s than those not integrating with the global economy. Such internal comparisons are important because, by holding national trade and macroeconomic policies constant, they reveal how important it is to complement trade liberalization with institutional reform so that integration can actually occur.

The accelerated growth rates of globalizing countries such as China, India, and Vietnam are consistent with cross-country comparisons that find openness going hand in hand with faster growth. The most that these studies can establish is that more trade and investment is highly correlated with higher growth, so one needs to be careful about drawing conclusions about causality. Still, the overall evidence from individual cases and cross-country correlation is persuasive. As economists Peter Lindert and Jeffrey Williamson have written, "even though no one study can establish that openness to trade has unambiguously helped the representative Third World economy, the preponderance of evidence supports this conclusion." They go on to note that "there are no antiglobal victories to report for the postwar Third World."

Contrary to the claims of the antiglobalization movement, therefore, greater openness to international trade and investment has in fact helped narrow the gap between rich and poor countries rather than widen it. During the 1990s, the economies of the globalizers, with a combined population of about 3 billion, grew more than twice as fast as the rich countries. The nonglobalizers, in contrast, grew only half as fast and nowadays lag further and further behind. Much of the discussion of global inequality assumes that there is growing divergence between the developing world and the rich world, but this is simply not true. The most important development in global inequality in recent decades is the growing divergence within the developing world, and it is directly related to whether countries take advantage of the economic benefits that globalization can offer.

The Path Out of Poverty

The antiglobalization movement also claims that economic integration is worsening inequality within countries as well as between them. Until the mid-1980s, there was insufficient evidence to support strong conclusions on this important topic. But now more and more developing countries have begun to conduct household income and consumption surveys of reasonable quality. (In low-income countries, these surveys typically track what households actually consume because so much of their real income is self-produced and not part of the money economy.) Good surveys now exist for 137 countries, and many go back far enough to measure changes in inequality over time.

One way of looking at inequality within countries is to focus on what happens to the bottom 20 percent of households as globalization and growth proceed apace. Across all countries, incomes of the poor grow at around the same rate as GDP. Of course, there is a great deal of variation around that average relationship. In some countries, income distribution has shifted in favor of the poor; in others, against them. But these shifts cannot be explained by any globalization-related variable. So it simply cannot be said that inequality necessarily rises with more trade, more foreign investment, and lower tariffs. For many globalizers, the overall change in distribution was small, and in some cases (such as the Philippines and Malaysia) it was even in favor of the poor. What changes in inequality do reflect are country-specific policies on education, taxes, and social protection.

It is important not to misunderstand this finding. China is an important example of a country that has had a large increase in inequality in the past decade, when the income of the bottom 20 percent has risen much less rapidly than per capita income. This trend may be related to greater openness, although domestic liberalization is a more likely cause. China started out in the 1970s with a highly equal distribution of income, and part of its reform has deliberately aimed at increasing the returns on education, which financially reward the better schooled. But the Chinese case is not typical; inequality has not increased in most of the developing countries that have opened up to foreign trade and investment. Furthermore, income distribution in China may have become more unequal, but the income of the poor in China has still risen rapidly. In fact, the country's progress in reducing poverty has been one of the most dramatic successes in history.

Because increased trade usually accompanies more rapid growth and does not systematically change household-income distribution, it generally is associated with improved well-being of the poor. Vietnam nicely illustrates this finding. As the nation has opened up, it has experienced a large increase in per capita income and no significant change in inequality. Thus the income of the poor has risen dramatically, and the number of Vietnamese living in absolute poverty dropped sharply from 75 percent of the population in 1988 to 37 percent in 1998. Of the poorest 5 percent of households in 1992, 98 percent were better off six years later. And the improved well-being is not just a matter of income. Child labor has declined, and school enrollment has increased. It should be no surprise that the vast majority of poor households in Vietnam benefited immediately from a more liberalized trading system, since the country's opening has resulted in exports of rice (produced by most of the poor farmers) and labor-intensive products such as footwear. But the experience of China and Vietnam is not unique. India and Uganda also enjoyed rapid poverty reduction as they grew along with their integration into the global economy. [. . .]

In sum, the integration of poor economies with richer ones over the past two decades has provided many opportunities for poor people to improve their lives. Examples of the beneficiaries of globalization can be found among Mexican migrants, Chinese factory workers, Vietnamese peasants, and Ugandan farmers. Many of the better-off in developing and rich countries alike also benefit. After all the rhetoric about globalization is stripped away, many of the policy questions come down to whether the rich world will make integrating with the world economy easy for those poor communities that want to do so. The world's poor have a large stake in how the rich countries answer.

22 Growth with Equity is Good for the Poor

Oxfam

[In 1997] the annual address given by World Bank President James Wolfensohn at the IMF-World Bank meeting was entitled *The challenge of inclusion*. It set out a clear commitment to growth with equity. While acknowledging that economic growth and globalisation was generating important benefits for many, Mr Wolfensohn spoke of 'the tragedy of exclusion'. The address set out a bold vision for the future, with the World Bank President calling on the international community to reduce the huge disparities in income and opportunity preventing the poor from participating in economic growth. 'In too many countries,' he said, 'the poorest 10 per cent of the population have less than 1 per cent of national income, while the richest 20 per cent enjoy over half.' Mr Wolfensohn concluded by pledging that the World Bank would work with others to change this picture and increase the share of wealth captured by the poor.

Today, this approach to development is under open attack, not least within the World Bank. The emphasis is shifting away from policies for achieving growth with equity, and towards policies geared toward growth alone. Distributional concerns are being removed from the political agenda. The highly-publicised report produced by David Dollar and Aart Kraay of the World Bank's Development Research Group, entitled *Growth is good for the poor*, is a recent example of the new trend. It represents an attempt to refute the case for more equitable patterns of distribution, as set out in early drafts of this year's World Development Report.

If *Growth is good for the poor* were just a research exercise, it could be dismissed as weak but largely irrelevant. Unfortunately, it comes with the imprimatur of the World Bank. The report represents a conscious attempt to shift the policy debate away from a concern with equity – and it will have a major bearing on policy choices made by southern governments and aid donors. This is of major concern because the specific choices it advocates are the wrong ones for poverty reduction.

Briefly summarised, *Growth is good for the poor* argues that existing patterns of globalisation are inherently good for poverty reduction. In place of Mr Wolfensohn's commitment to growth with equity, Dollar and Kraay are at one with their colleagues in some of the darker recesses of the IMF in arguing that 'standard pro-growth macroeconomic policies' are the most effective route to poverty reduction. The abysmal record of these policies in achieving poverty reduction in much of the developing world is ignored. Income distribution and public investment in health and education are regarded as peripheral to the core challenge of implementing policies to produce

Original publication details: Excerpted from Oxfam, "Growth with equity is good for the poor," *Oxfam Policy Papers* 6/00. Reproduced by permission from Oxfam Publishing, 274 Banbury Road, Oxford, OX2 7DZ.

high growth. The clear message to governments and donors is 'leave it to the market'. That message reflects an ideological hankering for a return to the 'golden era' of free market economics, and to the discredited 'trickle-down' approach to poverty reduction that guided World Bank and IMF policy advice to such disastrous effect in the 1980s.

In Oxfam's view, the Dollar and Kraay report suffers from two defects: it is 'anti-poor' and 'anti-growth'. It is anti-poor because it fails to address the key question of how to share the benefits of growth more equitably. And it is anti-growth because high levels of inequality are not just bad for poverty reduction, but also for economic efficiency. Extreme inequalities in land ownership, access to productive assets and income distribution serve to exclude poor people from access to market opportunities, and to undermine investment.

Contrary to claims advanced by Dollar and Kraay, few development agencies would contest the view that economic growth is a necessary requirement for poverty reduction. **But it is not the only requirement. The rate at which growth is converted into poverty reduction also matters. Growth associated with positive distributional changes in favour of the poor will have a greater impact on poverty than narrowly-based growth, in which the benefits are captured by the wealthy.** Crudely stated, the larger the share of any increment to growth captured by the poor, the faster the rate of poverty reduction. Conversely, the higher the level of inequality, the weaker the linkage between poverty reduction and growth.

The choice facing policy makers is not whether or not to go for growth – there is no alternative. It goes without saying that growth is necessary for poverty reduction and that the incomes of the poor will increase with growth. **The real question is how to convert growth into poverty reduction at the rate required to achieve the 2015 targets.** At a time when growth is increasingly associated with rising inequality in many countries, the challenge is to increase the share of growth captured by the poor. For policy makers concerned with poverty reduction, inequality does matter. If distribution can be improved without adverse implications for growth, then the rate of poverty reduction can be increased. In fact, there are good reasons why pro-poor distributional changes might have positive outcomes for growth. Where extreme inequality reinforces income poverty, it restricts investment by the poor and undermines the development of markets. Similarly, smallholder agriculture is more efficient than large-scale agriculture, in terms of both productivity and employment generation. For this reason redistribution of land has potential to be a pro-growth and pro-poor policy.

The relationship between economic growth and poverty reduction is of direct relevance to the challenge of meeting the 2015 target of halving income poverty. There is growing evidence that rising inequality is weakening the linkage between growth and poverty reduction. Parts of the developing world, such as Latin America, have succeeded in restoring macro-economic stability and growth, but with limited benefits for poverty reduction. In India, home to the largest number of people living below the poverty line, the impact of growth on poverty reduction is diminishing. By contrast, countries in East Asia have succeeded in combining high growth with rapid poverty reduction. If the world is to achieve the 2015 targets, developing countries need to grow on the East Asian pattern, rather than the highly unequal Latin American pattern. That is why it is essential that the quality of growth and distributional factors are given equal emphasis in the policy debate on growth and poverty reduction.

The World According to Dollar and Kraay

Much of the Dollar–Kraay report is spent caricaturing the arguments of others in order to create convenient straw men. The view (held by almost nobody but presented as widespread) that growth is bad for the poor is subjected to a withering critique. In the world of Dollar and Kraay, the choices are simple: if you are not 'pro-growth', you are 'anti-poor'. And if you are 'pro-growth', so the argument runs, then globalisation, liberalisation and free markets are the keys to success. Pro-poor distributional changes are seen as too slow, and too insignificant, to support poverty reduction on any scale. It follows that economic growth is the only effective route to poverty reduction.

For the benefit of the non-technical reader, the conclusions are stated in media-friendly sound-bites designed to send a clear message to policy makers. The basic argument can be summarised in three such sound-bites:

- **'Growth is good for the poor'.** The central contention is that the 'income of the poor rises one-to-one with overall growth' and that there is 'no apparent tendency for growth to be biased against poor income households'.
- **'Standard pro-growth macroeconomic policies are good for the poor'.** The report finds that 'private property rights, stability and openness directly create a good environment for poor households to increase their production and income'. Macro-economic stability and low inflation are not just pro-poor, they are 'super-pro-poor'. By contrast, the regression exercise purports to show that 'voice' and democratic institutions are statistically insignificant for growth and distribution. Primary education has small benefits for growth and no benefits for income distribution.
- **'Globalisation is good for the poor'.** This sub-divides into two propositions. First, 'trade openness is good for the poor' because it raises average incomes and the incomes of the poor in roughly equal proportion. Second, and more controversially, the report concludes: 'we do not find any evidence that capital account liberalisation is anti-poor'.

How Good for the Poor is Growth?

The principal 'discovery' made by Dollar and Kraay is that during periods of economic growth the average income of the poor increases by exactly the same proportion as overall income. They argue that income distribution patterns are irrelevant to poverty reduction. However, their report claims that there is no evidence of economic growth or greater openness being associated with rising inequality. The data upon which the latter conclusion is based is drawn principally from the 1970s and 1980s. Given that so much of the rapid trade liberalisation and capital account liberalisation associated with globalisation took place in the 1990s, there is a discrepancy between evidence and policy conclusions.

The purpose of this brief note is not to enter into a technical debate on econometric methods. However, it is worth noting that the Dollar and Kraay findings are inconsistent with other surveys. For instance, research carried out at the Institute for Development Studies in Sussex using data from 143 growth episodes found that the income share of the poorest 20 per cent fell in 69 cases.

The more serious problem with the Dollar and Kraay study is that it demonstrates the potential for absurd questions to produce absurd answers, even with the most sophisticated econometric models.

Even if it were true that economic growth raises the average income of the poor as much as the rich, policy makers with an interest in poverty reduction should be concerned with the share of the poor in national wealth. This is because for any given level of average income, the extent of poverty will depend on how income is distributed. Similarly, the distribution of any increment to growth will determine the rate at which growth is converted into poverty reduction. Highly unequal societies are bad at converting growth into poverty reduction. The rate of conversion – or 'the poverty reduction efficiency of growth' – matters because the more unequal the country, the faster the rate of growth needed to achieve any given level of poverty reduction.

The contrasting experiences of Latin America and East Asia illustrate the point. During 1990–1998, Latin America achieved real per capita economic growth rates of just under 2 per cent annually. But, despite this strong economic performance, the number of people living below the poverty line increased by 4.4 million, while the incidence of poverty fell by just over 1 per cent. By contrast, growth in East Asia lifted 174 million people out of poverty. Economic growth accounts for much of the difference, with per capita incomes in East Asia rising at 6 per cent per annum. But differences in the rate of growth are not the only factor. The rate of conversion from growth to poverty reduction is also critical. This can be expressed as the ratio of growth to changes in the incidence of poverty. The ratio of growth to poverty reduction in Latin America is 1:0.08, compared to 1:0.30 per cent in East Asia. **Every percentage point of growth in East Asia reduces the incidence of poverty at four times the rate achieved in Latin America.**

This difference matters. Even without an increase in economic growth, if Latin America had achieved East Asia's rate of conversion from growth to poverty reduction, there would be 3 million fewer people living below the poverty line. By contrast, if East Asia had been converting growth into poverty reduction at the Latin American rate, the incidence of poverty would be 9 per cent higher. This would translate into another 22 million people living below the poverty line. [. . .]

The Evidence

Contrary to the claims made by Dollar and Kraay, there is substantial evidence that current patterns of growth are reinforcing, rather than reducing, existing inequalities in income. This is true across a large spectrum of countries:

- In India, home to almost half of those living on less than $1 a day, the rate of poverty reduction has slowed in the 1990s, with the rural poor falling further behind, and the gap between richer and poorer states widening.
- In China, the number of poor increased by 2 million between 1997–1998, reversing a long-run trend. Widening income gaps between coastal and interior areas are largely responsible.
- In Vietnam, average income in the northern region increased by 31 per cent between 1993–1998 – less than half of the increase recorded in the south-east region. Poverty rates in the northern region are 59 per cent, compared to 8 per cent in the south-east.

- In Mexico, economic recovery has been associated with a widening income gap between rural populations in the poverty belt states of the South, and northern regions linked to the US economy. Between 1990–1996, the number of people in poverty increased by 11 million.
- In Eastern Europe and the Former Soviet Union historically unprecedented increases in inequality have reinforced the effects of slow growth, with the incidence of poverty increasing five-fold in the 1990s.
- In Latin America, the world's most unequal region, recent household survey evidence shows that inequality has increased in fifteen countries, including Peru, Brazil, Honduras and Nicaragua.
- In Britain, the proportion of the population with less than half average income trebled between 1979–1990, with the poorest 20–30 per cent failing to benefit from economic growth. Child poverty trebled in this period.

There is clear evidence from current and past experience that distributional changes do impact on poverty. Once again, the experience of Latin America is instructive. During the lost decade of the 1980s, an additional 100 million people in the region fell below the poverty line. Economic recession was an important factor, but it was reinforced by adverse distributional changes. According to the Inter-American Development Bank, the deteriorating patterns of income distribution were responsible for half of the increase in poverty.

It is not just during periods of economic recession that distribution influences poverty reduction. Research into growth periods under structural adjustment programmes has shown that worsening inequality acts as a brake on poverty reduction. Growth periods during the 1980s and 1990s in Kenya, Tanzania and Ghana were characterised by widening income gaps between rich and poor, between urban and rural areas, and between marginal and commercial rural areas. The point in all of these cases is not that growth has failed to reduce poverty, it is that adverse distributional shifts have weakened the effects of growth on poverty reduction. The key policy priority is to understand what measures are needed to enable poor people to participate more equitably in markets. Simplistic assertions to the effect that growth is ultimately good for everyone are not a helpful starting point. [. . .]

Standard Macro-Economic Policies and Globalisation Are Best for Poverty Reduction

Much of the Dollar and Kraay report is spent making a case for free markets, purportedly on the basis of data on the relationship between growth and distribution. Trade liberalisation, capital market liberalisation and economic globalisation are deemed to be inherently good. Dollar and Kraay are unable to find 'any evidence of a significant negative impact of openness to international trade on incomes of the poor', and they therefore jump in characteristic style to the conclusion that 'globalisation is good for the poor'. After reviewing a range of potential factors influencing growth and distribution, they claim that standard macro-economic policies, with an emphasis on low inflation and private property, are 'super-pro poor'. Public investment in health and education is presented as being only marginally relevant for growth and income distribution.

Part of the problem with the positive picture presented by Dollar and Kraay is that it contrasts so starkly with the experience of poor people in a large range of countries. There is a gulf between their assertions and the real experiences of many countries. In the Philippines, the liberalisation of agricultural markets left desperately poor producers in the island of Mindanao facing increased competition from subsidised imports from the United States. Producers in southern Mexico have faced similar problems. In Tanzania, the benefits of coffee market liberalisation have been unequally shared between richer and poorer coffee growing areas. In Zambia, maize market liberalisation undermined the position of producers in the most marginal areas. In China and Vietnam, increased openness has widened income gaps between regions, and between rich and poor. One recent World Bank report, cited in current drafts of the World Development Report, estimated that the benefits associated with trade liberalisation have been captured by the wealthiest 20 per cent, with the poorest 40 per cent becoming poorer.

The real issue here is not one of free trade versus protectionism. There are strong efficiency grounds for opening markets, especially in the importation of capital and intermediate goods. But the extravagent claims made about the benefits of openness in this area for poverty reduction are not warranted. Poor people are often excluded from market opportunities by a lack of productive assets, weak infrastructure, poor education and ill-health. **The degree to which trade liberalisation benefits the poor will depend in part on the extent to which government addresses these problems. But experience clearly demonstrates that the benefits are not automatic.** In fact, whether for growth or poverty reduction, openness per se is less significant than the complementary policies for managing growth that are developed by governments.

In the case of capital market liberalisation, Dollar and Kraay's claims are even less tenable, not least because their data does not extend to the period of financial crisis in East Asia. The liberalisation of capital markets in a context of weak financial regulation and volatile global markets contributed to a major recession in the region, with large-scale increases in poverty. The social costs have been enormous. In Thailand, the health budget has been cut by one-third. In Indonesia, the poverty rate increased by almost 50 per cent, with another 10 million people falling below the poverty line.

On the subject of education, Dollar and Kraay's findings run counter to those from a wide body of research, not to mention the views expressed by poor people themselves in participatory poverty assessments. Not surprisingly, there is clear evidence that the poorest households in Latin America have less education. In Mexico, the poorest 10 per cent of households receive on average two years of education, compared to 12 years for the wealthiest 10 per cent. According to the Inter-American Development Bank, education differences are the single biggest factor in explaining income inequality in the region. In Brazil and Mexico, workers with six years of education earn almost twice as much as workers with no education. Evidence from a large group of countries in the region suggests that returns to education are rising as demand for skilled labour, linked to education, increases. As in other regions – and in developed countries – inequalities in education are reinforcing income inequalities. Moreover, in almost all developing countries lack of education is a passport to low-income and poverty. Several studies using household data on education, poverty and income distribution provide grounds for questioning the results of the Dollar and Kraay study. For instance, panel data covering 2,678 Vietnamese households over the period 1993–98 found that the higher the level of education attained at the start of the period, the faster the subsequent income growth. On average, the expenditure levels of those with no education declined, while they increased for those with primary and secondary education. In Vietnam, the poverty rate in households

Table 22 *...gional poverty indicators*

	Number of poor (millions)		Headcount index		Required rate of poverty reduction to meet 2015 target	Actual rate of poverty reduction, 1990–1998
		1998	1990	1998		
East Asia	452	2 3	27.6	15.3	2	2.40
Latin America	74	78	16.8	15.6	2	0.15
South Asia	495	522	44.0	40.0	2	0.50
Sub-Saharan Africa	242	290	47.7	46.3	2	0.17
Total all developing and transition economies	1.276	1.190	29	24	2	0.62

headed by someone with no education is 68 per cent. In households headed by someone with a secondary education the figure falls to 41 per cent.

Making Markets Work for the Poor

For policy makers concerned with poverty reduction, the real challenge is that of making markets work for the poor. There is no blueprint. But there are some rules. Markets will not work for the poor where exclusion from educational opportunity or poor health restricts ability to generate income, or to raise productivity and wages. Similarly, market-reforms can create opportunities, but poor producers cannot take advantage of opportunities if they lack access to land, credit, skills, good health or to marketing infrastructure. The issue of power in the market place is also important. People do not enter markets as equals – and market outcomes reflect power relations. State intervention can compensate for unequal power relations, for instance by setting minimum employment and wage standards.

Achieving the patterns of growth with equity needed to meet the 2015 poverty reduction targets is not just about taxing growth and transferring income to the poor in the form of social welfare provision. Such transfers can play an important role in compensating for income inequality, as they have in several OECD countries. But for poor countries poverty reduction and enhanced equity requires a production-based approach. That is, the poor need to be provided with opportunities to produce and invest their way out of poverty, rather than to await the trickle down of wealth. This implies government commitment to the redistribution of opportunity through the transfer of assets, the prioritisation of the poor in public spending provision, and the management of market liberalisation to protect the livelihoods of vulnerable producers.

None of this is to argue against the primacy of growth as an engine for poverty reduction. But growth without equity is a prescription for deepening social divisions, the continuation of mass poverty and – ultimately – economic inefficiency. This is the model of the future offered by Dollar and Kraay. It is a model that deserves to be returned to the museum of failed economics.

23 Beyond Good Intentions: Corporate Citizenship for a New Century

Mary Robinson

[. . .]

Beyond Good Intentions

The title I have chosen for my lecture today is "Beyond Good Intentions: Corporate Citizenship for a New Century". I chose this title for two reasons:

First, to repeat a point which I made at the Albert Medal ceremony last year: business leaders don't have to wait – indeed, increasingly they can't afford to wait – for governments to pass and enforce legislation before they pursue "good practices" in support of international human rights, labour and environmental standards within their own operations and in the societies of which they are part. The public increasingly expects corporations to act in a socially responsible way. But it is also a business led debate, as the recent annual meeting of the Institute of Directors here in London illustrated.

With globalisation has come the growing sense that we are all responsible in some way for helping promote and protect the rights of our neighbours whether they live on the next street or on the next continent. The Universal Declaration of Human Rights is not simply a charter of rights, but speaks of duty in very broad terms. Article 29 provides: "Everyone has duties to the community . . ." What we need to do in the new century is to acknowledge that the community is no longer just our nearest neighbourhood but the global community.

Second, I wanted to indicate that good intentions clearly won't be enough. It is vital that the business community focuses not only on policies of good corporate citizenship but also their implementation in practice. If it really wants to prove to a growing number of sceptics that globalisation can be made to work not just for the privileged, but also for the powerless, it is practice that matters.

Despite the progress made at the policy level in recognising the links between profitable business and responsible social performance, many observers are still not convinced that company commitments are much more than window dressing in terms of the way business gets done around the world. Recent studies have shown that the

Original publication details: Excerpted from Mary Robinson (UN High Commissioner for Human Rights), "Beyond Good Intentions: Corporate Citizenship for a New Century," Royal Society of Arts World Leaders Lecture, May 7, 2002. Reprinted by permission of United Nations Publications.

business world has not succeeded in persuading the public that companies are serious about corporate social responsibility in practice.

Research published late last year by the *Observer* newspaper reveals high levels of scepticism among leaders from the voluntary sector, education, local government and media over companies' claims that they have improved their environmental and social performance. These leaders believe strongly that only legislation is effective. They want laws to compel companies to act responsibly. This significant sector of public opinion is convinced that voluntary approaches, though strongly favored by the private sector, are piece-meal and largely ineffective because only limited pressure for change can come from consumers, investors or campaigning groups.

On the environment, this debate is over whether or not business can "green itself from the inside". Environmental groups say it is not going to happen. Some of these groups are campaigning to have the Johannesburg Summit on Sustainable Development in August adopt proposals for an international convention to enforce responsible corporate behaviour. They seek an international regulatory framework on corporate activities as the best way to ensure proper respect for environmental and social standards around the world.

I would argue that it is not a simple case of choosing between voluntary or regulatory systems to induce corporate responsibility. If indeed we believe that universal principles in the areas of human rights, labour rights and the environment should become an integral part of business strategies and day-to-day operations, regulation alone will not be sufficient. It must be coupled with a concerted effort to stimulate good practices.

Regulation is crucial to minimize abuses and to enforce compliance with minimum norms. But regulation alone won't establish the business case for making necessary changes. To do so, we must provide incentives so that doing the right thing also makes good business sense. By focusing exclusively on regulation, business is driven toward the logic of managing the costs of compliance. The result is that society loses out on the power of business to innovate and establish new forms of behaviour that are so desperately needed.

Millions of people who are denied their rights today want to enjoy them now, not in some distant future. To achieve that goal we will have to embrace every good idea, every committed partner and every possible approach that can make a difference.

The Global Compact

One way of making progress is to engage the private sector in achieving public goals. Engagement between the UN and civil society in furthering international objectives is not new. Although the number, diversity and influence of civil society organizations and private enterprises has grown markedly over the past decade, they have been interacting with the United Nations since its founding. Several non-governmental organizations, including representatives of business associations, participated in the San Francisco Conference of 1945.

Today, the UN is pursuing its engagement with the private sector on corporate social responsibility issues through a number of different avenues. One of the key initiatives is the Global Compact. Formally launched by the Secretary-General in July 2000, the Global Compact calls on business leaders, trade unions and NGOs to join forces behind a set of core values in the areas of human rights, labour standards and the environment.

Let me outline briefly what we are asking corporations to do in these three areas. With respect to human rights, corporations should, first, ensure that they support and respect human rights within their sphere of influence as set out in the Universal Declaration of Human Rights and second, ensure they are not themselves complicit in human rights abuses. On labour standards, businesses should uphold freedom of association and collective bargaining and make sure they are not employing under-age children or forced labour, either directly or indirectly, and that, in their hiring and firing policies they do not discriminate on grounds of race, creed, gender or ethnic origin. And in relation to the environment, companies should support a precautionary approach to environmental challenges, promote greater environmental responsibility and encourage the development and diffusion of environmentally friendly technologies.

Several hundred companies from a wide range of countries North and South, such as Russia, China, Argentina, South Africa, Germany, Norway, Indonesia, Thailand, the United Kingdom, and the United States, have responded to the Global Compact and are working with trade unions, civil society and the UN to make its principles part of the strategic vision and everyday practices of companies in all regions. I have learned of local initiatives in discussion with business leaders of companies large and small in places as far apart as São Paulo, Brazil, organized by the Ethos Institute, and New Delhi, organized by the Institute of Indian Industry. It has been heartening to see women business leaders to the fore in these discussions.

What specifically are companies supporting the Global Compact being exhorted to do? As a first step, we are calling on them to:

publicly express support for the Compact and its principles in mission statements and annual reports; post on the Global Compact website concrete examples of progress made or lessons learned in implementing the Global Compact principles; undertake activities jointly with the United Nations that advance the implementation of the Compact's principles or support wider UN goals such as poverty eradication.

The Global Compact is a voluntary initiative to promote good corporate citizenship. I want to stress that it is not, and must not be, a mere public relations exercise. A commitment to the Global Compact has to lead to concrete actions in support of the core principles I have explained. Equally, when such actions are taken, a company deserves recognition.

But how will we know that real changes are happening? The Global Compact is developing a learning forum which will serve as an information bank of disparate experiences – some successful and some not – of company efforts to implement the Compact's nine principles. Through this learning approach we hope to develop the elements of good practice that address specific human rights, labour and environmental issues relevant to all industry sectors. The idea is to move toward a system of performance-based good practices, reflecting the judgment of the broader international community, rather than the situation of asking companies simply to adhere to varied and often weak local standards and legislation.

It is too early to say whether this initiative will bring about large-scale improvements in business practices around the world. But I believe it is an experiment worth trying.

Many NGOs have argued that without monitoring mechanisms in place to ensure adherence to its principles, there can be little hope that the Global Compact will produce real change in performance by companies. The Global Compact does not substitute for other approaches that rely on monitoring and enforcement. It is designed to complement such approaches by giving business and other sectors of society space to try out new ideas, and to make a difference through voluntary action. [. . .]

Turning to the second principle of the Global Compact – the obligation of companies to avoid complicity in human rights abuses – may I say that I do not underestimate the difficulties of defining the boundaries of business responsibility in this context. In order to draw those boundaries, it is important first to understand how the concept of complicity is being used today.

There can be no doubt that a corporation which knowingly assists a State in violating international human rights standards could be viewed as directly complicit in such a violation. For example, a company that promoted, or assisted with, the forced relocation of people in circumstances which would constitute a violation of international human rights could be considered directly complicit in the violation. The corporation could be legally responsible if it or its agents knew of the likely effects of their assistance.

But the contemporary notion of corporate complicity in human rights abuses is not confined to direct involvement in the execution of illegal acts by others. The complicity concept has also been used to describe the corporate position in relation to violations by government or rebel groups when the company benefits from these violations. Violations committed by security forces, such as the suppression of peaceful protest against business activities, or the use of repressive measures while guarding company facilities, are often cited as examples of corporate complicity in human rights abuses. In legal terms, where human rights violations occur in the context of a business operation, the company need not necessarily cause the harm directly for it to become implicated in the abuses.

Perhaps most challenging is the growing expectation that companies will raise systematic or continuous human rights abuses with the appropriate authorities. Indeed, it reflects the growing acceptance by the public, and by leading companies, that there is something culpable about failing to exercise influence in such circumstances. Whether or not such silent complicity would give rise to a finding of a breach of a legal obligation against a company in a court of law, it has become increasingly clear that the moral dimension of corporate action – or inaction – has taken on significant importance.

We have, I believe, made some progress in analyzing what is meant by the key phrases: "sphere of influence" and "complicity in human rights abuses". These concepts shape the expectations on companies. They can also reflect legal requirements now and in the future.

But corporate responsibility is only part of the picture. What I want to stress again is that, although I am confident that initiatives like the Global Compact can help to build consensus and reach practical solutions to contemporary human rights challenges, they do not imply that the role of government in ensuring respect for human rights has become any less important. Primary responsibility for the promotion and protection of human rights remains with governments. Voluntary initiatives are no substitute for government action. [. . .]

24 The Case Against 'Corporate Social Responsibility'

David Henderson

Issues concerning the social responsibilities of private businesses have been the subject of study and dispute for decades if not centuries. But in recent years a new way of thinking on the subject has arisen and taken hold. Both in the business world and outside it, there is wide and growing support for today's conception of Corporate Social Responsibility (CSR).

New Vistas

There is no universally agreed statement of just what CSR means and implies, and ideas on the subject are still evolving. All the same, a common body of doctrine has now taken shape and won general approval among those who favour the approach.

According to this way of thinking, a combination of recent changes on the world scene and pressures from public opinion now requires businesses to take on a new role, a newly-defined mission. They should play a leading part in achieving the shared objectives of public policy and making the world a better place. In doing so, they should embrace the notion of 'corporate citizenship'. They should run their affairs, in close conjunction with an array of different 'stakeholders', so as to pursue the common goal of 'sustainable development'. Sustainable development is said to have three dimensions – 'economic', 'environmental' and 'social'. Hence companies should set objectives, measure their performance, and have that performance independently audited, in relation to all three. They should aim to meet the 'triple bottom line', rather than focusing narrowly on profitability and shareholder value.

All this applies to privately-owned businesses in general, and in particular to large multinational enterprises (MNEs). Only by acting in this way (so the argument goes) can companies respond to 'society's expectations'. Making such a positive response is presented as the key to long-run commercial success for individual corporations in today's world. This is because profits depend on reputation, which in turn depends increasingly on being seen to act in a socially responsible way. Thus taking the path of CSR will in fact be good for enterprise profitability: it will bring and sustain support and custom from outside the firm, and make for greater loyalty and keenness from its employees. To embrace corporate citizenship represents enlightened self-interest on the part of business.

Original publication details: Excerpted from David Henderson, "The Case Against 'Corporate Social Responsibility'," *Policy*, 17, 2, Winter 2001. Copyright © 2001 by the Centre for Independent Studies, Sydney, www.cis.org.au Reprinted by permission of *Policy*. Based on David Henderson, *Misguided Virtue: False Notions of Corporate Social Responsibility* (New Zealand Business Roundtable and Institute of Economic Affairs, 2001).

There is also a wider dimension, going beyond the individual corporation. The adoption of CSR by businesses generally is seen as necessary to ensure continuing public support for the private enterprise system as a whole. For modern capitalism to be made acceptable and hence viable, it has to be given 'a human face'.

Today's consensus

CSR has caught on. It has been endorsed by a substantial and growing number of businesses, especially among the MNEs which are under close outside scrutiny and have in many cases been subject to hostile attacks or campaigns. Evidence of the spread of CSR among companies across the world is to be seen in the substantial and still-increasing membership of business organisations that are committed to it. Prominent among these are the World Business Council for Sustainable Development, the Prince of Wales Business Leaders Forum, and what was until recently the European Business Network for Social Inclusion and has just been renamed CSR Europe. In many industries, including in particular such exposed cases as mining, petroleum and pharmaceuticals, it is now unusual, and arguably imprudent, for a leading MNE to remain aloof from such CSR-oriented organisations. To join them provides a badge, a token, of corporate citizenship. [. . .]

Outside the business milieu, CSR is typically favoured, and often demanded, by so-called 'public interest' non-governmental organisations (NGOs), many of which are leading and forceful critics of businesses in general and MNEs in particular. In many cases, the endorsement of CSR by companies can be seen, in part at least, as a response to well publicised attacks on them as greedy, secretive, exploitative and concerned only with making money for their owners and managers. The development of the Internet has opened up new possibilities for NGOs to engage in effective worldwide campaigns against what they see as threats, abuses or non-responsible conduct on the part of businesses or others.

Last but far from least, many governments have endorsed the notion. For example, the present British government has appointed a minister formally charged with the duty of advancing the cause of corporate social responsibility in general. Again, the European Commission, with encouragement from ministers of the member governments of the European Union (EU), has just issued a 'green paper' on CSR specifically. This marks the beginning of a six-month 'consultative exercise', the aim of which is reported to be the establishment of a 'fully-fledged CSR policy' covering the EU as a whole. [. . .]

Twin objections

I believe that this consensus view is misguided, for two main related reasons. First, the doctrine of CSR rests on a false view of the world. Second, a general adherence to it will have damaging consequences for people in general, even though it may contribute to the profitability of individual businesses.

Oversimplifying the issues

The picture of reality that CSR presents is at fault in several respects. For one thing, it greatly oversimplifies issues, problems and choices. Its supporters characteristically take for granted the idea that the problems of today have known and agreed 'solutions'. In particular, they speak and write as though sustainable development were a well defined and obviously desirable objective: they imply that there is general agreement on what it involves and how it is to be achieved. This is not at all the case. Admittedly the notion is an appealing one, which has now gained wide support across the world: to raise doubts about sustainable development may appear as eccentric or perverse. All the same, there are both uncertainties and substantial differences of opinion as to its meaning, interpretation and usefulness as a guide to the conduct and policies of businesses – as also of governments. Again, the three-fold division into 'economic' 'environmental' and 'social' aspects, and with it the notion of a triple bottom line, is widely taken as well established but is in fact highly dubious.

The notion of 'society's expectations' is likewise open to question. Many supporters of CSR simply assume that these expectations are given authentic voice in what the leading critics of business – NGOs, commentators, parliamentarians and so on – are currently saying. But how far these critics are representative is debatable. It is in fact open to doubt whether what most people now expect of businesses is that they should work with stakeholders in pursuit of sustainable development and the triple bottom line, even though, as will be seen, this could well result in higher costs and prices for the products and services in question. In any case, not all public expectations, and the demands arising from them, are reasonable and well founded. Businesses have a right, and arguably a duty, to argue a case against views which they see as mistaken and proposed measures which they think could lead to harmful consequences. This aspect of corporate social responsibility is scarcely mentioned in the writings on CSR that I have seen. The emphasis is on appeasement of critics and compliance with demands on business.

Embracing global salvationism

Often though not always, CSR advocates, both in the business world and outside it, are adherents of what I call *global salvationism*. This goes with an acceptance of alarmist views on the state of the environment and the damage done to it by business-related activities, a belief that fateful choices now have to be made on behalf of humanity and the planet, and a distorted view of globalisation and its effects. In accepting these ideas, and by financing organisations that give currency to them, many businesses have joined forces with critics of the market economy, both in the NGOs and elsewhere.

Contrary to global salvationist assertions, it is not the case that globalisation has brought with it 'social exclusion', nor has it 'marginalised' poor countries. Again, it has not brought disproportionate benefits to MNEs in particular, nor has it increased their power to influence events while reducing that of governments. To the contrary: governments retain their capacity to act, while in recent years privatisation, deregulation and the freeing of cross-border trade and capital flows have combined to *reduce* the economic power of businesses by making markets more open and competitive. The idea that corporations now have to take on new and wider national and international responsibilities, because they have become more powerful while governments have become weaker, has no basis. Yet it has been uncritically repeated by business executives, business organisations, and others in the business world, as well as by outsiders.

But the trouble with CSR is not just that it rests on dubious or false assumptions. Putting it into effect is liable to do significant harm.

Reducing welfare

Within businesses, the adoption of CSR carries with it a high probability of cost increases and impaired performance. Managers have to take account of a wider range of goals and concerns, and to involve themselves in new and time-consuming processes of consultation with outside stakeholders. New systems of accounting, monitoring and auditing are called for. On top of all this, the adoption of more exacting self-chosen environmental and 'social' standards is liable to add to costs, all the more so if firms insist on observance of these same standards by their partners, suppliers and contractors.

There is no reason to believe that these various adverse effects on enterprise performance will be more than offset by gains. In particular, and contrary to what is often assumed by supporters of CSR, it is not the case that progress necessarily results from the adoption of 'higher' norms and standards. There are many instances where insistence on these has brought higher costs in exchange for benefits which were dubious or disproportionately small. There is an obvious risk that, in the name of CSR, and in the pursuit of questionable objectives such as 'eco-efficiency' and 'social justice' that are said to reflect 'society's expectations', businesses will find themselves going further down such a path. This would make everyone worse off.

There are also risks that go beyond individual firms. Insofar as 'socially responsible' businesses find that their new role is bringing with it higher costs and lower profits, they have a strong interest in ensuring that their unregenerate rivals are compelled to follow suit, whether through public pressure or government regulation. The effect of such enforced conformity is to limit competition and hence to worsen performance across the economy as a whole. The system effects of CSR, as well as the enterprise effects, will tend to make people in general poorer.

The greatest potential for harm of this latter kind arises from attempts, whether by governments or by businesses in the name of CSR and 'global corporate citizenship', to impose worldwide norms and standards. Since circumstances differ widely across countries, such official and unofficial regulatory actions would restrict the scope for mutually beneficial trade and investment flows. In particular, they would hold back the development of poor countries by suppressing employment opportunities within them.

Prominent businesses which have adhered to CSR have lent their support to dubious corporatist notions of 'global governance', in which businesses join hands with governments, international agencies and leading NGOs to raise standards across frontiers. A recent leading instance of this tendency is the so-called Global Compact, initiated by the Secretary-General of the United Nations. Besides carrying with them the danger of over-regulating the world economy, such collaborative ventures confer on organisations which are not politically accountable – both businesses and NGOs – powers and responsibilities that do not rightly belong to them.

Corporate irresponsibility

In embracing CSR, many corporations and business organisations have failed to contest, or have even endorsed, the arguments and demands of anti-business activist groups. They have treated these arguments and demands as reflecting the views of 'society'. They have accepted many of the leading ideas of global salvationism, and failed to make an effective case for the market economy. Many of their public statements show little regard for easily accessible facts, arguments and ideas. With few exceptions, the contribution of the business world to public debate on these broad issues of public policy has been, and continues to be, inadequate or worse. It is high time for those leading corporations that have retained a sense of proportion to consider how they could improve this state of affairs.

Strengthening the Market Economy

The advocates of CSR want to remake capitalism anew. They see defence of the market economy in terms of making businesses more popular and respected, through meeting 'society's expectations' which they identify with current radical programmes for change.

Such an attitude confuses ends and means. It may well be true, or become true as the doctrine prevails, that firms must take the path of CSR in the interests of survival and profitability in an unfriendly world. But insofar as their doing so weakens enterprise performance, limits economic freedom and restricts competition, it deprives private business of its distinctive virtues and rationale.

The case for private business, and its key role in contributing to the general welfare, does not depend on the willingness of those who direct it to embrace 'corporate citizenship'. It largely rests on the links between private ownership, competition and economic freedom within a largely market-directed economy. In such an economy, firms make profits, and can only make profits, by providing products that people wish to buy of their own free choice, and by being enterprising and innovative in doing so. The most effective way to improve the business contribution to society is to extend the scope and improve the functioning of markets. Among the advocates of CSR, there is little recognition of this aspect, and the role of profits as an essential signalling device is often disregarded or played down.

Striking a balance

None of this is to say that questions relating to the conduct of private businesses today, and the rules and conventions that bear on it, have simple answers. Now as in the past, there are unresolved issues of corporation law, corporate governance, business ethics, and the relationship between private profitability and the general welfare. Today as always, companies have moral as well as legal obligations. Now more than ever, they are under pressure to justify what they do, and need to be concerned with their public reputation. They have to show that they treat people in ways that are fair and humane, that their activities are not giving rise to seriously damaging external effects, and that, where current environmental and social concerns appear to them well founded, they are ready to contribute, in ways that are consistent with their primary purpose and obligations as commercial entities, to common efforts to deal with these.

But responsible conduct, in this sense, is not to be identified with adopting CSR. To the contrary, it is neither necessary nor wise for corporations to endorse dubious notions of 'sustainable development' and the 'triple bottom line'; to make questionable assumptions as to 'society's expectations', and to treat these supposed expectations as unchallengeable; to approve without qualification the principle of 'stakeholder engagement'; to accept, or acquiesce in, the tangle of false doctrines that makes up global salvationism; to go out of their way to appease anti-business groups; and to lend support to ill-conceived ventures in 'global governance'. In relation to any useful conception of corporate social responsibility, all these lines of thought and action are simply excess baggage. Yet all of them form an integral part of today's CSR.

Conclusion

Like sustainable development, corporate social responsibility is an appealing concept, and the general notion is – or was until recently – a helpful one. But the current widely-held doctrine of CSR is deeply flawed. It rests on a mistaken view of issues and events, and its general adoption by businesses would reduce welfare and under-mine the market economy.

25 Globalism's Discontents

Joseph E. Stiglitz

Few subjects have polarized people throughout the world as much as globalization. Some see it as the way of the future, bringing unprecedented prosperity to everyone, everywhere. Others, symbolized by the Seattle protestors of December 1999, fault globalization as the source of untold problems, from the destruction of native cultures to increasing poverty and immiseration. In this article, I want to sort out the different meanings of globalization. In many countries, globalization has brought huge benefits to a few with few benefits to the many. But in the case of a few countries, it has brought enormous benefit to the many. Why have there been these huge differences in experiences? The answer is that globalization has meant different things in different places.

The countries that have managed globalization on their own, such as those in East Asia, have, by and large, ensured that they reaped huge benefits and that those benefits were equitably shared; they were able substantially to control the terms on which they engaged with the global economy. By contrast, the countries that have, by and large, had globalization managed for them by the International Monetary Fund and other international economic institutions have not done so well. The problem is thus not with globalization but with how it has been managed.

The international financial institutions have pushed a particular ideology – market fundamentalism – that is both bad economics and bad politics; it is based on premises concerning how markets work that do not hold even for developed countries, much less for developing countries. The IMF has pushed these economics policies without a broader vision of society or the role of economics within society. And it has pushed these policies in ways that have undermined emerging democracies.

More generally, globalization itself has been governed in ways that are undemocratic and have been disadvantageous to developing countries, especially the poor within those countries. The Seattle protestors pointed to the absence of democracy and of transparency, the governance of the international economic institutions by and for special corporate and financial interests, and the absence of countervailing democratic checks to ensure that these informal and *public* institutions serve a general interest. In these complaints, there is more than a grain of truth.

Beneficial Globalization

Of the countries of the world, those in East Asia have grown the fastest and done most to reduce poverty. And they have done so, emphatically, via "globalization."

Original publication details: Excerpted from Joseph E. Stiglitz, "Globalism's Discontents," *The American Prospect*, 13, 1, January 1–14, 2002. Reprinted by permission of *The American Prospect*, 5 Broad Street, Boston, MA 02109, USA. All rights reserved.

Their growth has been based on exports – by taking advantage of the global market for exports and by closing the technology gap. It was not just gaps in capital and other resources that separated the developed from the less-developed countries, but differences in knowledge. East Asian countries took advantage of the "globalization of knowledge" to reduce these disparities. But while some of the countries in the region grew by opening themselves up to multinational companies, others, such as Korea and Taiwan, grew by creating their own enterprises. Here is the key distinction: Each of the most successful globalizing countries determined its own pace of change; each made sure as it grew that the benefits were shared equitably; each rejected the basic tenets of the "Washington Consensus," which argued for a minimalist role for government and rapid privatization and liberalization.

In East Asia, government took an active role in managing the economy. The steel industry that the Korean government created was among the most efficient in the world – performing far better than its private-sector rivals in the United States (which, though private, are constantly turning to the government for protection and for subsidies). Financial markets were highly regulated. My research shows that those regulations promoted growth. It was only when these countries stripped away the regulations, under pressure from the U.S. Treasury and the IMF, that they encountered problems.

During the 1960s, 1970s, and 1980s, the East Asian economies not only grew rapidly but were remarkably stable. Two of the countries most touched by the 1997–1998 economic crisis had had in the preceding three decades not a single year of negative growth; two had only one year – a better performance than the United States or the other wealthy nations that make up the Organization for Economic Cooperation and Development (OECD). The single most important factor leading to the troubles that several of the East Asian countries encountered in the late 1990s – the East Asia crisis – was the rapid liberalization of financial and capital markets. In short, the countries of East Asia benefited from globalization because they made globalization work for them; it was when they succumbed to the pressures from the outside that they ran into problems that were beyond their own capacity to manage well.

Globalization can yield immense benefits. Elsewhere in the developing world, globalization of knowledge has brought improved health, with life spans increasing at a rapid pace. How can one put a price on these benefits of globalization? Globalization has brought still other benefits: Today there is the beginning of a globalized civil society that has begun to succeed with such reforms as the Mine Ban Treaty and debt forgiveness for the poorest highly indebted countries (the Jubilee movement). The globalization protest movement itself would not have been possible without globalization.

The Darker Side of Globalization

How then could a trend with the power to have so many benefits have produced such opposition? Simply because it has not only failed to live up to its potential but frequently has had very adverse effects. But this forces us to ask, why has it had such adverse effects? The answer can be seen by looking at each of the economic elements of globalization as pursued by the international financial institutions and especially by the IMF.

The most adverse effects have arisen from the liberalization of financial and capital markets – which has posed risks to developing countries without commensurate rewards. The liberalization has left them prey to hot money pouring into the country, an influx that has fueled speculative real-estate booms; just as suddenly, as investor sentiment changes, the money is pulled out, leaving in its wake economic devastation. Early on, the IMF said that these countries were being rightly punished for pursuing bad economic policies. But as the crisis spread from country to country, even those that the IMF had given high marks found themselves ravaged.

The IMF often speaks about the importance of the discipline provided by capital markets. In doing so, it exhibits a certain paternalism, a new form of the old colonial mentality: "We in the establishment, we in the North who run our capital markets, know best. Do what we tell you to do, and you will prosper." The arrogance is offensive, but the objection is more than just to style. The position is highly undemocratic: There is an implied assumption that democracy by itself does not provide sufficient discipline. But if one is to have an external disciplinarian, one should choose a good disciplinarian who knows what is good for growth, who shares one's values. One doesn't want an arbitrary and capricious taskmaster who one moment praises you for your virtues and the next screams at you for being rotten to the core. But capital markets are just such a fickle taskmaster; even ardent advocates talk about their bouts of irrational exuberance followed by equally irrational pessimism.

Lessons of Crisis

Nowhere was the fickleness more evident than in the last global financial crisis. Historically, most of the disturbances in capital flows into and out of a country are not the result of factors inside the country. Major disturbances arise, rather, from influences outside the country. When Argentina suddenly faced high interest rates in 1998, it wasn't because of what Argentina did but because of what happened in Russia. Argentina cannot be blamed for Russia's crisis.

Small developing countries find it virtually impossible to withstand this volatility. I have described capital-market liberalization with a simple metaphor: Small countries are like small boats. Liberalizing capital markets is like setting them loose on a rough sea. Even if the boats are well captained, even if the boats are sound, they are likely to be hit broadside by a big wave and capsize. But the IMF pushed for the boats to set forth into the roughest parts of the sea before they were seaworthy, with untrained captains and crews, and without life vests. No wonder matters turned out so badly!

To see why it is important to choose a disciplinarian who shares one's values, consider a world in which there were free mobility of skilled labor. Skilled labor would then provide discipline. Today, a country that does not treat capital well will find capital quickly withdrawing; in a world of free labor mobility, if a country did not treat skilled labor well, it too would withdraw. Workers would worry about the quality of their children's education and their family's health care, the quality of their environment and of their own wages and working conditions. They would say to the government: If you fail to provide these essentials, we will move elsewhere. That is a far cry from the kind of discipline that free-flowing capital provides.

The liberalization of capital markets has not brought growth: How can one build factories or create jobs with money that can come in and out of a country overnight? And it gets worse: Prudential behavior requires countries to set aside reserves equal to the amount of short-term lending; so if a firm in a poor country borrows $100 million at, say, 20 percent interest rates short-term from a bank in the United States, the government must set aside a corresponding amount. The reserves are typically held in U.S. Treasury bills – a safe, liquid asset. In effect, the country is borrowing $100 million from the United States and lending $100 million to the United States. But when it borrows, it pays a high interest rate, 20 percent; when it lends, it receives a low interest rate, around 4 percent. This may be great for the United States, but it can hardly help the growth of the poor country. There is also a high *opportunity* cost of the reserves; the money could have been much better spent on building rural roads or constructing schools or health clinics. But instead, the country is, in effect, forced to lend money to the United States. [. . .]

The Costs of Volatility

Capital-market liberalization is inevitably accompanied by huge volatility, and this volatility impedes growth and increases poverty. It increases the risks of investing in the country, and thus investors demand a risk premium in the form of higher-than-normal profits. Not only is growth not enhanced but poverty is increased through several channels. The high volatility increases the likelihood of recessions – and the poor always bear the brunt of such downturns. Even in developed countries, safety nets are weak or nonexistent among the self-employed and in the rural sector. But these are the dominant sectors in developing countries. Without adequate safety nets, the recessions that follow from capital-market liberalization lead to impoverishment. In the name of imposing budget discipline and reassuring investors, the IMF invariably demands expenditure reductions, which almost inevitably result in cuts in outlays for safety nets that are already threadbare.

But matters are even worse – for under the doctrines of the "discipline of the capital markets," if countries try to tax capital, capital flees. Thus, the IMF doctrines inevitably lead to an increase in tax burdens on the poor and the middle classes. Thus, while IMF bailouts enable the rich to take their money out of the country at more favorable terms (at the overvalued exchange rates), the burden of repaying the loans lies with the workers who remain behind.

The reason that I emphasize capital-market liberalization is that the case against it – and against the IMF's stance in pushing it – is so compelling. It illustrates what can go wrong with globalization. Even economists like Jagdish Bhagwati, strong advocates of free trade, see the folly in liberalizing capital markets. Belatedly, so too has the IMF – at least in its official rhetoric, though less so in its policy stances – but too late for all those countries that have suffered so much from following the IMF's prescriptions.

But while the case for trade liberalization – when properly done – is quite compelling, the way it has been pushed by the IMF has been far more problematic. The basic logic is simple: Trade liberalization is supposed to result in resources moving from inefficient protected sectors to more efficient export sectors. The problem is not only that job destruction comes before the job creation – so that unemployment and poverty result – but that the IMF's "structural adjustment programs" (designed in ways that allegedly would reassure global investors) make job creation almost impossible. For these programs are often accompanied by high interest rates that are often justified by a single-minded focus on inflation. Sometimes that concern is deserved; often, though, it is carried to an extreme. In the United States, we worry that small increases in the interest rate will discourage investment.

The IMF has pushed for far higher interest rates in countries with a far less hospitable investment environment. The high interest rates mean that new jobs and enterprises are not created. What happens is that trade liberalization, rather than moving workers from low-productivity jobs to high-productivity ones, moves them from low-productivity jobs to unemployment. Rather than enhanced growth, the effect is increased poverty. To make matters even worse, the unfair trade-liberalization agenda forces poor countries to compete with highly subsidized American and European agriculture.

The Governance of Globalization

By contrast, [. . .] in the current process of globalization we have a system of what I call global governance without global government. International institutions like the World Trade Organization, the IMF, the World Bank, and others provide an ad hoc system of global governance, but it is a far cry from global government and lacks democratic accountability. Although it is perhaps better than not having any system of global governance, the system is structured not to serve general interests or assure equitable results. This not only raises issues of whether broader values are given short shrift; it does not even promote growth as much as an alternative might.

Governance through Ideology

Consider the contrast between how economic decisions are made inside the United States and how they are made in the international economic institutions. In this country, economic decisions within the administration are undertaken largely by the National Economic Council, which includes the secretary of labor, the secretary of commerce, the chairman of the Council of Economic Advisers, the treasury secretary, the assistant attorney general for antitrust, and the U.S. trade representative. The Treasury is only one vote and often gets voted down. All of these officials, of course, are part of an administration that must face Congress and the democratic electorate. But in the international arena, only the voices of the financial community are heard. The IMF reports to the ministers of finance and the governors of the central banks, and one of the important items on its agenda is to make these central banks more independent – and less democratically accountable. It might make little difference if the IMF dealt only with matters of concern to the financial community, such as the clearance of checks; but in fact, its policies affect every aspect of life. It forces countries to have tight monetary and fiscal policies: It evaluates the trade-off between inflation and unemployment, and in that trade-off it always puts far more weight on inflation than on jobs.

The problem with having the rules of the game dictated by the IMF – and thus by the financial community – is not just a question of values (though that is important) but also a question of ideology. The financial community's view of the world predominates – even when there is little evidence in its support. Indeed, beliefs on key issues are held so strongly that theoretical and empirical support of the positions is viewed as hardly necessary.

Recall again the IMF's position on liberalizing capital markets. As noted, the IMF pushed a set of policies that exposed countries to serious risk. One might have thought, given the evidence of the costs, that the IMF could offer plenty of evidence that the policies also did some good. In fact, there was no such evidence; the evidence that was available suggested that there was little if any positive effect on growth.

Ideology enabled IMF officials not only to ignore the absence of benefits but also to overlook the evidence of the huge costs imposed on countries.

An Unfair Trade Agenda

The trade-liberalization agenda has been set by the North, or more accurately, by special interests in the North. Consequently, a disproportionate part of the gains has accrued to the advanced industrial countries, and in some cases the less-developed countries have actually been worse off. After the last round of trade negotiations, the Uruguay Round that ended in 1994, the World Bank calculated the gains and losses to each of the regions of the world. The United States and Europe gained enormously. But sub-Saharan Africa, the poorest region of the world, lost by about 2 percent because of terms-of-trade effects: The trade negotiations opened their markets to manufactured goods produced by the industrialized countries but did not open up the markets of Europe and the United States to the agricultural goods in which poor countries often have a comparative advantage. Nor did the trade agreements eliminate the subsidies to agriculture that make it so hard for the developing countries to compete.

The U.S. negotiations with China over its membership in the WTO displayed a double standard bordering on the surreal. The U.S. trade representative, the chief negotiator for the United States, began by insisting that China was a developed country. Under WTO rules, developing countries are allowed longer transition periods in which state subsidies and other departures from the WTO strictures are permitted. China certainly wishes it were a developed country, with Western-style per capita incomes. And since China has a lot of "capitas," it's possible to multiply a huge number of people by very small average incomes and conclude that the People's Republic is a big economy. But China is not only a developing economy; it is a low-income developing country. Yet the United States insisted that China be treated like a developed country! China went along with the fiction; the negotiations dragged on so long that China got some extra time to adjust. But the true hypocrisy was shown when U.S. negotiators asked, in effect, for developing-country status for the United States to get extra time to shelter the American textile industry.

Trade negotiations in the service industries also illustrate the unlevel nature of the playing field. Which service industries did the United States say were *very* important? Financial services – industries in which Wall Street has a comparative advantage. Construction industries and maritime services were not on the agenda, because the developing countries would have a comparative advantage in these sectors.

Consider also intellectual-property rights, which are important if innovators are to have incentives to innovate (though many of the corporate advocates of intellectual property exaggerate its importance and fail to note that much of the most important research, as in basic science and mathematics, is not patentable). Intellectual-property rights, such as patents and trademarks, need to balance the interests of producers with those of users – not only users in developing countries, but researchers in developed countries. If we underprice the profitability of innovation to the inventor, we deter invention. If we overprice its cost to the research community and the end user, we retard its diffusion and beneficial effects on living standards.

In the final stages of the Uruguay negotiations, both the White House Office of Science and Technology Policy and the Council of Economic Advisers worried that we had not got the balance right – that the agreement put producers' interests over users'. We worried that, with this imbalance, the rate of progress and innovation might actually be impeded. After all, knowledge is the most important input into research, and overly strong intellectual-property rights can, in effect, increase the price of this input. We were also concerned about the consequences of denying life-saving medicines to the poor. This issue subsequently gained international attention in the context of the provision of AIDS medicines in South Africa. The international outrage forced the drug companies to back down – and it appears that, going forward, the most adverse consequences will be circumscribed. But it is worth noting that initially, even the Democratic U.S. administration supported the pharmaceutical companies.

What we were not fully aware of was another danger – what has come to be called "biopiracy," which involves international drug companies patenting traditional medicines. Not only do they seek to make money from "resources" and knowledge that rightfully belong to the developing countries, but in doing so they squelch domestic firms who long provided these traditional medicines. While it is not clear whether these patents would hold up in court if they were effectively challenged, it is clear that the less-developed countries may not have the legal and financial resources required to mount such a challenge. The issue has become the source of enormous emotional, and potentially economic, concern throughout the developing world. This fall, while I was in Ecuador visiting a village in the high Andes, the Indian mayor railed against how globalization had led to biopiracy. [. . .]

Global Social Justice

Today, in much of the developing world, globalization is being questioned. For instance, in Latin America, after a short burst of growth in the early 1990s, stagnation and recession have set in. The growth was not sustained – some might say, was not sustainable. Indeed, at this juncture, the growth record of the so-called post-reform era looks no better, and in some countries much worse, than in the widely criticized import-substitution period of the 1950s and 1960s when Latin countries tried to industrialize by discouraging imports. Indeed, reform critics point out that the burst of growth in the early 1990s was little more than a "catch-up" that did not even make up for the lost decade of the 1980s.

Throughout the region, people are asking: "Has reform failed or has globalization failed?" The distinction is perhaps artificial, for globalization was at the center of the reforms. Even in those countries that have managed to grow, such as Mexico, the benefits have accrued largely to the upper 30 percent and have been even more concentrated in the top 10 percent. Those at the bottom have gained little; many are even worse off. The reforms have exposed countries to greater risk, and the risks have been borne disproportionately by those least able to cope with them. Just as in many countries where the pacing and sequencing of reforms has resulted in job destruction outmatching job creation, so too has the exposure to risk outmatched the ability to create institutions for coping with risk, including effective safety nets.

In this bleak landscape, there are some positive signs. Those in the North have become more aware of the inequities of the global economic architecture. The agreement at Doha to hold a new round of trade negotiations – the "Development Round" – promises to rectify some of the imbalances of the past. There has been a marked change in the rhetoric of the international economic institutions – at least they talk about poverty. At the World Bank, there have been some real reforms; there has been some progress in translating the rhetoric into reality – in ensuring that the voices of the poor are heard and the concerns of the developing countries are listened to. But elsewhere, there is often a gap between the rhetoric and the reality. Serious reforms in governance, in who makes decisions and how they are made, are not on the table. If one of the problems at the IMF has been that ideology, interests, and perspectives of the financial community in the advanced industrialized countries have been given disproportionate weight (in matters whose effects go well beyond finance), then the prospects for success in the current discussions of reform, in which the same parties continue to predominate, are bleak. They are more likely to result in slight changes in the shape of the table, not changes in who is *at* the table or what is on the agenda.

September 11 has resulted in a global alliance against terrorism. What we now need is not just an alliance *against* evil, but an alliance *for* something positive – a global alliance for reducing poverty and for creating a better environment, an alliance for creating a global society with more social justice.

Questions

1   What did Malaysia do to become more integrated into the world economy? Why does Greider expect that "convergence" between rich and poor will lead to a global "jobs auction"? How does Motorola's presence in Malaysia illustrate the "high drama of globalization"?

2   What is a global "commodity chain"? What does the rise of such chains in many sectors tell you about the changing division of labor around the globe? Who benefits most from the work done in such chains? What lessons can you draw from Korzeniewicz's case study of the Nike Corporation?

3   Why is growth good for the poor, according to Dollar and Kraay, and how does globalization foster such growth? What beneficiaries do they cite? Does globalization also lessen inequality within or across countries?

4   Does Oxfam contest the view that growth is necessary for poverty reduction? Does trade liberalization benefit the poor? Overall, what evidence and arguments does Oxfam provide to challenge Dollar and Kraay's positive picture of globalization?

5   What should corporations take responsibility for, according to the Global Compact described by Robinson? Why does she think it is important for corporations to take on broad responsibility for dealing with global issues? How do voluntary initiatives such as the Global Compact relate to government action in addressing global problems?

6   Does Henderson think it is in the enlightened self-interest of private companies to take on the kind of corporate social responsibility advocated by Robinson? What effects might this have on businesses and on the market economy? Can business do as much good as people like Robinson expect? Why does Henderson describe advocates of corporate responsibility as adherents of "global salvationism"?

7   What are the "discontents" and the "darker side" of globalization, according to Stiglitz? How does he assess the consequences of market liberalization? What does he mean by "governance through ideology," and what should replace it?

Part V

Political Globalization I: The Demise of the Nation-State?

Introduction

In a world made up of powerful and highly stable nation-states, political globalization might seem like a contradiction in terms. A state (more commonly called "government" in the United States) is the sovereign authority in a specified territory, with the right to use force both to maintain internal order and to defend its territory against aggression. Sovereignty, in turn, implies that the state is the ultimate authority in its territory, exercising legal jurisdiction over its citizens and the groups and organizations they form in the conduct of daily life. The sovereign state is not subject to any higher authority – no state has the right to expect compliance from any other state, and no all-encompassing world state has emerged with authority over all national states. Sometimes the United Nations is described as the potential nucleus of a world state, but it has no compelling authority over its member states and it relies entirely on the action of its members to enforce compliance with its resolutions and sanctions against misbehaving states.

In times past, world maps contained many different kinds of political units, from small dukedoms and principalities to large empires ruled by powerful states. Nearly all of the small units have been absorbed in larger nation-states, and all but a few of the colonies held by former imperial powers like Britain and France have become independent sovereign states. With the dissolution of the last great empire, the Soviet Union, in the 1990s, the world is now composed almost entirely of sovereign nation-states.

What sense does it make, then, to speak of political globalization? First, the very fact that the entire world, with the exception of the Arctic areas and a few small colonies and dependencies, is organized by a single type of political unit, the nation-state, is a sign of globalization. Never before has the world been composed of only one type of political unit. The rapid decolonization of the twentieth century, when more than 130 colonies or dependencies became independent states, was a great political surprise, since most of these new states are far too small and weak to defend themselves effectively from more powerful states. This indicates that the principle of state sovereignty itself has become a central feature of global society, and that a particular model of political organization, the sovereign state, has achieved global status as the most desirable, viable, and legitimate way of structuring political life.

Second, political globalization is indicated by the considerable uniformity exhibited by sovereign states in terms of their goals, structures, programs, and internal operations. Almost all states assume responsibility for a wide range of activities, including education, health care, management of the economy and finance, welfare programs, retirement pensions, environmental protection, and poverty alleviation, alongside the classic core concerns of states, foreign policy, and military defense. Almost all states have elaborate bureaucratic structures to administer the many programs they operate to meet their responsibilities. And almost all states are formally structured (in their constitutions and legislation) as democracies in which all citizens have an equal right to vote in elections that determine the holders of executive and legislative positions. Thus, a common basic model of the state is in place everywhere in the world, though states vary considerably in how they implement the basic model in concrete terms.

A third dimension of political globalization is the emergence in the past hundred years of intergovernmental organizations (IGOs). IGOs are associations of states created to deal with problems and manage issues that affect many countries at once or involve high levels of interdependence among countries. Of the approximately three hundred global IGOs and more than a thousand regional or sub-regional IGOs, most are concerned with economic, technical, or political matters. Most prominent are the United Nations and its associated agencies (UNESCO, the World Health Organization, the International Labor Organization, ECOSOC, and so on), which constitute a central world political forum within which states conduct their international relations. Other prominent bodies include the World Trade Organization (WTO) and International Monetary Fund (IMF), which help manage the world economy; the International Telecommunications Union and INTELSAT, which manage global telecommunications and satellite systems; the International Organization for Standardization (known as ISO), and the International Electro-Technical Commission (IEC), which develop and promote global standards for manufacturing, materials, product safety, and so on; and the Universal Postal Union, which manages international postal services.

As economic globalization has increased, as technology and technical systems have become more encompassing and complex, as problems like pollution and narcotics trafficking and terrorism have also become global, the adequacy of states to cope with the rapidly integrating world has increasingly been called into question. Many transnational corporations (TNCs) have larger sales revenues than the entire economies of most countries, and daily global financial transactions routinely surpass the $1 trillion level – so the world economy is beyond the control of states. Global warming and environmental degradation are inevitable by-products of economic development, and states are too much concerned with their own development to take serious action about such problems. Religious and ethnic groups within countries are increasingly militant and well-armed, threatening the viability of the states they oppose. These and numerous other factors have led many observers to speak of repeated "crises" of the state and to predict the breakdown or irrelevance of states.

Other observers caution that the death of the state has been announced prematurely. Problems may be increasingly global in scale, but states are also larger and more capable than ever before. They take in a larger share of GNP as tax revenues than ever before; they have larger and better trained bureaucracies than ever before; they are remarkably effective in operating national health-care systems, pension plans, postal services, road and air transportation systems, and many other programs, at least in the more developed countries. The demands on states are certainly growing, perhaps even faster than states can keep up with them, but it is by no means certain that states are as incapable of dealing with their responsibilities as many critics claim. Only in some poorer countries do we find clearly weak states that fall far short of global expectations for their performance.

Our selections on political globalization begin with the widespread view, developed here by Kenichi Ohmae, that the institutions and boundaries of the nation-state are becoming increasingly irrelevant in an era of increased economic integration. Ohmae argues that the "4 I's" (Investment, Industry, Information, and Individual) render states powerless to do much more than stand by and watch as events spin out of their control. Susan Strange expands on such views by arguing that the power and authority of the state are declining due to technological change and the rapid escalation of capital costs for successful innovation. These factors force states to do the bidding of transnational corporations, whose massive resources are seen as necessary to maintain national competitiveness in the global economy. Strange notes the paradox that declining state effectiveness has been accompanied by growing state intervention into people's daily lives, but such intervention has less to do with fundamental responsibilities and increasingly focuses on marginal issues.

Dani Rodrik provides evidence that economic globalization may indeed have undermined the capacity of states to give adequate support to citizens. The problem, Rodrik says, is that companies in the developed countries can move their operations to places where labor costs are lower and unions are weak. This practice lowers wages, diminishes labor's bargaining power, and lowers government revenues so that welfare and social security programs become more difficult to support. The developed countries are also undercut by the low-cost imports available to consumers, which further intensifies this downward spiral. Rodrik argues that states should respond by being more skeptical of free trade and capital flows, so a balance can be struck between openness and social responsibility.

Geoffrey Garrett directly questions claims about the declining ability of states to manage the impact of economic integration. He argues that expanded state action to cushion the negative impact of free flows of goods and capital can produce higher economic growth and more balanced economies than would be achieved if states passively succumbed to global openness. The key is the improved morale and motivation of the labor force that results from knowing that a strong social support system is always available, along with the willingness of labor organizations to cooperate with employers to reach mutually acceptable compromises about state support programs and thereby avoid the disruptions of strikes and lockouts when issues come to a head.

Finally, a statement by UN Secretary General Kofi Annan addresses the role of the state in a globalizing world. Annan holds that effective, well-organized states are more, not less, necessary as problems become ever more global. Only effective states can provide crucial forms of security – physical, economic, and psychological – that their citizens expect. States must be strong to maintain domestic peace, ensure the rule of law, and enforce the implementation of solutions to such global problems as poverty, environmental degradation, climate change, terrorism, and crime. At the same time, states must be devoted champions of human rights, working with their citizens rather than coercing them, if a better world is to be achieved.

26   The End of the Nation State

Kenichi Ohmae

A funny – and, to many observers, a very troubling – thing has happened on the way to former US President Bush's so-called "new world order": the old world has fallen apart. Most visibly, with the ending of the Cold War, the long-familiar pattern of alliances and oppositions among industrialized nations has fractured beyond repair. Less visibly, but arguably far more important, the modern nation state itself – that artifact of the eighteenth and nineteenth centuries – has begun to crumble. [. . .]

In economics as in politics, the older patterns of nation-to-nation linkage have begun to lose their dominance. What is emerging in their place, however, is not a set of new channels based on culture instead of nations. Nor is it a simple realignment of previous flows of nation-based trade or investment.

In my view, what is really at stake is not really which party or policy agenda dominates the apparatus of a nation state's central government. Nor is it the number of new, independent units into which that old center, which has held through the upheavals of industrialization and the agonies of two world wars, is likely to decompose. Nor is it the cultural fault lines along which it is likely to fragment.

Instead, what we are witnessing is the cumulative effect of fundamental changes in the currents of economic activity around the globe. So powerful have these currents become that they have carved out entirely new channels for themselves – channels that owe nothing to the lines of demarcation on traditional political maps. Put simply, in terms of real flows of economic activity, nation states have *already* lost their role as meaningful units of participation in the global economy of today's borderless world.

In the first place, these long-established, politically defined units have much less to contribute – and much less freedom to make contributions. The painful irony is that, driven by a concern to boost overall economic well-being, their efforts to assert traditional forms of economic sovereignty over the peoples and regions lying within their borders are now having precisely the opposite effect. Reflexive twinges of sovereignty make the desired economic success impossible, because the global economy punishes twinging countries by diverting investment and information elsewhere.

The uncomfortable truth is that, in terms of the global economy, nation states have become little more than bit actors. They may originally have been, in their mercantilist phase, independent, powerfully efficient engines of wealth creation. More

Original publication details: Excerpted from Kenichi Ohmae, *The End of the Nation State: The Rise of Regional Economies* (The Free Press, 1995), pp. 7, 11–16, 141–2. Copyright © 1995 by McKinsey & Co., Inc. Reprinted with the permission of the Free Press, a division of Simon & Schuster Adult Publishing Group.

recently, however, as the downward-ratcheting logic of electoral politics has placed a death grip on their economies, they have become – first and foremost – remarkably inefficient engines of wealth distribution. Elected political leaders gain and keep power by giving voters what they want, and what they want rarely entails a substantial decrease in the benefits, services, or subsidies handed out by the state.

Moreover, as the workings of genuinely global capital markets dwarf their ability to control exchange rates or protect their currency, nation states have become inescapably vulnerable to the discipline imposed by economic choices made elsewhere by people and institutions over which they have no practical control. Witness, for example, the recent, Maastricht-related bout of speculation against the franc, the pound, and the kronor. Witness, also, the unsustainable but self-imposed burden of Europe's various social programs. Finally, witness the complete absence of any economic value creation, save for those around the world who stand to benefit from pork-barrel excesses, in such decisions as the Japanese Diet's commitment – copied from the New Deal policies of Franklin Roosevelt – to build unnecessary highways and bridges on the remote islands of Hokkaido and Okinawa.

Second, and more to the point, the nation state is increasingly a nostalgic fiction. It makes even less sense today, for example, than it did a few years ago to speak of Italy or Russia or China as a single economic unit. Each is a motley combination of territories with vastly different needs and vastly different abilities to contribute. For a private sector manager or a public sector official to treat them as if they represented a single economic entity is to operate on the basis of demonstrably false, implausible, and nonexistent averages. This may still be a political necessity, but it is a bald-faced economic lie.

Third, when you look closely at the goods and services now produced and traded around the world, as well as at the companies responsible for them, it is no easy matter to attach to them an accurate national label. Is an automobile sold under an American marque really a US product when a large percentage of its components comes from abroad? Is the performance of IBM's foreign subsidiaries or the performance of its R&D operations in Europe and Japan really a measure of US excellence in technology? For that matter, are the jobs created by Japanese plants and factories in the Mississippi Valley really a measure of the health of the Japanese, and not the US, economy? The barbershop on the corner may indisputably be a part of the domestic American economy. But it is just not possible to make the same claim, with the same degree of confidence, about the firms active on the global stage.

Finally, when economic activity aggressively wears a national label these days, that tag is usually present neither for the sake of accuracy nor out of concern for the economic well-being of individual consumers. It is there primarily as a mini-flag of cheap nationalism – that is, as a jingoistic celebration of nationhood that places far more value on emotion-grabbing symbols than on real, concrete improvements in quality of life. By contrast, we don't hear much about feverish waves of Hong Kong nationalism, but the people in Hong Kong seem to live rather well. With much fanfare, Ukraine and the Baltic states have now become independent, but do their people have more food to eat or more energy to keep them warm during the winter or more electricity for light to see by?

An arresting, if often overlooked, fact about today's borderless economy is that people often have better access to low-cost, high-quality products when they are not produced "at home." Singaporeans, for example, enjoy better and cheaper agricultural products than do the Japanese, although Singapore has no farmers – and no farms – of its own. Much the same is true of construction materials, which are much less expensive in Singapore, which produces none of them, than in Japan, which does.

Now, given this decline in the relevance of nation states as units of economic activity, as well as the recent burst of economic growth in Asia, the burgeoning political self-consciousness of Islam, and the fragmentation, real or threatened, of such "official" political entities as Italy, Spain, Somalia, Rwanda, Canada, South Africa, and the former Yugoslavia, Czechoslovakia, and Soviet Union – given all this, it is easy to see why observers like Huntington should look to cultural, religious, ethnic, even tribal affiliations as the only plausible stopping point of the centrifugal forces unleashed by the end of the Cold War.

Once bipolar discipline begins to lose its force, once traditional nation states no longer "hold," or so the argument goes, visionless leaders will start to give in to the fear that older fault lines will again make themselves felt. And given the bloody violence with which many of these lines have already begun to reappear, these leaders will find it hard to see where this process of backsliding can come to rest short of traditional groupings based on some sort of cultural affinity. In other words, in the absence of vision and the presence of slowly rising panic, the only groupings that seem to matter are based on civilizations, not nations.

But are cultures or civilizations meaningful aggregates in terms of which to understand economic activity? Think, for a moment, of the ASEAN countries. In what sense is it useful to talk about them as a single, culturally defined economic area? As they affect local patterns of work, trade, and industry, the internal differences among their Buddhist, Islamic, Catholic (in the Philippines and the Sabah state of Malaysia), and Confucian traditions are every bit as large as, if not larger than, the differences separating any one of these traditions from the dominant business cultures of New York or London or Paris.

But in ASEAN, at least, differences of this sort do not provoke the same kinds of conflicts that often arise elsewhere. Most Western observers know, for example, that Spanish and Portuguese speakers can converse with each other, if with some minor degree of difficulty. Many fewer, however, know that the same is true of Indonesians and Malaysians. Or that, in border regions between Thailand and Malaysia, such as Phuket, there are peaceful, economically linked villages, some of which have mainly Buddhist and some mainly Islamic populations. These on-the-ground realities have made it possible for ASEAN leaders to accept and to reinforce, with little fear of internal friction, the development of cross-border economic ties like those stretching across the Strait of Malacca which are represented by the Greater Growth Triangle of Phuket, Medan, and Penang.

Even more important than such cultural differences within a civilization, and what Huntington's line of thought leaves out, is the issue of historical context. The particular dissolution of bipolar, "great power" discipline that so greatly affects us today is not taking place in the 1790s or the 1890s, but the 1990s. And that means it is taking place in a world whose peoples, no matter how far-flung geographically or disparate culturally, are all linked to much the same sources of global information. The immediacy and completeness of their access may vary, of course, and governments may try to impose restrictions and control. Even if they do, however, the barriers will not last forever, and leakages will occur all along the way. Indeed, the basic fact of linkage to global flows of information is a – perhaps, *the* – central, distinguishing fact of our moment in history. Whatever the civilization to which a particular group of people belongs, they now get to hear about the way other groups of people live, the kinds of products they buy, the changing focus of their tastes and preferences as consumers, and the styles of life they aspire to lead.

But they also get something more. For more than a decade, some of us have been talking about the progressive globalization of markets for consumer goods like Levi's jeans, Nike athletic shoes, and Hermès scarves – a process, driven by global exposure to the same information, the same cultural icons, and the same advertisements, that I have elsewhere referred to as the "California-ization" of taste. Today, however, the process of convergence goes faster and deeper. It reaches well beyond taste to much more fundamental dimensions of worldview, mind-set, and even thought process. There are now, for example, tens of millions of teenagers around the world who, having been raised in a multimedia-rich environment, have a lot more in common with each other than they do with members of older generations in their own cultures. For these budding consumers, technology-driven convergence does not take place at the sluggish rate dictated by yesterday's media. It is instantaneous – a nanosecond migration of ideas and innovations.

The speed and immediacy of such migrations take us over an invisible political threshold. In the post-Cold War world, the information flows underlying economic activity in virtually all corners of the globe simply cannot be maintained as the possession of private elites or public officials. They are shared, increasingly, by all citizens and consumers. This sharing does not, of course, imply any necessary similarity in how local economic choices finally get made. But it does imply that there is a powerful centripetal force at work, counteracting and counterbalancing all the centrifugal forces noted above.

The emotional nexus of culture, in other words, is not the only web of shared interest able to contain the processes of disintegration unleashed by the reappearance of older fault lines. Information-driven participation in the global economy can do so, too, ahead of the fervid but empty posturing of both cheap nationalism and cultural messianism. The well-informed citizens of a global marketplace will not wait passively until nation states or cultural prophets deliver tangible improvements in lifestyle. They no longer trust them to do so. Instead, they want to build their own future, now, for themselves and by themselves. They want their own means of direct access to what has become a genuinely global economy. [. . .]

A Swing of the Pendulum

In the broad sweep of history, nation states have been a transitional form of organization for managing economic affairs. Their right – their prerogative – to manage them grew, in part, out of the control of military strength, but such strength is now an uncomfortably great burden to maintain. (It has also largely been exposed as a means to preserve the positions of those in power, not to advance the quality-of-life interests of their people.) Their right grew out of the control of natural resources and colonies, but the first is relatively unimportant as a source of value in a knowledge-intensive economy, and the second is less a source of low-cost resources than a bottomless drain on the home government's treasury. It grew out of the control of land, but prosperous economies can spread their influence through neighboring territories without any need for adjustment in formal divisions of sovereignty. And it grew out of the control of political independence, but such independence is of diminishing importance in a global economy that has less and less respect for national borders.

Moreover, as it grew, the nation state's organizational right to manage economic affairs fell victim to an inescapable cycle of decay. This should occasion no surprise. It comes as close to being a natural law as the messy universe of political economy allows. Whatever the form of government in power and whatever the political ideology that shapes it, demands for the civil minimum, for the support of special interests, and for the subsidization and protection of those left behind inexorably rise. In different circumstances, under different regimes, and during different eras, the speed of escalation varies. Good policy can slow the pace, bad policy can accelerate it. But no policy can stop it altogether. Nation states are political organisms, and in their economic bloodstreams cholesterol steadily builds up. Over time, arteries harden and the organism's vitality decays.

History, of course, also records the kinds of catastrophic, equilibrium-busting events that can stop or even reverse this aging process. Wars can do it, as can natural disasters like plagues, earthquakes, and volcanic eruptions. They have certainly done so in the past. But even for the most cold-blooded practitioners of *realpolitik*, these are hardly credible as purposeful instruments of economic policy.

Thus, in today's borderless economy, with its rapid cross-border [flows], there is really only one strategic degree of freedom that central governments have to counteract this remorseless buildup of economic cholesterol, only one legitimate instrument of policy to restore sustainable and self-reinforcing vitality, only one practical as well as morally acceptable way to meet their people's near-term needs without mortgaging the long-term prospects of their children and grandchildren. And that is to cede meaningful operational autonomy to the wealth-generating region states that lie within or across their borders, to catalyze the efforts of those region states to seek out global solutions, and to harness their distinctive ability to put global logic first and to function as ports of entry to the global economy. The only hope is to reverse the postfeudal, centralizing tendencies of the modern era and allow – or better, encourage – the economic pendulum to swing away from nations and back toward regions. [. . .]

27 The Declining Authority of States

Susan Strange

Today it seems that the heads of governments may be the last to recognise that they and their ministers have lost the authority over national societies and economies that they used to have. Their command over outcomes is not what it used to be. Politicians everywhere talk as though they have the answers to economic and social problems, as if they really are in charge of their country's destiny. People no longer believe them. Disillusion with national leaders brought down the leaders of the Soviet Union and the states of central Europe. But the disillusion is by no means confined to socialist systems. Popular contempt for ministers and for the head of state has grown in most of the capitalist countries – Italy, Britain, France and the United States are leading examples. Nor is the lack of confidence confined to those in office; opposition parties and their leaders are often no better thought of than those they wish to replace. In the last few years, the cartoonists and the tabloid press have been more bitter, less restrained critics of those in authority in government than at any other time this century. Although there are exceptions – mostly small countries – this seems to be a worldwide phenomenon of the closing years of the twentieth century, more evident in some places than others, but palpable enough to suggest that some common causes lie behind it.

[I write] in the firm belief that the perceptions of ordinary citizens are more to be trusted than the pretensions of national leaders and of the bureaucracies who serve them; that the commonsense of common people is a better guide to understanding than most of the academic theories being taught in universities. The social scientists, in politics and economics especially, cling to obsolete concepts and inappropriate theories. These theories belong to a more stable and orderly world than the one we live in. It was one in which the territorial borders of states really meant something. But it has been swept away by a pace of change more rapid than human society had ever before experienced.

For this reason I believe the time has come to reconsider a few of the entrenched ideas of some academic colleagues in economics, politics, sociology and international relations. The study of international political economy has convinced me that we have to rethink some of the assumptions of conventional social science, and especially of the study of international relations. These concern: firstly, the limits of politics as a social activity; secondly, the nature and sources of power in society; thirdly, the necessity and also the indivisibility of authority in a market economy; and fourthly, the anarchic nature of international society and the rational conduct of states as the

Original publication details: Excerpted from Susan Strange, The Retreat of the State: The Diffusion of Power in the World Economy (Cambridge University Press, 1996), pp. 3–8, 9–10, 12–14. Reprinted by permission of Cambridge University Press.

unitary actors within that society. The first and second are assumptions commonly taken for granted in political science. The third is an assumption of much liberal, or neo-classical economic science. And the last is an assumption of much so-called realist or neo-realist thinking in international relations. Each of these assumptions will be examined more closely later.

But first it may help to outline briefly the argument of the book as a whole. That will show the context in which these more fundamental questions about politics and power arise and have to be reconsidered. The argument put forward is that the impersonal forces of world markets, integrated over the postwar period more by private enterprise in finance, industry and trade than by the cooperative decisions of governments, are now more powerful than the states to whom ultimate political authority over society and economy is supposed to belong.

Where states were once the masters of markets, now it is the markets which, on many crucial issues, are the masters over the governments of states. And the declining authority of states is reflected in a growing diffusion of authority to other institutions and associations, and to local and regional bodies, and in a growing asymmetry between the larger states with structural power and weaker ones without it.

There are, to be sure, some striking paradoxes about this reversal of the state-market balance of power. One, which disguises from many people the overall decline of state power, is that the *intervention* of state authority and of the agencies of the state in the daily lives of the citizen appears to be growing. Where once it was left to the individual to look for work, to buy goods or services with caution in case they were unsafe or not what they seemed to be, to build or to pull down houses, to manage family relationships and so on, now governments pass laws, set up inspectorates and planning authorities, provide employment services, enforce customer protection against unclean water, unsafe food, faulty buildings or transport systems. The impression is conveyed that less and less of daily life is immune from the activities and decisions of government bureaucracies.

That is not necessarily inconsistent with my contention that state *power* is declining. It is less effective on those basic matters that the market, left to itself, has never been able to provide – security against violence, stable money for trade and investment, a clear system of law and the means to enforce it, and a sufficiency of public goods like drains, water supplies, infrastructures for transport and communications. Little wonder that it is less respected and lacks its erstwhile legitimacy. The need for a political authority of some kind, legitimated either by coercive force or by popular consent, or more often by a combination of the two, is the fundamental reason for the state's existence. But many states are coming to be deficient in these fundamentals. Their deficiency is not made good by greater activity in marginal matters, matters that are optional for society, and which are not absolutely necessary for the functioning of the market and the maintenance of social order. Trivialising government does not make its authority more respected; often, the contrary is true.

The second paradox is that while the governments of established states, most notably in North America and western Europe, are suffering this progressive loss of real authority, the queue of societies that want to have their own state is lengthening. This is true not only of ethnic groups that were forcibly suppressed by the single-party government of the former Soviet Union. It is true of literally hundreds of minorities and aboriginal peoples in every part of the world – in Canada and Australia, in India and Africa, even in the old so-called nation-states of Europe. Many – perhaps the majority – are suppressed by force, like the Kurds or the Basques.

Others – like the Scots or the Corsicans – are just not strong enough or angry enough to offer a serious challenge to the existing state. Still others such as the native Americans, the Aboriginals, the Samis or the Flemish are pacified by resource transfers or by half-measures that go some way to meet their perceived need for an independent identity. Only a few, such as the Greenlanders, the Slovaks or Slovenes or the unwanted, unviable Pacific island-states, have succeeded in getting what they wanted – statehood. But once achieved, it does not seem to give them any real control over the kind of society or the nature of their economy that they might have preferred. In short, the desire for ethnic or cultural autonomy is universal; the political means to satisfy that desire within an integrated world market economy is not. Many, perhaps most, societies have to be content with the mere appearance of autonomy, with a facade of statehood. The struggle for independence has often proved a pyrrhic victory.

The final paradox which can be brought as evidence against my basic contention about the hollowness of state authority at the end of this century is that this is a western, or even an Anglo-Saxon phenomenon, and is refuted by the Asian experience of the state. The Asian state, it is argued, has in fact been the means to achieve economic growth, industrialisation, a modernised infrastructure and rising living standards for the people. Singapore might be the prime example of a strong state achieving economic success. But Japan, Korea, Taiwan are all states which have had strong governments, governments which have successfully used the means to restrict and control foreign trade and foreign investment, and to allocate credit and to guide corporate development in the private sector. Is it not premature – just another instance of Eurocentrism therefore – to assume the declining authority of the state?

There are two answers to this third paradox. One is that all these Asian states were exceptionally fortunate. They profited in three ways from their geographical position on the western frontier of the United States during the Cold War. Their strategic importance in the 1950s and after was such that they could count on generous military and economic aid from the Americans, aid which was combined with their exceptionally high domestic savings and low patterns of consumption. The combination gave a head start to rapid economic development. Secondly, and also for strategic reasons, they could be – almost had to be – exempted from the pressure to conform to the norms of the open liberal economy. They were allowed, first formally and then informally, to limit foreign imports and also to restrict the entry of the foreign firms that might have proved too strong competitors for their local enterprises. At the same time, they were given relatively open access first to the large, rich US market for manufactures, and later, under some protest, to the European one. And thirdly, the technology necessary to their industrialisation was available to be bought on the market, either in the form of patents, or in the person of technical advisors from Europe and America or through corporate alliances which brought them the technology without the loss of managerial control.

Now, I would argue, these special dispensations are on the way out, and not only because the Cold War is over. The Asian governments will be under increasing pressure from Washington to adopt more liberal non-discriminatory policies on trade and investment. And they will also be under pressure from within to liberalise and to allow more competition, including foreign competition, for the benefit of consumers and of other producers. In short, the exceptionalism of the Asian state during the Cold War has already been substantially eroded, and will continue to be so. As it has been at other times, and in other places, there will be contests for control over the institutions and agencies of government in most of the Asian countries. There will be contests between factions of political parties, between vested interests both in the private sectors and in the public sector. There will be power struggles between branches of the state bureaucracy. Both the unity and the authority of government is bound to suffer.

The Neglected Factor – Technology

The argument depends a good deal on the accelerating pace of technological change as a prime cause of the shift in the state-market balance of power. Since social scientists are, not, by definition, natural scientists, they have a strong tendency to overlook the importance of technology which rests, ultimately, on advances in physics, in chemistry and related sciences like nuclear physics or industrial chemistry. In the last 100 years, there has been more rapid technological change than ever before in human history. On this the scientists themselves are generally agreed. It took hundreds – in some places, thousands – of years to domesticate animals so that horses could be used for transport and oxen (later heavy horses) could be used to replace manpower to plough and sow ground for the production of crops in agriculture. It has taken less than 100 years for the car and truck to replace the horse and for aircraft to partly take over from road and rail transport. The electric telegraph as a means of communication was invented in the 1840s and remained the dominant system in Europe until the 1920s. But in the next eighty years, the telegraph gave way to the telephone, the telephone gave way to radio, radio to television and cables to satellites and optic fibres linking computers to other computers. No one under the age of thirty or thirty-five today needs convincing that, just in their own lifetime, the pace of technological change has been getting faster and faster. The technically unsophisticated worlds of business, government and education of even the 1960s would be unrecognisable to them. No fax, no personal computers, no accessible copiers, no mobile phones, no video shops, no DNA tests, no cable TV, no satellite networks connecting distant markets, twenty-four hours a day. The world in which their grandparents grew up in the 1930s or 1940s is as alien to them as that of the Middle Ages. There is no reason to suppose that technological change in products and processes, driven by profit, will not continue to accelerate in future.

This simple, everyday, commonsense fact of modern life is important because it goes a long way to explaining both political and economic change. It illuminates the changes both in the power of states and in the power of markets. Its dynamism, in fact, is basic to my argument, because it is a continuing factor, not a once-for-all change.

For the sake of clarity, consider first the military aspects of technical change, and then the civilian aspects – although in reality each spills over into the other. In what are known as strategic studies circles, no one doubts that the development of the atom bomb in the middle of the twentieth century, and later of nuclear weapons carried by intercontinental missiles, has brought about a major change in the nature of warfare between states. Mutual assured destruction was a powerful reason for having nuclear weapons – but equally it was a good reason for not using them. After the paradoxical long peace of the Cold War, two things began to change. The expectation that, sooner or later, nuclear war would destroy life on the planet began to moderate. And confidence began to wane that the state could, by a defensive strategy, prevent this happening. Either it would or it wouldn't, and governments could do little to alter the probabilities. Thus, technology had undermined one of the primary reasons for the existence of the state – its capacity to repel attack by others, its responsibility for what Adam Smith called 'the defence of the realm'. [. . .]

The Second Neglect – Finance

Not the least of the TNC's attractions to host states is its ability to raise finance both for the investment itself and – even more important – for the development of new technology. Another key part of [my] argument is that, besides the accelerating pace of technological change, there has been an escalation in the capital cost of most technological innovations – in agriculture, in manufacturing and the provision of services, and in new products and in new processes. In all of these, the input of capital has risen while the relative input of labour has fallen. It is this increased cost which has raised the stakes, as it were, in the game of staying up with the competition. This is so whether we look at competition from other firms who are also striving for larger market shares, or whether we look at governments trying to make sure that the economies for whose performance they are held responsible stay up with the competition in wealth-creation coming from other economies. Thus, to the extent that a government can benefit from a TNC's past and future investments without itself bearing the main cost of it, there are strong reasons for forging such alliances.

But the escalating costs of technological change are also important for a more fundamental reason, and not just because it explains the changing policies of host states to TNCs. It has to do with change in the world system. The cost of new technology in the production structure has added to the salience of money in the international political economy. It is no exaggeration to say that, with a few notable exceptions, scholars in international relations for the past half-century have grossly neglected the political aspects of credit-creation, and of changes in the global financial structure. In much theorising about international relations or even international political economy there is no mention at all of the financial structure (as distinct from the international monetary order governing the exchange relations of national currencies.) Briefly, the escalating capital costs of new technologies could not have been covered at all without, firstly, some very fundamental changes in the volume and nature of credit created by the capitalist market economy; and secondly, without the added mobility that in recent years has characterised that created credit. The *supply* of capital to finance technological innovation (and for other purposes) has been as important in the international political economy as the *demand* from the innovators for more money to produce ever more sophisticated products by ever more capital-intensive processes of production.

These supply and demand changes take place, and take effect, in the market. And it is markets, rather than state–state relations that many leading texts in international political economy tend to overlook. Much more emphasis is put on international monetary relations between governments and their national currencies. To the extent that attention is paid at all to the institutions creating and marketing credit in the world economy, they are held to be important chiefly for the increased volatility they may cause to exchange rates, or to the impact they may have on the ability of governments to borrow abroad to finance development or the shortfall between revenue and spending, or between export earnings and import bills. [. . .]

Politics, Power and Legitimacy

There are three premises underlying [my] argument. Each relates directly to – indeed, challenges – some of the conventional assumptions of economics, social and political science and international relations. The first premise is that politics is a common activity; it is not confined to politicians and their officials. The second is that power over outcomes is exercised impersonally by markets and often unintentionally by those who buy and sell and deal in markets. The third is that authority in society and over economic transactions is legitimately exercised by agents other than states, and has come to be freely acknowledged by those who are subject to it.

. . . dealing with recent changes in international political economy, readers will encounter three general propositions about the patterns of legitimate authority now developing in the international political economy towards the end of the twentieth century. One is that there is growing asymmetry among allegedly sovereign states in the authority they exercise in society and economy. In international relations, back to Thucydides, there has always been some recognition of a difference between small states and great powers, in the way each behaves to others and in the options available to them in their relations with other states. But there has been a tendency all along to assume a certain uniformity in the nature and effectiveness of the control which each state has over social and economic relations within their respective territorial boundaries. The attributes of domestic sovereignty, in other words, were assumed automatically to go with the regulation accorded each state by its peers. Now, I shall argue, that assumption can no longer be sustained. What was regarded as an exceptional anomaly when in 1945 the United States conceded two extra votes in the UN General Assembly for the Soviet Union – one for the 'sovereign' republic of the Ukraine and one for Byelorussia – now hardly attracts comment. The micro-states of Vanuatu and the Republic of San Marino are admitted to the select circle of member-states of the United Nations. But no one really believes that recognition of their 'sovereignty' is more than a courteous pretence. It is understood that there is only a difference of degree between these and many of the smaller and poorer members of the international society of states who are established occupants of seats in the UN.

The second proposition is that the authority of the governments of all states, large and small, strong and weak, has been weakened as a result of technological and financial change and of the accelerated integration of national economies into one single global market economy. Their failure to manage the national economy, to maintain employment and sustain economic growth, to avoid imbalances of payments with other states, to control the rate of interest and the exchange rate is not a matter of technical incompetence, nor moral turpitude nor political maladroitness. It is neither in any direct sense their fault, nor the fault of others. None of these failures can be blamed on other countries or on other governments. They are, simply, the victims of the market economy.

The third proposition complements the second. It is that some of the fundamental responsibilities of the state in a market economy – responsibilities first recognised, described and discussed at considerable length by Adam Smith over 200 years ago – are not now being adequately discharged by anyone. At the heart of the international political economy, there is a vacuum, a vacuum not adequately filled by inter-governmental institutions or by a hegemonic power exercising leadership in the common interest. The polarisation of states between those who retain some control over their destinies and those who are effectively incapable of exercising any such control does not add up to a zero-sum game. What some have lost, others have not gained. The diffusion of authority away from national governments has left a yawning hole of non-authority, ungovernance it might be called. [. . .]

28 Has Globalization Gone Too Far?

Dani Rodrik

The process that has come to be called "globalization" is exposing a deep fault line between groups who have the skills and mobility to flourish in global markets and those who either don't have these advantages or perceive the expansion of unregulated markets as inimical to social stability and deeply held norms. The result is severe tension between the market and social groups such as workers, pensioners, and environmentalists, with governments stuck in the middle. [. . .]

While I share the idea that much of the opposition to trade is based on faulty premises, I also believe that economists have tended to take an excessively narrow view of the issues. To understand the impact of globalization on domestic social arrangements, we have to go beyond the question of what trade does to the skill premium. And even if we focus more narrowly on labor-market outcomes, there are additional channels, which have not yet come under close empirical scrutiny, through which increased economic integration works to the disadvantage of labor, and particularly of unskilled labor. This book attempts to offer such a broadened perspective. As we shall see, this perspective leads to a less benign outlook than the one economists commonly adopt. One side benefit, therefore, is that it serves to reduce the yawning gap that separates the views of most economists from the gut instincts of many laypeople.

Sources of Tension

I focus on three sources of tension between the global market and social stability and offer a brief overview of them here.

First, reduced barriers to trade and investment accentuate the asymmetry between groups that can cross international borders (either directly or indirectly, say through outsourcing) and those that cannot. In the first category are owners of capital, highly skilled workers, and many professionals, who are free to take their resources where they are most in demand. Unskilled and semiskilled workers and most middle managers belong in the second category. Putting the same point in more technical terms, globalization makes the demand for the services of individuals in the second category *more elastic* – that is, the services of large segments of the working population can be more easily substituted by the services of other people across national boundaries. Globalization therefore fundamentally transforms the employment relationship.

Original publication details: Excerpted from Dani Rodrik, *Has Globalization Gone Too Far?* (Institute for International Economics, 1997), pp. 2, 4–7, 77–81. Copyright © 1997 Institute for International Economics, Washington, DC. All rights reserved.

The fact that "workers" can be more easily substituted for each other across national boundaries undermines what many conceive to be a postwar social bargain between workers and employers, under which the former would receive a steady increase in wages and benefits in return for labor peace. This is because increased substitutability results in the following concrete consequences:

- Workers now have to pay a larger share of the cost of improvements in work conditions and benefits (that is, they bear a greater incidence of nonwage costs).
- They have to incur greater instability in earnings and hours worked in response to shocks to labor demand or labor productivity (that is, volatility and insecurity increase).
- Their bargaining power erodes, so they receive lower wages and benefits whenever bargaining is an element in setting the terms of employment.

These considerations have received insufficient attention in the recent academic literature on trade and wages, which has focused on the downward shift in demand for unskilled workers rather than the increase in the elasticity of that demand.

Second, globalization engenders conflicts within and between nations over domestic norms and the social institutions that embody them. As the technology for manufactured goods becomes standardized and diffused internationally, nations with very different sets of values, norms, institutions, and collective preferences begin to compete head on in markets for similar goods. And the spread of globalization creates opportunities for trade between countries at very different levels of development.

This is of no consequence under traditional multilateral trade policy of the WTO and the General Agreement on Tariffs and Trade (GATT): the "process" or "technology" through which goods are produced is immaterial, and so are the social institutions of the trading partners. Differences in national practices are treated just like differences in factor endowments or any other determinant of comparative advantage. However, introspection and empirical evidence both reveal that most people attach values to processes as well as outcomes. This is reflected in the norms that shape and constrain the domestic environment in which goods and services are produced – for example, workplace practices, legal rules, and social safety nets.

Trade becomes contentious when it unleashes forces that undermine the norms implicit in domestic practices. Many residents of advanced industrial countries are uncomfortable with the weakening of domestic institutions through the forces of trade, as when, for example, child labor in Honduras displaces workers in South Carolina or when pension benefits are cut in Europe in response to the requirements of the Maastricht treaty. This sense of unease is one way of interpreting the demands for "fair trade." Much of the discussion surrounding the "new" issues in trade policy – that is, labor standards, environment, competition policy, corruption – can be cast in this light of procedural fairness.

We cannot understand what is happening in these new areas until we take individual preferences for processes and the social arrangements that embody them seriously. In particular, by doing so we can start to make sense of people's uneasiness about the consequences of international economic integration and avoid the trap of automatically branding all concerned groups as self-interested protectionists. Indeed, since trade policy almost always has redistributive consequences (among sectors, income groups, and individuals), one cannot produce a principled defense of free trade without confronting the question of the fairness and legitimacy of the practices that generate these consequences. By the same token, one should not expect broad popular support for trade when trade involves exchanges that clash with (and erode) prevailing domestic social arrangements.

Third, globalization has made it exceedingly difficult for governments to provide social insurance – one of their central functions and one that has helped maintain social cohesion and domestic political support for ongoing liberalization throughout the postwar period. In essence, governments have used their fiscal powers to insulate domestic groups from excessive market risks, particularly those having an external origin. In fact, there is a striking correlation between an economy's exposure to foreign trade and the size of its welfare state. It is in the most open countries, such as Sweden, Denmark, and the Netherlands, that spending on income transfers has expanded the most. This is not to say that the government is the sole, or the best, provider of social insurance. The extended family, religious groups, and local communities often play similar roles. My point is that it is a hallmark of the postwar period that governments in the advanced countries have been expected to provide such insurance.

At the present, however, international economic integration is taking place against the background of receding governments and diminished social obligations. The welfare state has been under attack for two decades. Moreover, the increasing mobility of capital has rendered an important segment of the tax base footloose, leaving governments with the unappetizing option of increasing tax rates disproportionately on labor income. Yet the need for social insurance for the vast majority of the population that remains internationally immobile has not diminished. If anything, this need has become greater as a consequence of increased integration. The question therefore is how the tension between globalization and the pressures for socialization of risk can be eased. If the tension is not managed intelligently and creatively, the danger is that the domestic consensus in favor of open markets will ultimately erode to the point where a generalized resurgence of protectionism becomes a serious possibility.

Each of these arguments points to an important weakness in the manner in which advanced societies are handling – or are equipped to handle – the consequences of globalization. Collectively, they point to what is perhaps the greatest risk of all, namely that the cumulative consequence of the tensions mentioned above will be the solidifying of a new set of class divisions – between those who prosper in the globalized economy and those who do not, between those who share its values and those who would rather not, and between those who can diversify away its risks and those who cannot. This is not a pleasing prospect, even for individuals on the winning side of the divide who have little empathy for the other side. Social disintegration is not a spectator sport – those on the sidelines also get splashed with mud from the field. Ultimately, the deepening of social fissures can harm all. [. . .]

The Role of National Governments

Policymakers have to steer a difficult middle course between responding to the concerns discussed here and sheltering groups from foreign competition through protectionism. I can offer no hard-and-fast rules here, only some guiding principles.

Strike a balance between openness and domestic needs

There is often a trade-off between maintaining open borders to trade and maintaining social cohesion. When the conflict arises – when new liberalization initiatives are under discussion, for example – it makes little sense to sacrifice social concerns completely for the sake of liberalization. Put differently, as policymakers sort out economic and social objectives, free trade policies are not automatically entitled to first priority.

Thanks to many rounds of multilateral trade liberalization, tariff and nontariff restrictions on goods and many services are now at extremely low levels in the industrial countries. Most major developing countries have also slashed their trade barriers, often unilaterally and in conformity with their own domestic reforms. Most economists would agree that the efficiency benefits of further reductions in these existing barriers are unlikely to be large. Indeed, the dirty little secret of international economics is that a tiny bit of protection reduces efficiency only a tiny bit. A logical implication is that the case for further liberalization in the traditional area of manufactured goods is rather weak.

Moreover, there is a case for taking greater advantage of the World Trade Organization's existing escape clause, which allows countries to institute otherwise-illegal trade restrictions under specified conditions, as well as for broadening the scope of these multilateral safeguard actions. In recent years, trade policy in the United States and the European Union has gone in a rather different direction, with increased use of antidumping measures and limited recourse to escape clause actions. This is likely because WTO rules and domestic legislation make the petitioning industry's job much easier in antidumping cases: there are lower evidentiary hurdles than in escape clause actions, no determinate time limit, and no requirement for compensation for affected trade partners, as the escape clause provides. Also, escape clause actions, unlike antidumping duties, require presidential approval in the United States. This is an undesirable situation because antidumping rules are, on the whole, consistent neither with economics principles nor, as discussed below, with fairness. Tightening the rules on antidumping in conjunction with a reconsideration and reinvigoration of the escape clause mechanism would make a lot of sense.

Do not neglect social insurance

Policymakers have to bear in mind the important role that the provision of social insurance, through social programs, has played historically in enabling multilateral liberalization and an explosion of world trade. As the welfare state is being pruned, there is a real danger that this contribution will be forgotten.

This does not mean that fiscal policy has to be profligate and budget deficits large. Nor does it mean a bigger government role. Enhanced levels of social insurance, for better labor-market outcomes, can be provided in most countries within existing levels of spending. This can be done, for example, by shifting the composition of income transfers from old-age insurance (i.e., social security) to labor-market insurance (i.e., unemployment compensation, trade adjustment assistance, training programs). Because pensions typically constitute the largest item of social spending in the advanced industrial countries, better targeting of this sort is highly compatible with responsible fiscal policies. Gearing social insurance more directly toward labor markets, without increasing the overall tax burden, would be one key step toward alleviating the insecurities associated with globalization.

There is a widespread feeling in many countries that, in the words of Tanzi and Schuknecht, "[s]ocial safety nets have . . . been transformed into universal benefits with widespread free-riding behavior, and social insurance has frequently become an income support system with special interests making any effective reform very difficult." Further, "various government performance indicators suggest that the growth in spending after 1960 may not have brought about significantly improved economic performance or greater social progress." However, social spending has had the important function of buying social peace. Without disagreeing about the need to eliminate waste and reform in the welfare state more broadly, I would argue that the need for social insurance does not decline but rather increases as global integration increases. So the message to reformers of the social welfare system is, don't throw the baby out with the bath water.

Do not use "competitiveness" as an excuse for domestic reform

One of the reasons globalization gets a bad rap is that policymakers often fall into the trap of using "competitiveness" as an excuse for needed domestic reforms. Large fiscal deficits or lagging domestic productivity are problems that drag living standards down in many industrial countries and would do so even in closed economies. Indeed, the term "competitiveness" itself is largely meaningless when applied to whole economies, unless it is used to refer to things that already have a proper name – such as productivity, investment, and economic growth. Too often, however, the need to resolve fiscal or productivity problems is presented to the electorate as the consequence of global competitive pressures. This not only makes the required policies a harder sell – why should we adjust just for the sake of becoming better competitors against the Koreans or the Mexicans? – it also erodes the domestic support for international trade – if we have to do all these painful things because of trade, maybe trade isn't such a wonderful thing anyhow!

The French strikes of 1995 are a good case in point. What made the opposition to the proposed fiscal and pension reforms particularly salient was the perception that fundamental changes in the French way of life were being imposed for the sake of international economic integration. The French government presented the reforms as required by the Maastricht criteria, which they were. But presumably, the Maastricht criteria themselves reflected the policymakers' belief that a smaller welfare state would serve their economies better in the longer run. By and large, the French government did not make the case for reform on its own strengths. By using the Maastricht card, it turned the discussion into a debate on European economic integration. Hence the widespread public reaction, which extended beyond just those workers whose fates would be immediately affected.

The lesson for policymakers is, do not sell reforms that are good for the economy and the citizenry as reforms that are dictated by international economic integration.

Do not abuse "fairness" claims in trade

The notion of fairness in trade is not as vacuous as many economists think. Consequently, nations have the right – and should be allowed – to restrict trade when it conflicts with *widely held* norms at home or undermines domestic social arrangements that enjoy *broad* support.

But there is much that is done in the name of "fair trade" that falls far short of this criterion. There are two sets of practices in particular that should be immediately suspect. One concerns complaints made against other nations when very similar practices abound at home. Antidumping proceedings are a clear example: standard business practices, such as pricing over the life of a product or pricing over the business cycle, can result in duties being imposed on an exporting firm. There is nothing "unfair" about these business practices, as is made abundantly clear by the fact that domestic firms engage in them as well.

The second category concerns cases in which other nations are unilaterally asked to change *their* domestic practices so as to equalize competitive conditions. Japan is frequently at the receiving end of such demands from the United States and the European Union. A more recent example concerns the declaration by the US Trade Representative that corruption in foreign countries will henceforth be considered as unfair trade. While considerations of fairness and legitimacy will guide a country's own social arrangements, even by restricting imports if need be, such considerations should not allow one country to impose its own institutions on others. Proponents of fair trade must bear this key distinction in mind. Thus, it is perfectly legitimate for the United States to make it illegal for domestic firms to engage in corrupt practices abroad (as was done with the Foreign Corrupt Practices Act of 1977). It is also legitimate to negotiate a multilateral set of principles with other countries in the Organization for Economic Cooperation and Development (OECD) with broadly similar norms. It may also be legitimate to restrict imports from a country whose labor practices broad segments of the domestic population deem offensive. But it is not acceptable to unilaterally threaten retaliation against other countries because their business practices do not comply with domestic standards at home *in order to force these countries to alter their own standards*. Using claims of fairness to advance competitive aims is coercive and inherently contradictory. Trying to "export" norms by asking other countries to alter their social arrangements to match domestic ones is inappropriate for the same reason. [. . .]

29 Partisan Politics in the Global Economy

Geoffrey Garrett

Throughout the world today, politics lags behind economics, like a horse and buggy haplessly trailing a sports car. While politicians go through the motions of national elections – offering chimerical programs and slogans – world markets, the Internet and the furious pace of trade involve people in a global game in which elected representatives figure as little more than bit players. Hence the prevailing sense, in America and Europe, that politicians and ideologies are either uninteresting or irrelevant.

> Roger Cohen, "Global Forces Batter Politics," *The New York Times Week in Review*, November 17, 1996, p. 1.

[I] challenge the conventional wisdom about the effects of globalization on domestic politics in the industrial democracies. There is a glut of research claiming that the international integration of markets in goods, services, and above all capital has eroded national autonomy and, in particular, all but vitiated social democratic alternatives to the free market. In contrast, I argue that the relationship between the political power of the left and economic policies that reduce market-generated inequalities has not been weakened by globalization; indeed, it has been strengthened in important respects. Furthermore, macroeconomic outcomes in the era of global markets have been as good or better in countries where powerful left-wing parties are allied with broad and centrally organized labor movements ("social democratic corporatism") as they have where the left and labor are weaker.

These findings have broader implications for the relationship between democracy and capitalism in the contemporary period. People who propose dire scenarios based on visions either of the inexorable dominance of capital over labor or of radical autarkic and nationalist backlashes against markets overlook the ongoing history of social democratic corporatism. There is more than one path to competing successfully in the global economy. The impact of electoral politics has not been dwarfed by market dynamics. Globalized markets have not rendered immutable the efficiency–equality trade-off. These lessons from the industrial democracies should hearten advocates of social democracy throughout the world.

The conventional wisdom about the globalization of markets claims that the ever-increasing capacity of firms and investors to move production and capital around the world has precipitated a sea change away from the halcyon days of the postwar mixed economy. In this new environment of deep trade interdependence, multinational production regimes and global capital markets, government attempts to intervene in the

Original publication details: Excerpted from Geoffrey Garrett, "Introduction," from *Partisan Politics in the Global Economy* (Cambridge University Press, 1998), pp. 1–11. Reprinted by permission of Cambridge University Press.

economy are thought to be doomed to fail if they extend beyond minimal "market friendly" measures. The lesson for all governments is supposedly clear: The imperatives of the market impose heavy constraints on the bounds of democratic choice. Good government is market friendly government, and this effectively rules out most of the "welfare state" policies that the left labored long and hard to establish in the forty years following the Depression.

From this perspective, the age-old debate about the relative power of the capitalist economy and the democratic polity as social forces has been definitively settled in capital's favor. From the Depression until the 1970s, it was widely argued that government could (and should) intervene in the economy to reduce inequality without adversely affecting the macroeconomy. In the contemporary era of global markets, however, the trade-off between efficiency and welfare is considered to be harsh and direct. Even left-wing governments that would like to use the policy instruments of the state to redistribute wealth and risk in favor of the less fortunate have no choice but to bow to the demands of the market.

My portrayal of the globalization thesis is anything but a straw man. Consider the following gloomy predictions from recent and influential scholarly research on the future of social democracy. Paulette Kurzer concludes:

> [T]his book does not hold great promise for social democracy. . . . [L]eft-wing parties will continue to seek election and occasionally win power. However, these parties have little in common with their predecessors in terms of articulating progressive options and pursuing programs different from the conservative, or establishment view. . . . In the past decade, growth has been sluggish, and investments have stagnated. Unemployment and declining wages marked the 1980s. Governments could combat such situations by spending money on public programs, increasing public employment, or raising social transfer payments, but no governments can afford to do this today.

Fritz Scharpf's bottom line is very similar:

> Unlike the situation in the first three postwar decades, there is now no economically plausible Keynesian strategy that would permit the full realization of social democratic goals within a national context without violating the functional imperatives of the capitalist economy. Full employment, rising real wages, larger welfare transfers, and more and better public services can no longer all be had simultaneously. . . . For the foreseeable future . . . social democracy has a chance to influence economic policy only if it explicitly accepts the full harshness of world economic conditions and hence the constraints on domestic policy options.

The globalization thesis can, of course, be taken much further than claims about the demise of social democracy. Some have pointed to the rise of xenophobic nationalism as a profoundly destabilizing consequence of globalization. For example, Ethan Kapstein argues that there are disturbing similarities between the 1990s and the 1930s:

> While the world stands at a critical time in postwar history, it has a group of leaders who appear unwilling, like their predecessors in the 1930s, to provide the international leadership to meet economic dislocations. . . . Like the German elite in Weimar, they dismiss mounting worker dissatisfaction, fringe political movements, and the plight of the unemployed and working poor as marginal concerns compared with the unquestioned importance of a sound currency and balanced budget. Leaders need to recognize the policy

failures of the last 20 years and respond accordingly. If they do not, there are others waiting in the wings who will, perhaps on less pleasant terms.

Others argue that the nation-state itself, irrespective of how it is governed, is a dinosaur that is very poorly adapted to the global economy. Management theorist Kenichi Ohmae's description of the anachronistic and embattled nation state provides a vivid portrayal of this view:

> [T]he glue holding traditional nation states together, at least in economic terms, has begun to dissolve. Buffeted by sudden changes in industry dynamics, available information, consumer preferences, and flows of capital; burdened by demands for the civil minimum and for open-ended industrial subsidies in the name of the national interest; and hog-tied by political systems that prove ever-less responsive to new challenges, these political aggregations no longer make compelling sense as discrete, meaningful units on an up-to-date map of economic activity.

I, however, challenge the reasoning and conclusions that underpin all of these studies and many others like them. I do not wish to argue that analysts have exaggerated the extent to which goods, services, and capital markets are internationally integrated today. Others have made this case, but it is not necessary for my argument. Rather, I argue that existing studies have significantly underestimated the effects of domestic political conditions both on the way governments react to globalization and on their impact on the national economy. Posed in its starkest terms, my argument is that there remains a leftist alternative to free market capitalism in the era of global markets based on classic "big government" and corporatist principles that is viable both politically (in terms of winning elections) and economically (by promoting strong macroeconomic performance).

The first element of this argument concerns domestic political dynamics. Proponents of the globalization thesis focus almost exclusively on the increased "exit" threats of mobile asset holders. Despite and because of the reality of this phenomenon, market integration has also increased demands on government ("voice") to mitigate the insecurities, instabilities and inequalities it has generated. As Robert Keohane and Joseph Nye argued twenty years ago, globalization heightens the vulnerability of countries to the international economy – in terms of both the portion of society subject to global competition and the speed with which changes in market conditions are transmitted across borders. Even the OECD is well aware of this relationship:

> Reduced wage and employment security has extended to sectors and population segments that have been historically considered "safe", such as public sector employees and executive and managerial workers. In all countries the nature of employment is changing, with an increasing share of total employment accounted for by part-time work and temporary contracts . . . the share of involuntary part-time employment has been increasing in almost all countries.

These conditions have proved fertile ground for left-wing parties and for economic policies that ameliorate market-generated inequality and risk. Some conservative parties – notably in the Anglo-American countries – have chosen not to cultivate voters who benefit from government efforts to mitigate the dislocations of globalization. But most left-of-center parties have concentrated their efforts on this constituency.

The consequences of government efforts to compensate short-term market losers, however, are not necessarily benign. Indeed, most people would argue that they are bad for competitiveness and can only result in greater capital flight. Dani Rodrik makes this argument eloquently. He contends that the twin domestic consequences of globalization – increased exit options for mobile asset holders ("footloose capital") and increased voice among the less mobile (most citizens) for policies that cushion market forces – may be on a collision course that will do great harm to all. According to Rodrik:

> [T]he cumulative consequence of (globalization) will be the solidifying of a new set of class divisions – between those who prosper in the globalized economy and those who do not; between those who share its values and those who would rather not; and between those who can diversify away its risks and those who cannot. This is not a pleasing prospect even for the individuals on the winning side of the divide with little empathy for the other side. Social disintegration is not a spectator sport – those on the sidelines also get splashed with mud from the field. Ultimately, the deepening of social fissures can harm all.

The second element of my argument is that social democratic corporatism provides a way to avoid this collision course. Rodrik's argument makes explicit the common perception that government policies reducing inequality and social risk are antithetical to the interests of mobile asset holders. This view contends that whenever footloose capital sees powerful left-wing parties, strong labor market institutions, and interventionist big government, it will exercise its exit options. Not only will this make it increasingly difficult for government to tax business to fund its spending objective, but capital flight will also deal a body blow to economic performance.

There are numerous reasons to be skeptical of this argument. One, ultimately limited, reason follows from "new growth" theory. In recent years, many economists have argued that the ambit of market friendly government should be broadened to include policies that produce growth-enhancing collective goods undersupplied by the market. The clearest example of such goods is public education and training, but the label can also be applied to physical infrastructure. These collective goods are not only beneficial to citizens in terms of jobs and improving future life chances; they are also attractive to capital in terms of increasing investment returns. There are nonetheless clear limits to the types of government policies sanctioned by new growth theory. Most government spending, for example, is considered unproductive.

Indeed, it would be very hard to make the case that income transfer programs or in-kind benefits for the unemployed, the sick, or the old are "good for growth" in a direct sense. But this is precisely the argument I wish to make by taking a broad view of the positive externalities of big government. I contend that the types of redistributive economic policies associated with strong left-wing parties are compatible with strong economic performance in the global economy, provided labor market institutions are sufficiently "encompassing" to facilitate collective action among the bulk of the workforce.

Social democratic corporatist regimes are based on a virtuous circle in which government policies that cushion market dislocations are exchanged for the regulation of the national labor market by the leaders of encompassing trade union movements. The products of this virtuous circle include predictable patterns of wage setting that restrain real wage growth in accordance with productivity and competitiveness constraints, highly skilled and productive workers, cooperation between labor and business in the work place, and low levels of social strife more generally. These economic "goods" are attractive even to mobile asset holders in the volatile global economy, offsetting the disincentives to investment generated by big government and high labor costs highlighted by neoclassical economics. I thus contend that there is no good reason to believe that in the global economy, capital flight will be the knee-jerk response of mobile asset holders to social democratic corporatism.

This doesn't mean, of course, that contemporary social democratic corporatism doesn't face important challenges. For example, the graying of society in the context of generous public health and pension entitlements to retirees and the power of public sector trade unions are both significant problems that must be confronted. But there are solutions to these problems that do not violate the fundamental tenets of social democracy. More importantly for my purposes, these challenges have very little to do with globalization. Rather, they are better thought of as inherent products of the success of the social democratic project in the postwar period.

My primary claim is that globalization and national autonomy are not mutually exclusive options. The benefits of globalization can be reaped without undermining the economic sovereignty of nations, and without reducing the ability of citizens to choose how to distribute the benefits – and the costs – of the market. The experience of the social democratic corporatist countries should provide succor, not spawn regret, among advocates of social democracy as an equitable and efficient means for reconciling markets and democracy.

The Argument

The dominant view about the domestic effects of globalization accords a *deus ex machina* quality to market forces. If business occupies (in Charles Lindblom's famous terms) a "privileged position" in all capitalist economies, its position is even stronger where markets are global but politics is national. Capital can simply choose to exit the national economy if government pursues policies that business people disapprove of. The rubric of bad economic policies is presumed to cover all market "distortions," including government spending on goods and services that could be provided more efficiently by the market, and taxes to pay for them that treat different income sources unequally.

The notion that mobile asset holders in the industrial democracies today have credible exit threats is indisputable. Many firms have production regimes that cross national boundaries, and strategic alliances are increasingly common. The growth of international portfolio investment in equity, bond, and currency markets has been explosive in the past twenty years. Do these developments represent the death knell of social democracy? The conventional wisdom makes two implicit assumptions about the political economy of capitalist democracy. First, the state of the macroeconomy is considered the primary – if not the sole – determinant of a government's prospects for reelection. Second, government interventions in the economy beyond explicitly capital friendly measures precipitate downward spirals in economic performance. When combined with capital's exit options, these two assumptions lead to the conclusion that social democracy is incompatible with global markets.

I argue that both of these assumptions are inappropriate. There is ample evidence that macroeconomic outcomes significantly influence elections. But presiding over an expanding pie is not the only path to electoral success. Political parties can also attract support by distributing the social pie in ways that favor certain groups over others. Indeed, the short-term nature of democratic politics creates a bias in favor of distributional strategies: Governments cannot afford to do what is good for the economy in the long run if this immediately hurts their core electoral constituencies.

The most important distributional cleavage in the industrial democracies has long been between those who support the market allocation of wealth and risk – the natural constituency of right-wing parties – and those who favor government efforts to alter market outcomes – the left's core base of support. The welfare state – broadly construed to include not only income transfer programs such as unemployment insurance and public pensions but also the provision of social services such as education and health – is the basic policy instrument for redistribution. Left-wing and centrist Christian democratic parties have long been more willing to expand the welfare state than their counterparts on the right. Some have claimed that the electoral appeal of the welfare state has declined apace with the shrinking of the manufacturing working class. But even in the Anglo-American democracies, popular support for the welfare state grew at the same time as the traditional working class shrank. Broader cross-national surveys of public opinion also show that public support for the welfare state continues to be very strong in most countries.

The key to understanding the popularity of welfare programs in the global economy is recognizing that although market integration may benefit all segments of society in the longer run through the more efficient allocation of production and investment, the short-term effects of globalization are very different. Indeed, perhaps the most important immediate effect of globalization is to increase social dislocations and economic insecurity, as the distribution of incomes and jobs across firms and industries becomes increasingly unstable. The result is that increasing numbers of people have to spend evermore time and money trying to make their future more secure. Whatever the portion of the labor force that is directly affected by market dislocations, perceptions of growing economic insecurity will always be considerably more widespread. In the contemporary period, this constituency obviously extends well beyond the traditional manufacturing working class.

Given this nexus between globalization and economic insecurity, it is not surprising that government policies that cushion market dislocations by redistributing wealth and risk are at least as popular today as they have ever been. This does not mean that parties across the political spectrum will choose to expand the welfare state; ideological concerns will also play a role. Nonetheless, globalization has provided new and fertile ground for the social democratic agenda (and for more populist and xenophobic appeals for economic closure).

Critics might accept this part of my argument but dismiss it as irrelevant, claiming that the political incentives to pursue interventionist economic policies are overwhelmed by the macroeconomic costs of doing so in the global economy. If such policies only lead to disinvestment and recession, even voters who benefit in the short term from a large public economy will ultimately abandon governments that preside over its expansion. From this perspective, it is only a question of when, not whether, the left bows to the power of the market.

Careful analysis of the evidence about the macroeconomic consequences of big government, however, prompts more caution and less dogmatism. Joel Slemrod concludes in an exhaustive review of the empirical literature, for example, that there is no overall nor consistent relationship between the size of government and rates of economic growth. In a similar study on unemployment, Charles Bean argues that there is no clear link between government-generated rigidities in labor markets and rising unemployment in the industrial countries since the early 1980s.

The underlying message of these studies is that although it is easy to point to specific costs of discrete interventionist policies, big government seems to produce positive externalities that are overlooked by its critics. These externalities may take two forms. The first is quite specific and relates to new growth theory. Many economists now believe that government investments in infrastructure – from bridges and roads to research and development to education and training – are beneficial to the economy. Thus, government spending on human and physical capital is unlikely to provoke capital flight in global markets.

The second type of externality generated by big government is more general. It is also central to claims about the economic efficacy of social democratic corporatism. Where powerful left parties are allied with encompassing labor movements, policies that redistribute market allocations of wealth and risk are unlikely to provoke capital flight among mobile asset holders.

Consider the following hypothetical example of a left-wing government's decision to increase the duration of unemployment benefits. Even economists who argue that appropriately constructed unemployment insurance schemes are desirable look dimly on increasing the duration of benefits. The wages acceptable to those in employment, and especially those organized into trade unions, increase with declines in the material costs of unemployment. The government must borrow money or raise taxes to fund its new scheme. Thus, increasing the duration of benefits must slow output growth and job creation.

The flaw in this logic is that it ignores the impact of labor market institutions on the behavior of workers. I argue that where national labor market institutions are sufficiently encompassing to overcome labor's collective action problem, the benefits of leftist policies that mitigate the distributional asymmetries inherent in the market allocation of resources and risk offset the costs highlighted by the neoclassical perspective. In contrast, interventionist economic policies are likely to have deleterious macroeconomic consequences where labor movements are not encompassing, precisely because isolated groups of workers can be expected to take advantage of reduced market constraints to push up their wages.

In the scenario outlined above, the government's enhanced unemployment insurance policy helps all those at risk in the labor market. The direct effect of this policy reform is that the threat of unemployment is now less disciplining on the labor market, which could be detrimental to overall economic performance. Those currently in work could push up their wages, reducing demand for the currently unemployed. The result of this "insider–outsider" problem would be higher inflation and higher unemployment.

The leaders of encompassing labor movements, however, care about the welfare of the whole labor force, and they have the institutional clout to ensure that the behavior of certain groups of workers does not reduce the welfare of others. In my example, labor leaders have both the incentive and the capacity to mitigate the insider–outsider problem. They appreciate that the best path to increasing total employment at the highest possible level of disposable incomes (both wages and work-related benefits) is to constrain wage growth among those currently employed in accordance with productivity improvements. In so doing, labor as a whole can reap the benefits of the government's policy without incurring the costs that it might otherwise generate.

This argument can be made more general. Indeed, it is at the core of the vast literature on social democratic corporatism. All government programs that alter the market allocation of wealth and risk in favor of labor should prompt the leaders of encompassing organizations to "internalize" the costs of decentralized militancy for the economy as a whole. In addition to upward pressures on wages, these external-ities comprise all types of inefficiency and instability associated with groups of workers who have the organizational capacity to voice effectively their grievances. These range from the threat of strikes to unwillingness to cooperate with management at the workplace to more general social agitation.

The combination of left government and encompassing labor market institutions reduces these sources of inefficiency and instability. In turn, the strategic decisions of mobile asset holders will be affected not only by the direct costs of social democra-tic corporatism – a bigger public economy and higher total labor costs – but also by the benefits – higher productivity and economic, political, and social stability. A price must be paid for these desirable outcomes, but the return is considerable. There is thus no good a priori reason to think that mobile asset holders will choose to exit from social democratic corporatist regimes.

Let me now summarize the structure of the argument. I have suggested that the "class compromise" of capitalist democracy – in which asset holders accept redistributive government policies and governments accept the primacy of market mechanisms – is at least as important in the global economy as it has ever been. Glob-alization increases the potential long-run social benefits of markets, but it also height-ens political opposition to them in the short run. Governments face the daunting task of reconciling these two forces. Where the left is allied with encompassing labor markets, it is possible to reap the benefits of market integration without increasing the risk of damaging popular backlashes in the form of economic, political and social instability. Farsighted capital can be expected to understand the upside of social democratic corporatism and hence to forgo the temptation to use the threat or reality of exit. [. . .]

The Evidence

The empirical core of this argument can be distilled into three basic propositions about the interrelationships among globalization, partisan politics, and the economy that track the progression of the theoretical argument:

- Globalization has generated new political constituencies for left-of-center parties among the increasing ranks of the economically insecure that offset the shrink-ing of the manufacturing working class. As a result, enduring cross-national differences in the balance of power between left and right remain. So, too, do marked differences in labor market institutions.
- Globalization has increased the political incentives for left-wing parties to pursue economic policies that redistribute wealth and risk in favor of those adversely affected in the short term by market dislocations, especially in countries where organized labor is also strong. Thus, the historical relationship between left-labor power and big government has not weakened with market integration.
- Globalization has increased the importance of economic, political and social sta-bility to the investment decisions of mobile asset holders. Because the combina-

tion of powerful left-wing parties and encompassing labor market institutions promotes stability in the wage-setting process and in society more generally, macroeconomic performance under social democratic corporatism has been as good as
– if not better than – that under any other constellation of political power and
labor market institutions.

30   The Role of the State in the Age of Globalisation

Kofi Annan

[...] The United Nations was founded in 1945 as the centrepiece of a new international order, in which it was taken for granted that nation-states were the main actors. It was assumed that the main threat to world order would come from the aggression of one State against another. And the international economy was made up of separate national economies trading with each other.

The world of today is very different. In recent decades, far more people have been killed in civil wars, ethnic cleansing and acts of genocide than in conventional war between States. Even in the relatively prosperous and orderly parts of the world, what keeps people awake at night is less the threat of armed attack by another State than the fear of what might be done by a handful of fanatics – perhaps armed only with box-cutters, like those who attacked the United States last September, or, even more frighteningly, armed with weapons of mass destruction, purchased in an illicit arms bazaar that largely ignores State frontiers.

Similarly, the word "international" is no longer the best one to describe today's world economy. While international trade has increased spectacularly since 1945, it has been far outstripped by the growth of cross-border investment. As a result there are many companies, and a vast number of products, on which it is now hard to stick a meaningful national label. There really is a global economy.

And the speed and ubiquity of modern communications – with the same images appearing simultaneously on TV and computer screens throughout the world – have also given us the beginnings of a global society and culture.

All these phenomena are largely unimpeded by national frontiers. They challenge the authority, or even the relevance, of nation states. That means that they also present new challenges to the United Nations.

Some people imagine that the UN, as a global institution, is itself one of those global forces that are eroding the authority of States. But that is a misunderstanding. The United Nations, as its name implies, is primarily an association of nation states.

There is therefore no contradiction between my office and the thesis I wish to put before you today, which is that – in spite or even because of all the globalising forces I have mentioned – the sovereign State remains a highly relevant and necessary institution; indeed, the very linchpin of human security.

Look around you at this city of Geneva, which is so calm and prosperous. Do any of us imagine that it could be like that without the rule of law, enforced by a strong and effective State?

Original publication details: Excerpted from Kofi Annan, "The Role of the State in the Age of Globalisation," keynote address to Conference on Globalisation and International Relations in the 21st Century, June 2002. Reprinted by permission of United Nations Publications.

You may think I have chosen the wrong or a bad example, since in Geneva many state powers belong to the city or the Canton, while the strictly national authority of the Swiss Confederation has rather limited power. Moreover Switzerland, with its multiplicity of national languages, may seem an untypical nation State.

But I would argue the opposite. The only thing that makes Switzerland untypical is that it is unusually strong and successful. Over the centuries, the Swiss have forged a national identity that does not depend on sharing a single language or religion. And the confederal form of the State, which leaves so much power in the hands of the Cantons, is itself a central feature of that identity.

Whether they speak German, French, Italian or Romansch, whether they are Catholic, Protestant, Jewish, or of any other religion, the Swiss are proud to be Swiss and to belong to a Swiss state. Like the United States of America, they have found strength and unity through diversity. It is entirely fitting that they have now decided to join the United Nations, and I am sure they will feel at home there.

Now consider which people in the world are most unlike the citizens of Geneva, in the sense of being deprived of the advantages those citizens enjoy.

Are they not the people who live in the weakest States, where order has completely broken down and even the most rudimentary social services, such as primary health-care and education, are lacking – like Somalia, for instance, which, despite having a single language and culture, has sadly become the text book example of a "failed State"?

Or are they, perhaps, the people who have been completely deprived of their own State's protection and driven into exile in other States, where they are not citizens – and which therefore recognise few if any of their obligations towards them?

Whichever is the most unfortunate group – those who have fled their own country and become effectively stateless, or those who remain trapped in a country without an effective State – I do not think the citizens of Switzerland, or any other well-organized State, would wish to change places with them.

Indeed, those who are most cheerful about globalisation are invariably people who themselves enjoy the security of citizenship and the rule of law in a well organized and effective State. They may perhaps be living outside that State, and they may con-gratulate themselves on the freedom to roam the world that globalisation has brought them. But they do so with a national passport in their pocket, and the knowledge that, if things get rough, they have a State of their own to go back to or to go home to.

I say that, not as a critic of such people, but rather as one of them myself. I do believe that globalisation represents a great opportunity for the whole human race, and I have said so to many audiences who are less ready to accept that message than you here today.

But I always say in the next breath that at present the benefits of globalisation are far from being equitably shared. There are many, many people in the world who are not enjoying them, and one reason for that is that they do not live in well-organized States that are capable of managing the process.

Globalisation makes well-organized States if anything more necessary, not less. But even the best-organized States are not finding globalisation easy to manage. That is because globalisation challenges their ability to perform their historic function of pro-viding security to their citizens, in all three of its aspects – physical security, economic security, and psychological security.

This is most obvious in the case of economic security.

Globalisation is only partly the result of technological change. Equally important have been decisions, taken by States, to reduce the controls and restrictions they for-merly imposed on the economic life of their citizens.

On balance, and in the long term, I have no doubt that this move away from State control is beneficial. But its immediate effect is to deprive States of many of their traditional instruments for protecting vulnerable groups. It has become more difficult to finance social expenditure by raising taxes, or to enforce standards in such areas as environmental protection, working conditions, and even basic human rights, without being accused either of obstructing the free flow of trade, or of imposing unfair conditions on your own exporters, in a highly competitive global market.

But globalisation now challenges the ability of States to protect and provide the physical security of their citizens, too.

Weak States in the developing world – especially in Africa – find that they are no longer able to monopolise and control the flow of weapons in their societies, because groups within those societies are able to by-pass the State, financing weapons purchases on the global market through sales, on the same global market, of illicit crops or illicitly mined natural resources. For these countries, globalisation represents a return to some of the worst features of the pre-colonial or early colonial era.

But the same phenomena, or related ones, are also undermining security in developed countries. Neither crime nor terrorism is a new problem. But increasingly they are global problems, from which no country can feel safe.

In addition, few States can fully protect either the economic or the physical security of their citizens against environmental problems, which increasingly cut across frontiers – from acid rain and other forms of pollution to climate change, not to mention competition for water and other scarce resources, as population pressures increase and cultivable land shrinks.

As if these threats were not bad enough in themselves, their effects are magnified by a loss of psychological security. In many countries people feel that their traditional way of life, even their identity, is threatened.

Transmitted around the world, images of the ease and plenty enjoyed by a few societies can stimulate new appetites and temptations, new patterns of consumption, and new relationships. They can become a siren song, undermining family structures and challenging religious authorities.

And in many countries – especially, perhaps, those of the developed world – population movements bring people of different cultural backgrounds into formerly stable communities, prompting questions about how inclusive a nation should be, and what its identity is based on.

I believe all these different types of insecurity were reflected in recent election results in several European countries, where many voters supported fringe groups of right or left, or failed to vote at all. These voters were expressing their disillusionment with the failure of those in power to protect them against new threats.

Even the strongest States look weak, to many of their citizens, because they seem unable to respond to the challenges of unemployment, deteriorating services, rising crime levels, and intrusive social change. And so those citizens voice their nostalgia for what they remember, or imagine, as the good old days of the nation State.

Yet following the programmes of the fringe parties, or reverting to traditional methods of control, will not bring those good old days back.

One of the lessons of the twentieth century is that a strong State is not the same thing as a coercive State. States that were extremely coercive, like Nazi Germany and the Soviet Union, looked terrifyingly strong for a time, while liberal democracies appeared weak and decadent. But at the end of the century it was the liberal democracies that proved resilient.

So it would be a tragic mistake if, as the new century begins, States tried to assert themselves mainly by coercive methods.

Please understand: I am not advocating a passive approach. It was not through laissez-faire policies, nor yet by unilateral disarmament, that the liberal democracies outlasted Nazism and communism.

States need robust policies. They must have the capacity to resist aggression, to detect and punish crime, to protect their citizens against terrorism, and also to provide basic services and safety nets. And for all these things they need to raise revenue through taxation.

But they must reassert themselves by tapping new sources of legitimacy and strength. They need to broaden the base of their support.

Many of their objectives today can be achieved only by engaging other actors, not unwillingly but as true partners. The private sector, voluntary agencies and pressure groups, universities, research institutes, think tanks, foundations, and individuals: all will do much more to deliver what the community needs if they are inspired, cajoled, negotiated with – and, of course, listened to – than if governments attempt to coerce them.

The same applies even more clearly on the international level. There too, States need to work with all these various non-state actors, and also with each other. [. . .]

Questions

1   Identify several aspects of globalization that make it more difficult for states to manage their societies.

2   What happens to the territory of an empire when it collapses? Think about the case of the Soviet Union after 1989, when many new states appeared. Did any former Soviet republics choose not to become independent states? Can you explain why?

3   How can intergovernmental organizations (IGOs) help solve the problems states face in dealing with globalization?

4   Strange argues that rapid technological change and the extensive resources required for technological innovation force states to do the bidding of transnational corporations. Give the logic of this argument, while showing how technological change can also work to the benefit of states.

5   Ohmae says that "nation states have become little more than bit actors" with respect to the global economy. Explain what he means by this. Then discuss a variety of measures taken by states to ensure that they are not only "bit actors" on the global economic stage.

6   Garrett challenges the claim that expanded government interferes with economic growth. What are some of the "positive externalities" of expanded government that may help economic growth, despite the higher taxes and lowered flexibility that government expansion often entails?

7   The UN Secretary General, Kofi Annan, asserts that states need to be strong to deal with the impact of globalization. What kinds of problems and issues associated with globalization require efficient and effective states, in Annan's view? How is the state to provide the necessary forms of "security" that he mentions?

Part VI

Political Globalization II: Reorganizing the World

Introduction

The selections in this part turn to the impact of international nongovernmental organizations (INGOs), global social movements, and international conferences on world politics and global governance. While most analysts of world politics see states as the primary actors, stressing their jockeying for power as the driving force behind world development (or, as we saw in Part V, raising doubts about the capacity of states to meet the challenges posed by globalization), in these selections states are not so much "in the driver's seat" regarding world affairs. Instead, states are only one among many types of global actors, and they often are influenced substantially by other actors in ways they may hardly recognize. In addition, in many sectors of global development states are only marginally involved, and the past decade has witnessed a growing insistence on the importance and value of nongovernmental organizations and social movements as mechanisms for satisfying the needs and desires of the world's population, rather than the desires of often corrupt or power-hungry elites.

Until quite recently, researchers approached the study of social movements on a country-by-country basis, with movements in the United States receiving the lion's share of attention. Case studies have traced in great detail the origins, growth, and successes and failures of the civil rights movement, the women's movement, gay and lesbian rights organizations, environmentalism, and so on. Sometimes, a broader perspective has been added by bringing together case studies of, say, the anti-nuclear movements in the United States, Germany, and Japan, comparing the cases to identify common and dissimilar elements. Often unnoticed or little discussed is the striking fact that a great many social movements have emerged and flourished in a large number of countries simultaneously. This simultaneity, and the tendency of movements to form in countries of highly varied social conditions, leads some researchers to conclude that movements often are global in character, not simply national. Correspondingly, scholars have begun to identify the global and regional structures underlying social movements in many sectors.

These global and regional structures, it turns out, usually take the form of INGOs. INGOs are voluntary associations of individuals (and, sometimes, of other associations or corporations) banding together for specific purposes on a worldwide or regional basis. The best known INGOs are human rights organizations like Amnesty International and Human Rights Watch, environmental bodies like the World Wildlife Fund and Greenpeace, and relief and development organizations like the Red Cross and CARE. Human rights and environmental INGOs are good examples of global social movement organizations, working to improve conditions in countries all around the world and drawing on members from all continents and many countries. Many other global movements are also driven by INGOs, almost always in conjunction with domestic nongovernmental organizations (NGOs) – movements for women's rights and equality, for democracy and free elections, for the rights of indigenous peoples, for improved labor practices by global corporations like Nike or The Gap, for homosexual rights, and so on.

Social movement INGOs stand out because they engage extensively with and often challenge states, trying to change state policies or prompt state action on specific problems. They usually have little choice but to work through states because their own resources are meager and states are the only actors capable of and responsible for solving broad social problems. Many other types of INGOs pay little attention to states, however. Sports federations, professional associations, technical and standardization bodies, science and knowledge associations, and medical INGOs, among others, normally carry out their global governance activities quite autonomously, resisting state involvement. They may rely on state subsidies to some extent, but for the most part they draw on member fees, the sale of documents and publications, and individual donations to finance their work.

INGOs also become involved with intergovernmental organizations (IGOs), which were introduced in Part V. Of special importance are the United Nations and its agencies, which formally incorporate INGOs in their work through what is known as "consultative status." Thousands of INGOs now have consultative status with UN bodies, and they are key participants in many UN programs. UNAIDS (the Joint United Nations Programme on HIV/AIDS) even placed an INGO on its governing board, the first time an IGO permitted such direct INGO involvement.

The most important IGO, the United Nations, was formed after World War II as the successor to the League of Nations. Unlike the League, which the United States never joined, the UN mandate from the beginning was much broader than the issues of security and peace. Very quickly the UN became the focal point for global governance in many domains, and by the 1960s it had assumed a major role in promoting decolonization, the formation of new states in the former colonies, and the development of education, health care, and other modern systems in the less developed world. One of the UN's more striking activities has been its sponsorship of major world conferences on emerging issues, such as the conferences on women's issues during the UN Decade for Women (1976–85) and the more recent Beijing conference in 1995, as well as global conferences on the environment, including the highly publicized "Earth Summit" in Rio de Janeiro in 1992 and the follow-up World Summit on Sustainable Development in Johannesburg in 2002. In every instance, the official UN conferences, attended by delegates from states, have vied for attention with the parallel and much larger INGO/NGO conferences that speak not for governments but, in the broadest sense, for humanity as a whole.

As the twenty-first century unfolds, we therefore find a complex and highly decentralized global governance structure that involves much cooperation among INGOs, IGOs (led by the UN), and states – but also much divisiveness, disagreement, and controversy about specific policies, programs, and lines of development in many domains. Global consensus is often hard to reach, but the globalization of issues – the degree to which issues and policies are debated and settled at the global level – is continually on the rise.

In the first selection, Nitza Berkovitch discusses the global women's movement, which originated in the late nineteenth century and became an increasingly coherent and effective social movement after World War I as it concentrated its efforts on the International Labor Organization, a new IGO set up to promote and standardize labor law and policy. Berkovitch analyzes the rise of new sets of global rules and expectations pertaining to women, crystallizing after World War II in a powerful ideology calling for women's full equality with men. Sparked by the UN Decade for Women, women's INGOs have proliferated rapidly, making the movement both more global and more divided as the voices of Third World women have become increasingly prominent. The next selection, the Beijing Declaration from the Fourth World Conference on Women in 1995, provides a good encapsulated statement of the goals and demands of the world women's movement. It also neatly sidesteps some of the more controversial women's issues, such as female circumcision.

John Boli and George Thomas present a high-level overview of the entire population of international nongovernmental organizations since 1875. After charting the enormous increase in INGO formation and its ups and downs with the two world wars, they set INGOs in a world cultural context by showing how they foster and enact increasingly widespread global principles. Their article finds considerable evidence that INGOs can and do influence IGOs and states, though the extent of such influence varies greatly from issue to issue.

Peter Eigen, formerly an official at the World Bank, builds the case for global action to eliminate government corruption, including the bribing of public officials by companies seeking contracts or investment opportunities. As Chairman of Transparency International, the INGO he founded to identify and challenge corruption, he reviews the problems caused by corruption and the measures that TI believes can reduce its prevalence, if a strong partnership among INGOs, states, and such IGOs as the OECD can be mobilized effectively.

The fifth selection, by Jessica Mathews, brings domestic nongovernmental organizations (NGOs) into the picture. Mathews observes the enormous increase in voluntary citizen associations in many countries following the end of the Cold War, discerning a "power shift" in which NGOs supplement and, at times, supplant states in dealing with social problems, both nationally and globally. She points out both the promise and the pitfalls of a larger role for NGOs as the key elements of "civil society," welcoming the nimble flexibility of NGOs but cautioning that many problems still require focused state action.

Finally, Michael Bond elucidates the "backlash" that INGOs have encountered as their importance in global governance has become more obvious and widely recognized. Critics describe INGOs as self-interested, single-minded, and not accountable to the constituencies they claim to represent. INGOs working in international development aid are seen as fostering dependence on the part of governments and peoples in poor countries, and their projects are decried as overly expensive and not well adapted to local needs. These and other criticisms raise important issues for INGOs, whose ideological commitments often lead them to resist moving from a confrontational approach to a more conciliatory mode that involves cooperating with corporations and states and thus compromising their values and principles to some extent.

31 The Emergence and Transformation of the International Women's Movement

Nitza Berkovitch

The Interwar Period: Lobbying for Expansion of the World Agenda

The world polity after World War I differed markedly from that of the previous period. Earlier dreams of establishing permanent international cooperative bodies were realized with the creation of the League of Nations and the International Labor Organization (ILO), which ushered in a new phase of world-polity construction. The League and the ILO, both created at the Paris Peace Conference of 1919, constituted the first stable organizational basis for inter-state cooperation. They opened a new arena for women's mobilization by offering a central world focal point that theretofore had been lacking. In so doing, they changed the context in which women's organizations operated, consequently provoking changes in their modes of operation as well. Their main effort now targeted the newly created international bodies.

By turning their attention to the new world bodies, women's organizations conferred legitimacy on them and thus helped institutionalize their centrality. At the same time, the degree of organization and cooperation among women's groups increased. Many women's organizations moved their headquarters to Geneva to facilitate contacts with the various bodies of the League, while others established specialized bureaus expressly to deal with the League. In addition, a new type of organization emerged, the multi- or supra-international organization consisting of representatives of a number of international organizations. For example, in 1925 the Joint Committee of Representative Organizations was founded, and in 1931 ten of the largest women's groups formed the Liaison Committee of Women's International Organizations. Members of the Committee established close contacts with high officials in the League Secretariat, cooperating with the League on various welfare-related and other activities.

The increased global mobilization of women within the formally organized global arena sharpened tensions within the international women's movement. Bitter conflict

Original publication details: Excerpted from Nitza Berkovitch, "The Emergence and Transformation of the International Women's Movement," in John Boli and George M. Thomas (eds.), *Constructing World Culture: International Nongovernmental Organizations since 1875*, pp. 109–10, 119–21, 124–6. Copyright © 1999 by the Board of Trustees of the Leland Stanford Jr. University. Reprinted with the permission of Stanford University Press, www.sup.org

emerged between those who supported action on behalf of women's equality and those who favored laws that gave women special protection, especially in the area of work. Both camps focused their efforts on getting the League and ILO to take action on women's issues, but with quite different emphases.

The League's limited mandate did not allow women's issues to be considered in full; regulation of the relationships between states and their respective citizens was not included in its jurisdiction. Instead, the League concentrated on regulating relations among states. Individual "rights," a construct that had mobilized social movements for more than a century, were not considered an international concern that could be regulated by international standards. It was only through a sustained effort lasting almost two decades that women's international organizations were able to place the heart of their social concerns, the legal status of women, on the League's agenda.

The exclusion of the issue of women's rights from the League's jurisdiction was explicitly stipulated by officials during the Paris Peace Conference. Facing continuous pressure from women's organizations, however, and after much hesitation and deliberation on the part of the politicians, Conference officials agreed that "women's organizations could be heard," but only "by commissions occupying themselves especially with questions touching on women's interests." The women's delegation to the Conference presented seven resolutions covering moral, political, and educational issues. For the most part, they were ignored. [. . .]

Development Ideology

During the 1970s, the discourse of women's rights encountered that of development. This encounter was the result of the most significant event in global organizing on women's issues: the United Nation's Decade for Women (1976–1985). The Women's Decade coincided with the Second United Nations Development Decade, during which development started to dominate global discourse and activity. The two events melded into each other in the sense that a core dimension for grappling with women's issues became the concern for "incorporating women into development"; women's issues came to the fore in many development documents and projects. Framing women's issues in the context of development brought about qualitative and quantitative changes on both national and international fronts. It led to an intensification of world activity on women's issues that in turn had an enormous impact on nation-states, while it stimulated the establishment of women's movements in many countries and led most governments in the world to create an official state agency for the promotion of women's issues. Women's issues became a state concern.

Before discussing these interrelated developments, I should note that the catalyst for the Decade for Women is believed to have been a women's organization, not any of the UN bodies. Hilkka Pietila, who was herself involved in some of the activities she documents, refers to "an oral tradition in the UN family" that identifies the Women's International Democratic Federation (WIDF) as the source of the proposal for an International Women's Year. As observers on the UN Commission on the Status of Women, the WIDF's president and a number of other WINGO leaders drafted a proposal that the Commission recommended to the General Assembly. Despite initial resistance, the Assembly eventually endorsed the idea in 1972, proclaiming 1975 as International Women's Year (IWY) with the themes of equality, development, and peace.

In 1975 the World Conference of the International Women's Year was held in Mexico City. One hundred and thirty-three states participated, endorsing two major documents: the "Declaration of Mexico on the Equality of Women and Their

Contribution to Development and Peace" and the "World Plan of Action for the Implementation of the Objectives of IWY." The conference designated the 1976–1985 period as the UN Decade for Women. Representatives from 145 countries attended the 1980 Mid-Decade Conference in Copenhagen, convened as a "mid-point review of progress and obstacles in achieving the goals of the Decade," and adopted a Programme of Action. The end of the Decade was marked by the 1985 World Conference to Review and Appraise the Achievements of the UN Decade for Women, held in Nairobi. Drawing representatives from 157 countries, the conference adopted a document titled "The Nairobi Forward-Looking Strategies for the Advancement of Women."

It was during the Women's Decade that the status of women was linked to the development of their countries. As a result, both the form and content of global organizing has changed. Official bodies and the international women's movement shifted their focus from legal standards and international law to concrete projects, further organizational expansion, greater research efforts, and network enhancement to coordinate these numerous endeavors.

Within the new framework, elevating women's status and achieving equality between the sexes were conceptualized as necessary conditions for full national – economic and social – development. Women were now considered important human resources essential to comprehensive rationalization. Eradicating discrimination was an integral part of the global plan to improve the well-being of national societies and of the world as a whole. "Human rights" as a leading concept lost its prominence, though it did not disappear. Thus, for example, the sweepingly broad Convention for the Elimination of All Forms of Discrimination Against Women (adopted by the General Assembly in 1979) incorporates, side by side, the principles of abstract social justice and a more "instrumental" principle of development. In 1982, a commission under the same name was established to monitor the Convention's implementation. By 1990, this convention had been ratified by 101 countries, one of the highest rates of ratification of any UN convention. [. . .]

Summary

The story of "united womanhood" must be understood within the larger framework of the changing world polity. The existence of the international women's movement as such, its huge conferences, its plethora of documents and resolutions, and its ubiquitous lobbying visibly enact the concept of transnationalism and thus boost our tendency to see the world as a single global social system. As Roland Robertson notes: "Indeed this is one among many movements and organizations which have helped to compress the world as a whole." Thus, the international women's movement did not only reflect world culture but also helped shape its content and structure.

What started in earlier periods as moral crusades led by women's groups eventually culminated in highly legitimized and rationalized actions enacted by official world bodies on behalf of women. Around the turn of the century, the women's movement, being part of the transnational reform movement, reflected and reinforced the emphasis on moral reform and universalism. However, these early groups also promoted elements of equality, rights, and suffrage. One way of resolving the tension between the notions of individual rights and moral regeneration was subsuming the former in the latter. The international women's movement promoted women's rights as a necessary condition for enacting and bringing about desired changes in society. However, in the early period there were no world bodies to act on behalf of women.

With the establishment of the ILO as a global organization with the mandate to set international standards, the women's movement found a central target for its advocacy of the principle of equality alongside the principle of "protection," with growing tension between the two principles. The League of Nations also helped shape the mode of action and agenda of the women's groups when it became the focus for their lobbying efforts for and against an international equal rights treaty. However, it was only after World War II, when world-level organizing intensified and a more authoritative world center was established, that the principle of equality began to guide world activities regarding women. The changing agenda of the ILO regarding women's employment is striking. The sole focus on protective legislation was widened to include binding standards on equality in employment. Nation-states joined the campaign, and the majority of them revised their national labor codes to be consistent with the new spirit of women's rights.

In the 1970s another layer was added: an instrumental discourse of development that brought with it further rationalizing and organizing of world activities on women's issues. The encounter between the two discourses shaped much of the activity and spirit of the UN Decade for Women (1976–1985). The international women's movement began to operate in a much more complicated environment, with more options but also more constraints. Thanks to the initiatives of women's organizations, regular world women's conferences were held both during the Decade and after, the latest in Beijing in 1995.

The three UN conferences indicate a great deal about the worldwide construction of women's issues. First, official world organizing and activities regarding women's issues have expanded tremendously in comparison with previous periods. Second, the effects are not limited to the international level. Nation-states put "women" on their agenda, altering existing laws and establishing official bureaus and departments to deal with women's issues. Third, world-cultural ideas about women have penetrated developing countries as well, leading to the emergence of women's movements in almost every country in the world.

All the while, the international women's movement has expanded in size and transformed in content and composition. It became truly global as it grew to incorporate women from the Third World, with their specific concerns and perspectives. This process, however, was not unproblematic. Rather, it was accompanied by rising tension between women from the South and women from the North. This shows that, in contrast to conventionally held wisdom, transnational movements in general and the women's movement in particular cannot be reduced to the interests of one hegemonic region. National and regional factors can affect international organizing agenda, but the wider context affects, to large degree, the legitimacy and effectiveness of international organizing. Once international organizing emerges and gains a degree of legitimacy and operational capacity, however, new organizational dynamics are set in motion that reshape the wider context itself.

Women everywhere have been integrated into the ongoing global campaign. The international women's movement has emerged as a visible and viable global force. The overarching result is, indeed, a reconceptualization of feminism as

> a movement of people working for change across and despite national boundaries, not of representatives of nation states or national governments . . . we must be global, recognising that the oppression of women in one part of the world is often affected by what happens in another, and that no woman is free until the conditions of oppression of women are eliminated everywhere.

32   Beijing Declaration

UN Fourth World Conference on Women

Resolutions Adopted by the Conference

Resolution 1
Beijing Declaration and Platform for Action
The Fourth World Conference on Women,
Having met in Beijing from 4 to 15 September 1995,
1.   Adopts the Beijing Declaration and Platform for Action, which are annexed to the present resolution;
2.   Recommends to the General Assembly of the United Nations at its fiftieth session that it endorse the Beijing Declaration and Platform for Action as adopted by the Conference.

Annex I
BEIJING DECLARATION
1.   We, the Governments participating in the Fourth World Conference on Women,
2.   Gathered here in Beijing in September 1995, the year of the fiftieth anniversary of the founding of the United Nations,
3.   Determined to advance the goals of equality, development and peace for all women everywhere in the interest of all humanity,
4.   Acknowledging the voices of all women everywhere and taking note of the diversity of women and their roles and circumstances, honouring the women who paved the way and inspired by the hope present in the world's youth,
5.   Recognize that the status of women has advanced in some important respects in the past decade but that progress has been uneven, inequalities between women and men have persisted and major obstacles remain, with serious consequences for the well-being of all people,
6.   Also recognize that this situation is exacerbated by the increasing poverty that is affecting the lives of the majority of the world's people, in particular women and children, with origins in both the national and international domains,
7.   Dedicate ourselves unreservedly to addressing these constraints and obstacles and thus enhancing further the advancement and empowerment of women all over the world, and agree that this requires urgent action in the spirit of determination, hope, cooperation and solidarity, now and to carry us forward into the next century.
We reaffirm our commitment to:

Original publication details: Excerpted from the United Nations Fourth World Conference on Women, Beijing Declaration (1995), # 1–27, 35. Reprinted by permission of United Nations Publications.

8.   The equal rights and inherent human dignity of women and men and other purposes and principles enshrined in the Charter of the United Nations, to the Universal Declaration of Human Rights and other international human rights instruments, in particular the Convention on the Elimination of All Forms of Discrimination against Women and the Convention on the Rights of the Child, as well as the Declaration on the Elimination of Violence against Women and the Declaration on the Right to Development;

9.   Ensure the full implementation of the human rights of women and of the girl child as an inalienable, integral and indivisible part of all human rights and fundamental freedoms;

10.   Build on consensus and progress made at previous United Nations conferences and summits – on women in Nairobi in 1985, on children in New York in 1990, on environment and development in Rio de Janeiro in 1992, on human rights in Vienna in 1993, on population and development in Cairo in 1994 and on social development in Copenhagen in 1995 with the objective of achieving equality, development and peace;

11.   Achieve the full and effective implementation of the Nairobi Forward-looking Strategies for the Advancement of Women;

12.   The empowerment and advancement of women, including the right to freedom of thought, conscience, religion and belief, thus contributing to the moral, ethical, spiritual and intellectual needs of women and men, individually or in community with others and thereby guaranteeing them the possibility of realizing their full potential in society and shaping their lives in accordance with their own aspirations.

We are convinced that:

13.   Women's empowerment and their full participation on the basis of equality in all spheres of society, including participation in the decision-making process and access to power, are fundamental for the achievement of equality, development and peace;

14.   Women's rights are human rights;

15.   Equal rights, opportunities and access to resources, equal sharing of responsibilities for the family by men and women, and a harmonious partnership between them are critical to their well-being and that of their families as well as to the consolidation of democracy;

16.   Eradication of poverty based on sustained economic growth, social development, environmental protection and social justice requires the involvement of women in economic and social development, equal opportunities and the full and equal participation of women and men as agents and beneficiaries of people-centred sustainable development;

17.   The explicit recognition and reaffirmation of the right of all women to control all aspects of their health, in particular their own fertility, is basic to their empowerment;

18.   Local, national, regional and global peace is attainable and is inextricably linked with the advancement of women, who are a fundamental force for leadership, conflict resolution and the promotion of lasting peace at all levels;

19.   It is essential to design, implement and monitor, with the full participation of women, effective, efficient and mutually reinforcing gender-sensitive policies and programmes, including development policies and programmes, at all levels that will foster the empowerment and advancement of women;

20.   The participation and contribution of all actors of civil society, particularly women's groups and networks and other non-governmental organizations and

community-based organizations, with full respect for their autonomy, in cooperation with Governments, are important to the effective implementation and follow-up of the Platform for Action;

21. The implementation of the Platform for Action requires commitment from Governments and the international community. By making national and international commitments for action, including those made at the Conference, Governments and the international community recognize the need to take priority action for the empowerment and advancement of women.

We are determined to:

22. Intensify efforts and actions to achieve the goals of the Nairobi Forward-looking Strategies for the Advancement of Women by the end of this century;

23. Ensure the full enjoyment by women and the girl child of all human rights and fundamental freedoms and take effective action against violations of these rights and freedoms;

24. Take all necessary measures to eliminate all forms of discrimination against women and the girl child and remove all obstacles to gender equality and the advancement and empowerment of women;

25. Encourage men to participate fully in all actions towards equality;

26. Promote women's economic independence, including employment, and eradicate the persistent and increasing burden of poverty on women by addressing the structural causes of poverty through changes in economic structures, ensuring equal access for all women, including those in rural areas, as vital development agents, to productive resources, opportunities and public services;

27. Promote people-centred sustainable development, including sustained economic growth, through the provision of basic education, life-long education, literacy and training, and primary health care for girls and women; [. . .]

We are determined to:

35. Ensure women's equal access to economic resources, including land, credit, science and technology, vocational training, information, communication and markets, as a means to further the advancement and empowerment of women and girls, including through the enhancement of their capacities to enjoy the benefits of equal access to these resources, inter alia, by means of international cooperation. [. . .]

33 World Culture in the World Polity: A Century of International Non-Governmental Organization

John Boli and George M. Thomas

For a century and more, the world has constituted a singular polity. By this we mean that the world has been conceptualized as a unitary social system, increasingly integrated by networks of exchange, competition, and cooperation, such that actors have found it "natural" to view the whole world as their arena of action and discourse. Such a conceptualization reifies the world polity implicitly in the often unconscious adoption of this cultural frame by politicians, businesspeople, travelers, and activists, and explicitly in the discourse of intellectuals, policy analysts, and academicians.

Like all polities, the world polity is constituted by a distinct culture – a set of fundamental principles and models, mainly ontological and cognitive in character, defining the nature and purposes of social actors and action. Like all cultures, world culture becomes embedded in social organization, especially in organizations operating at the global level. Because most of these organizations are INGOs, we can identify fundamental principles of world culture by studying structures, purposes, and operations of INGOs. By studying INGOs across social sectors, we can make inferences about the structure of world culture. By studying the promotion of world-cultural principles that INGOs are centrally involved in developing, we can see how INGOs shape the frames that orient other actors, including states. [. . .]

An Historical Overview of the INGO Population

Data

Since 1850 more than 25,000 private, not-for-profit organizations with an international focus have debuted on the world stage. They include the Pan American Association of Ophthalmology, International Exhibitions Bureau, Commission for the Geological Map of the World, International Catholic Child Bureau, International Tin Council, and Tug of War International Federation. Most are highly specialized, drawing members worldwide from a particular occupation, technical field, branch of knowledge, industry, hobby, or sport to promote and regulate their respective areas

Original publication details: Excerpted from John Boli and George Thomas, "World Culture in the World Polity: A Century of International Non-Governmental Organization," *American Sociological Review*, April 1997, pp. 172–3, 174, 179–82, 187–8. Reprinted by permission of the American Sociological Association.

of concern. Only a few, such as the Scout Movement, International Olympic Committee, International Red Cross, and World Wildlife Fund, are widely known.

We analyze data on 5,983 organizations founded between 1875 and 1988. They constitute the entire population of INGOs classified as genuinely international bodies by the Union of International Associations (UIA) in its *Yearbook of International Organizations.* [. . .]

Data quality and coding issues

The UIA limits INGOs to not-for-profit, non-governmental organizations (TNCs and IGOs are excluded). They vary in size from a few dozen members from only three countries to millions of members from close to 200 countries. About half of the INGOs in our data base have members from at least 25 countries, 20 percent have members from 50 or more countries, and only 11 percent have members from fewer than eight countries. [. . .]

Basic historical patterns

Figure 33.1 presents the number of INGOs founded and dissolved in each year between 1875 and 1973. Not-for-profit international organizing grew rapidly in the latter part of the nineteenth century, with about 10 new organizations emerging each year during the 1890s. The population burgeoned after the turn of the century, reaching a peak of 51 foundings in 1910. The severe collapse after that point led to a low of four foundings in 1915. Swift recovery after World War I yielded a period of fairly steady growth followed by some decline during the 1930s that preceded another steep fall going into World War II.

Following the war, international organizing exploded. By 1947 over 90 organizations a year were being founded, a pace that was maintained and even surpassed through the 1960s. The pattern for dissolved INGOs is similar, indicating a generally steady proportion of INGOs that eventually dissolved, but revealing peaks of fragility among organizations founded just before each of the wars.

INGO foundings and dissolutions thus match the general "state of the world" rather well, rising in periods of expansion and declining rapidly in times of crisis, with the declines beginning shortly before the outbreaks of the world wars. [. . .]

World Development, INGOs, and Capitalist and Interstate Systems

Global organizing proceeds in mutually reinforcing tension with the expansion of the nation-state system. INGOs began to proliferate during the heyday of nationalism and European imperialism; bringing the last "unclaimed" regions of the globe into the world economy and under the jurisdiction of states made the notions of "one world" and "one history" structurally compelling.

This dialectic is further evident in the effects of the world wars. The precipitous decline in INGO foundings after 1910 reflects the dominance of states for most of that decade, but the war also strengthened the conception of the world as a single polity and prompted expanded INGO (and IGO) efforts to organize the world polity. After a similar cycle in the 1930s and 1940s, a much broader discursive space for INGOs opened up as global technical and infrastructural resources increased exponentially. World-polity organizing jumped to a higher level than ever before, just as the independent nation-state form was adopted by or imposed on the rest of the world.

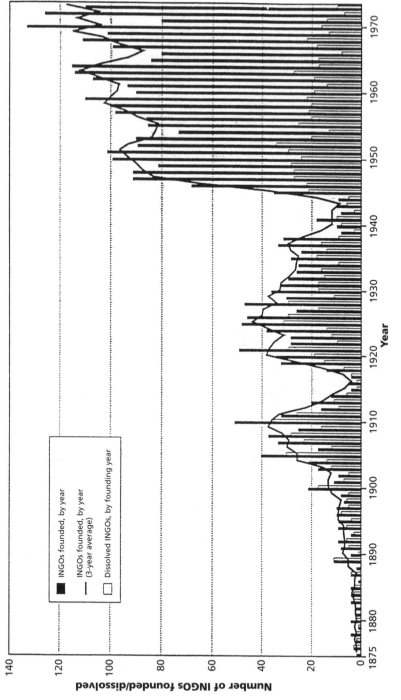

Figure 33.1 *International non-governmental organizations: INGOs founded and founding dates of dissolved INGOs, 1875 to 1973*
Source: Yearbook of International Organizations (Brussels: Union of International Associations, 24th edn. 1984–5, 27th edn. 1988–9).

The dialectic between world-polity and national-level organization is also evident in the relationship between IGOs and INGOs. Many IGOs were founded as INGOs and later co-opted by states, including such major bodies as the World Meteorological Organization, the International Labor Organization, and the World Tourism Organization. Moreover, INGOs have often been instrumental in founding new IGOs and shaping IGO activities. Thousands of INGOs have consultative status with agencies of the United Nations – over 900 with the Economic and Social Council alone – and most IGOs engage relevant INGOs as providers of information, expertise, and policy alternatives. IGO authority is not relinquished to INGOs, but IGO decisions are heavily influenced by INGO experts and lobbyists. [. . .]

INGOs as Enactors and Carriers of World Culture

Almost all INGOs originate and persist via voluntary action by individual actors. INGOs have explicit, rationalized goals. They operate under strong norms of open membership and democratic decision-making. They seek, in a general sense, to spread "progress" throughout the world: to encourage safer and more efficient technical systems, more powerful knowledge structures, better care of the body, friendly competition and fair play. To achieve their goals they emphasize communication, knowledge, consensual values and decision-making, and individual commitment. Following are five basic world-cultural principles that underlie INGO ideologies and structures: universalism, individualism, rational voluntaristic authority, human purposes of rationalizing progress, and world citizenship.

Universalism

Humans everywhere have similar needs and desires, can act in accordance with common principles of authority and action, and share common goals. In short, human nature, agency, and purpose are universal, and this universality underlies the many variations in social forms. Most INGOs are explicit about this – any interested person can become an active member, and everyone everywhere is a potential beneficiary of INGO activity.

Universalism is evident also in the breadth of INGOs' claims about what they do. Physics and pharmacology are presumed to be valid everywhere. Techniques for playing better chess are not country-specific. Red Cross aid will alleviate suffering in Africa as well as Asia. Across every sector, the purposes and means of action promoted by INGOs are assumed to be useful and meaningful everywhere.

A world not characterized by universalism does not coalesce as a singular polity; rather, it develops distinct subworld polities (societies, civilizations, empires) across which joint mobilization is unlikely. At the opposite extreme, a world state would thoroughly incorporate and regulate individuals and organizations – universalism would prevail but it would be bureaucratically absorbed.

The present world polity lies between these two extremes. Neither segmental nor ad hoc, neither is it *étatisée*; legal-bureaucratic authority is partitioned among multiple states. The principle of universalism that INGOs embody remains culturally autonomous because INGOs operate in the interstices of this decentralized structure.

Individualism

Most INGOs accept as members only individuals or associations of individuals; the main exceptions are trade and industry bodies, which often have firms as members. Individualism is also evident in their structures: INGOs use democratic, one-person–one-vote decision-making procedures, they assess fees on members individually, and they downplay national and other corporate identities in their conferences and publications. In the world-view embodied by INGOs, individuals are the only "real" actors; collectivities are essentially assemblages of individuals.

The combination of universalism and individualism may undermine traditional collectivities like the family or clan, but it also strengthens the one truly universalistic collectivity – humanity as a whole. INGOs habitually invoke the common good of humanity as a goal. The cultural dynamic at work parallels that characterizing national polities: As cultural constructs, the individual and the nation reinforce one another. In recent times, this centuries-old dynamic has shifted to the global level.

Rational voluntaristic authority

INGOs activate a particular cultural model when they organize globally, debate principles and models, and attempt to influence other actors. This model holds that responsible individuals acting collectively through rational procedures can determine cultural rules that are just, equitable, and efficient, and that no external authority is required for their legitimation. Such "self-authorization" runs counter to Weber's analysis of authority as forms of domination because INGOs cannot dominate in the conventional sense. INGOs have little sanctioning power, yet they act as if they were authorized in the strongest possible terms. They make rules and expect them to be followed; they plead their views with states or transnational corporations and express moral condemnation when their pleas go unheeded.

INGO authority is thus informal – cultural, not organizational. It is the agency presumed to inhere in rational individuals organizing for purposive action. Its basis can only be the diffuse principles of world culture, for INGO authority does not flow from any legal-bureaucratic or supernatural source.

Rational voluntarism is encouraged by the decentralized character of formal authority; at the world level, it is practiced by states and transnational corporations as well. For example, because sovereignty implies that no state has authority over any other, collective actions by states can occur only via rational voluntarism. This is why most IGOs, like INGOs, have resolutely democratic formal structures. It also helps explain why the legal-bureaucratic authority of states is brought into play to enforce INGO conceptions and rules.

Human purposes: dialectics of rationalizing progress

The rational character of INGOs is evident in their purposive orientation, formalized structures, and attention to procedures. INGOs in science, medicine, technical fields, and infrastructure activities are engaged in purely rationalized and rationalizing activity; almost all other INGOs rely on science, expertise, and professionalization in their operations and programs. What INGOs seek is, in essence, rational progress – not the crude nineteenth-century idea that steam engines and railroads would lead to heaven on earth, but the more diffuse and embedded concept of "development" that now prevails. This concept includes not only economic growth but also individual self-actualization, collective security, and justice.

At all levels, progress is assumed to depend on rationalization. Rational social action is the route to equality, comfort, and the good life. Rational production and distribution achieve all sorts of collective purposes. The scientific method, technique, monetarization, logical analysis – these are the favored *modi operandi*. These instruments of progress may often be criticized, but they are built into worldwide institutions and the ideology of development.

Rationalization, however, has another face. A tension operates between the rational and the irrational that strengthens both. Disenchantment of the world via rationalization endows the agents of disenchantment with increasing substance and sacredness; the apparent failure of actors to behave entirely rationally leads to theorizing about actors' irrational selves or cultures. Rationalized actors are thus culturally constituted as having complex "non-rational" subjectivities that are more primordial than objectified rationality. À la Nietzsche, the irrational becomes the arena of authenticity. Moreover, this face of rationalization launches wide-spread movements claiming to be anti-science, anti-Western, or postmodern: Western science, capitalism, and bureaucracy are imperialistic, dehumanizing forces against which authentic peoples must struggle to maintain their true, nonrational natures.

The rational/irrational tension thus generates conflict, but the irrational and subjective are continually channeled into rationalized activities and forms (e.g., revolution, UFO cults). Movements of self-exploration and expression, though rhetorically rejecting rationalism, also are rationalized (transcendental meditation becomes a test-improvement technique). Thus we find sports, leisure, spiritual, and psychological INGOs in abundance.

World citizenship

The principles discussed so far come together in the construct of world citizenship. Everyone is an individual endowed with certain rights and subject to certain obligations; everyone is capable of voluntaristic actions that seek rational solutions to social problems; therefore, everyone is a citizen of the world polity. World citizenship rules infuse each individual with the authority to pursue particularistic interests, preferably in organizations, while also authorizing individuals to promote collective goods defined in largely standardized ways.

World citizenship is strongly egalitarian. Individuals vary in their capacities, resources, and industry, but all have the same basic rights and duties. Correspondingly, only fully democratic governance structures are consistent with world citizenship. "Autocratic" tendencies are decried even within some INGOs (e.g., Greenpeace and the International Olympic Committee).

World citizenship is prominently codified in the Universal Declaration of Human Rights, which depicts a global citizen whose rights transcend national boundaries. The Declaration insists that states ensure the rights of their citizens and even that every human has the right to a national citizenship. In the absence of a world state, however, these obligations cannot be imposed on states. Acting as the primary carriers of world culture, INGOs translate the diffuse global identity and authority of world citizenship into specific rights, claims, and prescriptions for state behavior.

Here again we observe that states sometimes act as agents of informal world-polity authority. World citizens must turn to national states for protection of their rights, and INGOs back them up in the process. Increasingly, individuals need not be national citizens to make claims on the state; noncitizen residents of many countries have extensive rights almost equivalent to those of citizens, simply because they are human.

The cultural principles *re*-presented by INGOs are also integral to the world economy and state system, but INGOs push them to extremes. Their discourse is often critical of economic and political structures, stigmatizing "ethnocentric" (nonuniversalistic) nationalism and "exploitative" (inegalitarian) capitalism. INGOs dramatize violations of world-cultural principles, such as state maltreatment of citizens and corporate disregard for the sacredness of nature. Such examples illustrate the contested nature of these principles; they are widely known but by no means uncontroversial. [. . .]

Conclusion

INGOs are built on world-cultural principles of universalism, individualism, rational voluntaristic authority, progress, and world citizenship. Individuals and associations construct rationalized structures with defined goals, some diffuse (world peace, international understanding), but most quite specific and functional. Some INGOs, including sports, human rights, and environmental bodies, dramatically reify the world polity; human rights and environmental INGOs are especially prominent because of their conflicts with states over world-cultural principles. But most INGOs unobtrusively foster intellectual, technical, and economic rationalization that is so thoroughly institutionalized that they are hardly seen as actors, despite the enormous effects they have on definitions of reality, material infrastructure, household products, school texts, and much more.

The decentralization of authority among states facilitates transnational organizing (because centralized barriers to rational voluntarism are weak) and forces transnational organizations to focus their attention on states. Contrary to the claims of global neo-realist theories, states are not always leaders of social change; they can also be followers. In mobilizing around and elaborating world-cultural principles, INGOs lobby, criticize, and convince states to act on those principles, at least in some sectors and with respect to some issues.

How extensively this model of global change applies we cannot say. One of the central tasks for world-polity research is the development of a general theory about the conditions under which INGOs are able to take the initiative *vis-à-vis* states. A related task is the study of INGO relationships with the other major sets of reified world-polity actors, IGOs and transnational corporations. The literature contains many case studies touching on these relationships but little systematic analysis.

If a legal-rational world state emerges, much of the INGO population is likely to be co-opted to staff its bureaucracy and advise on policy decisions. To this point, we think of the operation of the world polity only as a world proto-state. A singular authority structure is lacking, states monopolize the legitimated use of violence, and states jealously guard their sovereignty. Nevertheless, the world as a proto-state has shared cultural categories, principles of authority, and universally constructed individuals who, as world proto-citizens, assume the authority to pursue goals that transcend national and local particularisms. More often than is commonly acknowledged, the resulting organizations prove to be effective. If they are absorbed in a formal global authority structure in the future, it may well be said that the road to a world state was paved by the rational voluntarism of INGOs.

34 Closing the Corruption Casino: The Imperatives of a Multilateral Approach

Peter Eigen

It is with very real pleasure that I accepted the invitation of our hosts to speak at this, the opening of Global Forum II, at a time when all the players in the battle against corruption face tremendous challenges.

In facing those challenges, it is imperative that we never forget the victims of corruption, from the plundering and misuse of rich oil resources by Sani Abacha to the wilful abuse of a siege economy by Slobodan Milosevic.

- While the world called for Milosevic to be arrested on war crimes, prosecutors in Serbia arrested him on charges of corruption and abuse of power. More than US $70 million has been located in Swiss bank accounts linked to the Milosevic regime. The people of Serbia have not only lost the lives of many of those closest to them, but have at the same time been swindled by his brutal regime.
- Abacha, who ruled Nigeria until his death in June 1998, stripped Nigeria of at least US $7 billion, a sum vast enough to begin to turn the tide of the HIV AIDS epidemic, a tragedy that is threatening the lives of a new generation in sub-Saharan Africa from the moment each child emerges from a mother's womb.

How can we not act when the proceeds of Abacha's money-laundering remain in the vaults of banks in Britain and Switzerland? This is a challenge we must address in The Hague this week. Another is to ensure that the launch of the Euro does not descend into a carnival of money-laundering.

To defeat the scourge of money-laundering, we must act together, and I speak from the standpoint of an NGO, Transparency International, which began with two simple beliefs.

First, that corruption – and the struggle against it – was an issue that stands above the divides of party politics, and so one on which all who are concerned for their country's future and the well-being of their people can and should come together.

Second, that the way to progress was through dialogue and involvement rather than the more traditional NGO approach of exposure and confrontation, that we had

Original publication details: Excerpted from Peter Eigen, "Closing the Corruption Casino: The Imperatives of a Multilateral Approach," opening address at Global Forum II, The Hague, Netherlands, May 28, 2001. Reprinted by permission of Peter Eigen, Chairman, Transparency International, http://www.transparency.org

to raise awareness and build a coalition of all three sectors – government, civil society and the private sector – both at the national and international level.

Today, this coalition approach has taken hold all over the world.

Yet at the outset we were viewed with suspicion from many sides. Despite the fact that many of our founders are from the south, critics in the south accused us of a "developed world agenda", of blaming corruption on the south. Critics in the north liked to imagine that – despite our name, Transparency – we had a hidden agenda and were captives of entrenched interests of one kind or another. Some governments were distinctly nervous at the thought of an NGO coming anywhere near the institutions of which they were members. Within the NGO community, it was said that we were siding with those we should be criticising in the streets. The then leadership of the World Bank wanted nothing whatsoever to do with us. Ours has been a delicate tightrope-walking act.

Our partnership with the government of the Netherlands and the Organising Committee of Global Forum II is further evidence of the way we can all work together effectively and creatively. And I hope to see this partnership given even more coherence in two years' time when the Global Forum and the International Anti-Corruption Conference will be held jointly in Seoul, as I very much hope they will be, rather than being split between different venues, The Hague and Prague (in October), as they are this year.

Looking at your agenda, it is important for all to recognise that there is even more at stake than fighting corruption alone. For the set of instruments we develop and use to combat corruption – accountability, transparency and the involvement of the private sector and civil society – are precisely the instruments that:

- build more efficient, effective and rational government;
- secure the state against infiltration by organised crime;
- protect human rights;
- alleviate poverty through unlocking the development process and access to essential services such as health and education;
- build public belief in the institutions that serve them; and
- forge public confidence in their governments and in the way in which they are governed.

So there is very much more at stake here this week than the essential tasks of containing the petty corruption of junior civil servants and pocket-lining by senior decision-makers. Because corruption is such a broad and cross-cutting issue, confronting corruption is about building a better, fairer and more just world.

And this is why it involves everyone. It is why a strategy built solely on enforcing law and order – important though this is – will never yield the results we all aspire to. No one, I suggest, wants a civil service cowered by fear and nervous about taking initiatives. Civil servants, too, need to feel that they are a part of the creative process.

Back in March, the chief notary of the Russian Federation, Anatoly Tikhenko, was gunned down near his house in Moscow in what was described by Moscow radio station Ekho Moskvy as a "paid killing", a reaction to his efforts to bring increased transparency and accountability to the corruption-ridden notary business. PricewaterhouseCoopers reckons that Russia loses US $10 billion a year in potential foreign investments because of corruption, inadequate accounting procedures, weaknesses in its legal system and lack of reliable financial information. And yet, as recently as March

2, Russia's Interior Minister Vladimir Rushailo denied allegations that 70 per cent of all Russian officials were corrupt with the response that "you should not confuse corruption with bribe taking". Only those with links to organised criminal gangs, he argued, should be regarded as corrupt.

Our movement is not, I repeat not, anti-governments. We do not argue that the problem of corruption rests solely with public servants. Far from it. The private sector, too, shares responsibility by using bribery in its interactions with officials; the public at large is part of the problem, willing to pay bribes or acquiescing in conduct it should not accept. The ethics of the public service reflect in large measure those of society as a whole. So that this is not a struggle of "us" against "them": rather it is a struggle of all of us together to build stronger ethics among society at large.

Nor is countering corruption only a priority for developing countries and for countries in transition. There is a need for continuous improvement in every society as, in a rapidly changing world, events either prove the fallibility of institutions or call into question the reliability of institutional arrangements that may have functioned in the past. Among the country reports TI has prepared for this gathering are two on countries in the north – the Netherlands and Canada – and each points to shortcomings in need of attention.

Responding to the challenge, and working with civil society, the private sector and the governments of Tanzania and Uganda, we developed the concept of the National Integrity System. Available here today is a new, expanded edition of the TI Source Book, which describes this in detail. It is entitled "Confronting Corruption: The Elements of a National Integrity System", and I commend it to each and every one of you.

The approach is an holistic way of looking at the institutions and practices that collectively assure a society of its basic integrity. By looking at these institutions – the executive, the legislature, the judiciary, the watchdog agencies, the mass media, the private sector and civil society – we have a framework within which to study the pluses and minuses in accountability and transparency. It enables us all to diagnose weaknesses and to address them in context and in a co-ordinated way. It provides, if you like, a road map for those who are serious about addressing their country's deficiencies.

This is why TI, with the encouragement and support of the Organising Committee and the countries concerned, has prepared some 19 "country studies" in which the national integrity system has been audited in countries as diverse as Canada and Colombia. Responding to the challenge, the government of Trinidad and Tobago even conducted an audit of its own system. Along with the civil society audits, this too is available here this week.

Let's take the Netherlands where most of the elements of Transparency International's National Integrity System are in place. Even here the country study identifies Dutch blind spots, such as "a broad reluctance concerning managing conflict-of-interest situations and monitoring assets, income, liabilities and business interests of politicians and civil servants as well as political parties". The Netherlands also lacks an adequate system of financial disclosure, and in the private sector there is very limited public involvement to secure integrity. "Business corruption gets no political or judicial attention."

The whole exercise comes together in an overview that draws out the common threads across the country studies, charting successes and shortcomings and setting an agenda for us all to address – all, north, south, east and west.

Why, you may ask, should an NGO like TI undertake such a mission? The answer is that we believe it is incumbent on modern NGOs to join in the search for solutions. Not to be content with identifying problems and calling for remedies, but entering the more challenging area of creative dialogue and doing what we can to assist the search for appropriate responses.

But corruption has no respect for national boundaries. In an increasingly globalised world, corruption seriously distorts economic activity and denies people at large the benefits of their efforts. The scourge of corruption has to be confronted through increased cross-border co-operation.

This is why the OECD Convention outlawing the bribing of foreign public officials to win or retain business is so important. Developing countries never stood a chance of confronting corruption until the exporting countries agreed – albeit for their own reasons – to co-operate to criminalise such conduct and to end the obscenity of granting tax deductions for bribes.

It is why there have to be faster and more effective ways of returning to their rightful owners the contents of national coffers looted by former leaders. And why there is concern that money frozen in European and US bank accounts still lingers there while limitation periods run.

It is why it is unacceptable for countries to grant "safe havens" to their citizens when they are accused of perpetrating serious acts of corruption elsewhere, the more so where that citizen has held a position of high responsibility. And why there is concern that countries that insist on immunity from extradition do not accept the obligation to prosecute such cases in their own courts.

I sincerely hope that the election of the Bush administration does not signal a sea-change in the US stance towards international co-operation against corruption and does not herald a new "unilateral" approach. The recent statement by Paul O'Neill, the US Treasury Secretary, that he has "had cause to re-evaluate the United States' participation in the OECD working group that targets 'harmful tax practices'" has raised alarm bells. I urge the US Government to consult promptly with the other OECD member-states, because US withdrawal from the effort to develop programmes to prevent the misuse of off-shore financial centers would represent a serious blow to effective international co-operation against corruption and money laundering.

Strong multilateral action is required to prevent corrupt officials from hiding their ill-gotten gains in unregulated off-shore accounts. Billions of laundered funds are at stake. Around US$1 trillion of criminal proceeds are laundered through banks worldwide each year, and about half of that is moved through American banks.

More effective international information-sharing regimes and improved mutual legal assistance procedures are required to return that money to its rightful owners in Africa and elsewhere. I would like to remind the Bush Administration that unilateral US efforts to combat corruption through the Foreign Corrupt Practices Act hurt US interests and did not improve the practices of its competitors. It was only when fighting corruption was internationalised in the mid-nineties that progress began to be made. And this was when it was realised that a principal objective was to help developing countries in their efforts to stem the devastation caused – and still being caused – by bribes from the industrial world. It is this concern – for the poor and the marginalised – that is central to the TI coalition.

International money-laundering arrangements are critical, as long as the proceeds of "grand corruption" are spirited away to safe havens. And why there is such concern when French parliamentarians contemplate lifting their anti-money-laundering laws for a period of six months' "grace" during the imminent conversion to the Euro – something that could well trigger the largest money-laundering exercise in the history of the human race.

It is clear that the rush to move dirty money from the Balkans and the CIS from Deutschmarks to US dollars has already begun – and many economists argue that the flood to the dollar of this underworld money accounts for the Euro's continued weakness. The current burst of economic activity in unlikely places across Europe points to a headlong rush to turn dirty money into bricks and mortar – a phenomenon that governments must surely monitor and investigate.

Clearly the proposed United Nations Convention can go some way towards extending the scope and effectiveness of international co-operation. But UN Conventions are less ideal for progressing an anti-corruption campaign. They tend to take years to produce and then only reflect the lowest common denominator. Thereafter they are not monitored and can simply lie in limbo.

This week we hope you will try to ensure that any UN Convention against corruption is limited to areas in which it can be really effective, and is negotiated without delay. Above all, it should not be used as a pretext by governments for failing to take remedial action in the meantime – or to oppose regional initiatives in this field.

The UN Convention could be used as an excuse for inaction. We look to Ministers when they meet on Thursday to recognise this danger and to lock and bolt the door against those who might exploit it.

There has been enough talking about corruption. The need today is for action. This is a government forum. In October, in Prague, the wider anti-corruption movement will come together. And it is not by your rhetoric but by your deeds that your work this week will be judged.

35 Power Shift

Jessica T. Mathews

The Rise of Global Civil Society

The end of the Cold War has brought no mere adjustment among states but a novel redistribution of power among states, markets, and civil society. National governments are not simply losing autonomy in a globalizing economy. They are sharing powers – including political, social, and security roles at the core of sovereignty – with businesses, with international organizations, and with a multitude of citizens groups, known as nongovernmental organizations (NGOs). The steady concentration of power in the hands of states that began in 648 with the Peace of Westphalia is over, at least for a while. The absolutes of the Westphalian system – territorially fixed states where everything of value lies within some state's borders; a single, secular authority governing each territory and representing it outside its borders; and no authority above states – are all dissolving. Increasingly, resources and threats that matter, including money, information, pollution, and popular culture, circulate and shape lives and economies with little regard for political boundaries. International standards of conduct are gradually beginning to override claims of national or regional singularity. Even the most powerful states find the marketplace and international public opinion compelling them more often to follow a particular course.

The state's central task of assuring security is the least affected, but still not exempt. War will not disappear, but with the shrinkage of U.S. and Russian nuclear arsenals, the transformation of the Nuclear Nonproliferation Treaty into a permanent covenant in 1995, agreement on the long-sought Comprehensive Test Ban treaty in 1996, and the likely entry into force of the Chemical Weapons Convention in 1997, the security threat to states from other states is on a downward course. Nontraditional threats, however, are rising terrorism, organized crime, drug trafficking, ethnic conflict, and the combination of rapid population growth, environmental decline, and poverty that breeds economic stagnation, political instability, and, sometimes, state collapse. The nearly 100 armed conflicts since the end of the Cold War have virtually all been intrastate affairs. Many began with governments acting against their own citizens, through extreme corruption, violence, incompetence, or complete breakdown, as in Somalia. These trends have fed a growing sense that individuals' security may not in fact reliably derive from their nation's security. A competing notion of "human security" is creeping around the edges of official thinking, suggesting that security be viewed as emerging from the conditions of daily life – food, shelter, employment,

Original publication details: Excerpted from Jessica T. Mathews, "Power Shift," *Foreign Affairs*, 76, 1, January/February 1997. Copyright © 1997 by the Council on Foreign Relations, Inc. Reprinted by permission of *Foreign Affairs*.

health, public safety – rather than flowing downward from a country's foreign relations and military strength. The most powerful engine of change in the relative decline of states and the rise of nonstate actors is the computer and telecommunications revolution, whose deep political and social consequences have been almost completely ignored. Widely accessible and affordable technology has broken governments' monopoly on the collection and management of large amounts of information and deprived governments of the deference they enjoyed because of it. In every sphere of activity, instantaneous access to information and the ability to put it to use multiplies the number of players who matter and reduces the number who command great authority. The effect on the loudest voice – which has been government's – has been the greatest. By drastically reducing the importance of proximity, the new technologies change people's perceptions of community. Fax machines, satellite hookups, and the Internet connect people across borders with exponentially growing ease while separating them from natural and historical associations within nations.

In this sense a powerful globalizing force, they can also have the opposite effect, amplifying political and social fragmentation by enabling more and more identities and interests scattered around the globe to coalesce and thrive. These technologies have the potential to divide society along new lines, separating ordinary people from elites with the wealth and education to command technology's power. Those elites are not only the rich but also citizens' groups with transnational interests and identities that frequently have more in common with counterparts in other countries, whether industrialized or developing, than with countrymen. Above all, the information technologies disrupt hierarchies, spreading power among more people and groups. In drastically lowering the costs of communication, consultation, and coordination, they favor decentralized networks over other modes of organization. In a network, individuals or groups link for joint action without building a physical or formal institutional presence. Networks have no person at the top and no center. Instead, they have multiple nodes where collections of individuals or groups interact for different purposes. Businesses, citizens' organizations, ethnic groups, and crime cartels have all readily adopted the network model. Governments, on the other hand, are quintessential hierarchies, wedded to an organizational form incompatible with all that the new technologies make possible. Today's powerful nonstate actors are not without precedent. The British East India Company ran a subcontinent, and a few influential NGOs go back more than a century. But these are exceptions. Both in numbers and in impact, nonstate actors have never before approached their current strength. And a still larger role likely lies ahead.

Dial Locally, Act Globally

No one knows how many NGOs there are or how fast the tally is growing. Published figures are badly misleading. One widely cited estimate claims there are 35,000 NGOs in the developing countries; another points to 12,000 irrigation cooperatives in South Asia alone. In fact, it is impossible to measure a swiftly growing universe that includes neighborhood, professional, service, and advocacy groups, both secular and church-based, promoting every conceivable cause and funded by donations, fees, foundations, governments, international oganizations, or the sale of products and services. The true number is certainly in the millions, from the tiniest village association to influential but modestly funded international groups like Amnesty International to larger global activist organizations like Greenpeace and giant service providers like CARE, which has an annual budget of nearly $400 million. Except in China, Japan, the Middle East, and a few other places where culture or authoritarian governments severely limit civil society, NGOs' role and influence have exploded in the last half-decade. Their financial resources and–often more important – their expertise, approximate and sometimes exceed those of smaller governments and of international organizations. "We have less money and fewer resources than Amnesty International, and we are the arm of the U.N. for human rights," noted Ibrahima Fall, head of the U.N. Center for Human Rights, in 1993. "This is clearly ridiculous."

Today NGOs deliver more official development assistance than the entire U.N. system (excluding the World Bank and the International Monetary Fund). In many countries they are delivering the services – in urban and rural community development, education, and health care – that faltering governments can no longer manage. The range of these groups' work is almost as broad as their interests. They breed new ideas; advocate, protest, and mobilize public support; do legal, scientific, technical, and policy analysis; provide services; shape, implement, monitor, and enforce national and international commitments; and change institutions and norms. Increasingly, NGOs are able to push around even the largest governments. When the United States and Mexico set out to reach a trade agreement, the two governments planned on the usual narrowly defined negotiations behind closed doors. But NGOs had a very different vision. Groups from Canada, the United States, and Mexico wanted to see provisions in the North American Free Trade Agreement on health and safety, transboundary pollution, consumer protection, immigration, labor mobility, child labor, sustainable agriculture, social charters, and debt relief. Coalitions of NGOs formed in each country and across both borders. The opposition they generated in early 1991 endangered congressional approval of the crucial "fast track" negotiating authority for the U.S. government. After months of resistance, the Bush administration capitulated, opening the agreement to environmental and labor concerns. Although progress in other trade venues will be slow, the tightly closed world of trade negotiations has been changed forever. Technology is fundamental to NGOs' new clout. The nonprofit Association for Progressive Communications provides 50,000 NGOs in 133 countries access to the tens of millions of Internet users for the price of a local call.

The dramatically lower costs of international communication have altered NGOs' goals and changed international outcomes. Within hours of the first gunshots of the Chiapas rebellion in southern Mexico in January 1994, for example, the Internet swarmed with messages from human rights activists. The worldwide media attention they and their groups focused on Chiapas, along with the influx of rights activists to the area, sharply limited the Mexican government's response. What in other times would have been a bloody insurgency turned out to be a largely nonviolent conflict. "The shots lasted ten days," Jose Angel Gurria, Mexico's foreign minister, later remarked, "and ever since, the war has been . . . a war on the Internet." NGOs' easy reach behind other states' borders forces governments to consider domestic public opinion in countries with which they are dealing, even on matters that governments have traditionally handled strictly between themselves. At the same time, cross-border NGO networks offer citizens' groups unprecedented channels of influence. Women's and human rights groups in many developing countries have linked up with more experienced, better funded, and more powerful groups in Europe and the United States. The latter work the global media and lobby their own governments to pressure leaders in developing countries, creating a circle of influence that is accelerating change in many parts of the world.

Out of the Hallway, Around the Table

In international organizations, as with governments at home, NGOs were once largely relegated to the hallways. Even when they were able to shape governments' agendas, as the Helsinki Watch human rights groups did in the Conference on Security and Cooperation in Europe in the 1980s, their influence was largely determined by how receptive their own government's delegation happened to be. Their only option was to work through governments. All that changed with the negotiation of the global climate treaty, culminating at the Earth Summit in Rio de Janeiro in 1992. With the broader independent base of public support that environmental groups command, NGOs set the original goal of negotiating an agreement to control greenhouse gases long before governments were ready to do so, proposed most of its structure and content, and lobbied and mobilized public pressure to force through a pact that virtually no one else thought possible when the talks began. More members of NGOs served on government delegations than ever before, and they penetrated deeply into official decision-making. They were allowed to attend the small working group meetings where the real decisions in international negotiations are made. The tiny nation of Vanuatu turned its delegation over to an NGO with expertise in international law (a group based in London and funded by an American foundation), thereby making itself and the other sea-level island states major players in the fight to control global warming. ECO, an NGO-published daily newspaper, was the negotiators' best source of information on the progress of the official talks and became the forum where governments tested ideas for breaking deadlocks.

Whether from developing or developed countries, NGOs were tightly organized in a global and half a dozen regional Climate Action Networks, which were able to bridge North-South differences among governments that many had expected would prevent an agreement. United in their passionate pursuit of a treaty, NGOs would fight out contentious issues among themselves, then take an agreed position to their respective delegations. When they could not agree, NGOs served as invaluable back channels, letting both sides know where the other's problems lay or where a compromise might be found. As a result, delegates completed the framework of a global climate accord in the blink of a diplomat's eye – 6 months – over the opposition of the three energy superpowers, the United States, Russia, and Saudi Arabia. The treaty entered into force in record time just two years later. Although only a framework accord whose binding requirements are still to be negotiated, the treaty could force sweeping changes in energy use, with potentially enormous implications for every economy. The influence of NGOs at the climate talks has not yet been matched in any other arena, and indeed has provoked a backlash among some governments. A handful of authoritarian regimes, most notably China, led the charge, but many others share their unease about the role NGOs are assuming. Nevertheless, NGOs have worked their way into the heart of international negotiations and into the day-to-day operations of international organizations, bringing new priorities, demands for procedures that give a voice to groups outside government, and new standards of accountability. [. . .]

For Better or Worse?

A world that is more adaptable and in which power is more diffused could mean more peace, justice, and capacity to manage the burgeoning list of humankind's interconnected problems. At a time of accelerating change, NGOs are quicker than governments to respond to new demands and opportunities. Internationally, in both the poorest and richest countries, NGOs, when adequately funded, can outperform government in the delivery of many public services. Their growth, along with that of the other elements of civil society, can strengthen the fabric of the many still-fragile democracies. And they are better than governments at dealing with problems that grow slowly and affect society through their cumulative effect on individuals – the "soft" threats of environmental degradation, denial of human rights, population growth, poverty, and lack of development that may already be causing more deaths in conflict than are traditional acts of aggression. As the computer and telecommunications revolution continues, NGOs will become more capable of large-scale activity across national borders. Their loyalties and orientation, like those of international civil servants and citizens of non-national entities like the EU, are better matched than those of governments to problems that demand transnational solutions. International NGOs and cross-border networks of local groups have bridged North-South differences that in earlier years paralyzed cooperation among countries.

On the economic front, expanding private markets can avoid economically destructive but politically seductive policies, such as excessive borrowing or overly burdensome taxation, to which governments succumb. Unhindered by ideology, private capital flows to where it is best treated and thus can do the most good. International organizations, given a longer rein by governments and connected to the grassroots by deepening ties with NGOs, could, with adequate funding, take on larger roles in global housekeeping (transportation, communications, environment, health), security (controlling weapons of mass destruction, preventive diplomacy, peacekeeping), human rights, and emergency relief. As various international panels have suggested, the funds could come from fees on international activities, such as currency transactions and air travel, independent of state appropriations. Finally, that new force on the global scene, international public opinion, informed by worldwide media coverage and mobilized by NGOs, can be extraordinarily potent in getting things done, and done quickly.

There are at least as many reasons, however, to believe that the continuing diffusion of power away from nation-states will mean more conflict and less problem-solving both within states and among them. For all their strengths, NGOs are special interests, albeit not motivated by personal profit. The best of them, the ablest and most passionate, often suffer most from tunnel vision, judging every public act by how it affects their particular interest. Generally, they have limited capacity for large-scale endeavors, and as they grow, the need to sustain growing budgets can compromise the independence of mind and approach that is their greatest asset. A society in which the piling up of special interests replaces a single strong voice for the common good is unlikely to fare well. Single-issue voters, as Americans know all too well, polarize and freeze public debate. In the longer run, a stronger civil society could also be more fragmented, producing a weakened sense of common identity and purpose and less willingness to invest in public goods, whether health and education or roads and ports. More and more groups promoting worthy but narrow causes could ultimately threaten democratic government. Internationally, excessive pluralism could have similar consequences. Two hundred nation-states is a barely manageable number. Add hundreds of influential nonstate forces – businesses, NGOs, international organizations, ethnic and religious groups – and the international system may represent more voices but be unable to advance any of them.

Moreover, there are roles that only the state – at least among today's polities – can perform. States are the only nonvoluntary political unit, the one that can impose order and is invested with the power to tax. Severely weakened states will encourage conflict, as they have in Africa, Central America, and elsewhere. Moreover, it may be that only the nation-state can meet crucial social needs that markets do not value. Providing a modicum of job security, avoiding higher unemployment, preserving a livable environment and a stable climate, and protecting consumer health and safety are but a few of the tasks that could be left dangling in a world of expanding markets and retreating states. More international decision-making will also exacerbate the so-called democratic deficit, as decisions that elected representatives once made shift to unelected international bodies; this is already a sore point for EU members. It also arises when legislatures are forced to make a single take-it-or-leave-it judgment on huge international agreements, like the several-thousand-page Uruguay Round trade accord. With citizens already feeling that their national governments do not hear individual voices, the trend could well provoke deeper and more dangerous alienation, which in turn could trigger new ethnic and even religious separatism. The end result could be a proliferation of states too weak for either individual economic success or effective international cooperation. Finally, fearsome dislocations are bound to accompany the weakening of the central institution of modern society. The prophets of an internetted world in which national identities gradually fade, proclaim its revolutionary nature and yet believe the changes will be wholly benign. They won't be. The shift from national to some other political allegiance, if it comes, will be an emotional, cultural, and political earthquake.

Dissolving and Evolving

Might the decline in state power prove transitory? Present disenchantment with national governments could dissipate as quickly as it arose. Continuing globalization may well spark a vigorous reassertion of economic or cultural nationalism. By helping solve problems governments cannot handle, business, NGOs, and international organizations may actually be strengthening the nation-state system. These are all possibilities, but the clash between the fixed geography of states and the nonterritorial nature of today's problems and solutions, which is only likely to escalate, strongly suggests that the relative power of states will continue to decline. Nation-states may simply no longer be the natural problem-solving unit. Local government addresses citizens' growing desire for a role in decision-making, while transnational, regional, and even global entities better fit the dimensions of trends in economics, resources, and security.

The evolution of information and communications technology, which has only just begun, will probably heavily favor nonstate entities, including those not yet envisaged, over states. The new technologies encourage noninstitutional, shifting networks over the fixed bureaucratic hierarchies that are the hallmark of the single-voiced sovereign state. They dissolve issues' and institutions' ties to a fixed place. And by greatly empowering individuals, they weaken the relative attachment to community, of which the preeminent one in modern society is the nation-state. If current trends continue, the international system 50 years hence will be profoundly different. During the transition, the Westphalian system and an evolving one will exist side by side. States will set the rules by which all other actors operate, but outside forces will increasingly make decisions for them. In using business, NGOs, and international organizations to address problems they cannot or do not want to take on, states will, more often than not, inadvertently weaken themselves further. Thus governments' unwillingness to adequately fund international organizations helped NGOs move from a peripheral to a central role in shaping multilateral agreements, since the NGOs provided expertise the international organizations lacked. At least for a time, the transition is likely to weaken rather than bolster the world's capacity to solve its problems. If states, with the overwhelming share of power, wealth, and capacity, can do less, less will get done. Whether the rise of nonstate actors ultimately turns out to be good news or bad will depend on whether humanity can launch itself on a course of rapid social innovation, as it did after World War II. Needed adaptations include a business sector that can shoulder a broader policy role, NGOs that are less parochial and better able to operate on a large scale, international institutions that can efficiently serve the dual masters of states and citizenry, and, above all, new institutions and political entities that match the transnational scope of today's challenges while meeting citizens' demands for accountable democratic governance.

36   The Backlash Against NGOs

Michael Bond

When 122 countries agreed to stop using and selling land mines in December 1997, the success was attributed not to the work of tireless government officials, but to the 1,000 or so non-governmental organisations (NGOs) in 60 countries which had lobbied ministers on the issue for years. At the signing ceremony in Ottawa, Jody Williams, the campaign's coordinator, remarked that NGOs had come into their own on the international stage. "Together," she said, "we are a superpower."

Her words have a significance far beyond the land mines treaty. They encompass a shift in the balance of power in international politics, unimaginable 30 years ago. Where once global politics were dictated exclusively by elected governments, now elected governments must compete with "civil society" – interest groups accountable only to themselves but often with significant financial resources, the management structure of a multinational company and a media image that governments can only envy.

Should we be worried about this shift? Is it safe to grant a mandate to change the world to unelected organisations which operate under the banner of democracy, but which answer only to their directors, fundholders or members, and are far less transparent than most political parties? The same question is asked by NGOs of multinational corporations. But are the champions of the oppressed in danger of mirroring some of the sins of the oppressor? More important, how responsible have NGOs been in wielding their newly-won power?

Filling the Global Gap

The turning-point in the fortunes of NGOs was the UN earth summit in Rio in 1992, where environmental pressure groups were directly involved in drawing up a treaty to control emissions of greenhouse gases. They had access to the official working groups and served on government delegations, and through lobbying and use of the media they greatly accelerated the negotiating process. For the first time, NGOs had moved from the spectators gallery to the decision-making table. Since then they have had considerable success: they have forced the World Bank to review its funding strategy; helped to create the post of UN high commissioner for human rights; scuppered the Multilateral Agreement on Investment (which aimed to liberalise foreign investment and immunise it from the interests of national governments); helped to derail the World Trade Organisation (WTO) talks in Seattle [in 1999]; and, at the end of 1999, helped to win a pledge from Britain (with other lenders expected to follow) to write off the debts of the world's 41 poorer countries. In January, at

Original publication details: Michael Bond, "The Backlash Against NGOs," originally published in *Prospect*, April 2000, www.prospect-magazine.co.uk

the World Economic Forum in Davos, representatives from 15 NGOs were for the first time invited to take part in debates on globalisation.

As finance and production become more global and increasingly important decisions are taken at an international level, where there is no political machinery to deal with citizens' concerns, NGOs are filling the "democratic deficit." "The same factors that have been eroding nation-states have also been promoting NGOs," says James Paul, executive director of the Global Policy Forum in New York. "NGOs have become the vehicle for the expression of popular concern in this transitional period as nation-states weaken and politics is not yet established at the transnational level."

The effectiveness of NGOs has been assisted by the internet. The collection and communication of large volumes of information is no longer the domain of governments alone. Pressure groups can link up across the world without moving from their desks – as the demonstrations in Seattle showed. "The difference between what you can do now and what you could do 15 years ago is enormous," says Jessica Mathews, co-founder of the World Resources Institute. "In the 1980s at the WRI it was impossible to deal with people in Africa – the phones didn't work well enough. The relative lowering of the cost of communication has made a huge difference for NGOs domestically and internationally."

Even if you exclude domestic NGOs (which number in the millions) it is difficult to estimate how many NGOs there are. One source estimates that during the 1990s the number of international NGOs increased from about 6,000 to more than 26,000. Many of the larger ones, such as CARE, control budgets worth more than $100m. Membership of the Worldwide Fund for Nature has increased nearly tenfold, to 5m, since the mid-1980s; it has 3,300 staff and an annual budget of more than $350m. Greenpeace has nearly 2.5m members and 1,142 staff. Amnesty International has 1m members in 162 countries. Friends of the Earth has 1m members in 58 countries. Membership of Britain's Royal Society for the Protection of Birds has risen from 10,000 in 1960, to 1m today. Several NGOs have stepped in to take up roles that the UN or national governments might once have been expected to fill. About 10 per cent of all development aid is channeled through NGOs, and that figure will rise. In the human rights field, the UN acknowledges that its entire programme would fall apart without the information-gathering and campaigning resources of NGOs. In his study *NGOs and the Universal Declaration of Human Rights* (1998), William Korey notes that when the Declaration was approved by the UN in 1948, 41 NGOs held consultative status. It has now been granted to more than 1,000. Amnesty International alone is better resourced than the human rights arm of the UN.

The big international NGOs cover three main areas: human rights, development and the environment. Some specialise in distributing aid, others in campaigning and propaganda. As advocates for change, NGOs are often far more effective than governments or international bodies: they are in touch with the grassroots, they can mobilise public opinion through the media and embarrass officialdom or businesses into action without fear of retaliation. In poor countries, foreign NGOs can provide assistance and poverty relief faster than bureaucratic government agencies. As the global economy takes hold, NGOs appear well-placed to act as transnational trouble-shooters and are thus natural allies of the UN. Kofi Annan, UN secretary-general, has called them "the conscience of humanity."

The Single Issue Problem

But there is another side to the NGOs. International civil society is not a homogeneous forum of altruistic groups fighting for a common outcome. As Jessica Mathews wrote in *Foreign Affairs* in 1997: "For all their strengths, NGOs are special interests. The best of them . . . often suffer most from tunnel vision, judging every public act by how it affects their particular interest. Generally, they have limited capacity for large-scale endeavours, and as they grow, the need to sustain growing budgets can compromise the independence of mind that is their greatest asset." The fact that NGOs do not have to think about policy trade-offs or the overall impact of their causes can even be harmful. "A society in which the piling up of special interests replaces a single strong voice for the common good is unlikely to fare well."

NGOs are like political parties in that they depend on their members for funding and answer to them for their policies. Since they could not survive without their "grassroots," much of their campaigning is geared towards expanding this base, sometimes in competition with other organisations. But NGOs are *unlike* political parties in that they are not accountable to the electorate. However much they claim to speak for the public, their main responsibility is always to themselves.

A tendency to play to the gallery, and straightforward infighting, is common among some NGOs desperate to maximise membership. This is most marked in the environmental sector. "There isn't a green movement," says Pete Wilkinson, a director of Greenpeace UK during the 1980s. "It's a bunch of self-interested organisations which generally don't get on." Tom Burke, director of Friends of the Earth from 1975–79, then adviser to three secretaries of state for the environment, and now an environmental policy consultant to BP and Rio Tinto, warns of a ghetto mentality. "One of the dangers is that you really do think you've got all the answers and anyone who doesn't agree with you is an idiot or evil."

Typical divisions include that between the Humane Society of the US, which wants to preserve wildlife at all costs, and organisations such as the Worldwide Fund for Nature which favour sustainable management and community involvement; or the division between advocates of a logging ban in North American forests and those promoting wood as a sustainable resource which could replace fossil fuels. Some NGOs measure their success in terms of new regulations passed by Congress or parliament; others favour decentralisation and a more market-orientated approach. And some green groups openly demonise others. In 1993 Greenpeace published a book of environmental enemies which included other organisations fighting for the same goals but using methods of which it did not approve.

For organisations which are not elected yet have a big influence on our lives, trust is usually crucial to their success. Monsanto has many enemies because it appears untrustworthy with its influence. But international NGOs are different, for now at least. If they fall down they are less likely to be penalised than a political party – which would lose an election – or a multinational – which would face a boycott of its products. NGO influence is thus open to abuse.

Aid NGOs carry a great responsibility because their work directly affects the world's poorest people. They also tend to attract most public money. (Of Oxfam's £98m budget, about 25 per cent was given by either the British government or the EU; Médecins Sans Frontières gets almost 50 per cent of its income from public sources.) They are given this responsibility because they are usually smaller and more flexible than government agencies. However, some groups are themselves now as large as a small government agency – and as bureaucratic. In many cases they have set up pervasive structures of aid provision in developing countries, taking over services such as healthcare and water supply which were previously run – however haphazardly – by the country's government. Because these structures often collapse when the foreign NGOs leave, this approach to aid provision can end up undermining the government.

NGOs are also expensive. A report written for Unicef in 1995, by Sussex University's Reginald Green and others, estimated that in Mozambique, health services set up by NGOs cost up to ten times as much as those provided by the government. Green recommends that foreign technical assistance should be reduced and the money used to support national or local government programmes instead. Joseph Hanlon, author of several books about aid to Mozambique, recalls that during a period in 1993 NGOs working in the health sector were spending more in two provinces than the entire national health budget – and that rather than use local doctors, they were flying in foreign experts. Hanlon calls NGOs "the new missionaries." A provincial governor in Mozambique once told him: "NGOs are trying to take the place of the government. They are trying to show that the old colonisers are really interested in the people after all; that they can bring you water today whereas the government can only give you a well tomorrow." Clare Short, Britain's secretary of state for international development, warned [in 1999] that aid agencies had concentrated too much on isolated projects instead of helping governments to provide essential services such as health and education. The success of aid agencies, she said, should be measured by how soon they leave a country, not by how long they stay.

Most large NGOs, such as Oxfam, the Red Cross, Cafod and Action Aid, are striving to make their aid provision more sustainable. But some, mostly in the US, are still exporting the ideologies of their backers. "They can be either evangelical in nature, or very traditional in approach, emphasising hand-outs and soup kitchens rather than trying both to provide relief and tackle the source of the problems," says Sarah Stewart of Christian Aid.

Yet however well intentioned, every NGO has to answer to the people who pay its bills. Accountability is central to the debate about NGOs' role in global decision-making. Critics claim that they are hardly a democratic substitute for governments. But James Paul says that campaigning groups may be no less representative than parliaments. After all, he says, democracies are often not very democratic.

Playing to the Gallery

Publicity is crucial to NGOs' success. At the earth summit in Rio, "civil society" became an international force mostly due to the presence of 9,000 journalists – more than twice as many as had attended any previous UN conference. This creates public relations temptations for NGOs. Stewart says that Christian Aid comes under pressure to pursue a certain goal not from its trustees so much as from the public, which wants to see action in response to a crisis. She cites the war in Kosovo, "where overwhelming media attention – to the detriment of equally severe crises in Africa – compelled agencies to respond, in some cases beyond their original remit."

The media also encourage NGOs to indulge in competitive posturing. When a Chinese government delegation visited Britain a few years ago to discuss human rights, at least one big pressure group declined to attend a meeting with the delegation because it wanted to preserve its purity in the struggle against human rights abuse in China. Last year the same organisation, during the visit to London of Chinese president Jiang Zemin, was able to hold up placards saying "All we want to do is talk."

NGOs cannot grow in membership, funding or power without the media. Thus the "difficult" issues, which are often those most in need of attention, are ignored. As Paul de Jongh, former Dutch deputy director-general for the environment, warns in his book *Our Common Journey*: "The fruits we have harvested were the lowest on the tree, and we have reached nearly all of them." Global warming is a perfect campaign issue because it affects everyone and has potentially catastrophic consequences. But issues such as nitrate leaching, forest biodiversity or soil erosion in Africa hardly get a look in. Hanlon says that in the aid industry, NGOs' dependency on their media image for funds can be damaging for the country they are trying to help. "They need a new fashion to help them raise more money. One year it's gender, another it's democracy, the next year it's age. The problem is that local organisations cannot move so fast."

Little White Lies

Environmental groups have often been accused of stretching facts to create a greater media impact. In the campaign to ban the ivory trade, environmental and animal rights groups peddled statistics on the decline of elephant populations in Africa. When Norway was targeted for killing whales, activist groups placed advertisements in national newspapers implying that all whales were threatened with extinction, when in fact the Norwegians were sustainably hunting just one species, the minke. When the Braer oil tanker went aground off Shetland in 1993 and spilled tens of thousands of tonnes of crude oil into the sea, wildlife groups predicted catastrophic effects on marine life which were never borne out. And in Greenpeace's (ultimately successful) campaign to prevent Shell abandoning the Brent Spar oil platform in the North Sea in 1995, the group overestimated by a factor of 37 the amount of hydrocarbons in the rig which might leak into the sea. Greenpeace later apologised for its mistake over the Brent Spar, but the incident underlined how scientific facts frequently play second fiddle to politics.

The row over genetically modified organisms (GMOs) is another example. When Greenpeace activists destroyed an experimental crop of GM maize near Norwich in summer [1999], effectively they were saying that they were rejecting GM crops irrespective of whether or not these had a detrimental effect on the environment. In this way Greenpeace can no longer strictly call itself an environmental group: it is fighting as much against global trade and the multinationals. Doug Parr, chief scientist at Greenpeace, acknowledges that the group no longer operates "wholly in the scientific domain," but claims that public perception of the environment has moved on. "There's a tendency among our critics to say that science is the only decision-making tool . . . but political and commercial interests are using science as a cover for getting their way."

Because of their big grassroots support, environmental groups have never been limited to working through government to achieve their ends – unlike aid agencies and human rights groups. Thus the green groups are responsible for most of the innovations in NGO tactics. Now that green groups have started to campaign beyond their original remit, NGOs in other sectors may follow suit. But are any of them really ready for this shift?

Richard Jefferson, a molecular biologist and executive director of Cambia, which helps farmers in the third world, thinks not. He believes that anti-GMO campaigns in the west have already done huge damage to farming in the developing world. European institutions which have been funding the development of GM technologies for third world farmers have been cutting back because they are worried about their public image. And yet, he says, western activists are ignorant of third world farming. "They are becoming as paternalistic as the multinationals they propose to save these farmers from. If people really knew how agriculture was done here they'd thank God we had some technologies that could save us from past mistakes. If the activists really cared for the environment they would be looking at lowering pesticides usage or reducing tillage."

Philip Burnham, a social anthropologist at University College London, who has worked for 30 years in central and west Africa, says that NGOs will often try to stifle development at any cost. He has recently been assessing the social impact of Exxon's proposed oil pipeline through Cameroon. Exxon, he says, has been surprisingly open about the project, and local people are for it. But various US and European environmental groups are against it because they claim it will destroy rainforest biodiversity – a claim Burnham says is based on poor science. Pete Wilkinson says the problem is bigger than faulty analysis; green groups have failed to move from the confrontational tactics of the 1980s to a more conciliatory approach required today when the issues have become more complex, and business and government have adopted much of the lexicon of the movement. "After Rio, I thought there'd be a major consolidation of the green movement, a rethinking of tactics and the emergence of a more mature green lobby. We haven't seen that." The failure of green groups to cooperate with other "players" spurred Jens Katjek, former head of policy with Friends of the Earth Germany, to move to the corporate sector two years ago. If NGOs want the best for the environment, he says, they have to learn to compromise. Richard Jefferson is more critical still. "They've got everything so mixed up now. In their anti-corporatism they've become anti-technology, anti-science, anti-informed discussion. They do not like complexity, just the black-and-white."

Questions

1   How can a social movement be global rather than national? Identify some of the factors that have made it easier since World War II for movements to coordinate their activities and pursue common goals in many countries simultaneously.

2   What international nongovernmental organizations (INGOs) can you name? Do they receive much attention in the media? Why are you more likely to hear about an organization like the Red Cross than the International Council for Science or the World Federation of Advertisers?

3   The United Nations and its agencies have given consultative status to thousands of INGOs. Would you expect INGOs always to support UN projects and programs? How might INGOs be critical of what UN agencies do?

4   For Berkovitch, the women's movement has become more complex and conflictual as Third World women have become more active participants in the movement. Does this mean that the status and role of women are becoming less globalized issues? Does globalization imply consensus, or is it more likely to lead to disagreement and controversy?

5   What strikes you as particularly important in the Beijing Declaration about women's rights and equality? What strikes you as controversial or provocative? Is the Declaration expressing only the views of western women, or does it also reflect the outlook and needs of women in the developing world?

6   In the Boli and Thomas selection, five principles that undergird most INGOs are identified. Explain these principles. Then identify at least two types of INGOs that are not likely to embrace these principles as fully as most INGOs do.

7   How does Transparency International identify corruption in the countries of the world? How does it try to lower the incidence of corruption? What factors make the job of rooting out corruption a difficult one?

8   What is the "power shift" that Mathews discusses? Does this shift imply that solutions to global problems are more likely to be forthcoming in future decades? What is the "backlash" discussed by Bond, and how might this affect the relative power of states, corporations, and nongovernmental organizations?

Part VII

Cultural Globalization I: The Role of Media

Introduction

Cultural globalization is familiar to almost everyone, though it may not always be recognized. Everyone knows that prominent icons of popular culture, like Coca-Cola, blue jeans, rock music, and McDonald's Golden Arches, can be found "everywhere." We are also all aware of the seeming sameness engendered by the diffusion of such cultural objects and genres. Add to the list such items as Hollywood movies, French philosophizing, and Japanese organizational techniques that have been widely adopted by American and European companies, and it is easy to believe that cultural globalization inevitably acts as a universal solvent that will dissolve all cultural differences in a dull and colorless homogeneity throughout the world.

Call it "Americanization," call it "westernization," call it cultural imperialism (and many have, both within and outside the West) – the driving forces behind this homogenization, critics claim, are the mass media. Controlled mainly by American and European companies, spreading their ethereal tentacles through the airwaves to the farthest reaches of the globe, the media impose their powerful images, sounds, and advertising on unprepared peoples who succumb meekly to their messages, which are designed to increase the profits of capitalist firms. Such is the kernel of one side of the debate on the role of the media in world society. But contrary voices can also be heard, and changes in the structure of the global news, television, radio, music, and film industries have changed much of the received wisdom about cultural imperialism.

The cultural imperialism debate picked up speed soon after decolonization began to produce dozens of new states in Africa, Asia, and the Pacific. Though colonialism was dead or dying, in its place scholars identified a new form of capitalist subjugation of the Third World (which term itself comes from the 1960s), more economic than political, more ideologically than militarily supported: neo-colonialism. As the argument goes, because direct politico-military control could no longer be practiced, neo-colonialist powers turned to symbolic and psychological means of control, conveniently facilitated by the rapid integration of global telecommunications systems and, especially, by the proliferation of television. Pushing mainly American culture that promoted ideologies of consumption, instant gratification, self-absorption, and the like, the expanded mass media fit neatly with the spread of global capitalism in its struggle with the Communist-dominated "Second World" led by the Soviet Union.

One prominent outcome of the cultural imperialism thesis was the strident call for a "New World Information Order" (NWIO). Less developed countries pleaded their case against the domination of western media in UNESCO and other UN forums, arguing that restrictions should be placed on western cultural propagation and that aid should flow to the former colonies to improve their nascent communications systems. A related issue was the purportedly biased view of the world presented by the major global news organizations, Associated Press (AP) and United Press International (UPI) from the United States, Agence France-Presse (AFP), and British-owned Reuters, which together accounted for the vast majority of stories entering the newsrooms of the world's newspapers and television stations. The NWIO debate led to few concrete actions, in part because the less developed countries lost interest as many new states took direct control of the broadcast media in their countries and turned radio, television, and major newspapers into mouthpieces of official government policy.

While the press wire services (AP, UPI, AFP, Reuters), all with their roots in the nineteenth century, represent a longstanding form of news globalization, it was only in the 1970s and 1980s that electronic media globalization assumed serious proportions. Mergers and acquisitions by aggressive media companies like Rupert Murdoch's News Corporation yielded massive conglomerates with truly global reach. Ted Turner's upstart Cable News Network (CNN) survived the struggles of its early days to become a ubiquitous, 24-hour news provider watched almost religiously by global business and political elites. At the same time, however, a steady process of decentralization of global media industries was underway, as major countries in different world regions became regional production centers: Mexico for Spanish-language television, India for film, Hong Kong for East Asian film and television, and so on. Alongside this development has been the "indigenization" of many television formats and genres that originated in the West. The once hugely popular "Dallas" has given way to local equivalents with local twists – Brazilian soaps, Mexican *telenovelas*, and many other forms. The net result is an undeniable global increase in the degree to which people's everyday lives are experienced through the media, but the homogenizing effects of media globalization are much less clear than was once supposed.

The first of our selections in this part, by Sean MacBride and Colleen Roach, presents the cultural imperialism thesis and an argument in favor of global governance structures to reduce western media domination. MacBride chaired the UNESCO International Commission for the Study of Communications Problems, appointed in 1976 to investigate global communications and information. He became a western spokesman for the mostly Third World countries that were demanding changes in global media industries. The Commission's MacBride Report of 1980 led UNESCO to call for a restructuring of global media along more egalitarian lines. The report also, however, was critical of restrictions on freedom of the press and broadcast media in many of the very countries that were demanding an end to cultural imperialism.

The next two selections challenge the cultural imperialism thesis. Referring to the growing variety of media content and the emergence of new regional centers for media production, John Sinclair, Elizabeth Jacka, and Stuart Cunningham question whether the "peripheral visions" of the media in the less developed countries are rightly described as products of imperial western design. As regional centers gain market share in exports to their regions, the authors are also led to question whether US media dominance has ever been as great as the cultural imperialism thesis supposed. The excerpt from John

Tomlinson's book on the issue, which provides a thorough analysis and critique of the cultural imperialism argument, leads to considerable doubt about the degree to which US television shows and pharmaceutical advertising in the Third World actually carry US values and improve the profits of US companies. Cultural homogenization is growing in some respects, Tomlinson suggests, but local transformations and interpretations of imported media products imply that cultural diversification is hardly at an end in global society.

Our last selection is Heather Tyrrell's sketch of the film industry in India ("Bollywood," centered in Bombay) as a major competitor to the long-term dominance of America's Hollywood. She describes Hollywood's difficulties in penetrating the Indian market and the strengths of Indian cinema as an emerging cultural force that explicitly challenges American themes and assumptions about the filmgoing public. Indian films have become symbols of successful resistance to western cultural imperialism even while incorporating elements of Hollywood commercialism, illustrating the culture clash and paradoxes of globalization that can also be found in rising film industries in other Third World countries such as Mexico, Hong Kong, Brazil, and China.

37 The New International Information Order

Sean MacBride and Colleen Roach

Resolutions, meetings, and manifestos calling for a "new order" in international information structures and policies became a feature of the world scene in the early 1970s and often generated intense dispute. The original impulse came from the nonaligned nations, many of which had gained independence in the postwar years. To many the euphoria of independence was turning to a sense of disillusionment. In spite of international assistance programs, the economic situation in many developing countries had not improved, and in some it had actually deteriorated. For certain countries foreign trade earnings could not cover interest due on foreign loans. These same years witnessed the rapid development of new communications media, and the era was constantly characterized as the Information Age – one in which information would be a key to power and affluence. To the developing countries it was increasingly clear that the "flow of information" (a term that seemed to subsume ideas and attitudes and followed a one-way direction from rich to poor countries) was dominated by multinational entities based in the most powerful nations. The resulting disparities tended to set the framework for discussion even within developing countries. Clearly political independence was not matched by independence in the economic and sociocultural spheres. A number of nonaligned countries saw themselves as victims of "cultural colonialism." The imbalances it involved, and what might be done about them, became the focus of debate for the nonaligned countries.

Evolution of the Debate

The nonaligned nations movement took form in 1955 at a meeting in Bandung, Indonesia, that brought together world leaders from Asia and Africa. Subsequent meetings – in some cases, summit meetings of nonaligned leaders – were held in Bangkok, Algiers, Tunis, Havana, and elsewhere. During the 1970s the membership grew to more than 90 countries plus several regional groups and represented a majority in various United Nations bodies, with strong influence over their agendas. These UN agencies embraced a "development ideology," meaning that high priority would be given to the development needs of the Third World.

A nonaligned summit held in Algiers in 1973 adopted a resolution calling for a "new international economic order," which was endorsed the following year by the UN General Assembly. This served as precedent and model for a similar resolution

Original publication details: Excerpted from Sean MacBride and Colleen Roach, "The New International Information Order," in Erik Barnouw, *International Encyclopedia of Communications*, 4 vols., pp. 3–10. Copyright © 1989 by Trustees of the University of Pennsylvania. Used by permission of Oxford University Press, Inc.

focusing on information, which was articulated at a 1976 nonaligned news symposium in Tunis. A leading figure at this meeting was Mustapha Masmoudi, Tunisian secretary of state for information, who demanded a "reorganization of existing communication channels that are a legacy of the colonial past." This "decolonization" of information, he said, must lead to a "new order in information matters." In subsequent meetings this phrase evolved into a *new international information order* and, at a later stage, into a *new world information and communication order.*

That same year UNESCO's General Conference in Nairobi also discussed information issues, in a context that produced sharp confrontation between the interests of developed and developing countries. The focus was on the free-flow-of-information doctrine. UNESCO's mandate in the area of communications is explicit in its constitution, adopted in 1946, which enjoined the agency to "collaborate in the work of advancing the mutual knowledge and understanding of peoples, through all means of mass communication and to that end recommend the free flow of ideas by word and image." The free-flow doctrine was developed by the United States and other Western nations after World War II. As viewed by supporters, the unhampered flow of information would be a means of promoting peace and understanding and spreading technical advances. The doctrine had ties with other Western libertarian principles such as freedom of the press. However, critics of the doctrine came to view it as part of a global strategy for domination of communication markets and for ideological control by the industrialized nations. They saw it as serving the interests of the most powerful countries and transnational corporations and helping them secure economic and cultural domination of less powerful nations. A rewording of the doctrine was urged by nonaligned spokespersons calling for a free *and balanced* flow of information. The suggestion stirred deep suspicion in developed countries. If it meant that Third World nations would ordain a proper balance, and control or limit the flow, this would be – according to Western spokespersons – the very antithesis of a free flow. "Free and balanced flow" and "free flow" seemed at this meeting to be irreconcilable concepts.

An important outcome of this 1976 UNESCO meeting was the appointment by Amadou-Mahtar M'Bow, Director-General of UNESCO, of a 16-person commission – broadly representative of the world's economic and geographic spectrum and headed by Sean MacBride of Ireland – to study "the totality of communication problems in modern societies." Its members held different opinions about what sort of new order was needed, but all were in agreement that the existing information order was far from satisfactory. They began their work late in 1977 and, after two years of fact-gathering, committee hearings, and debate, submitted their final report – known as the MacBride Report – to the 1980 UNESCO General Conference in Belgrade. Published in English as *Many Voices, One World*, it has been translated into many languages. Along with a resolution adopted at the same conference confirming UNESCO's support for a *new information and communication order* (see table 37.1), the report became the focus of debate during the following years – a rallying point as well as a target for attack.

Themes

The debate had at first centered on the news-flow question. The major Western international news services – AP and UPI of the United States, the French Agence France-Presse, and Reuters of the United Kingdom – were consistently described as having *monopoly* control over the flow of news to and from developing countries, and

Table 37.1 *Resolution 4/19 adopted by the Twenty-first Session of the UNESCO General Conference, Belgrade, 1980*

The General Conference considers that

(a) this new world information and communication order could be based, among other considerations, on:

   (i) elimination of the imbalances and inequalities which characterize the present situation;

   (ii) elimination of the negative effects of certain monopolies, public or private, and excessive concentrations;

   (iii) removal of the internal and external obstacles to a free flow and wider and better balanced dissemination of information and ideas;

   (iv) plurality of sources and channels of information;

   (v) freedom of the press and of information;

   (vi) the freedom of journalists and all professionals in the communication media, a freedom inseparable from responsibility;

   (vii) the capacity of developing countries to achieve improvement of their own situations, notably by providing their own equipment, by training their personnel, by improving their infrastructures and making their information and communication media suitable to their needs and aspirations;

   (viii) the sincere will of developed countries to help them attain these objectives;

   (ix) respect for each people's cultural identity and for the right of each nation to inform the world about its interests, its aspirations and its social and cultural values;

   (x) respect for the right of all peoples to participate in international exchanges of information on the basis of equality, justice and mutual benefit;

   (xi) respect for the right of the public, of ethnic and social groups and of individuals to have access to information sources and to participate actively in the communication process;

(b) this new world information and communication order should be based on the fundamental principles of international law, as laid down in the Charter of the United Nations;

(c) diverse solutions to information and communication problems are required because social, political, cultural and economic problems differ from one country to another and, within a given country, from one group to another.

---

exercising it from a limited perspective reflecting the economic and cultural interests of the industrialized nations. Expressions such as "coups and earthquakes" were frequently used to describe reporting of Third World events. In 1976 Indira Gandhi, the prime minister of India, expressed the prevailing view: "We want to hear Africans on events in Africa. You should similarly be able to get an Indian explanation of events in India. It is astonishing that we know so little about leading poets, novelists, historians, and editors of various Asian, African, and Latin American countries while we are familiar with minor authors and columnists of Europe and America." The need for policies and structures to develop communications between developing nations (sometimes referred to as "South–South dialogue") was constantly stressed.

The flow of television programming, including *entertainment* programming, was soon incorporated into the debate, in large measure owing to a study conducted by two Finnish researchers, Kaarle Nordenstreng and Tapio Varis, and published by

UNESCO in 1974. The study demonstrated that a few Western nations controlled the international flow of television programs, with the United States, the United Kingdom, France, and the Federal Republic of Germany accounting for the largest shares. The implications of this domination, in both financial and ideological terms, received increasing attention.

The integration of television with new technologies such as the communications *satellite* – including direct broadcast satellites – and telecommunications networks that were channels for an increasing volume of transborder data flow difficult or impossible to control, extended the range of topics covered in the debate. Here the questions also included imbalances in the assignment of spectrum frequencies and of orbital slots for future satellites.

The international flow of *advertising*, under similar multinational controls, was another issue that entered the debate. It was described by many as furthering not only products and services but also a way of life, generally centered on the acquisition of consumer goods. Some saw this as diverting attention from necessities to luxuries, and others saw it as a serious threat to indigenous culture.

In 1978 a new element was added to the debates with the passage of a UNESCO Declaration on the Mass Media. It was the result of six years of negotiation to achieve a consensus text, which finally carried the title *The Declaration of Fundamental Principles concerning the Contribution of the Mass Media to Strengthening Peace and International Understanding, to the Promotion of Human Rights and to Countering Racialism, Apartheid and Incitement to War*. Regarded by the nonaligned nations as furthering the *new order* movement, it was the first international instrument referring directly to moral, social, and professional responsibilities of mass media in the context of "the universally recognized principles of freedom of expression, information, and opinion." Hovering over the debate once again was the issue of the role of government. The final version of the resolution did not include – because of Western demands – proposals to make national governments responsible for the actions of communications companies working within their jurisdictions.

Collision Course

In the early 1980s the nature of the debate underwent decisive changes. Nonaligned nations were no longer as unified as they had been; amid a widespread economic recession some leaned toward a more militant, others toward a more conciliatory, stance. Differences in political systems came more sharply into focus. In the developed nations a trend toward *deregulation* of information media and privatization of public-sector enterprises was gaining momentum. The industrialized nations were increasingly attentive to information markets, including those in the Third World. Because the continued growth of the private sector seemed vital to this strategy, "government-controlled media" were viewed as particularly ominous.

The importance of this issue was evident at a 1981 UNESCO-sponsored meeting on the protection of journalists. For two decades attempts had been made by international organizations of journalists and publishers – such as the International Federation of Journalists, the International Federation of Newspaper Editors, and the International Press Institute – to draft and have adopted an international convention for the protection of journalists. At the UNESCO meeting the concerns of the journalists' organizations were quickly obscured by the recurring issue of the role of governments, this time revolving around licensing. Most governments were prepared to recognize the importance of safeguarding journalists, even though few seemed to cherish the activities of "investigative reporters." The status of journalists and the special protections proposed for them would presumably be based on professional credentials – but issued by whom? In raising this issue, Third World leaders were accused of wishing to license journalists, an idea that was anathema to Western nations.

Nonetheless, attempts were made during the early 1980s to steer the *new order* debates away from such divisive issues. This was especially evident in the creation of a new organization based on an earlier initiative of the United States: the International Program for the Development of Communication (IPDC). The IPDC was designed to be a key instrument for organizing international technical cooperation, helping in the creation and implementation of operational projects, and mobilizing the resources needed for those purposes. Although officially launched in 1980, its first meeting was not held until June 1981. It soon became apparent, however, that contributions from donor countries were much more limited than had been expected. The IPDC was faced with the same dilemma confronting a number of international development agencies: a necessary curtailment of expectations and plans.

The 1982 and 1983 UNESCO General Conferences, held in Paris, did not witness the heated polemics of similar meetings held in 1978 and 1980. At the 1983 conference the call for a new information and communication order was formally designated as "an evolving and continuous process" – a concession to Western interests intent on ensuring that the new order should not be viewed as requiring a sudden and radical transformation of existing communication structures.

A 1983 United Nations–UNESCO Round Table on a New World Information and Communication Order held in Igls, Austria, was another promising sign of dialogue. At the first official United Nations–UNESCO meeting on the issue, the Austrian round table was noteworthy for the absence of political rhetoric and the determination of participants to establish specific mechanisms for assisting the developing countries. Communications technology, rather than news flow alone, was now the primary concern of developing countries.

The year 1983 was to end with two paradoxical but not unrelated events. In early December the nonaligned nations movement held in New Delhi its first Media Conference. It opened with a call to intensify efforts to promote the proposed new order. Weeks later, as December came to a close, Secretary of State George P. Schultz of the United States sent a letter to the director-general of UNESCO informing him that, after the required one-year notification period, in December 1984 the United States would withdraw from UNESCO. An indirect reference to the *new order* campaign was evident in a passage referring to the necessity of maintaining "such goals as individual human rights and the free flow of information." The US decision to withdraw from UNESCO surprised observers who had taken note of the apparent absence of conflict in 1982 and 1983. However, it was clear that throughout the early 1980s there was significant bipartisan congressional opposition to UNESCO, not only because of its efforts to promote a new information order but also because of disputes relating to Israel, UNESCO's examination of the issues of peace and disarmament, and a new generation of "people's rights," as well as various financial and organizational reasons. This opposition was widely backed by the US press and other groups.

Challenges

Two decades of debates and resolutions had done little to solve underlying problems of the international flow of information, although they had made the world community more aware of the issues involved. Those issues would be a continuing presence, posing a diversity of challenges, many of which had been spelled out in the MacBride Commission's report. A notable aspect of the report was that it went beyond immediate needs and brought to the fore the overall significance of communications in modern society and the implications of media policies for the world's future.

Meanings of technology

The commission noted that technological needs had been a central concern at many meetings but urged that they not be allowed to overshadow the social, political, and economic implications. The importance of the new communications technologies was seen to lie to a large extent in the fundamental transformations they impose on society. Governments and private companies alike have long been inclined to think of technology as a means available to serve their particular needs without consideration of the impact on humanity at large. Use of technical developments cannot and should not be slowed, in the view of the commission, but their implications should be constantly assessed. Technology "is seldom neutral – its use is even less so" – for use is influenced by political, financial, and other considerations. Therefore, decisions about communications policies and priorities should not be made solely by technocrats but should involve wide public participation and discussion. "We must beware of the temptation to regard technology as an all-purpose tool capable of superseding social action." The commission noticed a widespread feeling that "technological progress is running ahead of man's capacity to interpret its implications and direct it into the most desirable channels," and cited the fear expressed by Albert Schweitzer that humankind has "lost the capacity to foresee and forestall the consequences" of its actions.

Ways of freedom

The commission noted the perilous status of freedom of expression around the world. The fact "that there is said to be freedom of expression in a country does not guarantee its existence in practice." The commission further noted that "even where freedom is not openly attacked by authority, it may be limited by self-censorship on the part of communicators themselves. Journalists may fail to publish facts which have come into their possession for several reasons: sheer timidity, an excessive respect for the power structure or in some instances lest they give offence to officialdom and thus risk losing access to their sources of information." Self-censorship, like censorship itself, was seen by the commission as a constantly distorting factor in the flow of communication.

The commission emphasized its view that the exercise of freedom in the communications field involves responsibilities. "We need to ask, moreover, on what grounds a claim for freedom is being made. The freedom of a citizen or social group to have access to communication, both as recipients and contributors, cannot be compared to the freedom of an investor to derive profits from the media. One protects a fundamental human right, the other permits the commercialization of a social need."

The report observed that because of the overwhelming importance of communication today, the state imposes some degree of regulation in virtually all societies. It can intervene in many diverse ways – through the allocation of broadcast licenses and newsprint and through visa policies, import restriction, and many other procedures. "Some governments find it natural to assume total control over the content of information, justifying themselves by the ideology in which they believe. Even on purely pragmatic standards, it is doubtful if this system can be called realistic."

Democratization of communication

Surveying the "spectrum of communication in modern society," the commission found that it almost defies description because of its immense variety. Barriers could readily be seen: monopolistic controls, technical disparities, restrictive media practices, exclusion of disadvantaged groups, blacklist, censorship. Nevertheless, a tendency toward democratization seemed to be taking place – for example, in the growing role of public opinion. Governments throughout the world were becoming increasingly aware that they must take into account not only national opinion but "world public opinion," because today's media are capable of diffusing "information on international questions to every part of the world." Occasionally opinion crystallizes on some issue with enough force to compel action. This happened, as the commission saw it, on the issues of colonialism, apartheid, and nuclear proliferation. But a meaningful process of opinion formation will in the long run require richer media fare, development of widespread "critical awareness," assertion of the "right to reply," the establishment of "alternative channels of communication," and public participation in decision making on media policies. The goal, the commission felt, should be that everyone would be both "producer and consumer of communication." [. . .]

38 Peripheral Vision

John Sinclair, Elizabeth Jacka, and Stuart Cunningham

Instead of the image of "the West" at the centre dominating the peripheral "Third World" with an outward flow of cultural products, we see the world as divided into a number of regions which each have their own internal dynamics as well as their global ties. Although primarily based on geographic realities, these regions are also defined by common cultural, linguistic, and historical connections which transcend physical space. Such a dynamic, regionalist view of the world helps us to analyse in a more nuanced way the intricate and multi-directional flows of television across the globe.

New Patterns of Television Flow

Public discourse about television and the media-studies literature are both replete with anxiety about the supposed cultural effects of the global spread of programmes like *Dallas* or, more recently, *Beverly Hills 90210*. The unquestioned basis for this anxiety is expressed in the orthodox critical paradigm for analysing the connection between international power relations and the media, the thesis of "cultural imperialism", or more particularly, "media imperialism". According to this view, world patterns of communication flow, both in density and in direction, mirror the system of domination in the economic and political order. Thus, world centres like New York, Los Angeles, London, and Tokyo are major nodes for international telecommunications traffic, as well as for other kinds of flows, such as television programmes. The media imperialism perspective more particularly sees that the major world sources for programme exports are located in the USA and secondarily in Europe, mainly the UK, and that these centres act as nodes through which all flows of cultural products must pass, including those from one peripheral part of the world to another.

The *locus classicus* of the cultural imperialism thesis is found in the work of Herbert Schiller. As recently as 1991, in an article tellingly entitled "Not Yet the Post-Imperialist Era", he has restated his position in the following way: "The role of television in the global arena of cultural domination has not diminished in the 1990s. Reinforced by new delivery systems – communication satellites and cable networks – the image flow is heavier than ever. Its source of origin also has not changed that much in the last quarter of the century". The classic study for UNESCO by

Original publication details: Excerpted from John Sinclair, Elizabeth Jacka, and Stuart Cunningham, "Peripheral Vision," in John Sinclair, Elizabeth Jacka, and Stuart Cunningham (eds.), *New Patterns in Global Television: Peripheral Vision* (Oxford University Press, 1996), pp. 5–10, 18–21, 25. Reprinted by permission of Oxford University Press.

Nordenstreng and Varis in 1974 documented the dominance of the USA in world television programme exports at that time. Television programme flows became an integral issue for the New World Information Order movement and its debate within UNESCO. As this continued into the 1980s, the cultural imperialism view of international domination stood challenged only by those who were seen as apologists for the USA and its demand for a "free flow" international regime for trade in cultural products. Neither critics nor apologists questioned the oft-quoted factoid that entertainment is second only to aerospace as an export industry for the USA.

Indeed, as long as the flows of television programme exports seemed to continue along the "one-way street" from the West (and the USA in particular) to the rest of the world, the critical discourse of cultural imperialism was a plausible theoretical response, at least in its more subtle variations, notably that of "cultural dependence" and "media imperialism". In an essential respect, the cultural imperialism perspective was the then-current neo-Marxist analysis of capitalist culture projected on to an international scale: the "dominant ideology" thesis writ large. As such, it had the all-embracing appeal of a comprehensive theory, and also provided the high moral ground from which the international activities of USA networks and the ideological content of their television programmes could be analysed, and then denounced.

However, by the mid-1980s it became evident that the cultural imperialism discourse had serious inadequacies, both as theory and in terms of the reality which the theory purported to explain. Actual transformation of the world television system made it less and less sustainable on the empirical level, and shifting theoretical paradigms, including postmodernism, postcolonialism, and theories of the "active" audience, made its conceptual foundations less secure. To take the empirical aspect first, Jeremy Tunstall had long since pointed out that the "television imperialism thesis" of such writers as Schiller and Wells was based on the quite incorrect assumption that the high levels of USA programme imports into Latin America in the 1960s were a permanent condition rather than a transitional stage in the development of television in these regions. The other empirical development which ought to have given pause to theorists of cultural imperialism was the research reported by Varis as an update of the original "one-way street" project, in which he noted "a trend toward greater regional exchanges", in spite of continued USA and European dominance in television programme flows. This finding was reinforced by other studies around the same time which, although absurdly exaggerated in their estimation of how far the flows had formed new patterns, were able nevertheless to document just how one such regional market was taking shape, in the case of Latin America.

Thus, even in Latin America, virtually the cradle of the theorization of cultural imperialism, USA imports were prominent only in the early stages. As the industry matured in Latin America, and as it developed "critical mass", USA imports were to some extent replaced by local products, a pattern that can be found repeated many times over around the world, and which is currently shaping Europe's new privately owned services. Of course, not all countries in Latin America have the capacity to develop sizeable indigenous television production industries. Rather, the pattern in Latin America, as in Asia and the Middle East, is that each "geolinguistic region", as we shall call them, is itself dominated by one or two centres of audiovisual production – Mexico and Brazil for Latin America, Hong Kong and Taiwan for the Chinese-speaking populations of Asia, Egypt for the Arab world, and India for the Indian populations of Africa and Asia. The Western optic through which the cultural imperialism thesis was developed literally did not see these non-Western systems of regional exchange, nor understand what they represented. Yet by the late 1980s,

Tracey could observe that the "very general picture of TV flows . . . is not a one-way street; rather there are a number of main thoroughfares, with a series of not unimportant smaller roads".

We have noted how, as theory, the cultural imperialism critique tended to identify the USA as the single centre of a process of mediacentric capitalist cultural influence which emanated out to the rest of the world in the form of television programmes. It also assumed that these programmes had an inevitable and self-sufficient ideological effect upon their helpless audiences in the periphery. Although this rationale established a theoretical connection between US television programmes and "consumerism", it did not address the question of just how such a mechanism of effect might work, nor how it could be observed in action upon actual audiences. In the discourse of cultural imperialism, the mystique of television entertainment's multivalent appeal for its audiences, and how specific audiences responded to it, were never on the agenda.

Other shortcomings arose from the theory's emphasis on external forces from the USA, and the corresponding disregard for the internal sociological factors within the countries seen to be subject to them. In its eagerness to hold US companies, and behind them, the US government, responsible for regressive sociocultural changes in the "Third World", the cultural imperialism critique neglected the internal historical and social dynamics within the countries susceptible to their influence. This left out of consideration the strategic social structural position of the individuals and interest groups who benefited from facilitating US market entry or even from taking their own initiatives. Some of these have subsequently built up their own international media empires, such as Mexico and Brazil. Other players have more recently joined the game, such as some Saudi investors, while investment in the new channels in India by expatriates shows that media entrepreneurism also can be widespread on a small scale. The cultural imperialism theory failed to see that, more fundamental than its supposed ideological influence, the legacy of the USA in world television development was in the implantation of its systemic model for television as a medium – the exploitation of entertainment content so as to attract audiences which could then be sold to advertisers. American content may have primed this process, but as the experience of many parts of the peripheral world shows, it is not required to sustain it.

We should also note that with its dichotomized view of "the West" versus the "Third World", the cultural imperialism theory was unable to give an adequate account of semi-peripheral settler societies such as Australia and Canada, where the experience of colonialism, and postcolonialism, has been quite distinct from that of nations in other former colonized zones, a distinctiveness manifest in the television systems which they developed.

The basic assumption of Western domination via television is worth further comment. Paradoxically, even though the cultural imperialism thesis has been articulated in the name of defending the "Third World" against domination by audiovisual products from the USA, it is more inclined to reinforce Western cultural influence by taking it as given, when it should be challenging it. A more postcolonial perspective in theory has forced us to realize that USA domination always was limited, either by cultural or political "screens", or both. A related weakness or "blind spot" of the cultural imperialism thesis has been its over-emphasis on the significance of imported *vis-à-vis* local television. Television has always been more of a local than a global medium, and remains so, although the increasingly multichannel and globalized nature of the industry may alter the balance at the margin in the longer term.

According to figures from 1989, the volume of purely domestic material in national markets is twenty-nine times higher than that which is traded. Television is still a gloriously hybrid medium, with a plethora of programming of an inescapably and essentially local, untranslatable nature.

Although US programmes might lead the world in their transportability across cultural boundaries, and even manage to dominate schedules on some channels in particular countries, they are rarely the most popular programmes where viewers have a reasonable menu of locally produced material to choose from. And even where there is imported content, it is no longer acceptable to read off from that fact alone any presumed effects of a cultural or political kind. Hamid Naficy captures this vividly in his brilliant study of television amongst Iranian exiles in Los Angeles. Describing how his exclusively English-speaking Iranian daughter, Shayda, and his exclusively German-speaking Iranian niece, Setarah, communicated through the Disney film *The Little Mermaid*, he goes on to comment:

> The globalization of American pop culture does not automatically translate into globalization of American control. This globalized culture provides a shared discursive space where transnationals such as Setarah and Shayda can localize it, make their own uses of it, domesticate and indigenize it. They may think with American cultural products but they do not think American. [. . .]

"Gatekeepers" and Cultural Industry Factors in Television Flows

Many cross-cultural studies emphasize the diverse, localized character of international audience responses, and are imbued with a sense of the viability and integrity of the cultures of peripheral or "small" nations. So it is somewhat ironic, because of the dominance of American programmes at highly visible though only provisionally premium places in schedules, that such studies should focus on US programmes almost exclusively. As Ellen Seiter argues strongly with regard to the theoretical field from which this position draws, "in our concern for audiences' pleasures . . . we run the risk of continually validating Hollywood's domination of the worldwide television market".

Far more than for the USA, the success or otherwise of peripheral nations' exports is contingent on factors other than those captured by established modes of audience study. This explains why so little audience reception research has been able to be conducted on their products in international markets, and why we need instead middle-range analysis to do so. In the middle range between political economy approaches and reception analysis, a number of factors are mediating. How are programmes acquired overseas? Who engages in their appraisal and acquisition and what perceptions have they formed of peripheral programming? This "primary audience" is the major source of informed "gatekeeping" which regulates (in the widest sense) the flow of peripheral programming in international markets. And what are the characteristics of the major territories which influence the success or failure of such programmes internationally? All these mediating factors embody legitimate, indeed central, aspects of cultural exchange, as virtually all the significant research on non-dominant nations' television production and reception indicates.

The actual structure of major international television trade markets is central to middle-range analysis. There is an ever-wider variety of modes of contracting for international programme production and exchange: offshore, co-production, official co-production, co-venture (including presales), and straight purchase of territorial rights for completed programmes in the major trade markets such as MIP-TV and MIPCOM. These run on annual cycles suited to the programming and scheduling patterns of the major northern hemisphere territories, but a notable shift in the patterns of global television traffic was indicated in 1994 when the first MIP-Asia was held, a trade market specifically for the Asian region. At such events, programming is often bought (or not bought) on the basis of company reputation or distributor clout, in job lots and sight-unseen. Very broad, rough-and-ready genre expectations are in play; judgements may seem highly "subjective" and arbitrary.

Universalist explanations may prove useful in accounting for the international successes of historically universal forms like US series drama, but there is solid evidence that cultural specificities, along with other middle-range industrial factors, are unavoidable and, at times, enabling factors for international success in peripheral countries' export activity. Studies which compare viewers' engagement with US as against other sources of television programming confirm that there tends to be a more distanced realm of "pure entertainment" within which US programmes are processed – as markers of modish modernity, as a "spectacular" world – compared to more culturally specific responses made to domestic and other sources.

The capacity for peripheral countries to export their programmes across diverse markets is to some extent based on their substitutability or non-substitutability for US material, although this also depends in part on the type of channel they are purchased for. Australian productions have provided useful models from which the protocols of commercial popularity may be learnt in rapidly commercializing European broadcasting environments, but the fact that Australian programmes are perceived as imitations of US formats constitutes a problem for both commentators and regulators in Europe.

To be sure, the structure of content and the form of internationally popular serial drama in particular are widely shared and may even be "borrowed" from US practice, as the *telenovela* was decades ago. But the "surface" differences, nevertheless, almost always are consequential, and contribute to the acceptance or rejection of non-US material, depending on whether the "primary audience" of gatekeepers and the viewing audience respond positively or negatively to those differences. As Anne Cooper-Chen has shown, even that most transparently internationalized of television formats, the game show, contains significant differences in the widely variant cultures in which it is popular. After looking at popular game shows in fifty countries, she regards them as having at least three structural variants – the East Asian, Western, and Latin models – and innumerable surface particularities. Hamid Mowlana and Mehdi Rad show that the Japanese programme *Oshin* found acceptance in Iran because its values of perseverance and long suffering were compatible with cultural codes prevalent in what might appear a distinctly different society. The evidence for the popularity of *Neighbours* in Britain demonstrates that, while Australian soaps arguably were brought into the market as substitutes for US material, their popularity built around textual factors based on projections and introjections of Australian "life-style". Australia has served in many ways as a kind of "other" to Britain – the younger, more upstart and hedonistic vision of how the British might like to see themselves.

The "export of meaning" is not just a matter of viewer reception. Many nations, both core and peripheral, place special importance on the international profile they can establish with their audiovisual exports. These are fostered both as a form of cultural diplomacy, and for intrinsic economic reasons, although national cultural objectives and audiovisual industry development are not always compatible, as

Australia and Canada have long been aware, and some Asian countries are now learning. In the case of the Middle East, one commentator has observed that the popularity of Egyptian television exports in the Arab states has a number of cultural and even political "multiplier effects". This popularity was preceded by the success of Egyptian films, and carries with it a potential acceptance and recognition of Egyptian accents and performers that can operate as "a soft-sell commercial for Egyptian values" which then carries over into indirect political leverage. While it might be difficult to isolate and measure them, it is not unreasonable to infer cultural, trade, and political multiplier effects from what can be seen of peripheral nations' products on the world's television screens. [. . .]

Even amongst the globalization theorists, it is becoming a commonplace to observe that the globalizing forces towards "homogenization", such as satellite television, exist in tension with contradictory tendencies towards "heterogenization", conceived pessimistically as fragmentation, or with postmodernist optimism, as pluralism. Thus, "identity and cultural affiliation are no longer matters open to the neat simplifications of traditional nationalism. They are matters of ambiguity and complexity, of overlapping loyalties and symbols with multiple meanings". To the extent that we can assume that television is in fact a source of identity, and that audiences for the same programme derive similar identities from it, it becomes possible to think of identities which are multiple, although also often contradictory, corresponding to the different levels from which the televisual environment is composed in a given market. An Egyptian immigrant in Britain, for example, might think of herself as a Glaswegian when she watches her local Scottish channel, a British resident when she switches over to the BBC, an Islamic Arab expatriate in Europe when she tunes in to the satellite service from the Middle East, and a world citizen when she channel surfs on to CNN. [. . .]

39 Cultural Imperialism

John Tomlinson

"Watching *Dallas*": The Imperialist Text and Audience Research

For many critics, the American TV series *Dallas* had become the byword for cultural imperialism in the 1980s. Ien Ang's study, *Watching Dallas* takes as its central question the tension between the massive international popularity of the Texan soap opera:

> ... in over ninety countries, ranging from Turkey to Australia, from Hong Kong to Great Britain ... with the proverbial empty streets and dramatic drop in water consumption when an episode of the series is going out ...

and the reaction of cultural commentators to this "success":

> *Dallas* was regarded as yet more evidence of the threat posed by American-style commercial culture against authentic national identities. In February 1983 for instance, Jack Lang, the French Minister for Culture ... had even proclaimed *Dallas* as the "symbol of American cultural imperialism".

Ang detects amongst European cultural critics an "ideology of mass culture" by which she means a generalised hostility towards the imported products of the American mass culture industry, which has fixed on *Dallas* as the focus of its contempt.

Ang quotes Michelle Mattelart:

> It is not for nothing that *Dallas* casts its ubiquitous shadow wherever the future of culture is discussed: it has become the perfect hate symbol, the cultural poverty ... against which one struggles.

The evident popularity of *Dallas* juxtaposed with its hostile critical reception amongst "professional intellectuals" and the linked charges of cultural imperialism poses for us nicely the problem of the audience in the discourse of media imperialism. For the cultural critics tend to condemn *Dallas* with scant regard to the way in which the audience may read the text.

Cultural imperialism is once more seen as an ideological property of the text itself. It is seen as inhering in the images of dazzling skyscrapers, expensive clothes and

Original publication details: Excerpted from John Tomlinson, *Cultural Imperialism: A Critical Introduction* (Pinter, 1991), pp. 45–50, 108–13. Reprinted by permission of Continuum International Publishing Group Ltd., The Tower Building, 11 York Road, London, SE1 7NX, England.

automobiles, lavish settings, the celebration in the narrative of power and wealth and so on. All this is seen to have an obvious ideological manipulative effect on the viewer. As Lealand has put it:

> There is an assumption that American TV imports do have an impact whenever and wherever they are shown, but actual investigation of this seldom occurs. Much of the evidence that is offered is merely anecdotal or circumstantial. Observations of . . . Algerian nomads watching *Dallas* in the heat of the desert are offered as sufficient proof.

However, encouraged by developments in British critical media theory, some writers have attempted to probe the audience reception of "imperialist texts" like *Dallas*. Ien Ang's study, although it is not primarily concerned with the issue of media imperialism, is one such.

Ang approaches the *Dallas* audience with the intention of investigating an hypothesis generated from her own experience of watching *Dallas*. She found that her own enjoyment of the show chafed against the awareness she had of its ideological content. Her critical penetration as "an intellectual and a feminist" of this ideology suggested to her that the pleasure she derived from the programme had little connection with, and certainly did not entail, an ideological effect. In reacting to the ideology in the text, she argues, the cultural critics overlook the crucial question in relation to the audience: "For we must accept one thing: *Dallas* is popular because a lot of people somehow *enjoy* watching it."

Ang saw the popularity of the show, which might be read as a sign of its imperialist ideological power, as a complex phenomenon without a single cause, but owing a good deal to the intrinsic pleasure to be derived from its melodramatic narrative structure. The show's ability to connect with "the melodramatic imagination" and the pleasure this provides were, Ang thought, the key to its success, and these had no necessary connection with the power of American culture or the values of consumer capitalism. What the cultural critics overlooked was the capacity of the audience to negotiate the possible contradictions between alien cultural values and the "pleasure of the text".

Ang's study was based on a fairly informal empirical procedure. She placed an advertisement in a Dutch women's magazine asking people to write to her describing what they liked or disliked about *Dallas*. Her correspondents revealed a complex set of reactions, including evidence that some did indeed, like Ang herself, manage to resolve a conflict between their distaste for the ideology of the show and a pleasure in watching it. For example:

> *Dallas*. . . . God, don't talk to me about it. I'm hooked on it! But you wouldn't believe the number of people who say to me, "Oh, I thought you were against Capitalism?" I am, but *Dallas* is just so tremendously exaggerated, it has nothing to do with capitalists any more, it's just sheer artistry to make up such nonsense.

Ang found such a high level of disapproval for the cultural values of *Dallas* in some of her correspondents that she speaks of their views being informed by the "ideology of mass culture" of the cultural critics. These viewers, she argues, have internalised what they perceive as the "correct" attitude towards mass-cultural imports – that of the disapproving professional intellectuals. They thus feel the need to justify their enjoyment of the show by, for example, adopting an ironic stance towards it.

Alternatively, she suggests, an opposing "anti-intellectual" ideological discourse of "populism" may allow the *Dallas* fan to refuse the ideology of mass culture as elitist and paternalist, and to insist (in such popular maxims as "there's no accounting for taste") on their right to their pleasure without cultural "guilt".

Ang's analysis of the ideological positioning and struggle around the text of *Dallas* is not without its problems. But her empirical work does at the very least suggest how naive and improbable is the simple notion of an immediate ideological effect arising from exposure to the imperialist text. The complex, reflective and self-conscious reactions of her correspondents suggest that cultural critics who assume this sort of effect massively underestimate the audience's active engagement with the text and the critical sophistication of the ordinary viewer/reader.

The same message comes from most recent studies of audience response. Katz and Liebes, for instance, also looked at reactions to *Dallas*, but in a rather more formal empirical study than Ang's. Their work involved a large-scale cross-cultural study of the impact of *Dallas*, comparing different ethnic groups in Israel with a group of American viewers. Katz and Liebes situate themselves within the growing perspective in media research which sees the audience as active and the process of meaning construction as one of "negotiation" with the text in a particular cultural context. They argue that this perspective:

> raises a question about the apparent ease with which American television programmes cross cultural and linguistic frontiers. Indeed, the phenomenon is so taken for granted that hardly any systematic research has been done to explain the reasons why these programmes are so successful. One wonders how such quintessentially American products are understood at all. The often-heard assertion that this phenomenon is part of the process of cultural imperialism presumes, first, that there is an American message in the content and form; second, that this message is somehow perceived by viewers; and, third, that it is perceived in the same way by viewers in different cultures.

Katz and Liebes, like Ang, are generally dubious about the way in which the media imperialism argument has been presented by its adherents:

> Since the effects attributed to a TV programme are often inferred from content analysis alone, it is of particular interest to examine the extent to which members of the audience absorb, explicitly or implicitly, the messages which critics and scholars allege they are receiving.

Their study of *Dallas* thus represents perhaps the most ambitious attempt so far to examine the media imperialism argument empirically from the perspective of audience response. In order to do this, they organised fifty "focus groups" consisting of three couples each to watch an episode of *Dallas*. The idea of watching the programme in groups was essential to one of their guiding premises, that the meanings of TV texts are arrived at via a *social* process of viewing and discursive interpretation. They believe, in common with other recent views, that TV viewing is not essentially an isolated individual practice, but one in which social interaction – "conversation with significant others" – is a vital part of the interpretative and evaluative process. This may be even more significant when the programme in question is the product of an alien culture and, thus, potentially more difficult to "decode".

The groups that Katz and Liebes arranged were all from similar class backgrounds – "lower middle class with high school education or less" – and each group was "ethnically homogeneous":

There were ten groups each of Israeli Arabs, new immigrants to Israel from Russia, first- and second-generation immigrants from Morocco and Kibbutz members. Taking these groups as a microcosm of the worldwide audience of *Dallas*, we are comparing their "readings" of the programme with ten groups of matched Americans in Los Angeles.

The groups followed their viewing of *Dallas* with an hour-long "open structured" discussion and a short individual questionnaire. The discussions were recorded and formed the basic data of the study, what Katz and Liebes refer to as "ethnosemiological data".

The groups were invited to discuss, first, simply what happened in the episode – "the narrative sequence, and the topics, issues and themes with which the programme deals". Even at this basic level Katz and Liebes found examples of divergent readings influenced, they argue, by the cultural background of the groups and reinforced by their interaction. One of the Arabic groups actually "misread" the information of the programme in a way which arguably made it more compatible with their cultural horizon. In the episode viewed, Sue Ellen had taken her baby and run away from her husband JR, moving into the house of her former lover and his father. However, the Arab group confirmed each other in the more conventional reading – in their terms – that she had actually gone to live in her *own* father's house. The implications of this radical translation of the events of the narrative must at least be to undermine the notion that texts cross cultural boundaries intact.

More importantly, perhaps, Katz and Liebes found that different ethnic groups brought their own values to a judgement of the programme's values. They quote a Moroccan Jew's assessment:

> *Machluf*: You see, I'm a Jew who wears a skullcap and I learned from this series to say, "Happy is our lot, goodly is our fate" that we're Jewish. Everything about JR and his baby, who has maybe four or five fathers, who knows? The mother is Sue Ellen, of course, and the brother of Pam left. Maybe he's the father. . . . I see that they're almost all bastards.

This sort of response, which seems to be not just a rejection of Western decadence, but an actual reinforcement of the audience's own cultural values, extended from issues of interpersonal and sexual morality to the programme's celebration of wealth: "With all that they have money, my life style is higher than theirs." However, here, at the "real foundations", Katz and Liebes found a more typical response to be an agreement on the importance of money:

> *Miriam*: Money will get you anything. That's why people view it. People sit at home and want to see how it looks.
> [. . .]
> *Yosef*: Everybody wants to be rich. Whatever he has, he wants more.
> *Zari*: Who doesn't want to be rich? The whole world does.

It scarcely needs saying that responses like these demonstrate no more than agreement with aspects of the perceived message of *Dallas* and cannot be taken as evidence of the programme's ideological effect. All cultures, we must surely assume, will generate their own set of basic attitudes on issues like the relationship between wealth and happiness. *Dallas* represents, perhaps, one very forceful statement of such an attitude, informed by a dominant global culture of capitalism. But it would be absurd to assume that people in any present-day culture do not have developed attitudes to such a central aspect of their lives quite independent of any televisual representations. We clearly cannot assume that simply watching *Dallas* makes people want to be rich! The most we can assume is that agreement here, as with disagreement elsewhere with the programme's message, represents the outcome of people's "negotiations" with the text.

Katz and Liebes are careful not to draw any premature conclusions from this complex data. But they do at least suggest that it supports their belief in the active social process of viewing and demonstrates a high level of sophistication in the discursive interpretations of ordinary people. They also make the interesting suggestion that the social and economic distance between the affluent denizens of the South-fork Range and their spectators around the globe is of less consequence than might be thought: "Unhappiness is the greatest leveller." This thought chimes with Ang's argument that it is the melodramatic nature of the narrative and its appeal to the "tragic structure of feeling", rather than its glimpses of consumer capitalism at its shiny leading edge that scores *Dallas*'s global ratings.

The general message of empirical studies – informal ones like Ang's and more large-scale formal projects like Katz and Liebes's – is that audiences are more active and critical, their responses more complex and reflective, and their cultural values more resistant to manipulation and "invasion" than many critical media theorists have assumed. [. . .]

Multinational Capitalism and Cultural Homogenisation

Critics of multinational capitalism frequently do complain of its tendency towards cultural convergence and homogenisation. This is the major criticism made in the discourse of cultural imperialism which takes capitalism as its target. A good example is Cees Hamelink's book, *Cultural Autonomy in Global Communications*. Hamelink, who acknowledges the co-operation of both Schiller and Salinas, places the issues of cultural autonomy and cultural homogenisation – or what he refers to as "cultural synchronisation" – at the centre of his analysis. He is broadly correct in identifying the processes of "cultural synchronization" (or homogenisation) as unprecedented in historical terms and in seeing these processes as closely connected to the spread of global capitalism. But he fails to show why cultural synchronisation should be objected to and, specifically, he fails to show that it should be objected to on the grounds of cultural autonomy.

In his opening chapter Hamelink lists a number of personal "experiences of the international scene" to illustrate his thesis. For example:

In a Mexican village the traditional ritual dance precedes a soccer match, but the performance features a gigantic Coca-Cola bottle.

In Singapore, a band dressed in traditional Malay costume offers a heart-breaking imitation of Fats Domino.

In Saudi Arabia, the television station performs only one local cultural function – the call for the Moslem prayer. Five times a day, North American cops and robbers yield to the traditional muezzin.

In its gigantic advertising campaign, IBM assures Navajo Indians that their cultural identity can be effectively protected if they use IBM typewriters equipped with the Navajo alphabet.

The first thing to note about these examples is precisely their significance as *personal* observations – and this is not to make any trivial point about their "subjective" nature. Hamelink expresses the cultural standpoint of the concerned Westerner confronting a perplexing set of global phenomena. We have to accept, at the level of the personal, the sincerity of his concern and also the validity of this personal discourse: it is valid for individuals to express their reaction to global tendencies. But we need to acknowledge that this globe-trotting instancing of cultural imperialism shapes the discourse in a particular way: to say "here is the *sameness* that capitalism brings – and here – and here . . ." is to assume, however liberal, radical or critical the intention, the role of the "tourist": the problem of homogenisation is likely to present itself to the Western intellectual who has a sense of the diversity and "richness" of global culture as a particular threat. For the people involved in each discrete instance Hamelink presents, the experience of Western capitalist culture will probably have quite different significance. Only if they can adopt the (privileged) role of the cultural tourist will the sense of the homogenisation of global culture have the same threatening aspect. The Kazakhstani tribesman who has no knowledge of (and, perhaps, no interest in) America or Europe is unlikely to see his cassette player as emblematic of creeping capitalist domination. And we cannot, without irony, argue that the Western intellectual's (informed?) concern is more valid: again much hangs on the question, "who speaks?"

This said, Hamelink does draw from these instances an empirical conclusion which is, I think, fairly uncontroversial:

> One conclusion still seems unanimously shared: the impressive variety of the world's cultural systems is waning due to a process of "cultural synchronisation" that is without historic precedent.

For those in a position to view the world as a cultural totality, it cannot be denied that certain processes of cultural convergence are under way, and that these are new processes. This last is an important point, for Hamelink is careful to acknowledge that cultures have always influenced one another and that this influence has often enriched the interacting communities – "the richest cultural traditions emerged at the actual meeting point of markedly different cultures, such as Sudan, Athens, the Indus Valley, and Mexico". Even where cultural interaction has been in the context of political and economic domination, Hamelink argues, there has been, in most cases a "two-way exchange" or at least a tolerance of cultural diversity. There is a sharp difference for him between these patterns and modern "cultural synchronization":

> In the second half of the twentieth century, a destructive process that differs significantly from the historical examples given above threatens the diversity of cultural systems. Never before has the synchronization with one particular cultural pattern been of such global dimensions and so comprehensive.

Let us be clear about what we are agreeing. It seems to me that Hamelink is right, broadly speaking, to identify cultural synchronisation as an unprecedented feature of global modernity. The evaluative implications of his use of the word "destructive", however, raises larger problems. It is one thing to say that cultural diversity is being destroyed, quite another to lament the fact. The latter position demands reasons which Hamelink cannot convincingly supply. The quotation continues in a way that raises part of the problem: "Never before has the process of cultural influence proceeded so subtly, without any blood being shed and with the receiving culture thinking it had sought such cultural influence." With his last phrase Hamelink slides towards the problematic of false consciousness. As we have seen more than once before, any critique which bases itself in the idea that cultural domination is taking place "behind people's backs" is heading for trouble. To acknowledge that a cultural community might have thought it had sought cultural influence is to acknowledge that such influence has at least *prima facie* attractions.

This thought could lead us to ask if the process of cultural homogenisation itself might not have its attractions. It is not difficult to think of examples of cultural practices which would probably attract a consensus in favour of their universal application: health care; food hygiene; educational provision; various "liberal" cultural attitudes towards honesty, toleration, compassion and so on; democratic public processes etc. This is not to say that any of these are indisputable "goods" under any description whatever, nor that they are all the "gifts" of an expanding capitalist modernity. But it is to say that there are plenty of aspects of "culture", broadly defined, that the severest critic of cultural homogenisation might wish to find the same in any area of the globe. Critics of cultural homogenisation are selective in the things they object to, and there is nothing wrong in this so long as we realise that it undermines the notion that homogenisation is a bad thing *in itself*. But then we enter a quite separate set of arguments – not about the uniformity of capitalist culture, but about the spread of its pernicious features – which require quite different criteria of judgement.

Engaging with the potentially attractive features of homogenisation brings us to see, pretty swiftly, the problems in its use as a critical concept. But there are other ways of approaching the issue, and one of Hamelink's arguments seems on the surface to avoid these problems. He argues that cultural synchronisation is to be deplored on the grounds that it is a threat to cultural autonomy. I would argue against both the notion of autonomy as applied to a "culture" in the holistic sense and against any logical connection between the concept of autonomy and any particular *outcome* of cultural practices. Autonomy, as I understand it, refers to the free and uncoerced choices and actions of agents. But Hamelink uses the notion of autonomy in what strikes me as a curious way, to suggest a feature of cultural practices which is necessary, indeed "critical", for the actual survival of a cultural community.

Hamelink's reasoning appears to be based on the idea that the cultural system of any society is an *adaptive* mechanism which enables the society to exist in its "environment", by which he seems to mean the physical and material features of its global location: "Different climatic conditions, for example, demand different ways of adapting to them (i.e., different types of food, shelter and clothing)." Again, there is nothing particularly controversial about this, except in the obvious sense that we might want to argue that many of the cultural practices of modernity are rather more "distanced" from the function of survival than those of more "primitive" systems. But from this point he argues that the "autonomous" development of cultural systems – the freedom from the processes of "cultural synchronization" – are necessary to the "survival" of societies. Why should this be so? Because "the adequacy of the cultural system can best be decided upon by the members of the society who face directly the problems of survival and adaptation".

There are a number of difficulties arising from this sort of argument. First, what does Hamelink mean by the "survival" of a society? In his reference to very basic adaptations to environmental conditions he seems to trade on the idea that a culture allows for the actual physical survival of its members. At times he explicitly refers to the physical survival of people. For example, he claims that the intensive promotion of milk-powder baby food in the Third World by companies like Nestlé and Cow and Gate is a practice that can have life-threatening consequences:

> Replacing breast-feeding by bottle feeding has had disastrous effects in many Third World countries. An effective, adequate, and cheap method has been exchanged for an expensive, inadequate and dangerous product. . . . Many illiterate mothers, unable to prepare the milk powder correctly, have not only used it improperly but have also inadvertently transformed the baby food into a lethal product by using it in unhygienic conditions.

There *are* important issues having to do with the "combined and unequal development" produced by the spread of capitalism of which this is a good example. But the incidence of illness and death Hamelink refers to here, deplorable though it is, will obviously not carry the weight of his argument about cultural synchronisation affecting the physical survival of whole populations in the Third World. He cannot, plausibly, claim that cultural synchronisation with capitalist modernity carries this direct threat. It is probably true that capitalist production has long-term consequences for the global environment, thus for physical survival on a global scale, but this is a separate argument.

At any rate, Hamelink's notion of survival seems to slide from that of physical survival to the *survival of the culture itself.* But this is a very different proposition, which cannot be sustained by the functional view of culture he takes as his premise. For the failure of a culture to "survive" in an "original" form may be taken itself as a process of adaptation to a new "environment" – that of capitalist industrial modernity. A certain circularity is therefore introduced into the argument. Hamelink claims that unique cultures arise as adaptive mechanisms to environments, so he deplores heteronomy since it threatens such adaptation. But what could cultural synchronisation mean if not an "adaptation" to the demands of the social environment of capitalism?

The incoherences of this account arise, I believe, from the attempt to circumvent the problems of autonomy in cultural terms by referring the holistic view to a functional logic of adaptation. Autonomy can only apply to agents, and cultures are not agents. Hamelink seeks to bypass these problems with an argument that reduces the ethical-political content of "autonomy" to make it a mere indicator of social efficiency – the guarantor of the "best" form of social organisation in a particular environment. His argument is incoherent precisely because autonomy cannot be so reduced: in cultural terms, "best" is not to be measured against a simple index of physical survival. Things are far more complicated than this. Cultural autonomy must address the autonomous choices of agents who make up a cultural community; there is no escaping this set of problems by appeal to functionality. Hamelink gives the game away in his reference, cited earlier, to a form of cultural "false consciousness" and elsewhere where he speaks of cultural synchronisation as cultural practices being "persuasively communicated to the receiving countries".

I do not believe the appeal to autonomy grounds Hamelink's critique of cultural synchronisation. Even if it did, this would be an objection to the inhibition of independence by manipulation, not to the resulting "sameness" of global culture. But Hamelink does want to object to "sameness": this is implicit in his constant references to the "rich diversity" of cultures under threat. What are the grounds for such an objection?

Adaptation to physical environments has, historically, produced a diversity in cultural practices across the globe. However, the *preservation* of this diversity – which is what Hamelink wants – seems to draw its justification from the idea that cultural diversity is a good thing in itself. But this depends on the position from which you speak. If the attractions of a uniform capitalist modernity outweigh the charms of diversity, as they well may for those from the outside looking in, it is difficult to insist on the priority of preserving differences. Indeed, the appeal to variety might well be turned back on the critic of capitalism. For it might be argued that individual cultures making up the rich mosaic that Hamelink surveys are lacking in a variety of cultural experience, being tied, as Marx observed, to the narrow demands of the struggle with nature for survival. Cultural synchronisation could in some cases increase variety in cultural experience.

It must be said immediately that arguments exist that the *nature* of such experience in capitalist modernity is in some sense deficient – shallow, "one-dimensional", "commodified", and so on. But this is not a criticism of homogenisation or synchronisation as such: it is a criticism of the sort of culture that synchronisation brings. It is quite different to object to the spread of something bad – uniform badness – than to object to the spread of uniformity itself. This demands quite separate arguments about capitalism as a culture. [. . .]

40 Bollywood versus Hollywood: Battle of the Dream Factories

Heather Tyrrell

Introduction

Theorisation around cinema and globalisation has largely been structured in terms of a basic opposition between Western commercial and culturally imperialist cinema, and Third World non-commercial, indigenous, politicised cinema. Much criticism of Hollywood and much support for alternative cinemas have been based on this understood opposition. 'Bollywood', North Indian popular commercial cinema, is an anomalous case which forces us to re-think the global map of cultural consumption and challenge the assumptions generally made concerning world cinema.

While India is not the only non-Western country with a commercial, popular, indigenous cinema – the cinemas of Hong Kong, China, Mexico and Brazil could be similarly described – its film industry is at this time experiencing rapid changes which make it a particularly pertinent subject for examination. ' "Bollywood" has become widespread [sic] nomenclature for the Indian movie industry in recent times' and amalgamates two names: 'Hollywood', and 'Bombay' (India's commercial hub, now renamed Mumbai). But is Bollywood named in imitation of Hollywood, or as a challenge to it? For many years commentators have assumed the former, but if Bollywood were simply a substitute for Western film while economic barriers prevented the import of the original, once those barriers collapsed it would be expected that Bollywood would collapse too.

However, Indian film culture has not been undermined or devalued by the recent influx of Western product as some expected, and multinational companies have not succeeded in dominating the prized Indian market. The role and the importance of popular Indian cinema culture has been misinterpreted or underestimated by external commentators, perhaps precisely because it does not fit easily into the theoretical model developed around the dichotomy of First World and Third World cinema.

This chapter will begin by situating Bollywood within and against the theories formulated around Third World film known as Third Cinema theory. I will then go on to relate theory to practice by looking at three aspects of the Bollywood film industry: first, the current volatile period of change in India's film and media culture, as the international film industry attempts to enter the Indian market; second, Bollywood itself as an international film industry, in terms of production, distribution and

Original publication details: Excerpted from Heather Tyrrell, "Bollywood versus Hollywood: Battle of the Dream Factories," in Tracey Skelton and Tim Allen (eds.), *Culture and Global Change* (Routledge, 1999), pp. 260–6, 272–3. Reprinted by permission of Taylor & Francis Books Ltd.

exhibition; and third, oppositions to Bollywood as a dominant cultural force in India. By focusing on these areas I hope to demonstrate why Bollywood is fertile theoretical ground for Development Studies and Cultural Studies alike, and may force us to rethink how Third World popular culture is read.

Bollywood and Third Cinema

'Third Cinema' is a term coined originally by Argentine film-makers Fernando Solanas and Octavio Gettino, and generally applied to the theory of cinemas opposed to imperialism and colonialism. Bollywood, as a commercial popular cinema, has a problematic relationship to theories of Third Cinema, which assume a non-commercial, minority cinema as their subject.

In discussions of world cinema, the mainstream is generally taken to be North American and European cinema, with others as oppositional, marginal, and most significantly, non-commercial. Bollywood, the most prolific film industry in the world, and one with an international commercial market, challenges this assumption. Bollywood films are not solely politically motivated, nor are they entirely devoid of nationalist/anti-colonialist content. They are at once 'escapist' and ideologically loaded.

In *Questions of Third Cinema*, Jim Pines and Paul Willemen (1989) talk about Third World films as 'physical acts of collective self-defence and resistance'. Bollywood can be read both as defending itself and Indian values against the West, and as a dangerous courier of Western values to the Indian audience, and is read in both these ways by the Indian popular film press. A constant process of negotiation between East and West takes place in Bollywood films, operating both in terms of style (narrative continuity, *mise-en-scène*, acting styles), and in terms of content (the values and ideas expressed in the films). Indian cinematic style negotiates the cinematic traditions of Classical Hollywood, while its content addresses the ideological heritage of colonisation; just as, in the 'picturisation' of a single film song, hero and heroine oscillate between Eastern and Western dress in a rapid series of costume swaps as they dance and mime to music which is itself a hybrid of Eastern and Western styles.

But does this negotiation, and its often overt anti-Western agenda, qualify Bollywood as Third Cinema? A cinema does not automatically qualify for the title because it is produced in and for the Third World. Argentine film-makers Fernando Solanas and Octavio Gettino, defined any 'big spectacle cinema' financed by big monopoly capital as First Cinema, 'likely to respond to the aspirations of big capital'. Third Cinema was 'democratic, national, popular cinema'. But both these statements can equally be applied to Bollywood, which, despite its prolific commercial profile, has always been refused industry status by the Indian government, and which, historically, received subsidies from Nehru's government to pursue an explicitly anti-colonial agenda.

Fidel Castro fiercely criticised Hollywood in his closing speech at the 1985 Havana Film Festival:

> They are poisoning the human mind in incredible doses through commercial cinematography, grossly commercial. [Third world cinema must be supported, because] if we do not survive culturally we will not survive economically or politically.

Compare this speech with an article by Shah Rukh Khan, India's top film star, in 1996, defending Bollywood's commercial film industry in an introduction to a feature on 100 years of Indian cinema in *Movie International* magazine.

I'd like to stress we are part of world cinema and we are making films – films we like, not for film festivals . . . Mark my words one day Indian cinema will rule the world. Once we get the technology we are going to kill them.

Khan's military metaphors are directed explicitly against the West, and not only against Hollywood and commercial cinema, but also against the independent, alternative cinema of 'film festivals' – cinema that could, in many cases, be described as 'Third Cinema'.

Bollywood seems both diametrically opposed to, and fiercely aligned to, Third Cinema. This confusion arises because commercialism has been exclusively identified with the West in cultural criticism, without taking into account a non-Western, even anti-Western commercialism. A cinema which is both commercial and concerned with 'decoding . . . the deemed superiority of the West' problematises established theoretical oppositions of East and West. Some of the strategies of Third Cinema can be applied to it, but so can some of the criticisms levelled at Hollywood. Vijay Mishra in his essay *The Texts of 'Mother India'* (1989) argues that Bollywood cannot be seen as Third Cinema, despite its 'defiantly subversive' stance, because it is ultimately conforming: 'popular Indian Cinema is so conservative and culture specific as to make a radical post colonial Indian Cinema impossible'.

Third Cinema is commonly perceived as 'serious' cinema, challenging in an aesthetic as well as a political sense. Bollywood films generally include light-hearted song-and-dance numbers, causing Tim Allen to dismiss them from the Third Cinema equation in his dossier on Third Cinema: 'In India serious films are not generally very popular at all. Most cinemas show jolly musicals . . .'

However, as Mira Reym Binford says in her essay *Innovation and Imitation in Indian Cinema*:

> the obligatory song-and-dance sequences of the Indian mainstream film are a striking example of indigenously based aesthetic principles [with remote antecedents in the traditional Sanskrit drama] shaping the use of imported technology.

These very song-and-dance sequences are a form of opposition to Western cultural imperialism. Also, Bollywood films are not musicals alone; they are an 'Omnibus' or a 'Masala' form, combining melodrama, action, comedy, social commentary and romance, violently juxtaposing intensely tragic scenes with jolly song and dance numbers, jolting the viewer from one extreme of feeling to another (an aesthetic similarly inherited from Sanskrit theatre).

However, if Bollywood has not developed, stylistically, as 'serious' Third Cinema, neither has its style much connection with Hollywood. Indian cinema has developed a film language which has little or nothing in common with the codes of classical Hollywood cinema and, ironically, this has caused some critics to dismiss Bollywood as escapist. Modes of presentation termed escapist according to the classical Hollywood mode, like the song-and-dance number, are, however, used to play on 'deep tensions – between wealth and poverty, old and new, hope and fear' in Indian films. For example, in the 1996 film *Army*, a song-and-dancer routine breaks out in a prison compound, and prisoners sing, while cartwheeling about the exercise yard, that poverty is so extreme in Indian society outside the prison walls that they are better off in jail, under a death sentence, because a death sentence hangs over them even outside prison.

Ironically, while, from the outside, Bollywood is popularly viewed as a more escapist cinema than even Western commercial cinema, it has absorbed within it as successful commercial product a number of challenging and 'serious' films that in the West achieved only a small, independent distribution. Shekhar Kapoor's *Bandit Queen* (1995) was among the top ten grossing films of 1996 in India, over a year after its small-scale, independent release in the UK, and made $1 million in its first week of Indian release. The harrowing film is based on the life of outlaw Phoolan Devi, and confronts head-on the abuse of women in Indian society: Bollywood's aesthetic evidently cannot be dismissed as 'frivolous' if a film this 'serious' can achieve such enormous commercial success.

'Hollywood Raises Hell in Bollywood'

Hollywood/Bollywood relations are at a moment of crux, as the lifting of the ban on dubbing foreign films into Hindi in 1992 has left Hollywood free to enter the Indian market. However, audiences have shown little interest in Western imported film product; the barriers against the West are revealed as cultural, not simply economic, and 'Hindi films' have, effectively, 'triumphed over Hollywood in India'. Media coverage taken from the British and American film press, of the attempts of Hollywood to dominate the last remaining world market, chart some of the assumptions made, and broken down, before and during the current surprising impasse for Hollywood in India. In comparison, the discourses around East and West, film and culture, that are used in the Indian press, are just as dismissive, even hostile, towards the West, and believe just as confidently in the greater merit of their own cinema.

The *Guardian's* film critic, Derek Malcolm, warned that 'a giant culture clash [was] looming' in India, as 'Spielberg's *Jurassic Park*, dubbed into Hindi, [had] given a fright to the massive Indian film industry'. An article in *The Sunday Times* in June 1995, 'Hollywood Raises Hell in Bollywood' predicted doom for the Indian film industry following the release of action movies such as Sylvester Stallone's *Cliffhanger* (1993), with its higher production values, and, as Lees quotes Indian sources as saying, 'machine guns instead of rifles'. However, the reception of Stallone's *First Blood* (1982), renamed *Blood* and released in July 1995 in India, was lukewarm. Trade reviews commented that 'the film holds appeal mainly for action film lovers', and judged its publicity and opening 'so so'.

Bollywood vs Hollywood

The reasons for Bollywood's resistance to colonisation by Hollywood are aesthetic and cultural as well as political. The formula for Bollywood films has been jokingly summarised as 'A star, six songs, three dances', and these Omnibus or Masala films must have the right mix of a diverse range of ingredients to satisfy their audiences. Without them a film 'lacks in entertainment value'.

However rigid this formula, adherence to it does not guarantee a film's success. Only one in ten films makes a profit, and whether a film is a hit or a flop depends on the unquantifiable judgement of the Bombay audience, who either fill or desert cinema houses in a film's first week of release. Films which imitate the formula of previous hits sink without a trace, while others appear from nowhere to become blockbusters. As Subhash K. Jha remarks in *g magazine*: 'The vagaries of the box-office have flummoxed film-makers and trade watchers forever'. If Indian film-makers are unable to guarantee audiences, Western film product is unlikely to do so.

The market for undubbed Western films in India before 1992 was very small, consisting only of an English speaking middle-class élite, and Western films had far shorter runs than Hindi films. Hollywood first attempted to attract Indian audiences after 1992 by dubbing major American hits into Hindi, but so far only a fraction of the films released have been commercially successful with the Hindi-speaking mass market. *Jurassic Park* (1993), *Speed* (1994) and *Dunston Checks In* (1995) – colloquially translated as 'A Monkey in a Hotel' – have been box office successes, but others, such as *Schindler's List* (1993), *The Flintstones* (1994) and *Casper* (1995), have 'bombed'. Even those films which did not 'bomb' achieved only a fraction of the success of domestic Indian films: in the same year that *Jurassic Park* grossed $6 million, *Hum Aapke Hain Koun . . . !* (1994) grossed $60 million. Hollywood has not yet discerned a pattern as to which films succeed and which 'flop' in India.

One significant factor in films' successes, which may be too culturally specific for Hollywood to duplicate, is their music. 'Popular music in India is synonymous with film music', and the popular film and music industries in India are interdependent. Not only does Indian popular film depend on music, Indian popular music also depends on film. Peter Manuel (1993), in his book *Cassette Culture*, explains the history of this symbiosis in economic terms; before the cassette revolution in the 1970s, the cinema was the most accessible way to hear popular music for many Indians. Film music is also culturally important; as Sanjeev Prakash (1984) notes in his article *La musique, la danse et le film populaire [Music, Dance and Popular Film]*, film music so pervades Indian culture that it is played even at marriages and religious festivals.

The star system too is a formidable force in India, and another factor excluding Western cinema. The earliest Indian films were known as 'mythological', portraying the adventures of Hindu gods such as Krishna, and the equation of actors with gods has remained. Many Indian film stars go on to become politicians and national icons, representing quintessential 'Indianness'. Nargis, 'the woman in white', was the personification of 'Mother India' in the 1950s; Amitabh Bachchan has been India's greatest cinema icon for thirty years, and his face has come to be used as a symbol for India itself (as we shall see later). Western stars cannot compete with such quasi-religious iconography. A recent Hindi film, *Rock Dancer* (1995), starring Samantha Fox, a British glamour model turned pop singer, singing all her own songs in Hindi, received very little press attention and no commercial success. Though the urban middle classes knew her name well enough to merit an aside in one film news column, to the mass Hindi film audience, she was an unknown.

Having largely failed to export Western product to India, Hollywood is now investing in Indian studios – putting money into Bollywood, not attempting to replace it with its own product. The Indian view of this seems to be of a cultural victory; as Shah Rukh Khan (1996) expresses in his piece, 'Soon Hollywood will come to us'; but economically this is no great victory for India over the West, since profits from what appears a quintessentially Indian product will now go back to the West.

The Indian cinema box office was not essentially diminished by the rise of video in the 1970s, but now Bollywood must accommodate satellite and cable expansion. Rupert Murdoch's Star network attempted to sell Western programmes in India, but could only attract élite minority audiences; but when an Indian company set up a Hindi satellite channel, Zee TV, they attracted a far larger market, and were the impetus for a whole industry of Indian satellite and cable channels, which Star have now bought into. As interviews with Zee TV and Star TV spokesmen (they were all men) showed, both Indian and Western companies interpreted this as a victory. The Indian company believed they had beaten Star at their own game and reaped the rewards. Star felt they had finally found a way to infiltrate the Indian market, by using an Indian figurehead company. The successful move of multinational media companies into the Indian market was ultimately demonstrated, however, when the 42nd Annual Filmfare Awards, otherwise known as 'the Indian Oscars', were screened exclusively on Sony Entertainment Television's Hindi Channel in March 1997.

Popular discourses of Hollywood/Bollywood opposition

Both Hollywood and Bollywood have made their direct opposition explicit in India, and their rivalry has passed into popular cultural vocabulary. The promotion poster for Stallone's *Cliffhanger* (1993) reads 'Hollywood challenges Bollywood'; Hollywood's decision to choose *Cliffhanger* as the vehicle for its challenge was perhaps based on a superficial reading of contemporary Indian film as high in action content, without taking into consideration its juxtaposition with other elements of the 'Masala' mix, such as song and emotional melodrama. *Cliffhanger*'s challenge failed. In contrast, as one Indian trade paper commented, a series of Indian music cassettes entitled 'Bollywood vs Hollywood' have been highly commercially successful.

Within Indian popular culture, the commercial success of Indian cinema has become emblematic of India's resistance to the West, and Bollywood stars have become figureheads in what is viewed as a battle against Westernisation. Actress Madhuri Dixit, known as Bollywood's 'queen bee', 'drew herself up and lectured the guy on patriotism' when a fan 'offered her a Canadian dollar for an autograph'. I have already mentioned the nationalist sentiments expressed by actor Shah Rukh Khan in a *Movie* magazine feature. Another instance is an advert for BPL (an Indian electrical hardware company) which appeared in *g magazine*, a leading Indian English-language film magazine, every month from October 1996 to January 1997. The advert combines a photograph of film star Amitabh Bachchan with discourses around national pride. December's advert concludes:

> Who would have guessed a few centuries ago that India would become a poor, Third-World country? And who knows what India will become in the next century? Who knows what may happen if we believe in ourselves?

Hollywood's failure to supersede Bollywood reveals that an existing Third World culture can be a crucial factor in halting Western cultural imperialism, even when political and economic barriers are lifted. Barnouw and Krishnaswamy (1963) describe in *The Indian Film* how Hollywood monopolised the world cinema market during the First World War, while other film producers were handicapped by the loss of resources and labour-power to the war effort, and successfully defined the cinematic experience for the rest of the world according to their product, so that, in effect, politics shaped economics shaped culture. However, Hollywood has not defined what makes a film work in India, where, conversely, cultural disparity, rather than any political or economic factor, has slowed Western commercial expansion. [. . .]

Conclusion

Bollywood is a wild-card in the globalisation process of the media. Its position is constantly shifting: influenced by its diasporic audiences, by Western moves into India, by newly emerging cultural dialogues between East and West, and by new technologies and their implications. Its relationship with the West has undergone radical changes in the last four years, which will no doubt change its future, although quite probably on its own terms rather than those of the West. Bollywood does not see itself as a minority cinema, but claims the right to be taken seriously as a commercial popular cinema. It demonstrates, finally, that the use of culture as a global force, and as a hegemonic force, is not confined to the West alone.

The existence of another economically imperialist international cinema outside Hollywood is in itself no cause for celebration simply because that cinema opposes Hollywood. Problematic issues around Bollywood and Hindu nationalism, élitism, censorship and corruption should not be glossed over. It has been my intention instead to suggest a reappraisal of current dichotomies of thought between East and West, between commercial and oppositional cinema, by highlighting how unstable these positions look when viewed from an entirely different perspective, a perspective taken, as far as possible, from within India.

A reappraisal of Indian cinema may challenge our assumptions not only about First World and Third World cultural politics, but also our assumptions about what constitutes commercial, and what oppositional, or 'art' cinema, for, as I have discussed, what has in the West been seen as 'difficult' independent cinema fare, has in India been consumed by mass audiences with greater enthusiasm than what we understand as overtly commercial Hollywood films.

I have left the issue of quality out of my discussion of Bollywood, largely because I do not presume to make value judgements on a cultural product designed for consumption by a culture relatively alien to my own experience. Bollywood films have, historically, been dismissed as formulaic and poor quality, and their audience, by inference, as unsophisticated. However, not only can the Bollywood audience watch a film for longer, generally, than a Western audience (Hindi films are uniformly three hours long), it is tolerant of, in fact hungry for, film which in the West is considered too 'challenging' for mainstream, commercial audiences. Which begs the question: which is, in fact, the more truly 'sophisticated' cinema audience? Hollywood's, or Bollywood's?

Questions

1   Discuss ways in which media globalization contributes to both homogenization and diversity in the countries of the world.

2   It is common to speak of the "Americanization" of countries influenced by the USA. What evidence do you see of "Japanization," "Africanization," and similar constructs in your culture – the borrowing and adaptation of cultural elements derived from other parts of the world?

3   Should the UN or UNESCO have the authority to regulate the global media, as the MacBride Report suggested? Identify positive and negative consequences of such regulation.

4   In the selection by Sinclair and colleagues, we see that media companies in less developed countries are producing "peripheral visions" ever more prolifically. Explain what this implies for the cultural imperialism argument about western domination. Does it suggest that we are now witnessing Mexican, Brazilian, and Indian cultural imperialism in some regions of the world instead?

5   For Tomlinson, any culture is a mélange of many other cultures. Does this mean that cultural imperialism is a meaningless concept? In responding, consider Tomlinson's emphasis on the survival of cultures as compared to their transformation and adaptation.

6   Bollywood is squaring off with Hollywood, according to Tyrrell. What does this article tell us about the capacity of non-western countries to resist western culture? Should we expect Hollywood's domination to decline further in the future? Why? What paradoxes about cultural globalization does Tyrrell illustrate through the case of the Indian cinema industry?

Part VIII

Cultural Globalization II: Fundamentalist Responses

Introduction

In 1979, conservative clerics and their followers established an Islamic Republic in Iran. This was the outcome of a long battle to depose the Shah of Iran, a battle clerics interpreted as an effort to vindicate the true Islamic faith and restore the rule of Islamic law. The Shah, they claimed, was an illegitimate tyrant who had tried to "modernize" the country in violation of Islamic norms. Supported by the evil, alien power of the United States, he had suppressed the social role of Islam. He had been an instrument of "Westoxication," the intrusion of foreign ideas, symbols, goods, and lifestyles that were infecting Iranians. To the victors, the overthrow of the Shah was a blow against a secular vision of society and against an American-influenced conception of the world. Indeed, the Islamic Republic aspired to become a platform for a broader revolution to slay the Great Satan. By returning to fundamentals of an indigenous tradition, it would be able to transform the world.

The success of the Islamic Revolution was a major world event. In Iran itself, which had longstanding ties to the West, the policies of the new Republic abruptly changed the course of public life, refashioning the national community along traditional lines. To western audiences, the event announced the puzzling arrival of a new cultural force that deliberately dissociated itself from western views. When Iranian students took hostages at the American embassy in Teheran in 1979, the cultural resistance turned into political defiance. To Muslim audiences, even those who did not share Iran's dominant Shi'ite faith, the revolution reversed years of Islamic decline. Iran showed that it was possible to build an ostensibly Islamic state under modern circumstances. Active "jihad" – in the sense of religiously motivated opposition to a secular, liberal global order – became a viable option. Symbolic of this jihad's global thrust was the Iranian response to the publication of Salman Rushdie's *Satanic Verses*: the book's fanciful treatment of the prophet Muhammad, justified as free artistic expression, earned the author a death sentence.

The Islamic Revolution thus put "fundamentalism" on the map. The term became a controversial global concept signifying a collective attempt to establish identity by restoring a sacred tradition in its original form. But what did it have to do with globalization? Our sketch of the impact of the Revolution already indicates some connections. While globalization was by no means the sole cause of Iranian fundamentalism, it helped set the conditions for its mobilization and provided targets for the Islamic program. Fundamentalists also took a stand on two questions raised by globalization as challenges to any society: What does it mean to live in world society? What is any one group's place in it? Globalization, in other words, challenges groups and societies to "identify" themselves.

Fundamentalism is but one solution to this global predicament. It signals that globalization is unlikely to lead to a single western-inspired culture that would prove universally dominant. The Iranian model and its offspring, in short, indicate that, while all must engage in deliberate identity construction, the process of reimagining communities is bound to take different forms around the world.

We use the fundamentalist case to illustrate what happens to collective identity under globalization. As indicated, globalization creates an identity "problem." But it also produces a common mold within which to address this problem, namely the nation-state. Collective identity generally takes the form of a national culture promoted by a state. Globalization also gives rise to common models and reference points that all societies now must take into account. Societies are further exposed to many cultural influences – transnational popular culture and religious movements, the cultures of business, of migrants, and of international organizations. Globalization makes difference problematic: as cross-cutting cultural ties and influences increase, any traditional understanding of tradition becomes tenuous. At the same time, globalization accentuates difference: each group must define its particular place and fashion its particular interpretation of universal precepts. Globalization, in short, unifies and separates, creating similarity and difference.

Frank Lechner describes fundamentalism as an ostensibly "antimodern" movement that is inevitably compromised by the very things it opposes. The search for the authentically sacred cannot be purely authentic. It is a distinctly modern project to create identity deliberately out of presumed fundamentals. But even as fundamentalisms become coopted, they nevertheless articulate a powerful oppositional stance within global culture. Even if they cannot reshape the world in their image, they sustain the ongoing contention about the direction of globalization. Mustafa Kamal Pasha reinforces this point by showing how Islamist movements resist the "unilinear" pathway of neoliberal globalization. He argues that unsuccessful decolonization and the failure of nationalist and Marxist programs turned many groups against westernizing elites in Muslim societies. Yet while Islamic social movements have a common thrust and meaning, they also vary greatly in local sources and impact. Bassam Tibi complements the Lechner and Pasha selections by arguing that Islamic fundamentalism is a form of political ideology rather than a mere expression of traditional Islamic religious belief. He argues that its advocates respond to a particular global predicament, namely the new conjunction of structural integration and cultural fragmentation. They revolt against the dominant world order by presenting Islam as the basis of an alternative universalist utopia. Tibi believes fundamentalism distorts Islamic tradition and exacerbates global cultural conflict.

The next two selections return to the Iranian case as an instructive and complex instance of collective identity-construction. Ann Elizabeth Mayer provides details about the actual purposes of Islamization in Iran. Islamization, she argues, was a by-product of the clerical takeover, not a conscious goal of a popular movement. Once initiated, it gave new authority to the clerics themselves and to precepts derived from Islamic law; it also made Iran firmly oppose "foreign devils." Yet the program had limited success: many western ideas and institutions remained in place, "moderate" opposition emerged in the late 1980s, and the effect on other Muslim countries was minimal. In one respect, Islamization had a significant impact, namely in the new government's treatment of women. As

Shahla Haeri shows, even as many Iranians supported the "plunge into an idealized past," the very mobilization of women in the revolution made it difficult to relegate them to second-class status. Fundamentalism sought to remove women from positions of authority and restrict their public roles. But Haeri argues that this inevitably provoked resistance.

Writing after the terrorist attack on the United States in 2001, Salman Rushdie argues that such violence is indeed connected to the Islamic tradition. For many Muslims, Islam has come to be associated with a loathing of modern society and the West; many organizations of Muslim men have turned Islam into a political project. But Rushdie also thinks that once Muslims forthrightly examine the faults within their societies and depoliticize their religious tradition, Islam can be reconciled with modernity. The recent experience of Iran offers some hope in this regard. The newly created Islamic Iranian identity is hardly the restoration of a world-transforming tradition. Iran is subject to multiple cultural flows and its brand of fundamentalism has run into global as well as local obstacles. In the way it deals with its dilemmas, Iran has carved out a distinct cultural stance, but this stance is under challenge from domestic reformers who draw on global symbolism. For most other societies, the Islamic Republic does not serve as an exemplar. They must create an identity of their own, fashioning their particular response to a universal predicament.

41   Global Fundamentalism

Frank J. Lechner

Fundamentalism is fashionable – as a problem for social analysis more than as a form of religious faith and activism. To be sure, the reemergence of a certain kind of religious traditionalism in the public arenas of some countries was sufficiently surprising to justify a major scholarly effort to account for it. For Western scholars, the puzzle to be solved went beyond the apparent influence and success of some seemingly archaic cultural movements. The very way in which those labeled "fundamentalist" tried to bring a sacred tradition to bear on the public affairs of their societies compelled scholars to reexamine their assumptions about the "normal" role of religion in modern societies and about the continued viability of religious traditions themselves. By virtue of its public character, fundamentalism seemed to point to a different future for religion from what many scholars had assumed. [. . .]

Global Perspectives

The "global turn" in sociology consists of sustained efforts by a number of researchers over the past few decades to treat the world as a social system in its own right. These efforts were obviously inspired by the simple realization that societies were becoming highly interdependent. Moreover, it became clear that the very processes in which sociologists were interested had an inherently global dimension. Nettl and Robertson argued, for example, that modernization consisted not of processes that simply occurred in similar fashion across the globe but rather of deliberate attempts by societal elites to place their society in a global hierarchy. Wallerstein saw this hierarchy as the product of long-term changes in the capitalist world economy, which had brought about not only a global division of labor but also a dominant world culture. This world culture became the primary concern of Meyer and his associates, who argued that modern institutions function according to global standards that are part of a "world polity." Robertson described such phenomena as aspects of "globalization" and specifically called attention to the importance of religious reactions against this process, brought forth by the tensions it has produced. An early attempt to link sociocultural movements to world-level changes was made by Wuthnow.

Given these scholarly precedents, what does it mean to speak of "global fundamentalism"? It means first of all that the predicament addressed by fundamentalist movements is a global one. Modernity is no longer a societal phenomenon, if it ever was. A reaction *against* modernity therefore necessarily has global implications: It

Original publication details: Excerpted from Frank J. Lechner, "Global Fundamentalism," in William H. Swatos (ed.), *A Future for Religion?*, pp. 19, 27–32. Copyright © 1993 by William H. Swatos. Reprinted by permission of Sage Publications, Inc.

entails a world-view in the literal sense of advocating a distinct view of "the world." For Islamic militants this includes an obligation to spread the Islamic revolution and defeat the dominant Western satan. A global culture, not simply local circumstances, becomes the target of fundamentalist movements. The defenders of God aspire to bringing the kingdom of God to the earth as a whole, and in this sense they become important actors on the global scene. As global antisystemic movements, they attempt to resolve literally worldwide problems in global fashion – changing both the actual balance of power in the world and the cultural terms on which global actors operate. The struggle in which they are engaged is not, or not only, against modernity abstractly defined, but also for a particular shape of the globe. The extent to which they pursue this ambition depends in large part on variations in global change, on the extent to which particular societies or regions are socially or culturally unsettled by forces beyond their control.

The changing global condition not only becomes a context and target of fundamentalism, but also serves as its primary precipitating factor. Yet apart from globally induced variations in the strength of fundamentalism, the very attempt to restore a sacred tradition as a basis for a meaningful social order is globally significant, as one effort among others to preserve or achieve a certain cultural authenticity in the face of a greedy, universalizing global culture. It is, in other words, a particular, albeit radical and problematic, form of striving for communal and societal identity under circumstances that make such deliberate identification a global expectation – a point Robertson has repeatedly emphasized. Indeed, fundamentalism itself has become a global category, part of the global repertoire of collective action available to discontented groups, but also a symbol in a global discourse about the shape of the world. For liberal Westerners concerned about further "progressive" change, fundamentalism is the global Other, that which "we" are not; for those taking issue with the meaning and structure of current, Western-inspired global culture, fundamentalism becomes a most radical form of resistance, a symbolic vehicle. Interpreting fundamentalism in this global fashion is to subsume, not to discard, the treatment of fundamentalism as a form of antimodernism. Indeed, of all the conventional approaches to fundamentalism, this may well have the most lasting value; global culture, after all, is still (though not only) the culture of modernity. Standard criticisms of this approach as ethnocentric appear increasingly misplaced, for it is one that touches on crucial features of the global condition and represents a form of sociological realism rather than Western wishful thinking. To see fundamentalists locked in a struggle about the shape of the world is to recognize part of their actual predicament, not to deny their particularity in imperialist fashion. In fact, those advocating a less analytical, more subjective approach to fundamentalism as well as other manifestations of religiosity or cultural difference now face the difficulty that doing justice to the other in his or her particularity forces one to take into account the other's relation to universal structures, the other's reaction to alien penetration, the other's distinctly modern assertions of particularity.

In other words, the otherness of the other is increasingly problematic as a consequence of globalization; fundamentalism, to put it most simply, is inevitably contaminated by the culture it opposes. Just as in any pluralistic culture, the other is always already within us, we are also already in the other, even when she or he puts forth a grand display of antipluralist authenticity. In the modern world system, no fundamentalist can simply reappropriate the sacred and live by its divine lights. The very reappropriation is a modern, global phenomenon, part of the shared experience of "creolization." To see it as such is to include the other as full participant in a common discourse, a common society, rather than to relegate him or her to the iron cage of otherness.

The global perspective on fundamentalism also makes comparisons in the conventional sense problematic. Such comparisons, after all, presuppose that one can isolate the units to be compared, in order to examine the differential effects of similar but independently occurring processes. Often carried out for the sake of historical sensitivity, such an exercise increasingly comes to seem artificially abstract. Societies are now inherently oriented toward each other; they are involved in processes that encompass all; even the object of the comparison, namely the propensity to engage in fundamentalism, is no longer an indigenously arising phenomenon. Of course, careful comparisons can still help to determine the causal weight of particular factors in social movements. But, beyond that, the new global condition has changed the terms of scholarly analysis as much as it has the terms of actual social action.

A Future for Fundamentalism?

The global turn in the study of fundamentalism was partly inspired by the concern about the possible public influence of fundamentalism mentioned at the outset. In the end, the scholarly and the public interest in fundamentalism converge on the question about the likely extent of this influence. I will briefly offer grounds for judging this influence relatively minor and for skepticism about the overall future of fundamentalism as we know it.

Of course, assessing the future of fundamentalism, a hazardous undertaking in any case, by no means exhausts the question of the future of religion as a whole. Indeed, from the point of view of nonfundamentalist believers, it may well be the case that the demise of fundamentalism is a condition for the revitalization of serious religiosity. Expressing skepticism about the future of fundamentalism also does not imply that there is no future for research about fundamentalism. There is work to be done, if only because the trends in social analysis sketched above have improved our understanding but not answered all questions. And precisely because its future is problematic and conflicted, fundamentalism will remain a fruitful subject for research.

Turning to substance: As I and others have argued over the years, fundamentalism is a quintessentially modern phenomenon. It actively strives to reorder society; it reasserts the validity of a tradition and uses it in new ways; it operates in a context that sets nontraditional standards; where it does not take decisive control, it reproduces the dilemmas it sets out to resolve; as one active force among others, it affirms the depth of modern pluralism; it takes on the tensions produced by the clash between a universalizing global culture and particular local conditions; it expresses fundamental uncertainty in a crisis setting, not traditional confidence about taken-for-granted truths; by defending God, who formerly needed no defense, it creates and recreates difference as part of a global cultural struggle. So compromised, fundamentalism becomes part of the fabric of modernity.

Being compromised in this way portends a problematic future for fundamentalism – problematic, that is, from a fundamentalist point of view. It indicates one of the ways in which fundamentalism, like any other cultural movement, engages and must engage in creolization, juxtaposing the seemingly alien and the seemingly indigenous into a worldview and identity that combine both in new seamless wholes. Of course, upon inspection traditions often display a hybrid character. But if Robertson is right, such hybridization now becomes a normal feature of globalization, robbing cultures of easy authenticity while making the search for the authentic a virtual obligation. If the point of fundamentalism is to restore an authentic sacred tradition, this means that fundamentalism must fail.

This failure is exacerbated by the modern circumstances fundamentalism must confront. In some respects, modernity does act as a solvent, undermining the thrust of fundamentalist movements. Insofar as a society becomes structurally differentiated, religion loses social significance; once that happens, restoration is difficult if not impossible. In differentiated, specialized institutions engaged in technical control of the world, religious distinctions have little role in any case; the very conception of infusing a perceived iron cage with religious meaning necessarily remains nebulous. If a culture becomes pluralistic and tears down its sacred canopy, those who would restore it are themselves only one group among others. Making claims for a fundamentalist project requires wider legitimation, except where there is overwhelming popular support; such wider legitimation entails watering down the message. Trying to act globally with some effectiveness presupposes the use of global means, technological and institutional; but satellite dishes and fighter planes and nation-states draw the would-be opposition farther into the culture it claims to disdain. Although its relative success varies according to the conditions sketched above, fundamentalism is inevitably coopted.

But being modern and becoming coopted presuppose that there is a viable modern order to be coopted into. The future of fundamentalism is thus closely linked to the future of modernity. One advantage of the analytical view of fundamentalism, starting by conceptualizing it as one form of antimodernism among others in order to expose its modern character, is that it draws research on the subject into the larger discourse about modernity, central not only to the social sciences but in the public arena as well. If modernity in anything like the liberal version I adopt here can be sustained, albeit transformed through globalization, then the life chances of large-scale public fundamentalism are correspondingly diminished. How strong, then, is the fabric of modernity? Contrary to conventional assertions of the imperialism inherent in modernization or the emptiness of liberal culture or the loss of meaning in advanced societies, liberal modernity offers a wide variety of cultural meanings. The usual jeremiads about the ills and weaknesses of imperially secular modernity notwithstanding, the latter offers considerable room for free religious expression and experience. In the actual struggles about the future direction of world society, it appears to this biased observer, the liberal-modern view of social order thus far has prevailed against challenges issued by various kinds of antimodern movements and regimes. Even after two world wars, the crises and conflicts of modern societies have not brought about the demise of the liberal modern project.

And yet, fundamentalism has its origins in real discontents experienced by real people; the mobilization factors that account for its relative strength in particular places have not disappeared everywhere; the tensions inherent in the globalization process cannot be resolved in any permanent fashion; in modern global culture, fundamentalism has found a place as part of a movement repertoire, to be activated when conditions are right. This does not enable us to make any clear-cut predictions about the reemergence of fundamentalism in the twenty-first century. It does enable us to say, more modestly if less informatively, that fundamentalism has a future – albeit one less bright than that of liberal modernity. [. . .]

42 Globalization, Islam and Resistance

Mustapha Kamal Pasha

[. . .] Globalization represents the high drama of world politics; opposition to globalization recedes into the background. Focusing on the Islamic cultural areas, this chapter proposes an alternative to hyperliberal notions of globalization and offers new understandings of resistance to economic globalization.

Assuming a basic cleavage between a global market project and a politics that is encoded in a religious idiom, one is likely to reproduce the universal–particular dualism which renders resistance merely as a mirror of localism. This dualism has been an integral part of thinking about economic, social, political, and cultural differences between rich and poor countries, the industrialized powers in the North and peripheral areas in the South.

Rather, if economic globalization is approached as a specific, uneven, incomplete, and contradictory phenomenon, the re-articulation of Islam acquires a more open-ended character, one with competing tendencies. This alternative vantage-point avoids the propensity to reify globalization, recognizing instead the practical consciousness of agents and their ability to constitute meaning in diverse ways. Despite the apparent inevitability of globalization, then, social processes can be seen as contested terrains. Similarly, the unidirectional thrust of economic globalization can be questioned. [. . .]

Islam and 'Resistance'

Global neoliberalism increasingly takes on the appearance of cultural homogenization, sustaining the fiction that allows Islamic politics *in its entirety* to appear as merely a *cultural* 'reaction' to globalization. With neither an internal centre nor agency, the re-articulation of Islam in the quotidian practices of Muslims across geographical frontiers, spanning varied local contexts, becomes subsumed under the common rubric of resistance to globalization. Ironically, by making the epithet of resistance fit every conceivable political and social practice in the Muslim World, the neoliberal view of globalization, gives actual resistance quixotic properties. Even critiques of globalization that stress the impact of flexible accumulation on human relations on a world-scale end up denying the *internality* of social processes in the Muslim world. In celebrating opposition to homogenization, resistance itself is *homogenized*. An indiscriminate mixing of diverse social movements, actors, attitudes, passions, and interests in the Muslim World produces the misguided effect of shifting focus away

Original publication details: Excerpted from Mustapha Kamal Pasha, "Globalization, Islam and Resistance," in Barry K. Gills (ed.), *Globalization and the Politics of Resistance* (Macmillan, 2000). Reproduced by permission of Palgrave Macmillan.

from contradictory social impulses in favour of elements that privilege religious affinities. Reducing politics to economic globalization, in turn, empties out the cultural content and its *particularized* expression in diverse local contexts.

Islam and Globalization

Islamic social movements are both a moment *of*, and a reaction *to*, neoliberal globalization. In either case, they are only an aspect of globalization. At base, these movements embody multilayered historical forces and currents; the sources and modalities of Islamic resistance to globalization are themselves diverse and complex. Invariably, they are conditioned by local circumstance, the form neoliberalism has embraced, and the relative strengths and weaknesses of social forces combating the materialist order. Thus, the character of Islamic politics offers a heterodox picture: Algeria, Iran, Turkey, or Pakistan, for instance, have demonstrably distinctive patterns. The conflict between Algeria's secular nationalists and the Islamic Salvation Front (FIS) may be interpreted as the culmination of a virtual cultural partition of the country, traceable to French colonialism and its uneven effects on Algerian society. The case of Iran on the other hand, is inexplicable without recognition and comprehension of notions of authority and legitimacy drawn from Shi'a Islamic constructions of political order, and the experience of the Shah's failed revolution from above. Turkey's political and cultural ambivalence is linked to Ottoman distemper as to the form modern or secular nationalism has taken. The sectarian character of Pakistan's numerically small, yet forceful, Islamic movement may represent local anxieties and political inheritance, rather than global concerns.

Recognizing the 'horizontal' and 'vertical' aspects of Islam, we need to recognize that the Muslim world is a complex of *living* societies. While there may be a broad agreement on the status of God's centrality in the Muslim worldview and the corresponding, subordinate role of human beings (the vertical dimension), there is tremendous variation within the world of Islam in the nature of social institutions and practice. The historically received awareness of a spatial (or horizontal) separation between the Islamic and the non-Islamic cultural areas, is also complemented *internally* by differences in wealth, power, and economic capacity. Islam, itself, is seen 'as a system of ideal social behaviour and as a path toward experiential knowledge of God'. Belief in a revealed scripture and vision of an ideal Muslim society produces complex permutations: the Islam of the *'ulama* and the Islam of the *sufis*, for instance, is quite different.

Yet, there are common signs of a basic rupture in the social lifeworld of Muslim countries. Ever since the decline of the Ottoman, Safavid, and Mughal empires and the consolidation of European power, Muslim states and society have been in the process of reconstitution. Crucial to this process was the inauguration of a cultural chasm *within* Muslim society over the nature of the ideal political community, legitimacy, and identity. Throughout the seventeenth and eighteenth centuries, Muslim society witnessed reformist, revivalist or 'scripturalist' movements. In part responses to endogenous problems, but largely an expression of a quest to establish new identities under conditions of foreign rule and subordination, these movements instituted a growing cultural divide. In vast regions of the Muslim lands, these movements became the basis of anti-colonial resistance, either in an India or an Indonesia, under the leadership of religious and spiritual authorities. A similar pattern was detectable in Central Asia and North Africa, where *sufi* movements waged struggles against Russian, Chinese, or West European expansion.

Key to an awareness of Islamic resurgence is the historical appreciation of the European colonial impact, especially in its role in eroding the traditional self-image of Muslims themselves, notably in the area of cultural self-sufficiency. In this vein, the current phase of resurgence can be viewed as the articulation of hidden or suppressed sensibilities in Muslim collective consciousness, but more accurately as a continuation of an unsuccessful process of decolonization. By projecting resurgence of a revolt against the West, a new 'national consciousness' can be created.

The roots of the re-articulation of Islam under globalizing conditions are, therefore, quite extensive and deep. But there is a marked difference in the character of 'political' Islam in the twilight of the twentieth century. Islamic movements are not simply a response to Western conquest and control, but a movement against western-centred globalization, promoted by factions *within* Muslim society, and a movement *for* realizing an alternative to secular-nationalism. To the extent that alternatives for building a (religious) community, society, and state do not emerge in a pure form, themselves shaped by the experience of subordination, they carry all the antinomies of a derivative discourse of modernity. With neoliberal globalization, the contradictions of Muslim society, which appear as cultural polarization, have acquired a new form.

Time-space compression reinforces the image of Islamic resurgence as a transnational volcano, ready to *simultaneously* erupt in different locales. To attempt to homogenize this phenomenon is to privilege the putative goals of its passionate adherents or its opponents rather than to acknowledge the silences that undergird its narrative. It is in the recognition of its own problems that Islamic resurgence under globalizing conditions is lent a true distinction. Economic dislocation, re-articulations of space and time, and dispersion of collective and personal identities are producing a heightened awareness of marginality in the midst of affluence; a condition now facing a 'universal culture of consumption and communication.' By rejecting the notion that social change necessitates secularization, one can encounter different forms of negotiations *in*, and not simply *with*, the modern world.

In short, the key to linking globalizing tendencies to 'resistance' in the Muslim world is a delineation of those material and symbolic intrusions that are affecting the *local* character, composition, and content of Islamic resurgence. Implicit in this thinking is an acknowledgement of the historical basis of Islamic movements, and their relative autonomy from homogenizing global currents. There is also the recognition of an analytical separation between local and *globalizing* processes, a separation ostensibly blurred by globalization. Resistance straddles the two, interlinked, worlds.

In breaking up communities built around principles of redistribution or reciprocity, global capitalism is no doubt an equal opportunity offender. Yet, there are multiple vectors of instituting the market and numerous patterns of defiance. Hence the need for recognizing the *differentiated* character of Islamic resurgence and the alleged forms of resistance to globalization. There is considerable temptation to lump heterodox phenomena under the heading 'Islamic fundamentalism', to bracket disparate forms of 'Islamic' consciousness as 'resistance to globalization', or to see Islam as 'an irrational and backward form of human consciousness'.

Generally, resistance to globalization has arisen in civil society. Seen as a 'moral defence' against alien values, Islam offers to its adherents the resources of an 'endogenous ideology with redeeming powers', but in the context of the failures of secular-nationalism, a site to conduct a 'war of position' in order to capture and reconstitute the state. Paradoxically, the major thrust of globalization also lies in civil society.

Taking civil society as an arena for realizing its promise and peril, neoliberal globalists undernourish the state. In this regard, civil society ends up playing a contradictory role: i.e. as the site of deepening globalizing tendencies and resistance to globalization. The Islamic movements embody the twin character of being both a moment of and resistance to globalization. The burden of welfare retrenchment and marginalization has fallen on those social sectors least capable of negotiating globalization. With major demographic shifts, migration flows, and the growth in the population of college-educated students, often without jobs, the scale of the problem is only getting larger. Growing inequities are undermining efforts to provide adequate schooling, and the character of education imbibes the neglect it has generally received in the Muslim world, except in Turkey and parts of Islamic South-east Asia. Without the development of educational infrastructures, knowledge production has increasingly assumed 'lumpen' forms of schooling, with obvious effects. Social and scientific truths are often sacrificed in favor of dogmatism.

For the sake of simplification, two sets of processes can be identified here: first, the insertion of an 'Islamic' texture into the social fabric of everyday life and the growth in religious centres, notably mosques, and pietist associations. Broadly viewed, this is the *zone of piety*. The basic thrust of Islamization here is a 'war of position' that takes cultural institutions as the bridgehead to the transformation of society and state. This 'civil' arena of Islamic politics offers a counter-discourse to the failed policies of secular nationalists, but it also underscores the withdrawal of the state from responsibility for welfare in the context of globalization. The role of the Muslim Brotherhood across the Middle East, for example, fits the characterization of Islamicists in this sphere.

The social world of the cities is invariably complex, indeterminate, and paradoxical. At one level, the ambivalence towards secular modernity, clearly more pronounced in the urban areas, may confirm the tensions inherent in an ongoing sexual (or gender) revolution in the world of Islam. Removed from established patterns of rural life, the vast majority of Muslim youth who now inhabit the congested cities, confront unexpected sexual encounters with the opposite sex. Both men and women now face the pressures to reconcile employment with social conservatism. From urban living to employment to mobility, the new social universe transmits multiplicities of sexual messages. Globalization has only accentuated communication. In this context, Islam serves as a coherent internal centre to filter out disturbing external tensions. The sexual revolution in the Islamic cultural areas is implicated in the zone of piety. By promising to transform society, that is, *Islamizing* it, an ideal city can be built. Vital to this promise is the notion of building a *'dar ul Islam'* (realm of Islam); the intrusion of 'impure' elements, mainly from the West, carried by secular nationalists, are recognized as ingredients of *'dar ul harb'* (realm of war).

Second, by contrast, the Muslim world is also the home of 'wars of manoeuvre' designed to strike an un-Islamic state and society directly, as in the case of the Iranian Revolution, and the recent Islamic movements in Algeria, the Sudan, and Afghanistan. Weakened by internal contradictions and with a weak political base, state structures in several Muslim states have become a target of assault from politically better organized social forces *outside* the state. This is mostly the case in the countries with more authoritarian rule. Facing threat of extinction, state managers here often rely on external support, notably from Western powers, to prop up their faltering regimes. Gravitation towards the West, usually in the name of secular and liberal alternatives, widens the gap between the westernizing elites and the rest of (Islamic) society.

Differences between the two strategies are not absolute. It would be a mistake to essentialize the difference between Islamic movements that are seeking to over-turn the status quo in society and those that want to capture political power. These movements are united by context, history, and memory. At the same time, the sources and compulsions of Islamic re-assertion are heterodox: the pattern shows con-siderable variation and diversity, since the social forces in local contexts originate from very different sets of historical conditions. From the near-success of the Islamic Salvation Front (FIS) in Algeria in capturing power, after an electoral victory in December 1991, to the growing assertion of religion in Central Asia, and South-east Asia, contemporary Islamic movements want to reconstitute both state and society. During the colonial period, the privileged and under-privileged parts of society pursued two radically opposed rhythms. The same appears to be the case in the Muslim world. However, with globalization, the character of polarization is now of a *hybrid* variety. [. . .]

Conclusion

Drawing its vitality from a wide spectrum of memory, resistance to neoliberal globalization is congealed in Islamicization movements that take the failure of the post-colonial state, but especially its incapacity to manage peripheral economies and preserve the lifelines of Islamic culture, as their starting-point. Islamic resurgence appears to have replaced the previously dominant ideologies of secular nationalisms and Marxism. Many Islamicists propose alternative forms of social engineering drawn from modernist assumptions of societal development and political power. While these views are often glossed over in covering Islam in the West, they guide policy and ideology. The terms of discourse and modes applied by Islamicists are quite distinct from the ones used by westernizing elites. But underpinning the Islamicist discourse is not only popular memory, with an autonomy of the sources of consciousness rooted in Islam, but also modernism.

An analysis of contemporary Islamic movements defies the hyper-liberal promise of a world unified by markets, telecommunications, or consumer culture. Although there are several homogenizing forces at work, the *social* context of change and trans-formation necessitates recognition of both the diversity of forms of life and the irre-ducible capacity of human beings to resist unilinear pathways towards the future. The re-articulation of Islam under globalizing conditions underscores the point that it is human beings that make their own history.

43 The Challenge of Fundamentalism

Bassam Tibi

[. . .] In what follows, I shall argue that Islamic fundamentalism is simply one variety of a new global phenomenon in world politics. At issue in each case is a political ideology, not the religion so cynically linked with that ideology. In my view, fundamentalism is an ideology symptomatic of the "clash of civilizations." It is not the cause of the current crisis of our world, but both an expression of it and a response to it. Fundamentalism, however, is not a solution. By inciting conflict and deepening the ongoing cultural fragmentation of the world, it leads to disorder. Many of the scholars who agree with me in stating that fundamentalist agitation leads to turmoil in the Islamic world stop short of conceding that this trend touches on world politics as well. I shall begin by establishing the argument that Islamic fundamentalism is not simply an intra-Islamic affair, but rather one of the pillars of an emerging new world disorder.

Long before the end of the Cold War, scholars had recognized the politicization of religion as a new global phenomenon. They proposed to describe and analyze the new tide as a *religious fundamentalism*. The term, of course, soon became highly charged, owing to its sensationalized application to the revolution of the Ayatollahs in Iran in 1979 and the ensuing climate of religious fanaticism and extremism there. A decade later, after the fall of the Berlin Wall, some observers, mostly on the left, argued that with the breakdown of communism the West had lost its arch-enemy. Ever since, of course, the West has been accused of being on the lookout for a substitute ogre, and Islamic fundamentalism seemed to have the right qualifications. The underlying argument is that the West needs to identify a new enemy so as to ensure the continuity of its political and military unity and hegemony. It is unfortunate that in this cynical climate the former NATO Secretary-General Willy Claes issued a statement that seemed to support this suspicion. Claes in fact proposed to view Islamic fundamentalism as the next major threat to Western civilization, and indeed the rhetoric of Islamic fundamentalists strongly supports NATO's taking such a position. But does rhetoric alone, unsupported by wherewithal, suffice for establishing trends in world politics?

Islamic fundamentalists do indeed attack the West, believing fervently that the world is already witnessing its decline and that they will therefore be in a position soon to proclaim a new order to supplant the discredited Western world order. Their view of a new order is based, so they say, on the political tenets of Islam, certainly as interpreted by them. One need not be an expert on Islamic movements to know

Original publication details: Excerpted from Bassam Tibi, *The Challenge of Fundamentalism: Political Islam and the New World Disorder* (University of California Press, 1998), pp. 2–3, 15–17, 65–7. Copyright © 1998 The Regents of the University of California. Reprinted by permission of the University of California Press.

how weak and divided these movements are, in relative terms, and to infer from their weakness their inability to bring about the new world order they proclaim with such electrifying rhetoric. To be sure, fundamentalists can engineer frightening levels of terrorism and otherwise throw the streets into turmoil, but it is difficult to imagine the diverse and rivalrous Islamic fundamentalist movements coming together long enough to create a new order, even had they the requisite economic, political, and military wherewithal. The argument of this book is that these movements can nonetheless create disorder within their own countries sufficient in the long run to lead to a combined regional and global disorder, addressed here as the new world disorder. My approach here is intended to be neither sensational nor accusatory. Rather, it describes an international trend. The analysis presented maintains that we are even now witnessing a simultaneity of structural globalization and national and international cultural fragmentation. The net effects of these simultaneous processes underlie the rise of religious fundamentalisms worldwide.

The new world disorder is, however, much more than turmoil; its broader ramifications are already made credible by the crisis of the nation-state in most countries of Asia and Africa. Again, fundamentalism is much more than extremism or terrorism; it is rather a powerful challenge to the existing order of the international system of secular nation-states. Given that this institution is Western in origin, the revolt against it is also a "revolt against the West."

What has Islam to do with this revolt, and why is a link being drawn between Islam and fundamentalism? In fact, Islam is both a world religion and a major civilization, embracing one-fifth of the people on the planet. In our age of the "clash of civilizations" world peace means accommodation between civilizations on grounds of mutual equality, respect, and recognition. To question the ongoing hegemony of the West is, from this point of view, not to claim a substitute for its hegemony, be it Islamic or whatever, but rather to argue for intercivilizational equality and justice, in preference to anyone's hegemony. A closer look, however, shows clearly that this is not the outlook of the Islamic fundamentalists, who envisage a new world order, in the twenty-first century, to be led by Islamic civilization. Again, it is crucial that a distinction be drawn between Islam as a religion and civilization and Islam as a political ideology, the latter characterized in this book and elsewhere as fundamentalism. These are two completely different issues. To offer enlightenment about Islamic fundamentalism is one thing, and to warn of a demonization of Islam and a reactionary anti-Islamism is quite another!

In the course of dismissing the perception of an "Islamic Threat," an effort that I share, some scholars nonetheless seem to confuse the two aspects of Islam. Islam as a religion is definitely not a threat, but Islamic fundamentalism is. It is a threat, however, only in the sense of creating disorder on a grand scale, not – as is often contended – in the sense of replacing communism as a "new global enemy for the Western alliance." [. . .]

I argue that Islam has become the West's leading challenger for one simple reason: in contrast to those of Hinduism, for example, Islamic perspectives are not restricted to national or regional boundaries. In this respect, Islam resembles Western civilization, in the sense that it is universal in both its claims and its outlook. It is thus easy to understand why Islam and the West clash, more consistently than do other competing civilizations. Unlike Western civilization, however, Islam, though universal, has not been able to spread the *da'wa*/Islamic mission throughout the modern world. The globalization process unfolding in the course of European expansion proved Western civilization to be more competitive, and severely challenged Islam.

Contemporary Muslims feel that the West has deprived Islam of its core function, that is, to lead humanity. Those who are familiar with the pronouncements of Muslim fundamentalists and have read the writings of Sayyid Qutb and Abu al-A'la al-Mawdudi know that this political movement does not arise simply from a nostalgia for past glory, or to foment a political revolt against Western hegemony. In fact, the concept of world order posed by these fundamentalists *competes* with Western universalism. I agree with Halliday that Islamic fundamentalists lack the capabilities needed for a broad implementation of their concepts, but their vision is not simply rhetoric, and they are already able to launch considerable disorder.

To make the issue more concrete, let me relate it to major political events. Many Muslims and even the CIA analyst Anthony Arnold share the view that Islam, owing to the repercussions of the Afghanistan war, has given its share to the breakdown of communism. These Muslims then ask, why not defeat the West, too? They asked this question during the Gulf War, and they continue to ask it, though that war led to an Islamic defeat. Saddam Hussein, in labeling the war a *jihad*/holy war, thus claiming to battle the West in the name of Islam, received the support of most of the fundamentalist movements in the Muslim world. Few in the West are aware that most Muslims outside the West view the Gulf War as a clash between their own civilization and that of the West. The fact that books and articles expounding this view are still being published by Muslims years after the Gulf War supports the observation that most Muslims continue to believe that the war was a "crusade of the West" against their civilization. As I have indicated, the war in Bosnia, too, is perceived by Muslims as a continuation of the same ongoing "crusade." To be sure, in both cases the perception runs counter to the hard facts of reality. Still, the perception alone is sufficient to incite the call for *jihad*, which is seen as the Islamic *response* to a powerful external threat, not an Islamic *initiative*.

This reading of the classical history of Islamic *jihad* and the Christian crusades into contemporary politics is designed to address the question, who will lead the world after the crumbling of the communist bloc? The question establishes a clear link between the breakdown of communism, the end of the Cold War, and the new boost given the *jihad* doctrine by Islamic fundamentalism after the Gulf War, despite the militarily shattering defeat it imposed. It would appear, in fact, that the West won the Gulf War militarily but lost it politically. Scholars of international relations preoccupied with international politics as inter-state relations can understand neither this phenomenon nor the "clash of civilizations" it brings to the fore. Indeed, the recent debate over the "clash of civilizations" provoked by the Harvard scholar Samuel P. Huntington indicates – despite its deplorable shortcomings – a welcome change in perspective among many in the international relations community. "Culture" and "civilization" are issues that had earlier been mostly ignored by scholars of international studies preoccupied with the "state."

In this context I have suggested that we might view fundamentalism as an ideology contributing to what I have called the "War of Civilizations." By "war" I do not address military issues, but rather a competition between worldviews seen as different frames of reference for dealing with politics. Certainly it is not the *term* that matters; French scholars, for instance, use their distinct term "*intégrisme*" in referring to the same process with the same meaning I allude to here. What matters is that in some of these cases a politicization of worldviews has linked religion to a variety of nationalisms. Serbian Orthodox fundamentalism, for example, which has politicized Eastern Orthodox Christianity, pursues in fact a nationalist strategy, albeit in a religious disguise. Thus the conflicts involved in these cases are seemingly domestic, with the avowed political goal of establishing a "Greater Serbia" in the Balkans, or a "Hindustan" as a Hindu state in India. Despite the fact that one can find similar mixes of religion and politics in other local cultures and civilizations, it does not seem to me appropriate to call this phenomenon in general "religious nationalism." In my view, "fundamentalism" is the more appropriate term for addressing the politicized worldviews of competing civilizations.

In the case of Islam, in fact, it is not "the nation" – in the sense of contemporary national boundaries – that is at stake. The revival of the Islamic notion of *umma* in the meaning of "universal Islamic community" differs significantly from the secular notion of *umma* in the meaning of "nation." Indeed, in the course of resisting the Western world order the Islamic revivalists direct their views and actions *against* the institution of the nation-state and the domestic Muslim elites who rule it. That is, Islamic fundamentalists accuse their rulers of fulfilling Western strategies aimed at dividing the universal *umma* into an array of secular nations along the Western model of the nation-state. Again, "fundamentalism" seems to me the most appropriate term to depict this ideological stance, because it suggests, on the level of civilization, the politicization of religion that is involved. [. . .]

Culture in World Politics: Globalized Structures and Cultural Fragmentation

. . . the attainments of structural globalization and cultural modernity have harbored a great confusion. What has been globalized through the European expansion and the ensuing mapping of the world into a Westernized international system was what Anthony Giddens called "the institutional dimension of modernity." This dimension of modernity is related to science, technology, and the achievements (that is, the modern institutions and instruments) resulting from them; it is not related to Western values and norms, and the latter are the real substance of cultural modernity. Clearly, the ongoing process of globalization has not universalized the cultural modernity that Habermas described in his masterpiece *The Philosophical Discourse of Modernity*. Cultural modernity has remained distinctly European, restricted largely to its heartland and the North American societies linked to it. Cultural modernity is based on the principle of subjectivity, that is, on the view that man (or woman) is an autonomous subject/individual free to discover and master nature and place it at the service of one's own society for fulfilling human needs. This worldview is both secular and man-centered, and as such required the replacing of the cosmological views of the world by a rational worldview based on modern science. To be sure, the more tangible and more useful products of modernity – in particular, science and technology – were transmitted to other civilizations as well, but were instrumentally confined; that is, they were adopted by the recipient civilizations without the cultural underpinning of the worldview they sprang from. In this sense, the more structurally globalized our world has become, the more culturally fragmented it has come to be. In this regard I coined the phrase "simultaneity of structural globalization and cultural fragmentation."

The project of modernization was driven by the almost missionary zeal of the universalist modernization approach that dominated American thought and Western approaches in general in the postcolonial period. The failure of modernization to travel beyond its original confines is the background for the ongoing process of cultural revival in non-Western civilizations. Although this spreading sentiment had been strong before the onset of the Cold War, it had not yet been internationally felt, and the end of the Cold War gave this sentiment its first great boost. As early as 1962 the great French sociologist Raymond Aron noted that the "heterogeneity of civilizations" is the major source of conflict in international politics. He added that the bipolar atmosphere of the Cold War contributed to "veiling" this source and predicted its unveiling in the aftermath of bipolarity. This is the historical background and the content of the de-Westernization of the world we are now witnessing; the process has moved to center stage. The issue is then no longer modernization, which had been proposed mainly by American social scientists, but de-Westernization. Western social scientists had been enlisted to address developments that would have the effect of promoting Westernization as modernization. In contrast, non-Westerners sought to promote modernization without Westernization. Fundamentalism is in fact not a traditionalism but rather a propensity to de-Westernization in the sense of dismissing cultural modernity while embracing instrumental modernization. I have depicted this propensity as an "Islamic dream of semi-modernity." [. . .]

In the current resurgence against the West, cultural references are becoming politically instrumental, serving as grist for a civilization-consciousness and a regional cross-cultural unity created for political ends. Religious fundamentalism is thus the political expression of the "Revolt against the West," but unlike the process of decolonization of past decades, this revolt is not purely political. Non-Western civilizations are increasingly exposed to a global matrix that projects cultural modernity as well as communication. For this reason the contemporary anti-Western revolt entails projecting, on political grounds, a cultural worldview. In other words, religious fundamentalism cannot be conceived properly as simply a political phenomenon – without reference, that is, to its sociocultural background. Nor is it simply a cultural revival. For despite their anti-modernity rhetoric, the fundamentalists are basically not traditionalists, but rather a product of modernity themselves. They seek to confront modern and secular institutions by reviving the worldviews of their own civilizations, all the while imprisoned in modernity and openly subscribing to its instruments.

This is the historical context of the phenomenon of religious fundamentalism that we encounter in most civilizations – most prominently, however, in Islam. Bearing this context in mind we are better able to realize how simplistic is the use of fundamentalism as a label synonymous with terrorism. To be sure, adherents of political Islam do undertake murder and other horrifying terrorist acts, as they have, for example, in Algeria, Turkey, Egypt, the Occupied Territories, Afghanistan, and Somalia. But these acts are only the surface manifestation of a historical phenomenon that cannot be grasped or explained by such primitive catchphrases as "Warriors of Allah" or "Islamic Terrorism." Terrorism reflects only a minor dimension of the global and all-encompassing phenomenon of fundamentalism. [. . .]

44 The Fundamentalist Impact on Law, Politics, and the Constitution in Iran

Ann Elizabeth Mayer

The Goals of Islamization in Iran

Any examination of the goals of fundamentalism in Iran entails an analysis of the goals of the Iranian Revolution of 1978–9, a complex phenomenon beyond the scope of this paper. At the very least, however, it should be noted that in Iran fundamentalist leaders and the fundamentalist program were linked in a variety of ways to a strong popular movement that culminated in a broad-based revolution. (This was not the case either in Pakistan or in the Sudan, where Islamization was imposed from above by military dictators.)

Iranian fundamentalists insist that the Iranian Revolution was led by them and fought on behalf of their cause, so that Islamization can be said to have been the goal of the revolution. It seems more accurate, however, to say that there was a fundamentalist takeover of a revolution that was fought primarily for secular political and economic goals. There was doubtless popular support for some of the broader fundamentalist goals, particularly among the lower middle and lower classes in urban areas, but it would be hard to establish that the Iranian Revolution was widely understood to have been waged on behalf of the specifics of the legislative program that emerged after powerful clerics seized control. Indeed, Ayatollah Khomeini, before consolidating his control, was evasive and vague in pronouncements about his objectives. It is possible that he realized that a candid revelation of the details of his fundamentalist agenda might weaken his position and undermine his popularity.

After the revolution the early focus of Iran's official Islamization program was on establishing an Islamic government, and one of the first tasks of the new regime was writing an Islamic constitution. This was a natural priority because of the prominence of Ayatollah Khomeini's leadership role in the struggle against the shah and his own preoccupation with setting up an Islamic government according to his model of *wilayat al-faqih*, or rule by the Islamic jurist. Khomeini's ideas for the Iranian constitution provoked much criticism by Iranians, including some prominent Shi'ite *ulama* who remained convinced that clerics should not play a role in governance. After a drafting process that was replete with disputes, in late 1979 Iran did succeed in promulgating a new constitution, in which the faqih was placed at the apex of

Original publication details: Excerpted from Ann Elizabeth Mayer, "The Fundamentalist Impact on Law, Politics, and Constitutions in Iran, Pakistan, and the Sudan," in Martin E. Marty and R. Scott Appleby (eds.), *Fundamentalisms and the State* (University of Chicago Press, 1993), pp. 115–23. Reproduced by permission of the University of Chicago Press.

the government (articles 5 and 107) and Islamic law was established as the supreme law of the land (article 4), which meant the law of the majority Twelver Shi'ite sect (article 12).

Once firmly ensconced in power, Ayatollah Khomeini and his allies worked toward a goal that they had not advertised prior to the revolution or even in its immediate aftermath: implementing a theocratic model of government in which Shi'ite clerics would play a dominant role in all important spheres and particularly in the legal domain. Shi'ite clerics allied with Khomeini proved eager to take political positions and to supplant the Western-trained or Western-oriented judges and lawyers who had come to dominate the legal establishment under the Pahlavis, under whom law and the legal profession had been largely reformed along French lines. The revolution gave clerics the opportunity to assume the central roles that they had played in the courts and in legal education prior to the secularizing reforms of the 1920s. In addition, clerics began to play a new and unfamiliar role, that of the dominant force in the Majlis, or parliament, which had been a thoroughly secular institution during the reign of Muhammad Reza Shah.

One could see the clerics' dislodging of Westernized professionals and secular-minded technocrats from the dominant positions that they had occupied under the shah as just one facet of the populist, anti-elitist dynamic of the revolution. The Westernized elite of the shah's era had grown estranged from Iranian traditions and had little in common with the values and outlooks of less affluent Iranians. Clerics were more in touch with the traditional culture of the average Iranian than the elite of the Pahlavi era. Nonetheless, this does not mean that the Iranians would have chosen a theocratic form of government had they been given the opportunity to choose between theocracy and democracy in free elections.

As a result of clerical ascendancy, postrevolutionary fundamentalist policies in Iran have been articulated by Shi'ite clerics. Iran's fundamentalist clerics had two bêtes noires on the domestic scene. Not surprisingly, these were the groups most dramatically affected by the Islamization program. The first target was Iranian women who rejected their traditional cloistered and subjugated role and demanded full equality with men. As Shahla Haeri [has pointed] out . . . , clerical ire had been aroused by the 1963 reform which granted women the right to vote and by the Iranian Family Protection Act of 1967, which significantly improved women's rights in the area of family law. The growing prominence of women in public roles and the professions in the last decades of the shah's regime was also profoundly disturbing to the clerics. A prime goal of the clerical regime was to discredit emancipated women as traitors to Islam, or "Western dolls," as they were often labeled. Once the clerics were in power, Islamic precepts were interpreted in ways that promoted sexual segregation and the exclusion of women from areas of education, employment, and public activity. Harsh criminal penalties were imposed to punish and deter any conduct by females that conservative clerics found indecent or immoral. Violating rules of modest dress was treated as a serious offense, with penalities such as seventy-four lashes being imposed on women if they appeared in public without proper veiling.

The other nemesis of the clergy was the sizable Baha'i community, which, not coincidentally, was ecumenically oriented, espoused liberal and humanistic values, and accorded full equality to women. Baha'ism had originated in Iran in the nineteenth century and had won many converts among Iran's Muslims. Clerics deemed that converts to Baha'ism and their descendants were apostates from Islam and deserving of capital punishment, the apostasy penalty set in premodern Shari'a jurisprudence.

Under the shah, despite intermittent persecutions, Baha'is had been able to achieve a measure of equality with Muslims. By neglecting to mention Baha'is as a recognized minority religion, the 1979 constitution denied them the measure of religious toleration that was accorded Zoroastrians, Jews, and Christians in article 13. To destroy Baha'ism and the values it stood for, the regime undertook persecutions, imprisonments, and executions of Baha'is and Baha'i institutions were dismantled. Enormous pressure was exerted on Baha'is to repent of their theological errors and return to the Islamic fold. The reasons for the persecution of the Baha'is are complex, but some may relate closely to the kinds of reactions fundamentalists have to the modern world in general. One of the most distinguished scholars of Shi'ism and modern Iran has opined that Baha'is are seen by Iranians much as Jews were seen by European anti-Semites and that anti-Baha'ism is comparable to anti-Semitism. Like Jews they are viewed as being cosmopolitan types. "Baha'is are seen to symbolize threatening aspects of modernity. . . . They adopt modern education and modern science with alacrity, producing large numbers of intellectuals, physicians, engineers, and business people. If modernity menaces Iran's identity, they are surely accomplices."

How Islamization Was Pursued

In Iran Islamization proceeded as a by-product of the clerical takeover of the government and the courts. The process entailed the unseating and eventual defeat of secular forces that were disposed to resist clerical rule. The regime was intolerant of criticism by dissident Shi'ite clerics, who risked being censored, harassed, and even placed under house arrest when they questioned the legitimacy of clerical rule or criticized the official Islamization line. Claiming to represent "Islam," the regime treated its foes as if their opposition to the government was tantamount to declaring war on the Islamic religion. Ruthless persecution, incarceration, torture, and mass execution of the regime's critics withered the opposition. About two million Iranians, actual and potential opponents of the regime, fled to foreign havens and wound up as exiles in the West and in neighboring Turkey.

There was no way to challenge the regime's oppressive scheme of Islamization in the courts, which meted out an arbitrary form of summary justice from which any semblance of due process was banished. Among other secular institutions, the Iranian Bar Association was destroyed and with it the modern legal profession and its members' commitment to legality.

Khomeini's Islamization policy was directed against various foreign devils, among which the United States was singled out for particularly strong vilification due to American support for the shah. In Khomeini's program the pursuit of Islamization became closely associated with a strident anti-Americanism, with the United States incessantly excoriated as the Great Satan and presented as the enemy of Islam. (This stands in remarkable contrast to the situation in Pakistan, where the United States was the primary backer of the Zia regime, and to the situation in the Sudan, where the United States was the sole foreign prop in the final stages of Numayri's regime.) Khomeini's demonizing of the regime of Iraqi president Saddam Hussein served a similar role within his Islamization program; the war with Iraq was in part a prolonged demonstration of revolutionary zeal against infidels on the doorstep. And once that war ended in the 1988 ceasefire, Khomeini kept the fires stoked by calling for the execution of Salman Rushdie as an apostate from Islam, while Iran's propagandists sought to tie Rushdie's work to an American and Israeli plot against Islam.

It is thus ironic that, while these battles were being fought, strikingly little lasting progress was made toward eradicating Western influences on the fundamental structure and institutions of the legal system. For example, in the 1979 Iranian constitution one finds borrowed Western institutions that lack Islamic antecedents such as the republican form of government, the division of the government into three separate branches, a directly elected president who functions as chief executive, a prime minister and a cabinet, the ideas of the independence of the judiciary and judicial review, the concept of legality, the notion of an elected legislative body, the need for the cabinet to obtain votes of confidence from the legislative branch, and the concept of national sovereignty. Even the distinctive institution of the faqih, as set forth in the 1979 constitution, is embedded in a matrix of relations with other, conventional Western governmental institutions. For example, according to article 110 the faqih's duties include appointing the chief of staff of Iran's armed forces, declaring war, organizing the Supreme Council for National Defense (the president, prime minister, minister of defense, and others), confirming the appointment of the president after his election, and dismissing the president in the interests of the country after a Supreme Court ruling that the president has violated his legal duties. Such principles have counterparts in Western political systems, but they have no relation to the traditional function of a Shi'ite faqih.

In many facets and in its general format, the Iranian constitution resembles the 1958 French constitution. The way Islamic content has been injected into provisions with French antecedents can be illustrated by comparing the treatment of national sovereignty in article 56 of the Iranian constitution with article 3 of the French constitution. The French version establishes that sovereignty rests on the will of the people as expressed through referendums and enjoins interference with the exercise of popular sovereignty. It begins: "National sovereignty belongs to the people, which shall exercise this sovereignty through its representatives by means of referendums. No section of the people, nor any individual, may attribute to themselves or himself the exercise thereof." In chapter 5 of the Iranian constitution under the heading "The Right of National Sovereignty and the Powers Derived from It" one sees in article 56 the Islamized version of the same provision, in which the theological tenet that God is the Supreme Ruler is inserted and the French provisions enjoining interference – this time with Divine Sovereignty – have been incongruously retained: "Absolute sovereignty over the world and mankind is God's and He alone has determined the social destiny of human beings. None shall take away this God-given right from another person or make use of it to serve his special personal or group interests." Wanting to retain the provision for popular referendums, the authors of the Iranian constitution relegated it to article 59, by which placement the clash between the idea that national sovereignty is exercised by the people via referendums and the idea that sovereignty is the exclusive province of the deity has been rendered less obvious. The incongruity remains: there is no room for popular sovereignty exercised via referendums in a system based on the theological premise of divine rule, which at the very least should mean that God's laws are binding and not subject to modification by any human agency, such as popular referendums involve.

A similar pattern of borrowing Western constitutional principles and then modifying them can be seen in chapter 3 of the Iranian constitution, where there are provisions for rights principles that are of Western derivation but with Islamic qualifications added to circumscribe them. Thus, for example, article 20 provides for human rights, a Western concept, but Islamizes them by indicating that they are to be enjoyed "according to Islamic standards." Again, there is a resultant incongruity, since the philosophy of human rights precludes curbing rights by reference to the standards of a particular religion.

Even though the making of laws via human agency is barred under traditional Islamic legal theory, according to which all laws are to be found in and derived from the Islamic sources, Iran's Islamic constitution provided for lawmaking by the Majlis in article 58, and laws continued to be enacted by the Majlis just as they had been under the shah.

The Iranian approach to legislation thus differed markedly from the approach to law in Saudi Arabia, where, in deference to Islamic tradition, there was officially no man-made law. Ayatollah Khomeini seems to have originally aspired to return to a similar system of jurists' law, asserting in 1970 in a speech: "The entire system of government and administration, together with the necessary laws, lies ready for you. There is no need for you, after establishing a government, to sit down and draw up laws, or, like rulers who worship foreigners and are infatuated with the West, run after others to borrow their laws. Everything is ready and waiting. All that remains is to draw up ministerial programs." However, modern legal institutions on Western lines proved firmly rooted and survived the Islamic revolution largely intact.

The ultimate guarantee that laws would be in conformity with the Shari'a lay in the provision in article 4 that Islamic law would be supreme, overriding not only any laws in conflict with it but even the constitution itself. The article also provided that clerics on the Council of Guardians would make the decisions in this regard. This represented the achievement of a goal of Iran's clerics, who had been determined to ensure that there would be effective clerical review of proposed legislation in order to ensure conformity with Shari'a requirements.

In practice, the Council of Guardians reviewed and invalidated proposed laws with such stringency and zeal that acute embarrassment resulted at times for the government. For example, economic reforms such as land reform laws enacted by the Majlis were needed to retain the political support of the poorer classes but were repeatedly nullified by the Council of Guardians on the grounds that they violated Islamic law. For nine years Khomeini avoided challenging these "Islamic" vetos of legislation that the regime deemed politically essential. However, Khomeini finally ruled on 7 January 1988 that the Islamic state had absolute power – like the power enjoyed by the Prophet Muhammad – and was permitted to adopt such measures as it deemed necessary for the interests of the Islamic state *even where these might conflict with Islamic law or a fundamental religious obligation like the pilgrimage to Mecca.* This ruling seemed to mean that measures passed by the Majlis and acceptable to the faqih would henceforth go into effect even if the Guardians believed that they contravened the requirements of the Shari'a. This ruling proved that fundamentalists were not actually concerned with restoring Shari'a law per se. As the Iranian experience showed, the commitment was actually to reinstate Shari'a rules insofar as they served fundamentalists' political agendas. Conversely, Shari'a rules could be discounted when they stood in the way of programs that served the fundamentalists' own political interests.

Thus, considerations of *raison d'état* were officially permitted to override Islamic criteria. This was, ultimately, embarrassing for a government officially committed to the implementation of Islamic law. A constitutional amendment adopted on 28 July 1989 attempted to deal with this problem by endorsing the establishment of a council that would mediate and consult when conflicts occurred between the Majlis and the Council of Guardians. Since the new council's members were to be appointed by the faqih, it seemed unlikely that they would be disposed to contradict his views. It is too early to say what role the council will actually be able to play in resolving conflicts between legislation and Shari'a law, but its establishment suggests that the position of the Council of Guardians has been downgraded.

How Successful has Islamization Been?

Islamization has gone far enough in Iran that it is destined to have a long-term impact. The government itself has been reconstituted, and the constitution rewritten to institutionalize clerical authority and the supremacy of Islamic law (however it might be interpreted). In the 1980s and early 1990s fundamentalist clerics were firmly ensconced in powerful positions and dominated the country's legal system. Laws were enacted that embodied the fundamentalists' policies of combating the erosion of the traditional social structure and value system. Even if the application of criminal laws to enforce Islamic morality was relaxed somewhat, as it appeared to be in 1991, the impact of these laws on Iranian society remained considerable. Pre-revolution advances in women's status were rolled back, the 1967 Family Protection Act repealed, and women relegated to subservient roles caring for their husbands and children. The Baha'i religion has been virtually persecuted out of existence in Iran.

At the same time, there have been detrimental side effects of fundamentalist policies that were not intended by the policymakers. In the wake of official efforts to confine women to domestic roles and encouraged by the regime's initial pronatalist policies, the birthrate soared to 3.9 percent a year. The population growth became so alarming that in 1990 fears were being publicly expressed in official circles that it could pose an obstacle to Iran's development. In a dramatic reversal, the regime began to support birth control measures. Another obstacle to development was the brain drain resulting from the mass exodus of highly trained professionals and technocrats who were alienated by the fundamentalist policies of the regime. By 1989 there was growing evidence that leaders of the regime felt that a policy of liberalization was essential to woo back members of the educated elite from exile. In hopes of attracting foreign investment and trade from Europe and Japan, a major project for a free-trade zone on Qeshm Island at the entrance to the Persian Gulf was approved by the Parliament in February of 1990, despite conservatives' vocal opposition to the plan for granting foreigners on Qeshm exemptions from Iranian law. In the prevailing climate of pragmatism, it was possible to hear a cleric, Hojjatulislam Hassan Ruhani, say openly in Parliament: "To install Islamic codes on Qeshm is in contradiction with reality. The more freedom we provide for investors, the more of them we can attract." Thus, to attract badly needed foreign capital, the regime was prepared to lift the application of its version of Islamic law. Ironically, this meant replicating the kind of scheme of extraterritorial treatment for foreign nationals that had been negotiated by Americans under the shah, which Ayatollah Khomeini had excoriated in a famous speech in 1964 as the work of traitors. Moreover, there were even some indications of official sentiment favoring liberalization of the veiling requirements for women.

Iran's clerics remain uneasy with Iranian nationalism, which has been generally espoused by secular-minded politicians and intellectuals unsympathetic to clerical interests. The late shah gave Iran's clerics special reasons for opposing Iranian nationalism, since his version of Iranian nationalism sought to revive pride in Iran's pre-Islamic heritage as a means of denigrating the Islamic contribution to Iranian culture.

In consequence, clerics have at various points since the revolution advocated measures like destroying the ancient ruins at Persepolis, banning the distinctive Iranian Nowruz (New Year) celebrations as pagan, and promoting Arabic as a replacement for Persian. That is, Iran's character as a nation-state, which survived the revolution, did so despite clerical and fundamentalist antipathy to aspects of Iranian nationalism. The failure of the fundamentalists to carry out their plans for eradicating a separate Iranian national identity and setting up a supranational polity on a religious basis was due to the great resistance from Iranians, who are for the most part profoundly nationalistic and proud of their distinctive culture.

The Iranian model has not been emulated by other countries. In the eyes of many fundamentalists, the Islamic Republic of Iran is a failure as an Islamic polity, because it has a specific, Iranian national character. Islamic fundamentalists, including some in Iran, have tended to favor the concept that in Islam the only legitimate political entity is the *umma*, or community of believers, and that the nation-state and nationalism are inherently un-Islamic. One of the issues that had proved contentious during the drafting of the constitution was whether or not it was permissible for a self-proclaimed Islamic state to have a national territory, a national language, and citizenship requirements like those of other nation-states. Although the final version of the Iranian constitution affirms Iran's character as a nation-state, Islamic fundamentalists have persisted in challenging its legitimacy.

The Iranian fundamentalist version of Islam is not an inclusive, ecumenical one but is fraught with distinctive Twelver Shi'ite characteristics, and this bias in favor of Twelver Shi'ism may eventually have an untoward effect on the political loyalties of the Sunni Baluchis, Kurds, and Turkomans inside Iran. Outside Iran this same Shi'ite bias has sharply limited the appeal of Iran's Islamic revolution, which was originally intended to be a model that would be emulated throughout the Muslim world but which has inspired scant emulation except in Twelver Shi'ite communities in places like Lebanon.

Future Prospects

The fortunes of fundamentalism in Iran will be strongly affected by which factions are ultimately successful in the power struggles that ensued after Khomeini's death. Politically active clerics in 1990 and 1991 differed significantly in the degree to which they were actually committed to the fundamentalist cause.

Before the Rushdie affair of February 1989 there were indications that powerful figures in the government were ready to adopt more moderate and conciliatory policies toward the opposition and the West and that they had become disenchanted with fundamentalist extremism. After the Rushdie affair exploded, the moderate Ayatollah Hossein Ali Montazeri, long Khomeini's chosen successor, came under siege. He was finally obliged to resign on 28 March after being attacked for having criticized government repression and for urging toleration of dissent. These manifestations of liberal sympathies led Montazeri to be characterized as one who had moved away from the Islamic system.

The June 1989 death of Ayatollah Khomeini placed the viability of his concept of governance by the leading jurist in jeopardy. No successor of equivalent prestige and charisma was available to serve as faqih. After the disgrace of Ayatollah Montazeri and his elimination from the succession, no distinguished, high ranking clerics remained who could be trusted to follow Khomeini's political line. Articles 107 and 109 of the constitution were amended in July of 1989 to downgrade the requirements for serving the office of faqih in order to accommodate Ayatollah 'Ali Khamene'i, a far less eminent cleric than Ayatollah Khomeini had been. In the aftermath of these changes, the importance of the office of faqih seemed destined to dwindle.

Constitutional amendments adopted in July of 1989 eliminated the office of prime minister and concentrated power in the presidency, a secular office, even though currently occupied by a cleric. Hojjatulislam Ali Akbar Hashemi Rafsanjani was able to win a pro forma election as president in July 1989. Rafsanjani's subsequent consolidation of his power signaled at least a temporary victory by a relatively moderate and pragmatic faction in the government at the expense of the fundamentalist hardliners. The original Islamic scheme of government seemed to be in the process of being transformed into a mundane presidential one.

Under the leadership of President Rafsanjani it seems that Iran's policies are being significantly liberalized in the political, economic, and social domains. One suspects that, if he did not have to fear a backlash from militant fundamentalist forces and could follow his own personal inclinations, Rafsanjani might be moving even faster toward liberalization. In a brave move for a cleric, he has supported the idea of allowing women greater freedoms and participation in public life and the professions than they enjoyed under Khomeini.

Like Prime Minister Nawaz Sharif of Pakistan, Rafsanjani seems to have little personal enthusiasm for the cultural dimensions of Islamization and appears primarily concerned with bold reforms to end his country's economic deterioration and to promote rapid development along free-market lines. This liberalization program entails improving Iran's relations with Europe and Japan and institutions like the IMF, which in turn necessitate hewing to a moderate political line. The trends justified a tentative conclusion that under President Rafsanjani and the pragmatists allied with him, and in the face of overwhelming need to extricate the country from an economic morass, the fundamentalist impulse faded in the early 1990s – at least at the governmental level, where it would shape politics, laws, and the constitution.

45 Obedience versus Autonomy: Women and Fundamentalism in Iran and Pakistan

Shahla Haeri

Islamic societies from Morocco to Indonesia were radically affected in the 1980s and early 1990s by movements advocating a return to the Islamic ideals, to the fundamentals, particularly in the area of family relations, marriage, and divorce. This chapter is set, however, within the broader context of an ongoing dialectical relationship between Islamic secular reformers of the 1950s and 1960s, and Islamic fundamentalists of the late 1970s and 1980s in Iran and Pakistan. The former, who initiated legal and social reforms, came under strong criticism by the latter who have argued that the laws and the ensuing reforms are un-Islamic and hence illegal. The fundamentalists contested the legitimacy of these reforms, claiming them to be inspired (or imposed) by the West rather than guided by Islamic law. The tension between the secularist governments and fundamentalists has mirrored the alienation from and disillusionment with ideals and promises of "modernity" in many Muslim societies.

Much of the debate between fundamentalists and secularists has centered on the issues of status of women, marriage, and family law. Islamic laws and commandments are spelled out in the Qur'an, the hadith, and other classical legal sources. They are believed to be divine and unchanging, and are understood to be central to the texture of social life in an Islamic society. Changes in Islamic marriage law were initiated by the colonial powers in the late nineteenth century in India and Egypt, setting the stage for later protests by Islamic groups, including the fundamentalists in Iran and Pakistan. On the whole, however, Islamic family law itself remained unchanged well into the twentieth century, and relative unanimity has existed among different schools of Islamic law regarding the contractual form of marriage *(nikah)*, the reciprocal rights and obligations of the spouses, divorce, and child custody.

Ironically, after centuries of resistance to changing Islamic family law, the Muslim reformers of the 1950s and 1960s adopted elements of Western law and applied them within an Islamic framework. They referred to the sources, to the Qur'an and Sunna of the Prophet Muhammad, to find an "Islamic rationale" for such adoptions, and an "Islamic methodology" to implement them. Nonetheless, a number of the ulama and their followers, including Maulana Maududi in Pakistan

Original publication details: Excerpted from Shahla Haeri, "Obedience versus Autonomy: Women and Fundamentalism in Iran and Pakistan," in Martin E. Marty and R. Scott Appleby (eds.), *Fundamentalisms and Society* (University of Chicago Press, 1993), pp. 182–91. Reproduced by permission of the University of Chicago Press.

and Ayatollah Khomeini in Iran, perceived such "reforms" as a form of capitulation to the West, as a thinly veiled apologetic, and as an all too eager attempt to find an "Islamic justification" for an essentially Western approach to the issue of interpersonal relations.

Within this context I discuss the interaction and exchange between fundamentalists, who continue to advocate structured gender relations, and Iranian and Pakistani urban middle-class women, who are articulating their own interpretations of personal laws as their knowledge of religious, legal, and political discourses grows. In the 1980s these women added a new voice to the decades-old debates between the fundamentalists and secularists.

The theoretical concepts underpinning my argument are those of *obedience* and *autonomy*, both of which are inextricably associated with the reciprocal rights of the spouses and derived from the contractual form of marriage in Islam. Though seminal to the historically dominant worldview of Islamic countries, both concepts are subject to new interpretations due to a heightened tension between secularists and fundamentalists. Whereas the former are more inclined to break through or improvise on the predetermined boundaries of the marriage contract, the latter are determined to return to a literal meaning of such concepts.

We must look to the broader logic of an Islamic marriage contract, and the historically maintained perception of its immutability, to understand some of the specificities of gender relations in Iran and Pakistan, historical resistance to the reform of personal laws, and hence the basis for the fundamentalists' objection to women's legal autonomy. Contracts constitute the dominant metaphor, or model, for marital relations in Islamic societies and belong to that category of concepts referred to as "root paradigms," that is, "as distinct from what is probably in each culture a wide range of quotidian or situational models for behavior under the sign of self or factual interest," and are "concerned with fundamental assumptions underlying the human bonds." Root paradigms provide people with "cultural maps" that can guide them through specific social "territories." Accordingly, the logic of a marriage contract necessitates a woman's obedience to her husband, while limiting her autonomy.

My concern is with the legal structure of the Islamic marriage contract. Wedding rituals, of course, vary greatly from one Islamic society to another, they take on local coloring and flavor, but the legal form of the Islamic marriage contract, nikah, is the same in almost all Islamic cultures. Moreover, although my focus is on women in Iran and Pakistan, the model of contractual marriage I am proposing is theoretically relevant to other Islamic cultures. Although both are Muslim societies, Pakistan is predominantly a Sunni and Iran mainly a Shi'ite society. Whereas Pakistan is within the South Asian cultural sphere, Iran shares the cultural area of the Middle East. Unlike the fundamentalists who represent the state in Iran and have appeared to be omnipotent within their domain, Pakistani fundamentalists are only a part of the ruling coalition and must compete for political and electoral power with other parties and interest groups. Their interpretation of the role and status of women, marriage, and family law is more contested than that of their counterparts in Iran, at least publicly. Despite years of apparent prosperity under Zia ul-Haq and their renewed prominence in the early 1990s, the fundamentalists' impact in Pakistan has been more limited, indirect, selective, and uneven than the Shi'ite fundamentalists' impact in Iran.

Obedience is a cornerstone of the Islamic vision of a just social order; the term "Islam" means, among other things, submission and obedience. The Qur'an enjoins believers to "Obey God, His Prophet, and those in authority among you." Like the concept of contract, the concept of obedience is paradigmatic in an Islamic culture. Obedience maintains the status quo, making the hierarchy of social relations culturally meaningful. In the context of family life and marriage, the observance of obedience *(tamkin)*, and avoidance of disobedience *(nushuz)*, are not just obligations with far-reaching legal and social ramifications for women; they are also a wife's divine obligation. A disobedient wife is known as *nashizih*, a rebellious one, who should be admonished because her action transgresses the divine command, and brings about discomfort to the husband and disorder to the family. She also sets a bad example for her own children and others. Within such a worldview, a wife cannot legally be autonomous; a man cannot be obedient to a woman; a woman cannot be the leader of a Muslim state.

Islamic Worldview: The Marriage Contract

The marriage contract maintained its legal form until the passage of the Family Law Ordinance (1961) in Pakistan and the Family Protection Law (1967) in Iran. These acts were intended to give women some judicial relief by granting them certain rights and minimizing a man's unilateral right to divorce. In legal form, an Islamic marriage is a contract of sale *('aqd)*, although contemporary Islamic legal scholars generally shy away from specifying the category of contracts to which it actually belongs. Such reluctance, or "misrecognition," is more pronounced in the case of the contemporary ulama, who have become increasingly conscious of the implications of the concepts of ownership and purchase that are embedded in a contract of marriage. There are nonetheless significant similarities between a contract of marriage and a contract of sale.

Like a contract of sale, an Islamic marriage involves an exchange of goods and services, each meticulously tied in with the proper functioning of the other. In exchange for brideprice *(mahr)* and daily maintenance *(nafaqih)*, which the wife receives, the husband gains exclusive ownership right *(tamlik)*, over his wife's sexuality and reproductive activities and, by extension, over her person. Significantly, Islamic marriage does not involve the purchase or exchange of women, at least not in the sense conceptualized by Lévi-Strauss. Initially, Islamic law upholds the right of a woman as partner, albeit an unequal one, to the marriage contract; this provision assumes she has some degree of autonomy and volition. According to Islamic law, the woman is to give her consent, however nominally, and it is the woman, not her father, who is to receive the full amount of brideprice (custom aside). However, the moment a woman agrees to a marriage contract, she is understood to relinquish "voluntarily" all control and autonomy she may have had over her own legal and social persona. Prior to signing the contract of marriage, an adult Muslim woman is accorded a degree of legal autonomy (though the extent differs among the Sunnis and the Shi'ites), but after the conclusion of the contract she is legally and conceptually associated with the object of exchange, and hence she comes under the jural authority of her husband.

Conceptually, within the structure of a marriage contract, a woman's sexual and reproductive organs are viewed as an object, a fetishized "commodity" – actually and/or symbolically – that is separated from her person and is at the core of an individual, social, and economic transaction. Though conceptually isolated from a woman's body, a woman's sexuality is in practice identified with her whole being. In this gender ideology, woman as person is conflated with woman as object. Furthermore, women are perceived not only as sexual beings but as the very embodiment of sex itself. In this sense veiling is an expression of the concealment of sexuality itself. This cultural/religious ideology leads to a particular pattern of interpersonal relations. Men view women as objects to be owned and jealously controlled; as objects of desire to seclude, to veil, and to discard; and, at the same time, as objects of indispensable value to men's sense of power and virility. This association of women with objects of exchange is at the heart of an ideological ambivalence toward women, inspiring a sustained resistance against granting women independent rights.

Within this ideological scheme, a man is legally empowered to engage in a dual relationship with his wife; in the one she is considered a person, and in the other a sexual and reproductive object. The woman, too, assumes the dual characteristics of a person and an object – characteristics that, though often subjectively blurred, nonetheless color her sense of self-perception. Theoretically, the relationship between husband and wife is mediated through the object of exchange, an object that has become a highly charged cultural symbol, a gift that bestows power on the woman who has it and authority on the man who has legal control over it.

The logic of this particular form of contract dictates a wife's obedience to her husband, while limiting her autonomy. The legal structure of a marriage contract obliges a wife to be obedient, while the divine verses in the Qur'an and the sociocultural beliefs regarding the "nature" of man and woman further entangle a wife in a web of obedience and surrender.

The comments of Ayatollah Khomeini and his Sunni counterparts in Pakistan are indicative of shared legal conceptualizations of the sexes, and the reciprocal rights and obligations of the spouses. "A permanent wife," argued Ayatollah Khomeini, "must not leave the house without her husband's permission, and must submit (*taslim*) herself for whatever pleasure he wants. . . . In this case her maintenance is incumbent upon her husband. If she does not obey him, she is a sinner (*gunahkar*) and has no right to clothing, housing, or sleeping." Similarly, citing a hadith, Maulana Maududi (1903–79), the founder of the most vocal fundamentalist movement in Pakistan and a renowned Sunni scholar, wrote: "When a woman steps out of her house against the will of her husband, she is cursed by every angel in the heavens and by everything other than men and jinn by which she passes, till she returns." Citing Bukhari and Muslim (two major sources of Sunni collections of hadith), Muhammad Imran, a member of the Jamaat-i-Islami, wrote in a similar vein: "As a rule, no wife should refuse her husband what he wants from her except on legitimate grounds, i.e., at the time of menstrual flow or fasting. Some theologians regard even this refusal unlawful as the husband may get enjoyment from his wife in other ways – embracing, kissing, etc. The duty of the wife to her husband is to give him pleasure in his bed whenever he wants her. . . . No woman should, therefore, cause anxiety or give trouble to her husband. If she acts otherwise, she will not be able to be his mate in Paradise. There the pure-eyed virgin maids will be his consorts."

The general secretary for the women's division of the Jamaat-i-Islami in Lahore, though not expressing her interpretation of marital obligations in exactly the same terms, reflected on the issue from a broader perspective shared by the public: "A man's primary duty is to 'provide' (or 'protect') for his family, and that of the wife's is to raise children, take care of her husband, and be obedient to him at all times."

A woman's obedience to her husband and to the larger social order is reciprocated with financial security in the family and prestige in society. A wife's disobedience, however, has legal ramifications that may lead to a severing of her daily support and maintenance, if not to her repudiation. "Women are sometimes murdered by their husbands," wrote Justice Javid Iqbal from Pakistan, "for being rude or disobedient. In such cases the man is not sentenced to death, he usually gets off with a sentence of ten years or life imprisonment." A disobedient wife is guilty of a double violation: reneging on her contractual promise by denying her husband access to that which he legally possesses, and transgressing God's will.

The underlying assumption here is twofold. First, as "purchasers" in a contract of marriage, men are "in charge" of their wives because they pay for them, and naturally they ought to be able to control their wives' activities. Second, women are required to submit that for which they have been paid – or promised to be paid. It follows, therefore, that women ought to be obedient to their husbands. The issue of child custody and the expectation of their unquestioned obedience to their father should be seen within this context as well. Given that a contract of marriage creates "some sort of ownership," it follows that any issue of this contract should automatically belong to the father. Although different schools of Islamic law have different minimum-age requirements, the custody of children is nonetheless a legal/divine right of a father.

By the same rationale, it is woman's autonomy and independence that pose a "problem" for the status quo within the family and the proper functioning of marital relations, and ultimately a challenge to the social order. Any expression of female autonomy can be construed as disobedience and an infringement on male prerogative, and by extension a deviation from the divinely ordained, legally upheld, and historically enforced duties of a wife. The ulama's fierce resistance to any legal/political changes in the status of women in Islamic societies and the moral and cultural ambivalence felt toward empowering women proceed from the assumptions undergirding the logic of the marriage contract.

Of course the legal requirement and cultural expectation that women obey their husbands does not mean that women always do so. Nor does it mean that marital relations necessarily lack partnership and romance. They do mean, however, that the contractual form of marriage provides the basis for a range of specific patterns of gender relations and expectations in Islamic societies. For example, the preoccupation with virginity and the obsession with veiling assume a certain coherence within the framework of the marriage contract and the worldview it enacts. And the potential insecurity embedded in marital relations, which can be manipulated at the moment of conflict, also stems from the set of rights and assumptions on which the contract rests. Recent ethnographic data emerging from the Middle East underscore the often subtle forms through which many women negotiate their wants and desires. Using the potential power that is tacitly perceived to be inherent in their being in possession of the object of desire, women exercise a degree of autonomy and self-assertion. The logic of the marriage contract sets the context, framing the outer boundaries for marital obligations and duties. Having contained the boundaries of marital relations accordingly, this same structure allows for a range of negotiated and improvisational social behavior by means of which both husband and wife, though departing from different junctures, can exercise control, negotiate power, "bargain reality," use or abuse each other.

Muslim women are intimately aware of the reciprocal implications of obedience and financial support: if they do not oblige their husbands' wishes, their very livelihood is in danger. At the same time they are aware, however vaguely at times, of the potential power inherent in their possession of an object that is tied to a man's sense of history and continuity, honor and virility. Theoretically, therefore, women have the power to be obedient (or disobedient) to their husbands; they can use that power judiciously, situationally, and strategically as leverage. A woman has little authority to force her husband to support her, however, should he decide to punish her for insubordination.

Fundamentalism Consolidated: The Case of Iran

The decade of the 1970s was a period of dramatic change and restlessness in Iran and Pakistan. Even though they were following different historical paths, both societies seemed poised for an upheaval. In the end, the financial deluge of the petrodollar brought about more destruction than development in Iran. It widened the gap between the haves and have-nots; disrupted the traditional patterns of social relation, expectation, and propriety; distorted the fabric of moral order; and created crises of identity. Personal privileges were abused and public trust was betrayed. The economic, political, and moral corruption that followed in the wake of the economic boom and development left many citizens disoriented, dislodged many from their physical environment and ideological beliefs, and perplexed others as to where the nation was heading and where they stood in the overall scheme of things. A sense of moral chaos prevailed, particularly in cities and urban centers.

As confusion and uncertainty in all spheres of public and private life intensified, the need to reassert oneself and hang on to the familiar also increased. Many Iranians were unable to internalize the "unveiling" of gender relations, or to tolerate the vagaries associated with modern life in Iran, or to focus on any one of the many voices that dictated new directions and orientations for citizens almost daily. An overwhelming majority of Iranians took a collective plunge into an idealized past, hoping to retrieve what they thought they could agree on, namely, an Islamic identity. The stunning victory of Ayatollah Khomeini is attributed, among other causes, to his unambiguous call for an Islamic identity that presumably once existed but had been seriously undermined by the policies of successive ruling monarchies, particularly by Muhammad Reza Pahlavi (1941–79).

Ayatollah Khomeini portrayed the latter as a usurper, an impostor, and a "false god," a *taghut*, who sold his soul and that of his nation to the "Great Satan." Khomeini regarded the shah's policies as inimical to a "genuine" Islamic society, and contrary to "God's purposeful creation to further the establishment of ethical order on earth." In the area of family and personal law Khomeini objected in particular to the Unveiling Act of 1936 and the Family Protection Law of 1967 that granted women some autonomy and rights in the family.

The most immediate and noticeable change in the status of women after the revolution was the requirement of veiling. The Islamic regime made wearing a veil (optional since 1941) mandatory and required all women to wear an "Islamic veil" while appearing in public. Despite this, however, a significant degree of continuity in the legal status of women and in the social beliefs associated with their role and status endured the revolutionary changes. What changed significantly was the rhetoric of the Islamic regime (matched at times by the "emancipation" rhetoric of the Pahlavi regime) regarding the high status accorded veiled women in an Islamic society. Caught in the exuberance of the moment, women initially donned the veil and participated en masse in the anti-shah demonstrations. Many women's reasons for wearing the veil were symbolic (a protest against its forced removal in the 1930s) or pragmatic (fear of recognition by the SAVAK, the shah's secret police) rather than motivated by religious conviction.

In response, the fundamentalists encouraged women to participate in demonstrations against the Pahlavi regime, to fight against oppression and demand justice in the spirit of Zainab, the Prophet Muhammad's granddaughter who defended her martyred brother, Imam Husain, in the aftermath of the tragedy of Karbala in 680 C.E. The Iranian revolution thus ushered in a new role model for women, one that proved to have widespread appeal to urban women, and also one that the regime began to retract soon after consolidating its power. Although for political purposes the Zainab model is still publicly supported, in the privacy of marital relations and in relation to men, the Fatimah model is the privileged one and the one encouraged by the government. However, the representation of Zainab as a patron saint of women sowed the seed of a new consciousness in the minds of many urban Iranian women. Here lies a locus of tension between the Islamic regime and women.

The Islamic fundamentalist regime found itself challenged to fulfill its revolutionary promises, made during the mobilization of 1978–9, to provide social justice, welfare, equal access to education, jobs, and other resources to women. For their part, with increasing sophistication, Iranian women have engaged the fundamentalist regime in frequent dialogues and debates during the 1980s and early 1990s, articulating their own interpretations of various Qur'anic commandments and injunctions, and sayings of the Prophet Muhammad. Individually and collectively, be they women leaders such as Mrs Zahra Rahnavard and Azam-i Taliqani or members of the editorial board of a popular weekly magazine (such as *Zan-i Ruz*), women have criticized and even scolded the regime, demanding that it live up to its promises and allow Iranian Muslim women to develop their full potential in a just and equitable Islamic state. They call for full participation of women in the public sphere and in education, demand the creation of opportunities for divorced and widowed women, and seek to curb men's unilateral right to divorce and polygamy.

The fundamentalists thus have been confronted with an unintended consequence of their success as revolutionaries – the heightened awareness and increased expectations of small but vocal segments of the urban female population. The fundamentalists responded by attempting to negotiate "new" boundaries of male–female relationships, rights, reciprocal obligations, and duties with an old "adversary" who is determined to assert herself – to be the Zainab of her time – and take her place on the sociopolitical hierarchy. The fundamentalists' dilemma has been how to deal with this "new woman" without themselves being dislodged from their traditional position of power and privilege, yet without appearing to undermine their own revolutionary Islamic rhetoric.

Although disgruntled women have not been able to challenge the legitimacy of the regime, they have endeavored to counter the cultural images and perceptions detrimental to its view of women in family and society. Having acquired knowledge of the Shi'ite Islamic discourse, educated urban Iranian women have engaged the fundamentalists in frequent debates, questioning publicly the images of "nagging," "weak," or "dependent" women portrayed on Iranian National Television. For example, a public debate occurred in 1989 between the editorial board of *Zan-i Ruz* (Modern Woman) and Hashemi Rafsanjani (the present Iranian president and then Speaker of the Parliament). Mr Rafsanjani apparently feared popular discontent with the high casualty rate of young men in the Iran–Iraq War, and the consequent frustration of many families with delays in arranging suitable marriages for their children. In one of his Friday sermons, Rafsanjani called on men to marry several wives (permanently or temporarily), telling women to put aside their inhibitions and selfishness. His recommendations prompted swift response from the editorial board of *Zan-i*

Ruz, leading him to revise and modify his comments. "Only in a true Islamic society," argued the editorial board of *Zan-i Ruz*, "can a man be a good enough Muslim to maintain justice between his wives. Until then, polygamy leads to more misery for women. That is why we object to polygamy [and recommend monogamy]."

The tension between the fundamentalist regime in Iran and the women who helped bring them to power is exacerbated by a number of issues affecting daily life.

Veiling

Veiling in the Islamic world is not monolithic and uniform, even within individual Islamic societies. Rather, veiling is a multifaceted and polysemic institution, involving a multiplicity of forms and meanings both domestically and internationally. Unlike in Iran, veiling is not universally prescribed in Pakistan. It is much more diverse in Pakistan than in Iran, ranging from the very thin and attractive scarf casually worn by female television newscasters (under Zia ul-Haq's regime, use of the scarf became mandatory for them), to the facial veils worn by some, to the *burqa* which covers all parts of the body except for a narrow rectangular "window" over the eyes (particularly worn by female beggars in urban areas). The particular garment prescribed for women in Iran after the revolution came to be known as "Islamic veiling" *(hijab-i Islami)*.

Despite the Islamic regime's attempt at uniformity, many urban women have learned to assert their "individuality" by improvising on the theme of Islamic veiling. Some reverted to wearing the traditional long black veil *(chador)* because underneath they can dress anyway they like. Others, rather than using the dull colors of black, brown, maroon, or gray prescribed by the government, use colorful scarfs interwoven with gold and silver threads; some wrap their scarves differently, and others show a few strands of highlighted hair. These variations of veiling have consistently provoked the ire of the more radical elements within the Islamic regime, toward whom the "moderates," such as President Rafsanjani, have had to defer.

Notwithstanding the differences of perception on veiling among the ruling fundamentalists themselves, the issue in Iran is no longer to veil or not to veil. It is, rather, to "veil well" or to "veil bad" *(bad hijabi)*, the former a sign of a good woman, one who obeys the regime's teachings and directives, and the latter a sign of a bad (autonomous) woman, one who holds on to the remnants of the old "decadent" and "Westoxicated" Pahlavi regime. In April 1989 the regime passed laws forbidding once again the "bad veiling" of women and threatening disobedient women with seventy-four lashes and internment for "rehabilitation." A woman's family would also be punished by being forced to pay all her expenses during internment.

That the Islamic regime found it necessary to pass yet another set of directives with harsh punishments is indicative of the regime's continued intolerance of any expressions of autonomy by women. It also indicates that there is a relentless, though submerged, struggle against the veiling directives of the Islamic regime. Although the veil itself is not subject to negotiation, what emerges from this continuous and subtle subversion of authority is a public and highly politicized debate about the particular way the veil is worn, the specific colors chosen, or the arena within which women can appear and work.

Iranian history is replete with unilateral orders and edicts issued by autocratic rulers. In 1936 Reza Shah Pahlavi (1925–41), responding to a growing ideology of modernity that was rapidly spreading across the globe, dramatically ordered Iranian women to appear in public unveiled. Any form of veiling was banned. Women caught disobeying the law were severely punished. The impact of law was felt strongly in the Iranian urban centers where traditionally women wore a chador, or long black veil.

Then as now some women obeyed the law. Some, though resenting it, did not take any action, but others felt obliged to challenge such unilateral laws. Many refused to leave their homes, not even to go to the public bath; some defied the regime and paid a heavy price for their insubordination. Only women who obeyed the law and packed their veils in their trunks could hope for any public recognition in the form of access to education, professional training, and employment. Similarly, after the Islamic revolution, only women who wore the veil were permitted to leave their homes, to enter government premises and agencies, and to have limited access to sociopolitical and economic resources.

In both situations obedience to the authorities was the key to access. The relationship between the dominant regime (in its autocratic as well as theocratic form) and women operates on two interconnected levels. On a more obvious level, women who obey the law are accorded certain concessions and given limited privileges. On a more subtle level, however, women quietly yet consistently challenge the premises of their oppression, while asserting a degree of their own will, however minimal, at times. In the early 1980s some women were openly defiant, which led to their punishment or incarceration. Later they changed their tactics to quiet resistance: while wearing the veil they attempted to subvert the law. Women disobey the law not only to defy the male authority, but also to protest their exclusion from decision-making processes, from having a choice in a matter so directly involving their lives. [. . .]

46   Yes, This is About Islam

Salman Rushdie

London – "This isn't about Islam." The world's leaders have been repeating this mantra for weeks, partly in the virtuous hope of deterring reprisal attacks on innocent Muslims living in the West, partly because if the United States is to maintain its coalition against terror it can't afford to suggest that Islam and terrorism are in any way related.

The trouble with this necessary disclaimer is that it isn't true. If this isn't about Islam, why the worldwide Muslim demonstrations in support of Osama bin Laden and Al Qaeda? Why did those 10,000 men armed with swords and axes mass on the Pakistan-Afghanistan frontier, answering some mullah's call to jihad? Why are the war's first British casualties three Muslim men who died fighting on the Taliban side?

Why the routine anti-Semitism of the much-repeated Islamic slander that "the Jews" arranged the hits on the World Trade Center and the Pentagon, with the oddly self-deprecating explanation offered by the Taliban leadership, among others, that Muslims could not have the technological know-how or organizational sophistication to pull off such a feat? Why does Imran Khan, the Pakistani ex-sports star turned politician, demand to be shown the evidence of Al Qaeda's guilt while apparently turning a deaf ear to the self-incriminating statements of Al Qaeda's own spokesmen (there will be a rain of aircraft from the skies, Muslims in the West are warned not to live or work in tall buildings)? Why all the talk about American military infidels desecrating the sacred soil of Saudi Arabia if some sort of definition of what is sacred is not at the heart of the present discontents?

Of course this is "about Islam." The question is, what exactly does that mean? After all, most religious belief isn't very theological. Most Muslims are not profound Koranic analysts. For a vast number of "believing" Muslim men, "Islam" stands, in a jumbled, half-examined way, not only for the fear of God – the fear more than the love, one suspects – but also for a cluster of customs, opinions and prejudices that include their dietary practices; the sequestration or near-sequestration of "their" women; the sermons delivered by their mullahs of choice; a loathing of modern society in general, riddled as it is with music, godlessness and sex; and a more particularized loathing (and fear) of the prospect that their own immediate surroundings could be taken over – "Westoxicated" – by the liberal Western-style way of life.

Highly motivated organizations of Muslim men (oh, for the voices of Muslim women to be heard!) have been engaged over the last 30 years or so in growing radical political movements out of this mulch of "belief." These Islamists – we must

Original publication details: Salman Rushdie, "Yes, This Is About Islam," *The New York Times*, November 2, 2001. © 2001 by Salman Rushdie. Reprinted by permission of the Wylie Agency, Inc., and the Wylie Agency (UK) Ltd.

get used to this word, "Islamists," meaning those who are engaged upon such political projects, and learn to distinguish it from the more general and politically neutral "Muslim" – include the Muslim Brotherhood in Egypt, the blood-soaked combatants of the Islamic Salvation Front and Armed Islamic Group in Algeria, the Shi'ite revolutionaries of Iran, and the Taliban. Poverty is their great helper, and the fruit of their efforts is paranoia. This paranoid Islam, which blames outsiders, "infidels," for all the ills of Muslim societies, and whose proposed remedy is the closing of those societies to the rival project of modernity, is presently the fastest growing version of Islam in the world.

This is not wholly to go along with Samuel Huntington's thesis about the clash of civilizations, for the simple reason that the Islamists' project is turned not only against the West and "the Jews," but also against their fellow Islamists. Whatever the public rhetoric, there's little love lost between the Taliban and Iranian regimes. Dissensions between Muslim nations run at least as deep, if not deeper, than those nations' resentment of the West. Nevertheless, it would be absurd to deny that this self-exculpatory, paranoiac Islam is an ideology with widespread appeal.

Twenty years ago, when I was writing a novel about power struggles in a fictionalized Pakistan, it was already de rigueur in the Muslim world to blame all its troubles on the West and, in particular, the United States. Then as now, some of these criticisms were well-founded; no room here to rehearse the geopolitics of the cold war and America's frequently damaging foreign policy "tilts," to use the Kissinger term, toward (or away from) this or that temporarily useful (or disapproved-of) nation-state, or America's role in the installation and deposition of sundry unsavory leaders and regimes. But I wanted then to ask a question that is no less important now: Suppose we say that the ills of our societies are not primarily America's fault, that we are to blame for our own failings? How would we understand them then? Might we not, by accepting our own responsibility for our problems, begin to learn to solve them for ourselves?

Many Muslims, as well as secularist analysts with roots in the Muslim world, are beginning to ask such questions now. In recent weeks Muslim voices have everywhere been raised against the obscurantist hijacking of their religion. Yesterday's hotheads (among them Yusuf Islam, a k a Cat Stevens) are improbably repackaging themselves as today's pussycats.

An Iraqi writer quotes an earlier Iraqi satirist: "The disease that is in us, is from us." A British Muslim writes, "Islam has become its own enemy." A Lebanese friend, returning from Beirut, tells me that in the aftermath of the attacks on Sept. 11, public criticism of Islamism has become much more outspoken. Many commentators have spoken of the need for a Reformation in the Muslim world.

I'm reminded of the way noncommunist socialists used to distance themselves from the tyrannical socialism of the Soviets; nevertheless, the first stirrings of this counterproject are of great significance. If Islam is to be reconciled with modernity, these voices must be encouraged until they swell into a roar. Many of them speak of another Islam, their personal, private faith.

The restoration of religion to the sphere of the personal, its depoliticization, is the nettle that all Muslim societies must grasp in order to become modern. The only aspect of modernity interesting to the terrorists is technology, which they see as a weapon that can be turned on its makers. If terrorism is to be defeated, the world of Islam must take on board the secularist-humanist principles on which the modern is based, and without which Muslim countries' freedom will remain a distant dream.

Questions

1   What makes fundamentalism a distinctly global phenomenon? How does Lechner assess its likely impact?

2   How and why do Islamic fundamentalists resist "global neoliberalism" and defy the "hyper-liberal promise" of a unified world, according to Pasha? How did economic globalization also help to foster this resistance movement? If economically based discontents are important to fundamentalism, would greater corporate responsibility or regulation of the kind discussed in Part IV diminish fundamentalism's appeal to Muslims?

3   Does Tibi agree that neoliberalism is the chief source and target of Islamic fundamentalism? What makes such fundamentalism more than a form of religious belief and practice? What is its likely impact? What is Tibi's own assessment of fundamentalism?

4   What were the goals and methods of Islamization in Iran? What impact did it have, according to Meyer? What effects on Iranian women does Haeri describe, and what tensions did these create? What did the Islamic republic appear to find most threatening about "Westoxication" and the West's "cultural imperialism"? What are its strengths and weaknesses as the core of a global antisystemic movement?

5   Against whom is Rushdie arguing when he says that the struggle against Islamist terrorism is also "about Islam"? How does he describe the influence of Islam on the worldview of many Muslims? What does he think must be done for Islam to be "reconciled with modernity"?

Part IX

Changing World Society: Environmentalism and the Globalization of Social Problems

Introduction

Over the past three decades, it has become routine to think of problems as being global in nature. Obviously, we tell ourselves, environmental degradation in the form of air pollution, acid rain, tropical deforestation, and the thinning of the ozone layer affect the entire globe, so it makes no sense for states or environmentalists to attempt anything less than a global approach to such problems. In historical perspective, though, it is difficult to avoid the conclusion that nothing inherent in a given problem, whether related to environmental degradation, human rights violations, inequality, authoritarian political regimes, or the oppression of women, automatically qualifies it as a global concern.

Take air pollution as an example. During the heyday of unregulated industrial capitalism in the nineteenth century, air pollution was far worse in most major cities than it was in the 1960s, when global environmentalism first became a major social movement. The reason the air was so bad is simple: in the days before electric heaters, natural gas furnaces, and centralized delivery of hot water for radiant heat, factories and homes directly burned enormous quantities of coal. Unlike today, however, the smoke belching from factory stacks often evoked not horrified criticism but almost lyrical praise as a sign of the glorious progress that industrialization was bringing to the blessed peoples of the ever-richer West. Not only was pollution not a global problem; for the most part, it was not a problem at all.

The same analysis applies to human rights violations, inequality, authoritarianism, and women's oppression: though the "problems" have long been widespread and often severe, either they have not been interpreted as problems or they have been treated primarily as local or national issues requiring only local or national responses. The sovereign authority of the state to manage its own society meant that critics and activists from outside the country were more likely to be told to mind their own business than to be heard or allowed to spread their critical views. Each state was to "put its own house in order," but international cooperation was neither needed nor desired.

By the twenty-first century, of course, much has changed. On the one hand, social problems of all sorts have proliferated wildly. No longer can inequality, oppression, or violations of rights be justified as "in the natural order of things" or "divinely ordained," and modern societies are filled with specialists of many stripes who make it their business to identify and publicize never-before-imagined problems. On the other hand, the ongoing integration of world society, and the thickening web of international organizations and social movements that cover the globe, have made it increasingly likely that social problems, new or old, will be cast in global terms and lifted up to the global agenda of major

IGOs and INGOs. Many INGOs in particular are dedicated to searching out problems and publicizing them so that IGOs, states, transnational corporations, and other INGOs will pay attention to them and begin to work toward global approaches to solving them.

What has emerged, then, is a global "civil society" largely analogous to the national civil societies that identify, publicize, and attempt to solve a growing array of social problems. As indicated in Part VI, by "civil society" we mean the vast network of organizations that are neither profit-oriented businesses nor government agencies. Operating "between states and markets," and often deliberately outside them, these organizations are usually voluntary associations with democratic structures and specific programs of action intended to meet the needs and interests of their members or effect change and improvement in some aspect of social life. They include charities, sports clubs, advocates for the homeless, women's rights groups, hobby associations, churches, endangered species protectors, and much more. Local and national organizations concentrate on local and national issues, but increasingly they are linked to INGOs and thereby to their counterparts in other countries. They thus form complex networks of ties, sharing information about problems, tactics, solutions, and coordinated action that can attract global attention to problems that appear to affect the entire globe or some large portion of it.

In this part we have chosen readings from a single sector of global civil society, environmentalism. By concentrating on environmentalism, we can illustrate some of the complex issues that arise when a social problem with far-reaching ramifications – for economic development, for the quality of life, for inequality, foreign investment, and interstate relations – enters the global arena and assumes a prominent place on the agenda of many global organizations. To a large extent, the messages these readings convey are applicable to many other global civil society sectors, such as those mentioned above dealing with human rights violations, inequality, political repression, and the subordination of women. Important differences will be found across these and other sectors, of course, and researchers are busily studying a great many sectors to learn more about the role of global civil society organizations in global governance (some examples are in Part VI).

It is tempting to believe that global civil society groups, most notably INGOs, hold out the promise of considerable progress in solving major social problems. Some successes are striking, such as the ability of two small but highly professional INGOs to win a 50-year moratorium on mineral exploitation in the 1991 revision of the Antarctic Treaty; the remarkable achievement of the International Campaign to Ban Landmines, a coalition of many INGOs and NGOs, in getting most countries of the world to agree to stop using or making anti-personnel mines; and the formation of the International Criminal Court, which was conceived and strongly pushed by a wide array of INGOs. Yet many problems are so large, and so deeply integrated into the structure of global economic and political development, that even modest improvements can come only over a period of decades. One critical issue is whether the global activists who make up the INGOs and NGOs working to ameliorate these stubbornly intractable problems will be able to sustain their efforts long enough to make a substantial difference. An equally critical issue, however, is whether world society will be able to avoid widespread catastrophes and collapses if they do not.

Our selections on world environmentalism begin with a statement from the influential World Commission on Environment and Development, established by the UN in 1983 as a body independent of states and even of the UN itself. The statement describes the successes and failures of global environmental action and the severe problems facing the world at the end of the twentieth century, making a plea for a model of "sustainable development" that balances economic growth with careful environmental management. We then present the final declaration from the 1992 Earth Summit, the world's largest IGO conference to date that was accompanied by the largest parallel nongovernmental conference ever. Though the principles enunciated in the declaration are stated in general and abstract terms, they spell out a high degree of responsibility for states and citizens to protect the natural environment from unregulated or careless development.

The selections by Paul Wapner, and by Margaret Keck and Kathryn Sikkink, analyze the impact of various nongovernmental groups in creating global concern about, and pressing for action on, the degradation and pollution of the natural world. Wapner discusses Greenpeace, which grew from a small band of activists protesting nuclear bomb tests in Alaska in 1969 to a massive transnational organization that can call on the contributions of millions of supporters to carry out a wide range of attention-grabbing actions all over the globe. Keck and Sikkink emphasize the growth and operation of environmental "advocacy networks" that link local NGOs and global INGOs in the effort to preserve the rainforests. We have chosen their discussion of the campaign in Sarawak, which was able to achieve some success but ultimately could not put an end to logging in this part of Borneo, because of the fine detail they provide about this case. Next, Abigail Abrash presents an in-depth study of local resistance to the operations of Freeport McMoRan, one of the largest mining companies in the world, in Irian Jaya (in Papua, a part of Indonesia). Two indigenous peoples, the Amungme and Kamoro, have struggled against Freeport and the Indonesian government to get compensation for the lands they have lost and to end the degradation of their remaining lands. This case has become something of a *cause célèbre* among environmentalists around the world, as it brings together many significant issues regarding the responsibility of companies toward not only the environment but also the people most directly affected by their activities.

In the last selection, prominent environmental analyst Wolfgang Sachs centers his discussion on the "image of the blue planet," that is, the Earth as seen from space. He identifies two increasingly irreconcilable interpretations associated with this powerful image: the environmentalist's sense of the finitude and limitations of the planet, which points to an ethic of conservation and careful stewardship; and corporate appropriation of the image to indicate the wonders of globally integrated technical, transportation, trade, and financial systems entailed in economic globalization. Sachs leads the reader to consider the global implications of everyday consumption activities and raises important questions about the prospects for sustainability – particularly in the developing countries, where an increasing share of "dirty" extractive and manufacturing industries are located – in a world of ever larger and more influential transnational corporations.

47 From One Earth to One World

World Commission on Environment and Development

In the middle of the twentieth century, we saw our planet from space for the first time. Historians may eventually find that this vision had a greater impact on thought than did the Copernican revolution of the sixteenth century, which upset the human self-image by revealing that the Earth is not the centre of the universe. From space, we see a small and fragile ball dominated not by human activity and edifice but by a pattern of clouds, oceans, greenery, and soils. Humanity's inability to fit its doings into that pattern is changing planetary systems, fundamentally. Many such changes are accompanied by life-threatening hazards. This new reality, from which there is no escape, must be recognized – and managed.

Fortunately, this new reality coincides with more positive developments new to this century. We can move information and goods faster around the globe than ever before; we can produce more food and more goods with less investment of resources; our technology and science gives us at least the potential to look deeper into and better understand natural systems. From space, we can see and study the Earth as an organism whose health depends on the health of all its parts. We have the power to reconcile human affairs with natural laws and to thrive in the process. In this our cultural and spiritual heritages can reinforce our economic interests and survival imperatives.

This Commission believes that people can build a future that is more prosperous, more just, and more secure. Our report, *Our Common Future*, is not a prediction of ever increasing environmental decay, poverty, and hardship in an ever more polluted world among ever decreasing resources. We see instead the possibility for a new era of economic growth, one that must be based on policies that sustain and expand the environmental resource base. And we believe such growth to be absolutely essential to relieve the great poverty that is deepening in much of the developing world.

But the Commission's hope for the future is conditional on decisive political action now to begin managing environmental resources to ensure both sustainable human progress and human survival. We are not forecasting a future; we are serving a notice – an urgent notice based on the latest and best scientific evidence – that the time has come to take the decisions needed to secure the resources to sustain this and coming generations. We do not offer a detailed blueprint for action, but instead a pathway by which the peoples of the world may enlarge their spheres of cooperation.

Original publication details: Excerpted from World Commission on Environment and Development, *Our Common Future* (Oxford University Press, 1987), pp. 1–9. Reprinted by permission of Oxford University Press.

The Global Challenge

Successes and failures

Those looking for success and signs of hope can find many: Infant mortality is falling; human life-expectancy is increasing; the proportion of the world's adults who can read and write is climbing; the proportion of children starting school is rising; and global food production increases faster than the population grows.

But the same processes that have produced these gains have given rise to trends that the planet and its people cannot long bear. These have traditionally been divided into failures of "development" and failures in the management of our human environment. On the development side, in terms of absolute numbers there are more hungry people in the world than ever before, and their numbers are increasing. So are the numbers who cannot read or write, the numbers without safe water or safe and sound homes, and the numbers short of woodfuel with which to cook and warm themselves. The gap between rich and poor nations is widening – not shrinking – and there is little prospect, given present trends and institutional arrangements, that this process will be reversed.

There are also environmental trends that threaten to radically alter the planet, that threaten the lives of many species upon it, including the human species. Each year another six million hectares of productive dryland turns into worthless desert. Over three decades, this would amount to an area roughly as large as Saudi Arabia. More than 11 million hectares of forests are destroyed yearly, and this, over three decades, would equal an area about the size of India. Much of this forest is converted to low-grade farmland unable to support the farmers who settle it. In Europe, acid precipitation kills forests and lakes and damages the artistic and architectural heritage of nations; it may have acidified vast tracts of soil beyond reasonable hope of repair. The burning of fossil fuels puts into the atmosphere carbon dioxide, which is causing gradual global warming. This "greenhouse effect" may by early next century have increased average global temperatures enough to shift agricultural production areas, raise sea levels to flood coastal cities, and disrupt national economies. Other industrial gases threaten to deplete the planet's protective ozone shield to such an extent that the number of human and animal cancers would rise sharply and the oceans' food chain would be disrupted. Industry and agriculture put toxic substances into the human food chain and into underground water tables beyond reach of cleansing.

There has been a growing realization in national governments and multilateral institutions that it is impossible to separate economic development issues from environment issues; many forms of development erode the environmental resources upon which they must be based, and environmental degradation can undermine economic development. Poverty is a major cause and effect of global environmental problems. It is therefore futile to attempt to deal with environmental problems without a broader perspective that encompasses the factors underlying world poverty and international inequality.

These concerns were behind the establishment in 1983 of the World Commission on Environment and Development by the UN General Assembly. The Commission is an independent body, linked to but outside the control of governments and the UN system. The Commission's mandate gave it three objectives: to re-examine the critical environment and development issues and to formulate realistic proposals for dealing with them; to propose new forms of international co-operation on these issues that will influence policies and events in the direction of needed changes; and to raise the levels of understanding and commitment to action of individuals, voluntary organizations, businesses, institutes, and governments.

Through our deliberations and the testimony of people at the public hearings we held on five continents, all the commissioners came to focus on one central theme: many present development trends leave increasing numbers of people poor and vulnerable, while at the same time degrading the environment. How can such development serve next century's world of twice as many people relying on the same environment? This realization broadened our view of development. We came to see it not in its restricted context of economic growth in developing countries. We came to see that a new development path was required, one that sustained human progress not just in a few places for a few years, but for the entire planet into the distant future. Thus "sustainable development" becomes a goal not just for the "developing" nations, but for industrial ones as well.

The interlocking crises

Until recently, the planet was a large world in which human activities and their effects were neatly compartmentalized within nations, within sectors (energy, agriculture, trade), and within broad areas of concern (environmental, economic, social). These compartments have begun to dissolve. This applies in particular to the various global "crises" that have seized public concern, particularly over the past decade. These are not separate crises: an environmental crisis, a development crisis, an energy crisis. They are all one.

The planet is passing through a period of dramatic growth and fundamental change. Our human world of 5 billion must make room in a finite environment for another human world. The population could stabilize at between 8 billion and 14 billion sometime next century, according to UN projections. More than 90 percent of the increase will occur in the poorest countries, and 90 percent of that growth in already bursting cities.

Economic activity has multiplied to create a $13 trillion world economy, and this could grow five- or tenfold in the coming half-century. Industrial production has grown more than fiftyfold over the past century, four-fifths of this growth since 1950. Such figures reflect and presage profound impacts upon the biosphere, as the world invests in houses, transport, farms, and industries. Much of the economic growth pulls raw material from forests, soils, seas, and waterways.

A mainspring of economic growth is new technology, and while this technology offers the potential for slowing the dangerously rapid consumption of finite resources, it also entails high risks, including new forms of pollution and the introduction to the planet of new variations of life forms that could change evolutionary pathways. Meanwhile, the industries most heavily reliant on environmental resources and most heavily polluting are growing most rapidly in the developing world, where there is both more urgency for growth and less capacity to minimize damaging side-effects.

These related changes have locked the global economy and global ecology together in new ways. We have in the past been concerned about the impacts of economic growth upon the environment. We are now forced to concern ourselves with the impacts of ecological stress – degradation of soils, water regimes, atmosphere, and forests – upon our economic prospects. We have in the more recent past been forced to face up to a sharp increase in economic interdependence among nations. We are now forced to accustom ourselves to an accelerating ecological interdependence among nations. Ecology and economy are becoming ever more interwoven – locally, regionally, nationally, and globally – into a seamless net of causes and effects.

Impoverishing the local resource base can impoverish wider areas: Deforestation by highland farmers causes flooding on lowland farms; factory pollution robs local fishermen of their catch. Such grim local cycles now operate nationally and regionally. Dryland degradation sends environmental refugees in their millions across national borders. Deforestation in Latin America and Asia is causing more floods, and more destructive floods, in downhill, downstream nations. Acid precipitation and nuclear fallout have spread across the borders of Europe. Similar phenomena are emerging on a global scale, such as global warming and loss of ozone. Internationally traded hazardous chemicals entering foods are themselves internationally traded. In the next century, the environmental pressure causing population movements may increase sharply, while barriers to that movement may be even firmer than they are now.

Over the past few decades, life-threatening environmental concerns have surfaced in the developing world. Countrysides are coming under pressure from increasing numbers of farmers and the landless. Cities are filling with people, cars, and factories. Yet at the same time these developing countries must operate in a world in which the resources gap between most developing and industrial nations is widening, in which the industrial world dominates in the rule-making of some key international bodies, and in which the industrial world has already used much of the planet's ecological capital. This inequality is the planet's main "environmental" problem; it is also its main "development" problem.

International economic relationships pose a particular problem for environmental management in many developing countries. Agriculture, forestry, energy production, and mining generate at least half the gross national product of many developing countries and account for even larger shares of livelihoods and employment. Exports of natural resources remain a large factor in their economies, especially for the least developed. Most of these countries face enormous economic pressures, both international and domestic, to overexploit their environmental resource base.

The recent crisis in Africa best and most tragically illustrates the ways in which economics and ecology can interact destructively and trip into disaster. Triggered by drought, its real causes lie deeper. They are to be found in part in national policies that gave too little attention, too late, to the needs of smallholder agriculture and to the threats posed by rapidly rising populations. Their roots extend also to a global economic system that takes more out of a poor continent than it puts in. Debts that they cannot pay force African nations relying on commodity sales to overuse their fragile soils, thus turning good land to desert. Trade barriers in the wealthy nations – and in many developing ones – make it hard for Africans to sell their goods for reasonable returns, putting yet more pressure on ecological systems. Aid from donor nations has not only been inadequate in scale, but too often has reflected the priorities of the nations giving the aid, rather than the needs of the recipients. The production base of other developing world areas suffers similarly both from local failures and from the workings of international economic systems. As a consequence of the "debt crisis" of Latin America, that region's natural resources are now being used not for development but to meet financial obligations to creditors abroad. This approach to the debt problem is short-sighted from several standpoints: economic, political, and environmental. It requires relatively poor countries simultaneously to accept growing poverty while exporting growing amounts of scarce resources.

A majority of developing countries now have lower per capita incomes than when the decade began. Rising poverty and unemployment have increased pressure on environmental resources as more people have been forced to rely more directly upon them. Many governments have cut back efforts to protect the environment and to bring ecological considerations into development planning.

The deepening and widening environmental crisis presents a threat to national security – and even survival – that may be greater than well-armed, ill-disposed neighbours and unfriendly alliances. Already in parts of Latin America, Asia, the Middle East, and Africa, environmental decline is becoming a source of political unrest and international tension. The recent destruction of much of Africa's dryland agricultural production was more severe than if an invading army had pursued a scorched-earth policy. Yet most of the affected governments still spend far more to protect their people from invading armies than from the invading desert.

Globally, military expenditures total about $1 trillion a year and continue to grow. In many countries, military spending consumes such a high proportion of gross national product that it itself does great damage to these societies' development efforts. Governments tend to base their approaches to "security" on traditional definitions. This is most obvious in the attempts to achieve security through the development of potentially planet-destroying nuclear weapons systems. Studies suggest that the cold and dark nuclear winter following even a limited nuclear war could destroy plant and animal ecosystems and leave any human survivors occupying a devastated planet very different from the one they inherited.

The arms race – in all parts of the world – pre-empts resources that might be used more productively to diminish the security threats created by environmental conflict and the resentments that are fuelled by widespread poverty.

Many present efforts to guard and maintain human progress, to meet human needs, and to realize human ambitions are simply unsustainable – in both the rich and poor nations. They draw too heavily, too quickly, on already overdrawn environmental resource accounts to be affordable far into the future without bankrupting those accounts. They may show profits on the balance sheets of our generation, but our children will inherit the losses. We borrow environmental capital from future generations with no intention or prospect of repaying. They may damn us for our spendthrift ways, but they can never collect on our debt to them. We act as we do because we can get away with it: future generations do not vote; they have no political or financial power; they cannot challenge our decisions.

But the results of the present profligacy are rapidly closing the options for future generations. Most of today's decision makers will be dead before the planet feels the heavier effects of acid precipitation, global warming, ozone depletion, or widespread desertification and species loss. Most of the young voters of today will still be alive. In the Commission's hearings it was the young, those who have the most to lose, who were the harshest critics of the planet's present management.

Sustainable development

Humanity has the ability to make development sustainable – to ensure that it meets the needs of the present without compromising the ability of future generations to

The World Commission on Environment and Development first met in October 1984, and published its report 900 days later, in April 1987. Over those few days:

- The drought-triggered, environment-development crisis in Africa peaked, putting 35 million people at risk, killing perhaps a million.
- A leak from a pesticides factory in Bhopal, India, killed more than 2,000 people and blinded and injured over 200,000 more.
- Liquid gas tanks exploded in Mexico City, killing 1,000 and leaving thousands more homeless.
- The Chernobyl nuclear reactor explosion sent nuclear fallout across Europe, increasing the risks of future human cancers.
- Agricultural chemicals, solvents, and mercury flowed into the Rhine River during a warehouse fire in Switzerland, killing millions of fish and threatening drinking water in the Federal Republic of Germany and the Netherlands.
- An estimated 60 million people died of diarrhoeal diseases related to unsafe drinking water and malnutrition; most of the victims were children.

The Commission has sought ways in which global development can be put on a sustainable path into the 21st century. Some 5,000 days will elapse between the publication of our report and the first day of the 21st century. What environmental crises lie in store over those 5,000 days?

During the 1970s, twice as many people suffered each year from "natural" disasters as during the 1960s. The disasters most directly associated with environment/development mismanagement – droughts and floods – affected the most people and increased most sharply in terms of numbers affected. Some 18.5 million people were affected by drought annually in the 1960s, 24.4 million in the 1970s. There were 5.2 million flood victims yearly in the 1960s, 15.4 million in the 1970s. Numbers of victims of cyclones and earthquakes also shot up as growing numbers of poor people built unsafe houses on dangerous ground.

The results are not in for the 1980s. But we have seen 35 million afflicted by drought in Africa alone and tens of millions affected by the better managed and thus less-publicized Indian drought. Floods have poured off the deforested Andes and Himalayas with increasing force. The 1980s seem destined to sweep this dire trend on into a crisis-filled 1990s.

meet their own needs. The concept of sustainable development does imply limits – not absolute limits but limitations imposed by the present state of technology and social organization on environmental resources and by the ability of the biosphere to absorb the effects of human activities. But technology and social organizations can be both managed and improved to make way for a new era of economic growth. The Commission believes that widespread poverty is no longer inevitable. Poverty is not only an evil in itself, but sustainable development requires meeting the basic needs of all and extending to all the opportunity to fulfil their aspirations for a better life. A world in which poverty is endemic will always be prone to ecological and other catastrophes.

Meeting essential needs requires not only a new era of economic growth for nations in which the majority are poor, but an assurance that those poor get their fair share of the resources required to sustain that growth. Such equity would be aided by political systems that secure effective citizen participation in decision making and by greater democracy in international decision making.

Sustainable global development requires that those who are more affluent adopt lifestyles within the planet's ecological means – in their use of energy, for example. Further, rapidly growing populations can increase the pressure on resources and slow any rise in living standards; thus sustainable development can only be pursued if population size and growth are in harmony with the changing productive potential of the ecosystem.

Yet in the end, sustainable development is not a fixed state of harmony, but rather a process of change in which the exploitation of resources, the direction of investments, the orientation of technological development, and institutional change are made consistent with future as well as present needs. We do not pretend that the process is easy or straightforward. Painful choices have to be made. Thus, in the final analysis, sustainable development must rest on political will. [. . .]

48 Rio Declaration on Environment and Development

UN Conference on Environment and Development

The UN Conference on Environment and Development,

Having met at Rio de Janeiro from 3 to 14 June 1992,

Reaffirming the Declaration of the United Nations Conference on the Human Environment, adopted at Stockholm on 16 June 1972, and seeking to build upon it,

With the goal of establishing a new and equitable global partnership through the creation of new levels of cooperation among States, key sectors of societies and people,

Working towards international agreements which respect the interests of all and protect the integrity of the global environmental and developmental system,

Recognizing the integral and interdependent nature of the Earth, our home,

Proclaims that:

Principle 1

Human beings are at the centre of concerns for sustainable development. They are entitled to a healthy and productive life in harmony with nature.

Principle 2

States have, in accordance with the Charter of the United Nations and the principles of international law, the sovereign right to exploit their own resources pursuant to their own environmental and developmental policies, and the responsibility to ensure that activities within their jurisdiction or control do not cause damage to the environment of other States or of areas beyond the limits of national jurisdiction.

Principle 3

The right to development must be fulfilled so as to equitably meet developmental and environmental needs of present and future generations.

Principle 4

In order to achieve sustainable development, environmental protection shall constitute an integral part of the development process and cannot be considered in isolation from it.

Original publication details: Excerpted from United Nations Conference on Environment and Development, "Rio Declaration on Environment and Development" and "Agenda 21" (1992), #1–25. Reprinted by permission of United Nations Publications.

Principle 5

All States and all people shall cooperate in the essential task of eradicating poverty as an indispensable requirement for sustainable development, in order to decrease the disparities in standards of living and better meet the needs of the majority of the people of the world.

Principle 6

The special situation and needs of developing countries, particularly the least developed and those most environmentally vulnerable, shall be given special priority. International actions in the field of environment and development should also address the interests and needs of all countries.

Principle 7

States shall cooperate in a spirit of global partnership to conserve, protect and restore the health and integrity of the Earth's ecosystem. In view of the different contributions to global environmental degradation, States have common but differentiated responsibilities. The developed countries acknowledge the responsibility that they bear in the international pursuit of sustainable development in view of the pressures their societies place on the global environment and of the technologies and financial resources they command.

Principle 8

To achieve sustainable development and a higher quality of life for all people, States should reduce and eliminate unsustainable patterns of production and consumption and promote appropriate demographic policies.

Principle 9

States should cooperate to strengthen endogenous capacity-building for sustainable development by improving scientific understanding through exchanges of scientific and technological knowledge, and by enhancing the development, adaptation, diffusion and transfer of technologies, including new and innovative technologies.

Principle 10

Environmental issues are best handled with the participation of all concerned citizens, at the relevant level. At the national level, each individual shall have appropriate access to information concerning the environment that is held by public authorities, including information on hazardous materials and activities in their communities, and the opportunity to participate in decision-making processes. States shall facilitate and encourage public awareness and participation by making information widely available. Effective access to judicial and administrative proceedings, including redress and remedy, shall be provided.

Principle 11

States shall enact effective environmental legislation. Environmental standards, management objectives and priorities should reflect the environmental and developmental context to which they apply. Standards applied by some countries may be inappropriate and of unwarranted economic and social cost to other countries, in particular developing countries.

Principle 12

States should cooperate to promote a supportive and open international economic system that would lead to economic growth and sustainable development in all countries, to better address the problems of environmental degradation. Trade policy measures for environmental purposes should not constitute a means of arbitrary or unjustifiable discrimination or a disguised restriction on international trade. Unilateral actions to deal with environmental challenges outside the jurisdiction of the importing country should be avoided. Environmental measures addressing transboundary or global environmental problems should, as far as possible, be based on an international consensus.

Principle 13

States shall develop national law regarding liability and compensation for the victims of pollution and other environmental damage. States shall also cooperate in an expeditious and more determined manner to develop further international law regarding liability and compensation for adverse effects of environmental damage caused by activities within their jurisdiction or control to areas beyond their jurisdiction.

Principle 14

States should effectively cooperate to discourage or prevent the relocation and transfer to other States of any activities and substances that cause severe environmental degradation or are found to be harmful to human health.

Principle 15

In order to protect the environment, the precautionary approach shall be widely applied by States according to their capabilities. Where there are threats of serious or irreversible damage, lack of full scientific certainty shall not be used as a reason for postponing cost-effective measures to prevent environmental degradation.

Principle 16

National authorities should endeavour to promote the internalization of environmental costs and the use of economic instruments, taking into account the approach that the polluter should, in principle, bear the cost of pollution, with due regard to the public interest and without distorting international trade and investment.

Principle 17

Environmental impact assessment, as a national instrument, shall be undertaken for proposed activities that are likely to have a significant adverse impact on the environment and are subject to a decision of a competent national authority.

Principle 18

States shall immediately notify other States of any natural disasters or other emergencies that are likely to produce sudden harmful effects on the environment of those States. Every effort shall be made by the international community to help States so afflicted.

Principle 19

States shall provide prior and timely notification and relevant information to potentially affected States on activities that may have a significant adverse transboundary environmental effect and shall consult with those States at an early stage and in good faith.

Principle 20

Women have a vital role in environmental management and development. Their full participation is therefore essential to achieve sustainable development.

Principle 21

The creativity, ideals and courage of the youth of the world should be mobilized to forge a global partnership in order to achieve sustainable development and ensure a better future for all.

Principle 22

Indigenous people and their communities and other local communities have a vital role in environmental management and development because of their knowledge and traditional practices. States should recognize and duly support their identity, culture and interests and enable their effective participation in the achievement of sustainable development.

Principle 23

The environment and natural resources of people under oppression, domination and occupation shall be protected.

Principle 24

Warfare is inherently destructive of sustainable development. States shall therefore respect international law providing protection for the environment in times of armed conflict and cooperate in its further development, as necessary.

Principle 25

Peace, development and environmental protection are interdependent and indivisible.

49   Greenpeace and Political Globalism

Paul Wapner

There are forces in the world which work, not in an arithmetical, but in a geometrical ratio of increase. Education, to use the expression of Plato, moves like a wheel with an ever multiplying rapidity. Nor can we say how great may be its influence, when it becomes universal.

Benjamin Jowett

Nonstate-oriented politics is nothing new. Since the dawn of social life, human beings have worked to shape and direct collective affairs independent of formal government. In recent years, however, scholars have begun thinking theoretically about this type of activity and, in so doing, have provided a degree of conceptual clarity to it. In particular, the contributions of social movement theory, post-structuralism, feminism, and critical thought have broadened understandings of power and thus have heightened our sensitivity to how politics takes place in the home, office, and marketplace, as well as in the halls of congresses and parliaments. Politics, in this sense, is much more subtle to notice than the conduct of governments but, according to proponents of these orientations, no less significant for political affairs.

It is with a more comprehensive notion of power that I wish to begin investigating the ways in which transnational environmental groups engage in world civic politics. By suspending judgment about what constitutes real politics, one can focus on diverse forms of agency that actually shape world environmental affairs. In this chapter, I describe the ways in which activists work outside of, around, or at the margins of governmental activity in their efforts to alleviate global environmental problems. This descriptive element will sensitize readers to genuinely alternative forms of political activism.

In addition to describing forms of nonstate environmental politics, one must still ask the political question about them: namely, do they make a difference? Does all the time, money, and human energy involved actually contribute to addressing and partly alleviating environmental problems? Specifically, in what ways does a non-state-oriented type of political action actually affect world environmental affairs? That activists employ such a politics is, as I will demonstrate, true; but does it really matter in terms of world politics? In this chapter, in addition to describing the work of transnational activists, I furnish evidence to suggest that their efforts actually do

Original publication details: Excerpted from Paul Wapner, "Greenpeace and Political Globalism," in Paul Wapner, *Environmental Activism and World Civic Politics*, pp. 41–3, 47–54. © 1996, State University of New York. Reprinted by permission of the State University of New York Press. All rights reserved.

matter in world political events. They create conditions that direct the actions of others within a world context.

To begin, I want to draw attention to a level of analysis that has a long history in the study of world politics but which is, at present, still underdeveloped and underappreciated. This is the level at which norms, values, and discourse operate in the global arena outside the domain of states. It is that dimension of world experience where widespread, shared understandings among people throughout the globe act as determinants for present conditions on the planet. It is part of, for want of a better phrase, the *cultural* school of thought which believes that ideas within societies at large structure human collective life. Working within this tradition, the key argument of this chapter is that transnational environmental groups contribute to addressing global environmental problems by heightening worldwide concern for the environment. They persuade vast numbers of people to care about and take actions to protect the earth's ecosystem. In short, they disseminate what I call an *ecological sensibility*. This serves an important political function in coming to terms with the environmental threat.

A sensibility operates as a political force insofar as it constrains and directs widespread behavior. It works at the ideational level to animate practices and is considered a form of *soft law* in contrast to the *hard law* of government directives, policies, and so forth. Scholars make it a habit of differentiating between hard and soft law insofar as they distinguish legal and cultural factors in their understanding of social change. On the one hand, there are those who claim that governmental action is the key to social change. Laws, policies, and directives drive social norms, and thus as they change, the entire configuration of social life will shift. Those who share this perspective see governmental action as the "base" with cultural and social life being the "superstructure." On the other hand, there are those who claim that social norms are central to social change. Governmental decrees, from this perspective, are not the source of change but merely reflections of it. Laws and policies arise out of, or give authoritative expression to, norms that already enjoy widespread acceptance. Scholars sharing this view see social norms as the "base" and governmental directives as the "superstructure."

Differentiating legal and cultural factors, while analytically helpful, is misguided when it forces a thinker to choose between them. When it comes to such large categories of social analysis, it is a mistake to assume that one dimension of social change is definitively more significant than the other. The obvious response to such differentiation is that both factors are important. Indeed, some argue that they are in dialectical relation to each other. As Christopher Stone writes, "in general, laws and cultural norms are mutually reinforcing. Formal laws arise from cultures, and command obedience in proportion to their coherence with the fundamental beliefs of the culture. Cultures, however, are not static. Law, and especially the activities of law making and legal reform, are among the forces that contribute to cultural evolution."

In this chapter, I do not weigh in on the ideational side and argue for its primacy nor celebrate the dialectical relationship. Rather, I simply emphasize the degree to which widely held conceptualizations animate large-scale practices and use this to show how efforts to disseminate an ecological sensibility have world political significance. What makes such efforts political, it should be clear, is not that they are ultimately codified into law or governmental decree but that they represent the use of power to influence and guide widespread behavior. An ecological sensibility, then, is not itself an answer to global environmental threats nor *the* agent for shifting one state of affairs to another. It is, however, an important part of any genuine response to environmental harm. Put simplistically for the moment, it creates an ideational context which inspires and motivates people to act in the service of environmental well-being and thus constitutes the milieu within which environmentally sound actions can arise and be undertaken. While not solely responsible for the *existence* of this sensibility, transnational environmental groups deserve substantial credit for *spreading* it throughout the world. [. . .]

Since 1972, Greenpeace has grown from having a single office in Vancouver to staffing offices in over thirty countries and, until recently, a base in Antarctica. Greenpeace has offices in the developed as well as the developing world, including Russia and Eastern Europe. Its eco-navy consists of eight ships, and it owns a helicopter and a hot-air balloon. It employs over 1,000 full-time staff members, plus hundreds of part-timers and thousands of volunteers. As of July 1994, it had over 6 million members worldwide and an estimated income of over $100 million. All money comes from voluntary donations, 90 percent of which is in the form of small contributions from individual members. Additionally, Greenpeace sends hundreds of canvassers out each night to raise funds and educate the general public about current environmental issues. Finally, it has expanded its area of concern. While originally focused on nuclear weapons testing, it is now concerned with all threats to the planetary ecosystem. In short, from 1972 to the present Greenpeace has grown into a full-scale, transnational environmental organization.

Transnational Organizational Structure

Greenpeace sees the bulk of global environmental problems falling into four categories: toxic substances, energy and atmosphere, nuclear issues, and ocean and terrestrial ecology. Greenpeace works for environmental protection by dividing its attention among these four issue areas, also called campaigns. Within each of these, Greenpeace works on numerous subissues. For example, under the rubric of its nuclear campaign, Greenpeace focuses on reprocessing and dumping of nuclear material, sea-based nuclear weapons and nuclear testing. Under the rubric of ocean ecology, Greenpeace concentrates on whales, sea turtles, fisheries, and dolphins.

As a transnational environmental group concerned with threats to the entire planet, Greenpeace undertakes its campaigns and projects worldwide. The problems associated with toxic substances, energy, and atmosphere and so forth are not limited to individual countries. Almost all parts of the world are vulnerable to the environmental consequences involved. Greenpeace is organized to allow it to address these dilemmas on a global scale.

The top tiers of the organization are made up of the Greenpeace Council, an executive board, and regional trustees. The council is made up of representatives from all the countries where Greenpeace has offices and meets once a year to decide on organizational policy. The council is one of the ways Greenpeace coordinates its diverse activities. The council sets guidelines for the general operation of Greenpeace, approves the international budget, and develops long-term goals. Because council members come from around the world, decisions can reflect a sensitivity to differing regional and local aspects of environmental problems. To provide greater efficiency in day-to-day operations, and to emphasize coordination among campaigns and projects, there is an executive board that ratifies all council resolutions and makes significant decisions for Greenpeace throughout the year when the council is not in session. The board consists of both voting and nonvoting members and is elected by the Greenpeace Council.

In addition to the council and the executive board, there are regional trustees that provide the final stamp of approval for Greenpeace's overall operations. Trustees are representatives of the areas of the world where Greenpeace has offices. These include Latin America, the Pacific, North America, and Europe. While the trustees generally approve all decisions put forward by the council and the executive board, it serves as the final arbiter of Greenpeace policies. Because individual trustees represent diverse regions of the world, as a whole the trustees advance a global rather than a national or even regional orientation within Greenpeace.

Aside from the council and executive board, Greenpeace organizes itself worldwide along the lines of its four campaign areas. Heading each campaign is an international coordinator. He or she designs the way specific campaigns play themselves out in different regional and national contexts. For example, the campaign coordinator of toxic substances orchestrates all Greenpeace projects that contribute to achieving the aims of the toxics campaign. She or he provides the global perspective to different projects.

Underneath international campaign coordinators are project directors. Project directors are scattered across the globe and work on subissues of the larger campaigns. For example, there are nine projects currently being undertaken by the toxics campaign. One of these focuses on the pulp and paper industry. The pulp and paper industry is responsible for 50 percent of all organchlorine discharges into the earth's waterways. Organchlorine is dangerous to both humans and the natural environment; it is known to cause sterility and cancer in mammals. The project's aim is to change the production process of the industry away from bleaching procedures that use chlorine. The bulk of the pulp and paper industry is located in a number of countries, and Greenpeace pursues the project in each of them. The project director oversees all these efforts. Project directors, like campaign coordinators, take a global perspective on their respective projects. They make sure that separate Greenpeace activities throughout the world support each other and fit together to advance the cause of their specific project.

Working under the project coordinators are regional and national campaigners. Campaigners devise specific Greenpeace activities. They identify what they take to be the most effective ways to communicate with people and change environmentally destructive practices. For purposes of this chapter, one should think of campaigners as organizers of concrete activities that aim to alter people's perceptions of particular environmental threats. To use the pulp and paper example, there are campaigners in a number of countries including the United States, Canada, Sweden, and Germany. Campaigners focus on the pulp and paper industries in their respective countries, taking into account the governmental, cultural, and industrial attributes of each country to address the problem. Regional and national campaigners are key to Greenpeace's global efforts because they understand the particular contexts within which environmental damage is being caused and fashion appropriate responses. They take the general intentions of projects and overall campaigns and translate them into concrete actions that are tailored for specific geographical and political contexts.

Working with campaigners are a host of assistants and volunteers who help carry out specific activities. There are literally thousands of these people throughout the world. They paint banners, circulate petitions, research issues, organize protests, and take part in direct, nonviolent actions. All levels of activity are designed, at least in theory, to advance the goals of specific campaigns.

Greenpeace's Politics

Key to all Greenpeace's efforts is the insight that people do not damage the ecosystem as a matter of course. Rather, they operate in an ideational context that motivates them to do so. People are not machines; they do not respond directly to situations. In the words of Harry Eckstein, people are moved by "predispositions which pattern behavior." In the language of social science, human behavior is a matter of "oriented action." People process experience into action through general conceptions or interpretations of the world. At the most general level, but also the most important, then, an important step toward protecting the earth is to change the way vast numbers of people understand the world. It involves persuading them to abandon their anti-ecological or non-ecological attitudes and practices, and to be concerned about the environmental well-being of the planet. In short, it requires disseminating an ecological sensibility.

People respond to situations through interpretive categories that reflect a particular understanding of everyday circumstances. Such mediating orientations are cultural in character. They reflect customary, socially transmitted understandings that are embedded in the prevailing values, norms, and modes of discourse. Greenpeace targets and tries to alter these dispositions. It literally attempts to manipulate values, norms, and modes of discourse; it seeks to alter people's conceptions of reality. Greenpeace hopes that in so doing, people will undertake actions that are more respectful of the ecological integrity of the planet.

Central to Greenpeace's efforts is the practice of "bearing witness." This is a type of political action, originating with the Quakers, which links moral sensitivities with political responsibility. Having observed a morally objectionable act, one cannot turn away in avoidance. One must either take action to prevent further injustice or stand by and attest to its occurrence. While bearing witness often works to stop specific instances of environmental destruction, in general, it aims simply to present ecological injustice to the world. This offers as many people as possible an alternative understanding of contemporary affairs and sets them in motion against such practices. One way Greenpeace does this is by engaging in direct, nonviolent action and advertising it through the media worldwide.

Direct, nonviolent action is a form of political practice that shares much with the passive resistance of Mahatma Gandhi and Martin Luther King. It is a vehicle for confrontation and an outreach to other citizens. For Greenpeace, such action includes climbing aboard whaling ships, parachuting from the top of smokestacks, plugging up industrial discharge pipes, and floating a hot-air balloon into a nuclear test site. Such actions create images that can be broadcasted through the media to spark interest and concern of the largest audience.

Greenpeace is able to capture media attention because its actions are visually spectacular. According to political theorist J. Glenn Gray, human beings have what the New Testament calls "the lust of the eye." This is a primitive urge for visual stimulation; it describes the aesthetic impulse. The urge is lustful because it requires the novel, the unusual, the spectacular. The eye cannot satiate itself on the familiar, the everyday, the normal. Greenpeace actions excite the eye. They portray people taking dangerous risks. These grab attention and thus receive media coverage. By offering spectacular images to the media, Greenpeace invites the public to bear witness; it enables people throughout the world to know about environmental dangers and tries to pique their sense of outrage.

A number of years ago it was difficult to use direct, nonviolent action to change political conditions around the globe. While direct action has always been a political tool for those seeking change, the technology did not exist to publicize specific actions to a global audience. Recent innovations in communication technologies have allowed information to whip around the globe within seconds, linking distant corners of the world. Greenpeace plugs into this planetwide communication system to advertise its direct actions.

For example, in the 1970s Greenpeace ships used Morse code to communicate with their offices on land. Information from sailing expeditions would be translated in a central office and then sent out to other offices and onto the media via the telephone. This was cumbersome and expensive and compromised much of the information that could prove persuasive to public audiences. After weeks at sea, ships would return with still photographs, and these would be the most convincing images Greenpeace could use to communicate about environmental destruction taking place on the high seas.

With the advent of affordable innovations in the field of communications, Greenpeace has been able to update its ability to reach diverse and numerous audiences. Instead of Morse code, Greenpeace ships now use telephones, fax machines, and satellite uplinks to communicate with home offices. This allows for instantaneous information to be communicated and verified. Moreover, Greenpeace uses video cameras to capture its actions. Footage can be taken of whaling expeditions, ocean dumping of nuclear wastes, and discharging of toxic substances into streams and waterways. This documents more accurately actual instances of environmental destruction and the risks that Greenpeace members undertake to protect the environment. Once Greenpeace has footage and photographs of such abuse, it sends them into peoples' homes across the world through the planetwide mass communication system. Greenpeace has its own media facilities and uses these to get its information out to the public. Aside from attracting journalists and television crews to their actions, Greenpeace provides its own photographs to picture editors and has facilities to distribute edited, scripted, and narrated video news spots to television stations in eighty-eight countries within hours.

To see how Greenpeace uses direct, nonviolent action to make the world bear witness, consider its whale campaign. For years, Greenpeace has been trying to preserve whale populations and guard them from extinction. This is part of a larger campaign to generate more awareness and concern for the mass depletion of species currently taking place throughout the world. One technique Greenpeace uses to do this is direct action on the high seas. In one of its early expeditions, for instance, Greenpeace sent a ship to pursue a Russian whaling fleet. One of Greenpeace's first actions was to document the fleet's activities. Greenpeace found that the Russians were killing whales that were smaller than the official allowable size, as designated by the International Whaling Commission. To record this, Greenpeace filmed the killing of an undersized whale and took still photographs of a human being perched over it to demonstrate that it was merely a whale calf. Greenpeace noticed, moreover, that the sheer size and capability of the fleet enabled it to take large catches and thus threaten the sperm whale population in the area. To dramatize this, Greenpeace members boarded inflatable dinghies and positioned themselves between harpoon ships and pods of whales. In essence, they tried to discourage harpooners from firing by threatening to die for the cause. This proved effective as numerous times Russian whalers did not shoot their harpoons for fear of killing Greenpeace members. What turned out to be crucial was that Greenpeace captured this on film. Footage was broadcasted on television stations and still photographs were reproduced in newspapers and magazines worldwide. Greenpeace has engaged in numerous similar actions since then and continues to use such strategies.

A second example of direct action is Greenpeace's campaign to stop ozone depletion. In 1989, Greenpeace members infiltrated a DuPont manufacturing plant in Deepwater, New Jersey. Activists climbed the plant's 180-foot water tower and hung a huge, blue-ribbon banner awarding DuPont a prize for being the world's number-one ozone destroyer. (At the time, DuPont produced half of the chlorofluorocarbons (CFCs) used in the US and 25 percent of world annual production.) The following day, Greenpeace bolted a steel box – with two people inside – onto the plant's railroad tracks and blocked the export of CFCs from the plant. Greenpeace draped the box with a banner that read, "Stop Ozone Destruction Now," with a picture of the earth in the background and used it to stage an 8-hour blockade holding up rail cars carrying 44,000 gallons of CFCs.

What is curious is that, according to Greenpeace, within minutes of removing the blockade, business proceeded as usual. The plant continued to function, producing and sending out substances that are proven to erode the stratospheric ozone layer. Nonetheless, something had happened in those brief 8 hours; something had changed. While DuPont workers continued to manufacture CFCs, they now did so knowing that others knew about and were concerned with the environmental effects. Moreover, because Greenpeace captured its actions on film and distributed video news spots to television stations throughout the world, vast numbers of people were now able to understand the connection between the production of CFCs and ozone depletion. In short, the utility of Greenpeace's activity in this case had less to do with the blocking action and more to do with the message that was conveyed. Greenpeace gave the ozone issue form and used the image of disrupting DuPont's operations to send out a message of concern. As Paul Watson, an early member of Greenpeace put it, "When you do an action it goes through the camera and into the minds of people. The things that were previously out of sight and out of mind now become commonplace. Therefore you use the media as a weapon."

Political Strategies

Greenpeace obviously does more than perform direct actions. It also lobbies government officials, gathers information, organizes protests and boycotts, produces record albums and other educational merchandise, and carries out scientific research. While many of these endeavors, especially lobbying, are directed specifically at states, a large percentage of Greenpeace's work is not meant to change states' policies per se but is aimed at changing the attitudes and behavior of the more general public. It seeks to change prevailing, and at times internationally shared, values, norms, and modes of discourse. It strives to "sting people with an ecological sensibility regardless of occupation, geographical location, or access to government officials. [. . .]

50 Environmental Advocacy Networks

Margaret E. Keck and Kathryn Sikkink

The Campaign against Deforestation in Sarawak

A case of deforestation that began to receive considerable attention in the late 1980s was the extremely rapid logging of tropical timber in the Malaysian state of Sarawak, on the island of Borneo. Logging had already decimated the forests of neighboring Sabah, but received little public attention. Sarawak was different, for three reasons: (1) a change in the international institutional context for discussion of tropical forestry issues, with establishment of the International Tropical Timber Organization, provided a new campaign focus, following upon a relatively successful effort to target a similar organization on the whaling issue; (2) strong connections between deforestation and native land rights issues brought environmental and indigenous rights campaigners together, especially in Europe, and the actions of Bruno Manser, an amateur anthropologist who had lived with a nomadic people in Sarawak called the Penan, dramatized their plight; and (3) the case was taken up vigorously by a Malaysian organization, Sahabat Alam Malaysia, that was already a member of Friends of the Earth International as well as several other mainly southern, transnational networks.

Background

Sarawak and Sabah are the two Malaysian states located on the northern coast of Borneo. They enjoy significant autonomy under the country's federal system, with the ability to control customs, civil service, and immigration (Sarawak requires a passport for visitors from peninsular Malaysia). Sarawak also controls the revenues from timber concessions, the result of an agreement at the time of joining the federation that gave peninsular Malaysia, in return, control over oil revenues. As a result of this deal, the federal government in Kuala Lumpur has been able to deny responsibility for logging practices in Sarawak.

With the exception of a severe recession in 1986, Malaysia's GNP has grown at 6–8 percent per annum since the early 1970s. A series of five-year plans have worked toward the goal, articulated in Prime Minister Mahathir Mohamad's "Vision 2020" program, of being a fully industrialized economy by the year 2020. Industry currently represents around 70 percent of the nation's exports. Timber is second to oil as a revenue producer in the primary sector.

Original publication details: Excerpted from Margaret E. Keck and Kathryn Sikkink, "Environmental Advocacy Networks," in Margaret E. Keck and Kathryn Sikkink (eds.), *Activists Beyond Borders: Advocacy Networks in International Politics* (Cornell University Press, 1998), pp. 150–62. Copyright © 1998 by Cornell University. Used by permission of the publisher, Cornell University Press.

The country is a multi-ethnic state. The shadow of ethnic conflict has hung heavily over Malaysia since an explosion of violence in 1969. Although preferential treatment is given to Malays, the benefits of development are very widely distributed. Given the image of rapid modernization which is currently a central component of Malaysia's political identity, the idea that Dayak (indigenous) land rights should be secured in part to preserve traditional lifeways commonly portrayed as backward does not fit with the image of a country racing toward the twenty-first century. Malaysia has been ruled by a large multi-party coalition headed by the UMNO-Baru (United Malays National Organization), a Muslim–Malay party, since independence in 1957, and overtly ethnic politics is seen by dominant groups as potentially destabilizing.

Logging in peninsular Malaysia declined significantly between 1975 and 1985 as a conservationist National Forestry Policy (which does not affect Sarawak and Sabah) came into effect. At the same time, log output in Sarawak increased from 4.4 million cubic meters in 1976 to 12.2 million in 1985. Although in theory logging in Sarawak was tightly controlled from the outset, enforcement has been practically nonexistent; both the geographical constraints of hill logging and the economic incentives for cutting beyond the targets are very strong. Briefly, timber concessions under the control of state politicians are granted (sold) for short-term logging licences to timber companies, whose motivation to log selectively and with care in areas designated for protection is virtually nil.

Logging decimated traditional forms of livelihood, meanwhile accelerating the integration of Dayak communities into the state's cash economy. Although logging brought short-term jobs to native communities, it eroded soils, polluted rivers and reduced fish stocks, eliminated wildlife formerly hunted for food, and increased flooding. Employment benefits ended when the logging companies moved on to the next area. Attempts by Dayak communities to gain the rights to log in their own areas have been unsuccessful, as have most attempts to have areas declared communal forests and thus protected from the loggers. Making land rights effective has been a losing struggle in the state. Logging hit especially hard for the still partially nomadic Penan people of the Baram region, for whom the forest provided food and home.

Dayak resistance came to international attention beginning in March 1987, when the Penan set up barricades on logging roads in the Upper Baram. Use of this tactic quickly spread throughout the region to other Dayak groups (the Kenyah, Kayan, Lambawang, and Kelabit). Activities in at least sixteen logging camps were halted. Although this is not the first time that barricades were used against loggers, it is the first time they were part of a sustained campaign, and the first time the resistance received so much attention.

What elements projected the Sarawak conflicts onto a broader stage in 1987? First, interrelated political crises at the national and state levels amplified their importance. Malaysia had undergone a severe recession in 1986, with per capita income declining by 15.7 percent. Criticism of the government became pervasive both in the governing coalition and the opposition, mainly concerning access to decision-making. Within Sarawak, rising Dayak nationalism since 1983 had spawned the first explicitly ethnic political party in the state (Parti Bansa Dayak Sarawak – PBDS). Prime Minister Mahathir began to fear for his coalition. In addition, by early March 1987 Sarawak was in the midst of its own political crisis, significant for the present story because of revelations about official corruption in granting timber concessions. This multifaceted crisis formed the backdrop for the logging blockades.

Second, tropical forests had become increasingly visible on the international agenda by the mid-1980s. In March 1983 sixty-four countries had agreed to establish an International Tropical Timber Organization (ITTO). Composed of producers and consumers of tropical timber, the new group was given a mandate to consider global resource management issues. Then in 1985, declared the International Year of the Forest, the UN Food and Agriculture Organization, the World Bank, and the UN Development Program, working with the World Resources Institute, produced the Tropical Forestry Action Plan and published "Tropical Forests: A Call for Action." The resulting International Tropical Forest Timber Agreement and Action Plan, passed in June 1986 in Geneva, was to be implemented by the International Tropical Timber Organization, headquartered in Yokohama, Japan. The ITTO council met for the first time in March 1987, at the same time that the blockades of logging roads began to spread throughout the Baram region of Sarawak. [. . .]

The third factor that brought Sarawak logging wide attention was that local protests were linked to international publics through two different network nodes. One was the charismatic (and enigmatic) Bruno Manser, a Swiss national who had lived with the Penan for a number of years and who apparently helped to organize the blockade; and the other was Sahabat Alam Malaysia, one of a set of interrelated organizations based in Penang. Involved in a variety of environmental campaigns in peninsular Malaysia, SAM had an office in Marudi, Sarawak, run by Harrison Ngau, a Kayan from the Baram region. SAM was also the Malaysian member of Friends of the Earth International. SAM provided logistical support for the blockades, and arranged for twelve native representatives to go to Kuala Lumpur, where they met with the acting prime minister and a variety of high government officials. Although Dayak customary rights to land were recognized in law, the state government continued to violate them.

Before the blockades in 1987, forest campaigners had already begun to mount an international campaign involving deforestation in the region. At a meeting of FOE International in Penang in September 1986, everyone was looking for a way to influence the tropical timber trade, especially with regard to Japan. FOE–UK promoted the view that a campaign needed an institutional lever such as International Tropical Timber Organization. Experience with the International Whaling Commission in the antiwhaling campaign was undoubtedly a factor in that assessment. Others preferred to work for export bans and timber boycotts. Although organizations in the network concentrated on different aspects of the campaign, these were not seen as mutually exclusive. [. . .]

Despite passages of a forest amendment bill in late 1987 that made interfering with logging operations a criminal act punishable with a heavy fine and imprisonment, the blockades were repeated. From 1988 into the 1990s, they offered a powerful symbol of resistance and a continuing stimulus to network activities though they were of little value in producing concessions from state officials. Although the Penan Association and longhouse organizations continued to try to gain land titles or communal forest designations, the logging went on.

Framing the Sarawak conflict

The Sarawak campaign has different meanings for different groups of proponents. For people influenced by the experiences of Bruno Manser, who emerged from his hiding place in the forest and somehow returned to Europe in 1990, the nomadic

Penan tribesmen were the symbolic center of the story. Organizing with the Penan at the center has created powerful images of an exotic and lost people fighting a heroic battle for the forest in the interest, it is implied, of all of us. Not surprisingly, this vision of the conflict has generated the most powerful media images. Filmmakers, journalists, and photographers have in the main placed the Penan at the center of their accounts. Although the Penan are indeed an important part of the Sarawak story, several other frames have produced different kinds of strategies and engaged different constellations of actors.

Some organizations, including the World Rainforest Movement's Forest Peoples' Program, SAM, Survival International, and *The Ecologist*, have placed primary emphasis on indigenous land rights, which is also a central issue in Evelyne Hong's influential book *Natives of Sarawak*. Without secure land title, they argue, the structural inequalities that prevent Dayak populations from resisting timber interests can never be addressed. This cogent vision of the problem is less resonant internationally than the Penan story, and one with which transnational networks have more difficulty organizing. The causal chain is fairly long, and the remedies difficult to devise.

The other main transnational strategy that emerged from the Sarawak case was its embedding in a broader campaign around tropical or rainforest timber (and in some cases temperate and boreal timber as well). This decentralized strategy has allowed space for considerable variation in organizational activities. Its main components have been consumer boycotts, targeting corporations and particular kinds of businesses (Mitsubishi, Do-it-Yourself stores, for example), persuading local or state governments to refrain from using tropical timber in construction projects, pressuring national governments and the European Union for tropical timber bans, pressuring ITTO members to develop sustainability requirements, and, increasingly, "eco-labeling." A large number of organizations have adopted these strategies, shared information, and collaborated on certain activities, though sometimes disagreeing over where to direct energies at particular stages.

This campaign involves a number of loosely connected subcampaigns with different organizational sponsors. A central role, though not always a coordinating one, has belonged to the constellation of organizations headquartered in Penang – SAM, the Asian-Pacific People's Environmental Network, the Third World Network, and the World Rainforest Movement. By the early 1990s the campaign was focused on logging in Papua New Guinea, Guyana, and Brazil (in all of which Sarawak logging companies have expanded their operations). [. . .]

Campaign strategies around Sarawak's forests

The Sarawak campaign's efforts to set in motion a boomerang strategy had some effect, but fell far short of success. From taking Dayak representatives to meet with officials in Kuala Lumpur and foreign capitals to contesting the information Malaysian representatives presented in international forums, the network mobilized vast quantities of information and testimony. Repeated barricades of logging roads were powerful symbols of resistance. Demanding that the Malaysian federal government intervene to control or block log exports from Sarawak, the network hoped to exert moral leverage. No effective material leverage was available – no World Bank loans in relevant areas, for example, or strategically placed aid programs. However, because Malaysia aspired to leadership in the Southeast Asian region, the idea that it would respond to moral leverage seemed a credible one. Moral leverage proved insufficient, however, to overcome Prime Minister Mahathir's dependence on the votes of Sarawak's political elites to maintain his broad coalition government. Moreover, there is some evidence that Mahathir's willingness to stand up to US and European critics on this issue may even have enhanced his regional prestige.

Beyond the matter of leverage, however, the tropical timber campaign implicitly proposed a different kind of relationship between north and south than existed in the Brazilian case. From the perspective of most of the Sarawak campaigners, the blame for overexploitation of timber in the region belonged even more to importers than it did to the exporter. Without demand, went the argument, there would be no supply. Thus the campaign was framed and focused quite differently from those waged around World Bank projects; instead of focusing the energies of activists in developed countries on a developing country target, it asked them to target their efforts at home.

The reasons for the difference were both ideological and logistical. First, there was no single source of leverage that provided the same purchase over the Sarawak situation that the World Bank seemed to offer in Rondônia. The central government's insistence that it had no authority over timber extraction in Sarawak was not a fiction; the tradeoff between centralizing oil revenues and leaving timber revenues to the states of East Malaysia had been a crucial compromise at the time of federation. For Sarawak's politicians, growing rich from timber concessions, there was simply no incentive – positive or negative – to stop logging. Because of Mahathir's dependence on a very broad coalition, the political costs of attempting to intervene might have been very high. Furthermore, the Malaysian NGOs that provided the bridge between the Dayak populations in Sarawak and the transnational network were not anti-development – though they wanted to see development's fruits distributed more justly – and believed that first-world governments and NGOs should not use the environmental issue as a weapon to prevent third-world countries from developing autonomously. This argument was especially salient in international debates during the preparatory process for the 1992 UN Conference on Environment and Development in Rio de Janeiro. The tropical timber campaign therefore focused attention on the industrialized world, that rabidly consumed Sarawak's tropical hardwoods.

The tropical timber campaign and its effects

Campaigning around tropical timber had the advantage of decentralization, which allowed for a variety of activities and styles – from Rainforest Action Network activists climbing Mitsubishi office buildings to hang boycott banners and parading with huge Godzilla figures to protest Japanese tropical hardwood imports, to WWF's more sober negotiations over sustainability guidelines with corporations.

Organizations in Germany, the United Kingdom, and the Netherlands launched boycotts in 1988. On a motion from a Dutch Green party delegate, the European Parliament voted in 1988 to recommend Malaysian timber bans to European Union (EU) members until its logging became sustainable. The EU Commission subsequently overturned that recommendation, but as a symbol of protest it garnered much publicity. In May 1989 Australia's Rainforest Action Group, which had already called for a boycott, deployed swimmers and kayaks to Malaysian timber-bearing ships. The Rainforest Action Network in the United States declared a boycott of Mitsubishi, and Friends of the Earth did the same in Europe.

In addition to corporate boycotts, environmental organizations organized hundreds of local government boycotts of the use of tropical timber in municipal construction. This strategy was very successful in Europe; by November 1990 local boycotts had so incensed Malaysians and Indonesians that they threatened trade retaliations. In 1993 and 1994 Japanese activists stepped up a similar local campaign.

These protests had little effect on logging. In 1990, timber operators in Sarawak cut a record eighteen million cubic meters of tropical hardwood logs. In early 1990, angry at foreign pressure, the Malaysian government had asked the ITTO to assess the question of sustainability. The ITTO team reported in May 1990 that Sarawak was logging at eight to ten times a sustainable level. The report recommended a reduction in log output by 1.5 million cubic meters a year. In 1992 the Sarawak government claimed it would comply with the recommendation, but regulations continued to be weakly enforced, and illegal logging is common.

But the trade issue had clearly become a serious one. In October 1991 Prime Minister Mahathir gave the keynote address at the meeting of the Association of Southeast Asian Nations (ASEAN) economy ministers, saying that ASEAN countries must speak with one voice against campaigns linking trade and environmental issues, and that the threats these posed to development had reached serious proportions. [. . .]

Measuring the impact of the tropical timber campaign requires that we define clearly the goals the campaign intended to reach. For those who wanted to preserve the nomadic lifeways of the Penan and the forest in which they lived, the campaign failed. Only a few hundred Penan remain in the forest. The rest live in longhouses, many work in timber camps and others suffer from the chronic unemployment that has beset communities throughout the region as the loggers move on. For those who wanted to fuel a struggle for land rights, the campaign continues. SAM has helped to organize several hundred community associations, for which security of tenure remains the precondition for any kind of community development activity. Although the transnational network does not exert direct leverage over this question, the campaign nonetheless provides some degree of protection to local efforts. For those who wanted to stop tropical timber logging in Sarawak, the campaign also failed. Sarawak will be logged out in five years, and Sarawakian timber companies are now repeating the process in Guyana and Papua New Guinea. The substantive goals of the Sarawak campaign, in other words, were not met.

In some respects, though, the efforts of the NGO networks and activists were remarkably successful. The Malaysian newspaper *Business Times* reported in October 1995, "Malaysia's timber exports to Europe have fallen by half since 1992 due to pressures from environmental groups on local and municipal governments in Europe to boycott or ban tropical timber products." Tropical timber imports into the Netherlands fell by 50 percent between 1990 and 1995, "mainly as a result of an NGO boycott campaign." Everyone seems to agree that the campaign succeeded in reducing consumption of tropical timber in some of the major importing countries.

If we see the tropical timber campaign as pursuing procedural rather than substantive goals, that is, a change in the international timber trading regime, then it has had some limited success. Campaign activities raised the salience of the issue and eventually placed it on the trade agenda. Unlike subsequent environmentalist attempts to use the trade agenda, as in the dispute over the effects of tuna fishing on dolphins, a forum was in place in which the issues could be ajudicated – the ITTO.

Within the ITTO, beyond pressuring the institution to send investigative missions to logging areas and holding states accountable to their commitments, activists in the network have forced debates on the social dimensions of logging and on customary and common property arrangements. However, the new international tropical timber agreement negotiated in 1994 was far weaker than expected. [. . .]

Conclusions

More than other network campaigns, rainforest campaigns are built on the tensions between recognizing structural causes and designing strategies that seek remedies by placing blame on, and influencing the behavior of, particular actors. Furthermore, the struggles they entail over meaning, power, and access to resources highlight the north–south dimension found in many network campaigns. The campaigns include participants whose understandings have been changed by their ongoing conversation with what anthropologist Anna Tsing calls people in out-of-the-way-places. And, since these are stories about the real world, the campaigns include participants whose understandings have not been changed at all.

Environmental advocacy networks have not so much gotten the tropical forest issue onto the agenda – it was already there – as they have changed the tone of the debate. To the frequent consternation of the epistemic community of scientists and policymakers who had succeeded in placing it on the agenda initially, the advocacy networks deliberately politicized the issues. While the epistemic community had sought to design sound policies and tried on the basis of their authoritative knowledge to persuade governments to adopt them, advocacy networks looked for leverage over actors and institutions capable of making the desired changes. Advocacy networks also insisted on different criteria of expertise. Although they did not deny the expertise of the scientists, they demanded equal time for direct testimony about experience. And within the networks they also cultivated the strategic expertise of good organizers. The issue, especially for the multilateral bank campaigners, was not ultimately forests, or dams, or any other particular environmental issue, but leverage over institutions that make a difference.

The advocacy networks helped to broaden the definition of which information and whose knowledge should shape the agenda on tropical forest issues. In the process, they won seats at the bargaining table for new actors. Their campaigns created a new script for sustainable forest management projects, with roles for "local people," "NGOs," and so forth. We must be careful not to exaggerate the power of the individuals and groups that play these roles, relative to that of states, economic actors like corporations, or multilateral organizations (the Planafloro deliberative council is a good example). Nonetheless, once these roles have been legitimized, organizations like the World Bank must address them.

How much change have transnational advocacy networks produced in the tropical forest issue? Because the networks are not the only reform-minded actors engaged, exact attributions of influence are difficult. The multilateral development bank campaign would certainly not have had much success without the collaboration of network members inside the bank. At the levels of both discursive and procedural change the network has been remarkably successful. Multilateral development banks increasingly claim to be addressing environmental objectives in loans, and there is some evidence that they have begun to eliminate high-risk projects much earlier in the project evaluation cycle. Besides having adopted the discourse of sustainable development, the bank has also implemented important procedural changes, including the information policy. Under increased pressure from the United States after the 1989 Pelosi amendment, all of the multilateral banks are taking the environmental assessment process more seriously.

Similarly, though less dramatically, the tropical timber campaign has had considerable success in promoting discursive change and some success with procedural change as well. Malaysia, as well as other tropical forest states, has begun at least to use the discourse of sustainable forestry, whether or not much has changed in practice. Malaysia has also adopted action plans phasing out unsustainable logging, and has begun to encourage local wood processing. The ITTO has adopted somewhat more stringent standards for movement toward demonstrably sustainable forestry practices. Green labeling, about which forest campaign advocates are quite divided, has not yet proved itself; should it change behavior in the ways that its proponents hope, this may stimulate further steps from the ITTO.

Among the people whose testimony generated the sharpest images of the impact of deforestation on lives, signs of success are harder to find. In Sarawak the transnational advocacy campaign has had very little impact. Logging goes on with its ecological and human impacts. [. . .]

51 The Amungme, Kamoro & Freeport: How Indigenous Papuans Have Resisted the World's Largest Gold and Copper Mine

Abigail Abrash

The story of the Amungme and Kamoro peoples and U.S. mining corporation Freeport McMoRan Copper & Gold ("Freeport") offers one of the best-documented examples of how local communities have experienced and resisted the seizure of their traditional lands by government-backed multinational mining enterprises.

The Amungme and Kamoro are the original indigenous landowners of the areas that now comprise Freeport's copper and gold mining operations and infrastructure in the Timika area of Papua (Irian Jaya/West Papua), Indonesia. At the time of Freeport's arrival in 1967, the two communities numbered several thousand people, organized in clan-based village social and governance structures. With lands encompassing the area's tropical rainforest, coastal lowlands, and glacial mountains and river valleys, the Kamoro (lowlanders) and Amungme (highlanders) practiced a subsistence economy based on sustainable agriculture and forest products, fishing, and hunting; their cultures intimately entwined with the surrounding landscape.

Westerners and other outsiders had visited Kamoro and Amungme lands prior to Freeport's arrival. These included, during the twentieth century, British naturalist expeditions, mountaineering teams, Japanese troops, Catholic and Protestant missionaries, and officials of the Dutch colonial administration. Unlike previous visitors to the area, however, Freeport's presence caused a massive, permanent, and escalating disruption to the lives of the Amungme and Kamoro.

Alien Invasion

Freeport's seizure, control, and despoilation of Kamoro and Amungme lands and natural resources has circumscribed or destroyed local communities' economies and livelihoods, and caused the internal displacement – often forcibly – of entire villages. The Amungme and Kamoro have been further displaced and marginalized – economically, politically, socially, and culturally – by the outsiders who swarmed to

Original publication details: Excerpted from Abigail Abrash, "The Amungme, Kamoro & Freeport: How Indigenous Papuans Have Resisted the World's Largest Gold and Copper Mine," *Cultural Survival Quarterly*, Spring 2001. Reprinted by permission of Cultural Survival.

the economic "boom" town created by the mine and its infrastructure. The new arrivals include thousands of primarily Javanese settlers sponsored by the Indonesian government's discredited transmigration program, "spontaneous" migrants such as traders from Sulawesi, thousands of Papuans from other parts of the territory, and North American and Australian employees of Freeport. By the 1990s, the area's population had exploded to more than 60,000 people, making Timika the fastest-growing "economic zone" in the entire Indonesian archipelago.

In defense of their lands, lives, and livelihoods, community members have protested Freeport's uninvited invasion and occupation – and the overwhelming influx of migrants and often-brutal Indonesian military force accompanying it – using a variety of nonviolent strategies and tactics grounded in strong community organizing.

The fact that their struggle continues, now in its fourth decade, underscores the urgent need for more successful mechanisms for safeguarding the rights of indigenous communities who face assaults by large-scale mining operations in Indonesia and worldwide. [. . .]

Seeds of Conflict

The Amungme and Kamoro tell us that their conflict with Freeport began, in 1967, with the company's confiscation of indigenous communities' territory without consultation with or consent by local landowners.

The 1967 COW [contract], drafted by Freeport, gave the company broad powers over the local population and resources, including the right to take, on a tax-free basis, land, timber, water, and other natural resources, and to resettle indigenous inhabitants while providing "reasonable compensation" only for dwellings and permanent improvements.

Freeport was not required to compensate the Amungme and Kamoro for the loss of their food gardens, hunting and fishing grounds, drinking water, forest products, sacred sites, and other elements of the natural environment upon which their cultures and livelihoods depend. Under the new Indonesian regime, the indigenous population had no rights of refusal or of informed consent, nor any right to adequate compensation. A sign of the time, no social or environmental impact assessment was done.

The Amungme have themselves emphasized their respect for the land. One Amungme author writes, "[The Amungme's] respect toward nature restrains them from causing any destruction to their environment. To destroy the environment is akin to their [own] destruction." He states, "To the Amungme, the most important thing is to maintain the harmony among the three elements of life: humankind, the natural environment, and the spirit of the ancestors." Another Amungme declares, "The land is ourselves. The land is our mother." Amungme cosmology depicts the mountain that Freeport is mining as the sacred head of their mother and its rivers as her milk. To the Amungme, Freeport's mining activities are killing their mother and polluting the milk on which they depend for sustenance.

Disregarding indigenous Papuans' deeply held connections to and reliance upon the natural environment, the dominant powers – Freeport and the Indonesian central government, military, and police – have imposed a cash/wage-economy paradigm in which land and other resources are exploitable commodities. Subsumed into a capitalist, consumer-oriented, earth-exploiting system in which "property rights" and "freedom of choice" are doctrine, the Amungme and Kamoro have discovered that the system offers them neither.

As in other countries, Indonesia's national laws do not comply with international human rights standards; they offer no adequate respect for community land rights and no effective protection for traditional livelihoods and cultures. The legal regime governing authority over land, water, and other natural resources grants near-total control to the state government. This system has siphoned the vast majority of short-term resource profits to foreign stockholders and the national elite, leaving local people dispossessed, displaced, and marginalized.

Indonesian authorities have treated opposition to economic "development" as a crime of subversion, often acting with aggression against indigenous communities seeking to retain their customary lands or to participate in decision-making regarding use or management of natural resources.

Human Rights Concerns

In order to fight local Papuan resistance in obscurity, the Indonesian government has vigorously obstructed international scrutiny of human rights conditions in the Freeport COW areas (and Papua, generally). It has repeatedly blocked access by human rights monitors, including the U.N. Working Group on Arbitrary Detention (1999), the U.N. Special Rapporteur on Violence Against Women (1998), and a joint NGO Indonesian-international independent assessment team (1999).

While research remains incomplete, well-documented evidence of human rights abuses against the indigenous Papuan communities in Freeport's COW areas has included:

- Torture; rape; indiscriminate, summary, and extrajudicial killings; disappearances; arbitrary detention; surveillance and intimidation; employment discrimination; and severe restrictions on freedom of movement;
- Interference with access to legal representation;
- Violation of subsistence and livelihood rights resulting from seizure and destruction of thousands of acres of rainforest – including community hunting grounds and forest gardens – and contamination of water supplies and fishing grounds;
- Violation of cultural rights, including the destruction of a mountain and other spiritually significant sites held sacred by the Amungme; and
- Forced resettlement of communities and destruction of housing, churches, and other shelters.

Some of these violations – such as those caused by environmental destruction – are the by-products of Freeport's mining operations. Others – such as physical attacks – are the results of the illegal, indiscriminate, and disproportionate use of force against civilians by the Indonesian military and police. [. . .]

Defending their Rights

The earliest Amungme protests against Freeport involved, in 1967, positioning of traditional taboo sticks around Freeport's highlands base camp. Later acts have included public demonstrations, sit-ins, and raisings of the Papuan national independence Morning Star flag, adopted in 1961 by the territory's elected New Guinea Council.

Community members have also repeatedly sought to resolve problems through open dialogue. Seven years after Freeport's arrival, for example, Amungme, Freeport, and the provincial government met – at the insistence of the Amungme community – to discuss local concerns. This meeting resulted in the 1974 January Agreement, in which Freeport pledged to construct facilities, including a school and health clinic, for those communities in exchange for approval by indigenous landowners of mining activities.

A lack of transparency in the land acquisition process continued, however. Kamoro and Amungme leaders report that as late as 1995, community members understood for the first time that according to government records they had ceded all ancestral lands in the Timika area (nearly one million hectares) to the government for transmigration settlements, the town of Timika, and Freeport's company town, Kuala Kencana.

Dissatisfied with the dominant powers' commitment to addressing their concerns, Amungme community members in 1996 brought two civil lawsuits against Freeport in the United States, one in U.S. federal court, the other in the state court of Louisiana, where Freeport is headquartered. Filed on grounds of human rights abuse, personal injury, environmental damages, and cultural genocide, the suits were ultimately unsuccessful. Still, thousands of indigenous community members formally supported the suits, viewing them as the only available means of effective legal redress.

The Amungme and Kamoro have increasingly sought to defend their rights by chronicling and communicating their concerns and demands in a variety of letters, resolutions, public statements, and media interviews. They have appealed to the Indonesian government, military, and civil society institutions, the U.N., U.S. courts and policy-makers, and directly to Freeport and Rio Tinto management and shareholders in an effort to be heard and to have their concerns effectively addressed.

They have expressed clear demands:

- compensation by Freeport for all lands that have been confiscated;
- independent environmental and human rights assessments to determine the extent of damages;
- accountability for military personnel who have perpetrated human rights abuses;
- explanations by Freeport and the Indonesian government of the company's mining plans and activities under its COW;
- community-led development programs;
- cessation by the government of the transmigration program and of "spontaneous" migration;
- responsibility by Freeport for reclamation of land degraded by mining activities;
- cessation by Freeport of tailings deposition into local river systems;
- compensation to the communities by Freeport for pollution-related suffering;
- cessation by the government of military involvement in the management of natural resources;
- compensation by the government for past losses suffered as a result of land seizures and exploitation of Amungme lands;
- the return by the government and Freeport of traditional Amungme lands confiscated without the community's permission; and
- Amungme permission and consent for all activity on Amungme land. This includes sitting on Freeport's Board of Directors and participating in shareholder meetings.

The response, by the Indonesian government and by Freeport, has been inadequate. [. . .]

Community Development?

As noted, a fundamental source of conflict between the Amungme, Kamoro, and Freeport has been the exclusion of local people from the economic, political, environmental, social and cultural decisions that affect their lives. Rather than recognizing the Kamoro and Amungme as original landowners and local sovereigns – or even working with them as equal partners – Freeport and the Indonesian government have treated community members like criminals, serfs, or nuisances. Viewing them as "backward" people without skills or rights, the dominant powers have too often responded to community concerns paternalistically or with violence.

Freeport has taken steps to address concerns through the construction of schools and a clinic, job training and scholarships, special land recognition payments to the Amungme and Kamoro, and special preference for supporting local businesses developed by those communities. Some of these measures have been required by the company's 1991 contract; most have been taken in response to community pressure or external critiques.

Freeport's "One Percent Trust Fund Offer," which designates one percent of annual revenues for development programs, has been one of the most controversial and damaging responses. LEMASA (the Amungme Tribal Council) and the area's three Christian churches denounced the offer for having a divisive impact amongst indigenous communities and for encouraging a welfare/dependency mentality. In a June 1996 resolution, LEMASA "unconditionally and absolutely" rejected Freeport's "One Percent Offer," declaring that "with the help of God we shall never [succumb] to the offer of bribes, intimidation or [be] dishonestly induced into accepting PT Freeport Indonesia's 'Settlement Agreement.'" Despite efforts to address the acknowledged failures of its community development programs, Freeport's overall involvement in financing and structuring these projects remains problematic.

Amungme leader Tom Beanal has written with some bitterness about his acceptance – with LEMASA's backing – of positions as a PT Freeport Commissioner and as Vice President of the People's Development Foundation – Irian Jaya (LPM-IRJA), the organization established with Freeport's One Percent funding. Citing the devastation to local communities caused by Freeport's provision of monies through the One Percent Offer, including the deaths of 18 indigenous people because of inter-ethnic conflict, Beanal describes these decisions as the only option left to him in defending the rights of his people. He states: What Freeport has done to me is to present me with a single limited choice, prepared by the company, so that I was not able to choose freely, but was always obliged to choose what was desired by Freeport. People see me as working with Freeport now. Perhaps it's true! Nevertheless, in the depths of my heart, I feel that I must do what is best for my people. (Dodd, 2000)

The recent Memorandum of Understanding signed by Beanal, a Kamoro community member, and Freeport – publicized in August 2000 by the company as representing a watershed in community–company relations – must be considered in light of these comments. While the announcement of the MOU helped to boost Freeport's stock rating, there is no indication that it represents a retreat from the local communities' commitment to holding Freeport accountable for its social and environmental impact.

Beanal remains critical of the continuing dynamic of exploitation that Amungme and Kamoro experience. He recently told a journalist, "The Indonesian Government eats at the table with Freeport, they throw the leftover food on the floor and we Papuans have to fight for it."

Closure

The Kamoro and Amungme experience typifies that of so many local people who find themselves at the mercy of unregulated global capital in the extractive industries. Their story asks us to consider what sustainable development really is, and whether it is possible to achieve via economic strategies based on large-scale mineral extraction designed and imposed by multinationals and governments. It demonstrates the egregious harm to human life – and to the health of politically disempowered communities – that results when those who control the means of force allow economic interests to trump democratic public policy-making and the protection of basic human rights and the environment.

Due in part to the experience of the Amungme and Kamoro and other communities similarly situated, standards regarding the rights of indigenous peoples, corporate responsibility, and stakeholder consultation have advanced considerably during the past decade. Yet until governments – and extraction-industry corporations – respect the universal human right to development and abandon neo-colonial approaches to natural resources and indigenous people, conflicts will continue between multinational mining companies like Freeport and the peoples whose lands they take. [. . .]

52　Globalization and Sustainability

Wolfgang Sachs

Symbols are the more powerful the more meanings they are able to admit. They actually live on ambivalence. The Cross, for instance, counted both as a token of victory for conquerors and as a token of hope for the vanquished. That ambivalence raised it above the fray; a single clear message would have meant that it divided rather than united. The same may be said of the image of the blue planet, now a symbol unchallenged by either Left or Right, conservative or liberal. Whatever their differences, they are all fond of adorning themselves with this symbol of our epoch. To fall in with it is to announce that one is abreast of the times, in tune with the world, focused on the future, truly prepared to set off into the new century. In this picture are condensed the opposing ambitions of our age. It is hoisted like a flag by troops from enemy camps, and its prominence results from this plurality of meaning. The photography of the globe contains the contradictions of globalization. That is why it could become an all-weather icon.

No sooner had it become available, in the late 1960s, than the international environmental movement recognized itself in it. For nothing stands out from the picture as clearly as the round margin that sets it off from the dark cosmos. Clouds, oceans and land masses gleam in the wan light; the earth appears to the observer as a cosy island in a universe unfriendly to life, holding all the continents, seas and living species. For the environmental movement the picture's message was plain: it revealed the earth in its finitude. That circular object made it obvious that the ecological costs of industrial progress could not be shifted forever to Noplace, that they were slowly building up into a threat to all within a closed system. In the end, the externalization of costs belonged to the realm of the impossible. In a finite world, where everyone was affected by everyone else, there was an urgent need for mutual care and attention, for more thought about the consequences of one's actions. Such was the holistic message – and, certainly, it was not without some effect. Since the days when a few minorities launched their appeal so full of foreboding, the image of the planet as a closed system has steadily gained currency and even recognition in international law. The conventions on ozone, world climate and biodiversity prove that the perception of the earth's bio-physical limits has attained the supreme political consecration.

For some time, however, ecologists have no longer had a monopoly on the image. At various airports, in the endless passageways between check-in and exit, a well-lit publicity board has been visible in recent years that strikingly expresses a

Original publication details: Excerpted from Wolfgang Sachs, *Planet Dialectics: Explorations in Environment and Development* (Zed Books, 1999), pp. 129–31, 149–55. Reprinted by permission of Zed Books Ltd., London.

different view of globalization. It shows the blue planet pushing itself on the observer from its blue-black background, with a laconic text: 'MasterCard. The World in Your Hands.' The hurrying passengers are being told that, wherever they fly in this big wide world, they can count on the services of their cards and slot themselves into a global credit and debit network. The credit-card empire stretches out across all frontiers, with purchasing power in any location and accounting in real time, and its electronic money transfers ensure that the traveller is always provided for. In these and numerous other variations, the image of the planet has turned since the 1980s into an emblem of transnational business; hardly any company in telecommunications or tourism – not to speak of the news industry – seems able to manage without it.

This has been possible because the picture also contains quite a different message. In its detachment from the pitch-black cosmos, the terrestrial sphere stands out as a unified area whose continuous physical reality causes the frontiers between nations and polities to disappear – hence the visual message that what counts is the boundaries of the earth. Only oceans, continents and islands can be seen, with no trace of nations, cultures or states.

In the picture of the globe, distances are measured exclusively in geographical units of miles or kilometres, not in social units of closeness and foreignness. The satellite photographs generally look like renaturalized maps, seeming to confirm the old cartographical postulate that places are nothing more than intersections of two lines – the lines of longitude and latitude. In marked contrast to the globes of the nineteenth century, which sharply delineate political frontiers and often use different colours for different territories, any social reality is here dissipated into morphology. The earth is depicted as a homogeneous area offering no resistance to transit – or only resistance caused by geographical features, not to human communities and their laws, customs or purposes. Every point of the hemisphere turned towards the observer can be seen at the same moment, and this simultaneous access of the human gaze suggests the idea of unobstructed access on the ground too. The image of the planet offers the world up for unrestricted movement, promises access in every direction, and seems to present no obstacle to expansionism other than the limits of the globe itself. Open, continuous and controllable – there is an imperial message too in the photographs of the earth.

The image symbolizes limitation in the physical sense and expansion in the political sense. Little wonder, then, that it can serve as a banner for both environmental groups and transnational corporations. It has become the symbol of our times across all the rival world views, because it brings to life both sides of the basic conflict that runs through our epoch. On the one hand, the ecological limits of the earth stand out more clearly than ever before; on the other hand, the dynamic of economic globalization pushes for the removal of all boundaries associated with political and cultural space. The two narratives of globalization – limitation and expansion – have acquired a clearer form over the past three decades and fight it out in both the arena of theory and the arena of politics. The outcome of this struggle will decide the shape of the new century. [. . .]

How Economic Globalization Changes the Geography of Environmental Stress

In recent years, more and more salmon dishes – fresh, smoked or grilled – have been appearing on German menus, almost as if it were a fish from local waters. By now

Germans consume nearly 70 million kilos a year of the favoured fish, which is brought from farms in Norway or Scotland to supermarket displays. But as in the mass farming of any other creature, large quantities of feed have to be supplied – to be precise, five kilos of wild deep-water fish have to be processed into one kilo of fishmeal, which is then used to feed salmon for consumption. This raw material is mostly caught off the Pacific coast of South America, where catches are declining because of overfishing, and it is then turned into meal in Peruvian harbour towns that are in danger of suffocating in the gaseous, liquid and solid waste matter that results from the process. While German consumers can feast themselves on fresh low-calorie (and rather expensive) fish, people in Peru are left with pillaged seas and filthy dirty towns.

This example shows how a lengthening of the supply chain can shift the ecological division of labour between countries of the South (and East) and those of the North. For economic globalization does not mean that the costs and benefits of economic activity are globalized. On the contrary, it is more likely that extension of the value-creation chain to different locations around the world will bring a new allocation of advantage and disadvantage. When a production process is divided up among different countries and regions, a tendency soon appears to separate costs and benefits by redistributing them up and down the chain. Anyway it would be wrong to imagine that the worldwide networking of offices, factories, farms and banks is accompanied by a decentralization of all functions from production and planning to finance, not to speak of the collection of profits. Despite many attempts to increase the autonomy of sub-units, the opposite is generally the case: that is, the diversification of economic activities leads to a concentration of control and profit at the nodal points of the network economy. The flux of investment into distant countries is offset by a reflux of power and profits to the originating country, or, more precisely, to the 'global cities' of the North. As special export zones multiply in Bangladesh, Egypt or Mexico, where cheap labour, tax breaks and lax environmental norms considerably reduce production costs, the sky is the limit for the towers of banks and company offices in Hong Kong, Frankfurt or London.

The changed distribution of economic power goes together with a change in how the pressure on the environment is distributed across geographical space. If power, in an ecological sense, is defined as the capacity to internalize environmental advantages while externalizing environmental costs, then it may be supposed that the lengthening of economic chains will start a process that concentrates advantages at the upper end and disadvantages at the lower end. In other words, the environmental costs incurred within the transnational value-creation chains will become especially high in the countries of the South and East, while the post-industrial economies will become ever more environmentally friendly. Or to use an analogy (with the salmon example in mind), the rich countries will increasingly occupy the upper positions in the food chain (where larger volumes of low-value inputs have step-by-step been converted into smaller volumes of high-value food), while the developing or poorer countries will occupy the middle and lower positions. In fact, along with numerous individual examples, a series of highly aggregated data on international flows of materials lend credence to this interpretation. Thus, 35 per cent of total resource consumption is incurred abroad in the case of Germany, 50 per cent in Japan, 70 per cent in the Netherlands, and so on. The smaller the area of an industrialized country, the greater seems to be the geographical separation between the sites of pressure on the environment and the sites of consumption benefit. In all these countries, there has been a tendency over the past 15 years for a growing proportion of environmental consumption to take place abroad (involving not so much raw materials as semi-finished products).

In agriculture, Southern regions of the world no longer supply only agrarian mass produce as in the days of colonialism, but also supply goods with a high dollar value per unit of weight for affluent consumers in the North. Highly perishable items such as tomatoes, lettuce, fruit, vegetables and flowers come as air freight to Europe from Senegal or Morocco, to Japan from the Philippines, or to the United States from Colombia or Costa Rica. As in the case of salmon, health-conscious shoppers with an average to high income are only too pleased to have a supply that does not depend on the season, while plantations and glasshouses in the areas of origin impose irrigation, pesticide use and the repression of local farmers. Nor are things much different with shrimp or meat production. The breeding of shrimps and prawns in Thailand or India for the Japanese and European markets means that people have to wade through toxic residue to catch them and that many a mangrove forest has to disappear from the scene. More refined consumption in the North at the price of the environment and subsistence economics in the South: this pattern has rooted itself deeply in the food-produce market since the 1970s. The raising of cattle and pigs in Europe draws in manioc or soya both from the United States and from countries such as Brazil, Paraguay, Argentina, Indonesia, Malaysia or Thailand. The old law that the market puts purchasing power before human need asserts itself still more powerfully in a world economy beyond frontiers.

Of course, the expansion of the fossil development model into one or two dozen aspiring economies in the South and East has done most to change the geography of environmental stress. As the newly industrialized nations entered the age fuelled by fossil resources, the possibility presented itself of stretching the industrial production chains beyond the OECD countries. The South's share of world output has thus been growing (and the OECD's slowly declining) in primary industry, metalworking and chemicals, rising in the last of these from 17 per cent in 1990 to 25 per cent in 1996. What is happening is not so much migration for environmental reasons as a redistribution of functions within the world economy. The stages of an international production chain that put most pressure on the environment are usually in less-developed regions, while the cleaner and less material stages tend to be in the G-7 countries. In the aluminium industry, for instance, the quarrying of bauxite takes place in Guyana, Brazil, Jamaica and Guinea (along with Australia). The actual smelting of the aluminium, which is the next stage along, moved more and more in the 1980s from the North to countries such as Brazil, Venezuela, Indonesia or Bahrain, while the research and development stage remained chiefly located in the OECD area. Despite higher use overall, the production of aluminium grew strongly in Japan and weakly in Europe; imports from the South filled the gap.

A look at the computer branch further along shows just how much high-tech industry lives off the new ecological division of labour. In the case of 22 computer companies in the industrialized countries, more than half of their (mostly toxic) microchip production is located in developing countries. Does this not show in outline the future restructuring of the world economy? The software economies of the North will pride themselves on their plans for a cleaner environment, while the newly industrialized economies will do the manufacturing and contend with classical forms of water, air and soil pollution, and the poorer primary economies will do the extracting and undermine the subsistence basis of the third of humanity that lives directly from nature.

Which and Whose Globalization?

Globalization is not a monopoly of the neo-liberals: the most varied actors, with the most varied philosophies, are also caught up in the transnationalization of social relations; indeed the ecological movement is one of the most important agents of global thinking. Accordingly, the image of the blue planet – that symbol of globalization – conveys more than just one message. The imperial message of collapsing frontiers always found itself confronted with the holistic message of the planet's finite unity. A clear line can be drawn from Earth Day 1970 (often seen as the beginning of the American ecological movement) to the United Nations conference on world climate held in Kyoto in 1997. In the squares where people assembled on that first Earth Day, speakers and demonstrators underpinned their demands for comprehensive environmental protection with photographs of the earth taken less than a year before from the surface of the moon. And nearly thirty years later, the emblem of the planet was prominently displayed on the front of the conference hall where, for the first time, the world's governments entered into legally binding commitments to limit pollution levels. That picture shows the earth as a single natural body binding human beings and other forms of life to a common destiny; it globalizes our perception both of nature and of the human story. Only with that image did it become possible to speak of 'one earth' or 'one world' in the true sense of the term. For neither the name of Friends of the Earth, nor the title of the Brundtland Report, *Our Common Future*, would have meant much without that photo of the planet.

But the 'blue planet effect' and its message of finitude go deeper still: they produce a way of seeing that places local action within a global framework. The picture shows the outer limits of the living space of everyone who looks at it. Does not everyone know that, if only the image were sufficiently enlarged, he or she would be able to find himself or herself on it? For the observing subject cannot be separated there from the observed object; in scarcely any other example is self-reference so inextricably woven into the image. This visual superimposition of global and individual existence has shifted the cognitive and moral coordinates of our perception of ourselves. The consequences of an action, it suggests, may extend to the edges of the earth – and everyone is responsible for them. All of a sudden, car drivers and meat buyers are linked to the greenhouse effect, and even a hairspray or an air ticket is seen as having overstepped the global boundaries. 'Think globally, act locally': this electoral slogan of the ecological movement has played its part in creating a 'global citizen' who internalizes the earth's limits within his or her own thinking and action. The narrative of limitation derives its moral force from this association of planet and subject in a common drama. The ecological experience is thus undoubtedly one dimension of the experience of globalization, because it overturns people's conventional notion that they live and act in national political and social spaces that are clearly demarcated and separated from one another.

Yet the ecological movement cannot escape the fact that, however provisionally, the imperial message has won through. One sign of this is the way in which multinational corporations have almost completely seized for themselves the image of the blue planet. The perception of the world as a homogeneous space, visible and accessible all the way across, has everywhere become hegemonic. This vision is imperial, because it claims the right to roam the world unhindered and to grab whatever it fancies – exactly as if there were no places, no communities, no nations. The mechanisms of GATT, NAFTA and the WTO were born in the spirit of frontier demolition. They codify the world as a freely accessible economic arena, in which economics enjoys the right of way. The newly established rules are designed to proclaim transnational corporations as sovereign subjects within global space, exempt from any obligation to regions or national governments. State protectionism is thereby abolished, only to be replaced by a new protectionism that favours corporations. Transnational partnerships are entitled to claim all sorts of freedoms and rights, while territorial states – not to mention citizens or civic associations – have to take second place.

When people look back on the last century of this millennium, they will be forced to conclude that Rio de Janeiro was pretty good on rhetoric, but Marrakesh was taken in real earnest. Here the UN conference on the environment held in Rio in 1992 stands for a long series of international agreements – notably the conventions on climate and biodiversity – that were supposed to steer the world economy in less ecologically harmful directions. Marrakesh stands for the founding of the World Trade Organization after the end of the GATT Uruguay Round, and for the growing importance of the IMF as a shadow government in many countries. There the basis was laid for an economic regime in which the investment activity of transnational actors would be free of regulation anywhere on the globe. These transnational regimes – the environmental and the economic – are attempts to give a political–legal foundation to transnational economic society, but the two stand in marked contradiction to each other. The environmental regime is concerned with protection of the natural heritage, the economic regime with equal rights to exploit it; the environmental agreements are based on respect for natural limits, the economic agreements on the right to carry through economic expansion successfully. Paradoxically, moreover, they wager on different systems of responsibility and accountability. On the one hand, the environmental agreements appeal to sovereign states as responsible entities that are supposed to uphold the public good in their territory. On the other hand, the economic agreements assume sovereign, transnationally active corporations that belong to no territory and are therefore responsible to no state. Already today the world's hundred largest economies comprise 49 countries and 51 corporations.

It is therefore not clear how the conflicting messages that appropriate the image of the blue planet can be reconciled with each other. Each transnational civil society has succeeded only on specific occasions in confronting corporations with their responsibility towards nature and the overwhelming majority of the world's citizens. If the holistic message stands for 'sustainability' and the imperial message for 'economic globalization', then it would seem necessary to suppose that, however great the synergies at a micro-level, the chasm between the two is continuing to widen. But that is the greatness of a symbol: it can hold together divergent truths within a single visual form.

Questions

1. What makes a social problem global? Discuss features of the contemporary world that make it increasingly likely that problems will be considered global rather than national, regional, or local in character.

2. Given that global civil society organizations have no formal authority and, often, not much money either, why do states and IGOs pay any attention to them? What is it about INGOs and similar organizations that makes them influential with respect to global issues?

3. Are global environmental organizations necessary? How do you think transnational corporations would behave if they were not being constantly scrutinized by groups like EarthAction, Greenpeace, and the World Wildlife Fund? Is there reason to believe that corporations would try to limit the environmental damage they do if there were no environmental INGOs?

4. In light of the selection from the World Commission on Environment and Development, explain what the concept of "sustainable development" means. Do you feel that the way of life in your country is consistent with this concept? Give examples to amplify your response.

5. Despite the participation of almost all governments in the Earth Summit in Rio, tropical deforestation continues, waterways remain badly polluted, and smog plagues many cities. Is the Rio Declaration therefore a meaningless document? Give arguments suggesting that it is. Also give arguments suggesting that the Declaration will have important long-term effects.

6. Wapner says that Greenpeace depends on "visually spectacular" actions to get attention and put environmental problems on the global agenda. Do such actions have any drawbacks? Think about how they may both promote environmentalism and hurt the environmentalist cause.

7. The anti-logging campaign in Sarawak was not able to protect the rainforests there, according to Keck and Sikkink. Abrash shows that the Amungme and Kamaro peoples have suffered many losses from the mining operations of Freeport McMoRan in their lands. What lessons can you draw from these cases about how environmental action becomes effective? What else could have been done that might have led to more success for these movements?

8. Develop Sachs's analysis of the way the "image of the blue planet" is used to support both environmentalism and economic globalization. What does his analysis imply about the prospects for sustainability? Are the prospects for sustainability better in the developed countries than in the rest of the world? Explain.

Part X

Resisting Globalization: Critique and Action

Introduction

Since the 1999 World Trade Organization conference in Seattle, meetings of international financial institutions have become the target of protests by people and groups opposed to their policies and large demonstrations against globalization have been organized across Europe. In 2001, groups opposed to globalization gathered in Porto Alegre, Brazil, for the World Social Forum, a deliberate counterpoint to the elite World Economic Forum held in Davos, Switzerland. As such events attest, the anti-globalization movement has itself become a broad and varied global phenomenon. Globalization has provoked a global backlash. For groups engaged in this backlash, globalization has a particular meaning: It is primarily an economic force, emanating from the West, that imposes an unjust, unequal, and environmentally harmful capitalist system on the world to the detriment of local cultures and democratic self-control. This critical view has shaped the global discourse of globalization. To some extent, globalization now is what its critics make of it.

The anti-globalization movement encompasses many groups, from students protesting athletic apparel produced in sweatshops to peasants resisting multinationals' control of their land and seeds; from indigenous groups defending their forest habitat to religious leaders seeking debt relief for developing countries; from labor unions concerned about the impact of free trade to feminists opposed to trafficking in young women. Resisting globalization can take many forms, and the anti-globalization movement is nothing if not diverse. This diversity reflects the fact that, for many people, "globalization" has become an all-purpose pejorative term. As a result, a wide range of problems are now routinely attributed to globalization, and groups pursuing quite specific goals increasingly unite behind a single anti-globalization banner. The very diversity of the movement makes articulating a widely supported alternative more difficult. But as the readings in this part confirm, to describe their efforts simply as resistance to globalization or a global backlash underestimates the global intent they share, which is to remake world society in accordance with principles that often conflict with established institutions. At least some of those principles, such as equality and justice, derive from a longstanding socialist and social-democratic tradition of opposition to the harsh consequences of modernizing change. In many ways, that tradition has been absorbed into the global backlash, which also includes radical nationalist and fundamentalist groups more commonly associated with the political right. Though the anti-globalization agenda is broader than that of older leftist movements, that agenda has served to inspire such older groups and their successors to become the vanguard of the anti-globalization effort. The critical idea that "another world is possible" has become the rallying cry of left-leaning groups everywhere.

As our examples above and readings in Part VI and Part IX already indicate, INGOs are especially prominent in the anti-globalization movement. Much critical energy is generated by border-crossing voluntary associations that involve experts, activists, and dues-paying members. Such groups typically attempt to focus public attention on new global problems and to build support for new policies to resolve them. Though globalization as such is a primary target, movement INGOs also aim their fire at states, IGOs, and MNCs. For example, the group Jubilee 2000 put pressure on developed countries to forgive the debts of developing countries; the French-based group ATTAC has advocated that countries impose the so-called "Tobin tax" on short-term capital movements across borders; the Seattle protesters demanded new rules for international trade from the WTO; and the sweatshop apparel campaign has targeted the labor practices used by corporations such as Nike. These examples further indicate that the anti-globalization movement is hardly limited to highly rhetorical symbolic politics; its various component groups and supporters have also proposed numerous specific policies. A common denominator in their proposals is the idea that global justice requires global governance, especially greater regulation of global economic activity.

Throughout this book we have presented examples of scholars, activists, and organizations critical of globalization. For example, John Gray's objections to the false dawn of neoliberal globalization and Joseph Stiglitz's opposition to "market fundamentalism" are widely shared views. Amartya Sen's and Oxfam's concern for a more equitable distribution of resources is a key goal for the overall movement as well. The readings in Part IX on the environment similarly express themes that resonate with anti-globalization activists. In this part we offer selections that further illustrate the resistance to globalization.

Gustavo Esteva and Madhu Suri Prakash describe how growing coalitions of grassroots activists effectively counteract the damage done by nefarious global ideas and institutions. The key to their success is the way they think and act locally instead of striving to engage in a grand globalized effort. Esteva and Prakash believe that, out of the "pluriverse" of thought and action by marginalized communities offering their own deeply rooted "cosmovisions," a better world order can emerge. Next, James Harding, of the pro-globalization *Financial Times*, analyzes anti-globalization activism more skeptically as a diverse counter-capitalist "movement of movements" without a unified agenda. But he also notes that activists are becoming well coordinated, well informed, and influential. Instead of a locally based pluriverse of voices, Harding describes a globally swelling "swarm" of globalization opponents deliberately constructing global symbols and networks.

Vandana Shiva, a prominent Indian activist, speaks for many critics when she describes globalization as a normative and political process forced on the weak by the powerful. "Liberalizing" the world economy actually means enhancing state and corporate power. Globalization also leads to a kind of environmental apartheid, as the North relocates pollution-intensive and hazardous-waste industries in the South. But Shiva finds hope in "people's movements" for community rights and biodiversity. Subcomandante Marcos represents one such movement, the Zapatista rebel group in southern Mexico. Addressing a gathering of supporters, he frames his group's struggle as "for humanity and against neoliberalism" – for "plural, different, inclusive" humanity, against the "brutal, universal, complete world war" of neoliberal globalization. He calls for a "network of voices" engaged in rebellion against global Power. One key node in that network is the World Social Forum. Its "Call for Mobilisation" attacks "the hegemony of finance, the destruction of cultures, the monopolization of knowledge, mass media and communication, [and] the degradation of nature" brought about by neoliberal globalization. The Forum aims to energize a broad movement that works for global "equity, social justice, democracy and security for everyone" through "participative democratic experiences." Citing the main slogan of the anti-globalization movement, our final selection, by the International Forum on Globalization, seeks to show more specifically how "another world is possible." Rejecting unbridled liberalization and the commodification of the global commons, it envisions a new form of global economic democracy built on principles of subsidiarity, human rights, common heritage, diversity, and equity.

53 From Global to Local: Beyond Neoliberalism to the International of Hope

Gustavo Esteva and Madhu Suri Prakash

[. . .] The policies and political slogans which emerged at the end of the Cold War, usually associated with "free trade," "neoliberalism" and other key words, have rapidly become effective *emblems* for selling the promises of a new era. New political, economic and social paradigms are once again in the process of being imposed by a few upon the many. Some of those emblems and paradigms are being transformed into *presuppositions*, as the constitutive elements of the myths of the "social minorities" of the world. These minorities are celebrating the opportunities being created by the Internet, World Wide Web or other global communications networks, as new forms of "global democracy." They are presuming that such "advances" will stimulate multiculturalism, through human "communication" inconceivable only a few years ago. They are assuming that the "New World Order" being established by the World Trade Organization and other institutions will finally materialize the most cherished dreams of humankind, dreamed by the few for the many. The unprecedented global exchange of goods and services, maintain the makers of the global *mythos*, will give access to the best that modern technology and civilization can offer to every man and woman on Earth.

None of these policy and political approaches, emblems or presuppositions go completely unchallenged. Not everyone shares the spirit of celebration they seek to promote. Since the very beginning of these campaigns for globalization (of education, citizenship, language, currency, religion and all other aspects of social life) multiple voices have expressed alarm about the new marvels and paradigms being promoted through media-hype. Even the most enthusiastic fans of Bill Gates and his Windows '97 experience misgivings and doubts when they observe the peculiar behaviors of their children emerging for brief moments out of the "virtual reality" in which they are being raised. Even the most single-minded and ambitious free trade advocates cannot fail to recognize the social and human costs of the policies they are promoting. More and more voices are raising alarms about their growing sense of powerlessness, tugged and pulled by "global forces."

Original publication details: Excerpted from Gustavo Esteva and Madhu Suri Prakash, *Grassroots Post-Modernism: Remaking the Soil of Cultures* (Zed Books, 1998), pp. 19–26, 27–8, 32–3. Reprinted by permission of Zed Books Ltd., London.

Until now, however, it appears as if most of the social movements or campaigns trying to resist the new "global" phenomena have proven to be highly ineffective. Some of them are even counterproductive, getting the opposite of what they are looking for; rooting and deepening in people and society the very evils against which they are struggling. True, many workers' strikes do succeed in protecting jobs or pension plans. At the same time, however, they also legitimize and consolidate the policies and orientations creating unemployment or dismantling the welfare state. Amongst the people struggling for some security in their lives, many assume that they have no more than one political option: that the best they can do is to protect their own situation; get some compensation for what they are losing; and hope that the promises offered in exchange for their sacrifices will one day be fulfilled. Such beliefs reinforce the "Global Project."

This chapter first explores the impossibility of regaining the experience of human agency and autonomy by supposedly "thinking" on the global scale to contend with the oppression of "global forces." No challenge to the proliferating experiences of people's powerlessness succeeds when conceived and implemented inside the institutional and intellectual framework which produced it. After closing the door to the fantasy of global thinking, we reflect on the multiplicity of local escape routes being invented or created daily to move out of the disabling global framework. These grass-roots counterforces of liberation remain invisible to the mainstream world of media and scholarship.

The earliest alarm signals about the new global paradigms encroaching upon the minds and lives of ordinary people were expressed in the slogan "Think globally, act locally," supposedly formulated by René Dubos some decades ago. It is not only a popular bumper sticker today; it increasingly captures the moral imagination of millions of people across the globe. Our analysis for moving beyond the "global framework" to local autonomy exposes the successes and strengths of the social philosophy underlying the slogan, while going beyond it in exploring the measure to which it can also be counterproductive.

Often, those supporting this slogan embrace several "certainties": first, the modern age forces everyone to live today in a global village; second, therefore, across the globe, people face shared predicaments and common enemies, like Cargill, Coca Cola, the World Bank, Nestlé, and other transnational corporations, as well as oppressive nation-states; third, only a clear awareness of the global nature of such problems could help forge the coalitions of "human solidarity" and "global consciousness" needed for struggling successfully against these all-pervasive global enemies; fourth, this global consciousness includes the recognition that every decent human being must be morally committed to the active global defense of "basic needs" or universal human rights (to schooling, health, nutrition, housing, livelihood, etc.) and human freedoms (from torture, oppression, etc.).

The slogan reveals the illusion of engaging in global action. This is not mere realism: ordinary people lack the centralized power required for "global action." It is a warning against the arrogance, the far-fetched and dangerous fantasy of "acting globally." Urging respect for the limits of "local action," it resists the Promethean lust to be godlike: omnipresent. By clearly defining the limits of intelligent, sensible action, it encourages decentralized, communal power. To make "a difference," actions should not be grandiosely global, but humbly local.

Extending the valuable insights contained in the second part of the slogan to the first part, we urge the replacement of "global thinking" with the "local thinking" practiced at the grassroots. We begin by presenting a synopsis of Wendell Berry's

. . . well-elaborated argument, warning not only against the dangerous arrogance of "global thinkers," but also of the human impossibility of this form of thought. Next, we debunk the other "certainties" that today pressure millions of modern, developed, "global citizens" into believing that they have the moral obligation to engage in global thinking. They disparage "think local"; for they suffer the modern illusion that local thinking must necessarily be not only ineffective in front of the global Goliath, but also parochial, taking humankind back to the dark ages when each was taught only to look after his/her own, letting "the devil take the hindmost." We reveal, instead, both the parochialism of "global thinking" and global action as well as the open nature of "local thinking" and local action, practiced "down below," at "the margins" of modern society.

Global Thinking is Impossible

The modern "gaze" . . . can distinguish less and less between reality and the image broadcast on the TV screen. It has shrunk the earth into a little blue bauble, a mere Christmas tree ornament, all too often viewed on a TV set. Forgetting its mystery, immensity and grandeur, modern men and women succumb to the arrogance of "thinking globally" to manage planet Earth . . .

We can only think wisely about what we actually know well. And no person, however sophisticated, intelligent and overloaded with the information age state-of-the-art technologies, can ever "know" the Earth – except by reducing it statistically, as all modern institutions tend to do today, supported by reductionist scientists. Since none of us can ever really know more than a minuscule part of the earth, "global thinking" is at its best only an illusion, and at its worst the grounds for the kinds of destructive and dangerous actions perpetrated by global "think tanks" like the World Bank, or their more benign counterparts – the watchdogs in the global environmental and human rights movements.

Bringing his contemporaries "down to earth" from out-of-space or spacy "thinking," teaching us to stand once again on our own feet (as did our ancestors), Wendell Berry helps us to rediscover human finiteness, and to debunk another "fact" of TV manufactured reality: the "global village." The transnational reach of *Dallas* and the sexual escapades of the British Royal Family or the Bosnian bloodbath, like the international proliferation of McDonald's, Benetton or Sheraton establishments, strengthen the modern prejudice that all people on Earth live in "One World." McLuhan's . . . unfortunate metaphor of the "global village" now operates as a presupposition, completely depleting critical consciousness. Contemporary arrogance suggests that modern man and woman can know the globe, just as pre-moderns knew their village. Rebutting this nonsense, Berry confesses that he still has much to learn in order to "husband" with thought and wisdom the small family farm which he has tilled and harvested for the past forty years in his ancestral Kentucky. His honesty about his ignorance in caring for his minuscule piece of our Earth renders naked the dangerousness of those who claim to "think globally" and aspire to monitor and manage the "global village."

Once environmental "problems" are reduced to the ozone layer or to global warming, to planetary "sources" and "sinks," faith in the futility of local efforts is fed by global experts; while their conferences, campaigns and institutions present the fabulous apparition of solutions "scientifically" pulled out of the "global hat." Both a global consciousness and a global government (such as the Global Environmental Facility "masterminded" at the Earth Summit) appear as badly needed to manage the planet's "scarce resources" and "the masses" irresponsibly chopping "green sinks" for their daily tortillas or chappatis, threatening the "experts'" planetary designs for eco-development. The "ozone layer" or "global warming" are abstract hypotheses, offered by some scientists as an explanation of recent phenomena. Even in that condition, they could prove to be very useful for fostering critical awareness of the folly of the "social minorities." But they are promoted as "a fact," reality itself; and all the socio-political and ecological dangers inherent in the illusion of the "Global Management" of planet Earth are hidden from "the people." Excluded, for example, from critical scrutiny is the reflection that in order for "global thinking" to be feasible, we should be able to "think" from within every culture on Earth and come away from this excursion single-minded – clearly a logical and practical impossibility, once it is critically de-mythologized. For it requires the supra-cultural criteria of "thinking" – implying the dissolution of the subject who "thinks"; or assuming that it is possible to "think" outside of the culture in which every man and woman on Earth is immersed. The human condition does not allow such operations. We celebrate the hopefulness of common men and women, saved from the hubris of "scientific man," unchastened by all his failures at playing God.

The Wisdom of Thinking Small

With the traditional humility of Gandhi, Ivan Illich, Leopold Kohr, Fritz Schumacher, and others of their ilk, Berry warns of the many harmful consequences of "Thinking Big": pushing all human enterprises beyond the human scale. Appreciating the genuine limits of human intelligence and capacities, Berry celebrates the age-old wisdom of "thinking little" or small: on the proportion and scale that humans can really understand, know and assume responsibility for the consequences of their actions and decisions upon others.

Afraid that local thinking weakens and isolates people, localizing them into parochialism, the "alternative" global thinkers forget that Goliath did in fact meet his match in David. Forgetting this biblical moral insight, they place their faith in the countervailing force of a competing or "alternative" Goliath of their own, whose global thinking encompasses the supra-morality of "planetary consciousness." Assuming that "Global Man" (the grown-ups' version of Superman) has more or less conquered every space on Earth (and is now moving beyond, into the extraterrestrial), they think he is now advancing towards a collective conscience: one conscience, one transcultural consciousness, one humanity – the great human family. "It is the planetary conscience that takes us to a 'world society' with a 'planetary citizenship'," says Leonardo Boff, the Brazilian theologian, describing a hope now shared by a wide variety of "globalists." Hunger in Ethiopia, bloody civil wars in Somalia or Yugoslavia, human rights violations in Mexico thus become the personal responsibilities of all good, non-parochial citizens of Main Street; supposedly complementing their local involvement in reducing garbage, homelessness or junk food in their own neighborhoods. Global Samaritans may fail to see that when their local actions are informed, shaped and determined by a "global frame of mind," they become as uprooted as those of the globalists they explicitly criticize.

To relearn how to "think little," Berry recommends starting with the "basics" of life: food, for example. He suggests discovering ways to eat which take us beyond "global thinking and action" towards "local thinking and action." Global thinkers and think tanks, like the World Bank, disregard this wisdom at the level of both thought and action. Declaring that current food problems, among others, are global in their nature, they seek to impose global solutions. Aware of the threats perpetrated by such "solutions," the proponents of "Think globally, act locally" take recourse to the tradition of Kohr et al. only at the level of action, as a sensible strategy to struggle against the "global forces." By refusing to "think little," given their engagement with global campaigns, the World Watch Institute and other "alternative" globalists of their ilk inadvertently function on their enemies' turf.

How do we defeat the five Goliath companies now controlling 85 percent of the world trade of grains and around half of its world production? Or the four controlling the American consumption of chicken? Or those few that have cornered the beverage market? The needed changes will wait for ever if they require forging equally gigantic transnational consumers' coalitions, or a global consciousness about the right way to eat. In accepting the illusory nature of the efforts to struggle against "global forces" in their own territory, on a global scale, we are not suggesting the abandonment of effective coalitions for specific purposes, like the Pesticides Action Network, trying to exert political pressure to ban specific threats. Even less are we suggesting that people give up their struggles to put a halt to the dangerous advances of those "global forces." Quite the opposite. In putting our eggs in the local basket, we are simply emphasizing the merits of the politics of "No" for dealing with global Goliaths: affirming a rich diversity of attitudes and ideals, while sharing a common rejection of the same evils. Such a common "No" does not need a "global consciousness." It expresses the opposite: a pluriverse of thought, action and reflection.

All global institutions, including the World Bank or Coca Cola, have to locate their transnational operations in actions that are always necessarily local; they cannot exist otherwise. Since "global forces" can only achieve concrete existence at some local level, it is only there – at the local grassroots – that they can most effectively and wisely be opposed. People at the grassroots are realizing that there is no need to "Think Big" in order to begin releasing themselves from the clutches of the monopolistic food economy; that they can, in fact, free themselves in the same voluntary ways as they entered it. They are learning to simply say "No" to Coke and other industrial junk, while looking for local alternatives that are healthy, ecologically sound, as well as decentralized in terms of social control. Among the more promising reactions in the industrial world is the movement towards Community Supported Agriculture (CSAs), inspired by both local thinking and action. This growing grassroots movement is teaching urban people how to support small local farmers who farm with wisdom, caring for local soils, waters and intestines. In doing so, local communities simultaneously ensure that unknown farmers from faraway places like Costa Rica or Brazil are not exploited with inhuman wages and left sick with cancer or infertility. By taking care of our own local food, farms and farmers, those of us who are members of CSAs are slowly learning to overcome the parochialism of "industrial eaters": who are "educated" to be oblivious to the harm done by purchasing from multinational agribusiness and others who "Think Big," destroying millions of small family farms across the globe.

Those of us supporting CSAs are trying to abandon the global thinking with which "industrial eaters" enter their local grocery stores: buying "goods" from any and every part of the earth, motivated solely by the desire to get the "best" return for their dollar. Of course, relearning to think locally about food (among other "basics") we are also frugal: we also want the best return for our dollar. But for us this means much more than maximizing the number of eggs or the gallons of milk with which we can fill our grocery bags. We are interested in knowing about the kinds of lives lived by the hens whose eggs we eat; we want to know what type of soil our lettuce springs from. And we want to ensure that not only were the animals and plants we bring to our palate treated well; we are critically examining our eating habits so that the farmers who work for us will not die of deadly diseases or become infertile because of the chemicals they were forced to spray on their fields. We have now read enough to know why these ills occur every time we buy grapes from California or bananas from Costa Rica. We also know that when our food comes from so far away, we will never know the whole story of suffering perpetrated unintentionally by us, despite the valiant efforts of journals like *The Ecologist* or scholars like Frances Moore Lappé . . . nor, for that matter, once we get a partial picture, will we be able to do much about it. Therefore, by decreasing the number of kilometers which we eat, bringing our food closer and closer to our local homes, we know we are "empowering" ourselves to be neither oppressed by the big and powerful, nor oppressors of *campesinos* and small farmers who live across the globe; and we are also reskilling ourselves to look after the well-being of members of our local community, who, in their turn, are similarly committed to our well-being. In doing so, we are discovering that we are also saving money, while being more productive and efficient: saving on manufactured pesticides, fertilizers, packaging, refrigeration or transportation over long distances.

Self-sufficiency and autonomy are now new political demands, well rooted in the experience of millions of Indians, *campesinos,* "urban marginals" and many other groups in the southern part of the globe. Rerooting and regenerating themselves in their own spaces, they are creating effective responses to the "global forces" trying to displace them. [. . .]

Escaping Parochialism

Global proposals are necessarily parochial: they inevitably express the specific vision and interests of a small group of people, even when they are supposedly formulated in the interest of humanity. . . . In contrast, if they are conceived by communities well rooted in specific places, local proposals reflect the unique "cosmovision" that defines, differentiates and distinguishes every culture: an awareness of the place and responsibilities of humans in the cosmos. Those who think locally do not twist the humble satisfaction of belonging to the cosmos into the arrogance of pretending to know what is good for everyone and to attempt to control the world.

There is a legitimate claim to "universality" intrinsic in every affirmation of truth. However, people who dwell in their places do not identify the limits of their own vision with that of the human horizon itself. Among Indian peoples, for example, all over the American continent, the notion of "territory" is not associated with ownership, but with responsibility. If the Earth is the mother, how can anyone own her? Indian peoples feel a genuine obligation to care for the portion of the cosmos where they have settled and they affirm the truth of their notion of human relations with their Mother, the Earth. But they do not transform that conviction into the arrogance of knowing, controlling and managing planet Earth, seeking to impose their own view on everyone.

Growing coalitions of local thinkers/activists are learning to effectively counteract the damage of global thinking and action through a shared rejection. Their shared "No" to their "common enemies" (whether a nuclear plant, dam or Wal-Mart) simultaneously affirms their culturally differentiated perceptions, their locally rooted initiatives and modes of being. When their shared "No" interweaves cross-cultural agreements or commitments, they retain their pluralism, without falling into cultural relativism. They successfully oppose globalism and plurality with radical pluralism, conceived for going beyond western monoculturalism – now cosmeticized and disguised as "multiculturalism" inside as well as outside the quintessentially western settings: the classroom or the office. And they find, in their concrete practices, that all "global powers" are built on shaky foundations (as the Soviet Union so ably demonstrated in the recent past); and may, therefore, be effectively opposed through modest local actions. The very size of gargantuan, disproportionate and oversized "systems" make them out of balance and extremely fragile. Saying "No," in contrast, may be one of the most complete and vigorous forms of self-affirmation for communities and organizations of real men and women. A unifying "No," expressing a shared opposition, is but the other side of a radical affirmation of the heterogeneous and differentiated beings and hopes of all the real men and women involved in resisting any global monoculture. Saying "No, thanks" to mindless jobs or the medicalization of society is the negative aspect of the affirmation of a wide variety of autonomous ways to cope with globalist or nationalist aggressions upon people's communal spaces. [. . .]

The Power of Thinking and Acting Locally

Local initiatives, no matter how wisely conceived, *prima facie* seem too small to counteract the "global forces" now daily invading our lives and environments. The whole history of economic development, in its colonialist, socialist or capitalist forms, is a terrible true tale of violent interventions by brutal forces "persuading" – with the use of weapons, economic lures and "education" – small communities to surrender. Furthermore, some of the contemporary threats, as Chernobyl illustrated in a horrifying way, do not respect any frontier – national, communal or ideological. The wise decision taken by the Austrians, to ban nuclear plants in their own territory, becomes irrelevant when some are operating 50 kilometers from their frontiers.

Innumerable similar cases give ample proof that local peoples often need outside allies to create a critical mass of political opposition capable of stopping those forces. But the solidarity of coalitions and alliances does not call for "thinking globally." In fact what is needed is exactly the opposite: people thinking and acting locally, while forging solidarity with other local forces that share this opposition to the "global thinking" and "global forces" threatening local spaces. For its strength, the struggle against Goliath enemies does not need to abandon its local inspiration and firmly rooted local thought. When local movements or initiatives lose the ground under their feet, moving their struggle into the enemy's territory – global arenas constructed by global thinking – they become minor players in the global game, doomed to lose their battles.

The Earth Summit is perhaps the best contemporary illustration of this sequence. Motivated by global thinking, thousands of local groups flew across the world to Rio only to see their valuable initiatives transmogrified into nothing more than a footnote to the global agreements, conceived and now being implemented by the Big and the Powerful. Prescient of this failure of "Thinking Big" or global, Berry accurately predicted that the global environmental movement, following the "grand highways" taken by the peace and civil rights movements, would lose its vitality and strength, uprooted out of its natural ground: the immediate spaces of real men and women who think and act locally. [. . .]

54   Counter-Capitalism: Globalisation's Children Strike Back

James Harding

Part One: The Mosquitoes Begin to Swarm

Just on the outskirts of respectable Washington DC, across town from the steel and glass headquarters of the World Bank, there is a clapboard two-storey house. On the ground floor, a neighbourhood lawyer offers "divorce specials", personal injury suits and "walk-in deals for car wrecks". Up the flimsy wooden staircase to the side of the building, Soren Ambrose is trying to dismantle the world's financial architecture.

Ambrose, a chubby 38-year-old with sandy hair and a scruffy blond beard, does not look like much of a threat to the world order. He wears creased olive-green khakis with a red, black and turquoise shirt of African cloth, which in another part of Washington might be used as ethnic cushion covers. The second-hand computer on his desk is surrounded by newspaper clippings, a pile of old campaign leaflets and a scattering of print-outs off the internet. The only son of a suburban Chicago couple – his father is a management consultant and his mother is a retired librarian – Ambrose came late to activism. He flirted with protest at junior high school in the late 1970s, but in 1981 swapped politics for partying: "I went to college and took drugs and drank," he laughs. When Ambrose was working on a doctorate in African literature, he went for a fortnight to Nigeria: "I met writers at the university there who did not have enough money to buy their own books. They were not so interested in language. They were interested in economics."

Ken Saro-Wiwa, the playright leading what was to become a global fight against Shell's oil operations in his native Ogoniland, was his host. Ambrose abandoned his dissertation half-written. He returned to the US and took up full-time campaigning. Initially with the Nicaragua Network, he was soon involved with 50 Years is Enough, a coalition put together by a handful of development economists, ex-aid workers, former missionaries and environmentalists seeking to combat the World Bank and the International Monetary Fund.

The sequel to Seattle

From half a dozen groups five years ago, it now draws support from more than 200 member organisations. Next week, from the converted bedrooms which serve as offices, Ambrose and the 50 Years director who also happens to be his wife, Njoki Njoroge Njehu, will put together the final plans for what is shaping up to be the

Original publication details: Excerpted from James Harding, "Counter-Capitalism: Globalisation's Children Strike Back," *Financial Times*, September 2001. Reprinted by permission of the *Financial Times*.

sequel to Seattle: a protest by tens of thousands of people against the World Bank and the IMF in Washington on the weekend of September 29–30 [, 2001]. "I was only in Nigeria for two weeks," says Ambrose, with an infectious chuckle, "but it turned into this big thing."

Soren Ambrose is what most people would call an anti-globalisation activist. To some world leaders, people like him are part of a movement that can no longer be ignored. Lionel Jospin, the French prime minister manoeuvring to become president, reached out to anti-globalisation activists by offering support for the so-called Tobin tax. Gerhard Schroder, the German chancellor, has since said he too is interested in the nearly 30-year-old idea of putting a levy on foreign exchange transactions to pass on to the world's poor. For the bosses of giant companies who have had to come to terms with life under constant attack, such as Phil Knight of Nike and Lord Browne of BP, the campaigners are forcing fundamental changes to corporate life.

To others, Ambrose is the new enemy. He is put in the bracket of what Peter Sutherland, the former European Commissioner, calls "foolish protesters". He is one of those campaigners against further free trade who President George W. Bush says threatens to wreck global prosperity. He participates in the kinds of demonstrations overrun by riotous thugs that British prime minister Tony Blair says are an attack on democracy. Either way, people in business and politics are right to take the likes of Ambrose seriously. He is one of tens of thousands of committed activists at the nexus of a global political movement embracing tens of millions of people.

Just over a decade after the fall of the Berlin Wall and the "End of History" promised by Francis Fukuyama, who argued free market liberalism had triumphed forever, there is a growing sense that global capitalism is once again fighting to win the argument. In the last 18 months, a million people have taken to the streets in what has become a rolling mobilisation. In 1999, just 25 turned up to protest at the World Bank/IMF annual meetings in Washington. Last year, it was 30,000. At the end of this month, activists are predicting more than 50,000.

Taken together, the string of protests since Seattle in 1999, which have torn through Washington, Melbourne, Prague, Seoul, Nice, Barcelona, Washington DC, Quebec City, Gothenburg and Genoa, have cost more than $250m in security precautions, damage and lost business. Hundreds have been injured, several shot and one young man has been killed.

Largest petition in history

Campaigners for debt relief for the world's poorest countries last year put together the largest petition in history, gathering 24 m[illion] names – more than the number of people who signed the condolence books for Princess Diana worldwide. Voter turnout may be plummetting in Europe and the US, but political activism is enjoying a resurgence not seen since the Vietnam War. At Attac, the Tobin tax advocates who have 30,000 paid-up followers across Europe, the intellectual campaigners say "the demonstrations make one think very much of the days of May 1968 in Paris". Tom Hayden, the ideologue of the American left who was one of the Chicago Seven accused of conspiring to incite a riot at the 1968 Democratic National Convention, says: "There is a spirit which I have not seen since 1960. People are emerging from invisibility after many years."

Protests now threaten to halt the global momentum of open markets and free capital, stopping the World Trade Organisation's effort to launch a new trade round for the second time in Doha, Qatar, in November. The world's most powerful politicians are in retreat, withdrawing to remote spots such as Kananaskis in the Canadian Rockies for the next Group of Eight summit.

The irony, of course, is that anti-globalisation activism is gathering momentum just as global capitalism looks prone to a bout of cyclical weakness. Anti-globalisation has been a backlash against a surging world economy. A recession could change the nature of activism, fuelling counter-capitalist feeling among some while making others more defensive about the companies which put food on the family table. "The big risk," according to Anne Krueger, deputy managing director of the IMF, is that "a slackening or slowdown in the rate of economic growth could lead to a sufficient downturn in economic activity to trigger a backlash among those who are now silent, but not necessarily supportive, of globalisation. Protectionism, in the guise of anti-globalisation, could return and reverse liberalisation and "the long period of successful economic growth that the world has enjoyed". [. . .]

It [anti-globalisation] turns out to be a formidable movement. Or, to be precise, a movement of movements. Anti-globalisation activism is diverse and inchoate, without a unified agenda or a traditional leadership.

Increasingly well-funded

It is, however, well co-ordinated. It is well-informed. It is increasingly well-funded. And, perhaps most alarming for elected politicians and corporate leaders, a growing number of people think it has mainstream values and a mass appeal. It is not, as Mr Blair has described the protesters, a "travelling circus of anarchists", although, to be sure, there are clowns, arsonists and Molotov-cocktail throwing thugs within the movement. Nor is it just society's green fringe of unwashed hippies and Luddite reactionaries, although there are plenty of vegan spiritualists, unreconstructed communists, regressive utopians and smoked-out dreamers. And, while there is plenty of fuzzy thinking and fast-and-loose abuse of economic statistics, there is also a critique backed by respected economists, businesspeople and politicians.

Nor is it strictly speaking "anti-globalisation". The vast majority of activists are pro-globalisation, indeed products of it. The movement was welded together by the internet. Mass mobilisations, in Europe in particular, have been made possible by mobile phones. The unprecedented pitch of public feeling in the North for people in the South has coincided with cheap air fares between the two. Instead, this is counter-capitalism. The new wave of political activism has coalesced around the simple idea that capitalism has gone too far. It is as much a mood as a movement, something counter-cultural. It is driven by the suspicion that companies, forced by the stock markets to strive for ever greater profits, are pillaging the environment, destroying lives and failing to enrich the poor as they promised. And it is fueled by the fear that democracy has become powerless to stop them, as politicians are thought to be in the pockets of companies and international political institutions are slaves to a corporate agenda.

A survey this summer in *Le Monde*, the French newspaper, showed 56 per cent of people in France thought multinational corporations had been the beneficiaries of globalisation. Just 1 per cent thought consumers and citizens had benefited. Such surveys have given the movement the sense that it is astride a mass mood. Elsewhere, there has been evidence that it has sympathisers within the corridors of power. It goes further than just the politicians who back the Tobin tax. Joseph Stiglitz, former chief economist of the IMF published a comprehensive critique of the Bretton

Woods institutions, and Jeffrey Sachs, the Harvard professor who has also been a fierce critic of the Fund, have reinforced the activists' sense of their own credibility. As one Bank official puts it: "There is a feeling that the shouts on the streets are echoed by murmurs inside the institutions."

Activism has been drawing people from the ranks of business, too. Craig Cohon, who today counts himself as part of the movement alongside No Logo author Naomi Klein, was one of the top marketing executives for Coca-Cola in Europe until last year. He went to Davos, the annual gathering of CEOs in Switzerland, and decided to quit his job. He has started working on Global Legacy, an effort to raise $100m to fight urban poverty around the world.

Some in the developing countries of the South say that what is happening in the industrial North is misguided. Anti-globalisation activists claim to speak for the poor in developing countries, but do not understand the issues. Worse still, a few even suggest anti-globalisation activism is the means by which the First World can pursue a protectionist agenda, denying the Third World the benefits of economic growth. Jerry Mander, an advertising executive-turned-anti-globalisation activist, however, argues that thanks to the "struggles in the South" the shortcomings of corporate-led globalisation are now evident to everyone. He reads out a quote: "'The rising tide of the global economy will create many economic winners, but it will not lift all boats. [It will] span conflicts at home and abroad . . . [Its] evolution will be rocky, marked by chronic financial volatility and a widening economic divide. [Those] left behind will face deepening economic stagnation, political instability and cultural alienation. They will foster political, ethnic, ideological and religious extremism, along with the violence that often accompanies it.' And," he says, "that's not me talking, that is the CIA."

This queasiness about capitalism, activists say, has been fed from many directions. There is a sense of growing inequality, stoked by mass redundancies, widespread job insecurity and the disgust at soaring executive pay. There is discomfort over the commercialisation of public space, reinforced by the idea that Starbucks, McDonald's and The Gap have overrun every high street in the industrialised world. It is, perhaps, no surprise that the gradual but seismic upheaval in the world economy of the last 20 years has generated mass anxiety. Foreign direct investment flows averaged $115.4bn a year in the late 1980s. By 1999 they had reached $865.5bn. The European single market, the North American Free Trade Association and the Uruguay Round have created supranational authorities that override national and local governments.

To some extent, the response is emotional, even spiritual. Bruce Rich, a senior attorney at Environmental Defense in the US, suggests there is an ennui of affluence: "The kids who grow up with everything say 'There must be more to life than this.' In the 50s, you had the silent generation and then in the 60s you had great activism. In the 80s you had the me generation and then in the 90s the start of this movement."

The campaigners have what they call many "asks". Most of them are negative. A cutback in carbon dioxide emissions. The abolition of Third World debt. The end of World Bank support to fossil fuel and mining projects. The withdrawal of Unocal from Burma. No more exploitation of Florida tomato farmers by fast-food chain Taco Bell. A stop to Occidental's oil projects in the U'wa region of Colombia. The list goes on. So far, the efforts to put together a positive programme for change have been fraught and unconvincing. In their efforts to come up with a bumper-sticker ideology, the activists have rallied around the slogan: "Another world is possible".

As yet, though, they have struggled to come up with a vision of what that other world would look like.

Instead, they have been brought together most singularly by the WTO. To many, the WTO has promoted trade, spread prosperity, extended consumer choice. As a result, trade liberalisation has been a stalking horse for democracy in countries where closed markets were the counterparts to closed governments. But the activists see the WTO as the corporate world's tool to turn more high streets into homogeneous shopping malls, to engineer the privatisation of more public services, to annul environmental protection laws in the name of free trade and to open more countries to the whimsical forces of Wall Street.

"With the WTO, they have handed us a huge target. They were seen to be meddling everywhere. They were trying to create a world for corporations. It has helped us unify. We were individual mosquitoes, which have become a swarm," says Kevin Danaher, a slimmer version of Jesse "The Body" Ventura, who runs Global Exchange. Outside Danaher's office on the corner of 16th Street and Mission, where San Francisco's crack addicts and homeless folks mill around, a truck delivers beer to the local grocery store. A panhandler begs for change outside McDonald's. The world does not look as though it is quite ready to rise up in revolution.

Like the coursing rivers the movement itself so loves, the counter-capitalist current cannot easily be pinned down. It does not have one voice, or one message. It keeps changing, morphing from one campaign to the next. It is wide in its tactics and ambitions, violent and revolutionary on the edges, peaceful and reformist in the main. It rushes in often contradictory directions, anti-corporate and entrepreneurial, anarchist and nostalgic, technophobic and futuristic, revolutionary and conservative all at the same time. And it does not have one source. Many tributaries have swollen counter-capitalism: the anti-apartheid movement, the campaigns against US intervention in central America, environmentalism, the emergence of protest movements in the Third World, famine relief in Africa, the Asian financial crisis, human rights protection, Acid House raves in Europe, road rallies organised by Reclaim the Streets and hip-hop music in the US.

For Soren Ambrose, his journey began in the Niger Delta with Ken Saro-Wiwa. In the early 1990s, Saro-Wiwa said the operations of Shell in Ogoniland had left people dead and huge stretches of land destroyed. His concerns were to define a new kind of activism in Europe and the US: a protest which is about "them, not us", which is focused on corporations and economic principles, not war and civil rights. And he touched lives which have since carried his concerns into campaigns against companies and institutions that were unscathed by protest five years ago. It was a meeting with Saro-Wiwa in the early 1990s that inspired Steve Kretzman to set up Project Underground, the Berkeley-based group which has become a permanent irritant to mining companies. John Sellers' meeting with Saro-Wiwa when he visited Greenpeace at the same time has helped impassion his leadership of the Ruckus Society, the group which next week hosts a training camp at Middleburg, Virginia, to prepare for mass civil disobedience in Washington this month. The message of Saro-Wiwa remains the inspiration behind Platform, which works from a tiny office on the Thames and seeks to turn public attitudes against BP and Shell. And it was Saro-Wiwa who prompted Soren Ambrose to quit a life of academia for activism.

When the Nigerian authorities hanged Saro-Wiwa in Port Harcourt on November 10, 1995, they created the first martyr of the counter-capitalist movement.

55 Ecological Balance in an Era of Globalization

Vandana Shiva

In 1992, the Earth Summit in Rio marked the maturing of ecological awareness on a global scale. The world was poised to make a shift to sustainability. However, the Rio process and the sustainability agenda were subverted by the free-trade agenda. In 1993, the Uruguay Round of the General Agreement on Tariffs and Trade (GATT) was completed, in 1995 the World Trade Organization (WTO) was established, and world affairs grew increasingly dictated by trade and commerce. The normative political commitment to sustainability and justice was replaced by the rule of trade and the elevation of exploitation, greed, and profit maximization as the organizing principles of the market, the state, and society. Instead of the state regulating the market for the good of society, global economic powers and commercial forces are now regulating the state and society for the benefit of corporations. Instead of commerce being accountable to state and society, economic globalization is making citizens and their governments accountable to corporations and global economic bodies.

Economic globalization is not merely an economic phenomenon related to reduction of tariff barriers and removal of "protectionist" policies. It is in fact a normative process that reduces all value by commercial value. Free trade is, in reality, the rule of commerce. Both GATT and WTO basically undo the Rio agenda. Five years after Rio, we do not have Rio plus five but Rio minus five.

On the one hand, the search for ecological balance in an era of globalization requires an assessment of the social and ecological impact of globalization. On the other hand, it requires an imagination and a realization of an alternative order that puts ecological balance and social and economic justice rather than trade at the center of economic policy.

Globlization is not a natural, evolutionary, or inevitable phenomenon, as is often argued. Globalization is a political process that has been forced on the weak by the powerful. Globalization is not the cross-cultural interaction of diverse societies. It is the imposition of a particular culture on all others. Nor is globalization the search for ecological balance on a planetary scale. It is the predation of one class, one race, and often one gender of a single species on all others. "Global" in the dominant discourse is the political space in which the dominant local seeks control, freeing itself from local, regional, and global sources of accountability arising from the imperatives of ecological sustainability and social justice. "Global" in this sense

Original publication details: Excerpted from Vandana Shiva, "Ecological Balance in an Era of Globalization," in Paul Wapner and Lester Edwin J. Ruiz (eds.), *Principled World Politics: The Challenge of Normative International Relations* (Rowman & Littlefield, 2000), pp. 130–1, 132–3, 135–7, 139–41, 145–7, 148–9. Reprinted by permission of the Rowman & Littlefield Publishing Group.

does not represent the universal human interest; it represents a particular local and parochial interest and culture that has been globalized through its reach and control, irresponsibility, and lack of reciprocity.

The Three Waves of Globalization

Globalization has come in three waves. The first wave was the colonization of the Americas, Africa, Asia, and Australia by European powers over the course of 1,500 years. The second wave was the imposition of the West's idea of "development" on non-Western cultures in the postcolonial era of the past five decades. The third wave of globalization was unleashed approximately five years ago as the era of "free trade," which for some commentators implies an end to history, but for us in the Third World is a repeat of history through recolonization. Each wave of globalization is cumulative in its impact, even while it creates a discontinuity in the dominant metaphors and actors. Each wave of globalization has served Western interests, and each wave has created deeper colonization of other cultures and of the planet's life. [. . .]

The Community, the State, and the Corporation

Globalization has distorted the relationship between the community, the state, and the economy, or, to use Marc Nerfin's more colorful categories, the relationship between the citizen, the prince, and the merchant. It is privileging the economy and its key actor, the corporation, insofar as the state and the community are increasingly becoming mere instruments of global capital.

The appeal of globalization is usually based on the idea that it implies less red tape, less centralization, and less bureaucratic control. It is celebrated because it implies the erosion of those bureaucratic impediments that drive up the ecological costs of trade and exchange in general.

During the past fifty years, the state has increasingly taken over the functions of the community and the self-organizing capacity of citizens. Through globalization, corporations are taking over the functions of the state and citizens. Food provisioning, health care, education, and social security are all being transformed into corporate projects under the code words of "competitiveness" and "efficiency." People's rights and the public domain are being eroded by exporting the economic label of "protectionism" to cover all domains: ethical, social, and political. The protection of the environment and the protection of people's security are treated as nontariff trade barriers that need to be dismantled.

While the state is being required to step back from the regulation of trade and commerce, it is being increasingly called in to regulate citizens and remove communities that are an "obstruction" to free trade. Thus, the state is becoming leaner in dealing with big business and global industry, and it is becoming meaner in dealing with people.

In the North and in the South, the principle of "eminent domain" is still applied to the state takeover of people's land and resources, which are then handed over to global corporations. For example, in India, under the new infrastructure policies, foreign companies can enjoy up to 100 percent equity participation, but the government will acquire the land, displace people, and deal with "law and order" problems created by displacements.

In the United States, the federal, state, and local governments are appropriating citizens' homes and farms to hand over to large corporations. In Hurst, Texas, a suburb of Fort Worth, the government appropriated the land of more than 100 home owners, handing it over to its largest taxpayer, the Northeast Mall. Additionally, 4,200 residences were destroyed in Detroit, Michigan, so that General Motors could build a new plant. Quite clearly, it is the property of the powerful corporations that is being protected by the state in every part of the world under the new free-trade regimes, while the property of the ordinary citizen has no protection.

Another area in which the role of the state is actually increasing is in intellectual property rights (IPRs). As larger areas are being converted into "intellectual property" through patents – from microbes to mice, from seeds to human cell lines – the state is being increasingly called on to police citizens to prevent them from engaging in everyday activities, such as saving seeds and exchanging knowledge. Our most human acts have been criminalized – in relationship to ourselves, to one anther, and to other species through IPR legislation that is being forced on all countries and all people. [. . .]

Globalization as Environmental Apartheid

"Apartheid" literally means "separate development." However, in practice, apartheid is more appropriately a regime of exclusion. It is based on legislation that protects a privileged minority and that excludes the majority. It is characterized by the appropriation of the resources and wealth of society by a small minority based on privileges of race or class. The majority is then pushed into a marginalized existence without access to resources necessary for well-being and survival.

Erstwhile South Africa is the most dramatic example of a society based on racial apartheid. Globalization has in a deep sense been a globalization of apartheid. This apartheid is especially glaring in the context of the environment. Globalization is restructuring the control over resources in such a way that the natural resources of the poor are systematically taken over by the rich and the pollution of the rich is systematically dumped on the poor.

In the pre-Rio period, it was the North that contributed most to the destruction of the environment. For example, 90 percent of historic carbon dioxide emissions have been by the industrialized countries. The developed countries produce 90 percent of the hazardous wastes produced around the world every year. Global free trade has globalized this environmental destruction in an asymmetric pattern. While the economy is controlled by Northern corporations, they are increasingly exploiting Third World resources for their global activities. It is the South that is disproportionately bearing the environmental burden of the globalized economy. Globalization is thus leading to an environmental apartheid.

The current environmental and social crisis demands that the world economy adjust to ecological limits and the needs of human survival. Instead, global institutions, such as the World Bank and the International Monetary Fund and the WTO, are forcing the costs of adjustment on nature and women and the Third World. Across the Third World, structural adjustment and trade liberalization measures are becoming the most serious threat to the survival of the people.

While the last five decades have been characterized by the "globalization" of maldevelopment and the spread of a nonsustainable Western industrial paradigm in the name of development, the recent trends are toward an environmental apartheid in which, through global policy set by the holy trinity, the Western TNCs, supported by the governments of the economically powerful countries, attempt to maintain the North's economic power and wasteful lifestyles of the rich by exporting the environmental costs to the Third World. Resource- and pollution-intensive industries are being relocated in the South through the economics of free trade.

Lawrence Summers, who was the World Bank's chief economist and was responsible for the *1992 World Development Report*, which was devoted to the economics of the environment, actually suggested that it makes economic sense to shift polluting industries to Third World countries. In a memo dated December 12, 1991, to senior World Bank staff, he wrote, "Just between you and me, shouldn't the World Bank be encouraging more migration of the dirty industries to the LDC?" Summers justified his economic logic of increasing pollution in the Third World on three grounds. First, since wages are low in the Third World, the economic costs of pollution arising from increased illness and death are the least in the poorest countries. According to Summers, "Relocation of pollutants to the lowest wage country is impeccable and we should face up to that." Second, since in large parts of the Third World pollution is still low, it makes economic sense to Summers to introduce pollution: "I've always thought that countries in Africa are vastly under polluted; their air quality is probably vastly inefficiently low compared to Los Angeles or Mexico City." Finally, since the poor are poor, they cannot possibly worry about environmental problems: "The concern over an agent that causes a one in a million change in the odds of prostate cancer is obviously going to be much higher in a country where people survive to get prostate cancer than in a country where under five mortality is 200 per thousand." He recommended the relocation of hazardous and polluting industries to the Third World because, in narrow economic terms, life is cheaper in the poorer countries. The economists' logic might value life differentially in the rich North and the poor South. However, all life is precious. It is equally precious to the rich and the poor, to the white and the black, to men and women.

In this context, recent attempts of the North to link trade conditionalities with the environment in platforms such as WTO need to be viewed as an attempt to build on environmental and economic apartheid. The destruction of ecosystems and livelihoods as a result of trade liberalization is a major environmental and social subsidy to global trade and commerce and those who control it. The main mantra of globalization is "international competitiveness." In the context of the environment, this translates into the largest corporations competing for the natural resources that the poor people in the Third World need for their survival. This competition is highly unequal not only because the corporations are powerful and the poor are not but also because the rules of free trade allow corporations to use the machinery of the nation-state to appropriate resources from the people and prevent people from asserting and exercising their rights.

It is often argued that globalization will create more trade, which will create growth, which will remove poverty. What is overlooked in this myth is that globalization and liberalized trade and investment create growth by destroying the environment and local, sustainable livelihoods. They, therefore, create poverty instead of removing it. The new globalization policies have accelerated and expanded environmental destruction and displaced millions of people from their homes and their sustenance base. [. . .]

Northern Dumping in the South

The United States generates more than 275 million tons of toxic waste every year and is the leading waste-exporting country in the world. The United States is one of the 161 countries that has signed the Basel International Convention but has not ratified it (along with fifty-eight other countries); parties to the convention, such as India, are not allowed to trade in hazardous wastes with nonparties to the convention. However, notwithstanding the convention, the United States continues its long tradition of exporting its toxic wastes, finding loopholes for dumping them on the South. The United States is thus violating international law in sending shipments of its waste, often mislabeled as recyclables, to India.

In the first half of 1996, approximately 1,500 tons of lead wastes were imported to India. Greenpeace findings state that the amount of toxic lead waste imported from industrialized countries into India has doubled since 1995. Imports from the United States, Australia, South Korea, Germany, the Netherlands, France, Japan, and the United Kingdom account for about 67 percent of the total import of lead wastes to India. The Organization of Economic Cooperation and Development (OECD) accounted for 98 percent of the 400 million metric tons of toxic waste generated worldwide.

Toxic waste such as cyanide, mercury, and arsenic is being shipped as "recyclable waste" – a deliberate attempt to mislead and disguise the true nature of the wastes. In reality, there is no such use or demand to recover such toxic chemicals because it is pure waste. The imported waste often ends up in backyard smelting organizations, not the commercial sector as stated by the government. Many of the importing units do not possess the technology or the expertise to process the chemicals they are importing; therefore, they inadvertently cause more harm to the environment and their communities because of their ignorance concerning the chemicals that they are dealing with. Eight-five hundred such units operate in Maharashtra alone.

Developed countries are offering lucrative prices (in Indian terms) to Indian "recycling" companies to take their material for "processing." India is being used as a dumping ground by the Northern industrialized countries because the cost of treating and disposing waste in a sustainable manner in the North has become highly expensive. Costs have become so high because of stringent laws that ban dumping, burning, and burying waste. Dumping in the developing world therefore becomes justified on grounds of economic efficiency.

The cost of burying one ton of hazardous waste in the United States rose from $15 in 1980 to $350 in 1992. In Germany, it is cheaper, by $2,500, to ship a ton of waste to a developing country than to dispose of it in Europe. Countries such as Germany find it cheaper to export their waste to a landfill than to recycle it themselves. Because India does not charge any landfill costs, the profits made in waste trade has made the industry even more attractive.

In 1966, the Research Foundation for Science, Technology and Ecology (RFSTE) filed public interest litigation seeking a ban on all hazardous and toxic wastes into India. In response, on May 6, 1997, the Supreme Court of India imposed a blanket ban on the import of all kinds of hazardous and toxic wastes into the country. The court also directed state governments to show cause why immediate orders should not be passed for the closure of more than 2,000 unauthorized waste-handling units identified by the central government in various parts of the country. The Supreme Court directed that no import be made or permitted of any hazardous waste that is already banned under the Basel International Convention, or to be banned after the date specified therein by the court.

A court statement established that 2,000 tons of hazardous wastes were being generated every day in India without adequate safe disposal sites. This ban applies to state governments as well as the central government to give authorization for the importation of hazardous wastes.

Today, toxic waste dumping has become a national issue, and several nongovernmental organizations are working specifically on the banning of toxic waste import and dumping and related issues. Srishti, Greenpeace, Toxics Link Exchange, Public Interest Research Group, WWF-India, and the RFSTE are Delhi-based movements that are concerned with hazardous wastes and toxics issues and that, in particular, are opposing the importation of toxic wastes. Furthermore, some of us are involved in creating awareness within India as to the actions of transnational and local industries who often openly defy existing environmental laws regarding importation, treatment, handling, and disposal of hazardous wastes. [. . .]

People's Movements for the Protection of Biodiversity and Collective Rights

New social and environmental movements are emerging everywhere in response to the widespread destruction of the environment and of the livelihoods that depend on biodiversity and in response to piracy of our indigenous resources and indigenous innovation. In India, the intricate link between people's livelihoods and biodiversity has evolved over centuries. Economic liberalization is threatening to sever this link by treating biodiversity as a raw material for exploitation of life forms as property and of people's livelihoods as an inevitable sacrifice for national economic growth and development. It is also eroding the level of governing control that people have over their lives.

In February 1995, the tribal people from different parts of India were in Delhi on an indefinite fast to force the government to recognize their declaration of "self-rule." The National Front for Tribal Self-Rule, a national organization of organizations of tribal people, has conducted a civil disobedience movement since October 2, 1995, for the establishment of self-rule. As they state,

> We have carried the cross of virtual slavery for much too long in spite of independence. Other rural folks are also in a similar state. Yet, now that everything is clear and there is unanimity in the establishment as also among members of parliament and experts, the change must not be delayed. We will not tolerate this. Even otherwise, on the issue of self-governance we need not be solicitous. It is a natural right. In the hierarchy of democratic institutions gram-sabha is above all, even parliament. This is what Gandhi preached; we will not obey any law which compromises the position of gram-sabha. In any case we resolve to establish self-rule with effect from October 2, 1995. We will have command over our resources and will manage our affairs thereafter. (Declaration, "Front for Tribal Self-Rule," Delhi, February 1995)

The struggle of the tribal people was successful.

The passing of the Provisions of the Panchayats (Extension to the Scheduled Areas) Act that came into effect in December 1996 represents a landmark piece of legislation as far as acknowledging the legal rights to self-rule of the tribal people are concerned. Section 4(b) and (d) of the act state the following:

- A village shall ordinarily consist of a habitation or a group of habitations, or a hamlet or a group of hamlets comprising a community and managing its affairs in accordance with traditions and customs.
- Each gram-sabha shall be competent to safeguard and preserve the traditions and customs of the people, their cultural identity, community resources and the customary mode of dispute resolution.

The implementation of the Panchayati Raj Act in Scheduled Areas has already set the precedent for the recognition of communities as competent authorities for decision making on resource use, cultural values and traditions, and community rights to common resources as the building block of a decentralized democracy (Research Foundation for Science, Technology and Ecology 1997).

More than 100 villages in and around the thick forests of Nagarhole in Karnataka have established self-governments to safeguard their livelihood under the provisions of a law passed by the Parliament that came into effect on December 24, 1996: the Provisions of the Panchayats (Extension to the Scheduled Areas) Act, 1996. However, this law has yet to be passed by the Karnataka Assembly to implement it in that state.

The people have formed gram-sabhas and established task forces to implement the self-rule program. In some of the villages, they have erected gates at the entrance, and only the chief of the tribal community/village has been entrusted with the power to give permission to any outsider to enter their village. The villagers are freely collecting the minor forest produce, and even they are adjudicating the problems themselves rather than going to the police or court.

The Movement for Declaration of Community Rights to Biodiversity: The Case of Pattuvam Panchayat

Nationwide people's movements have succeeded to date in stalling any legislation passing parliament that would promote IPRs over biodiversity. Such opposition signifies the degree of democratic dissent being generated at the grassroots level to laws affecting people's livelihoods and rights over their resources. People's movements against erosion, exploitation, and usurpation of biodiversity are numerous and widespread throughout the country. A small community in southern Kerala has taken a bold step to protect its biodiversity. On April 9, 1997, in a remote part of Kerala, hundreds of local people gathered to declare their local biodiversity as a community-owned resource that they will collectively protect and that they will not allow to be privatized through patents on derived products or varieties.

The community is known as the Pattuvam Panchayat. The Panchayat has set up its own biodiversity register to record all biodiversity of species in the region. It has stated that no individual, TNC, or state or central government can use their biodiversity without the permission of the Pattuvam Panchayat. The people of Pattuvam have taken a pathbreaking step by declaring their biodiversity a community resource over which the community as a whole has rights. This step demonstrates a commitment to rejuvenating and protecting their biodiversity and knowledge systems from the exploitative forces of economic liberalization.

Movements are occurring in other parts of India as well whereby communities are declaring the biodiversity and knowledge as the common heritage of local communities. For example, in Dharward in Karnataka and in Chattisgarh, Madhya Pradesh, declaration ceremonies have been held announcing that biodiversity is a community resource and that privatization of biodiversity and indigenous knowledge through patents is theft. [. . .]

Navdanya: Seeds of Freedom

I have started a national movement for the recovery of the biological and intellectual commons by saving native seeds from extinction. Seed is the first link in the food chain. It is also the first step toward freedom in food. Globalization is leading to total control over what we eat and what we grow. The tiny seed is becoming an instrument of freedom in this emerging era of total control. Our slogan is, "Native seed – indigenous agriculture – local markets."

Through saving the native seed, we are becoming free of chemicals. By practicing a "free" agriculture, we are saying no to patents on life and to biopiracy. Gandhi called such resistance "Satyagraha": the struggle for truth. Navdanya is a "Seed Satyagraha" in which it is the most marginal and poor peasants who are finding new hope.

A central part of the Seed Satyagraha is to declare the "common intellectual rights" of Third World communities who have gifted the world the knowledge of the rich bounties of nature's diversity. The innovations of Third World communities might differ in process and objectives from the innovations in the commercial world of the West, but they cannot be discounted just because they are different. But we are going beyond just saying no. We are creating alternatives by building community seed banks, strengthening farmers' seed supplies, and searching for sustainable agriculture options that are suitable for different regions.

The seed has become, for us, the site and the symbol of freedom in the age of manipulation and monopoly of its diversity. It plays the role of Gandhi's spinning wheel in this period of recolonization through free trade. The "Charkha" (spinning wheel) became an important symbol of freedom not because it was big and powerful but because it was small and could come alive as a sign of resistance and creativity in the smallest of huts and poorest of families. In smallness lay its power. The seed too is small. It embodies diversity. It embodies the freedom to stay alive. And seed is still the common property of small farmers in India. In the seed, cultural diversity converges with biological diversity. Ecological issues combine with social justice, peace, and democracy.

Conclusion

The dynamics of globalization and their associated violence are posing some of the most severe challenges to ordinary people in India and throughout the world. While this chapter has been pessimistic, outlining the character and strength of globalization and its ability to thwart citizen accountability, I take heart in the resistance movements mentioned in the last few sections. Continuous globalizing efforts may threaten democracy, the vibrancy and diversity of life forms, and ecological well-being in general. However, the human spirit, inspired by justice and environmental protection, can never be fully repressed. Despite the brutal violence of globalization, we have hope because we build alternatives in partnership with nature and people. [. . .]

56 Tomorrow Begins Today

Subcomandante Marcos

Through my voice speaks the voice of the EZLN.

Brothers and sisters of the whole world
Brothers and sisters of Africa, America, Asia, Europe, and Oceania
Brothers and sisters attending the First Intercontinental Encuentro for Humanity and against Neoliberalism:

WELCOME TO THE ZAPATISTA LA REALIDAD.
Welcome to this territory in struggle for humanity.
Welcome to this territory in rebellion against neoliberalism.[. . .]
Welcome, all men, women, children, and elders from the five continents who have responded to the invitation of the Zapatista indigenous to search for hope, for humanity, and to struggle against neoliberalism.[. . .]

In the world of those who live and kill for Power, there is no room for human beings. There is no space for hope, no place for tomorrow. Slavery or death is the choice that their world offers all worlds. The world of money, their world, governs from the stock exchanges. Today, speculation is the principal source of enrichment, and at the same time the best demonstration of the atrophy of our capacity to work. Work is no longer necessary in order to produce wealth; now all that is needed is speculation.

Crimes and wars are carried out so that the global stock exchanges may be pillaged by one or the other.

Meanwhile, millions of women, millions of youths, millions of indigenous, millions of homosexuals, millions of human beings of all races and colors, participate in the financial markets only as a devalued currency, always worth less and less, the currency of their blood turning a profit.

The globalization of markets erases borders for speculation and crime and multiplies them for human beings. Countries are obliged to erase their national borders for money to circulate, but to multiply their internal borders.

Original publication details: Excerpted from Subcomandante Marcos, *Our Word is Our Weapon* ("Tomorrow Begins Today"), Closing Remarks at the First Intercontinental *Encuentro* for Humanity and against Neoliberalism, August 3, 1996 (Seven Stories Press, 2001), pp. 115–23. Reprinted by permission of Seven Stories Press.

Neoliberalism doesn't turn many countries into one country; it turns each country into many countries.

The lie of unipolarity and internationalization turns itself into a nightmare of war, a fragmented war, again and again, so many times that nations are pulverized. In this world, Power globalizes to overcome the obstacles to its war of conquest. National governments are turned into the military underlings of a new world war against humanity.

From the stupid course of nuclear armament – destined to annihilate humanity in one blow – it has turned to the absurd militarization of every aspect in the life of national societies – a militarization destined to annihilate humanity in many blows, in many places, and in many ways. What were formerly known as "national armies" are turning into mere units of a greater army, one that neoliberalism arms to lead against humanity. The end of the so-called Cold War didn't stop the global arms race, it only changed the model for the merchandising of mortality: weapons of all kinds and sizes for all kinds of criminal tastes. More and more, not only are the so-called institutional armies armed, but also the armies' drug-trafficking builds up to ensure its reign. More or less rapidly, national societies are being militarized, and armies – supposedly created to protect their borders from foreign enemies – are turning their cannons and rifles around and aiming them inward.

It is not possible for neoliberalism to become the world's reality without the argument of death served up by institutional and private armies, without the gag served up by prisons, without the blows and assassinations served up by the military and the police. National repression is a necessary premise of the globalization neoliberalism imposes.

The more neoliberalism advances as a global system, the more numerous grow the weapons and the ranks of the armies and national police. The numbers of the imprisoned, the disappeared, and the assassinated in different countries also grows.

A world war:
the most brutal,
the most complete,
the most universal,
the most effective.

Each country,
each city,
each countryside,
each house,
each person,
each is a large or small battleground.

On the one side is neoliberalism, with all its repressive power and all its machinery of death; on the other side is the human being.

There are those who resign themselves to being one more number in the huge exchange of Power. There are those who resign themselves to being slaves. He who is himself master to slaves also cynically walks the slave's horizontal ladder. In exchange for the bad life and crumbs that Power hands out, there are those who sell themselves, resign themselves, surrender themselves.

In any part of the world, there are slaves who say they are happy being slaves. In any part of the world, there are men and women who stop being human and take their place in the gigantic market that trades in dignities.

But there are those who do not resign themselves, there are those who decide not to conform, there are those who do not sell themselves, there are those who do not surrender themselves. Around the world, there are those who resist being annihilated in this war. There are those who decide to fight. In any place in the world, anytime, any man or any woman rebels to the point of tearing off the clothes resignation has woven for them and cynicism has dyed gray. Any man or woman, of whatever color, in whatever tongue, speaks and says to himself or to herself: Enough is enough! – ¡ Ya Basta!

> Enough is enough of lies.
> Enough is enough of crime.
> Enough is enough of death.
> Enough is enough of war, says any man or woman.

Any man or woman, in whatever part of any of the five continents, eagerly decides to resist Power and to construct his or her own path that doesn't lead to the loss of dignity and hope.

Any man or woman decides to live and struggle for his or her part in history. No longer does Power dictate his or her steps. No longer does Power administer life and decide death.

Any man or woman responds to death with life, and responds to the nightmare by dreaming and struggling against war, against neoliberalism, for humanity . . .

For struggling for a better world, all of us are fenced in and threatened with death. The fence is reproduced globally. In every continent, every city, every countryside, every house. Power's fence of war closes in on the rebels, for whom humanity is always grateful.

> But fences are broken,
> in every house,
> in every countryside,
> in every city,
> in every state,
> in every country,
> in every continent,
> the rebels, whom history repeatedly has given us the length of its long trajectory, struggle and the fence is broken.

The rebels search each other out. They walk toward one another.

They find each other and together break other fences.

In the countryside and cities, in the states, in the nations, on the continents, the rebels begin to recognize each other, to know themselves as equals and different. They continue on their fatiguing walk, walking as it is now necessary to walk, that is to say, struggling . . . [. . .]

A world made of many worlds found itself these days in the mountains of the Mexican Southeast.

A world made of many worlds opened a space and established its right to exist, raised the banner of being necessary, stuck itself in the middle of the earth's reality to announce a better future.

A world of all the worlds that rebel and resist Power.

A world of all the worlds that inhabit this world, opposing cynicism.

A world that struggles for humanity and against neoliberalism.

This was the world that we lived these days.

This is the world that we found here.

This *encuentro* wasn't to end in La Realidad. Now it must search for a place to carry on.

But what next?

A new number in the useless enumeration of the numerous international orders?

A new scheme for calming and easing the anguish of having no solution?

A global program for world revolution?

A utopian theory so that it can maintain a prudent distance from the reality that anguishes us?

A scheme that assures each of us a position, a task, a title, and no work?

The echo goes, a reflected image of the possible and forgotten: the possibility and necessity of speaking and listening; not an echo that fades away, or a force that decreases after reaching its apogee.

Let it be an echo that breaks barriers and re-echoes.

Let it be an echo of our own smallness, of the local and particular, which reverberates in an echo of our own greatness, the intercontinental and galactic.

An echo that recognizes the existence of the other and does not overpower or attempt to silence it.

An echo that takes its place and speaks its own voice, yet speaks the voice of the other.

An echo that reproduces its own sound, yet opens itself to the sound of the other.

An echo of this rebel voice transforming itself and renewing itself in other voices.

An echo that turns itself into many voices, into a network of voices that, before Power's deafness, opts to speak to itself, knowing itself to be one and many, acknowledging itself to be equal in its desire to listen and be listened to, recognizing itself as diverse in the tones and levels of voices forming it.

Let it be a network of voices that resist the war Power wages on them.

A network of voices that not only speak, but also struggle and resist for humanity and against neoliberalism.

A network of voices that are born resisting, reproducing their resistance in other quiet and solitary voices.

A network that covers the five continents and helps to resist the death that Power promises us.

In the great pocket of voices, sounds continue to search for their place, fitting in with others.

The great pocket, ripped, continues to keep the best of itself, yet opens itself to what is better.

The great pocket continues to mirror voices; it is a world in which sounds may be listened to separately, recognizing their specificity; it is a world in which sounds can include themselves in one great sound.

The multiplication of resistances, the "I am not resigned," the "I am a rebel," continues.

The world, with the many worlds that the world needs, continues.

Humanity, recognizing itself to be plural, different, inclusive, tolerant of itself, full of hope, continues.

The human and rebel voice, consulted on the five continents in order to become a network of voices and resistance, continues.

57 Porto Alegre Call for Mobilization

World Social Forum

Social forces from around the world have gathered here at the World Social Forum in Porto Alegre. Unions and NGOs, movements and organizations, intellectuals and artists, together we are building a great alliance to create a new society, different from the dominant logic wherein the free-market and money are considered the only measure of worth. Davos represents the concentration of wealth, the globalization of poverty and the destruction of our earth. Porto Alegre represents the hope that a new world is possible, where human beings and nature are the center of our concern.

We are part of a movement which has grown since Seattle. We challenge the elite and their undemocratic processes, symbolised by the World Economic Forum in Davos. We came to share our experiences, build our solidarity, and demonstrate our total rejection of the neoliberal policies of globalisation.

We are women and men, farmers, workers, unemployed, professionals, students, blacks and indigenous peoples, coming from the South and from the North, committed to struggle for peoples' rights, freedom, security, employment and education. We are fighting against the hegemony of finance, the destruction of our cultures, the monopolization of knowledge, mass media, and communication, the degradation of nature, and the destruction of the quality of life by multinational corporations and anti-democratic policies. Participative democratic experiences – like that of Porto Alegre – show us that a concrete alternative is possible. We reaffirm the supremacy of human, ecological and social rights over the demands of finance and investors.

At the same time that we strengthen our movements, we resist the global elite and work for equity, social justice, democracy and security for everyone, without distinction. Our methodology and alternatives stand in stark contrast to the destructive policies of neo-liberalism.

Globalisation reinforces a sexist and patriarchal system. It increases the feminisation of poverty and exacerbates all forms of violence against women. Equality between women and men is central to our struggle. Without this, another world will never be possible.

Neoliberal globalization increases racism, continuing the veritable genocide of centuries of slavery and colonialism which destroyed the bases of black African civilizations. We call on all movements to be in solidarity with African peoples in the continent and outside, in defense of their rights to land, citizenship, freedom, peace, and equality, through the reparation of historical and social debts. Slave trade and slavery are crimes against humanity.

Original publication details: Excerpted from World Social Forum, "Porto Alegre Call for Mobilization," 2001. Reprinted by permission of World Social Forum, www.movsoc.org

We express our special recognition and solidarity with indigenous peoples in their historic struggle against genocide and ethnocide and in defense of their rights, natural resources, culture, autonomy, land, and territory.

Neoliberal globalisation destroys the environment, health and people's living environment. Air, water, land and peoples have become commodities. Life and health must be recognized as fundamental rights which must not be subordinated to economic policies.

The external debt of the countries of the South has been repaid several times over. Illegitimate, unjust and fraudulent, it functions as an instrument of domination, depriving people of their fundamental human rights with the sole aim of increasing international usury. We demand its unconditional cancellation and the reparation of historical, social, and ecological debts, as immediate steps toward a definitive resolution of the crisis this Debt provokes.

Financial markets extract resources and wealth from communities and nations, and subject national economies to the whims of speculators. We call for the closure of tax havens and the introduction of taxes on financial transactions.

Privatisation is a mechanism for transferring public wealth and natural resources to the private sector. We oppose all forms of privatisation of natural resources and public services. We call for the protection of access to resources and public goods necessary for a decent life.

Multinational corporations organise global production with massive unemployment, low wages and unqualified labour and by refusing to recognise the fundamental worker's rights as defined by the ILO. We demand the genuine recognition of the right to organise and negotiate for unions, and new rights for workers to face the globalisation strategy. While goods and money are free to cross borders, the restrictions on the movement of people exacerbate exploitation and repression. We demand an end to such restrictions.

We call for a trading system which guarantees full employment, food security, fair terms of trade and local prosperity. Free trade is anything but free. Global trade rules ensure the accelerated accumulation of wealth and power by multinational corporations and the further marginalisation and impoverishment of small farmers, workers and local enterprises. We demand that governments respect their obligations to the international human rights instruments and multilateral environmental agreements. We call on people everywhere to support the mobilizations against the creation of the Free Trade Area in the Americas, an initiative which means the recolonization of Latin America and the destruction of fundamental social, economic, cultural and environmental human rights.

The IMF, the World Bank and regional banks, the WTO, NATO and other military alliances are some of the multilateral agents of neoliberal globalisation. We call for an end to their interference in national policy. These institutions have no legitimacy in the eyes of the people and we will continue to protest against their measures.

Neoliberal globalization has led to the concentration of land ownership and favored corporate agricultural systems which are environmentally and socially destructive. It is based on export oriented growth backed by large scale infrastructure development, such as dams, which displaces people from their land and destroys their livelihoods. Their loss must be restored. We call for a democratic agrarian reform. Land, water and seeds must be in the hands of the peasants. We promote sustainable agricultural processes. Seeds and genetic stocks are the heritage of humanity. We demand that the use of transgenics and the patenting of life be abolished.

Militarism and corporate globalisation reinforce each other to undermine democracy and peace. We totally refuse war as a way to solve conflicts and we oppose the arms race and the arms trade. We call for an end to the repression and criminalisation of social protest. We condemn foreign military intervention in the internal affairs of our countries. We demand the lifting of embargoes and sanctions used as instruments of aggression, and express our solidarity with those who suffer their consequences. We reject US military intervention in Latin American through the Plan Colombia.

We call for a strengthening of alliances, and the implementation of common actions, on these principal concerns. We will continue to mobilize on them until the next Forum. We recognize that we are now in a better position to undertake the struggle for a different world, a world without misery, hunger, discrimination and violence, with quality of life, equity, respect and peace. [. . .]

The proposals formulated are part of the alternatives being elaborated by social movements around the world. They are based on the principle that human beings and life are not commodities, and in the commitment to the welfare and human rights of all.

Our involvement in the World Social Forum has enriched understanding of each of our struggles and we have been strengthened. We call on all peoples around the world to join in this struggle to build a better future. The World Social Forum of Porto Alegre is a way to achieve peoples' sovereignty and a just world.

[180 organizations listed as endorsing the Call, from 28 countries]

58 A Better World Is Possible!

International Forum on Globalization

Introduction

A. Global Resistance

Society is at a crucial crossroads. A peaceful, equitable and sustainable future depends on the outcome of escalating conflicts between two competing visions: one corporate, one democratic. The schism has been caught by media images and stories accompanying recent meetings of global bureaucracies like the World Trade Organization (WTO), the International Monetary Fund (IMF), the World Bank, the Free Trade Area of the Americas (FTAA), and numerous other gatherings of corporate and economic elites, such as the World Economic Forum at Davos, Switzerland, (although in 2002 it will meet in New York City).

Over the past five to ten years, millions of people have taken to the streets in India, the Philippines, Indonesia, Brazil, Bolivia, the United States, Canada, Mexico, Argentina, Venezuela, France, Germany, Italy, the Czech Republic, Spain, Sweden, England, New Zealand, Australia, Kenya, South Africa, Thailand, Malaysia and elsewhere in massive demonstrations against the institutions and policies of corporate globalization. All too often the corporate media have done more to mislead than to inform the public on the issues behind the protests. Thomas Friedman, *The New York Times* foreign affairs columnist, is typical of journalists who characterize the demonstrators as "ignorant protectionists" who offer no alternatives and are unworthy of serious attention.

The claim that the protestors have no alternatives is as false as the claims that they are anti-poor, xenophobic, anti-trade, and have no analysis. In addition to countless books, periodicals, conferences, and individual articles and presentations setting forth alternatives, numerous consensus statements have been carefully crafted by civil society groups over the past two decades that set forth a wealth of alternatives with a striking convergence in their beliefs about the underlying values human societies can and should serve. Such consensus statements include a collection of citizen treaties drafted in Rio de Janeiro in 1992 by the 18,000 representatives of global civil society who met in parallel to the official meetings of the United Nations Conference on Environment and Development (UNCED). A subsequent initiative produced The Earth Charter, scheduled for ratification by the UN General Assembly in 2002 – the product of a global process that involved thousands of people. In 2001 and 2002, tens of thousands more gathered in Porto Alegre, Brazil, for the first annual World Social Forum on the theme "Another World Is Possible"

Original publication details: Excerpted from the International Forum on Globalization, *A Better World Is Possible!*, report summary, 2002. Reprinted by permission of the International Forum on Globalization.

to carry forward this process of popular consensus building toward a world that works for all.

B. Different Worlds

The corporate globalists who meet in posh gatherings to chart the course of corporate globalization in the name of private profits, and the citizen movements who organize to thwart them in the name of democracy and diversity are separated by deep differences in values, world view, and definitions of progress. At times it seems they must be living in wholly different worlds – which in many respects they are.

Corporate globalists inhabit a world of power and privilege. They see progress everywhere because from their vantage point the drive to privatize public assets and free the market from governmental interference appears to be spreading freedom and prosperity throughout the world, improving the lives of people everywhere, and creating the financial and material wealth necessary to end poverty and protect the environment. They see themselves as champions of an inexorable and beneficial historical process toward erasing the economic and political borders that hinder corporate expansion, eliminating the tyranny of inefficient and meddlesome public bureaucracies, and unleashing the enormous innovation and wealth-creating power of competition and private enterprise.

Citizen movements see a starkly different reality. Focused on people and the environment, they see a world in deepening crisis of such magnitude as to threaten the fabric of civilization and the survival of the species – a world of rapidly growing inequality, erosion of relationships of trust, and failing planetary life support systems. Where corporate globalists see the spread of democracy and vibrant market economies, citizen movements see the power to govern shifting away from people and communities to financial speculators and global corporations dedicated to the pursuit of short-term profit. They see corporations replacing democracies of people with democracies of money, self-organizing markets with centrally planned corporate economies, and diverse ethical cultures with cultures of greed and materialism.

C. Transformational Imperative

In a world in which a few enjoy unimaginable wealth, 200 million children under five are underweight due to a lack of food. Fourteen million children die each year from hunger-related disease. A hundred million children are living or working on the streets. Three hundred thousand children were conscripted as soldiers during the 1990s and six million were injured in armed conflicts. Eight hundred million people go to bed hungry each night. Human activity – most particularly fossil fuel combustion is estimated to have increased atmospheric concentrations of carbon dioxide to their highest levels in 20 million years. According to the WorldWatch Institute, natural disasters – including weather related disasters such as storms, floods, and fires – affected more than two billion people and caused in excess of $608 billion in economic losses worldwide during the decade of the 1990s – more than the previous four decades combined.

D. Economic Democracy

Humanity has reached the limits of an era of centralized institutional power and control. The global corporation, the WTO, the IMF, and the World Bank are structured to concentrate power in the hands of ruling elites shielded from public accountability. They represent an outmoded, undemocratic, inefficient and ultimately destructive way of organizing human affairs that is as out of step with the needs and values of healthy, sustainable and democratic societies as the institution of monarchy. The current and future well being of humanity depends on transforming the relationships of power within and between human societies toward more democratic and mutually accountable modes of managing human affairs that are self-organizing, power-sharing, and minimize the need for coercive central authority.

E.   Global Governance

The concern for local self-reliance and self-determination have important implications for global governance. For example, in a self-reliant and localized system the primary authority to set and enforce rules must rest with the national and local governments of the jurisdictions to which they apply. The proper role of global institutions is to facilitate the cooperative coordination of national policies on matters where the interests of nations are inherently intertwined – as with action on global warming.

F.   Building Momentum

Growing public consciousness of the pervasive abuse of corporate power has fueled the growth of a powerful opposition movement with an increasingly impressive list of achievements. Unified by a deep commitment to universal values of democracy, justice, and respect for life this alliance functions with growing effectiveness without a central organization, charismatic leader, or defining ideology – taking different forms in different settings.

In India, popular movements seek to empower local people through the democratic community control of resources under the banner of a million strong Living Democracy Movement (*Jaiv Panchayat*). In Canada, hundreds of organizations have joined in alliance to articulate a Citizens' Agenda that seeks to wrest control of governmental institutions back away from corporations. In Chile, coalitions of environmental groups have created a powerful Sustainable Chile (*Sustainable Chile*) movement that seeks to reverse Chile's drift toward neoliberalism and re-assert popular democratic control over national priorities and resources. The focus in Brazil is on the rights of the poor and landless. In Bolivia it takes the form of a mass movement of peasants and workers who have successfully blocked the privatization of water. In Mexico, the Mayan people have revived the spirit of Zapata in a movement to confirm the rights of indigenous people to land and resources. Farmers in France have risen up in revolt against trade rules that threaten to destroy small farms. The construction of new highways in England has brought out hundreds of thousands of people who oppose this desecration of the countryside in response to globalization's relentless demand for ever more high speed transport.

These are only a few examples of the popular initiatives and actions in defense of democratic rights that are emerging all around the world. Together these many initiatives are unleashing ever more of the creative energy of humanity toward building cooperative systems of sustainable societies that work for all.

Chapter I   Critique of Economic Globalization

The alternatives offered in this report grow from the widespread damage inflicted by economic globalization over the past five centuries as it passed from colonialism and imperialism through post-colonial, export-led development models. The driving force of economic globalization since World War II has been several hundred large private corporations and banks that have increasingly woven webs of production, consumption, finance, and culture across borders. Indeed, today most of what we eat, drink, wear, drive, and entertain ourselves with is the product of globe-girdling corporations.

A. Key Ingredients and General Effects

Economic globalization (sometimes referred to as corporate-led globalization), features several key ingredients:

- Corporate deregulation and the unrestricted movement of capital;
- Privatization and commodification of public services, and remaining aspects of the global and community commons, such as bulk water and genetic resources;
- Integration and conversion of national economies (including some that were largely self-reliant) to environmentally and socially harmful export-oriented production;
- Promotion of hyper-growth and unrestricted exploitation of the planet's resources to fuel the growth;
- Dramatically increased corporate concentration;
- Undermining of national social, health and environmental programs;
- Erosion of traditional powers and policies of democratic nation-states and local communities by global corporate bureaucracies;
- Global cultural homogenization, and the intensive promotion of unbridled consumerism.

1. Pillars of Globalization: The first tenet of economic globalization, as now designed, is the need to integrate and merge all economic activity of all countries within a single, homogenized model of development; a single centralized system. A second tenet of the globalization design is that primary importance is given to the achievement of ever more rapid, and never ending corporate economic growth – hyper growth – fueled by the constant search for access to natural resources, new and cheaper labor sources, and new markets. A third tenet concerns privatization and commodification of as many traditionally non-commodified nooks and crannies of existence as possible – seeds and genes for example. A fourth important tenet of economic globalization is its strong emphasis on a global conversion to export-oriented production and trade as an economic and social nirvana.

2. Beneficiaries of Globalization: The actual beneficiaries of this model have become all too obvious. In the United States, for example, we know that during the period of the most rapid globalization, top corporate executives of the largest global companies have been making salaries and options in the many millions of dollars, often in the hundreds of millions, while real wages of ordinary workers have been declining. The Institute for Policy Studies reports that American CEOs are now paid, on average, 517 times more than production workers, with that rate increasing yearly. The Economic Policy Institute's 1999 report says that median hourly wages are actually down by 10 percent in real wages over the last 25 years. As for lifting the global poor, the U.N. Development Program's 1999 *Human Development Report* indicated that the gap between the wealthy and the poor within and among countries of the world is getting steadily larger, and it named inequities in the global trade system as being one of the key factors.

B. Bureaucratic Expressions of Globalization

Creating a world that works for all must begin with an effort to undo the enormous damage inflicted by the corporate globalization policies that so badly distort economic relationships among people and countries. The thrust of those policies is perhaps most dramatically revealed in the structural adjustment programs imposed on low and intermediate income countries by the IMF and the World Bank – two institutions that bear responsibility for enormous social and environmental devastation and human suffering. Structural adjustment requires governments to:

- Cut government spending on education, healthcare, the environment, and price subsidies for basic necessities such as food grains, and cooking oils in favor of servicing foreign debt.
- Devalue the national currency and increase exports by accelerating the plunder of natural resources, reducing real wages, and subsidizing export-oriented foreign investments.
- Liberalize financial markets to attract speculative short-term portfolio investments that create enormous financial instability and foreign liabilities while serving little, if any, useful purpose.
- Increase interest rates to attract foreign speculative capital, thereby increasing bankruptcies of domestic businesses and imposing new hardships on indebted individuals.
- Eliminate tariffs, quotas and other controls on imports, thereby increasing the import of consumer goods purchased with borrowed foreign exchange, undermining local industry and agricultural producers unable to compete with cheap imports, which increases the strain on foreign exchange accounts, and deepening external indebtedness.

The World Bank and the IMF, along with the General Agreement on Tariffs and Trade/World Trade Organization (GATT/WTO) are together known as the Bretton Woods institutions – the collective product of agreements reached at an international gathering held in Bretton Woods, New Hampshire, in July, 1944, to create an institutional framework for the post-World War II global economy.

C. Conclusions

The Bretton Woods institutions have a wholly distorted view of economic progress and relationships. Their embrace of unlimited expansion of trade and foreign investment as measures of economic progress suggests that they consider the most advanced state of development to be one in which all productive assets are owned by foreign corporations producing for export; the currency that facilitates day-to-day transactions is borrowed from foreign banks; education and health services are operated by global corporations on a for-profit, fee-for-service basis; and most that people consume is imported. When placed in such stark terms, the absurdity of the "neoliberal" ideology of the Bretton Woods institutions becomes obvious. It also becomes clear who such policies serve. Rather than enhance the life of people and planet, they consolidate and secure the wealth and power of a small corporate elite, the only evident beneficiaries, at the expense of humanity and nature. In the following section, we outline the principles of alternative systems that posit democracy and rights as the means toward sustainable communities, dignified work, and a healthy environment.

Chapter II Ten Principles for Democratic and Sustainable Societies

The current organizing principles of the institutions that govern the global economy are narrow and serve the few at the expense of the many and the environment. Yet, it is within our collective ability to create healthy, sustainable societies that work for all. The time has come to make that possibility a reality. Sustainable societies are rooted in certain core principles. The following ten core principles have been put forward in various combinations in citizen programs that are emerging around the world.

A. New Democracy

The rallying cry of the amazing diversity of civil society that converged in Seattle in late 1999 was the simple word "democracy." Democracy flourishes when people organize to protect their communities and rights and hold their elected officials accountable. For the past two decades, global corporations and global bureaucracies have grabbed much of the power once held by governments. We advocate a shift from governments serving corporations to governments serving people and communities, a process that is easier at the local level but vital at all levels of government.

B. Subsidiarity

Economic globalization results first, and foremost, in de-localization and disempowerment of communities and local economies. It is therefore necessary to reverse direction and create new rules and structures that consciously favor the local, and follow the principle of subsidiarity, i.e., whatever decisions and activities can be undertaken locally should be. Whatever power can reside at the local level should reside there. Only when additional activity is required that cannot be satisfied locally, should power and activity move to the next higher level: region, nation, and finally the world.

C. Ecological Sustainability

Economic activity needs to be ecologically sustainable. It should enable us to meet humans' genuine needs in the present without compromising the ability of future generations to meet theirs, and without diminishing the natural diversity of life on Earth or the viability of the planet's natural life-support systems.

D. Common Heritage

There exist common heritage resources that should constitute a collective birthright of the whole species to be shared equitably among all. We assert that there are three categories of such resources. The first consists of the shared natural heritage of the water, land, air, forests, and fisheries on which our lives depend. These physical resources are in finite supply, essential to life, and existed long before any human. A second category includes the heritage of culture and knowledge that is the collective creation of our species. Finally, basic public services relating to health, education, public safety, and social security are "modern" common heritage resources representing the collective efforts of whole societies. They are also as essential to life in modern societies as are air and water. Justice therefore demands that they be readily available to all who need them. Any attempt by persons or corporations to monopolize ownership control of an essential common heritage resource for exclusive private gain to the exclusion of the needs of others is morally unconscionable and politically unacceptable.

E. Human Rights

In 1948, governments of the world came together to adopt the United Nations Universal Declaration on Human Rights, which established certain core rights, such as "a standard of living adequate for . . . health and well-being . . . , including food, clothing, housing and medical care, and necessary social services, and the right to security in the event of unemployment." Traditionally, most of the human rights debate in the United States and other rich nations has focused on civil and political rights as paramount. We believe that it is the duty of governments to ensure these rights, but also to guarantee the economic, social and cultural rights of all people.

F. Jobs/Livelihood/Employment

A livelihood is a means of living. The right to a means of livelihood is therefore the most basic of all human rights. Sustainable societies must both protect the rights of workers in the formal sector and address the livelihood needs of the larger share of people who subsist in what has become known as the non-material, or "informal sector" (including small-scale, indigenous, and artisanal activities) as well as those who have no work or are seriously underemployed. Empowering workers to organize for basic rights and fair wages is vital to curb footloose corporations that pit workers against each other in a lose-lose race to the bottom. And, the reversal of globalization policies that displace small farmers from their land and fisherfolk from their coastal ecosystems are central to the goal of a world where all can live and work in dignity.

G. Food Security and Food Safety

Communities and nations are stable and secure when people have enough food, particularly when nations can produce their own food. People also want safe food, a commodity that is increasingly scarce as global agribusiness firms spread chemical- and biotech-intensive agriculture around the world.

H. Equity

Economic globalization, under the current rules, has widened the gap between rich and poor countries and between rich and poor within most countries. The resulting social dislocation and tension are among the greatest threats to peace and security the world over. Greater equity both among nations and within them would reinforce both democracy and sustainable communities. Reducing the growing gap between rich and poor nations requires first and foremost the cancellation of the illegitimate debts of poor countries. And, it requires the replacement of the current institutions of global governance with new ones that include global fairness among their operating principles.

I. Diversity

A few decades ago, it was still possible to leave home and go somewhere else where the architecture was different, the landscape was different, the language, lifestyle, food, dress, and values were different. Today, farmers and filmmakers in France and India, indigenous communities worldwide, and millions of people elsewhere, are protesting to maintain that diversity. Tens of thousands of communities around the world have perfected local resource management systems that work, but they are now being undermined by corporate-led globalization. Cultural, biological, social, and economic diversity are central to a viable, dignified, and healthy life.

J. Precautionary Principle

All activity should abide by the precautionary principle. When a practice or product raises potentially significant threats of harm to human health or the environment, precautionary action should be taken to restrict or ban it even if scientific uncertainty remains about whether or how it is actually causing that harm. Because it can take years for scientific proof of harm to be established – during which time undesirable or irreversible effects may continue to be inflicted – the proponents of a practice or product should bear the burden of proving that it is safe, before it is implemented.

Chapter III   Issues on Commodification of the Commons

This section grapples with one of the most pioneering yet difficult arenas in the alternatives dialogue: the question of whether certain goods and services should not be traded or subject to trade agreements, patents or commodification. Lengthy discussions among IFG members have clarified a lot of issues, but discussion is ongoing. The section will lay out the categories of goods and services that the drafters believe should be subject to different kinds of restrictions in global economic commerce: goods that come from the global or local commons, and goods which fulfill basic rights and needs. The section will then offer categories of proposed restrictions.

In a world where many resources have already been over-exploited and seriously depleted, there is constant pressure by global corporations and the public bureau-cracies that serve them to privatize and monopolize the full range of common heritage resources from water to genetic codes that have thus far remained off limits to commodification and management as corporate profit centers. Indeed, the more essential the good or service in question to the maintenance of life, the greater its potential for generating monopoly profits and the more attractive its ownership and control becomes to global corporations.

Water, a commonly shared, irreplaceable, and fundamental requirement for the survival of all life, is a leading example. Everywhere around the world, global corporations are seeking to consolidate their ownership and monopoly control of the fresh water resources of rivers, lakes and streams for promotion as an export commodity – like computer memory or car tires. The rules of many new trade agreements directly assist this commodification process.

Another formerly pristine area – one that most human beings had never thought could or ought to be a commodity bought and sold for corporate profits – is the genetic structure of living beings, including humans, which is now falling rapidly within the control of "life science" industries (biotechnology), and coming increasingly under the purview of global trade agreements. A third area concerns indigenous knowledge of plant varieties, seeds, products of the forest, medicinal herbs, and biodiversity itself, which has been vital in successfully sustaining traditional societies for millennia. A fourth area is bioprospecting currently underway by global corporations seeking genetic materials from the skin and other body parts among native peoples. Several of these latter areas, and others, are subject to patenting (monopoly control) by large global corporations, protected under the Trade Related Intellectual Property Rights Agreement (TRIPS) of the WTO and a similar North American Free Trade Agreement (NAFTA) chapter. The net result of these new corporate protections and rights over formerly non-commodified biological materials is to make it costly, difficult or impossible for agricultural or indigenous communities to avail themselves of biological resources that they formerly freely enjoyed.

Parallel to such efforts at privatizing and commodifying areas of the global commons is the tremendous effort to privatize and commodify as many public services that were once taken care of within communities and then performed by local, state and national governments on behalf of all people. These services may address such basic needs as public health and hospital care; public education; public safety and protection; welfare and social security; water delivery and purity; sanitation; public broadcasting, museums and national cultural expressions; food safety systems; and prisons. While these areas may not have been traditionally defined as part of "the commons," in the same way as water, land, air, forests, pasture or other natural expressions of the earth that have been freely shared within communities for millennia, in the modern world these public services have nonetheless been generally understood to fall within the vital fundamental rights and needs of citizens living in any nominally successful, responsible society.

If the corporate globalists have their way in negotiations at the General Agreement on Trade in Services (GATS) of the WTO, or within the FTAA, the way will be cleared for many of these essential services to move directly into the hands of global corporations to be operated as corporate profit centers accountable only to the interests of their shareholders. As with corporatized healthcare in the United States, the rich may be well served, but the vast majority of people will be unsatisfied, overcharged, or abandoned.

In the view of the drafters of this document, this process of privatizing, monopolizing, and commodifying common heritage resources and turning public services into corporate profit centers and the protection of this process within global trade agreements, must be halted at once. There is an appropriate place for private ownership and markets to play in the management, allocation, and delivery of certain common heritage resources, as for example land, within a framework of effective democratically accountable public regulation that guarantees fair pricing, equitable access, quality, and public stewardship. There is no rightful place in any public body, process, or international agreement to facilitate the unaccountable private monopolization of common heritage resources and public services essential to life or to otherwise exclude any person from equitable access to such essential resources and services.

Chapter IV   The Case for Subsidiarity: Bias Away From the Global Toward the Local

It is the major conceit or gamble of the corporate globalists that by removing economic control from the places where it has traditionally resided – in nations, states, sub-regions, communities or indigenous societies – and placing that control into absentee authorities that operate globally via giant corporations and bureaucracies, that all levels of society will benefit. As we have seen, this is not true, and it is a principal reason why so many millions of people are angrily protesting.

The central modus operandi of the globalization model is to delocalize all controls over economic and political activity; a systematic, complete appropriation on the powers, decisions, options and functions that through prior history were fulfilled by the community, region or state. When sovereign powers are finally removed from the local and put into distant bureaucracies, local politics must also be redesigned to conform to the rules and practices of distant bureaucracies. Communities and nations that formerly operated in a relatively self-reliant manner, in the interests of their own peoples, are converted into unwilling subjects of this much larger, undemocratic, unaccountable global structure.

If democracy is based upon the idea that people must participate in the great decisions affecting their lives, then the system we find today of moving basic life decisions to distant venues of centralized, international institutions, which display a disregard for democratic participation, openness, accountability, and transparency, brings the death of democracy. We have reached the end of the road for that process. It's time to change directions.

A.   Understanding Subsidiarity

As globalization is the intractable problem, then logically a turn toward the local is inevitable; a reinvigoration of the conditions by which local communities regain the powers to determine and control their economic and political paths. Instead of shaping all systems to conform to a global model that emphasizes specialization of production, comparative advantage, export-oriented growth, monoculture, and homogenization of economic, cultural and political forms under the direction of transnational corporate institutions, we must reshape our institutions to favor exactly the opposite.

The operating principle for this turnaround is the concept of subsidiarity, i.e., favoring the local whenever a choice exists. In practice this means that all decisions should be made at the lowest level of governing authority competent to deal with it. Global health crises and global pollution issues often require cooperative international decisions. But most economic, cultural and political decisions should not be international; they should be made at the national, regional or local levels, depending on what they are. Power should be encouraged to evolve downward, not upward. Decisions should constantly move closer to the people most affected by them.

Economic systems should favor local production and markets rather than invariably being designed to serve long distance trade. This means shortening the length of lines for economic activity: fewer food miles; fewer oil supply miles; fewer travel-to-work miles. Technologies should also be chosen that best serve local control, rather than mega-technologies that operate globally.

B.　The Road to the Local

Localization attempts to reverse the trend toward the global by discriminating actively in favor of the local in all policies. Depending on the context, the "local" is defined as a subgrouping within a nation-state; it can also be the nation-state itself or occasionally a regional grouping of nation-states. The overall idea is for power to devolve to the lowest unit appropriate for a particular goal.

Policies that bring about localization are ones that increase democratic control of the economy by communities and/or nation-states, taking it back from global institutions that have appropriated them: bureaucracies and global corporations. These may enable nations, local governments and communities to reclaim their economies; to make them as diverse as possible; and to rebuild stability into community life – to achieve a maximum self-reliance nationally and regionally in a way that ensures sustainable forms of development. [. . .]

Questions

1   Why do Esteva and Prakash think that opponents of globalization should not simply "think globally, act locally"? Why do they call engaging in global action an "illusion"? Why do they find wisdom in "thinking small" and power in "acting locally"? What examples do they cite in support of their view?

2   What makes the anti-globalization movement "formidable," according to Harding? What are some of the key groups that make up the movement, and what are their main activities? How did Ken Saro-Wiwa become a "martyr" of the movement?

3   Why does Shiva describe economic globalization as a "normative" and "political" process? What negative consequences does the latest "wave" of globalization have, and how does Shiva denounce these? How does native seed become a symbol of freedom for some anti-globalization groups?

4   Why does Marcos believe that neoliberal globalization causes "world war" and turns each country into a "battleground"? What must "rebels" do in their struggle against "the fence [that] is reproduced globally"? Does Marcos propose an alternative kind of globalization? Does Marcos's call for a "network of voices" fit Esteva and Prakash's argument?

5   How do both the World Social Forum and the International Forum on Globalization indict the current form of globalization? What specific demands does the WSF issue? What principles should guide institutions to govern the world economy, according to the IFG? Do the WSF and IFG readings show that a common worldview unites the anti-globalization movement?

Index